Monographs in Computer Science

Editors

David Gries
Fred B. Schneider

Springer
New York
Berlin
Heidelberg
Barcelona
Hong Kong
London
Milan
Paris
Singapore
Tokyo

Monographs in Computer Science

Abadi and Cardelli, **A Theory of Objects**

Brzozowski and Seger, **Asynchronous Circuits**

Selig, **Geometrical Methods in Robotics**

Nielson [editor], **ML with Concurrency**

Castillo, Gutiérrez, and Hadi, **Expert Systems and Probabilistic Network Models**

Paton [editor], **Active Rules in Database Systems**

Downey and Fellows, **Parameterized Complexity**

Leiss, **Language Equations**

Feijen and van Gasteren, **On a Method of Multiprogramming**

Broy and Stølen, **Specification and Development of Interactive Systems: FOCUS on Streams, Interfaces, and Refinement**

Benosman and Kang [editors], **Panoramic Vision: Sensors, Theory, and Applications**

Ryad Benosman
Sing Bing Kang
Editors

Panoramic Vision

Sensors, Theory, and Applications

Foreword by Olivier Faugeras

With 267 Illustrations

Springer

Ryad Benosman
Laboratoire des Instruments
et Systems
University Pierre et Marie Curie
4, place jussieu,75252
Paris cedex 05, boite 164
France
rbo@lis.jussieu.fr

Sing Bing Kang
Microsoft Corporation
One Microsoft Way
Redmond, WA 98052
USA
sbkang@microsoft.com

Series Editors:
David Gries
Department of Computer Science
Cornell University
Upson Hall
Ithaca, NY 14853-7501
USA

Fred B. Schneider
Department of Computer Science
Cornell University
Upson Hall
Ithaca, NY 14853-7501
USA

Library of Congress Cataloging-in-Publication Data
Panoramic Vision: sensors, theory, and applications/editors, Ryad Benosman, Sing Bing Kang.
p. cm.
Includes bibliographical references.
ISBN 0-387-95111-3 (alk. paper)
1. Photography, Panoramic. 2. Computer vision. I. Benosman, Ryad. II. Kang, Sing Bing.
TR661.P37 2001
778.3'6—dc21 00-053770

Printed on acid-free paper.

Production managed by Frank McGuckin; manufacturing supervised by Jacqui Ashri.
Camera-ready copy prepared from the authors' LaTeX2e files using Springer's macros.
Printed and bound by Maple-Vail Book Manufacturing Group, York, PA.
Printed in the United States of America.

9 8 7 6 5 4 3 2 1

ISBN 0-387-95111-3 SPIN 10774457

Springer-Verlag New York Berlin Heidelberg
A member of BertelsmannSpringer Science+Business Media GmbH

Foreword

Current cameras are poor imitations of the human eye and close descendants in their design of ideas and a technology that are more than a century old. People in computer vision have traditionally used off-the-shelf cameras that were not meant for the uses they were intended for by these researchers: off-the-shelf cameras are designed to capture images to be printed on paper or looked at on a television screen, not for guiding robots or making 3D models of the environment or even surveilling a large area where very large field of views, high geometric and photometric accuracies are necessary.

Quite a significant part of the efforts in computer vision has been targeted at overcoming *algorithmically* these problems. The authors of this book convince us that it is possible to abandon the traditional route of using standard cameras and to follow the path of designing new cameras explicitly for solving the tasks at hand in computer vision applications. This leads to different design concepts and allows to alleviate many of the difficulties encountered in the processing of the images taken with the "traditional" cameras.

This book addresses first in great depth the problem of designing new generations of cameras that output panoramic views of the scene, i.e., images with very large fields of view. It turns out that the design of such cameras opens up a great deal of new interesting research areas that are characterized by an intricate mixture of optics and geometry as exemplified in the first section of the book.

Once these new panoramic sensors are available it is possible to revisit one of the oldest problems in machine vision, i.e., the stereo problem. The combination of several of these new sensors introduces the new exciting possibility of producing much larger chunks of 3D representations of the environment much faster and much more easily than what is possible with standard cameras. This is the subject of the second section of the book.

Despite the fact that many of these new sensors are now becoming available, there are still quite a few standard cameras around and it is also important to explore ways in which algorithms and software can be used to simulate the new sensors with the old ones. This is the subject of the third section of the book.

In the final section we return to the original motivation for the design of the new sensors, i.e., the applications. We discover in four different cases how a clever use of the ideas and the technology that are featured in the first three parts of the book make simpler and/or possible exciting applications in such areas as robotics, 3D modelling, surveillance and video processing.

The book covers in depth a very new, active and promising area of computer vision. It is written by the world's leading vision researchers that have pioneered this new area. The presentation is consistent and the parts fit well together. Anyone who claims to be serious about research and applications in this domain absolutely must be aware of this work.

INRIA, MIT

Olivier Faugeras
June 2000

Preface

Computer vision as a field has come a long way since its humble beginnings in the 1960's. A significant amount of research work in computer vision has been biologically-inspired, using the human eye and visual perception as the model for binocular vision systems. There are even systems that are designed to mimic the human foveal and peripheral senses of vision.

The classical stereo system, no doubt influenced by the human visual system, comprises two narrow-field-of-view cameras placed side by side. The spatial coverage of this stereo system is obviously limited, and the resulting 3D data recovery at any given pose alone may be inadequate for many practical applications.

With the advancement of autocalibration and registration techniques, reasonably accurate 3D reconstruction of wide views is possible using a moving camera. This, however, is accomplished at a high computational cost. In addition, there are still some remaining stability and robustness issues associated with narrow fields-of-view to contend with.

We subscribe to the notion of simplifying analysis by capturing as widely as possible the appearance of the surrounding environment at any instant early in the pipeline. This is our primary motivation of this book on panoramic vision, which has important implications in both robotics and computer vision. This book features representative work in the design of panoramic image capturing systems, the theory involved in the imaging process, software techniques for creating panoramic images, and applications that use panoramic images. The intended audience is anyone who wishes to become familiar with panoramic vision and its latest research work. The contents of this book allow the reader to understand the more technical aspects of panoramic vision, such as sensor design and imaging techniques. Researchers and instructors will especially find this book useful.

University Pierre et Marie Curie *Ryad Benosman*
Microsoft Corporation *Sing Bing Kang*
May 2000

Contents

Contributors

Padmanabhan Anandan
Microsoft Corporation
One Microsoft Way
Redmond, WA 98052
USA
Email: anandan@microsoft.com
Homepage: http://www.research.microsoft.com/~anandan/

Lourdes de Agapito
Department of Engineering Science
University of Oxford
Parks Road
Oxford, OX1 3PJ
UK
Email: lourdes@robots.ox.ac.uk
Homepage: http://www.robots.ox.ac.uk/~lourdes

Simon Baker
The Robotics Institute
Carnegie Mellon University
Pittsburgh, PA 15213
Email: simonb@cs.cmu.edu
Homepage: http://www.ri.cmu.edu/people/baker_simon.html

Jonathan Baldwin
Department Of Computing Science
University of Alberta
Edmonton, Alberta
Canada T6G 2H1
Email: baldwin@cs.ualberta.ca
Homepage: http://www.cs.ualberta.ca/~baldwin/

Matthew Barth
Marlan and Rosemary Bourns College of Engineering
Center for Environmental Research and Technology
University of California, Riverside
Riverside, CA 92521
USA
Email: barth@ee.ucr.edu
Homepage: http://www.engr.ucr.edu/faculty/ee/barth.html

Anup Basu
Department Of Computing Science
University of Alberta
Edmonton, Alberta
Canada T6G 2H1
Email: anup@cs.ualberta.ca
Homepage: http://www.cs.ualberta.ca/~anup/

Moshe Ben-Ezra
School of Computer Science and Engineering
The Hebrew University of Jerusalem
91904 Jerusalem
Israel
Email: moshe@cs.huji.ac.il
Homepage: http://www.cs.huji.ac.il/~moshe/

Ryad Benosman
University Pierre et Marie Curie (Paris 6)
Laboratoire des Instruments et Systémes
4, place Jussieu, boite 164
75252 Paris Cedex 05
France
Email: rbo@lis.jussieu.fr
Homepage: http://www.robo.jussieu.fr/rbo/ryad_benosman.htm

Jean Devars
University Pierre et Marie Curie (Paris 6)
Laboratoire des Instruments et Systémes
4, place Jussieu, boite 164
75252 Paris Cedex 05
France
Email : devars@ccr.jussieu.fr

Richard I. Hartley
G.E. Corporate Research and Development
1 Research Circle
Niskayuna, NY 12309
USA
Email: hartley@crd.ge.com

Eric Hayman
Department of Engineering Science
University of Oxford
Parks Road
Oxford OX1 3PJ
UK
Email: hayman@robots.ox.ac.uk
Homepage: www.robots.ox.ac.uk/∼hayman

Václav Hlaváč
Czech Technical University, Faculty of Electrical Engineering
Department of Cybernetics, Center for Machine Perception
CZ 121 35 Prague 2, Karlovo náměstí 13
Czech Republic
Email: hlavac@cmp.felk.cvut.cz
Homepage: http://cmp.felk.cvut.cz/∼hlavac/

Michal Irani
Department of Computer Science and Applied Mathematics
The Weizmann Institute of Science
Rehovot
Israel
Email: irani@wisdom.weizmann.ac.il
Homepage: http://www.wisdom.weizmann.ac.il/∼irani

Hiroshi Ishiguro
Department of Computer and Communication Sciences
Wakayama University
Sakaedani 930, Wakayama 640-8501
Japan
E-mail: ishiguro@sys.wakayama-u.ac.jp
Homepage: http://www.lab7.kuis.kyoto-u.ac.jp/∼ishiguro/

Sing Bing Kang
Microsoft Corporation
One Microsoft Way
Redmond, WA 98052
USA
Email: sbkang@microsoft.com
Homepage: http://research.microsoft.com/Users/sbkang/

Amruta D. Karmarkar
Motorola Inc.
1501 West Shure Drive
Arlington Heights, IL 60004-1469
USA
Email: AKARMAR1@email.mot.com

Koji Kato
Division Department of Mechatronics and Precision Engineering
Tohoku University
Tribology Laboratory
Room No. Mechanical Engineering Building 2-517
Japan
Email: koji@tribo.mech.tohoku.ac.jp
Homepage: http://www.mech.tohoku.ac.jp/1999/kojiEng.html

Shree K. Nayar
Department of Computer Science
Columbia University
New York, NY 10027
USA
Email: nayar@cs.columbia.edu
Homepage: http://www.cs.columbia.edu/~nayar/

Tomáš Pajdla
Czech Technical University, Faculty of Electrical Engineering
Department of Cybernetics, Center for Machine Perception
CZ 121 35 Prague 2, Karlovo náměstí 13
Czech Republic
Email: pajdla@cmp.felk.cvut.cz
Homepage: http://cmp.felk.cvut.cz/~pajdla/

Shmuel Peleg
School of Computer Science and Engineering
The Hebrew University of Jerusalem
91904 Jerusalem
Israel
Email: peleg@cs.huji.ac.il
Homepage: http://www.cs.huji.ac.il/~peleg/

Venkata Peri
RemoteReality
295 Madison Ave.
New York, NY 10017
USA
Email: vperi@remotereality.com

Yael Pritch
School of Computer Science and Engineering
The Hebrew University of Jerusalem
91904 Jerusalem
Israel
Email: yaelpri@cs.huji.ac.il
Homepage: http://www.cs.huji.ac.il/~yaelpri/

Alex Rav-Acha
School of Computer Science and Engineering
The Hebrew University of Jerusalem
91904 Jerusalem
Israel
Email: alexis@cs.huji.ac.il

Ian Reid
Department of Engineering Science
University of Oxford
Parks Road
Oxford, OX1 3PJ
UK
Email: ian@robots.oxford.ac.uk
Homepage: http://www.robots.ox.ac.uk/~ian/

Benny Rousso
Impulse Dynamics
3 Haetgar Street, Carmel Building
P.O. Box 2044
Tirat Hacarmel 39120
Israel
Email: bennyr@impulse.co.il

Heung-Yeung Shum
Microsoft Research China
5/F, Beijing Sigma Center
Zhichun Road No. 49, Hai Dian District
Beijing China 100080
Email: hshum@microsoft.com

Takushi Sogo
Department of Social Informatics, Kyoto University
Sakyo-ku, Kyoto 606-8501
Japan
Email: sogo@kuis.kyoto-u.ac.jp
Homepage: http://www.lab7.kuis.kyoto-u.ac.jp/services/members/sogo.html

Tomáš Svoboda
Czech Technical University, Faculty of Electrical Engineering
Department of Cybernetics, Center for Machine Perception
CZ 121 35 Prague 2, Karlovo náměstí 13
Czech Republic
Email: svoboda@cmp.felk.cvut.cz
Homepage: http://cmp.felk.cvut.cz/~svoboda/

Richard Szeliski
Microsoft Corporation
One Microsoft Way
Redmond, WA 98052
USA
Email: szeliski@microsoft.com
Homepage: http://research.microsoft.com/~szeliski/

Mohan Trivedi
Department of Electrical and Computer Engineering
9500 Gilman Drive, Mail Code 0407
University of California, San Diego
La Jolla, CA 92093-0407
USA
Email: trivedi@ece.ucsd.edu
Homepage: http://swiftlet.ucsd.edu/~trivedi/

Assaf Zomet
School of Computer Science and Engineering
The Hebrew University of Jerusalem
91904 Jerusalem
Israel
Email: zomet@cs.huji.ac.il
Homepage: http://www.cs.huji.ac.il/~zomet/

1

Introduction

R. Benosman and S.B. Kang

1.1 Omnidirectional Vision in Nature

Man has always been curious about nature, and the fact that certain animals are capable of panoramic sight is particularly intriguing. Over the years, three types of compound eyes that permit this special ability have been identified. They exist in diurnal and nocturnal insects and some species of crustaceans such as lobsters, shrimps and crawfish.

Diurnal insect eyes are often made of a pattern of photoreceptive cells (see Figure 1.1) which allow panoramic sight. In fact, each eye of these insects comprises a collection of lenticular element and elementary vision sensor pairs, each of which covering a specific direction.

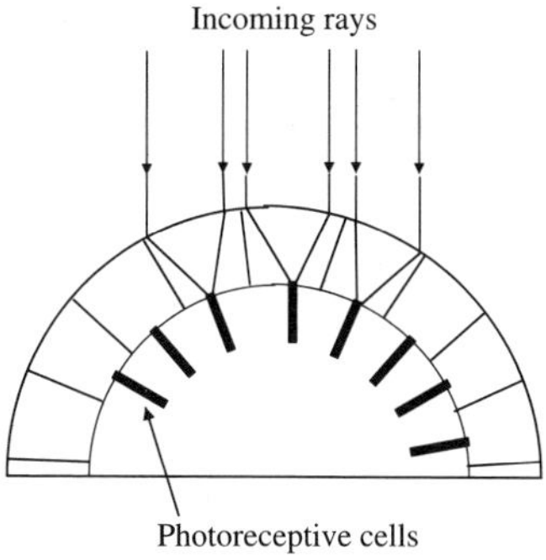

FIGURE 1.1. Diurnal insect vision system.

For nocturnal insects, the lenticular elements are arranged in a space-efficient hexagonal pattern. The refraction index in each lens changes radially in such as way that incident rays converge at one focal point on the retina. This has the effect of enhancing night vision. There is also a spatial gap between the lenticular elements and the retina. This enables the incident rays to be refracted to form an image (see Figure 1.2).

Each crustacean eye comprises a set of square, mirror-like surfaces as part of the lenticular elements. This allows rays to be reflected and converge at different unique points on the retina. Since these eyes also contain a spatial

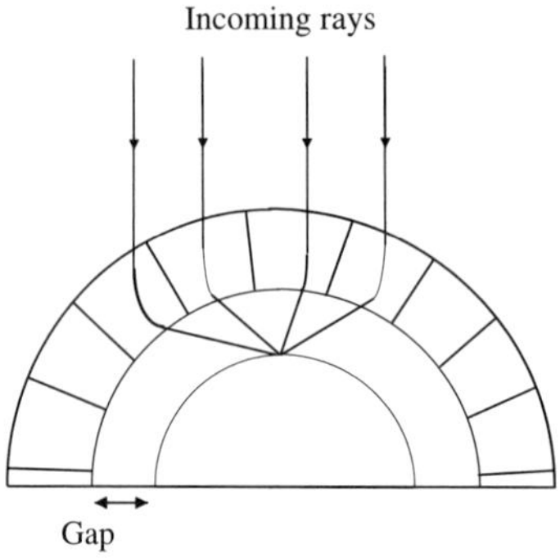

FIGURE 1.2. Nocturnal insect vision system.

gap, some entomologists in the past have mistakenly equated them with those of nocturnal insects. It was only in 1975 that the difference between the two types of eyes was found, i.e., the image formed in the crustacean eye is primarily through a set of juxtaposed mirrors (Figure 1.3).

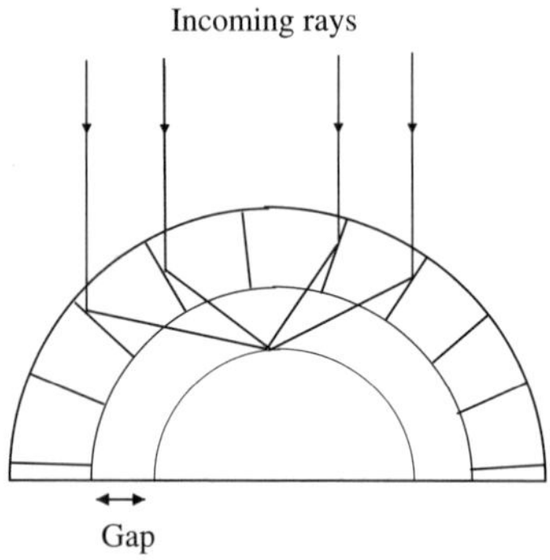

FIGURE 1.3. Crustacean vision system.

A particularly interesting case is the deep sea crutacean *Gigantocypris*, which has large eyes with reflectors that are similar to the optics in telescopes. This characteristic allows it to see under very dim conditions at depths of the order of thousands of feet. While this orange-red creature is only about half an inch long, its head occupies half of the body. Its two eyes are covered by a transparent lid. The optics of the eye with reflection is actually rather complex; its horizontal cross-section reveals the shape of the mirrors at the back of the eye to be parabolic, with a focal point situated at a small distance from the peak of the mirror (Figure 1.4). The mirror focuses the reflected light onto the retina, and while the image formed at the retina is not sharp, it is about 17 times brighter than when the image is formed in the eye with lenses.

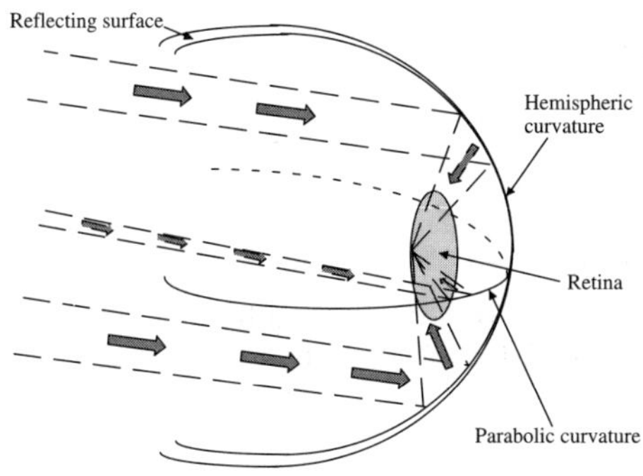

FIGURE 1.4. The reflecting eye of the *Gigantocypris*.

1.2 Man-Made Panoramic Vision

Man's first attempts at replicating panoramic vision, as described in Chapter 2, were mostly as a particular art form designed to provide an immersive experience. The concern then was primarily to create photorealistic wide imagery of landscapes or historical occurrences. Creating such panoramic art in those days required a great amount of capital.

As the popularity of panoramic art faded away, more scientific attempts were made at providing panoramic vision using a much more compact system. In doing so, nature was often imitated, either consciously or unconsciously. As an example, some of today's omnidirectional cameras are basically inside-out versions of the reflecting eye of the *Gigantocypris* shown in Figure 1.4.

1.3 Organization of Book

This book contains a good cross-section of more recent work on omnidirectional imaging and analysis. It is divided into four sections: The first two sections are on hardware systems, the third on software techniques, and the fourth on applications. In a little more detail:

- **Section I: Catadioptric panoramic systems**
  This section focuses on image capture systems that are designed to cover a wide field of view with just a single image capture and with no parallax. The word "catadioptric" refers to the use of glass elements and mirrors in an imaging system.

- **Section II: Panoramic stereo vision systems**
  In this section, different hardware-based approaches to produce stereo

panoramic images are described. These systems enable both wide-angle visualization with parallax and depth recovery.

- **Section III: Techniques for generating panoramic images**
The chapters in this section focus on software approaches for generating panoramic images. In addition, all approaches except one use just conventional off-the-shelf cameras. The types of panoramic images described here range from cylindrical ones (with 360° horizontal field of view) to spherical ones to those with arbitrary coverage.

- **Section IV: Applications**
In this final section, a diverse sample of applications that makes use of or are faciliated by panoramic imaging are featured. The areas covered by these applications are computer vision, robotics, and image/video processing as well. More specifically, the applications detailed here are 3D environment modeling, identification and recognition of robots, human tracking, and video representation.

This division allows the reader to quickly and easily access a particular area of interest. Each chapter is mostly self-contained, as is each section, so that the order in which chapters are read is not very important.

1.4 Acknowledgment

Section 1.1 is based on the following sources:

1. M. F. Land and T. S. Collett, A survey of active vision in invertebrates, *From Living Eyes to Seeing Machines*, M. V. Srinivasan and S. Venkatesh (eds.), Oxford University Press, 1997, pp. 16-36.

2. M. F. Land, L'Oeil et la Vision, *Traite de Zoologie VII (Dir: Grassé P-P) Crustacés*, vol. 2, J. Forest (ed.), Paris: Masson, 1996, pp. 1-42.

3. G. A. Kerkut and L. I. Gilbert (eds.), Chapters 4-8, The Eye, *Comprehensive Insect Physiology, Biochemistry and Pharmacology Vol. 6: Nervous System Sensory*, Pergamon Press, Oxford, 1985.

4. A. Horridge and D. Blest, The compound eye, *Insect Biology in the Future*, M. Locke and D. S. Smith (eds.), Academic Press, New York, 1980, pp. 705-733.

5. H. Autrum (series ed.) *et al.*, *Handbook of Sensory Physiology*, Springer-Verlag, 1971-1981.

2

A Brief Historical Perspective on Panorama

R. Benosman and S.B. Kang

According to Merriam-Webster's dictionary, the word "panorama" is a combination of two Greek terms, namely the suffix *pan* ($\pi\alpha\nu$), meaning "all," and *horama* ($\acute{o}\rho\alpha\mu\alpha$), meaning "sight." The dictionary also listed the year of its conception or start of popular usage as 1796. A more technical term used synonymously is "omnidirectional." In both cases, the meaning of wide field of view visibility is conveyed. This chapter traces some of the historical developments of the panorama, in both art and technology.

Robert Barker was arguably the first person who conceived the idea of the panorama; he had received a patent for it on June 17, 1767. The patent described an artistic format of paintings that practically surrounds the viewer. As such, this chapter would not be complete without a description of the panorama as it had originally started: as an art form. An authoritative book on panorama as an art form is Stephan Oettermann's "The Panorama: History of a Mass Medium" (translated by Deborah Schneider); the reader should consult it for more details and many more examples than those provided here.

2.1 Panorama in the Beginning

The first detailed report on panorama dated back to 1794, in the form of the Gottigen Pocket Book. It contained a full description of the picture exhibited by Barker in 1793, under the title of "A Painting Without Equal." It was only by the 1800s that the word "panorama" became part of the vocabulary of every European language. This can be attributed to the exhibits of the paintings themselves and publicity that they received through many newspapers and magazine articles. Panoramic art became the rage in Paris in the 1820s because of its novelty in presenting visual experience.

The most popular form of panoramic art was that of a large round painting, which provides a visual overview of a landscape or cityscape. Figure 2.1 shows the concept of this. It was one of the first genuine visual mass media, and what Robert Barker had intended was to depict a landscape in a full circle of 360° as realistically as possible. The art of circular panoramic painting allowed people to look at nature in a different way. Panoramic

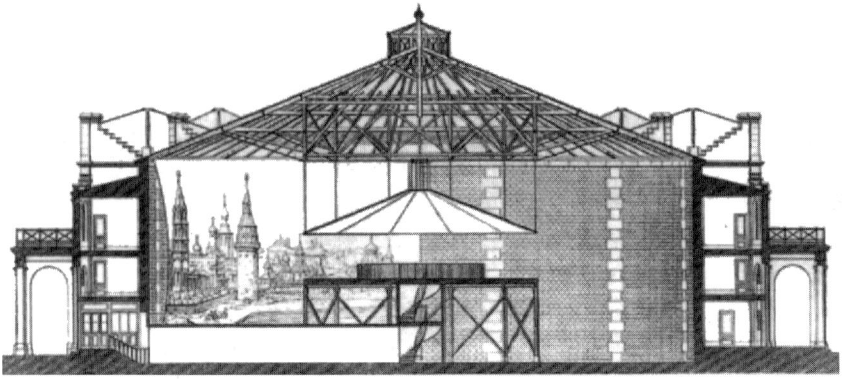

FIGURE 2.1. Cross section of the panorama at Champs-Elysées (1840). Gravure from a drawing of Jacques-Ignace Hittorff (courtesy of Bibliothèque Nationale, Paris).

paintings became a pattern for organizing visual experience and panoramic vision became a means for providing a visual sensurround experience.

2.2 From Panorama Exhibits to Photography

A panorama painter's goal was to reproduce the real world so realistically that onlookers could believe that what they were seeing was real. This illusion was achieved by new techniques of painting and more importantly by creating a physically immersive environment. The latter involves literally surrounding the spectators with the painting. The steps typically involved in creating such an immersive environment (an example is shown in Figure 2.2) are:

- Preliminary sketches on large sheets of paper using any of these equipment:
  - Obscura camera (Latin for "dark room"),
  - Panoramagraph (invented by Chaix in 1803),
  - Camera lucida (Latin for "light room", invented by William Wollaston, an English physicist, in 1806), which is more compact and portable than the camera obscura,
  - Diagraph (invented by Gavard in 1830), which is an extension of the camera lucida that includes the use of a curved ruler to compensate for panoramic curvature distortion.
- Preparation of the rotunda,
- Transfer of the sketch to the canvas, followed by

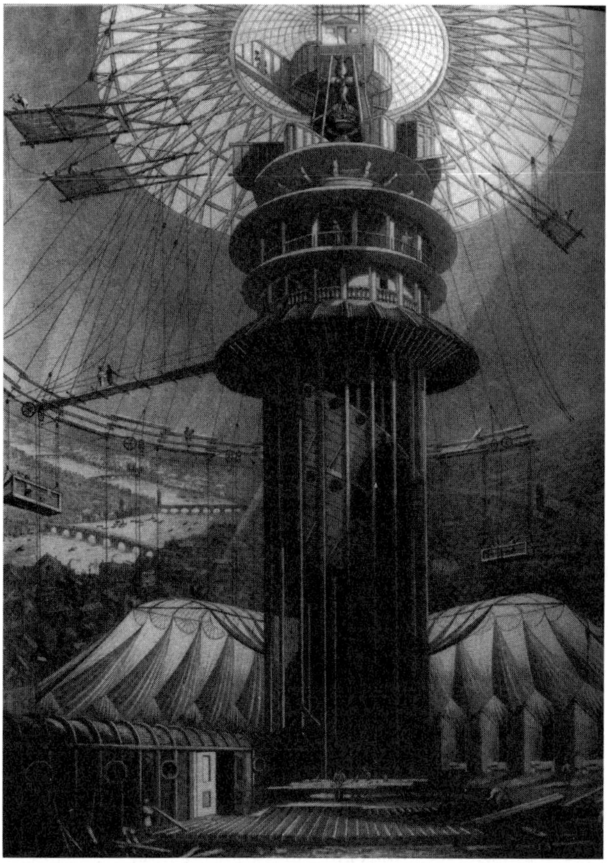

FIGURE 2.2. Inside view of the Colosseum with the panorama of London, shortly before its completion (courtesy of Guildhall Library, Corporation of London).

- Painting.

Visitors to these panoramic exhibits were often given a brochure that explains this form of art, and they were able to buy a small format panorama as a souvenir. The circular panorama was followed by the extended panorama, the double extended panorama, the scene panorama, the myriorama (from the Greek word *myrias*, which means "ten thousand"), the landscape kaleidoscope, the cosmorama, the diorama and finally the double effect diorama, which provides motion effects on a two-dimensional surface (invented by Jacob Philip Hackert and Louis Jacques Mande Daguerre). The success of this last invention in 1844 was even reported by the media.

An attempt was made by Friederich Von Martens to create a photographic panorama, but because of photographic deficiencies, the results were quite poor. When George Eastman introduced celluloid film in 1888, the flexibility of the improved device opened up new possiblities, thanks to further innovations in the field. Sutton Moessard succeeded in assembling multiple photographs to form a full panorama by using four projectors in a circular room. Subsequent higher field-of-view cameras were constructed, but their fields of view were still limited to 160-170°.

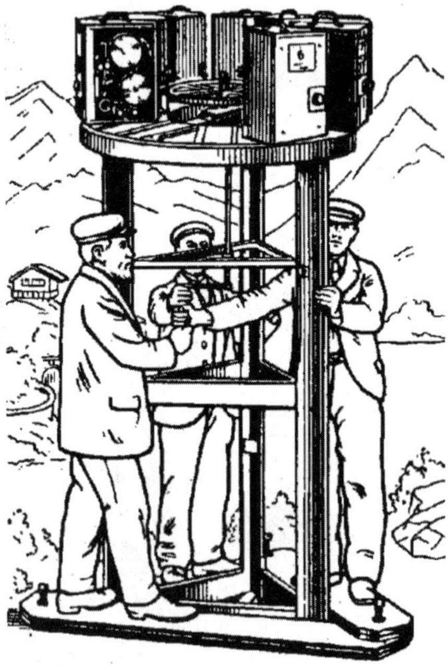

FIGURE 2.3. Camera configuration for Raoul Grimoin-Sanson's cineorama.

In 1894, Charles A. Chase demonstrated his Stereopticon-Cyclorama, which comprised of eight projectors projecting sixteen slides onto a circular screen. This invention was later improved by Raoul Grimoin-Sanson's Cineorama (Figure 2.3), which was highly successful at the 1900 World's Fair in Paris. A number of further technical improvements and inventions in panoramic feature filming took place, including Abel E. Gance's Magnoscope, Fred Waller's Cinerama, and Walt Disney's Circorama. Their success was unfortunately short-lived; it was speculated that viewers got frustrated when they found they are unable to view everything simultaneously during the feature film showing. This speculation is not true today, as it can easily be refuted by the popularity of OmniMax theaters[1].

[1] http://www.imax.com/

2.3 Panorama in Europe and the United States

The reception and development of the panorama were somewhat varied from country to country. Here we summarize some of the highlights that occurred in Great Britain, France, Germany, and the United States. Many more details can be found in Oettermann's book.

2.3.1 Panorama in Britain

Britain is where the panorama was first introduced as a popular art form. Robert Barker, an Irishman, was the first person to popularize the panorama. His first panoramic painting, that of Carton Hill, spanned half a circle, but full circular panoramas were to follow. The panorama of London (1792) was a success; this was followed by the construction of the Leicester Square rotunda in 1793, which housed other successes such as "London Howe's Victory" and "Glorious First of June" (1795).

One of Barker's sons, Henry Aston, who was a graduate from the Royal Academy of Art and a frequent traveller, followed his footsteps. Henry Barker's more significant successes were "The Battle of Waterloo" (1815) and "The Coronation of George IV" (1822). He was also the business co-owner with John Burdford at the Strand, which later became the Strand Theatre in 1831.

The success of the panorama had attracted a number of competitors such as Robert Ker Porter and John Thomas Serres. However, after the panorama fad in London had subsided, only two permanent rotundas remained, with one in Leicester Square and the other being the Strand.

No new panoramas were painted in England between 1880 and 1900. By 1900, there was only one single panorama left in London, namely "The Battle of Trafalgar," which still exists today. That piece of work measures forty feet by twelve feet and was painted in the years 1828-29 by W.L. Wyllie.

2.3.2 Panorama in France

It was Robert Fulton, an American artist, inventor, and entrepreneur, who introduced the panorama to France. On April 26, 1799 he was granted a patent giving him exclusive rights to panoramic painting for the next decade (Figure 2.4). At the same time, the construction of two rotundas started in "Le Jardin des Capucines" which became one of the most popular places in Paris. One of the rotundas opened in September 1799, and was shortly followed by the other. The exhibits there became popular with the Parisians. Such was the popularity of the panorama that the Institute of France had appointed a commission to gauge the cultural value of this new art form; the resulting report was a highly positive one.

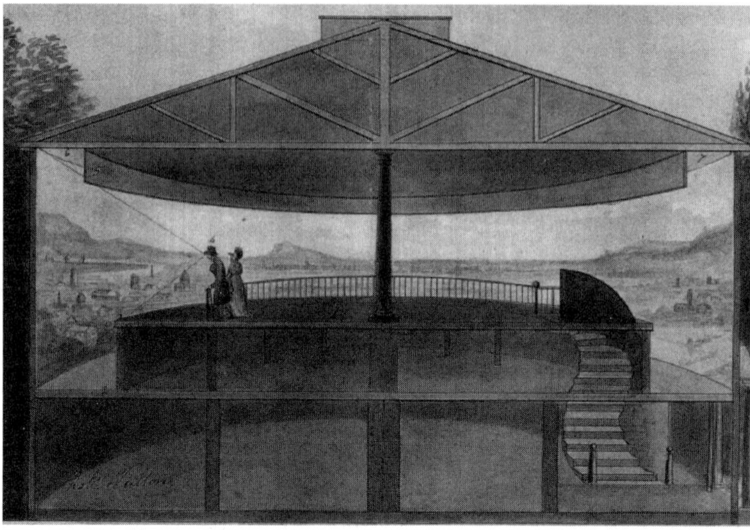

FIGURE 2.4. Robert Fulton's detailed description of the panorama or the art of drawing, painting and exhibiting a circular picture (1799 certificate, coloured pencil, National Institute of the Industrial Property, Paris).

In 1799, Robert Fulton sold all his rights to his fellow American J.W. Thayer and his wife. On April 26, 1801 Fulton secured a second panorama-related patent, which was valid for fifteen years. Meanwhile, in 1808, James Thayer and P. Prevost constructed a third rotunda which was twice the size of the two former rotundas. In 1810, the first exhibit opened, showing a view of Tilsit. The panorama of the battle of Wagram was later exhibited in the rotunda. This particular exhibition pleased Napoleon so much that he gave orders to produce more panoramas that depict French victories and exhibiting them not only in France, but also in conquered territories. However, the fateful events of 1811 had put an end to this project and even the cultural life of the capital till 1816.

A succession of "orama"s appeared in the late 1820s: cosmoramas, georamas, dioramas, uranoramas, neoramas, to name a few more prominent ones. Among all these, the neorama was most closely related to the original circular paintings. Pierre Alaux, as a panorama painter, worked with Prevost, Bouton and Daguerre, took up the diorama idea and combined it with the panorama to give birth to the neorama. His first picture showed St. Peter's interior in Rome. Companies were founded and more rotundas built, thanks to the panorama business.

One of the more curious exhibits was the panorama "Le Vengeur," which was unveiled the 26 May 1892 (Figure 2.5). It features the battle of Queffant (an event which took place a hundred years earlier), and was set up at the rotunda Davious at the Champs Elysees. What was interesting was that the platform was a reproduction of the deck of the ship, and during the

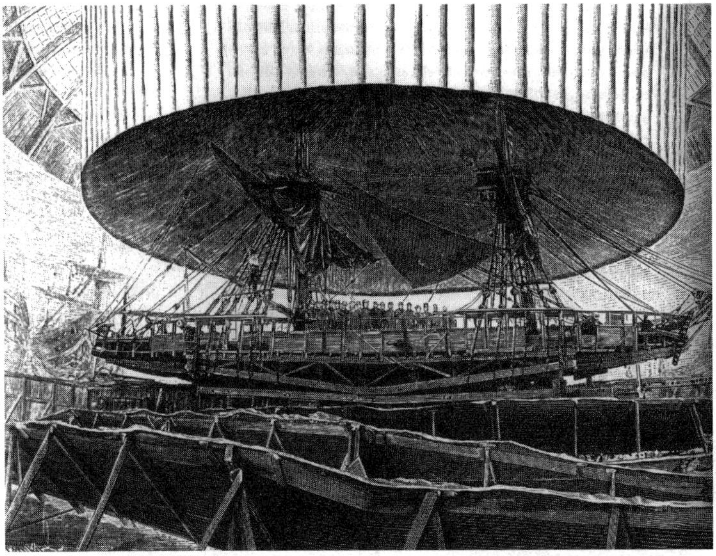

FIGURE 2.5. Platform of the panorama "Le Vengeur," from *La Nature* 20, July 20, 1892.

exhibition, it was moved using hydraulic jacks to give the feeling of rolling and pitching.

The 1900 Universal Exposition held in Paris featured innovations such as the photorama of the Lumiere Brothers, the cineorama of Grimoin-Sanson, the stereorama, the pleorama, and the mareorama (the last also known as "illusive voyage"). Unfortunately, decreasing public interest in the panorama in the ensuing years led to its disappearance.

2.3.3 Panorama in Germany

The first exhibit which took place in Germany was the Panorama of London in 1799. It was held in Berlin and Leipzig, and received extensive press coverage. In the same year, Johan Ada Breysig, a German painter, claimed in one of his books that he and not Robert Barker was the first to invent the panorama. The Panorama of London was quickly followed by the Nausorama, which was a slightly altered picture of Robert Barker's "The Grand Fleet at Spithead." Other exhibits such as "The Battle of Abukir" and "The Panorama of Toulon" also generated a significant amount of public interest.

Germany had lagged behind France in terms of artistic output because of the lack of money and sizeable taxes imposed on artists. In addition, the German infrastructure for panorama exhibits at that time could not handle huge panoramas. To compensate, the artists there reduced the panorama format, giving birth to the miniature panorama. These new formats are more portable and can be exhibited in smaller spaces, which was more cost-efficient. Unfortunately, as more and more amateurs were lured by the lucrative side of miniatures, quality suffered and contributed to its downfall.

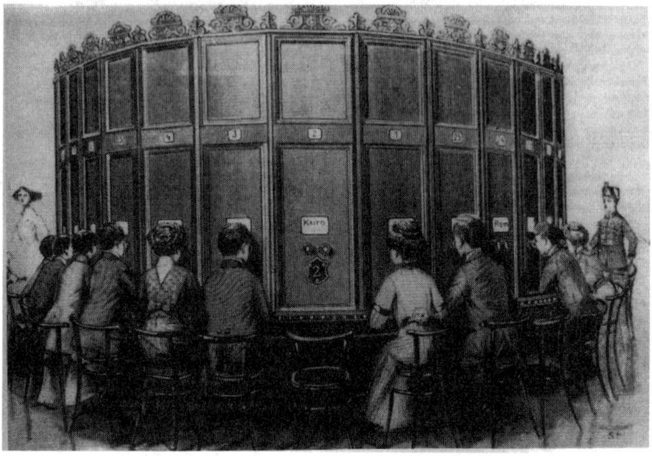

FIGURE 2.6. The Kaiser panorama.

The new technique of photography which gave the public a visual information on distant places and important events eventually replaced painted panoramas. This technique, implemented in the form of the Kaiser panorama (Figure 2.6), was created by a physicist named August Fuhrmann in 1883. Its success was tremendous and it lasted until 1939; several such shows were also held outside of Germany, such as Bavaria and Austria.

Fuhrmann founded an enterprise based on this show. Individual franchisers bought the rights to use the name and equipment, and photographers were sent to exotic places to film events and locations. This type of photojournalism was not only popular, but was deemed to be the most accurate visual account of people and events at that time. War had unfortunately put an end to popularity of the Kaiser panorama. The panorama rotundas, which were huge structures, were initially left vacant, and then were demolished and replaced with apartments.

2.3.4 Panorama in the United States

John Vanderlyn (1776-1852) was one of the first American artists to study in Paris. He brought back with him the idea of panoramic art, and built the first rotunda in 1818 at his own expense on land leased from the city of New York. The first exhibit, "The Battle of Paris," did not fare well. A year later, he exhibited his own painting "Palace and Gardens of Versailles," whose circular length measured an impressive 3,000 feet. However, it was not long before this exhibit was replaced by another, called "View of Hell."

Frederick Cartherwood built the second rotunda in New York City, and he had better success than Vanderlyn; his Panorama of Jerusalem was a huge success. This encouraged him to purchase three pictures that depicted Niagara Falls, Lima, and Thebes. Since he was fond of the Mayan ruins, he embarked on an expedition trip with Stephens to Central America in 1839. Upon their return in 1842, they exhibited their treasures in a form of a panoramic painting that depict carvings, vases, and sculptures. This exhibition did not last long, as it was soon destroyed by a fire.

At that time, Americans have more local tastes; they preferred paintings that depict the vast American frontiers over those that feature ruins and castles from faraway places. They liked the moving panoramas, which also tend to be more easily transportable and set up than their huge European counterparts. Clarkson Stanfield and David Roberts popularized these moving pictures which glorified the river and its banks, e.g., Samuel Adams Hudson's "Panorama of Ohio."

The popularity of the moving panorama and financial success that it enjoyed attracted imitators. In spite of this, the moving panoramas continued to interest the public and artists could exhibit their works. Among the more prominent panoramas were "The Battle of Gettysburg" (1886), "Paradise Lost" (1891), and "The Destruction of Babylon" (1893). The only panoramas that have survived in the United States are "The Battle of Atlanta" (currently in Atlanta) and "The Battle of Gettysburg" (currently being exhibited in a rotunda at a New York park).

2.4 From Panoramic Art to Panoramic Technology

Historically, the panoramic paintings as described in Sections 2.1 and 2.3 were basically regarded as an art form to be appreciated and enjoyed by the masses. Occasionally, they were used as a medium to inform and educate. Their creation was very laborious and they often require very large structures to house them. Exhibiting them was a very expensive proposition. This particular art form was initially intriguing as a novelty, but like any other fad, fell out of favor after a while.

As time passed, people found progressively more and more ingenious means of capturing panoramic images of real scenes without the painstaking manual process of painting or the use of elaborate structures to house multiple photographs or projectors. As indicated earlier in Section 2.2, one of the more promising developments is the use of higher fields-of-view cameras.

2.4.1 Panoramic Cameras

The first panoramic camera was invented by P. Puchberger of Austria in 1843. It was a handcrank driven swing lens panoramic camera capable of capturing a 150° image. The rotating camera invention of M. Garella of England in 1857 extended the field of view of capture to a full 360°.

Puchberger's camera belongs to a class of *swing lens cameras*. The lens of a swing lens camera is constructed so that it pivots around an axis of rotation while the rest remains stationary. Because the camera is stationary, however, the maximum field of view is typically limited to be between 120° and 150°. On the other hand, *rotating cameras*, of which Garella's camera is the first of its kind, do not have this limitation.

The classes of swing lens and rotating camera involve moving parts; another class of cameras, namely *extra wide angle cameras*, does not rely on moving parts for panoramic capture. One of the earliest camera with very wide angle capture is T. Sutton's Panoramic Camera that was invented in 1858. It uses a spherical lens filled with water to achieve the field of view of 120°.

The advent of computers and digitizable video cameras opened up possibilities for more kinds of configurations that allow omnidirectional capture. This is because distortions that may result can be digitally corrected either off-line or on the fly rather easily, once the warping parameters are known. Many of the more recent non-moving camera configurations are *catadioptric*, i.e., they use a combination of mirrors and lenses. In the next section, we describe a sample of different omnidirectional camera systems. This section will be necessarily brief because descriptions of such systems can be found in subsequent chapters in this book.

2.4.2 Omnidirectional Vision Sensors

D.W. Rees is probably the first to patent an omnidirectional capturing system using a hyperboloid mirror and a normal perspective camera in 1970 [224]. Once the mirror shape and camera parameters are known, parts of the captured image can be unwarped to yield correct perspective views. This configuration, which has a unique center of projection, has also been used in other more recent systems [306, 265]. Another system which yields a unique center of projection is the paraboloid mirror and telecentric lens combination (Chapter 4). A conic mirror setup has also been used [302], but this unfortunately does not produce images with a single unique virtual projection center. As a result, images taken with such a conic mirror setup contain parallax. Ishiguro and his colleagues have worked on different designs, as described in Chapter 3. Rotating cameras have also been used to create panoramic images, and many examples exist (e.g., Chapters 13 and 17). There are currently many companies which offer products to create digital panoramic images from rotated cameras (e.g., QuickTimeVR[2], Enroute Imaging's QuickStitch and PowerStitch[3], Panoscan[4], and Picture-Works' Spin Panorama and VideoBrush[5], just to name a few).

So far all the omnidirectional systems mentioned in this section are those of single camera. There are also multiple camera systems as well, and they have the advantage of being able to produce higher resolution panoramic images than their single camera counterparts. For example, D. McCutchen described a dodecahedral imaging system in his 1991 patent. In principle, the twelve cameras are located in the centers of the pentagonal surfaces and positioned to look outwards, thus covering the entire visual sphere. In 1996, V.S. Nalwa patented a system of cameras and mirrors that result in a single virtual projection center. The implemented system has four cameras looking up to an inverted pyramid whose four sides are mirrors. On the other hand, iMove[6] uses an outward-looking six-camera configuration to capture spherical video, in the same spirit as McCutchen's design. Of course, multiple rotating camera configurations also exist, such as that described in Chapter 9.

2.5 The Use of Mirrors in Paintings

Present day omnidirectional imaging systems use a wide variety of mirrors to provide panoramic fields of view. Long before such imaging systems existed, the fascination with reflections and light effects were manifested in paintings that feature or require non-planar mirrors. In this section, we provide a short overview of such paintings. Of course, these paintings were inspired by actual mirrors.

2.5.1 The Evolution of Mirrors

In ancient times, mirrors were created out of polished thin metal sheets, and had wooden handles. These mirrors were very small, between 15 to 20 cm, and were usually decorated with depictions of mythological scenes. Egypt, Greece and ancient Rome used these mirrors made of bronze, silver and sometimes gold; the mirrors were for personal use and for decoration. At that time, the ancients also knew how to make glass mirrors coated with lead. Such excavated items were convex and very small, between 2 to 7 cm

[2]http://www.apple.com/quicktime/qtvr/
[3]http://www.enroute.com/
[4]http://www.panoscan.com/
[5]http://www.pictureworks.com/dphome.html
[6]http://www.imoveinc.com

in diameter. Historians think that these were used more as jewelry than as mirrors.

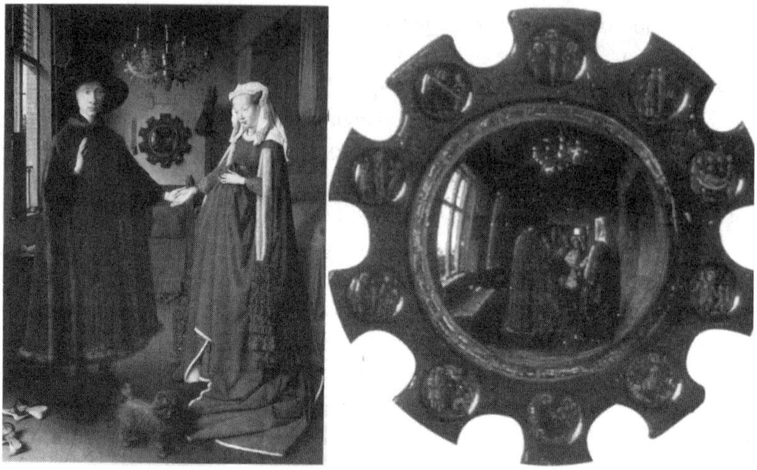

FIGURE 2.7. Left: "The wedding of Giovanni Arnolfini," oil on wood (Jan van Eyck, 1390-1441), National Gallery, London. The mirror can be seen between the two figures. Right: Mirror, magnified. The image of the painter holding the hand of a child can be seen in the mirror. The mirror represents both "the eye of the artist and the eye of God."

The medieval mirrors as depicted by painters of that time were small and domed, with poor reflective qualities but nevertheless still considered better than the metal counterparts. These small mirrors, called "witch mirrors," were depicted in paintings such as the famous van Eyck painting "Wedding of Giovanni Arnolfini" (Figure 2.7) and the painting "The praetor and his wife" of Quentin Metsys (Figure 2.8).

These mirrors were typically built by blowing to create a ball of glass and then, once the mirror is cold, applying a thin coat of lead. Lead was replaced by tin and in the 16th century, mercury replaced both metals. While these mirrors were far from being perfect and never did replace the metal mirrors during that period, they can be made bigger and easier to handle. However, their increased use amongst the rich made them popular.

2.5.2 *Mirrors in Paintings*

It was not long before it became tradition to make the mirror a metaphor in a painting. Through mirrors, the painter ponders about the nature of the image, on its genesis and relation to reality. The mirror, in the history of art, has become a tool for abstract reflection.

Up until the 16th century, the glass mirror was very small, rare, expensive, and imperfect. Throughout the subsequent centuries, its use had

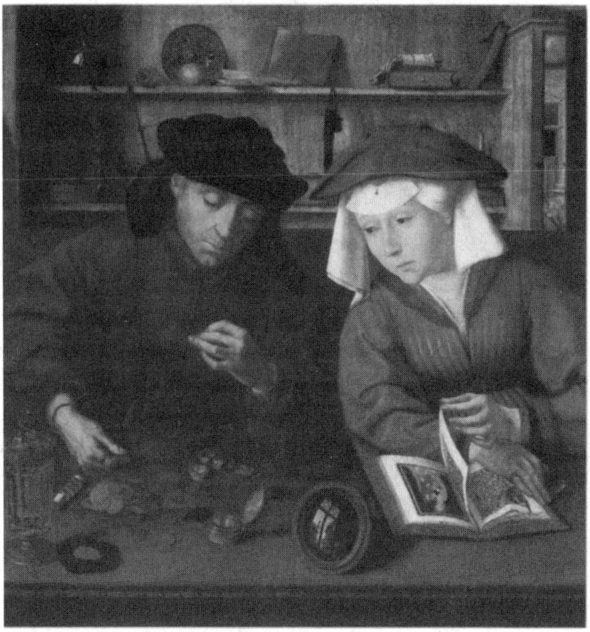

FIGURE 2.8. "The praetor and his wife," oil on wood (Quentin Metsys, 1466-1530). The mirror provides a reflected view of a larger scene not captured elsewhere in the painting. Courtesy of Louvres Museum, Paris.

changed, from the initial work of the medieval painter dedicated to the worship of God, to the one of the Renaissance working on establishing the rules of perspective, and finally to current artists experimenting with its reflective properties. A mirror has been regarded as a "prosthetic" eye that allows the painter to see or convey what is normally hidden, or to create illusions.

During the medieval period, the mirror became a highly religious symbol; God is compared to a pure mirror that contains everything before it was even created. Subsequently, in the Renaissance period, such religious symbolism faded, to be replaced by a regard of the mirror as an instrument of separation and distance. While the Flamand and Italian painters do not use mirrors in the same way, they both regard the mirror as a mediatory between the material and the spiritual. In the painting "The praetor and his wife" (Figure 2.8), Quentin Metsys placed at the center of the painting a small spherical mirror that illustrates the ability of the painter to reproduce the real and to change the scale of the observed space.

For a long time, mirrors were rare and expensive, but they are always used as a tool for painters. Since the 15th century, the artist had been using it to find the best vantage point to visualize the subject. By moving the mirror, he can recenter the viewpoint relative to his subject. In the painting itself, the mirror can enlarge space and allows visualization outside the normal field of view. This is true for convex mirrors. Mirrors can also be used to breach the limits of space and time in a painting, as well as change the rules of perspective. In the painting "The praetor and his wife," two perspectives can be seen; the first one is linear and the other one is curvilinear (in the mirror). The rest of the room can be seen within the painting.

2.5.3 Anamorphosis

An *anamorphosis* is a distorted image that can only appear as undistorted if viewed using a strategically placed mirror of a certain shape. The anamorphosis is a result of a very simple idea. Just as correct shapes can look distorted when reflected on a nonplanar mirror, by applying certain rules of reflection, it is possible to distort the correct shapes so that their reflection is "correct." Secret messages and pictures have been encrypted in this manner.

The anamorphosis is based on elementary geometry, and uses the fact that the appearance of objects changes from one position to another. The catoptric[7] anamorphosis is fascinating not only because it reveals what is hidden, but it also offers two contradictory ways of perceiving reality. In fact, the eye perceives the distorted and its correction version on the mirror, and simultaneously understands both the illusion and the mechanism of the illusion.

2.6 Concluding Remarks

We have highlighted what we regard as interesting and significant panoramic-related events and creations over time, starting with panoramic art, moving on to recent inventions of omnidirectional cameras and methods, and ending with use of mirrors in art. It is clear that there were many different innovations that have brought us to this current state-of-the-art in omnidirectional imaging. It is also instructive for us to learn about past developments in this area so that we can forge ahead using (the many) learned lessons of the past.

In this digital age, panoramas are created almost effortlessly. We have high resolution digital cameras, specialized wide-angle imaging devices, and sophisticated stitching software to help us create such panoramas. These, with web-enabled computers, have brought digital panoramas into our homes. There are, however, important questions that relate to the problems

[7]The word catoptric means "being or using a mirror to focus light" (from Merriam-Webster's dictionary).

of limited bandwidth and computational power to perform more sophisticated 3D-related functions, as well as the issue of representation. There are also the less technical and more sociological issues that relate to changing the mindset of consumers to fully embrace the use of panoramic visualization.

The remaining chapters in this book do not really address these bandwidth and sociological issues. Rather, they describe a variety of recent, innovative work that enable present-day digital panoramic images to be created and used.

2.7 Additional Online Resources

A website that provides interesting information and related online links on the cyclorama, cineorama, mareorama, and myriorama is www.cinemedia.net/SFCV-RMIT-Annex/rnaughton/CYCLORAMA.html. For more information on the art of anamorphosis, the reader can refer to websites such as www.anamorphosis.com/, www.kellyhoule.com/explanation.htm, and www.skillteam.com/skillteam/SKTWeb.ns4/all/Anamor_What_Ana_ana.html.

A good resource for panoramic photographers is the International Association of Panoramic Photographers' website panphoto.com. It has links to stitching products, articles, and information on cameras. An informative article on the historical development of panoramic cameras can be found in panphoto.com/TimeLine.html, while a description of the types of panoramic cameras can be found in ally.ios.com/~sstern29/cameras.html. The website www.cis.upenn.edu/~kostas/omni.html has a comprehensive list of omnidirectional-related projects and companies.

2.8 Acknowledgment

The sources for this chapter are:

1. E. Michaux (Coll. Champs Visuels), Du Panorama Pictural Au Cinéma Circulaire, *Origines et histoire d'un autre cinéma 1785-1998*, Paris, France, 1998.

2. S. Ottermann, *Das Panorama, Die Geschichte eines Massenmediums*, Francfort, Syndikat, 1980. Also available in English as: *The Panorama: History of a Mass Medium*, D. L. Schneider, Zone Books, New York, 1997.

3. "Le XIX siécle des Panorama," Bernard Comment, Ed Adam Biro, Paris, 1993.

4. “La Peinture en cinémascope,” Beaux Art Magazine, Paris, no. 115, 1995, pp. 140-143.

5. Encyclopedia Britannica.

6. “L’art de depeindre: la peinture hollandaise au XVII sciécle,” Alpers Svetlana, Gallimard 1990, Paris.

7. “Le miroir,” Baltrusaitis Jurgis, Ed Le seuil, 1978, Paris.

8. “Les miroirs 1650-1900,” Child Graham, Ed Flammarion 1990, Paris.

9. “Anamorphoses,” Baltrusaitis Jurgis, Ed Flammarion 1990, Paris.

10. “Anamorphoses,” Mathey François and Levie S.H., catalogue d’exposition, 27 February-9 May 1976, Museum des Arts Decoratifs, Paris.

11. “A Cache cache avec l’art,” Bolton Linda, Ed Circonflexe, 1994, Paris.

12. W. McBride, http://panphoto.com/TimeLine.html

13. S. Stern, http://ally.ios.com/~sstern29/cameras.html

In addition, Shree Nayar and Pal Greguss have been very helpful in identifying many of the patents on panoramic imaging technology described in this chapter. Shree Nayar also pointed out the interesting area of art using mirrors.

Section I

Catadioptric Panoramic Systems

The word "catadioptric" merely refers to the use of glass elements and mirrors in an imaging system. In photography, a catadioptric lens is also known as a *mirror lens.* In the next two sections, hardware-oriented solutions to generating panoramic images are described. This section focuses on *central, single-capture systems* that are designed to cover a wide field of view with just a single image capture and with no parallax.

Chapter 3 (Ishiguro) starts with a historical overview of catadioptric panoramic sensors; it also discusses the features and design problems of previously developed omnidirectional vision sensors. Subsequently, it details the design of a low-cost and compact omnidirectional vision sensor and describes a new application that uses such a sensor.

Chapter 4 (Baker and Nayar) examines the theoretical problem of determining the shapes of the mirrors that result in a single effective center of projection, i.e., a parallax-free configuration. This allows pure perspective images to be derived from the images captured using such a configuration. More specifically, the class of single-lens, single-mirror cameras is analyzed. A description of all solutions, with reference to many of the previous catadioptric systems, is given. The analysis of spatial resolution is also provided in this chapter. Finally, several implementations of a possible design, which comprises a telecentric lens and paraboloid mirror, is described.

There are basically two lens-mirror combinations that result in an imaging configuration with a unique point of projection (hence the use of the term "central panoramic catadioptric cameras"). They are the telecentric lens and paraboloid mirror combination, and the perspective lens and hyperboloid mirror combination. The first combination has been analyzed to a certain degree in Chapter 4 (Baker and Nayar). Chapter 5 (Pajdla, Svoboda, and Hlaváč), on the other hand, tackles the issue of epipolar geometry for both these combinations. This chapter also suggests normalizing image coordinates when omnidirectional cameras are used to ensure non-bias in computing camera parameters.

The last chapter in this section, namely Chapter 6 (Nayar and Peri), presents a framework for the design and analysis of central catadioptric cameras that use two or more mirrors. The use of multiple mirrors permits folding of the optics, which leads to more compact camera designs than those that use a single mirror. A dictionary of camera designs that use two conic mirrors is presented. This chapter shows that any folded system that uses conic mirrors has a geometrically equivalent system that uses a single conic mirror. This result makes it easy to determine the scene-to-image mapping of a conic-folded system. In addition, it discusses the optical benefits of using folded systems. The chapter concludes with a description of an implemented camera system that provides a hemispherical field of view.

Additional Notes on Chapters

Chapter 3 has originally appeared in the *International Conference on Information Systems, Analysis and Synthesis* in 1998. Parts of Chapter 4 were previously published in the *International Journal of Computer Vision* and the proceedings of the 1997 *IEEE Computer Vision and Pattern Recognition Conference.* A previous version of Chapter 6 was published in the proceedings of the *IEEE Conference on Computer Vision and Pattern Recognition* held in June 1999. The ideas in Chapter 5 have been presented in the *5th European Conference on Computer Vision* held in Freiburg, Germany, and can be found in volume 1406 of *Lecture Notes in Computer Science*, pages 218–232, Springer, June 1998.

3

Development of Low-Cost Compact Omnidirectional Vision Sensors

H. Ishiguro

3.1 Introduction

Physical agents living in complex environments, such as humans and animals, need two types of visual sensing abilities. One is to focus on particular objects with a precise but small retina, the other is to look around the environment with a wide but coarse retina. Both visual sensing mechanisms are required to enable robust and flexible visual behaviors. In particular, the omnidirectional visual information obtained by looking around is necessary to monitor wide areas and to avoid dangerous situations.

On the other hand, cameras developed for TV broadcasting so far are being used for monitoring systems and vision systems of robots in previous computer and robot vision studies. The standard TV cameras, which has a limited visual field of about 30-60°, is suitable for observing local areas, but it cannot be used to observe wide areas all at once. In order to extend the TV camera applications and develop robust and flexible vision systems like those of animals, special cameras which are capable of capturing omnidirectional visual information are needed.

Such *OmniDirectional Vision Sensors* (ODVSs) (or omnidirectional cameras) have been proposed by Rees [224] in the patent submitted to US government in 1970. Then, they have been developed again by Yagi [301], Hong [110] Yamazawa [306] in 1990, 1991 and 1993, respectively. Recently, Nayar [198] has geometrically analyzed the complete class of single-lens single-mirror catadioptric imaging systems and developed an ideal ODVS using a parabola mirror.

However, in the previous works, the researchers developed the ODVSs for the purposes to prototype themselves and to investigate properties of the *OmniDirectional Images* (ODIs) taken with the ODVSs. Therefore, the developed ODVSs were not so compact and their costs were expensive. This paper discusses features of previously developed ODVSs and their designs, then proposes ideas to solve problems of the previous ODVSs. Based on the discussions, this paper also shows designs for *low-cost and*

Compact ODVSs (C-ODVSs). Further, novel vision systems realized by using multiple C-ODVSs are discussed.

3.2 Previous Work

3.2.1 Omnidirectional Vision Sensors

The History

The original idea of the ODVSs using a mirror in combination with a conventional imaging system has been proposed by Rees in U.S. Patent No. 3,505,465 in 1970 [224] (see Figure 3.1(c)). The idea is to use a hyperboloidal mirror for acquiring an ODI which has a single center of projection. That is, the ODI can be transformed into normal perspective images.

In 1990, progress of computer technologies enabled real-time process of vision data and researchers made again several types of ODVSs as vision systems for computers and robots. Yagi and Kawato [301] made an omnidirectional vision sensor using a conic mirror (see Figure 3.1(a)). Hong and others [110] made an omnidirectional vision sensor using a spherical mirror (see Figure 3.1(b)). Their purpose was to navigate mobile robots with the ODVS. The omnidirectional vision of a robot is convenient for detecting moving obstacles around the robot and for localizing itself. Then, Yamazawa and others [306] made again an ODVS using a hyperboloidal mirror. By utilizing the merit of the hyperboloidal mirror that the ODI can be transformed into perspective images, they proposed a monitoring system with the ODVS.

Nayar and Baker [198] theoretically analyzed imaging systems for ODVSs and developed an ideal ODVS using a parabola mirror and a telecentric lens. The ODVS using a hyperboloidal mirror can generate an image taken from a single center of projection in combination with a standard perspective camera. Unfortunately, one of the two focal points of the hyperboloid has to be coincident with the camera center as shown in Figure 3.1(c). This feature makes it difficult to design the ODVS. On the other hand, the imaging system proposed by Nayar and Baker does not have such a demerit since it is using the telecentric lens as shown in Figure 3.1(d). It is well-known that the parabola mirror has a focal point for incident light that is parallel to the main axis of the parabola mirror. Furthermore, the imaging system is superior in acquisition of non-blurred images and it can eliminate internal reflections of a hollow cylindrical or spherical glass which supports the mirror.

Another Method to Acquire ODIs

The ODVSs using mirrors acquire ODIs in real time. However, the resolution is not so high. In order to acquire high resolution ODIs, methods swiveling a camera have been proposed by Sarachik [234] and Ishiguro [136]. The original idea has been given by the panorama camera which takes panoramic scene photographs by swiveling a slit camera. For taking images in a static environment, this method is very effective and it is being recently used in multimedia applications. Another problem of the ODVSs is control of camera parameters, especially control of iris. In the method to swiveling a camera, the camera observes the local environment, but the ODVS observes a wide environment and the ODI taken with the ODVS contains various intensities. Therefore, the camera used in the ODVS need a wide dynamic range.

As discussed here, the ODVS which can take an ODI has several advantages against the previous vision sensors, but it has also two major demerits, the low resolution and the requirement of a wide dynamic range. With current CCD sensors, it is difficult to obtain high resolution ODIs and its dynamic range is not so wide. We need to improve the CCD itself.

3.2.2 Omnidirectional Images

The History

The origin of the methods to acquire an ODI was a panoramic camera which takes omnidirectional photographs though a slit filter attached in the front of the camera lens while swiveling the camera. Zheng and Tsuji [312] used this idea with a CCD camera. The image obtained by arranging image data along a vertical line on the image center is called *Panoramic Image*. They analyzed the features of the panoramic images and proposed applications for mobile robot navigation. When the camera moves along a circular path in the method for acquiring panoramic images, an ODI is obtained. The ODIs is a cylindrical projection and it can contains precise angular information if the camera precisely moves.

Early studies on the ODIs were mainly done by Nelson, Zheng and Ishiguro. Zheng and others [312] proposed a *Circular Dynamic Programming* for identifying features between two ODIs. The circular dynamic programming robustly finds correspondences by iterating a conventional dynamic programming method based on the periodicity of the ODIs. Ishiguro and others [136] proposed two types of *Omnidirectional Stereo*. By rotating a camera along a circular path, motion pallarax is observed by tracking feature points on the image plane and omnidirectional range information can be obtained. This stereo method does not have any blind spots outside the circular path. Another stereo is realized with two ODIs taken at different locations. Although the method using two ODIs has a problem of feature identification, it can obtain more precise omnidirectional range information.

The Optical Flow Field

The flow field of ODIs is also interesting properties. Nelson and others [200] analyzed the flow field of the Gauss sphere retina and proposed methods to estimate camera motion parameters. On the other hand, Ishiguro and others focused upon just the FOEs and proposed methods to precisely navigate mobile robots [136] and to estimate robot motion parameters [134] based on the important feature of the ODIs that two FOEs, or FOE and FOC, are observed in the flow field and the angle between them is 180°.

The Periodicity

An ODI is a periodical signal around the rotation axis. That is, Fourier transform of the ODI does not require window functions. This means the transform is precise and efficient data compression is possible for the ODIs. By applying the Fourier transform, an ODI can be divided into magnitude and phase components. The magnitude and phase components depend on the location of the ODVS and the direction of the reference axis of the ODVS, respectively.

Based on the magnitude and phase components, mobile robot navigation which does not refer to the internal sensor data can be realized [133]. First, the robot moves randomly in the environment and takes ODIs at various locations. Then, it executes Fourier transform for the ODIs and divides them into magnitude and phase components. By comparing the magnitude components of the ODIs, positions where the ODIs are taken can be estimated. The positions cannot be precisely estimated but it is topologically correct. The map which represents the topological positions of the observation points can be used for the robot navigation. Here, in order to use the map, the robot needs to know the its direction against the environment. The direction can be estimated from the phase components of the ODIs. That is, the robot can memorize locations as a map and navigate itself by using it only with the ODVS.

3.3 Designs of ODVSs

An ODVS is consists of two major components, a mirror which is symmetrical on rotation and an apparatus which supports the mirror. This section discusses merits and demerits on various designs of the two major components of previously developed ODVSs

3.3.1 Designs of Mirrors

There are four types of the previously developed mirrors as shown in Figure 3.1. Merits and demerits of the mirrors can be discussed from the following viewing points:

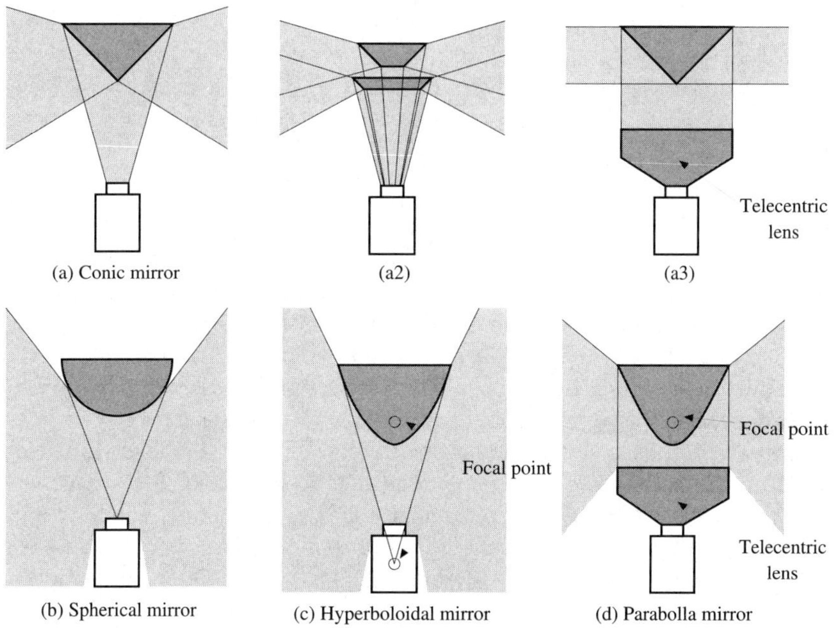

FIGURE 3.1. Omnidirectional mirrors

- Whether the mirror can generate an ODI which has a single center of projection. (The ODI can be transformed to normal perspective images.)
- How small the astigmatism of the optical system consisting of the mirror and a camera is.
- Whether the optical system uses a standard lens and camera.
- How large the vertical viewing angle is.

Spherical Mirror

Generally, mirrors are made by depositing aluminum film onto a shaped glass. An important issue in the machining is how easy it is to process the glass. A normal lens is a part of a spherical glass, therefore it is easy to make spherical mirrors with the conventional lens process.

In addition to the merit in the machining, another important merit of the spherical mirror is the astigmatism. Comparing with other mirrors as shown in Figure 3.1, the astigmatism is rather small since it can be considered as a flat surface near the optical axis of the camera (of course, it is not small in the peripheral). Further, as discussed in the next section, the spherical mirror does not require a long focal depth for acquiring a focused image. That is, the spherical mirror is superior to making low cost ODVSs which can acquire clear images.

However, the ODI acquired with the spherical mirror does not have a single center of projection and cannot be transformed into normal perspective images. The vertical viewing angle is also so large. Although the ODVS can observe over the horizontal plane, the image is distorted in the peripheral of the ODI.

Conic Mirror

A conic mirror is second to the spherical mirror in the easy machining. The feature of the conic mirror is to have normal reflection in the vertical direction. Therefore, it is easy to combine several mirrors. For example, stereo images can be acquired as shown in Figure 3.1(a2). Further, the conic mirror enables a special optical system which observes horizontally in combination with a telcentric lens as shown in Figure 3.1(a3).

However, the astigmatism is large and the ODI cannot be transformed into normal perspective images. Further, it needs a long focal depth to acquire focused ODIs. A spherical mirror has a focal point like a normal lens, on the other hand, the conic mirror does not have it and needs a lens which is close to a pinhole (the details are discussed in the next section).

Hyperboloidal Mirror

Machining of a hyperbolidal mirror is difficult, but it has a single center of projection. An ODI taken with the hyperboloidal mirror can be transformed to normal perspective images, cylindrical images, and so on. Further, if the curvature is small, the astigmatism is not so large.

The hyperboloidal mirror is the best for optical systems using normal cameras. However, it has a serious demerits that the design is not so flexible since the focal point of the hyperboloid needs to be set on the camera center.

Parabola Mirror

An ideal optical system can be realized with a parabola mirror and telecentric lens. The optical system has a single center of projection and the astigmatism is small for a small curvature. Further, the parabola mirror is the best for acquiring focused ODIs. The telecentric lens also brings two merits. Since the projection is orthogonal, the distance between the mirror and the lens can be set flexibly in the design and the lens eliminates internal reflections of a glass cylinder or sphere which supports the mirror (the details are discussed in the next subsection).

However, it is a demerit for making a compact and low-cost system to use the telecentric lens. The telecentric lens is generally expensive and the size is not so small.

Table 3.1 summarizes features of the four mirrors. In the table, the focal depth means the range in which the camera should be able to acquire non-blurred images for the mirror. The vertical viewing ranges are based on

	Machining cost	Astigmatism	Focal depth	Vertical viewing range	Single center of projection	Lens
S	*Low*	*Small*	*Short*	-90 ... 10	No	N.
C	*Low*	Large	Long	-45 ... 45	No	N.
HS	High	*Small*	*Short*	-90 ... 10	*Yes*	N.
HL	High	Large	Long	-90 ... 45	*Yes*	N.
PS	High	*Small*	*Short*	-90 ... 10	*Yes*	T.
PL	High	Large	*Short*	-90 ... 45	*Yes*	T.

S: Spherical mirror
C: Conic mirror
HS: Hyperboloidal mirror with a small curvature
HL: Hyperboloidal mirror with a large curvature
PS: Parabola mirror with a small curvature
PL: Parabola mirror with a large curvature
N.: Normal, T.: Telecentric

TABLE 3.1. Comparison between various mirrors.

our experience. -90 *degrees* and 0 *degrees* are directions to observe downward and horizontally, respectively. From the view point of applications, a summary is given as follows:

Spherical mirror ODVSs using spherical mirrors are suitable for observing objects which locate in the same height as the ODVSs or acquiring clear ODIs of objects locating under the ODVS. Further, since the cost of machining is low, the mass production can be performed.

Conic mirror The conic mirror is useful for acquire ODIs of which vertical visual field is limited.

Hyperboloidal mirror In combination with a normal lens, the mirror can generate ODIs which can be transformed to normal perspective images. Therefore, it can be applied to monitoring applications.

Parabola mirror The machining cost and the cost of the telecentric lens is, generally, high. However, it is an ideal optical system to acquire ODIs.

3.3.2 Design of a Supporting Apparatus

Another important component of the ODVS is an apparatus which supports the mirror as shown in Figure 3.1. For the supporting apparatus, there are two requirements:

1. Eliminating internal reflections by the supporting apparatus.

2. Precise surface finish for acquiring non-distorted ODIs.

In previous works, the following three types of the supporting apparatuses were used:

- Clear cylinder made from glass or plastic
- Clear sphere made from glass or plastic
- Clear cylinder/sphere and a telecentric lens

Many types of ready-made clear hollow cylinders made from glass and plastic are available and the surface precision is high. However, the clear hollow cylinder has a serious problem of internal reflections as shown in Figure 3.2. One of the ideas to solve this problem is to use a telecentric lens. Since the optical array of the telecentric lens is parallel to the surface of the cylinder, there is no projections of the internal reflections on the ODI.

Another idea is to support the mirror with a clear hollow sphere of which center locates on the focal point of the mirror. This idea has been proposed by Yamazawa and others [306] and applied to an ODVS using a hyperboloidal mirror. However, the problem is in the precision of the surface. Generally, precise machining for the clear hollow sphere is difficult.

As discussed here, there are two solutions: clear hollow cylinder with a telecentric lens and clear hollow sphere with a hyperboloidal mirror. But, these can be applied to particular ODVSs. More general idea is needed. The next section proposes such an idea.

3.4 Trial Production of C-ODVSs

Based on the discussion in the previous sections, this section proposes low-cost and compact ODVSs (C-ODVSs). The author considers ODVSs which can be used in various applications should satisfy the following requirements:

1. Small size including the camera
2. Low machining cost
3. Small astigmatism
4. Short focal depth
5. Using standard lenses and cameras

For the requirements, the authors originally developed the following two methods:

- **General optical mechanism to eliminate the internal reflection.**
- **A process to make mirrors from metal**

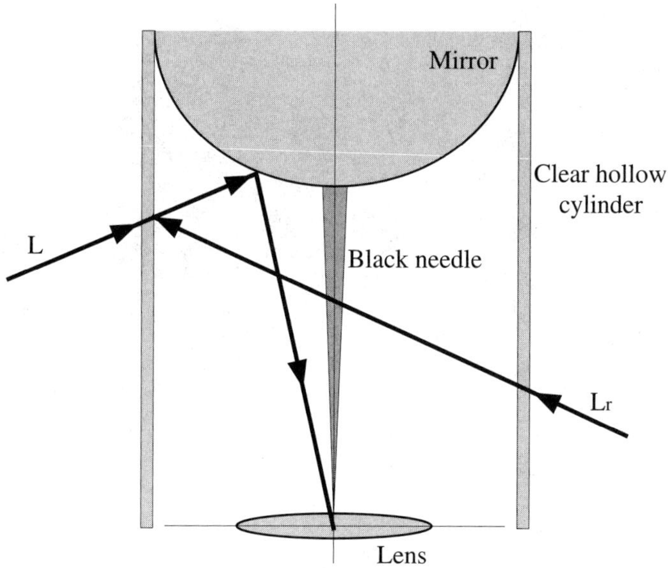

FIGURE 3.2. Elimination of the internal reflections with a black needle.

3.4.1 Eliminating Internal Reflections

From the view point of precision, the clear hollow cylinder is the best, however, it has a problem of internal reflections. And further, utilization of the telecentric lens make the size of the ODVS large and the cost is also high.

An idea to eliminate internal reflections by the clear hollow cylinder is to equip a black needle along the main axis of the cylinder. As shown in Figure 3.2, the light, which reflects on the internal surface of the clear hollow cylinder and then passes through the camera center, closes the main axis of the cylinder. Therefore, the black needle equipped along the main axis completely eliminates internal reflections. The idea is very simple but very effective as shown in Figure 3.3. In Figure 3.3(a), several double projections of fluorescent lamps are observed. On the other hand, the ODI taken with the black needle does not have such double projections as shown in Figure 3.3(b).

3.4.2 Making Mirrors from Metal

A standard process to make mirrors from glass is iterative polishing of a glass block and coating with aluminum. Therefore, it takes much time and cost for making a large-curvature mirror.

Another method is to make the mirrors from metal by using a precise NC machine. The major problem in this case is the precision of the surface. In order to make a precise mirror, careful selection of metal materials and

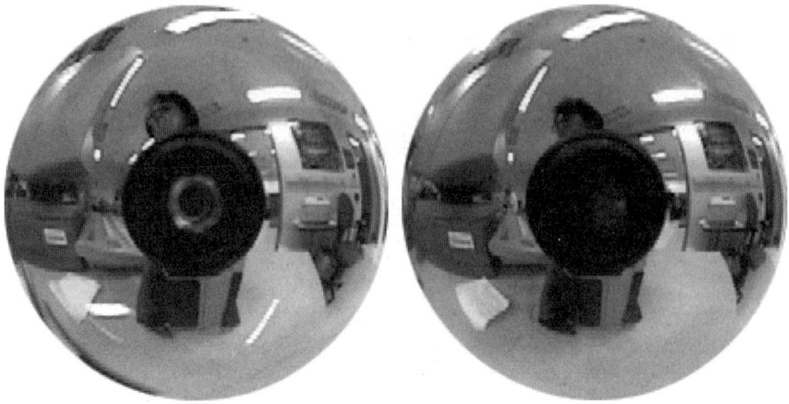

(a) Without the black needle (b) Withthe black needle

FIGURE 3.3. Experimentation on internal reflections.

control of the NC machine is required. With several trials, the author and others have determined to use brass as the metal material and learned empirical knowledge to precisely control the NC machine.

After the machining with the NC machine, coating is performed. Aluminum coating is precise but expensive. Therefore, in spite of aluminum coating, the author has performed iterative thin chrome plating and determined the number of the iteration through many trials.

3.4.3 Focusing in an ODVS

For previously developed ODVSs, cameras which have a short focal length are used in order to acquire focused ODIs. That is, the mirror is attached with the closest distance Dm under a condition that the camera acquires focused images for objects locating at infinity, as shown in Figure 3.4(a). And the minimum size of the ODVSs is restricted with the closest distance Dm. For instance, it is difficult to find a ready-made camera which has the closest distance of 10 cm.

For making smaller ODVSs, the mirror needs to be attached with a shorter distance. Actually, the focal depth (or object depth) of standard lens is not zero, and if it is possible to set all focal planes of the mirror for all objects locating with various distances in the focal depth $O_1 - O_2$, the ODVS can acquire focused ODIs with the mirror attached with a close distance D from the camera as shown in Figure 3.4(b).

Let us consider the focal planes of a spherical mirror as an example. As well known, the parallel light is focused with the spherical mirror but the focal point is not single. The focal point describes an epicycloid L_A, which pass through the point F, for the parallel light L_0, L_1 and L_2 in a direction as shown in Figure 3.5(a). In Figure 3.5(a), R is the radius of the spher-

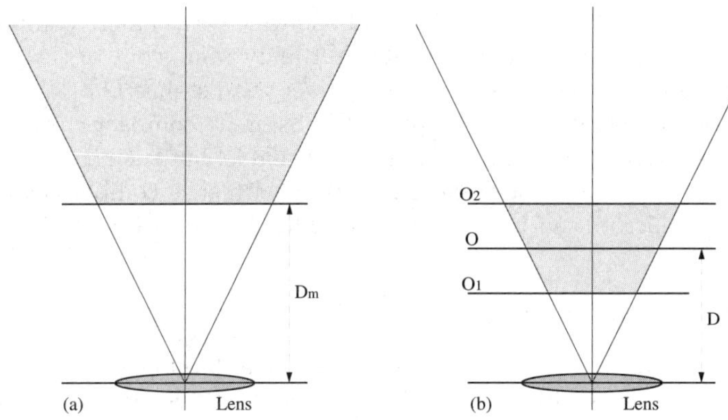

FIGURE 3.4. Focal depth of a camera

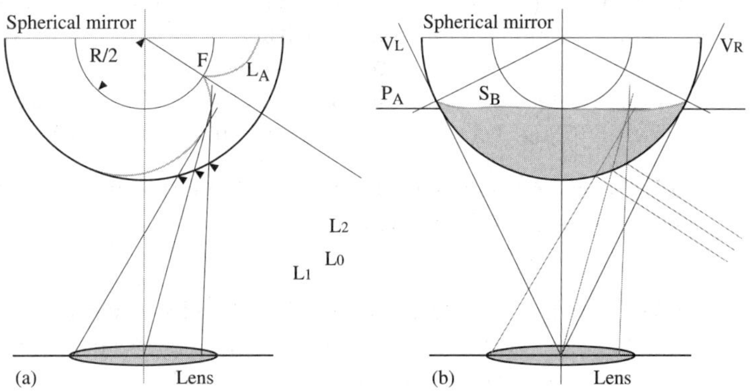

FIGURE 3.5. Focusing on a spherical mirror.

ical mirror. Therefore, images of all objects locating various locations are focused within the gray region encircled with the surface of the spherical mirror and the surface S_B as shown in Figure 3.5(b). In conclusion, if the focal depth covers the gray region, the camera focuses clear images for all objects through the spherical mirror. Especially, in the case of the spherical mirror, the gray region almost locates between the horizontal plane on P_A and the surface of the spherical mirror. In cases of the hyperboloidal and parabola mirrors with little curvatures, they can be considered to be identical with the spherical mirror. However, in cases of the conic, hyperboloidal and parabola mirrors with large curvatures, the gray region is extended along the surfaces of the mirrors and the camera needs a long focal depth for focusing clear ODIs. In order to making compact ODVSs, the spherical mirror is and small-curvature hyperboloidal and parabola mirrors are suitable.

Proper camera selection is also an important issue. For making compact ODVSs, a cameras which has a short distance of Dm shown in Figure 3.4(a) is required. As such a camera, SONY EVI-330 which is a camera component of a standard handy video recorder SONY HandyCam is one of the proper candidates. Although the size is not so compact the distance Dm is less than 10 cm. In order to make more compact ODVSs, more compact cameras are required. Recently, many such cameras are available, but their distance Dm is not sufficiently short. For designing ODVSs with such compact cameras, the spherical mirrors can be used with the idea shown in Figure 3.4(b).

3.4.4 Developed C-ODVSs

Based on the above discussions, the author have developed four types of C-ODVSs as shown in Figure 3.6. Each of the C-ODVSs has the following features:

C-ODVS with a hyperboloidal mirror The second from the left in Figure 3.6. A hyperboloidal mirror with a large curvature is used. The vertical viewing range is about 270 degrees. A black needle is attached for eliminating the internal reflections. It is designed for SONY EVI-330 and the overview is shown in Figure 3.7(a).

C-ODVS with a spherical mirror The third from the left in Figure 3.6. It is designed for SONY EVI-330. The height and diameter are 15 cm and 7cm, respectively.

Ultra C-ODVS with a hyperboloidal mirror The first from the left in Figure 3.6. The curvature of the mirror is small for acquiring clear images and the viewing range is about 190°. It is designed for a camera of RF Co. Ltd. The height and diameter are 3 cm and 4 cm, respectively.

Ultra C-ODVS with a spherical mirror The fourth from the left in Figure 3.6. It is designed for a camera of RF Co. Ltd. and the overview is shown in Figure 3.7(b).

Figure 3.8(a) and (b) show ODIs taken by the C-ODVS with a hyperboloidal mirror and the C-ODVS with a spherical mirror, respectively.

3.5 Applications of ODVSs

3.5.1 Multimedia Applications

In the recording of round table meeting scenes, the previous camera cannot acquire images which contains faces of all participants. The ODVS attached at the center of the table makes it possible. Nishimura and others [203] used the ODVS for recognizing human gestures in a round table meeting. Their

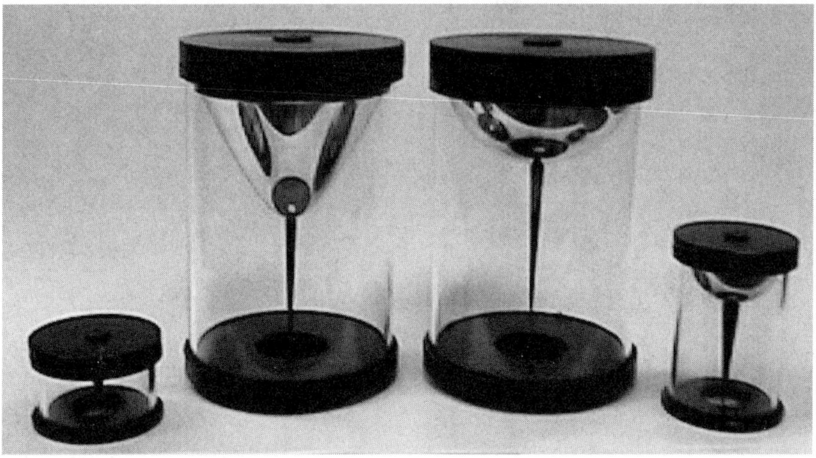

FIGURE 3.6. Four types of C-ODVs.

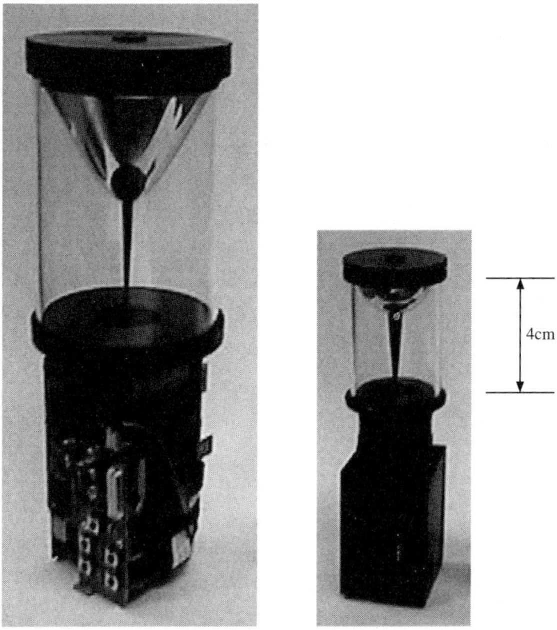

(a) C-ODVS with a hyperboloidal mirror (b) Ultra C-ODVS with a spherical mirror

FIGURE 3.7. C-ODVSs with cameras.

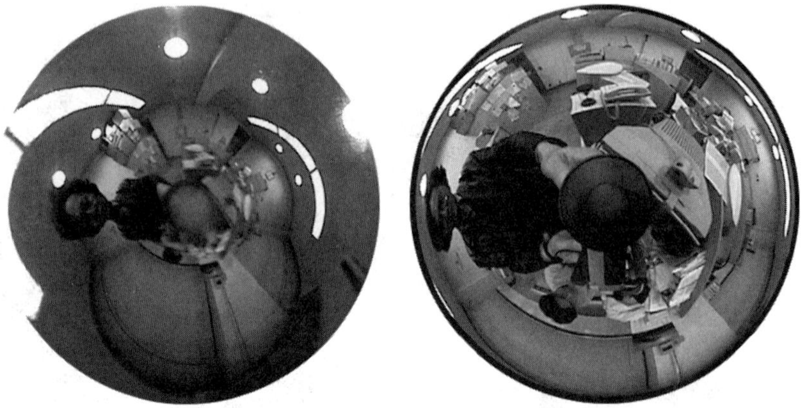

(a) With a hyperboloidal mirror (b) With a spherical mirror

FIGURE 3.8. ODIs.

approach can be extended for several applications. For example, indexed database of round table meetings with the simple human behavior recognition and tele-conference systems which enable communications between groups can be considered.

3.5.2 Monitoring Applications

The ODVS with a hyperboloidal or parabola mirror can be used in spite of the conventional camera system using a pan-tilt gaze controller. The ODI taken with the ODVS can be transformed into perspective images taken in any directions. Although there exist several problems, especially the resolution of the images, the ODVSs can be used as gaze control camera systems. The systems with the ODVSs is very compact and it can change the gaze direction in real time with a powerful computer.

The ODVS has a demerits of the low image resolution, therefore the author considers ODVSs should not be used as TV cameras, but as vision sensors. As an application in which ODVSs are used as vision sensors, a moving object tracking system using multiple ODVSs can be considered [132]. Figure 3.9 shows an overview of the system.

The use of multiple ODVSs solves the following problems of vision systems with the wide viewing range.

1. The wide environment can be covered with a smaller number of ODVSs.

2. The ODVSs can be observed each other, therefore the relative positions of the ODVSs can be precisely estimated with error minimization methods, such as a least square method.

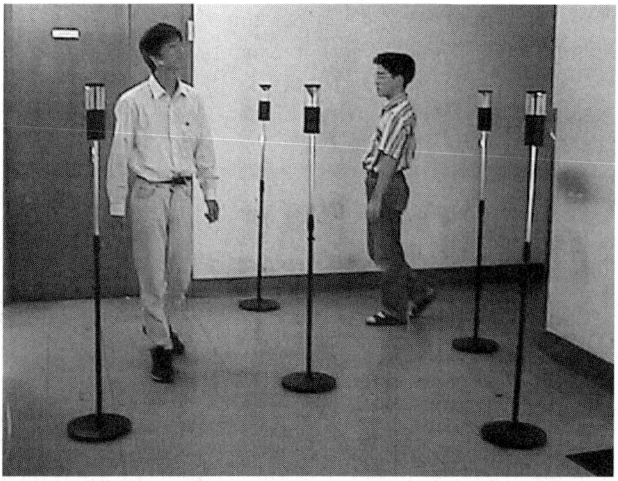

FIGURE 3.9. Distributed vision system for recognizing human behaviors

3. Extended trinocular vision, namely *N-ocular vision* can be realized. With the N-ocular vision, multiple ODVSs can robustly identifies objects between the ODIs.

The robust and real-time tracking system can be developed by using constraints of the environment in addition to the above fundamental merits. For example, this system can be used for human behavior recognition. Previous research approaches for human behavior recognition focused upon rather local behavior, such as facial expressions and gestures. The system which recognizes global behaviors of humans in a room gives useful information to the previous system for recognizing local behaviors.

3.5.3 Mobile Robot Navigation

Other major applications of the ODVS are in mobile robot navigation. The wide viewing range is useful for predicting collisions with moving obstacles. Yagi and others [301] proposed a method to avoid collisions with moving obstacles by continuous observation with the ODVS. In the case where both the robot and obstacles move along linear paths with constant velocities and they collide each other, the viewing angle from the robot to the obstacles is constant. By feeding the viewing angle to the steering, the robot can avoid the collision.

The ODIs are also useful for memorizing particular locations. Hong and others [110] proposed a method for image-based homing. The robot memorizes the goal location with a vertical edge image observed by the ODVS. Then, the robot goes from a distant location toward the goal by comparing input images with the memorized image. This approach is interesting as a method which shows rich properties of ODIs.

Further, ODVSs can be used for other functions of robots, such as pose stabilization and so on. The author considers the most serious problem of previous vision-guided mobile robots is in the limited visual field of the vision sensors. The ODVSs are expected as key tools for solving such difficulties.

3.6 Conclusion

This chapter has discussed features of previously developed omnidirectional vision sensors and proposed designs of low-cost and compact ODVSs. Further, their novel applications have been briefly discussed. Although a few problems are still remained for the ODVSs, the author considers utilization of omnidirectional vision sensor will be a key issue in Computer Vision and Multimedia applications. The detailed information on the ODVSs can be found in http://www.pluto.dti.ne.jp/~accowle1/index.html.

4

Single Viewpoint Catadioptric Cameras

S. Baker and S.K. Nayar

4.1 Introduction

Many applications in computational vision require that a large field of view is imaged. Examples include surveillance, teleconferencing, and model acquisition for virtual reality. A number of other applications, such as ego-motion estimation and tracking, would also benefit from enhanced fields of view. Unfortunately, conventional imaging systems are severely limited in their fields of view. Both researchers and practitioners have therefore had to resort to using either multiple or rotating cameras in order to image the entire scene.

One effective way to enhance the field of view is to use mirrors in conjunction with lenses. See, for example, [224], [47], [197], [301], [110], [85], [306], [28], [194], [195], and [44]. We refer to the approach of using mirrors in combination with conventional imaging systems as *catadioptric* image formation. *Dioptrics* is the science of refracting elements (lenses) whereas *catoptrics* is the science of reflecting surfaces (mirrors) [104]. The combination of refracting and reflecting elements is therefore referred to as catadioptrics.

As noted in [224], [307], [194], and [198], it is highly desirable that a catadioptric system (or, in fact, any imaging system) have a single viewpoint (center of projection). The reason a single viewpoint is so desirable is that it permits the generation of geometrically correct perspective images from the images captured by the catadioptric cameras. This is possible because, under the single viewpoint constraint, every pixel in the sensed images measures the irradiance of the light passing through the viewpoint in one particular direction. Since we know the geometry of the catadioptric system, we can precompute this direction for each pixel. Therefore, we can map the irradiance value measured by each pixel onto a plane at any distance from the viewpoint to form a planar perspective image. These perspective images can subsequently be processed using the vast array of techniques developed in the field of computational vision that assume perspective projection. Moreover, if the image is to be presented to a human, as in [216], it needs to be a perspective image not to appear distorted. Naturally, when the catadioptric imaging system is omnidirectional in its field of view, a single effective viewpoint permits the construction of panoramic images as well as perspective ones.

In this chapter, we take the view that having a single viewpoint is the primary design goal for the catadioptric camera and restrict attention to catadioptric cameras with a single effective viewpoint [12] [13]. However, for many applications, such as robot navigation, having a single viewpoint may not be a strict requirement [302]. In these cases, cameras that do not obey the single viewpoint requirement can also be used. Then, other design issues become more important, such as spatial resolution, camera size, and the ease of mapping between the catadioptric images and the scene [307]. Naturally, it is also possible to investigate these other design issues. For example, Chahl and Srinivassan recently studied the class of mirror shapes that yield a linear relationship between the angle of incidence onto the mirror surface and the angle of reflection into the camera [44].

We begin this chapter by deriving the entire class of catadioptric systems with a single effective viewpoint, and which can be constructed using just a single conventional lens and a single mirror. As we will show, the 2-parameter family of mirrors that can be used is exactly the class of rotated (swept) conic sections. Within this class of solutions, several swept conics are degenerate solutions that cannot, in fact, be used to construct cameras with a single effective viewpoint. Many of these solutions have, however, been used to construct wide field of view cameras with non-constant viewpoints. Some of the non-degenerate solutions have also been used in cameras proposed in the literature. In both cases, we mention all of the designs that we are aware of. A different derivation of the fact that only swept conic sections yield a single effective viewpoint was recently suggested by Drucker and Locke [65].

A very important property of a camera that images a large field of view is its resolution. The resolution of a catadioptric camera is not, in general, the same as that of any of the cameras used to construct it. In Section 4.3, we study why this is the case, and derive a simple expression for the relationship between the resolution of a conventional imaging system and the resolution of a derived single-viewpoint catadioptric camera. We specialize this result to the mirror shapes derived in the previous section. This expression should be carefully considered when constructing a catadioptric imaging system in order to ensure that the final camera has sufficient resolution. Another use of the relationship is to design conventional cameras with non-uniform resolution, which when used in an appropriate catadioptric system have a specified (e.g. uniform) resolution.

Another optical property which is affected by the use of a catadioptric system is focusing. It is well known that a curved mirror increases image blur [104]. In Section 4.4, we analyze this effect for catadioptric cameras. Two factors combine to cause additional blur in catadioptric systems: (1) the finite size of the lens aperture, and (2) the curvature of the mirror.

We first analyze how the interaction of these two factors causes defocus blur and then present numerical results for three different mirror shapes: the hyperboloid, the ellipsoid, and the paraboloid. The results show that the focal setting of a catadioptric camera using a curved mirror may be substantially different from that needed in a conventional camera. Moreover, even for a scene of constant depth, significantly different focal settings may be needed for different points in the scene. This effect, known as *field curvature*, can be partially corrected using additional lenses [104].

As a case study, in Section 4.5 we describe several implementations of single viewpoint catadioptric cameras using paraboloid mirrors. We outline the construction of the cameras, their calibration, and the real-time software that we developed to unwarp the catadioptric images to give perspective images. We conclude this chapter with a discussion of the design issues involved when building single viewpoint catadioptric cameras.

4.2 The Fixed Viewpoint Constraint

The fixed viewpoint constraint is the requirement that a catadioptric camera only measure the intensity of light passing through a single point in 3-D space. The direction of the light passing through this point may vary, but that is all. In other words, the catadioptric camera must sample the 5-D plenoptic function [1] [84] at a single point in 3-D space. The fixed 3-D point at which a catadioptric camera samples the plenoptic function is known as the *effective viewpoint*.

Suppose we use a single conventional camera as the only sensing element and a single mirror as the only reflecting surface. If the camera is an ideal perspective camera and we ignore defocus blur, it can be modeled by the point through which the perspective projection is performed; i.e. the *effective pinhole*. Then, the fixed viewpoint constraint requires that each ray of light passing through the effective pinhole of the camera (that was reflected by the mirror) would have passed through the effective viewpoint if it had not been reflected by the mirror. We now derive this constraint algebraically.

4.2.1 Derivation of the Fixed Viewpoint Constraint Equation

Without loss of generality we can assume that the effective viewpoint $\mathbf{v}$ of the catadioptric system lies at the origin of a Cartesian coordinate system. Suppose that the effective pinhole is located at the point $\mathbf{p}$. Then, again without loss of generality, we can assume that the z-axis $\hat{\mathbf{z}}$ lies in the direction $\mathbf{vp}$. Moreover, since perspective projection is rotationally symmetric about any line through $\mathbf{p}$, the mirror can be assumed to be a surface of revolution about the z-axis $\hat{\mathbf{z}}$. Therefore, we work in the 2-D Cartesian frame $(\mathbf{v}, \hat{\mathbf{r}}, \hat{\mathbf{z}})$ where $\hat{\mathbf{r}}$ is a unit vector orthogonal to $\hat{\mathbf{z}}$, and try to find the 2-dimensional profile of the mirror $z(r) = z(x, y)$ where $r = \sqrt{x^2 + y^2}$. Finally, if the distance from $\mathbf{v}$ to $\mathbf{p}$ is denoted by the parameter c, we have $\hat{\mathbf{v}} = (0, 0)$ and $\hat{\mathbf{p}} = (0, c)$. See Figure 4.1 for an illustration[1] of the coordinate frame.

We begin the translation of the fixed viewpoint constraint into symbols by denoting the angle between an incoming ray from a world point and the r-axis by θ. Suppose that this ray intersects the mirror at the point (z, r). Then, since we assume that it also passes through the origin $\mathbf{v} = (0, 0)$ we have the relationship:

$$\tan\theta = \frac{z}{r}. \tag{4.1}$$

If we denote the angle between the reflected ray and the (negative) r-axis by α, we also have:

$$\tan\alpha = \frac{c - z}{r} \tag{4.2}$$

since the reflected ray must pass through the pinhole $\mathbf{p} = (0, c)$. Next, if β is the angle between the z-axis and the normal to the mirror at the point (r, z), we have:

$$\frac{\mathrm{dz}}{\mathrm{dr}} = -\tan\beta. \tag{4.3}$$

Our final geometric relationship is due to the fact that we can assume the mirror to be specular. This means that the angle of incidence must equal the angle of reflection. So, if γ is the angle between the reflected ray and the z-axis, we have $\gamma = 90^{\circ} - \alpha$ and $\theta + \alpha + 2\beta + 2\gamma = 180^{\circ}$. (See Figure 4.1 for an illustration of this constraint.) Eliminating γ from these two expressions and rearranging gives:

$$2\beta = \alpha - \theta. \tag{4.4}$$

Then, taking the tangent of both sides and using the standard rules for expanding the tangent of a sum:

$$\tan(\mathrm{A} \pm \mathrm{B}) = \frac{\tan\mathrm{A} \pm \tan\mathrm{B}}{1 \mp \tan\mathrm{A}\tan\mathrm{B}} \tag{4.5}$$

we have:

$$\frac{2\tan\beta}{1 - \tan^2\beta} = \frac{\tan\alpha - \tan\theta}{1 + \tan\alpha\tan\theta}. \tag{4.6}$$

---

[1] In Figure 4.1 we have drawn the image plane as though it were orthogonal to the z-axis $\hat{\mathbf{z}}$ indicating that the optical axis of the camera is (anti) parallel to $\hat{\mathbf{z}}$. In fact, the effective viewpoint $\mathbf{v}$ and the axis of symmetry of the mirror profile $z(r)$ need not necessarily lie on the optical axis. Since perspective projection is rotationally symmetric with respect to any ray that passes through the pinhole $\mathbf{p}$, the camera could be rotated about $\mathbf{p}$ so that the optical axis is not parallel to the z-axis. Moreover, the image plane can be rotated independently so that it is no longer orthogonal to $\hat{\mathbf{z}}$.

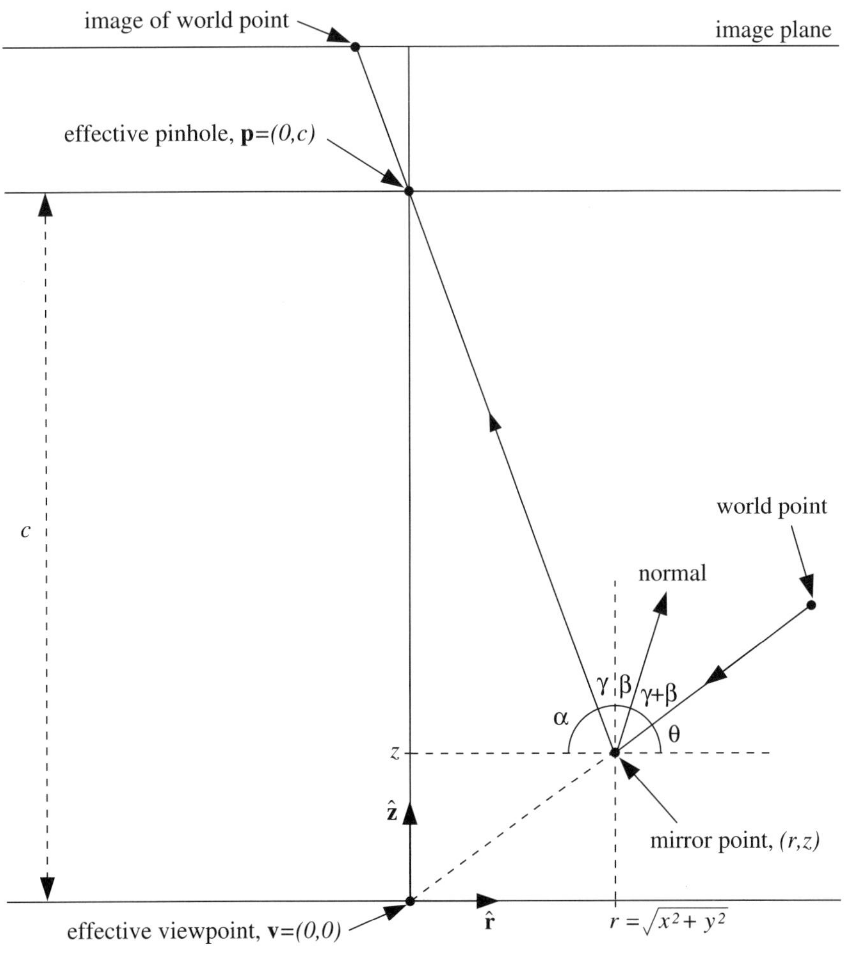

FIGURE 4.1. The geometry used to derive the fixed viewpoint constraint equation. The viewpoint $\mathbf{v} = (0,0)$ is located at the origin of a 2-D coordinate frame $(\mathbf{v}, \hat{\mathbf{r}}, \hat{\mathbf{z}})$, and the pinhole of the camera $\mathbf{p} = (0,c)$ is located at a distance c from $\mathbf{v}$ along the z-axis $\hat{\mathbf{z}}$. If a ray of light, which was about to pass through $\mathbf{v}$, is reflected at the mirror point (r,z), the angle between the ray of light and $\hat{\mathbf{r}}$ is $\theta = \tan^{-1}\frac{z}{r}$. If the ray is then reflected and passes through the pinhole $\mathbf{p}$, the angle it makes with $\hat{\mathbf{r}}$ is $\alpha = \tan^{-1}\frac{c-z}{r}$, and the angle it makes with $\hat{\mathbf{z}}$ is $\gamma = 90^\circ - \alpha$. Finally, if $\beta = \tan^{-1}\left(-\frac{\mathrm{dz}}{\mathrm{dr}}\right)$ is the angle between the normal to the mirror at (r,z) and $\hat{\mathbf{z}}$, then by the fact that the angle of incidence equals the angle of reflection, we have the constraint that $\alpha + \theta + 2\gamma + 2\beta = 180^\circ$.

Substituting from Equations (4.1), (4.2), and (4.3) yields the *fixed viewpoint constraint* equation:

$$\frac{-2\frac{\mathrm{dz}}{\mathrm{dr}}}{1-\left(\frac{\mathrm{dz}}{\mathrm{dr}}\right)^2} = \frac{(c-2z)r}{r^2+cz-z^2} \tag{4.7}$$

which when rearranged is seen to be a quadratic first-order ordinary differential equation:

$$r(c-2z)\left(\frac{\mathrm{dz}}{\mathrm{dr}}\right)^2 - 2(r^2+cz-z^2)\frac{\mathrm{dz}}{\mathrm{dr}} + r(2z-c) = 0. \tag{4.8}$$

4.2.2 General Solution of the Constraint Equation

The first step in the solution of the fixed viewpoint constraint equation is to solve it as a quadratic to yield an expression for the surface slope:

$$\frac{\mathrm{dz}}{\mathrm{dr}} = \frac{(z^2-r^2-cz)\pm\sqrt{r^2c^2+(z^2+r^2-cz)^2}}{r(2z-c)}. \tag{4.9}$$

The next step is to substitute $y = z - \frac{c}{2}$ and set $b = \frac{c}{2}$ which yields:

$$\frac{\mathrm{dy}}{\mathrm{dr}} = \frac{(y^2-r^2-b^2)\pm\sqrt{4r^2b^2+(y^2+r^2-b^2)^2}}{2ry}. \tag{4.10}$$

Then, we substitute $2rx = y^2 + r^2 - b^2$, which when differentiated gives:

$$2y\frac{\mathrm{dy}}{\mathrm{dr}} = 2x + 2r\frac{\mathrm{dx}}{\mathrm{dr}} - 2r \tag{4.11}$$

and so we have:

$$2x + 2r\frac{\mathrm{dx}}{\mathrm{dr}} - 2r = \frac{2rx - 2r^2 \pm \sqrt{4r^2b^2+4r^2x^2}}{r}. \tag{4.12}$$

Rearranging this equation yields:

$$\frac{1}{\sqrt{b^2+x^2}}\frac{\mathrm{dx}}{\mathrm{dr}} = \pm\frac{1}{r}. \tag{4.13}$$

Integrating both sides with respect to r results in:

$$\ln\left(x+\sqrt{b^2+x^2}\right) = \pm\ln r + C \tag{4.14}$$

where C is the constant of integration. Hence,

$$x+\sqrt{b^2+x^2} = \frac{k}{2}r^{\pm 1} \tag{4.15}$$

where $k = 2e^C > 0$ is a constant. By back substituting, rearranging, and simplifying we arrive at the two equations which comprise the general solution of the fixed viewpoint constraint equation:

$$\left(z - \frac{c}{2}\right)^2 - r^2\left(\frac{k}{2} - 1\right) = \frac{c^2}{4}\left(\frac{k-2}{k}\right) \qquad (k \geq 2) \qquad (4.16)$$

$$\left(z - \frac{c}{2}\right)^2 + r^2\left(1 + \frac{c^2}{2k}\right) = \left(\frac{2k + c^2}{4}\right) \qquad (k > 0). \qquad (4.17)$$

In the first of these two equations, the constant parameter k is constrained by $k \geq 2$ (rather than $k > 0$) since $0 < k < 2$ leads to complex solutions.

4.2.3 Specific Solutions of the Constraint Equation

Together, Equations (4.16) and (4.17) define the complete class of mirrors that satisfy the fixed viewpoint constraint. A quick glance at the form of these equations reveals that the mirror profiles form a 2-parameter (c and k) family of conic sections. Hence, the shapes of the 3-D mirrors are all swept conic sections. As we shall see, however, although every conic section is theoretically a solution of one of the two equations, a number of the solutions are degenerate and cannot be used to construct real cameras with a single effective viewpoint.

We will now describe the solutions in detail. For each solution, we demonstrate whether it is degenerate or not. Some of the non-degenerate solutions have actually been used in real cameras. For these solutions, we mention all of the existing designs that we are aware of which use that mirror shape. Several of the degenerate solutions have also been used to construct cameras with a wide field of view, but with no fixed viewpoint.

4.2.3.1 Planar Mirrors

In Equation (4.16), if we set $k = 2$ and $c > 0$, we get the cross-section of a planar mirror:

$$z = \frac{c}{2}. \qquad (4.18)$$

As shown in Figure 4.2, this plane is the one which bisects the line segment $\mathbf{vp}$ joining the viewpoint and the pinhole.

The converse of this result is that for a fixed viewpoint $\mathbf{v}$ and pinhole $\mathbf{p}$, there is only one planar solution of the fixed viewpoint constraint equation. The unique solution is the perpendicular bisector of the line joining the pinhole to the viewpoint:

$$\left[\mathbf{x} - \left(\frac{\mathbf{p} + \mathbf{v}}{2}\right)\right] \cdot (\mathbf{p} - \mathbf{v}) = 0. \qquad (4.19)$$

To prove this, it is sufficient to consider a fixed pinhole $\mathbf{p}$, a planar mirror with unit normal $\hat{\mathbf{n}}$, and a point $\mathbf{q}$ on the mirror. Then, the fact that the

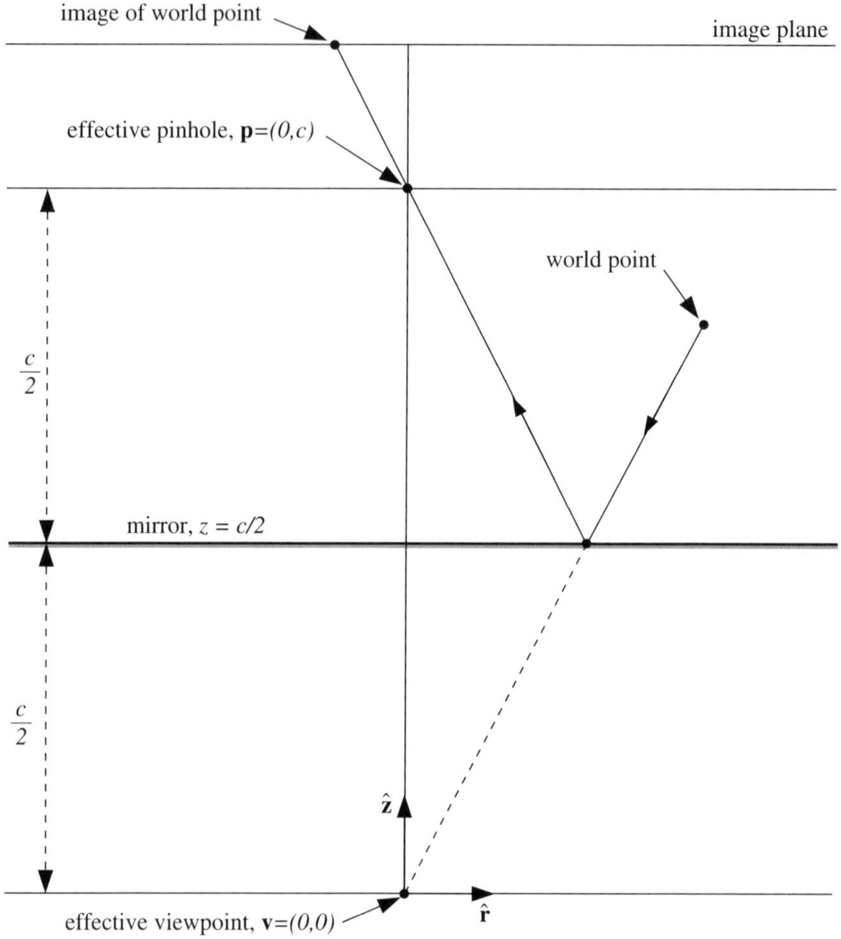

FIGURE 4.2. The plane $z = \frac{c}{2}$ is a solution of the fixed viewpoint constraint equation. Conversely, it is possible to show that, given a fixed viewpoint and pinhole, the only planar solution is the perpendicular bisector of the line joining the pinhole to the viewpoint. Hence, for a fixed pinhole, two different planar mirrors cannot share the same effective viewpoint. For each such plane the effective viewpoint is the reflection of the pinhole in the plane. This means that it is impossible to enhance the field of view using a single perspective camera and an *arbitrary number* of planar mirrors, while still respecting the fixed viewpoint constraint. If multiple cameras are used then solutions using multiple planar mirrors are possible [194].

plane is a solution of the fixed viewpoint constraint implies that there is a single effective viewpoint $\mathbf{v} = \mathbf{v}(\hat{\mathbf{n}}, \mathbf{q})$. To be more precise, the effective viewpoint is the reflection of the pinhole $\mathbf{p}$ in the mirror; i.e. the single effective viewpoint is:

$$\mathbf{v}(\hat{\mathbf{n}}, \mathbf{q}) \quad = \quad \mathbf{p} - 2\left[(\mathbf{p} - \mathbf{q}) \cdot \hat{\mathbf{n}}\right] \hat{\mathbf{n}}. \tag{4.20}$$

Since the reflection of a single point in two different planes is always two different points, the perpendicular bisector is the unique planar solution.

An immediate corollary of this result is that for a single fixed pinhole, no two different planar mirrors can share the same viewpoint. Unfortunately, a single planar mirror does not enhance the field of view, since, discounting occlusions, the same camera moved from $\mathbf{p}$ to $\mathbf{v}$ and reflected in the mirror would have exactly the same field of view. It follows that it is impossible to increase the field of view by packing an *arbitrary number* of planar mirrors (pointing in different directions) in front of a conventional imaging system, while still respecting the fixed viewpoint constraint. On the other hand, in applications such as stereo where multiple viewpoints are a necessary requirement, the multiple views of a scene can be captured by a single camera using multiple planar mirrors. See, for example, [85], [115], and [201].

This brings us to the panoramic camera proposed by Nalwa [194]. To ensure a single viewpoint while using multiple planar mirrors, Nalwa [194] arrived at a design that uses four separate imaging systems. Four planar mirrors are arranged in a square-based pyramid, and each of the four cameras is placed above one of the faces of the pyramid. The effective pinholes of the cameras are moved until the four effective viewpoints (i.e. the reflections of the pinholes in the mirrors) coincide. The result is a camera that has a single effective viewpoint and a panoramic field of view of approximately $360° \times 50°$. The panoramic image is of relatively high resolution since it is generated from the four images captured by the four cameras. This camera is straightforward to implement, but requires four of each component: i.e. four cameras, four lenses, and four digitizers. (It is, of course, possible to use only one digitizer but at a reduced frame rate.)

4.2.3.2 Conical Mirrors

In Equation (4.16), if we set $c = 0$ and $k \geq 2$, we get a conical mirror with circular cross section:

$$z \quad = \quad \sqrt{\frac{k-2}{2} r^2}. \tag{4.21}$$

See Figure 4.3 for an illustration of this solution. The angle at the apex of the cone is 2τ where:

$$\tan \tau \quad = \quad \sqrt{\frac{2}{k-2}}. \tag{4.22}$$

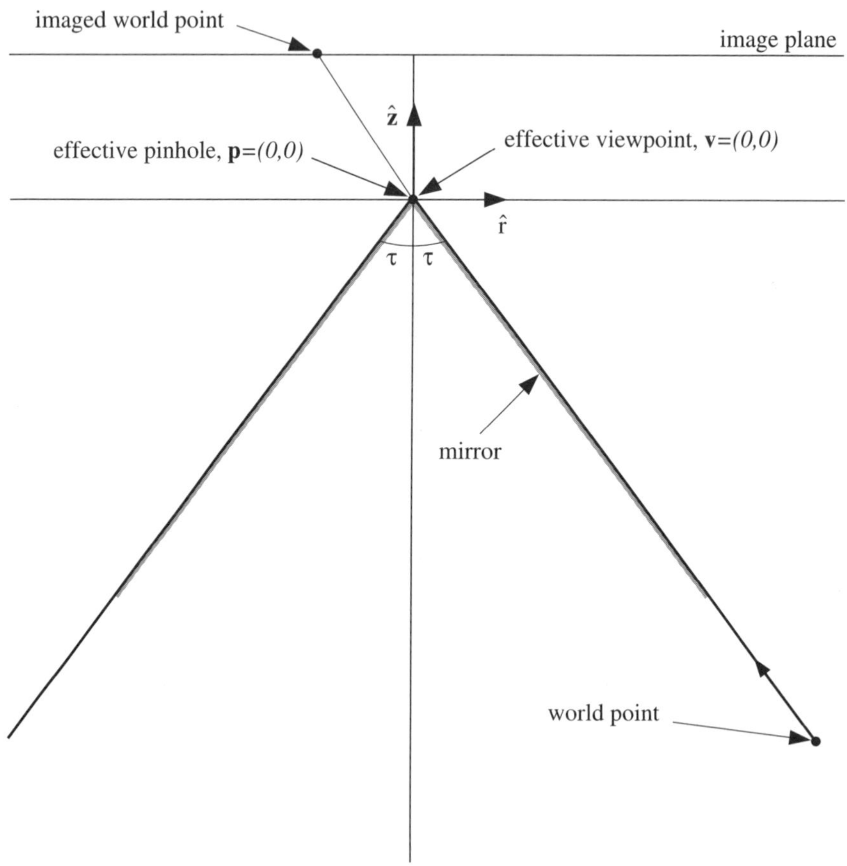

FIGURE 4.3. The conical mirror is a solution of the fixed viewpoint constraint equation. Since the pinhole is located at the apex of the cone, this is a degenerate solution that cannot be used to construct a wide field of view camera with a single viewpoint. If the pinhole is moved away from the apex of the cone (along the axis of the cone), the viewpoint is no longer a single point but rather lies on a circular locus [194] [12].

This might seem like a reasonable solution, but since $c = 0$ the pinhole of the camera must be at the apex of the cone. This implies that the only rays of light entering the pinhole from the mirror are the ones which graze the cone and so do not originate from objects in the world (see Figure 4.3.) Hence, the cone with the pinhole at the vertex is a degenerate solution that cannot be used to construct a wide field of view camera with a single effective viewpoint.

In spite of this fact, the cone has been used in wide-angle imaging systems several times [301] [304] [28]. In these implementations the pinhole is placed some distance from the apex of the cone. It is easy to show that in such cases the viewpoint is no longer a single point [194] [12]. In some applications such as robot navigation, the single viewpoint constraint is not vital. Conical mirrors can be used to build practical cameras for such applications. See, for example, the designs in [302] and [28].

4.2.3.3 Spherical Mirrors

In Equation (4.17), if we set $c = 0$ and $k > 0$, we get the spherical mirror:

$$z^2 + r^2 = \frac{k}{2}. \tag{4.23}$$

Like the cone, this is a degenerate solution which cannot be used to construct a wide field of view camera with a single viewpoint. Since the viewpoint and pinhole coincide at the center of the sphere, the observer would see itself and nothing else, as is illustrated in Figure 4.4.

The sphere has also been used to build wide field of view cameras several times [110] [28] [191]. In these implementations, the pinhole is placed outside the sphere and so there is no single effective viewpoint. The locus of the effective viewpoint can be computed in a straightforward manner using a symbolic mathematics package [12]. Like multiple planes, spheres have also been used to construct stereo rigs [197] [201], but as described before, multiple viewpoints are a requirement for stereo.

4.2.3.4 Ellipsoidal Mirrors

In Equation (4.17), when $k > 0$ and $c > 0$, we get the ellipsoidal mirror:

$$\frac{1}{a_e^2}\left(z - \frac{c}{2}\right)^2 + \frac{1}{b_e^2} r^2 = 1 \tag{4.24}$$

where:

$$a_e = \sqrt{\frac{2k + c^2}{4}} \quad \text{and} \quad \mathrm{b_e} = \sqrt{\frac{\mathrm{k}}{2}}. \tag{4.25}$$

The ellipsoid is the first solution that can actually be used to enhance the field of view of a camera while retaining a single effective viewpoint. As shown in Figure 4.5, if the viewpoint and pinhole are at the foci of the

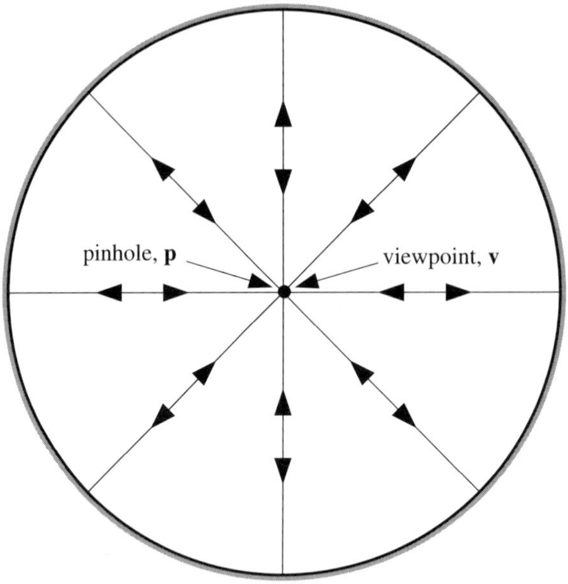

FIGURE 4.4. The spherical mirror satisfies the fixed viewpoint constraint when the pinhole lies at the center of the sphere. (Since $c = 0$ the viewpoint also lies at the center of the sphere.) Like the conical mirror, the sphere cannot actually be used to construct a wide field of view camera with a single viewpoint because the observer can only see itself; rays of light emitted from the center of the sphere are reflected back at the surface of the sphere directly towards the center of the sphere.

ellipsoid and the mirror is taken to be the section of the ellipsoid that lies below the viewpoint (i.e. $z < 0$), the effective field of view is the entire upper hemisphere $z \geq 0$.

4.2.3.5 Hyperboloidal Mirrors

In Equation (4.16), when $k > 2$ and $c > 0$, we get the hyperboloidal mirror:

$$\frac{1}{a_h^2}\left(z - \frac{c}{2}\right)^2 - \frac{1}{b_h^2}r^2 = 1 \tag{4.26}$$

where:

$$a_h = \frac{c}{2}\sqrt{\frac{k-2}{k}} \quad \text{and} \quad \mathrm{b_h} = \frac{\mathrm{c}}{2}\sqrt{\frac{2}{\mathrm{k}}}. \tag{4.27}$$

As seen in Figure 4.6, the hyperboloid also yields a realizable solution. The curvature of the mirror and the field of view both increase with k. In the other direction (in the limit $k \to 2$) the hyperboloid flattens out to the planar mirror of Section 4.2.3.1.

Rees [224] appears to have been first to use a hyperboloidal mirror with a perspective lens to achieve a large field of view camera system with a

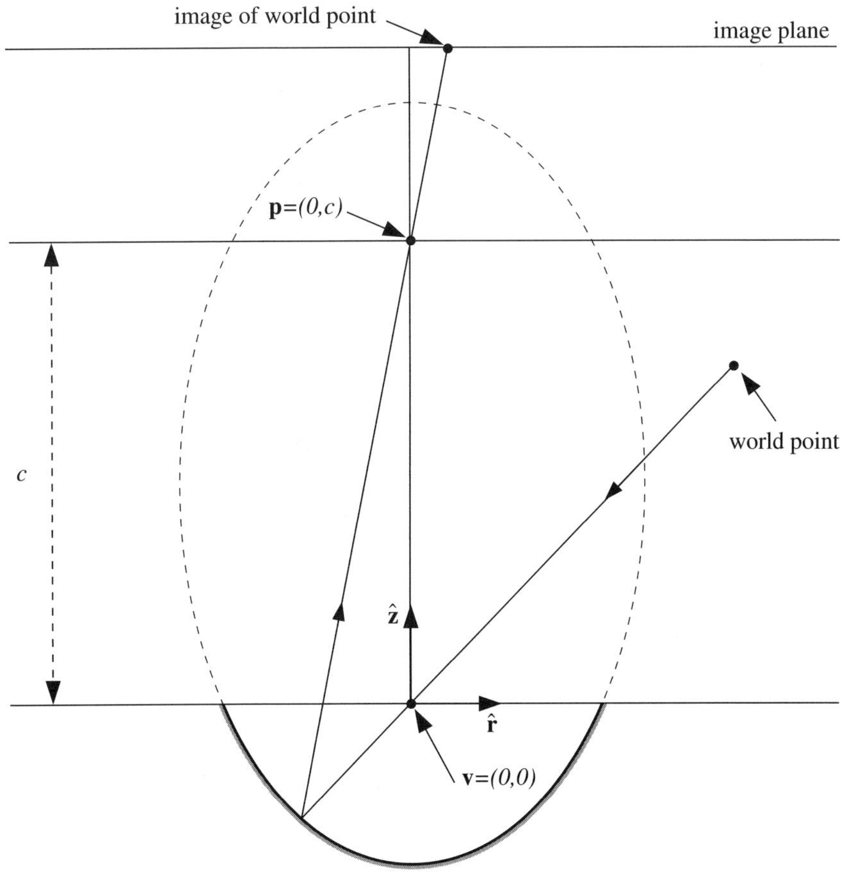

FIGURE 4.5. The ellipsoidal mirror satisfies the fixed viewpoint constraint when the pinhole and viewpoint are located at the two foci of the ellipsoid. If the ellipsoid is terminated by the horizontal plane passing through the viewpoint $z = 0$, the field of view is the entire upper hemisphere $z > 0$. It is also possible to cut the ellipsoid with other planes passing through $\mathbf{v}$.

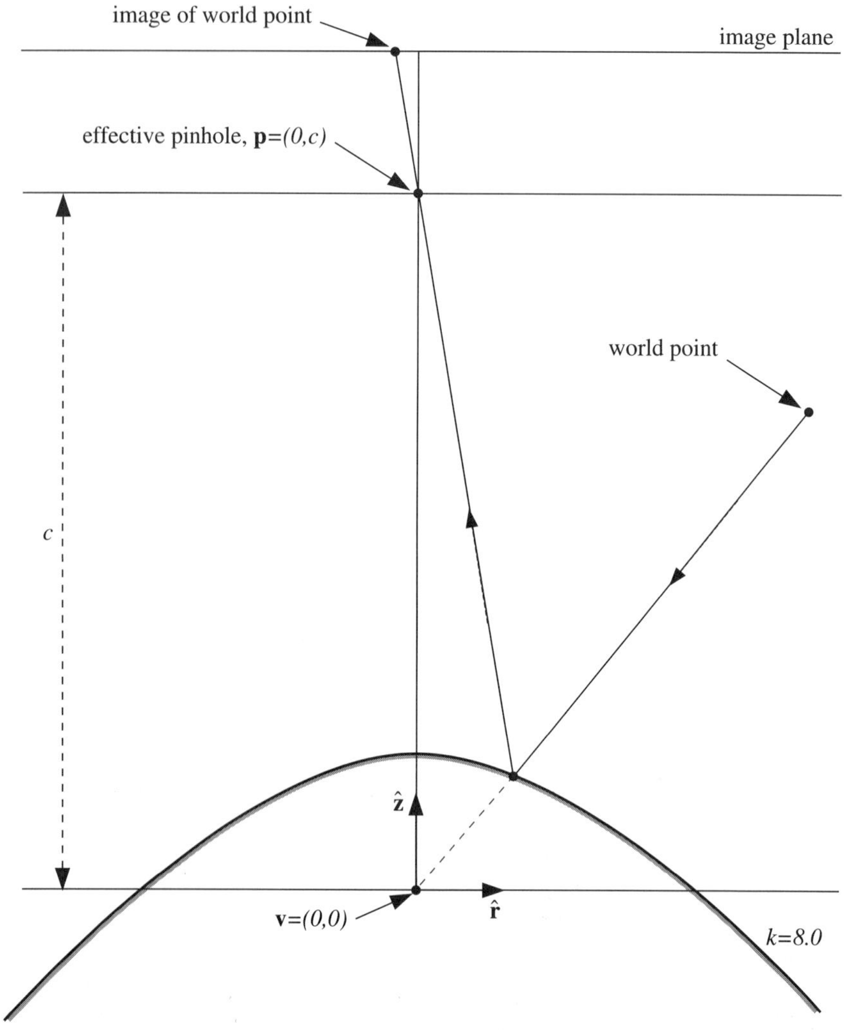

FIGURE 4.6. The hyperboloidal mirror satisfies the fixed viewpoint constraint when the pinhole and the viewpoint are located at the two foci of the hyperboloid. This solution does produce the desired increase in field of view. The curvature of the mirror and hence the field of view increase with k. In the limit $k \to 2$, the hyperboloid flattens to the planar mirror of Section 4.2.3.1.

single viewpoint. Later, Yamazawa *et al.* [306] [307] also recognized that the hyperboloid is indeed a practical solution and implemented a camera designed for autonomous navigation.

4.2.4 The Orthographic Case: Paraboloidal Mirrors

There is one conic section that we have not mentioned: the parabola. Although the parabola is not a solution of either equation for finite values of c and k, it is a solution of Equation (4.16) in the limit that $c \to \infty$, $k \to \infty$, and $\frac{c}{k} = h$, a constant. These limiting conditions correspond to orthographic projection.

Orthographic projection can be modeled by setting $\alpha = 90°$ in Figure 4.1; the direction of projection is then along the axis of symmetry $\hat{\mathbf{z}}$. Equation (4.6) then simplifies to:

$$\frac{2\tan\beta}{1-\tan^2\beta} = \frac{1}{\tan\theta}. \tag{4.28}$$

The *fixed viewpoint constraint* equation for orthographic projection is therefore:

$$\frac{-2\frac{dz}{dr}}{1-(\frac{dz}{dr})^2} = \frac{r}{z}. \tag{4.29}$$

As above, the first step in determining the shape of the mirror is to solve this quadratic equation for the surface slope:

$$\frac{dz}{dr} = \frac{z}{r} \mp \sqrt{1+(\frac{r}{z})^2}. \tag{4.30}$$

This first-order differential equation can be solved using similar transformations to those used above to obtain the following expression for the reflecting surface:

$$z = \pm\frac{h^2 - r^2}{2h}, \tag{4.31}$$

where, $h > 0$ is the constant of integration.

Not surprisingly, the mirror that guarantees a single viewpoint for orthographic projection is a paraboloid. Paraboloidal mirrors are frequently used to converge an incoming set of parallel rays at a single point (the focus), or to generate a collimated light source from a point source (placed at the focus). In both these cases, the paraboloid is a concave mirror that is reflective on its inner surface. This corresponds to the negative solution in Equation (4.31). In our case, the more natural solution to use is the positive one. Here, the paraboloid is reflective on its outer surface (a convex mirror) as is shown in Figure 4.7.

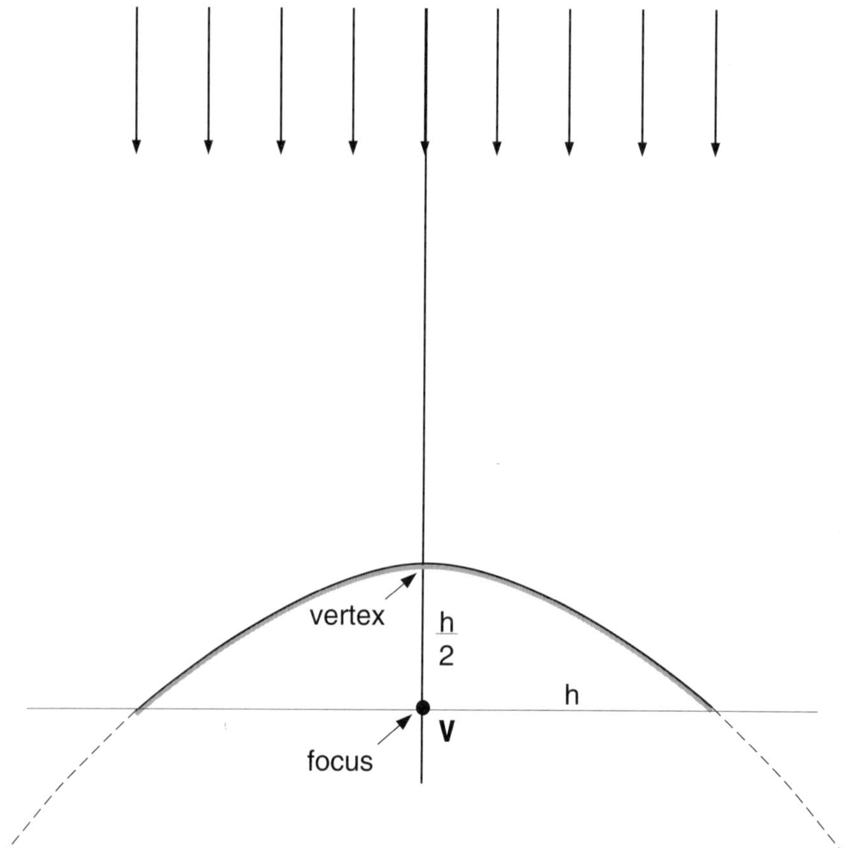

FIGURE 4.7. Under orthographic projection the only solution is a paraboloid with the effective viewpoint at the focus. Here we show one of the two possible paraboloids; the other is similar to the ellipse shown in Figure 4.5 and is the reflection of the one shown in the plane $z = 0$.

4.3 Resolution of a Catadioptric Camera

In this section, we assume that the conventional camera used in the catadioptric camera has a frontal image plane located at a distance u from the pinhole, and that the optical axis of the camera is aligned with the axis of symmetry of the mirror. See Figure 4.8 for an illustration of this scenario. Then, the definition of resolution that we will use is the following. Consider an infinitesimal area $\mathrm{d}A$ on the image plane. If this infinitesimal pixel images an infinitesimal solid angle $\mathrm{d}\nu$ of the world, the *resolution* of the camera as a function of the point on the image plane at the center of the infinitesimal area $\mathrm{d}A$ is:

$$\frac{\mathrm{d}A}{\mathrm{d}\nu}. \tag{4.32}$$

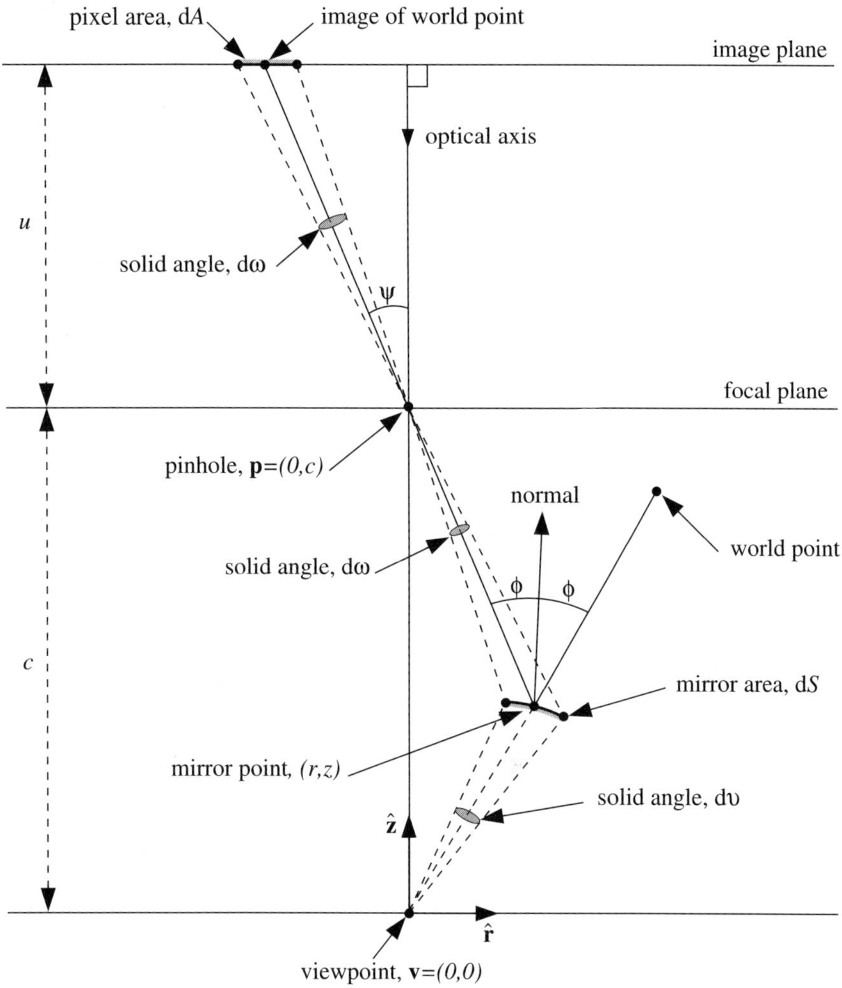

FIGURE 4.8. The geometry used to derive the spatial resolution of a catadioptric camera. Assuming the conventional camera has a frontal image plane which is located at a distance u from the pinhole and the optical axis is aligned with the z-axis $\hat{\mathbf{z}}$, the spatial resolution of the conventional camera is $\frac{\mathrm{d}A}{\mathrm{d}\omega} = \frac{u^2}{\cos^3\psi}$. Therefore the area of the mirror imaged by the infinitesimal image plane area $\mathrm{d}A$ is $\mathrm{d}S = \frac{(c-z)^2 \cdot \cos\psi}{u^2 \cos\phi} \cdot \mathrm{d}A$. So, the solid angle of the world imaged by the infinitesimal area $\mathrm{d}A$ on the image plane is $\mathrm{d}\nu = \frac{(c-z)^2 \cdot \cos\psi}{u^2(r^2+z^2)} \cdot \mathrm{d}A$. Hence, the spatial resolution of the catadioptric camera is $\frac{\mathrm{d}A}{\mathrm{d}\nu} = \frac{u^2(r^2+z^2)}{(c-z)^2 \cdot \cos\psi} = \frac{r^2+z^2}{r^2+(c-z)^2} \cdot \frac{\mathrm{d}A}{\mathrm{d}\omega}$ since $\cos^2\psi = \frac{(c-z)^2}{(c-z)^2+r^2}$.

If ψ is the angle made between the optical axis and the line joining the pinhole to the center of the infinitesimal area $\mathrm{d}A$ (see Figure 4.8), the solid angle subtended by the infinitesimal area $\mathrm{d}A$ at the pinhole is:

$$\mathrm{d}\omega = \frac{\mathrm{d}A \cdot \cos\psi}{u^2 / \cos^2\psi} = \frac{\mathrm{d}A \cdot \cos^3\psi}{u^2}. \tag{4.33}$$

Therefore, the resolution of the conventional camera is:

$$\frac{\mathrm{d}A}{\mathrm{d}\omega} = \frac{u^2}{\cos^3\psi}. \tag{4.34}$$

Then, the area of the mirror imaged by the infinitesimal area $\mathrm{d}A$ is:

$$\mathrm{d}S = \frac{\mathrm{d}\omega \cdot (c-z)^2}{\cos\phi \cos^2\psi} = \frac{\mathrm{d}A \cdot (c-z)^2 \cdot \cos\psi}{u^2 \cos\phi} \tag{4.35}$$

where ϕ is the angle between the normal to the mirror at (r, z) and the line joining the pinhole to the mirror point (r, z). Since reflection at the mirror is specular, the solid angle of the world imaged by the catadioptric camera is:

$$\mathrm{d}\nu = \frac{\mathrm{d}S \cdot \cos\phi}{r^2 + z^2} = \frac{\mathrm{d}A \cdot (c-z)^2 \cdot \cos\psi}{u^2(r^2+z^2)}. \tag{4.36}$$

Therefore, the resolution of the catadioptric camera is:

$$\frac{\mathrm{d}A}{\mathrm{d}\nu} = \frac{u^2(r^2+z^2)}{(c-z)^2 \cdot \cos\psi} = \left[\frac{(r^2+z^2)\cos^2\psi}{(c-z)^2}\right] \frac{\mathrm{d}A}{\mathrm{d}\omega}. \tag{4.37}$$

But, since:

$$\cos^2\psi = \frac{(c-z)^2}{(c-z)^2 + r^2} \tag{4.38}$$

we have:

$$\frac{\mathrm{d}A}{\mathrm{d}\nu} = \left[\frac{r^2+z^2}{(c-z)^2 + r^2}\right] \frac{\mathrm{d}A}{\mathrm{d}\omega}. \tag{4.39}$$

Hence, the resolution of the catadioptric camera is the resolution of the conventional camera used to construct it multiplied by a factor of:

$$\frac{r^2+z^2}{(c-z)^2 + r^2} \tag{4.40}$$

where (r, z) is the point on the mirror being imaged.

The first thing to note from Equation (4.39) is that for the planar mirror $z = \frac{c}{2}$, the resolution of the catadioptric camera is the same as that of the conventional camera used to construct it. This is as expected by symmetry. Secondly, note that the factor in Equation (4.40) is the square of the distance from the point (r, z) to the effective viewpoint $\mathbf{v} = (0, 0)$, divided by the square of the distance to the pinhole $\mathbf{p} = (0, c)$. Let $d_{\mathbf{v}}$ denote the distance from the viewpoint to (r, z) and $d_{\mathbf{p}}$ the distance of (r, z) from the pinhole. Then, the factor in Equation (4.40) is $\frac{d_{\mathbf{v}}^2}{d_{\mathbf{p}}^2}$. For the ellipsoid, $d_{\mathbf{p}} + d_{\mathbf{v}} = K_e$ for some constant $K_e > d_{\mathbf{p}}$. Therefore, for the ellipsoid the factor is:

$$\left(\frac{K_e}{d_{\mathbf{p}}} - 1\right)^2 \tag{4.41}$$

which increases as $d_{\mathbf{p}}$ decreases and $d_{\mathbf{v}}$ increases. For the hyperboloid, $d_{\mathbf{p}} - d_{\mathbf{v}} = K_h$ for some constant $0 < K_h < d_{\mathbf{p}}$. Therefore, for the hyperboloid the factor is:

$$\left(1 - \frac{K_h}{d_{\mathbf{p}}}\right)^2 \tag{4.42}$$

which increases as $d_{\mathbf{p}}$ increases and $d_{\mathbf{v}}$ increases. So, for both ellipsoids and hyperboloids, the factor in Equation (4.40) increases with r. Hence, both hyperboloidal and ellipsoidal catadioptric cameras constructed with a uniform resolution camera will have their highest resolution around the periphery, a useful property for applications such as teleconferencing.

4.3.1 The Orthographic Case

The orthographic case is slightly simpler than the projective case and is illustrated in Figure 4.9. Again, we assume that the image plane is frontal; i.e. perpendicular to the direction of orthographic projection. Then, the resolution of the conventional orthographic camera is:

$$\frac{\mathrm{d}A}{\mathrm{d}\omega} = M^2 \tag{4.43}$$

where the constant M is the linear magnification of the camera. If the solid angle $\mathrm{d}\omega$ images the area $\mathrm{d}S$ of the mirror and ϕ is the angle between the mirror normal and the direction of orthographic projection, we have:

$$\mathrm{d}\omega = \cos\phi \cdot \mathrm{d}S. \tag{4.44}$$

Combining Equations (4.36), (4.43), and (4.44) yields:

$$\frac{\mathrm{d}A}{\mathrm{d}\nu} = \left[r^2 + z^2\right] \frac{\mathrm{d}A}{\mathrm{d}\omega}. \tag{4.45}$$

For the paraboloid $z = \frac{h^2 - r^2}{2h}$, the multiplicative factor $r^2 + z^2$ simplifies to:

$$\left[\frac{h^2 + r^2}{2h}\right]^2. \tag{4.46}$$

Hence, as for both the ellipsoid and the hyperboloid, the resolution of paraboloid based catadioptric cameras increases with r, the distance from the center of the mirror.

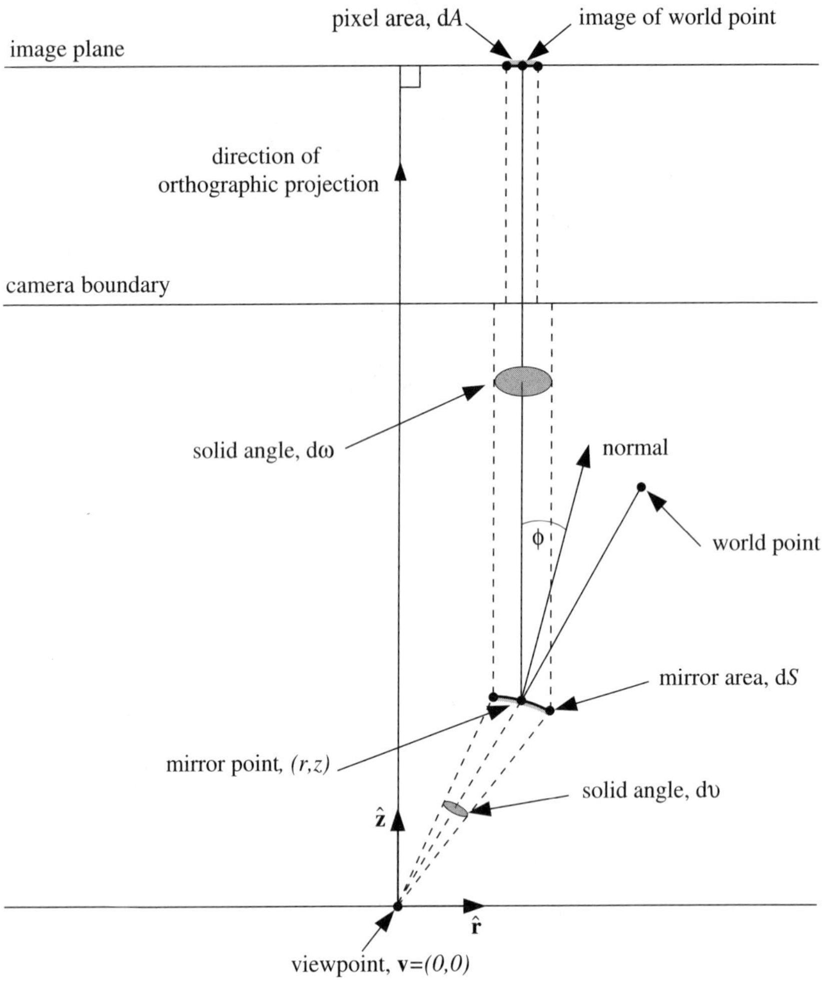

FIGURE 4.9. The geometry used to derive the spatial resolution of a catadioptric camera in the orthographic case. Again, assuming that the image plane is frontal and the conventional orthographic camera has a linear magnification M, its spatial resolution is $\frac{\mathrm{d}A}{\mathrm{d}\omega} = M^2$. The solid angle $\mathrm{d}\omega$ equals $\cos\phi \cdot \mathrm{d}S$, where $\mathrm{d}S$ is the area of the mirror imaged and ϕ is the angle between the mirror normal and the direction of orthographic projection. Combining this information with Equation (4.36) yields the spatial resolution of the orthographic catadioptric camera as $\frac{\mathrm{d}A}{\mathrm{d}\nu} = \left[r^2 + z^2\right] \frac{\mathrm{d}A}{\mathrm{d}\omega}$.

4.4 Defocus Blur of a Catadioptric Camera

In addition to the normal causes present in conventional dioptric systems, such as diffraction and lens aberrations, two factors combine to cause defocus blur in catadioptric sensors. They are: (1) the finite size of the lens aperture, and (2) the curvature of the mirror. To analyze how these two factors cause defocus blur, we first consider a fixed point in the world and a fixed point in the lens aperture. We then find the point on the mirror which reflects a ray of light from the world point through that lens point. Next, we compute where on the image plane this mirror point is imaged. By considering the locus of imaged mirror points as the lens point varies, we can compute the area of the image plane onto which a fixed world point is imaged. In Section 4.4.1, we derive the constraints on the mirror point at which the light is reflected, and show how it can be projected onto the image plane. In Section 4.4.2, we extend the analysis to the orthographic case. Finally, in Section 4.4.3, we present numerical results for hyperboloid.

4.4.1 Analysis of Defocus Blur

To analyze defocus blur, we need to work in 3-D. We use the 3-D cartesian frame $(\mathbf{v}, \hat{\mathbf{x}}, \hat{\mathbf{y}}, \hat{\mathbf{z}})$ where $\mathbf{v}$ is the location of the effective viewpoint, $\mathbf{p}$ is the location of the effective pinhole, $\hat{\mathbf{z}}$ is a unit vector in the direction $\mathbf{vp}$, the effective pinhole is located at a distance c from the effective viewpoint, and the vectors $\hat{\mathbf{x}}$ and $\hat{\mathbf{y}}$ are orthogonal unit vectors in the plane $z = 0$. As in Section 4.3, we also assume that the conventional camera used in the catadioptric sensor has a frontal image plane located at a distance u from the pinhole and that the optical axis of the camera is aligned with the z-axis. In addition to the previous assumptions, we assume that the effective pinhole of the lens is located at the center of the lens, and that the lens has a circular aperture. See Figure 4.10 for an illustration of this configuration.

Consider a point $\mathbf{m} = (x, y, z)$ on the mirror and a point $\mathbf{w} = \frac{l}{\|\mathbf{m}\|}(x, y, z)$ in the world, where $l > \|\mathbf{m}\|$. Then, since the hyperboloid mirror satisfies the fixed viewpoint constraint, a ray of light from $\mathbf{w}$ which is reflected by the mirror at $\mathbf{m}$ passes directly through the center of the lens (i.e. the effective pinhole.) This ray of light is known as the *principal ray* [104]. Next, suppose a ray of light from the world point $\mathbf{w}$ is reflected at the point $\mathbf{m}_1 = (x_1, y_1, z_1)$ on the mirror and then passes through the lens aperture point $\mathbf{l} = (d \cdot \cos\lambda, d \cdot \sin\lambda, c)$. In general, this ray of light will not be imaged at the same point on the image plane as the principal ray. When this happens there is defocus blur. The locus of the intersection of the incoming rays through $\mathbf{l}$ and the image plane as $\mathbf{l}$ varies over the lens aperture is known as the *blur region* or *region of confusion* [104]. For an

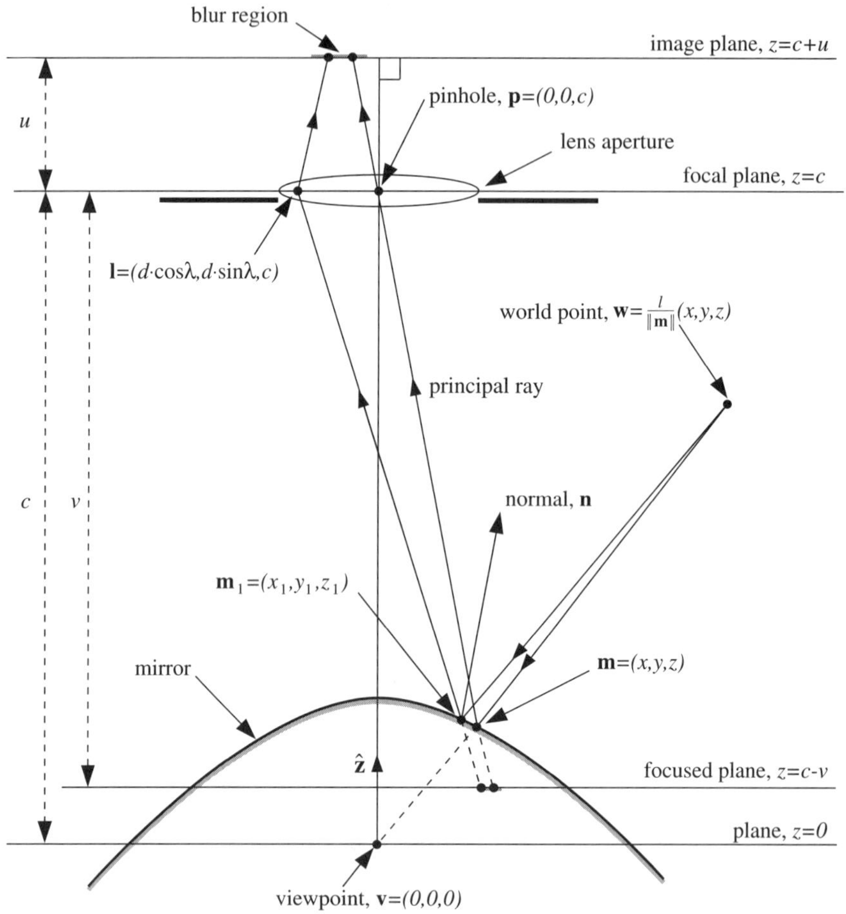

FIGURE 4.10. The geometry used to analyze the defocus blur. We work in the 3-D cartesian frame $(\mathbf{v}, \hat{\mathbf{x}}, \hat{\mathbf{y}}, \hat{\mathbf{z}})$ where $\hat{\mathbf{x}}$ and $\hat{\mathbf{y}}$ are orthogonal unit vectors in the plane $z = 0$. In addition to the assumptions of Section 4.3, we also assume that the effective pinhole is located at the center of the lens and that the lens has a circular aperture. If a ray of light from the world point $\mathbf{w} = \frac{l}{\|\mathbf{m}\|}(x, y, z)$ is reflected at the mirror point $\mathbf{m}_1 = (x_1, y_1, z_1)$ and then passes through the lens point $\mathbf{l} = (d \cdot \cos\lambda, d \cdot \sin\lambda, c)$, there are three constraints on $\mathbf{m}_1$: (1) it must lie on the mirror, (2) the angle of incidence must equal the angle of reflection, and (3) the normal $\mathbf{n}$ to the mirror at $\mathbf{m}_1$, and the two vectors $\mathbf{l} - \mathbf{m}_1$ and $\mathbf{w} - \mathbf{m}_1$ must be coplanar.

ideal thin lens in isolation, the blur region is circular and so is often referred to as the *blur circle* [104].

If we know the points $\mathbf{m}_1$ and $\mathbf{l}$, we can find the point on the image plane where the ray of light through these points is imaged. First, the line through $\mathbf{m}_1$ in the direction $\mathbf{lm}_1$ is extended to intersect the *focused plane.* By the thin lens law [104] the focused plane is:

$$z = c - v = c - \frac{f \cdot u}{u - f} \tag{4.47}$$

where f is the focal length of the lens and u is the distance from the focal plane to the image plane. Since all points on the focused plane are perfectly focused, the point of intersection on the focused plane can be mapped onto the image plane using perspective projection. Hence, the x and y coordinates of the intersection of the ray through $\mathbf{l}$ and the image plane are the x and y coordinates of:

$$-\frac{u}{v}\left(\mathbf{l} + \frac{v}{c - z_1}(\mathbf{m}_1 - \mathbf{l})\right) \tag{4.48}$$

and the z coordinate is the z coordinate of the image plane $c + u$.

Given the lens point $\mathbf{l} = (d \cdot \cos\lambda, d \cdot \sin\lambda, c)$ and the world point $\mathbf{w} = \frac{l}{\|\mathbf{m}\|}(x, y, z)$, there are three constraints on the point $\mathbf{m}_1 = (x_1, y_1, z_1)$. First, $\mathbf{m}_1$ must lie on the mirror and so (for the hyperboloid) we have:

$$\left(z_1 - \frac{c}{2}\right)^2 - \left(x_1^2 + y_1^2\right)\left(\frac{k}{2} - 1\right) = \frac{c^2}{4}\left(\frac{k-2}{k}\right). \tag{4.49}$$

Secondly, the incident ray $(\mathbf{w} - \mathbf{m}_1)$, the reflected ray $(\mathbf{m}_1 - \mathbf{l})$, and the normal to the mirror at $\mathbf{m}_1$ must lie in the same plane. The normal to the mirror at $\mathbf{m}_1$ lies in the direction:

$$\mathbf{n} = ([k-2]x_1, [k-2]y_1, c - 2z_1) \tag{4.50}$$

for the hyperboloid. Hence, the second constraint is:

$$\mathbf{n} \cdot (\mathbf{w} - \mathbf{m}_1) \wedge (\mathbf{l} - \mathbf{m}_1) = 0. \tag{4.51}$$

Finally, the angle of incidence must equal the angle of reflection and so the third constraint on the point $\mathbf{m}_1$ is:

$$\frac{\mathbf{n} \cdot (\mathbf{w} - \mathbf{m}_1)}{\|\mathbf{w} - \mathbf{m}_1\|} = \frac{\mathbf{n} \cdot (\mathbf{l} - \mathbf{m}_1)}{\|\mathbf{l} - \mathbf{m}_1\|}. \tag{4.52}$$

These three constraints on $\mathbf{m}_1$ are all multivariate polynomials in x_1, y_1, and z_1: Equation (4.49) and Equation (4.51) are both of order 2, and Equation (4.52) is of order 5. We were unable to find a closed form solution to these three equations (Equation (4.52) has 25 terms in general and so it is probable that none exists) but we did investigate numerical solutions. Before we present the results, we briefly describe the orthographic case.

4.4.2 Defocus Blur in the Orthographic Case

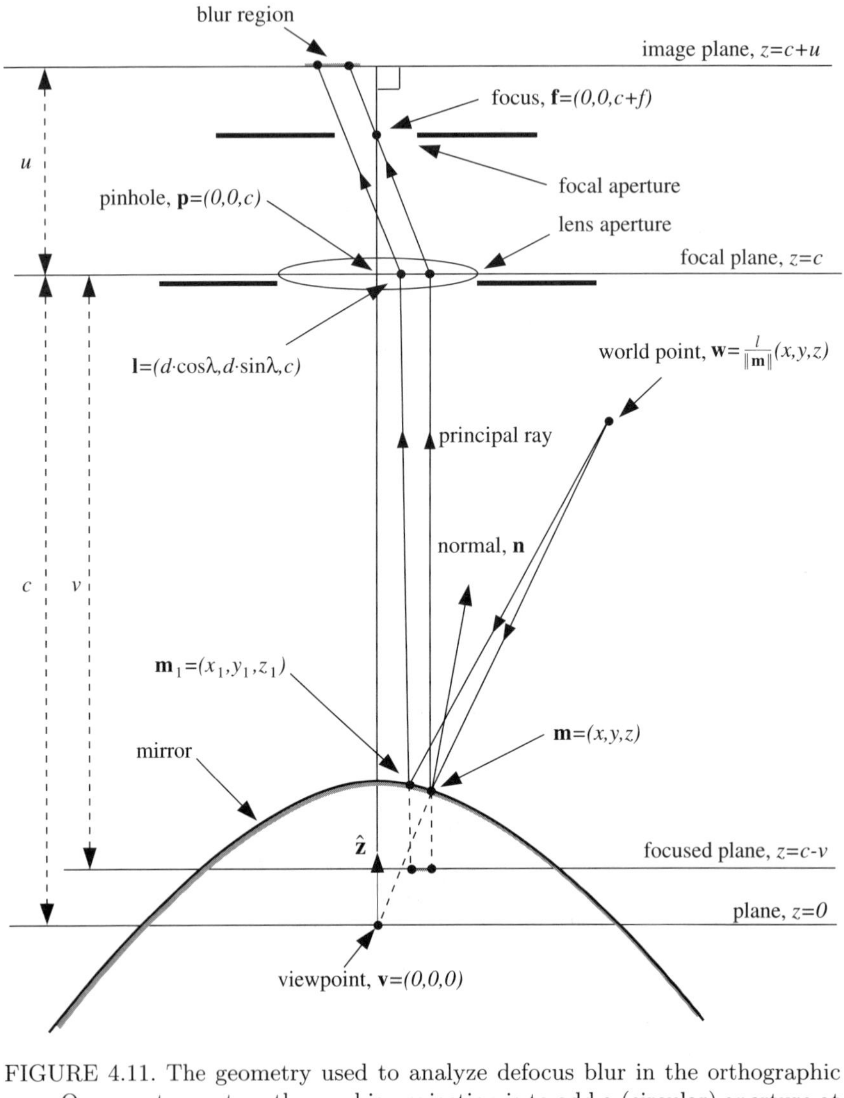

FIGURE 4.11. The geometry used to analyze defocus blur in the orthographic case. One way to create orthographic projection is to add a (circular) aperture at the rear focal point (the one behind the lens) [196]. Then, the only rays of light that reach the image plane are those which are (approximately) parallel to the optical axis. The analysis of defocus blur is then essentially the same as in the perspective case except that we need to check whether each ray of light passes through this aperture when computing the blur region.

The orthographic case is slightly different, as is illustrated in Figure 4.11. One way to convert a thin lens to produce orthographic projection is to place an aperture at the focal point behind the lens [196]. Then, the only rays of light that reach the image plane are those that are (approximately) parallel to the optical axis. For the orthographic case, there is therefore only one difference to the analysis. When estimating the blur region, we need to check that the ray of light actually passes through the (circular) aperture at the rear focal point. This task is straightforward. The intersection of the ray of light with the rear focal plane is computed using linear interpolation of the lens point and the point where the mirror point is imaged on the image plane. It is then checked whether this point lies close enough to the optical axis to pass through the aperture.

4.4.3 Numerical Results

It is possible to use the constraints derived in the previous two sections to investigate how the shape and size of the blur areas varies with the focal setting. For lack of space, however, we are unable to present these results. The reader is referred to [12] for the full details. Instead, we investigate how the focus setting that minimizes the area of the blur region for points a fixed distance away in the world varies with the angle which the world point $\mathbf{w}$ makes with the plane $z = 0$. The results are presented in Figures 4.12–4.14.

In our numerical experiments we set the distance between the effective viewpoint and the pinhole to be $c = 1$ meter, and the distance from the viewpoint to the world point $\mathbf{w}$ to be $l = 5$ meters. For the hyperboloidal and ellipsoidal mirrors, we set the radius of the lens aperture to be 10 mm. For the paraboloidal mirror, the limiting aperture is the one at the focal point. We chose the size of this aperture so that it lets through exactly the same rays of light that the front 10 mm one would for a point 1 meter away on the optical axis. We assumed the focal length to be 10 cm and therefore set the aperture to be 1 mm. With these settings, the F-stop for the paraboloidal mirror is $2 \times 10/100 = 1/5$. The results for the other two mirrors are independent of the focal length, and hence the F-stop.

To allow the three mirror shapes to be compared on an equal basis, we used values for k and h that correspond to the same mirror radii. The radius of the mirror is taken to be the radius of the mirror cut off by the plane $z = 0$; i.e. the mirrors are all taken to image the entire upper hemisphere. Some values of k and h are plotted in Table 4.1 against the corresponding mirror radius, for $c = 1$ meter.

From Figures 4.12–4.14, we see that the best focus setting varies considerably across the mirror for all of the mirror shapes. Moreover, the variation is roughly comparable for all three mirrors (of equal sizes.) In practice, these results, often referred to as "field curvature" [104], mean that it can sometimes be difficult to focus the entire scene at the same time. Either the center of the mirror is well focused or the points around the periphery are focused, but not both. Fortunately, it is possible to introduce additional lenses which compensate for the field curvature [104]. Also note that as

TABLE 4.1. The mirror radius as a function of the mirror parameters (k and h) for $c = 1$ meter.

Mirror Radius	Hyperboloid (k)	Ellipsoid (k)	Paraboloid (h)
20 cm	6.1	0.24	0.2
10 cm	11.0	0.11	0.1
5 cm	21.0	0.05	0.05
2 cm	51.0	0.02	0.02

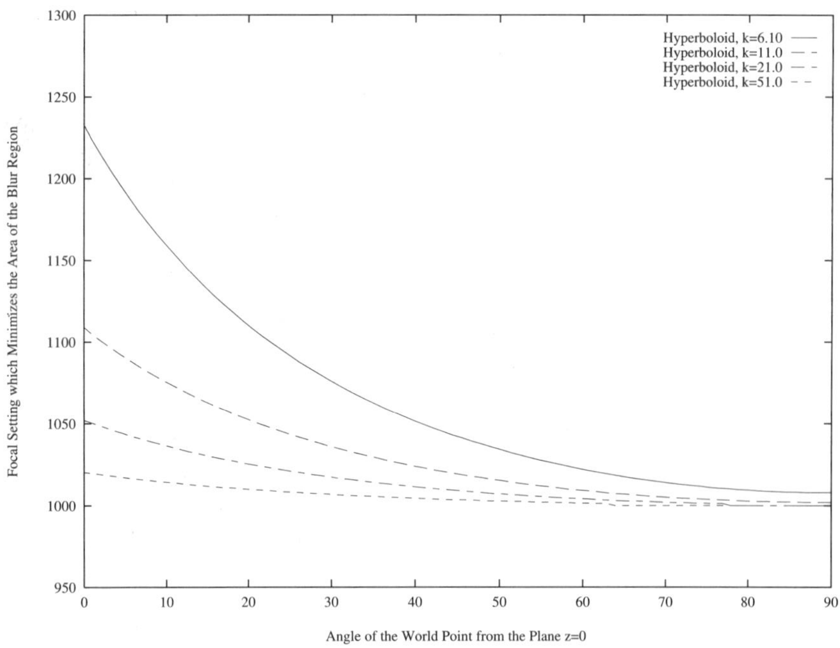

FIGURE 4.12. The focus setting which minimizes the area of the blur region plotted against the angle θ which the world point $\mathbf{w}$ makes with the plane $z = 0$. Four separate curves are plotted for different values of the parameter k. See Table 4.1 for the corresponding radii of the mirrors. We see that the best focus setting for $\mathbf{w}$ varies considerably across the mirror. In practice, these results mean that it can sometimes be difficult to focus the entire scene at the same time, unless additional compensating lenses are used to compensate for the field curvature [104]. Also, note that this effect becomes less important as k increases and the mirror gets smaller.

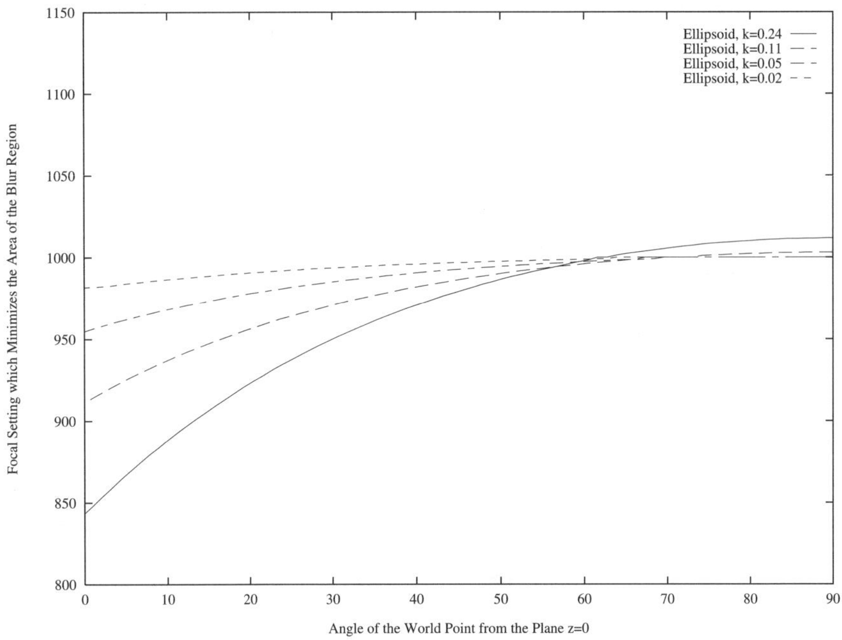

FIGURE 4.13. The focus setting which minimizes the area of the blur region plotted against the angle θ which the world point $\mathbf{w}$ makes with the plane $z = 0$. Four separate curves are plotted for different values of the parameter k. See Table 4.1 for the corresponding radii of the mirrors. The field curvature for the ellipsoidal mirror is roughly comparable to that for the hyperboloidal, and also decreases rapidly as the mirror is made smaller.

the mirrors become smaller in size (k increases for the hyperboloid, k decreases for ellipsoid, and h decreases for the paraboloid) the effect becomes significantly less pronounced.

4.5 Case Study: Parabolic Omnidirectional Cameras

As a case study, we describe the design and implementation of a parabolic omnidirectional camera [197]. As described above, such a camera requires an orthographic camera. There are several ways to achieve orthographic projection. The most obvious of these is to use commercially available telecentric lenses [66] that are designed to be orthographic. It has also been shown [289] that precise orthography can be achieved by simply placing an aperture [153] at the back focal plane of an off-the-shelf lens. Further, several zoom lenses can be adjusted to produce orthographic projection. Yet another approach is to mount an inexpensive relay lens onto an off-the-shelf

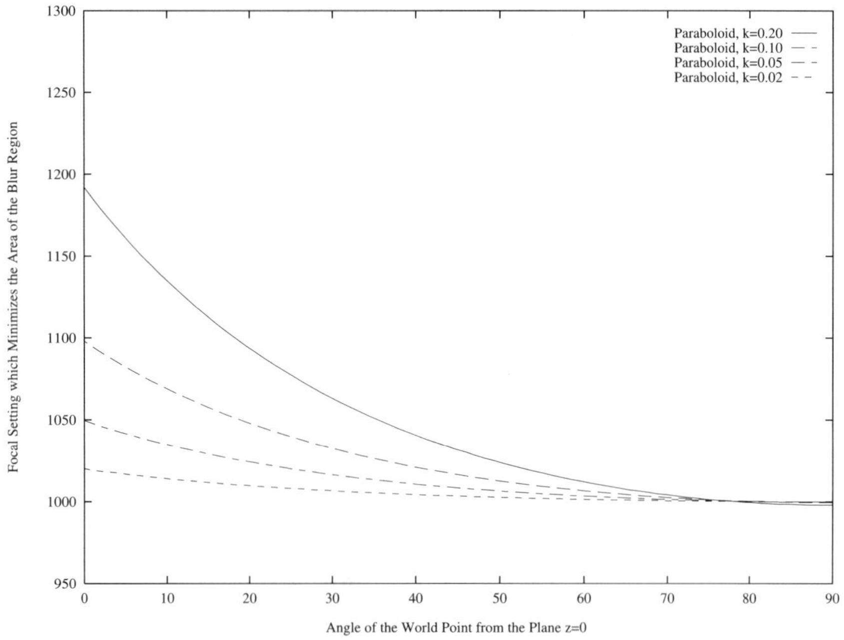

FIGURE 4.14. The focus setting which minimizes the area of the blur region plotted against the angle θ which the world point $\mathbf{w}$ makes with the plane $z = 0$. Four separate curves are plotted for different values of the parameter h. See Table 4.1 for the corresponding radii of the mirrors. The field curvature for the paraboloidal mirror is roughly comparable to that for the hyperboloidal, and also decreases rapidly as the mirror is made smaller.

perspective lens. The relay lens not only converts the imaging system to an orthographic one but can also be used to reduce more subtle optical effects such as coma and astigmatism [30] produced by curved mirrors. In short, the implementation of pure orthographic projection is viable and easy to implement.

One advantage of using an orthographic camera is that it can make the calibration of the catadioptric system far easier. Calibration is simpler because, so long as the direction of orthographic projection remains parallel to the axis of the paraboloid, any size of paraboloid is a solution. The paraboloid constant and physical size of the mirror therefore do not need to be determined during calibration. Moreover, the mirror can be translated arbitrarily and still remain a solution. Implementation of the camera is therefore also much easier because the camera does not need to be positioned precisely. By the same token, the fact that the mirror may be translated arbitrarily can be used to set up simple configurations where the camera zooms in on part of the paraboloid mirror to achieve higher resolution (with a reduced field of view), but without the complication of having to compensate for the additional non-linear distortion caused by the rotation of the camera that would be needed to achieve the same effect in the perspective case.

4.5.1 Selection of the Field of View

As the extent of the paraboloid increases, so does the field of view of the catadioptric camera. It is not possible, however, to acquire the entire sphere of view since the paraboloid itself must occlude the world beneath it. This brings us to an interesting practical consideration: Where should the paraboloid be terminated? Note that

$$\left| \frac{dz}{dr} \right| \Bigg|_{z=0} = 1 \,. \tag{4.53}$$

Hence, if we cut the paraboloid at the plane $z = 0$, the field of view exactly equals the upper hemisphere (minus the solid angle subtended by the imaging system itself). If a field of view greater than a hemisphere is desired, the paraboloid can be terminated below the $z = 0$ plane. If only a panorama is of interest, an annular section of the paraboloid may be obtained by truncating it below and above the $z = 0$ plane. For that matter, given any desired field of view, the the corresponding section of the parabola can be used and the entire resolution of the imaging device can be dedicated to that section. In other words, for an orthographic imaging system of given magnification, the parabolic mirror can be resized and translated horizontally to obtain any desired field of view. Note that the resulting imaging system also adheres to the single viewpoint constraint.

For the prototypes we present here, we have chosen to terminate the parabola at the $z = 0$ plane. This proves advantageous in applications in which the complete sphere of view is desired, as shown in Figure 4.15. Since the paraboloid is terminated at the focus, it is possible to place two identical catadioptric cameras back-to-back such that their foci (viewpoints) coincide. The shaded regions represents a small part of the field that is lost due to obstruction by the imaging system itself. Thus, we have a truly omnidirectional camera, one that is capable of acquiring an entire sphere of view at video rate.

4.5.2 Implementations of Parabolic Systems

Several versions of the catadioptric design based on the paraboloidal mirror have been implemented at Columbia University [197]. These sensors were designed keeping specific specific applications in mind. The applications we have in mind include video teleconferencing, remote surveillance and autonomous navigation. Figure 4.16 shows and details the different cameras and their components. The basic components of all the cameras are

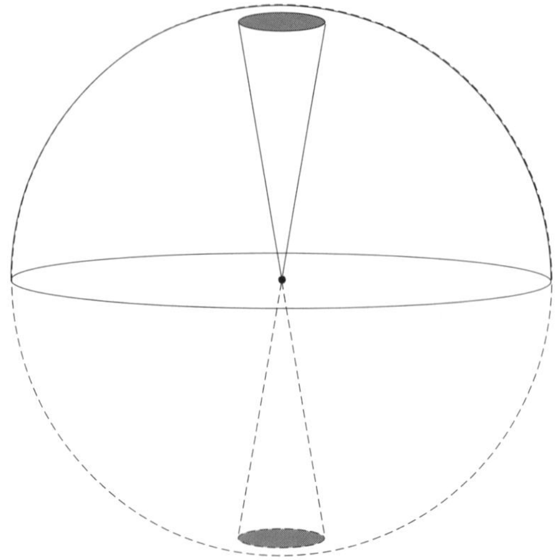

FIGURE 4.15. If the paraboloid is cut by the horizontal plane that passes through its focus, the field of view of the catadioptric system exactly equals the upper hemisphere. This allows us to place two catadioptric cameras back-to-back such that their foci (viewpoints) coincide. The result is a truly omnidirectional camera that can acquire the entire sphere of view. The shaded regions are parts of the field of view where the camera sees itself.

the same; each one includes a paraboloidal mirror, an orthographic lens system and a CCD video camera. The cameras differ primarily in the their mechanical designs and their attachments. For instance, the cameras in Figures 4.16(a) and 4.16(c) have transparent spherical domes that minimize self-obstruction of their hemispherical fields of view. Figure 4.16(d) shows a back-to-back implementation that is capable of acquiring the complete sphere of view.

The use of paraboloidal mirrors virtually obviates calibration. All that is needed are the image coordinates of the center of the paraboloid and its radius h. Both these quantities are measured in pixels from a single omnidirectional image. We have implemented software for the generation of perspective images. First, the user specifies the viewing direction, the image size and effective focal length (zoom) of the desired perspective image. Again, all these quantities are specified in pixels. For each three-dimensional pixel location (x_p, y_p, z_p) on the desired perspective image plane, its line of sight with respect to the viewpoint is computed in terms of its polar and azimuthal angles:

$$\theta = \cos^{-1} \frac{z_p}{\sqrt{{x_p}^2 + {y_p}^2 + {z_p}^2}}, \quad \phi = \tan^{-1} \frac{y_p}{x_p}. \tag{4.54}$$

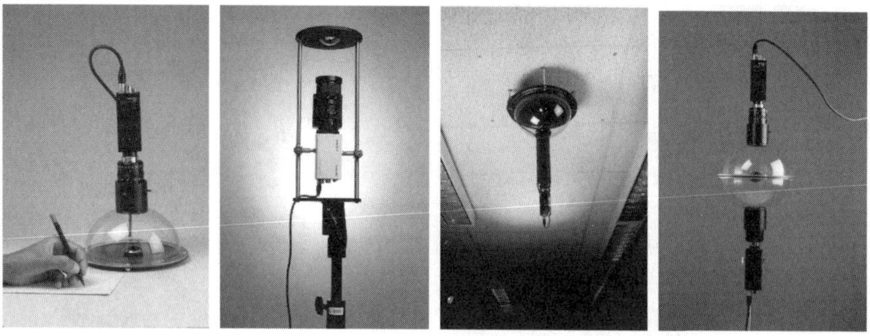

(a) (b) (c) (d)

FIGURE 4.16. Four implementations of catadioptric omnidirectional video cameras that use paraboloidal mirrors. (a) This compact camera for *teleconferencing* uses a 1.1 inch diameter paraboloidal mirror, a Panasonic GP-KR222 color camera, and Cosmicar/Pentax C6Z1218 zoom and close-up lenses to achieve orthography. The transparent spherical dome minimizes self-obstruction of the field of view. (b) This camera for *navigation* uses a 2.2 inch diameter mirror, a DXC-950 Sony color camera, and a Fujinon CVL-713 zoom lens. The base plate has an attachment that facilitates easy mounting on mobile platforms. (c) This camera for *surveillance* uses a 1.6 inch diameter mirror, an Edmund Scientific 55mm F/2.8 telecentric (orthographic) lens and a Sony XR-77 black and white camera. The camera is lightweight and suitable for mounting on ceilings and walls. (d) This camera is a back-to-back configuration that enables it to sense the entire sphere of view. Each of its two units is identical to the camera in (a).

This line of sight intersects the paraboloid at a distance ρ from its focus (origin), which is computed using the following spherical expression for the paraboloid:

$$\rho = \frac{h}{(1 + \cos\theta)} . \tag{4.55}$$

The brightness (or color) at the perspective image point (x_p,y_p,z_p) is then the same as that at the omnidirectional image point

$$x_i = \rho \sin\theta \cos\phi , \qquad y_i = \rho \sin\theta \sin\phi . \tag{4.56}$$

The above computation is repeated for all points in the desired perspective image. Figure 4.17 shows an omnidirectional image (512x480 pixels) and several perspective images (200x200 pixels each) computed from it. It is worth noting that perspective projection is indeed preserved. For instance, straight lines in the scene map to straight lines in the perspective images while they appear as curved lines in the omnidirectional image. A video-rate version of the above described image generation was developed as an interactive software system called OmniVideo [216]. This system can generate about a dozen perspective image streams at 30 Hz using no more than a standard PC.

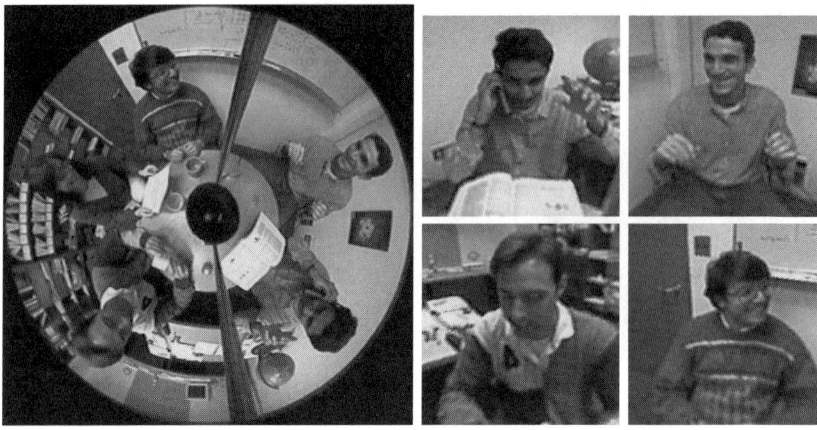

(a) (b)

FIGURE 4.17. Software generation of (b) perspective images from an (a) omnidirectional image. Each perspective image is generated using user-selected parameters, including, viewing direction (line of sight from the viewpoint to the center of the desired image), effective focal length (distance of the perspective image plane from the viewpoint of the camera), and image size (number of desired pixels in each of the two dimensions). It is clear that the computed images are indeed perspective; for instance, straight lines are seen to appear as straight lines even though they appear as curved lines in the omnidirectional image.

4.6 Conclusion

In this chapter, we have studied three design criteria for catadioptric cameras: (1) the shape of the mirrors, (2) the resolution of the cameras, and (3) the focus settings of the cameras. In particular, we have derived the complete class of mirrors that can be used with one camera to give a single effective viewpoint, found an expression for the resolution of a catadioptric camera in terms of the resolution of the conventional camera used to construct it, and presented detailed analysis of the defocus blur caused by the use of a curved mirror.

We have described a large number of mirror shapes in this chapter, including cones, spheres, planes, hyperboloids, ellipsoids, and paraboloids. Practical catadioptric cameras have been constructed using most of these mirror shapes. See, for example, [224], [47], [197], [301], [110], [85], [306], [28], [194], and [195]. As described in [44], even more mirror shapes are possible if we relax the single-viewpoint constraint. Which then is the "best" mirror shape to use?

Unfortunately, there is no simple answer to this question. If the application requires exact perspective projection, there are three alternatives: (1) the ellipsoid, (2) the hyperboloid, and (3) the paraboloid. The major limitation of the ellipsoid is that only a hemisphere can be imaged. As far as the choice between the paraboloid and the hyperboloid goes, using an orthographic imaging system does require extra effort on behalf of the optical designer, but makes construction and calibration of the entire catadioptric system far easier. No careful positioning of the camera relative to the mirror is needed. Moreover, all that is required to calibrate the camera is the image of the circle formed by the circumference of the mirror; no physical distances or other parameters are needed to obtain accurate perspective images.

Acknowledgment

This work was conducted at the Computer Vision Laboratory (CAVE) at Columbia University. It was supported in parts by an ONR/DARPA MURI grant under ONR contract No. N00014-97-1-0553, an NSF National Young Invenstigator Award and a David and Lucile Packard Fellowship.

5

Epipolar Geometry of Central Panoramic Catadioptric Cameras

T. Pajdla, T. Svoboda, and V. Hlaváč

5.1 Introduction

Epipolar geometry [67] describes relationship between positions of the corresponding points in a pair of images acquired by cameras with single viewpoints. Epipolar geometry can be established from a few image correspondences and used to simplify the search for more correspondences, to compute the displacement between the cameras, and to reconstruct the scene.

Ideal omnidirectional cameras would provide images covering the whole view-sphere and therefore they would be image sensors with no self-occlusion. However, ideal omnidirectional cameras are difficult to realize because a part of the scene is often occluded by an image sensor. Recently, a number of panoramic cameras appeared. They do not cover the whole view-sphere but most of it. A wide field of view eases the search for correspondences as corresponding points do not so often disappear from the field of view and helps to stabilize ego-motion estimation algorithms so that the rotation of the camera can be well distinguished from its translation [33]. As the panoramic cameras see a large part of the scene around them in each image, they can provide more complete reconstructions from fewer images.

Epipolar geometry is a property of the cameras with a central projection. It can be formulated for all cameras which have a single viewpoint. As there exist panoramic cameras which have single viewpoints, the epipolar geometry can be formulated for them too. An analysis of the epipolar geometry of panoramic catadioptric cameras which use hyperbolic mirrors was, for the first time, presented in [265]. In this work, a complete characterization of epipolar geometry of central panoramic catadioptric cameras is given by extending work [265] to the catadioptric cameras with parabolic mirrors.

The text is organized as follows. The specific terminology is defined in Section 5.2 where various cameras are classified with respect to their projection model, field of view, and construction. Section 5.3 overviews different panoramic cameras described in the literature and the way how they were

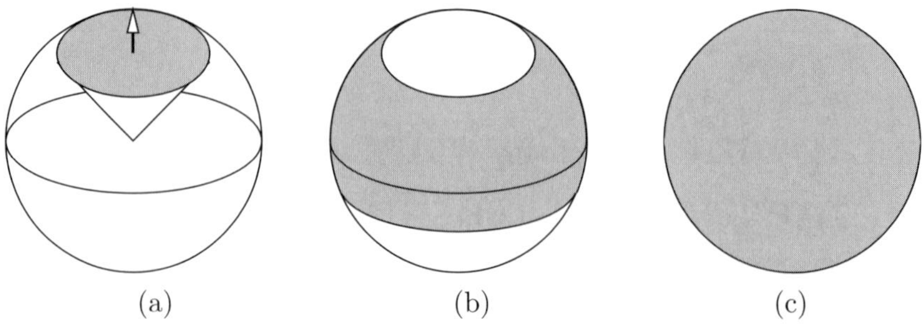

FIGURE 5.1. (a) The field of view of a directional camera is contained in a hemisphere. (b) The field of view of a panoramic camera contains at least one great circle. (c) The field of view of an omnidirectional camera covers the whole view-sphere.

applied. In Section 5.4, central panoramic catadioptric cameras are introduced. Section 5.5 defines the mathematical model of central panoramic catadioptric cameras. Examples of real cameras are given in Section 5.6 and their correct composition is discussed there. The epipolar geometry of central panoramic catadioptric cameras is described in Section 5.7. In Section 5.8, the estimation of the epipolar geometry for conventional and central panoramic cameras is compared. The work is summarized in Section 5.10.

5.2 Terminology and Notation

We say that the mirror is *convex* if rays reflect from the convex side of its surface. We say that it is *concave* if the rays reflect from the concave side. A planar mirror is neither convex nor concave.

All what can be seen from a single viewpoint can be represented by an omnidirectional image mapped on a *view-sphere*. We assume that all cameras have symmetrical fields of view so that the boundary of each field of view is a circle on the view-sphere.

By the *camera* (C) we shall henceforth understand any ray-based sensing device. For an unconstrained camera, the rays may be completely independent, in particular, they do not have to intersect in a single point. The field of view of an unconstrained camera may be arbitrary.

With respect to whether the rays intersect or not, cameras can be classified as *central* (Ce) and *non-central* (Nc). We say that the camera is *central* or has a *single viewpoint* or a *projection center* if all rays intersect in a single point.

With respect to the field of view, cameras can be classified as *directional* (Dr), Figure 5.1(a), *panoramic* (Pa), Figure 5.1(b), and *omnidirectional*

(*Od*), Figure 5.1(c). We say that the camera is *omnidirectional* if it has a complete field of view and its image covers the whole view-sphere. We say that the camera is *directional* if its field of view is a proper subset of a hemisphere on the view-sphere. For a directional camera, there exist a plane which does not contain any ray, hence the camera is pointed into the direction given by the normal of that plane. We say that the camera is *panoramic* if its field of view contains at least one great circle on the view-sphere. A panorama is seen around that great circle.

With respect to the construction, cameras can be classified as *dioptric* (*Di*) and *catadioptric* (*Ca*). The dioptric cameras use only lenses. The catadioptric cameras use at least one mirror but may also use lenses.

Our classification is by no means complete. Other cameras can still be found. For instance, there are cameras which look into different directions so that their field of view is not contained in a hemisphere, it does not contain a great circle, nor it covers the view-sphere completely.

The most common cameras will be called conventional. We say that the camera is *conventional* if it is a central directional dioptric camera, in other words it is a pinhole camera which has the field of view contained in a hemisphere. In this work, we shall concentrate on the *Central Panoramic Catadioptric Camera* (*CePaCaC*) which can be obtained by a combination of a convex mirror with a conventional camera.

5.3 Overview of Existing Panoramic Cameras

We give an overview of various principles used to obtain panoramic images which appeared in literature.

5.3.0.1 Mosaic-based Cameras

Panoramic images can be created from conventional images by mosaicing. The QTVR system[1] allows to create panoramic images by stitching together conventional images taken by a rotating camera. Peleg et. al [214] presented a method for creating mosaics from images acquired by a freely moving camera[2]. Similarly, the mosaicing method proposed by Shum and Szelisky [257, 273] does not require controlled motions or constraints on how the images are taken as long as there is no strong motion parallax.

5.3.0.2 Cameras with Rotating Parts

To speed up the acquisition of panoramic images, Benosman et al. [22, 24] use a line-scan camera rotating around a vertical axis. A similar system

---

[1]`http://www.qtvrworld.com/`

[2]Panoramic images can also be produced by Spin Panorama software `http://www.videobrush.com/` using the camera moving on a circle.

was described by Murray in [192] who used panoramic images to measure depth. In [217], Petty et al. investigated a rotating stereoscopic imaging system consisting of two line-scan cameras.

5.3.0.3 Cameras with a Single Lens

"Fish-eye" lenses provide wide angle of view and can directly be used for panoramic imaging. A panoramic imaging system using a fish-eye lens was described by Hall et al. in [91]. A different example of an imaging system using wide-angle lens was presented in [204] where the panoramic camera was used to find targets in the scene. Fleck [72] and Basu et al. [18] studied imaging models of fish-eye lenses suitable for panoramic imaging. Shah and Aggarwal [248] extended the conventional camera model by including additional lens distortions.

5.3.0.4 Cameras with a Single Mirror

In 1970's, Charles [45] designed a mirror system for the Single Lens Reflex camera. He proposed a darkroom process to transform a panoramic image into a cylindrical projection. Later, he designed a mirror so that the tripod holding the mirror was not seen in the image [46]. Various approaches how to get panoramic images using different types of mirrors were described by Hamit [92]. Greguss [87, 88] proposed a special lens to get a cylindrical projection directly without any image transformation. Chahl and Srinivasan [44] designed a convex mirror to optimize the quality of imaging. They derived a family of surfaces which preserve linear relationship between the angle of incidence of light onto the surface and the angle of reflection into the conventional camera. Yagi et al. [303] used a conic-shaped mirror for a mobile vehicle navigation. Similarly, Yamazawa *et al.* [307] detected obstacles using a panoramic sensor with a hyperbolic mirror. Nayar et al. [195] presented several prototypes of panoramic cameras using a parabolic mirror in combination with an orthographic cameras. Svoboda *et al.* [265] used a hyperbolic mirror imaged by a conventional camera to obtain a panoramic camera with a single viewpoint and presented epipolar geometry for the hyperbolic cameras. Geb [78] proposed a panoramic camera with a spherical mirror for navigating a mobile vehicle. Recently, Hicks and Bajcsy [108] presented a family of reflective surfaces which provide a large field of view while preserving the geometry of a plane perpendicular to the mirror symmetry axis.

5.3.0.5 Cameras with Multiple Mirrors

Kawanishi *et al.* proposed an omnidirectional sensor covering the whole view-sphere [149] consisting from two catadioptric panoramic cameras. Nalwa [286] proposed a panoramic camera consisting of four-sided spire and four conventional cameras. Two planar mirrors placed in front of a conventional camera were used to compute depth by Arnspang *et al.* [6], Gosthasby *et al.* [85], and most recently by Gluckman *et al.* [81]. A double-lobed mirror and a conventional camera were used by Southwell *et al.* [262]. They used mirrors with conic profiles to create a real time panoramic stereo. Nayar *et al.* [199] introduced a folded catadioptric camera that uses two mirrors and a special optics allowing for a very compact design. It was shown the the folded cameras with two conic mirrors are geometrically equivalent to cameras with one conic mirror.

5.3.1 Stereo and Depth from Panoramic Images

A number of works used multiple mirrors and multiple conventional cameras to create compact [6, 81, 85] or omnidirectional [201, 217, 262] stereo heads. Often, simplified camera models as well as the arrangements of the mirrors and cameras were used to avoid the derivation of general epipolar geometry. In particular, Nene and Nayar [201] studied the epipolar geometry for the limited case of a pure rotation of a hyperbolic mirror around the center of a conventional camera or equivalently a pure translation of a parabolic mirror with respect to an orthographic camera. Gluckman and Nayar [80] estimate ego-motion of the omnidirectional cameras by an optical flow algorithm. In [265], Svoboda et. al derived the epipolar geometry for a camera with a single hyperbolic mirror.

5.3.2 Classification of Existing Cameras and Comparison of Their Principles

Table 5.1 compares the cameras described in Section 5.3 with respect to the classification of cameras defined in Section 5.2. It can be concluded that only the cameras with a single mirror provide a single viewpoint. The camera from [199] is not an exception because it is designed to be equivalent to a camera with one mirror.

The table also compares the approaches with respect to the number of conventional images needed to create a single panoramic image and with respect to the resolution of the final panoramic image.

It can be concluded that mosaic based cameras are characterized by no single viewpoint, long acquisition time, and high resolution. They are therefore suitable for getting high quality panoramic images for visualization but they are not useful for an acquisition of dynamic scenes or for a computing a scene reconstruction. A similar situation holds for the cameras with rotating parts with that exception that the images are captured faster, though still not in real time.

Cameras with wide-angle lenses have no single viewpoint, are real-time, and have low resolution. The exception is the camera from [248], which has a single effective viewpoint but that is not a panoramic camera, only

Principle	**Camera**	**Type**[1]	**Imgs**[2]	**Res**[3]
Mosaics	QTVR	*NcPaDiC*	many	high
	VideoBrush, [214]	*NcPaDiC*	many	high
Rotating parts	Line-scan cameras [22, 192, 217]	*NcPa—C*	many	high
Wide-angle lenses	Fish-eye [18, 91]	*NcPaDiC*	1	low
	Wide-angle lens [248]	*CeDrDiC*	1	low
Multiple mirrors	Multiple planar mirrors with multiple cameras [149, 286]	*NcPaCdC*	a few	medium
	Two planar mirrors with one camera [6, 81, 85]	*NcDrCdC*	1	low
	Multiple conic mirrors with one camera [199]	*CePaCdC*	1	low
Single mirror	Mirror for SLR camera [46]	*NcPaCdC*	1	low
	Convex mirror with constant angular gain [44]	*NcPaCdC*	1	low
	Parabolic mirror [195]	*CePaCdC*	1	low
	Hyperbolic mirror [265, 307]	*CePaCdC*	1	low
	Special mirror preserving plane geometry [108]	*NcPaCdC*	1	low
	A special lens [87]	*NcPaCdC*	1	low

TABLE 5.1. The comparison of the existing cameras. [1]**Type** stands for the camera type, (*C*) Camera, (*Nc*) Non-central, (*Ce*) Central, (*Cd*) Catadioptric, (*Di*) Dioptric, (*Od*) Omnidirectional, (*Pa*) Panoramic, (*Dr*) Directional. [2]**Imgs** gives the number of conventional images needed to create one panoramic image. [3]**Res** gives the resolution of the resulting panoramic image. The panoramic cameras with a single viewpoint are underlined.

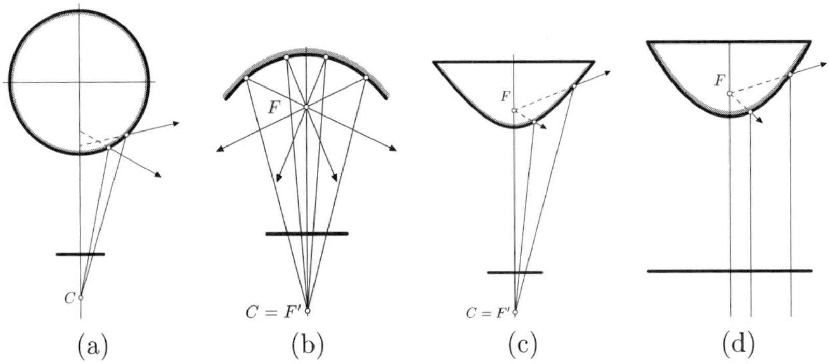

FIGURE 5.2. The combinations of a conventional central camera with (a) a spherical mirror (b), an elliptic mirror (c), a parabolic mirror (d), and a hyperbolic mirror. For elliptic (b) and hyperbolic (c) mirrors, there is a single viewpoint in F if the conventional camera center C is at F'. For parabolic mirrors (d), there is a single viewpoint in F if the mirror is imaged by an orthographic camera. There is no single viewpoint for a convex spherical mirror (a).

a directional one. Wide-angle lens cameras are suitable for fast panoramic image acquisition and processing, e.g. obstacle detection or mobile robot localization but are not suitable for doing a scene reconstruction. A similar situation holds for the cameras with multiple mirrors.

Cameras with a single mirror are real-time and provide low-resolution images. Only cameras with conic mirrors have a single viewpoint as it will be explained in the next section. These cameras are useful for low resolution dynamic scene reconstruction and ego-motion estimation. They are the only cameras for which epipolar geometry can be simply generalized.

5.4 Central Panoramic Catadioptric Camera

Figure 5.2 depicts geometry of light rays for the catadioptric cameras consisting of conventional perspective cameras and curved conic mirrors. The rays pass through a camera center C and then reflect from a mirror. The reflected rays may, see Figure 5.2(b, c, d), but do not have to, see Figure 5.2(a), intersect in a single point F.

If they do intersect, the projection of a space point into the image can be modeled by a composition of *two central projections*. The first one projects a space point onto the mirror, the second one projects the mirror point into the image. The geometry of multiple catadioptric cameras depends only on the first projection. The second projection is not so important as far as it is a one-to-one mapping. It can be seen as just an invertible image transform.

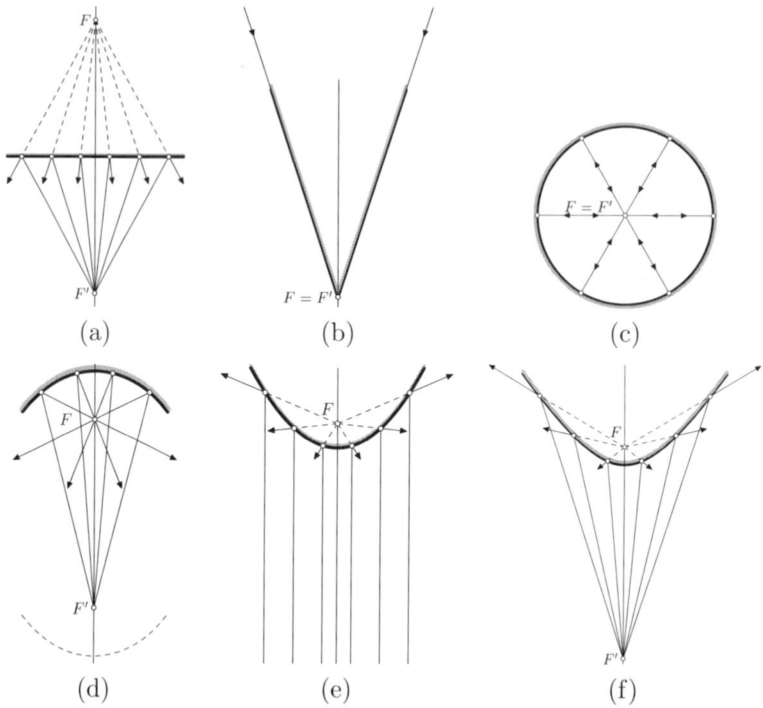

FIGURE 5.3. The mirrors which preserve a single viewpoint: (a) plane, (b) sphere, (c) cone, (d) ellipsoid, (e) paraboloid, (f) hyperboloid. The viewpoint is in F if the camera center is in F'.

If the first projection is a central projection, the catadioptric camera has the same – perspective – mathematical model as any conventional perspective camera and all the theory developed for conventional cameras [67] can be used. Thus, the images from a central catadioptric camera can be directly used e.g. to reconstruct the scene or to estimate the camera displacement.

In 1637 René Descartes presented an analysis of the geometry of mirrors an lenses in *Discours de la Methode* [62]. He showed that refractive as well as reflective "ovals" (conical lenses and mirrors) focus light into a single point if they are illuminated from other properly chosen point [103]. In computer vision, the characterization of curved mirrors preserving a single viewpoint was given by Baker and Nayar [12].

It can be shown [12] that the mirrors which preserve a single viewpoint are those and only those shown in Figure 5.3. All the shapes are rotationally symmetric quadrics: plane, sphere, cone, ellipsoid, paraboloid, or one sheet of a hyperboloid of two sheets. However, only two mirror shapes can be used to construct a central panoramic catadioptric camera.

Theorem:

Convex hyperbolic and convex parabolic mirror are the only mirrors which can be combined with a conventional (central directional dioptric) camera to obtain a (one-mirror) central panoramic catadioptric camera.

Proof:

Planar mirrors do not enlarge the field of view. Spherical and conical mirrors provide degenerate solutions of no practical use for panoramic imaging. For the sphere, the camera has to be inside of the mirror so that its center is in the center of the sphere. A conical mirror has the single viewpoint at its apex and only the rays which graze the cone enter the camera. An elliptic mirror cannot be used to make a panoramic camera because its field of view is smaller than a hemisphere due to the self-occlusion caused by the mirror if that is made large enough to reflect rays in angle larger than π. Parabolic and hyperbolic mirrors provide a single viewpoint as well as their field of view contains a great circle on the view-sphere. □

5.5 Camera Model

In this section, we study the geometry of image formation of central panoramic catadioptric cameras. Points in 3D space are represented by upper case letters, such as X or by bold upper case letters, such as $\mathbf{X}$, if we refer to their coordinates. Homogeneous vectors, corresponding to image points or rays, are represented by bold lower case letters, such as $\mathbf{x}$. The symbol $\|\mathbf{x}\|$ stands for the length of a vector $\mathbf{x}$.

By the camera model we understand the relationship between the coordinates of a 3D point $\mathbf{X}$ and its projection, $\mathbf{u}$, in the image. The following model of a conventional camera is used

$$\alpha\,\mathbf{x} = [R, -R\,\mathbf{t}]\,\mathbf{X}, \quad \alpha \in \mathsf{R}, \tag{5.1}$$

$$\mathbf{u} = K\mathbf{x}, \tag{5.2}$$

where $\mathbf{X} = [X, Y, Z, 1]^T$ is a 4-vector representing a 3D point, $\mathbf{t}$ is the position of the camera center, $R \in SO(3)$ is the rotation between the camera and a world coordinate system. Matrix K is a 3×3 upper triangular camera calibration matrix with $K_{33} = 1$ and α stands for a nonzero scale. Vector $\mathbf{x} = [x, y, 1]^T$ represents normalized homogeneous image coordinates whereas $\mathbf{u} = [u, v, 1]^T$ represents homogeneous pixel image coordinates which are measured in the image. See [67] for more details about the model of a conventional camera.

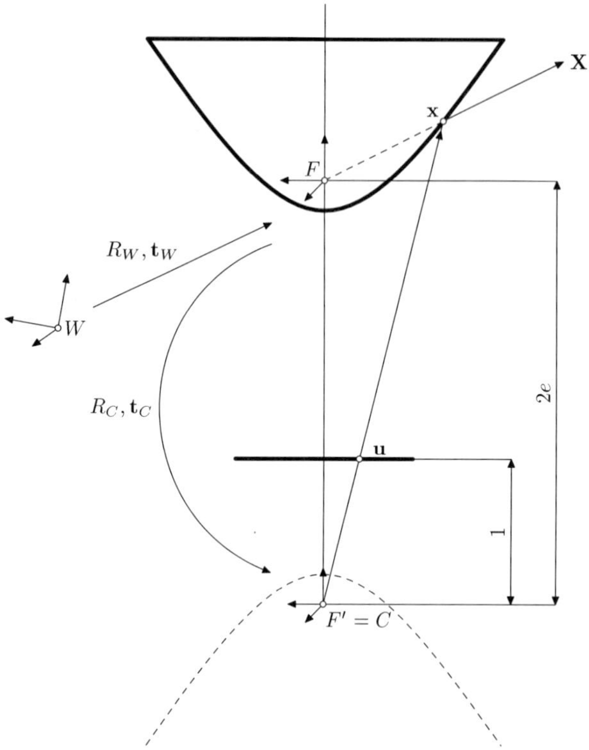

FIGURE 5.4. A conventional camera assembled with a hyperbolic mirror so that the camera center C coincides with the focal point of the mirror F'. The rays reflected from the mirror intersect in F.

5.5.1 Hyperbolic Mirror

Let us find the camera model of a central panoramic catadioptric camera with a hyperbolic mirror. Figure 5.4 depicts a conventional camera assembled with a hyperbolic mirror so that the camera center C coincides with the focal point of the mirror F'.

Three important Cartesian coordinate systems can be defined, see Figure 5.4: (1) the world system centered at W, henceforth called W; (2) the mirror system centered at F so that its z axis coincides with the symmetry axis of the mirror, henceforth called F; and (3) the conventional camera coordinate system centered in the camera center C (which coincides with the second focal point F'), henceforth called C. The mirror coordinate system F is the most crucial one. Therefore, all equations will be expressed in the coordinates of the system F if not stated otherwise. Coordinates without subscripts refer to the coordinate system F. Entities with subscript W, such as vector $\mathbf{X}_W$, refer to the world coordinate system W. Likewise, entities with subscript C, such as vector $\mathbf{x}_C$, refer to the coordinate system C.

The equation of a hyperboloid of two sheets in the coordinate system F reads as

$$\frac{(z+e)^2}{a^2} - \frac{x^2+y^2}{b^2} = 1\,, \tag{5.3}$$

where a, b are *mirror parameters* and $e = \sqrt{a^2+b^2}$ stands for mirror *eccentricity*.

The geometry of panoramic image formation can be expressed as a composition of coordinate transformations and projections. Let the point $\mathbf{X}_W$ be expressed in the world system W. Vector $\mathbf{X}_W$ is transformed to the mirror coordinate system F by the translation $\mathbf{t}_W$ and the rotation R_W

$$\mathbf{X} = R_W(\mathbf{X}_W - \mathbf{t}_W)\,. \tag{5.4}$$

Point $\mathbf{X}$ is projected by a central projection onto the surface of the mirror into a point $\mathbf{x}$ in the following way. Line

$$\nu_1 = \{\mathbf{v} \mid \mathbf{v} = \lambda[X,Y,Z]^T = \lambda\mathbf{X},\ \lambda \in \mathsf{R}\} \tag{5.5}$$

leads from F to the point $\mathbf{X}_W$ for λ going from 0 to 1. The λ for which the line ν_1 intersects the mirror is found by solving the quadratic equation

$$\lambda^2(b^2Z^2 - a^2X^2 - a^2Y^2) + \lambda\,(2b^2eZ) + b^4 = 0$$

(which is obtained by substituting $\mathbf{v}$ from (5.5) into (5.3)) as

$$\lambda_{1,2} = \frac{b^2(-eZ \pm a\|\mathbf{X}\|)}{b^2Z^2 - a^2X^2 - a^2Y^2}\,. \tag{5.6}$$

Line ν_1 always intersects the hyperboloid in two points. It can be verified that $\lambda_{1,2}$ are real and never equal 0 for $\mathbf{X}_W \neq F$. Let us choose the λ that corresponds to the intersection which lies between the points F and $\mathbf{X}_W$.

The signs of $\lambda_{1,2}$ depend on the position of the point $\mathbf{X}_W$ with respect to F. There are three combinations of the signs (as $\lambda_1 > \lambda_2$) which partition space of $\mathbf{X}_W$ into three areas, Figure 5.5. Firstly, the points from the area $\pi_{-,-}$ for which $\lambda_{1,2} < 0$ cannot be seen because they are inside of the mirror. Secondly, for $\mathbf{X}_W \in \pi_{+,+}$, the intersection with the sheet which corresponds to the mirror is given by $\lambda = \min(\lambda_{1,2})$. Finally, for $\mathbf{X}_W \in \pi_{+,-}$ the correct intersection is given by $\lambda = \max(\lambda_{1,2})$ to obtain a point between F and $\mathbf{X}_W$ When the correct λ is chosen, $\mathbf{x}$ is obtained as

$$\mathbf{x} = \lambda\mathbf{X}. \tag{5.7}$$

Vector $\mathbf{x}$ is expressed in the coordinate system C as

$$\mathbf{x}_C = R_C(\mathbf{x} - \mathbf{t}_C)\,, \tag{5.8}$$

where R_C stands for the rotation and $\mathbf{t}_C$ for the translation between the systems F and C. The translation $\mathbf{t}_C$ cannot be arbitrary because the

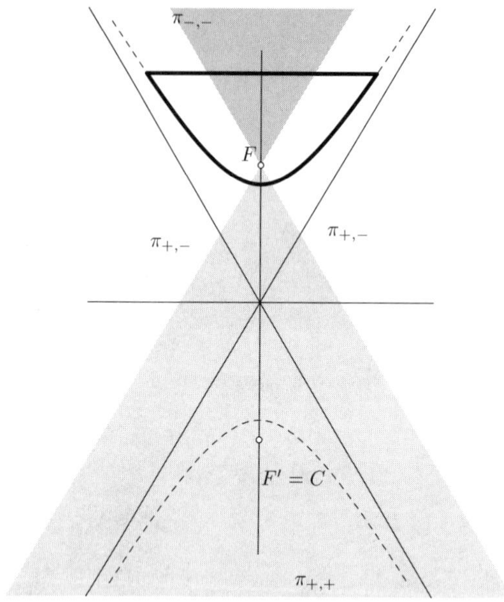

FIGURE 5.5. The signs of $\lambda_{1,2}$ partition space into three areas.

conventional camera center C has to coincide with F' to have a projection center in F. The translation thus must be $\mathbf{t}_C = [0, 0, -2e]^T$. The rotation R_C, on the other hand, can be any such that the mirror is seen in the conventional image even though Figure 5.4 shows the situation when R_C is identity.

Point $\mathbf{x}_C$ projects along the line $\mathbf{x}C$ into the image point with pixel coordinates

$$\mathbf{u} = K \frac{1}{z_C} \mathbf{x}_C, \text{ with } \mathbf{x}_C = [x_C, y_C, z_C]^T . \tag{5.9}$$

Putting (5.9), (5.8), (5.7), and (5.4) together, the complete model of a central panoramic catadioptric camera can be concisely rewritten as

$$\mathbf{u} = K \frac{1}{z_C} R_C \Big(\lambda R_W (\mathbf{X}_W - \mathbf{t}_W) - \mathbf{t}_C \Big) , \tag{5.10}$$

where λ is one of $\lambda_{1,2}$ from (5.6) and z_C is defined by (5.9) and (5.8).

There are 6 free external calibration parameters (3 for $\mathbf{t}_W$ and 3 for R_W) and 10 free internal parameters (2 for the mirror, 3 for the rotation matrix R_C, and 5 for K).

Let us show how $\mathbf{x}$ is obtained from $\mathbf{u}$. The line ν_2 going from the center C in the direction $\mathbf{u}$, see Figure 5.4, consists of points

$$\nu_2 = \{\mathbf{w} \mid \mathbf{w} = \lambda \begin{bmatrix} r \\ s \\ t \end{bmatrix} - \begin{bmatrix} 0 \\ 0 \\ 2e \end{bmatrix} = \lambda \mathbf{v} + \mathbf{t}_C = \lambda R_C^T K^{-1} \mathbf{u} + \mathbf{t}_C, \ \lambda \in \mathsf{R}\} . \tag{5.11}$$

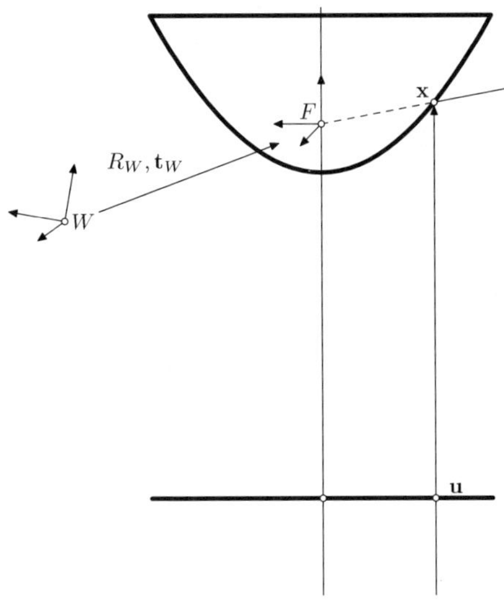

FIGURE 5.6. An orthographic camera with a parabolic mirror assembled so that rays of the conventional camera are parallel to the mirror symmetry axis. The reflected rays intersect in F.

Substituting $\mathbf{w}$ from (5.11) into the mirror equation (5.3) yields

$$\lambda^2(b^2t^2 - a^2r^2 - a^2s^2) - \lambda\,(2b^2et) + b^4 = 0\,.$$

Solving this quadratic equation gives

$$\lambda_{1,2} = \frac{b^2(et \pm a\|\mathbf{v}\|)}{b^2t^2 - a^2r^2 - a^2s^2}\,. \tag{5.12}$$

The decision which λ corresponds to the correct intersection is straightforward. Going from C in direction $\mathbf{u}$, Figure 5.4, we are interested in the intersection which is farther from the point C, hence $\lambda = \lambda_1$. The complete transformation from $\mathbf{u}$ to $\mathbf{x}$ can be concisely written as

$$\mathbf{x} = \mathcal{F}(R_C^T K^{-1}\mathbf{u}) R_C^T K^{-1}\mathbf{u} + \mathbf{t}_C\,, \tag{5.13}$$

with

$$\mathcal{F}(\mathbf{v}) = \frac{b^2(et + a\|\mathbf{v}\|)}{b^2t - a^2r^2 - a^2s^2}\,, \quad \text{where } \mathbf{v} = [r, s, t]^T = R_C^T K^{-1}\mathbf{u}. \tag{5.14}$$

5.5.2 Parabolic Mirror

The model of a central panoramic catadioptric camera with a parabolic mirror is simpler because a parabola is the limiting case of a hyperbola when F'

goes to infinity. There are two important coordinate systems shown in Figure 5.6: (1) the world coordinate system W and (2) the mirror coordinate system F.

The equation of a paraboloid in the system F reads as

$$z = \frac{x^2 + y^2}{2a} - \frac{a}{2}, \tag{5.15}$$

where a is the mirror parameter. Point $\mathbf{X}_W$ is transformed to the point $\mathbf{X} = [X, Y, Z]^T$ according to (5.4) and then projected by a central projection onto the surface of the mirror into a point $\mathbf{x}$. Likewise for the hyperbolic mirror, the intersection of the ray in the direction of $\mathbf{X}$ with the mirror gives the $\mathbf{x}$ in the form

$$\mathbf{x} = \lambda \mathbf{X}, \tag{5.16}$$

where

$$\lambda = \frac{a(Z + \|\mathbf{X}\|)}{X^2 + Y^2} \tag{5.17}$$

is obtained by solving the quadratic equation

$$\lambda^2 (X^2 + Y^2) - 2aZ\lambda - a^2 = 0,$$

which is obtained by substituting $\mathbf{x}$ from (5.16) into (5.15). There are two solutions for λ if $x_F \neq 0$ and $y_F \neq 0$. Since there is only one mirror, the positive λ is always the right one.

Point $\mathbf{x}$ is orthographically projected along the rays parallel with the mirror symmetry axis into the image plane to the point with pixel coordinates

$$\mathbf{u} = K R_C \begin{bmatrix} \begin{bmatrix} 1 & 0 & 0 \\ 0 & 1 & 0 \end{bmatrix} \mathbf{x} \\ 1 \end{bmatrix}, \quad \text{where } R_C = \begin{bmatrix} r_{11} & r_{12} & 0 \\ r_{21} & r_{22} & 0 \\ 0 & 0 & 1 \end{bmatrix} \tag{5.18}$$

is a rotation matrix. The image plane can be rotated in 3D with respect to the system F as well as the image axes can be rotated and skewed in the image plane. Since the projection rays are parallel, the transformation which has to be composed with the projection is an affine transformation and therefore product KR_C must be an affine transformation. With a triangular K, it is possible only if the rotation R_C is in the form given by (5.18).

Combining (5.18), (5.16), and (5.4), the complete camera model can be concisely rewritten as

$$\mathbf{u} = K R_C \begin{bmatrix} \lambda \begin{bmatrix} 1 & 0 & 0 \\ 0 & 1 & 0 \end{bmatrix} R_W (\mathbf{X}_W - \mathbf{t}_W) \\ 1 \end{bmatrix}, \tag{5.19}$$

where λ is defined by (5.17).

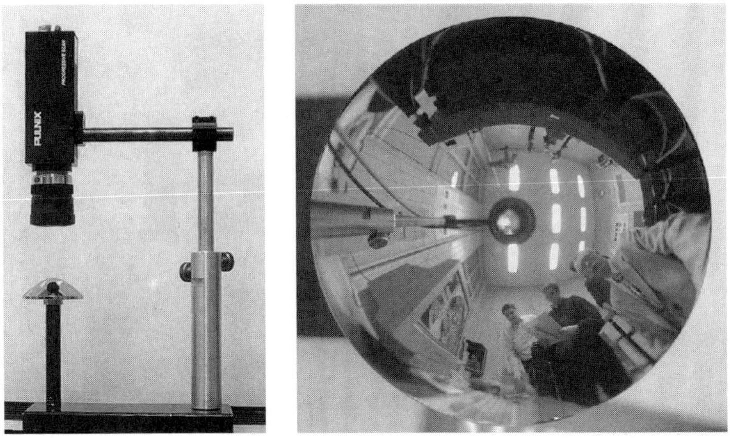

(a) (b)

FIGURE 5.7. (a) A central panoramic catadioptric camera consists of a hyperbolic mirror and a conventional perspective lens. The mirror has been designed at the Center for Machine Perception and manufactured by Neovision Ltd., www.neovision.cz. (b) A panoramic image.

The inverse mapping from $\mathbf{u}$ to $\mathbf{x}$ is rather straightforward. The formula for the coordinates of $\mathbf{x}$ follows directly from (5.18) and (5.15)

$$\mathbf{x} = \begin{bmatrix} x \\ y \\ \frac{x^2+y^2}{2a} - \frac{a}{2} \end{bmatrix}, \text{ where } \begin{bmatrix} x \\ y \\ 1 \end{bmatrix} = R_C^T K^{-1} \mathbf{u}\,. \tag{5.20}$$

There are 6 external calibration parameters (3 for $\mathbf{t}_W$ and 3 for R_W) and 7 internal calibration parameters (1 for the mirror, 1 for R_C, and 5 for K).

5.6 Examples of Real Central Panoramic Catadioptric Cameras

Figure 5.7 shows a central panoramic catadioptric camera consisting of a hyperbolic mirror and a conventional perspective camera. Figure 5.8 shows the central catadioptric camera consisting of a parabolic mirror and an orthographic camera. The orthographic camera is realized by telecentric optics.

For a hyperbolic central panoramic catadioptric camera, $C = F'$ must hold. Therefore, the mirror has to be assembled with a conventional camera so that the camera center coincides with the focal point F' of the mirror. The panoramic camera shown on Figure 5.7 was assembled using the knowledge how a correctly placed mirror must project into the image.

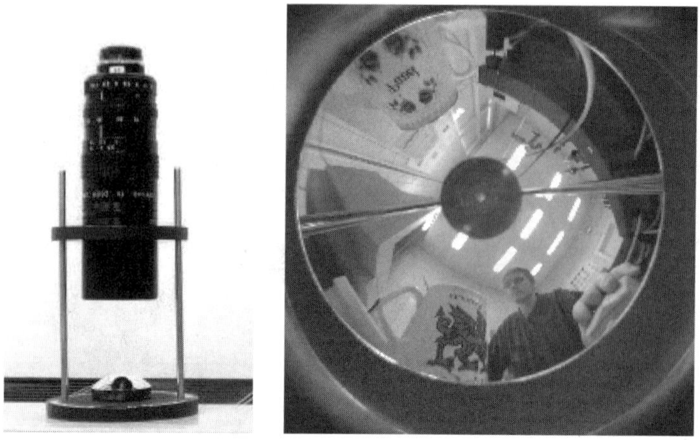

(a) (b)

FIGURE 5.8. (a) A central panoramic catadioptric camera consists of a parabolic mirror and a telecentric lens. The camera ParaCam was produced by Cyclovision Technologies, www.cyclovision.com. (b) A panoramic image.

Figure 5.9 shows the circle drawn in the image where the rim of the mirror and the point where the mirror tip must project if the mirror is placed correctly with respect to the conventional camera. The position of the circle and of the point in the image were computed using known mirror parameters a, b, the camera calibration matrix K obtained by a standard camera calibration technique [208], and for $R_C = I$. Therefore, if the mirror is placed so that it projects into the image as required, it is not only guaranteed that the reflected rays intersect in a single point, but also that the mirror symmetry axis and the lens optical axis coincide.

In order to obtain a parabolic central panoramic catadioptric camera, it is necessary to align the rays of the orthographic camera to be parallel with the symmetry axis of the mirror. It can also be done by the method described above. Let us note that Geyer and Daniilidis [79] recently presented a method for computing the calibration matrix K of a parabolic camera from panoramic images of a calibration target. They assume that the parabolic mirror was correctly assembled with an orthographic camera.

5.7 Epipolar Geometry

Epipolar geometry describes geometric relationship between the positions of the corresponding points in two images acquired by central cameras [67].

Let a scene point $\mathbf{X}$ project into two images as two image points $\mathbf{u}_1$, $\mathbf{u}_2$, see Figure 5.10. In a general situation, the point $\mathbf{X}$, the camera center C_1, and the camera center C_2 define an epipolar plane which intersects the

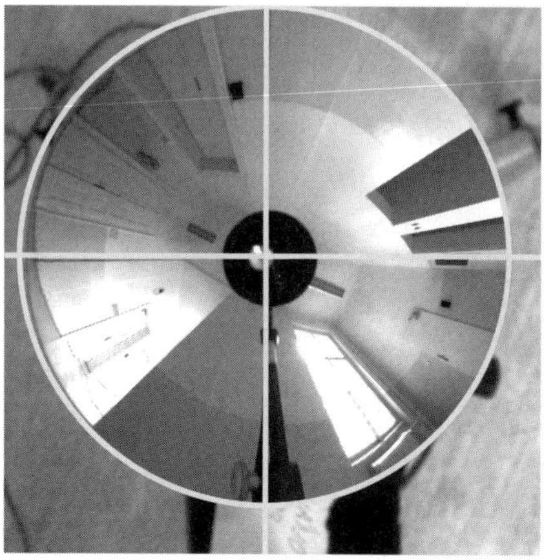

FIGURE 5.9. If the rim of the mirror projects onto the circle shown and the tip of the mirror projects onto the center of the circle, than $C = F'$.

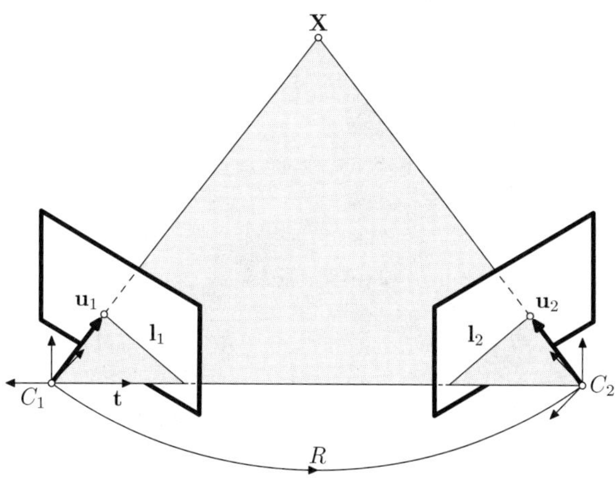

FIGURE 5.10. The epipolar geometry of two conventional cameras.

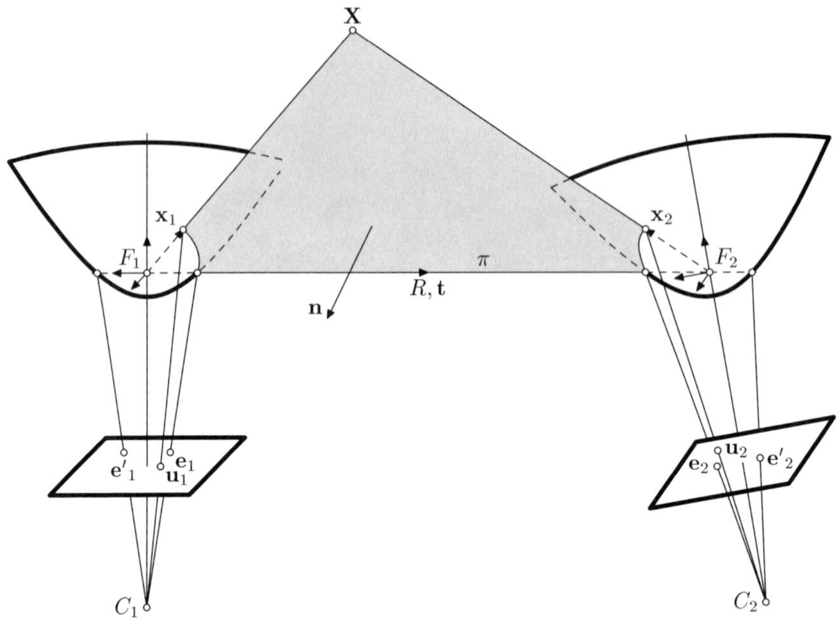

FIGURE 5.11. The epipolar geometry of two central panoramic catadioptric cameras with hyperbolic mirrors.

image planes in epipolar lines $\mathbf{l}_1$, $\mathbf{l}_2$. A pair of the corresponding points $\mathbf{u}_1$, $\mathbf{u}_2$ lie on the epipolar lines $\mathbf{l}_1^T \mathbf{u}_1 = 0$, $\mathbf{l}_2^T \mathbf{u}_2 = 0$. This constraint can be reformulated for points by using the fundamental matrix [67] as

$$\mathbf{u}_2^T F \mathbf{u}_1 = 0 \,. \tag{5.21}$$

The fundamental matrix F can be estimated from a few image correspondences [67].

If the camera calibration matrices K_1, K_2 are known, F can be written in the form

$$F = K_2^{-T} E K_1^{-1} \,, \tag{5.22}$$

where E is the *essential matrix* introduced by Longuett-Higgins in [170].

Epipolar geometry is a property of central cameras, therefore it also exists for central catadioptric cameras, see Figure 5.11. The shape of the epipolar curves as well as the constraint given by equation (5.21) and the epipolar geometry estimation algorithm may vary case to case depending on the type of the central camera.

Let us study how the epipolar curves look like for the central panoramic cameras with conic mirrors. Let the translation $\mathbf{t}$ and the rotation R relate the coordinate systems F_1 and F_2, see Figure 5.11. Let the projection of a 3D point $\mathbf{X}$ onto the mirror be denoted $\mathbf{x}_1$ resp. $\mathbf{x}_2$. The co-planarity of vectors $\mathbf{x}_1$, $\mathbf{x}_2$, and $\mathbf{t} = [t_x, t_y, t_z]^T$ can be expressed in the coordinate system F_2 as

$$\mathbf{x}_2^T R(\mathbf{t} \times \mathbf{x}_1) = 0\,, \tag{5.23}$$

where $\times$ denotes the vector product. Introducing an antisymmetric matrix S

$$S = \begin{bmatrix} 0 & -t_z & t_y \\ t_z & 0 & -t_x \\ -t_y & t_x & 0 \end{bmatrix}, \tag{5.24}$$

the co-planarity constraint (5.23) rewrites in the matrix form as

$$\mathbf{x}_2^T E \mathbf{x}_1 \;=\; 0, \tag{5.25}$$

where

$$E \;=\; RS\,, \tag{5.26}$$

stands for the essential matrix. Vectors $\mathbf{x}_1$, $\mathbf{x}_2$, and $\mathbf{t}$ form the *epipolar plane* π.

The epipolar plane π intersects the mirrors in intersection conics which are projected by a central projection into conics in the image planes. To each point $\mathbf{u}_1$ in one image, an epipolar conic is uniquely assigned in the other image. Expressed algebraically, it bring us the *fundamental constraint* on the corresponding points in two panoramic images

$$\mathbf{u}_2^T A_2(E, \mathbf{u}_1)\; \mathbf{u}_2 = 0\,. \tag{5.27}$$

In a general situation, matrix $A_2(E, \mathbf{u}_1)$ is a nonlinear function of the essential matrix E, of the point $\mathbf{u}_1$, and of the calibration parameters of a central panoramic catadioptric camera.

The shape of the conics, i.e., whether they are lines, circles, ellipses, parabolas, or hyperbolas, depends on the shape of the mirrors, on the motion of the cameras, as well as on which point in the image is considered. It holds that there is at least one line among all epipolar conics in each image. It is the line which corresponds to the epipolar plane containing the axis of the mirror. The corresponding epipolar curves are both lines if the motion is a translation keeping the axes of the mirrors parallel. Moreover, if the translation is along the axis of the mirror, all epipolar curves become lines. It is clear that the epipolar curves form a one-parameter family of conics which is parameterized by the angle of rotation of the epipolar plane around the vector $\mathbf{t}$.

All epipolar conics pass through two points which are the images of the intersections of the mirrors with the line F_1F_2. These points are two epipoles, denoted $\mathbf{e}_1$ and $\mathbf{e}_1'$, resp. $\mathbf{e}_2$ and $\mathbf{e}_2'$, in Figure 5.11. The epipoles can degenerate into a double epipole if the camera is translated along the symmetry axis of the mirror.

In the next two sections, we analyze the epipolar geometry of central panoramic catadioptric cameras with one mirror. We derive a fundamental equation of epipolar geometry and equations for epipolar conics in image coordinates.

5.7.1 Hyperbolic Mirror

Let us look for $A_2(E, \mathbf{u}_1)$ from equation (5.27) for the panoramic camera with a hyperbolic mirror. In order to do so, let us first find the equation of an orthographic projection of the intersection conic on the mirror to the xy plane of the coordinate system F_2. The intersection conic on the mirror is obtained by intersecting the epipolar plane with the mirror, see Figure 5.11. The equation of the conic, expressed in an orthographic projection to the xy plane, reads as

$$\bar{\mathbf{x}}_2^T A_{\bar{\mathbf{x}}_2} \bar{\mathbf{x}}_2 = 0 , \tag{5.28}$$

where

$$\bar{\mathbf{x}}_2 = [x, y, 1]^T \text{ and } \mathbf{x}_2 = [x, y, z]^T . \tag{5.29}$$

Let us find $A_{\bar{\mathbf{x}}_2}$. The focal point of the first mirror F_1, the vector $\mathbf{x}_1$, and the vector $\mathbf{t}$ define the epipolar plane π. The normal vector of the plane π, expressed in the coordinate system F_1, reads as

$$\mathbf{n}_1 = \mathbf{t} \times \mathbf{x}_1 . \tag{5.30}$$

The normal vector $\mathbf{n}_1$ can be expressed in the coordinate system F_2 by using E as

$$\mathbf{n}_2 = R\mathbf{n}_1 = R(\mathbf{t} \times \mathbf{x}_1) = RS\mathbf{x}_1 = E\mathbf{x}_1 . \tag{5.31}$$

Denoting

$$\mathbf{n}_2 = [p, q, s]^T , \tag{5.32}$$

the equation of the plane π can be written in the coordinate system F_2 as

$$px + qy + sz = 0 . \tag{5.33}$$

Assume that $s \neq 0$, i.e., the epipolar plane does not contain the axis of the second mirror. We can express z as a function of x, y from equation (5.33) and substitute it into the mirror equation (5.3) to obtain a second order polynomial in x, y

$$(p^2b_2^2 - s^2a_2^2)x^2 + 2pqb_2^2xy + (q^2b_2^2 - s^2a_2^2)y^2 - 2spb_2^2e_2x - 2sqb_2^2e_2y + s^2b_2^4 = 0 \tag{5.34}$$

which is actually the quadratic form of the conic defined by equation (5.28). Parameters a_2, b_2 in equation (5.34) are related to the second mirror since we are interested in the intersection of the epipolar plane with the second mirror. Consequently, the matrix $A_{\bar{\mathbf{x}}_2}$ from (5.28) has the form

$$A_{\bar{\mathbf{x}}_2} = \begin{bmatrix} p^2b_2^2 - s^2a_2^2 & pqb_2^2 & -pse_2b_2^2 \\ pqb_2^2 & q^2b_2^2 - s^2a_2^2 & -qse_2b_2^2 \\ -pseb_2^2 & -qse_2b_2^2 & s^2b_2^4 \end{bmatrix} . \tag{5.35}$$

The corresponding point on the second mirror, $\mathbf{x}_2$, lies on the epipolar plane π. Using equation (5.33), coordinates of $\mathbf{x}_2$ can be expressed as a linear function of $\bar{\mathbf{x}}_2$,

$$\mathbf{x}_2 = \begin{bmatrix} x \\ y \\ \frac{-px-qy}{s} \end{bmatrix} = \begin{bmatrix} 1 & 0 & 0 \\ 0 & 1 & 0 \\ -\frac{p}{s} & -\frac{q}{s} & 0 \end{bmatrix} \bar{\mathbf{x}}_2 \,. \tag{5.36}$$

It follows from equation (5.13) (for $a = a_2$, $b = b_2$) and equation (5.36) that[3] the relation between $\bar{\mathbf{u}}_2$ and $\bar{\mathbf{x}}_2$ is given by

$$\mathcal{F}(R_{C2}^T K_2^{-1}\mathbf{u}_2) R_{C2}^T K_2^{-1}\mathbf{u}_2 = \left(\mathbf{x}_2 + \begin{bmatrix} 0 \\ 0 \\ 2e_2 \end{bmatrix}\right) = \begin{bmatrix} 1 & 0 & 0 \\ 0 & 1 & 0 \\ -\frac{p}{s} & -\frac{q}{s} & 2e_2 \end{bmatrix} \bar{\mathbf{x}}_2 \,. \tag{5.37}$$

Since $\mathcal{F}(R_{C2}^T K_2^{-1}\mathbf{u}_2) \neq 0$ for $s \neq 0$, we can write

$$\bar{\mathbf{x}}_2 \simeq N R_{C2}^T K_2^{-1}\mathbf{u}_2, \text{ where } N = \begin{bmatrix} 1 & 0 & 0 \\ 0 & 1 & 0 \\ \frac{p}{2se_2} & \frac{q}{2se_2} & \frac{1}{2e_2} \end{bmatrix} \tag{5.38}$$

and the symbol $\simeq$ denotes "equality up to a scale". Vector $\bar{\mathbf{x}}_2$ given by equation (5.38) can be substituted into equation (5.28) yielding the desired equation of the epipolar conic in the image plane

$$\mathbf{u}_2^T K_2^{-T} R_{C2} N_2^T A_{\bar{\mathbf{x}}_2} N_2 R_{C2}^T K_2^{-1}\mathbf{u}_2 = 0 \tag{5.39}$$

and leaving us finally with $A_2 = K_2^{-T} R_{C2} B_2 R_{C2}^T K_2^{-1}$, where

$$\begin{aligned} B_2 &= N^T A_{\bar{\mathbf{x}}_2} N \qquad (5.40) \\ &= \begin{bmatrix} -4s^2a_2^2e_2^2 + p^2b_2^4 & pqb_2^4 & psb_2^2(-2e_2^2 + b_2^2) \\ pqb_2^4 & -4s^2a_2^2e_2^2 + q^2b_2^4 & qsb_2^2(-2e_2^2 + b_2^2) \\ psb_2^2(-2e_2^2 + b_2^2) & qsb_2^2(-2e_2^2 + b_2^2) & s^2b_2^4 \end{bmatrix} \end{aligned}$$

is a nonlinear function of a_2, b_2, and

$$[p, q, s]^T = E\left([\mathcal{F}(R_{C1}^T K_1^{-1}\mathbf{u}_1) R_{C1}^T K_1^{-1}\mathbf{u}_1]^T - [0, 0, 2e_1]^T\right) \tag{5.41}$$

with $\mathcal{F}(R_{C1}^T K_1^{-1}\mathbf{u}_1)$ defined by equation (5.14) for $a = a_1, b = b_1$. Equation (5.39) defines the curve on which the projected corresponding point has to lie and it is, indeed, an equation of a conic as alleged by equation (5.27).

Equation (5.39) holds even for $s = 0$ though it was derived for $s \neq 0$. When $s = 0$, the epipolar plane contains the axis of the mirror. It intersects the mirror in hyperbolas which project into lines. Substituting $s = 0$ into equation (5.40) reveals that B_2 is singular in this case and equation (5.39) describes a line.

---

[3]We use $\mathbf{t}_C = [0, 0, -2e_2]^T$ since the center C has to coincide with the focal point F'.

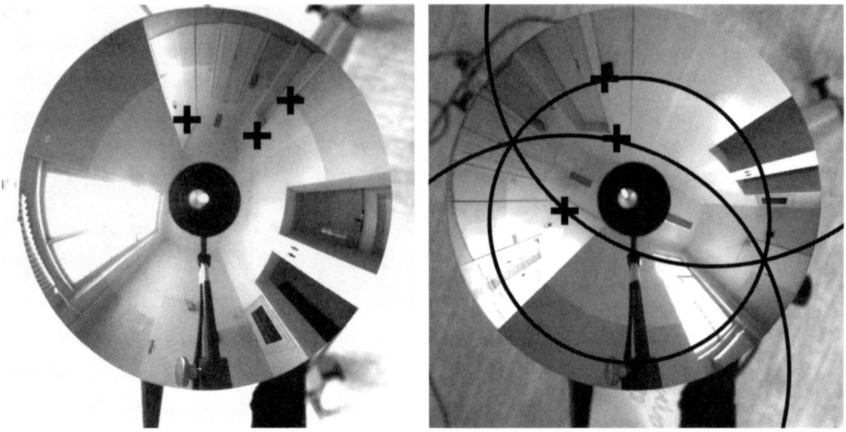

FIGURE 5.12. The illustration of the epipolar geometry of a central panoramic catadioptric camera with a hyperbolic mirror. Three points are chosen in the left panoramic image. Their corresponding epipolar conics are shown in the right panoramic image. The conics intersect in two epipoles and pass through the corresponding points.

Observation 1:

The epipolar conics of a central panoramic catadioptric camera with a hyperbolic mirror are ellipses, hyperbolas, parabolas, or lines. The shape depends on the angle between the epipolar plane and the mirror symmetry axis as well as on the orientation of the conventional perspective camera with respect to the mirror.

Proof 1:

A hyperboloid is intersected by a plane which passes through its focal point in a planar intersection conic. The shape of the conic depends on the angle between the plane and the rotation axis of the hyperboloid. In particular, it is a hyperbola for zero angle between the plane and the axis. The conic is projected into the image by a homography which maps conics to conics. The intersection conic is projected into the image as a line if the epipolar plane contains the mirror symmetry axis. See [264] for more details. □

Figure 5.12 shows an example of the epipolar geometry between a pair of panoramic images obtained by a camera with a hyperbolic mirror. Three corresponding points are marked in the left and in the right image. There are three epipolar conics shown in the right image which correctly pass through the corresponding points. The conics intersect in two epipoles.

5.7.2 Parabolic Mirror

The derivation of $A_2(E, \mathbf{u}_1)$ from equation (5.27) is the same as for the hyperbolic mirror until equation (5.33). Then, the shape of the parabolic mirror enters. Assuming $s \neq 0$, we substitute z from equation (5.33) into the equation of a parabolic mirror (5.15) and obtain the equation of epipolar conics

$$sx^2 + 2a_2px + sy^2 + 2a_2qy - sa_2^2 = 0\,, \tag{5.42}$$

where a_2 is the mirror parameter and p, q, s are defined by equation (5.32). Matrix $A_{\bar{\mathbf{x}}_2}$ from equation (5.28) now becomes

$$A_{\bar{\mathbf{x}}_2} = \begin{bmatrix} s & 0 & ap \\ 0 & s & a_2q \\ a_2p & a_2q & -a_2^2s \end{bmatrix}, \tag{5.43}$$

with

$$\begin{bmatrix} p \\ q \\ s \end{bmatrix} = E \begin{bmatrix} x \\ y \\ \frac{x^2+y^2}{2a_1} \end{bmatrix}, \quad \begin{bmatrix} x \\ y \\ 1 \end{bmatrix} = R_{C1}^T K_1^{-1} \mathbf{u}_1 \tag{5.44}$$

following from equation (5.20) and equation (5.31).

It follows from equation (5.18) that $\bar{\mathbf{x}}_2$ is related to $\mathbf{u}_2$ by a linear transform (compare to equation (5.38))

$$\bar{\mathbf{x}}_2 = R_{C2}^T K_2^{-1} \mathbf{u}_2\,. \tag{5.45}$$

Substituting (5.45) and (5.43) into (5.28) yields the fundamental epipolar constraint for the parabolic mirror

$$\mathbf{u}_2^T K_2^{-T} R_{C2} A_{\bar{\mathbf{x}}_2} R_{C2}{}^T K_2^{-1} \mathbf{u}_2 = 0\,, \tag{5.46}$$

and therefore

$$A_2 = K_2^{-T} R_{C2} A_{\bar{\mathbf{x}}_2} R_{C2}^T K_2^{-1}\,, \tag{5.47}$$

where $A_{\bar{\mathbf{x}}_2}$ is defined by equation (5.43).

Observation 2:

Epipolar conics of a central panoramic catadioptric camera with a parabolic mirror are ellipses, lines, or a point at infinity. In a physical image, only ellipses or lines can appear. The shape depends on the angle between the epipolar plane and the mirror symmetry axis as well as on the angle between the image plane and the axis.

Proof 2:

The epipolar plane intersects the parabolic mirror in an intersection conic. It is a parabola if the angle between the epipolar plane and the axis is zero. It is an ellipse otherwise.

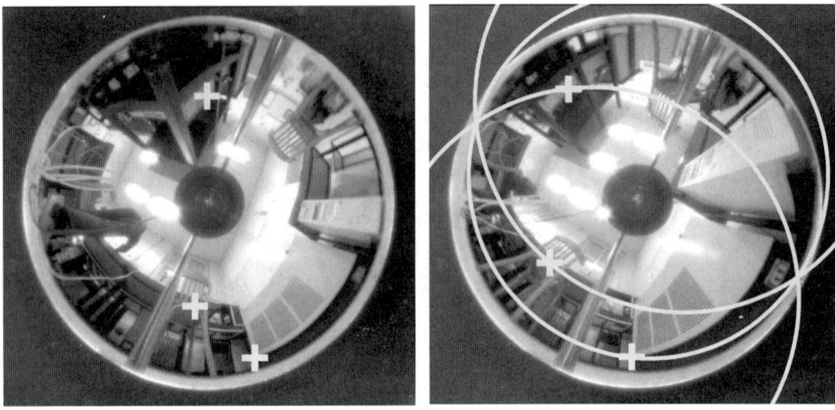

FIGURE 5.13. The illustration of the epipolar geometry of a central panoramic catadioptric camera with a parabolic mirror. Three points are chosen in the left panoramic image. Their corresponding epipolar conics are shown in the right panoramic image. The conics intersect in two epipoles and pass through the corresponding points.

Let the intersection conic be an ellipse. It can be shown that the intersection ellipse always projects into a circle in the xy plane of the coordinate system F [264]. Therefore, the parallel rays which project the ellipse into the image form an cylinder with a circular cross-section. The conic in the image plane results from the intersection of the cylinder with the image plane. A plane and a cylinder always intersect. The intersection is an ellipse if the angle between the plane and the axis of the cylinder is not zero. If it is zero, then the intersection can be either a line, a pair of lines, or a point at infinity on the axis. It is one line or a pair of lines if the plane has a finite intersection with the cylinder. It is a point at infinity if there is no finite intersection of the plane and the cylinder. Point at infinity cannot appear at a finite image.

Let the intersection conic be a parabola. The parallel rays which project the parabola into the image form a plane. The conic in the image results from the intersection of two planes. Two distinct planes always intersect in a line. If the planes are parallel, then the line is at infinity. There is no image conic if the planes are identical. □

Figure 5.13 shows an example of the epipolar geometry between a pair of two panoramic images obtained by a camera with a parabolic mirror. Three corresponding points are marked in the left and in the right image. There are three epipolar conics shown in the right image which pass through the corresponding points. The conics intersect in two epipoles.

5.8 Estimation of Epipolar Geometry

Epipolar geometry can be established from correspondences in images [170]. We shortly recapitulate the state of the art in the epipolar geometry estimation and point out where is a difference arising from using central panoramic catadioptric cameras instead of the conventional ones.

In this section, i numbers cameras and j numbers 3D points. Let $\mathbf{x}_{ij}$ denotes the vector in direction of the j-th ray reflected from the mirror of the i-th central panoramic catadioptric camera. As we have pointed out before, all reflected rays intersect in a single point and therefore the vectors $\mathbf{x}_{ij}$ can be used directly for computing the epipolar geometry of the central panoramic catadioptric cameras.

The fundamental equation of the epipolar geometry, expressed for $\mathbf{x}_{ij}$, reads as

$$\mathbf{x}_{2j}^T E \mathbf{x}_{1j} = 0 . \tag{5.48}$$

Equation (5.48) is a homogeneous linear equation in elements of E. It can be rearranged into the form

$$A\mathbf{e} = 0 , \tag{5.49}$$

where $\mathbf{e} = [E_{11}, E_{12}, \ldots, E_{33}]^T$ and the rows of matrix A are in the form

$$[x_1x_2, y_1x_2, z_1x_2, x_1y_2, v_1y_2, z_1y_2, x_1z_2, y_1z_2, z_1z_2] .$$

Equation (5.49) has a non-zero solution only if A is singular. Then, the vector $\mathbf{e}$ lies in a null space of A and can be recovered up to a nonzero scale. Using the Singular Value Decomposition (SVD) [83] of A, $\mathbf{e}$ is obtained as the right singular vector corresponding to the smallest singular value.

A similar epipolar geometry estimation algorithm was introduced by Longuett-Higgins [170] and it is known as *the 8-point algorithm*, though usually more than 8 correspondences are used. It is known to be susceptible to even small amount of noise. Hartley in [94, 94] and recently also Mühlich and Mester [190] showed that the above SVD-based method performs almost as well as much more complicated nonlinear methods [173] if coordinates of points $\mathbf{x}_{1j}$ and $\mathbf{x}_{2j}$ are normalized by a proper linear transformation so that the average point $\mathbf{x}_{ij}$ has coordinates $[1, 1, 1]^T$ [94].

The essential matrix E has six free parameters [67] while the solution obtained via SVD leaves eight free parameters. It is because the estimate of E, $\hat{E}$, obtained by solving equation (5.49), does not have to satisfy all the constraints valid for a true essential matrix due to noise in data. A true E, closest to $\hat{E}$ such that the Frobenius norm of $E - \hat{E}$ is minimal, can be found by the algorithm given by Hartley [96]. Similarly to the estimation of A, finding true E according to [96] has to be done in the normalized coordinates [94] to avoid sensitivity to noise.

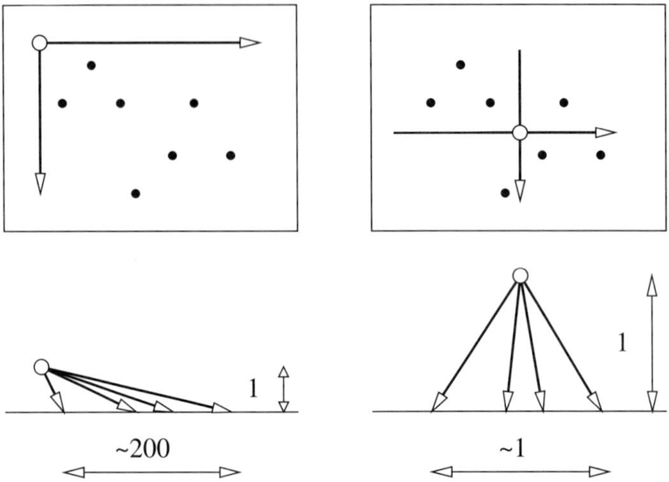

FIGURE 5.14. The normalization of image data for conventional cameras moves the center of the new coordinate system to the centroid of the points. The image coordinates are scaled so that their average equals $\sqrt{2}$.

5.9 Normalization for Estimation of Epipolar Geometry

We want to show that a different normalization of image coordinates has to be applied if omnidirectional cameras are used. Let us first shortly recapitulate how the normalization for conventional cameras [94, 94, 190] is done.

5.9.1 Normalization for Conventional Cameras

It is most critical to do the normalization for uncalibrated conventional cameras because the vectors $\mathbf{u}_{ij} = [u_{ij}, v_{ij}, 1]^T$, are measured in pixels. As the calibration matrices K_1, K_2 are unknown in this case, only a fundamental matrix F from equation (5.21) can be recovered from image data. The equation (5.49) therefore becomes

$$B\,\mathbf{f} = 0\,, \tag{5.50}$$

where $\mathbf{f} = [F_{11}, F_{12}, \ldots, F_{33}]^T$.

Let $\mathbf{u}_{ij} = [100, 100, 1]^T$ be a typical point in a pair of uncalibrated images. Then, the row of B will be in the form

$$\bar{\mathbf{b}}_i^T = [10^4, 10^4, 10^2, 10^4, 10^4, 10^2, 10^2, 10^2, 1]\,.$$

Large variations in the magnitudes of the elements of $\bar{\mathbf{b}}_i^T$ cause (5.50) to be ill-conditioned, hence incorrect F is obtained. The condition number of B in equation (5.50) can be improved by the following procedure [94]

1. Transform the image coordinates $\mathbf{u}_{ij}$ by a linear transform

$$\mathbf{u}'_{ij} = T_i \mathbf{u}_{ij} \tag{5.51}$$

so that the mean of $\mathbf{u}'_{1j}$ and the mean of $\mathbf{u}'_{2j}$ equal 0 and the average distance of the points in image from the origin equals $\sqrt{2}$, see Figure 5.14.

2. Find the fundamental matrix F' corresponding to the points $\mathbf{u}'_{ij}$.

3. Set $F = T_2^T F' T_1$.

Mühlich and Mester [190] show that the above procedure provides an unbiased estimate of F if pixel coordinates of points in the first image are affected by identically distributed zero-mean Gaussian noise while the coordinates in the second image are noise-free. They require that the transformation T_1 accounts for a translation and an isotropic scaling of pixel coordinates while T_2 accounts for a translation and an non-isotropic scaling. Thus, the distribution of noise in $\mathbf{u}'_{1j}$ is the same as the distribution of noise in $\mathbf{u}_{1j}$. It is mainly the autocorrelation matrix of $\mathbf{u}'_{ij}$ which is normalized. Since all $\mathbf{u}_{ij}$ lie in an (image) plane, the normalization can be done for all points by one linear transform.

Let us also remark that if conventional cameras are calibrated, a part of the normalization effect can be achieved by multiplying $\mathbf{u}_{ij}$ by inverses of the camera calibration matrices K_1, K_2. Then, the coordinates of vectors $\mathbf{u}'_{ij}$ are all in the same units and usually have less different magnitudes. Therefore, the condition number of B improves. However, using the inverses of the camera calibration matrices may be less optimal than the normalization proposed in [94, 190].

5.9.2 Normalization for Omnidirectional Cameras

The central panoramic catadioptric cameras described in this work are calibrated but the vectors $\mathbf{x}_{ij}$ from equation (5.48) can have quite large variations of lengths. It is therefore not possible to use them directly.

Moreover, vectors $\mathbf{x}_{ij}$ usually span more than a hemisphere and therefore cannot be modeled as vectors in plane with the first two coordinates affected by identically distributed noise. Instead, for a omnidirectional camera, it is more appropriate to expect that all the coordinates are affected by identically distributed Gaussian noise. Thus, the previous conventional normalization cannot be used. Instead, the following normalization

$$\mathbf{x}'_{ij} = \frac{\mathbf{x}_{ij}}{\|\mathbf{x}_{ij}\|}, \tag{5.52}$$

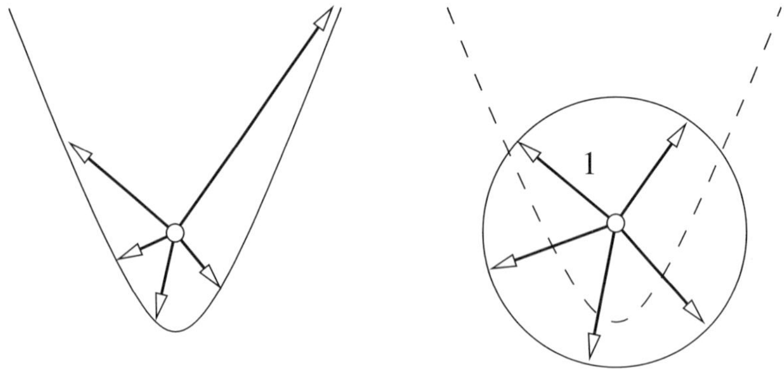

FIGURE 5.15. The normalization for omnidirectional cameras for identically distributed Gaussian noise in all coordinates transforms $\mathbf{x}_{ij} \to \mathbf{x}'_{ij}$ so that $\|\mathbf{x}'_{ij}\| = 1$.

so that $\|\mathbf{x}'_{ij}\| = 1$, see Figure 5.15, can be used to improve the condition number of A in equation (5.49).

Figure 5.16 shows the difference in the estimate of E when it is estimated directly from the vectors $\mathbf{x}_{ij}$ or from the vectors $\mathbf{x}'_{ij}$ normalized by (5.52). The dark epipolar conics are shown for the estimate $\hat{E}$ *without enforcing any constraints*. It is done so to see if the conics intersect in a consistent epipole. Assuming zero noise, $\hat{E} = E$. Therefore the conics intersect even without enforcing the constraints. An ideal estimation method has to be immune to noise and therefore it must provide a consistent $\hat{E}$. The light epipolar conics correspond to the true E which has been computed from a known camera motion and known camera parameters. Figure 5.16 shows that the consistency as well as the precision of the estimate improved when the normalization given by equation (5.52) was applied. Note that, though only 17 correspondences were used in the estimation, the estimated epipolar geometry is very close to the correct one. Two bottom images are details taken from image pair shown in Figure 5.12. Both images are with the same scale. The intersection of conics estimated from normalized points is much more compact than that one estimated from points without normalization.

Mühlich and Mester showed that the normalization (5.51) provides an unbiased estimate of E for identically distributed zero-mean Gaussian noise in pixel coordinates. The noise distribution in $\mathbf{x}_{ij}$ for a panoramic catadioptric camera does not have to be identical as $\mathbf{x}_{ij}$ are obtained as a nonlinear functions of $\mathbf{u}_{ij}$. Therefore, a general unbiased estimator of the epipolar geometry of central omnidirectional (not only panoramic) cameras has the following structure

1. Transform $\mathbf{x}_{ij}$ to $\mathbf{x}'_{ij} = N(\mathbf{x}_{ij})$ by a nonlinear mapping N so that (i) error in $\mathbf{x}'_{ij}$ is identically distributed and (ii) the epipolar con-

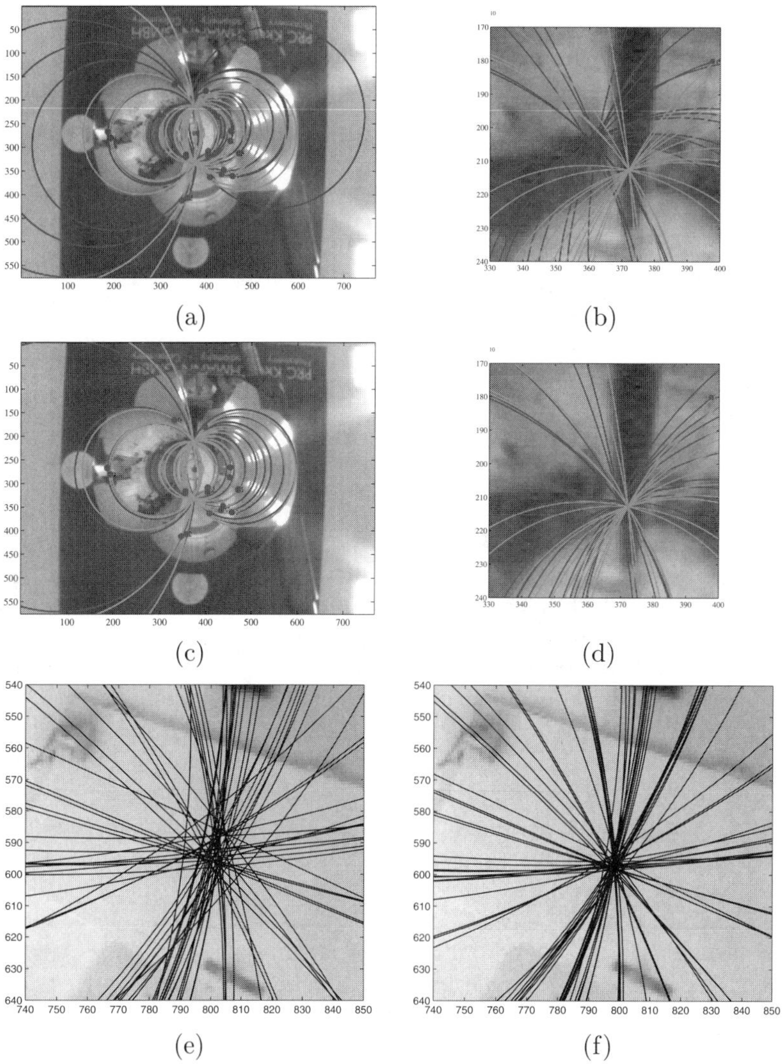

FIGURE 5.16. The light conics correspond to the actual ground-truth E while the dark ones are estimated from image data for (a) non-normalized $\mathbf{x}_{ij}$ and (b) normalized $\mathbf{x}'_{ij}$ so that $\|\mathbf{x}'_{ij}\| = 1$. Images (c) and (d) show detail views of an epipole. The normalization provides more consistent and more accurate epipolar geometry. Images (e) and (f) are detailed images of conic intersection taken from image pair shown in Figure 5.12. Both images are with the same scale. The intersection of conics estimated with the point normalization (f) is much more consistent than the one estimated without normalization (e).

straint still holds for exact data, i.e., $\forall \mathbf{x}_{ij}, \mathbf{x}_{2j}^T E \mathbf{x}_{1j} = 0$ holds that $\exists E', \forall \mathbf{x}'_{ij}, {\mathbf{x}'_{2j}}^T E' \mathbf{x}'_{1j} = 0$.

2. Find the estimate of the essential matrix, $\bar{E}'$ corresponding to the points $\mathbf{x}'_{ij}$ satisfying all the constraints of a true essential matrix.
3. Correct the points $\mathbf{x}'_{ij} \rightarrow \bar{\mathbf{x}}'_{ij}$ using $\bar{E}'$ so that $\bar{\mathbf{x}}'_{ij}$ satisfy the epipolar constraint defined by $\bar{E}'$ exactly.
4. Set $\bar{\mathbf{x}}_{ij} = N^{-1}(\bar{\mathbf{x}}'_{ij})$.
5. Recompute E from $\bar{\mathbf{x}}_{ij}$.

Different camera-mirror arrangements require different form of the normalization N. It is a matter of further research to work out unbiased estimators for various cases.

5.10 Summary

We have shown that the hyperbolic and parabolic catadioptric cameras are the only panoramic catadioptric cameras with a single mirror which have a single viewpoint. It was stressed that (i) a conventional camera center has to coincide with the focal point of the hyperbolic mirror to obtain a single viewpoint for the hyperbolic mirror; (ii) an orthographic camera has to have the rays parallel to the mirror symmetry axis to obtain a single viewpoint for the parabolic mirror. A complete characterization of epipolar geometry of central panoramic catadioptric cameras with one mirror was presented. Explicit formulas for the epipolar conics in panoramic images were given. It was shown that epipolar curves are (i) general conics for a hyperbolic camera; (ii) ellipses or lines for a parabolic camera. It was explained that the difference between the conventional and the panoramic epipolar geometry estimation algorithms based on SVD consists in image data normalization only. A normalization suitable for omnidirectional cameras was proposed and its performance was demonstrated. The need for an unbiased estimator of the epipolar geometry of panoramic cameras was pronounced.

Acknowledgment

This research was supported by the Grant Agency of the Czech Republic under the grants 102/97/0480, 102/97/0855, and 201/97/0437, and by the Czech Ministry of Education under the grant OCAMS and the grant VS96049.

6

Folded Catadioptric Cameras

S.K. Nayar and V. Peri

6.1 Introduction

Catadioptric cameras use a combination of mirrors and lenses to image the scene of interest. In recent years, several lens-mirror combinations have been proposed for the capture of panoramic images (for examples, see [46], [301], [110], [306], [28], [191], [194], [198], [43], [31], [157], [265], [21]. [35], [300], [13], [52]). Catadioptric systems have also been developed for the projection of stereo views onto a single image detector (see [197], [85], [115], [262], [309], [201], [82], [24], [81]).

Of particular interest to us here are wide-angle cameras that satisfy the single viewpoint constraint; if a catadioptric system is capable of viewing the world from a single point in space, the captured image can be mapped to distortion-free images. Since such mapped images adhere to perspective projection, a variety of existing results in vision can be directly applied. Surveys of existing single-mirror catadioptric systems have been presented in [194], [198] and [300]. The complete class of single-mirror, single-lens imaging systems that satisfy the single viewpoint constraint have been analyzed in [13].

A major issue with catadioptric imaging systems is that they tend to be physically large when compared with conventional ones. This is due to the fact that the capture of a wide unobstructed field of view requires the lens and the mirror to be adequately separated from each other. To work around this problem, the well-known method of optical folding is used. A simple example is the use of a planar mirror to fold the optical path between a curved mirror and an imaging lens (see [31]). The folding can be in any direction; a $90°$ fold may help conceal some of the optical elements in an outdoor application and a $180°$ fold reduces the size of the entire system. Folding by means of a curved mirror can result in greater size reduction. More importantly, curved folding mirrors can serve to reduce undesirable optical effects such as field curvature.

In the context of wide-angle imaging, a few folded systems have been implemented in the past. Here, we will focus on coaxial systems where the axes of the all the optical components are coincident. Buchele and Buchele [36] designed a single optical unit (a refractive solid) with a concave spherical mirror and a planar mirror attached to (or coated on) the solid.

This idea was extended by Greguss [88] who used a similar refractive solid with convex and concave aspherical mirrors. Powell [219] further improved the design by using a different shape for the refractive solid and convex and concave conics for the reflectors. Rees [224] has implemented a system that includes a convex hyperbolic primary mirror and a convex spherical secondary mirror. Rees has also developed an imaging lens that would compensate for undesirable optical aberrations generated by these curved mirrors. Rosendahl and Dykes [227] described an implementation that uses convex and concave hyperbolic mirrors and accompanying imaging optics for correction of field curvature. Charles [46] proposed a simple design in which the primary mirror is curved and the secondary one is planar. More recently, Davis et al. [57] described a system that uses three mirrors for redirection and folding. Several variants of the above designs have been suggested in the last few years (for examples, see [28], [191], [21]. [35]).

The previous work described above has not paid much attention to the single viewpoint constraint; the main objective has been to develop systems that produce high quality images of large fields of view. In this chapter, we first look at the general problem of designing folded catadioptric cameras that have a single viewpoint. Geometric tools used in telescope design [176] and microwave optics [53] are invoked in the context of wide-angle imaging. This leads to a general framework for designing multiple-mirror systems with single viewpoints. However, the resulting mirror shapes are shown to be arbitrarily complex. Such mirrors make it difficult for the designer to minimize optical aberrations over the entire field of view. Hence, we restrict ourselves to designs that use conic mirrors whose optical manifestations are better understood and easier to correct. A complete dictionary of conic systems is presented within which some of the existing designs lie. In addition, we show that any folded system that uses conics can be geometrically represented by an equivalent system that uses a single conic. This result makes is easy to determine the scene-to-image mapping for any folded system that uses conic mirrors.

Finally, as an example, we choose a specific design from our dictionary and implement a folded catadioptric video camera that is 9 cm tall, 5 cm wide and has a hemispherical field of view. The performance of the camera is described in terms of its spatially varying point blur function and enclosed energy plots. Perspective and panoramic images are shown that are computed from the hemispherical video using software.

6.2 Background: Single Mirror Systems

We briefly summarize the use of a single mirror and a single lens to capture a large field of view that is observed from a fixed viewpoint. In [12] the general problem of deriving mirror shapes that satisfy the fixed viewpoint constraint was studied. If $z(r)$ is the profile of the mirror shape, the complete class of solutions is given by

$$\left(z-\frac{c}{2}\right)^2+r^2\left(1-\frac{t}{2}\right) = \frac{c^2}{4}\left(\frac{t-2}{t}\right),$$

$$\left(z-\frac{c}{2}\right)^2+r^2\left(1+\frac{c^2}{2t}\right) = \left(\frac{2t+c^2}{4}\right), \tag{6.1}$$

where, c is the distance between the desired viewpoint and the entrance pupil of the imaging lens, and t is a constant of integration. This solution reveals that, to ensure a fixed viewpoint, the mirror must be a plane, ellipsoid, hyperboloid, or paraboloid (see [12] for details).

6.3 Geometry of Folded Systems

As stated earlier, optical folding allows us to develop catadioptric cameras with significantly better packaging and optical performance. As we shall see later, folding using mirrors can also serve to reduce undesirable optical effects that are inherent in most complex imaging systems.

6.3.1 The General Problem of Folding

As always, we will impose the constraint that the complete folded system must have a single fixed viewpoint. Interestingly, this does not imply that each mirror used in the system must satisfy the fixed viewpoint constraint. The general problem of designing folded imaging systems can be stated as follows: Given a desired viewpoint location and a desired field of view, determine the mirrors (shapes, positions and orientations) that would reflect the scene through a single point, namely, the center of projection of the imaging lens. Though this problem has not be addressed in the context of wide-angle imaging, valuable theory has been developed for the construction of multiple-mirror telescopes and microwave devices [53]. These are essentially imaging systems with very narrow fields of view (typically a couple of degrees). This theory is truly attractive in that it provides a suite of geometric tools for constructing folded systems (see [53]). Here, we will outline the approach in the context of single-viewpoint, wide-angle systems.

Figure 6.1 shows a sketch of the problem. Let us assume that shape of the *primary mirror* is arbitrarily chosen and positioned with respect to the desired viewpoint O. Since the mirror has an arbitrary shape, the rays of light that travel from the scene towards the viewpoint O, after reflection by the mirror, do not necessarily converge at a single point. Instead, they can be viewed as tangents to a surface that is called a *caustic*[1]. We would like to design a *secondary mirror* that would reflect these rays such that they intersect at a single point P, where the entrance pupil of the lens is located. For this, consider a string (dotted in Figure 6.1) with one end wound around and fixed to the caustic and the other end attached to the lens location P. Now, consider the point L that pulls on the string to keep it taut. As L moves along the string (while keeping it taut) in the direction shown in Figure 6.1, the string will wrap around the caustic and the locus of L is the required shape of the secondary mirror.

It is worth noting that this elegant method for deriving mirror shapes from caustics can be applied repeatedly to design systems with more than two mirrors. It is a general technique for designing mirrors that transforms one caustic to another. In our case, the second caustic happens to be a point (P). If the camera lens itself is not perspective but instead has a locus of viewpoints (yet another non-point caustic), it is possible to determine the secondary mirror that would map the first caustic to the second one [53], while ensuring that the complete system maintains a single viewpoint.

Clearly, the shape of the secondary mirror depends on the shape of the first caustic, which in turn depends on the shape of the primary mirror. Even for simple mirrors the caustics can have complex shapes such as nephroids, cardioids, cycloids, astroids, etc. For instance, in the case of collimated rays incident on a sphere, the caustic is a nephroid, which is rather complex [53].

6.3.2 The Simpler World of Conics

As we have seen, a variety of exotic mirror pairs can be used to construct folded imaging systems with single viewpoints. However, complex mirror shapes tend to produce severe optical aberrations that cause image quality to vary dramatically over the field of view.

To keep geometrical and optical analysis simple we return to the conic mirrors given by equation (6.1). Note that each conic has well-defined foci that essentially serve as "point caustics" in relation to Figure 6.1. It is therefore easy to combine two (or more) conic mirrors to ensure a fixed viewpoint. To further simplify matters, we will restrict ourselves to coaxial imaging systems where the axes of the mirrors and the optical axis of the imaging lens coincide. A dictionary of the various configurations that result from using conic mirrors is show in Figure 6.2. Figure 6.2(a) shows a primary hyperboloidal mirror and a secondary planar mirror. Rays from the scene in the direction of near focus F_1 of the hyperboloidal mirror are reflected in the direction of its far foucs F_1'. The system is folded by

[1]Caustics have been used in vision for the recovery of specular shapes from highlights (see [207]).

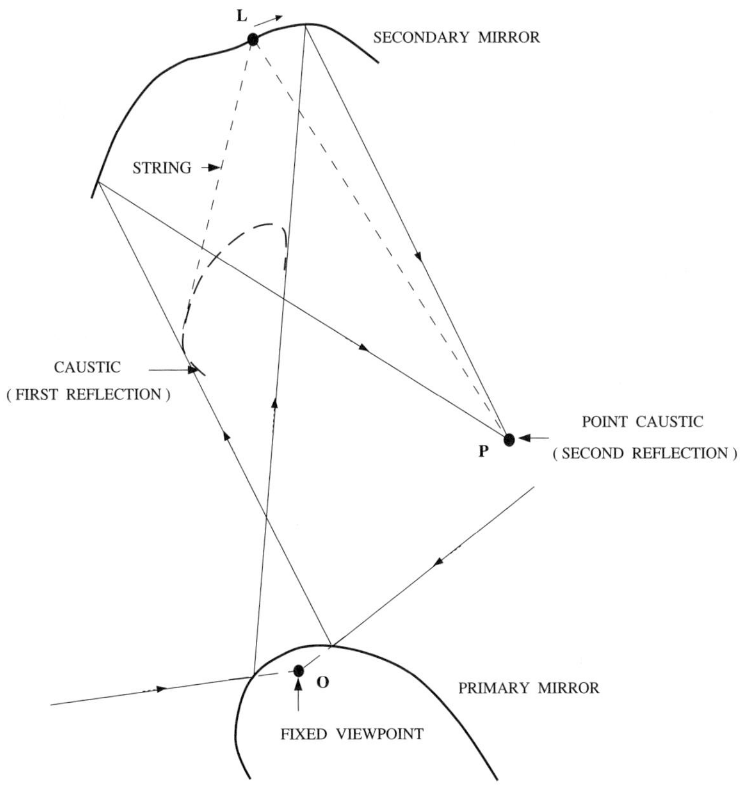

FIGURE 6.1. Geometrical construction of a wide-angle two-mirror imaging system. For any chosen primary mirror, a secondary mirror can be found that maps scene rays in the direction of a chosen viewpoint O to a chosen imaging pupil P. The rays of light in the direction of the viewpoint O are reflected by the primary mirror. The reflected rays are tangents to a surface called the caustic. The secondary mirror that would reflect these rays in the direction of the entrance pupil of the lens P is determined as the locus of the point L that slides along a taut string that is attached to the point P and wound around the caustic.

placing the planar mirror between the near and far foci such that the far focus F_1' is reflected to the point P where the imaging lens is positioned, facing upward. The imaging lens and camera can therefore be placed inside the hyperboloidal mirror, further aiding compact packaging. Similarly, in Figure 6.2(b) the far focus of an ellipsoidal primary mirror is reflected by the planar mirror to P.

More sophisticated systems can be found in Figures 6.2(c)-(f) where the primary and secondary mirrors are hyperboloids and ellipsoids[2]. In each case, the near focus of the secondary mirror is made to coincide with the far focus of the primary mirror. The entrance pupil of the imaging system is then placed at the far focus of the secondary mirror. Figure 6.2(g) shows how a concave hyperboloid may be used. A few more systems that use concave hyperboloids and convex ellipsoids exist but are omitted for brevity.

Finally, in Figure 6.2(h) and (i) paraboloidal primary and secondary mirrors are used. In these cases, the primary mirror orthographically reflects all rays of light incident in the direction of its focus F_1. These rays are collected by a secondary paraboloid and reflected so as to converge at its focus F_2, where the lens is positioned. In effect, the secondary mirror and the imaging lens together serve as a telecentric imaging system as used in [198]. Note that the secondary mirror has a significantly larger focal length than the first one. Similar designs were proposed in [35], where the pinhole of the camera is placed between the primary and secondary parabolic mirrors.

6.3.3 *Equivalent Single Mirror Systems*

Here, we show that any folded system with two conic mirrors can be geometrically represented by an equivalent system with a single conic mirror, where the scene-to-image mapping of the original system is preserved by the equivalent one. It should be noted that geometrical equivalence does not imply optical equivalence; a folded system can be designed to have better optical performance than its single-mirror equivalent. Even so, the geometrical equivalence is valuable in that it enables one to easily determine the relation between scene points and image coordinates, which is needed to map images produced by a folded system to perspective or panoramic ones.

Figure 6.3 shows a sketch of a folded system with two conic mirrors. Since the system has axial symmetry, the equivalence need be established only for a one-dimensional cross-section. Let the primary mirror C_1 have conic constant k_1, radius of curvature R_1, and near and far foci F_1 and F_1'. The shape of the mirror is fully determined by its conic constant: $k_1 = 0$

[2]Some of these combinations were pointed out by Sergey Trubko [283] at CycloVision Technologies.

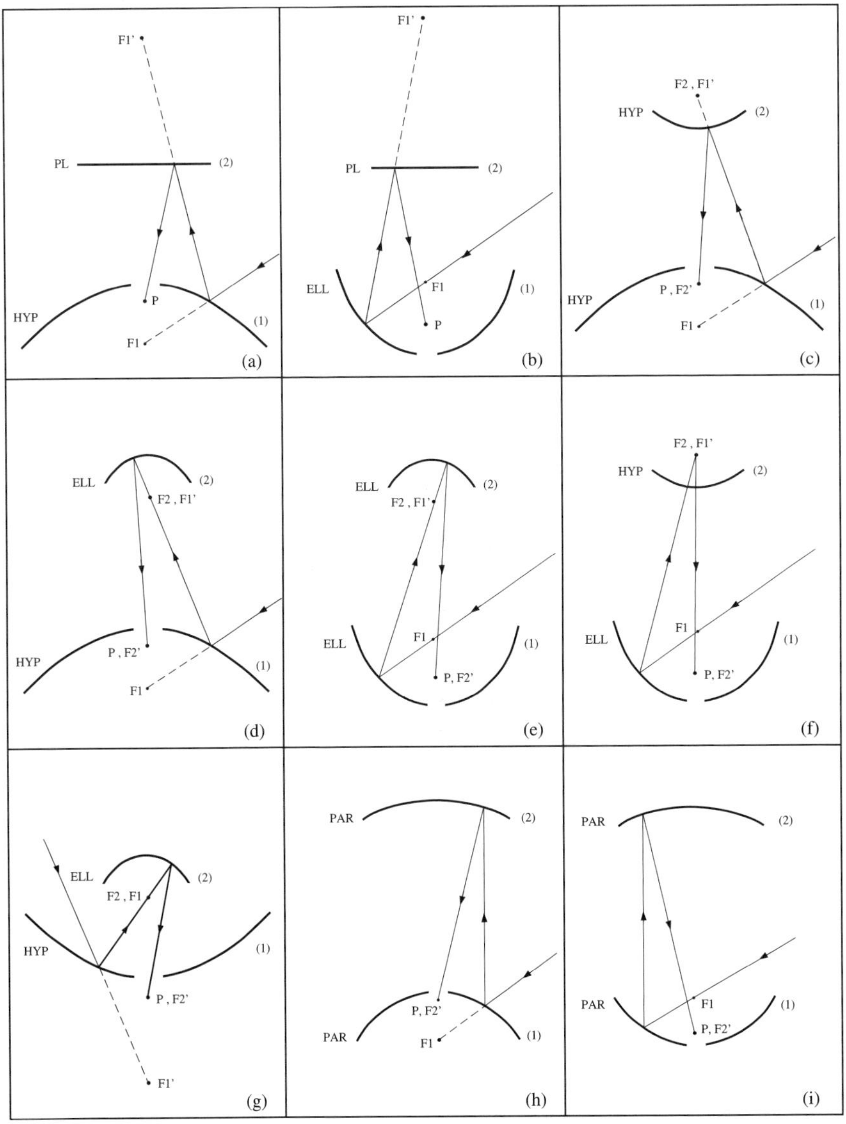

FIGURE 6.2. A dictionary of two-mirror folded catadioptric camera designs that satisfy the single viewpoint assumption. In this dictionary only mirrors with conic cross-sections are shown. Mirrors with the following shapes are used: planar (PL), hyperboloidal (HYP), ellipsoidal (ELL) and paraboloidal (PAR). The primary and secondary mirrors are denoted by (1) and (2), respectively. The near and far foci of the primary mirror are denoted by $F1$ and $F1'$, and those of the secondary mirror by $F2$ and $F2'$. The entrance pupil of the imaging lens is positioned at P.

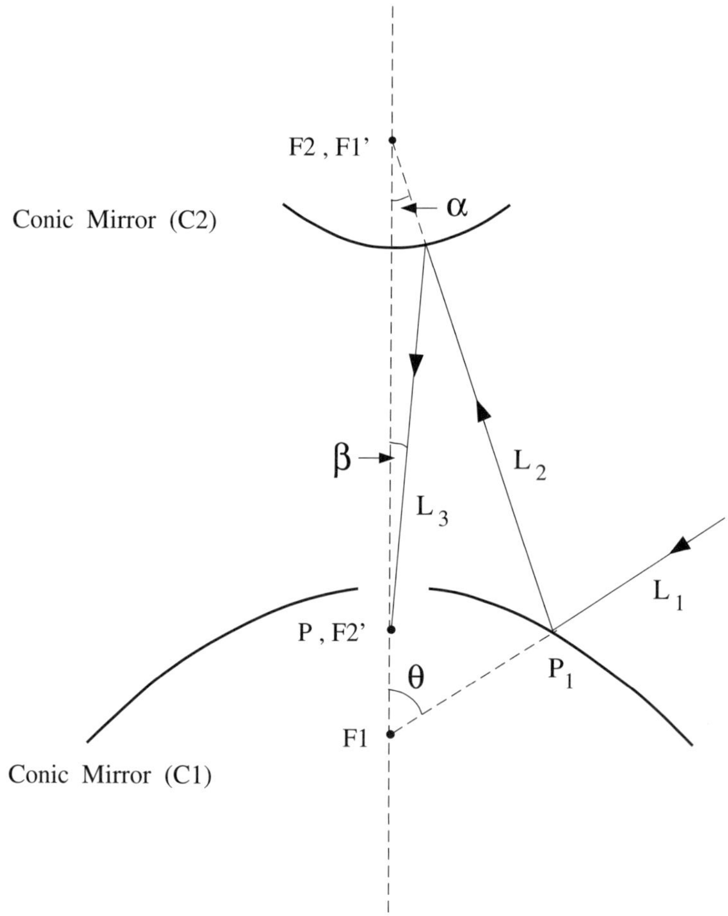

FIGURE 6.3. Any single-viewpoint folded system that uses two or more conic mirrors has an equivalent single mirror system with the same compression, which is the relation between the directions of scene points (θ) and their image coordinates (determined by β).

gives a sphere, $0 > k_1 > -1$ yields an ellipsoid, $k_1 = -1$ gives a paraboloid and $k_1 < -1$ results in a hyperboloid. The distance between its foci is $2R_1\sqrt{-k_1}/(1+k_1)$.

While the conics in equation (6.1) are defined with the near focus at the origin, we can move the origin to the apex (or vertex) of the mirror to get the simpler form:

$$r^2 = -2R_1 z - (1+k_1)z^2 . \tag{6.2}$$

Alternatively, one can write the expression of the conic in polar coordinates with the origin at the near focus F_1 as

$$\rho = \frac{R_1}{1+\sqrt{-k_1}\cos\theta} , \tag{6.3}$$

where

$$z = \rho\cos\theta - R_1/(1+\sqrt{-k_1}) , \quad r = \rho\sin\theta . \tag{6.4}$$

The scene ray L_1 in the direction of F_1 strikes the primary mirror C_1 at P_1. The slope of the mirror at P_1 is

$$m_1 = \frac{dr}{dz} = \frac{-R_1 - (1+k_1)z}{r} . \tag{6.5}$$

Using (6.4), we can substitute for z and r to get

$$m_1 = -\frac{\sqrt{-k_1}+\cos\theta}{\sin\theta} . \tag{6.6}$$

From this expression for the slope and the specular reflection constraint (incidence angle equals reflection angle), we get the following simple relation between the angle θ of an incoming scene ray L_1 and the angle α of the reflected ray L_2:

$$\tan\alpha = \frac{(1+k_1)\sin\theta}{2\sqrt{-k_1}+(1-k_1)\cos\theta} . \tag{6.7}$$

The above expression determines the *compression* of rays due to the primary mirror. The secondary mirror C_2 is also a conic (with constant k_2). Since its near focus F_2 coincides with the far focus F_1' of the primary mirror C_1, the rays reflected by C_1 are directed towards F_2. Hence, the above compression equation can be used to relate the angle α of an incoming ray L_2 to the angle β of the reflected ray L_3:

$$\tan\beta = \frac{(1+k_2)\sin\alpha}{2\sqrt{-k_2}+(1-k_2)\cos\alpha} . \tag{6.8}$$

From equations (6.7) and (6.8) we get the compression of the complete folded system:

$$\tan\beta = \frac{(1+k_1)(1+k_2)\sin\theta}{[\,2(\tilde{k_1}+\tilde{k_2}-k_1\tilde{k_2}-\tilde{k_1}k_2)+(1+k_1(k_2-1)+4\tilde{k_1}\tilde{k_2}-k_2)\cos\theta\,]} \tag{6.9}$$

where $\tilde{k_1} = \sqrt{-k_1}$ and $\tilde{k_2} = \sqrt{-k_2}$. If neither mirror is a paraboloid, i.e. $k_1 \neq -1$ and $k_2 \neq -1$, the above compression is the same as that produced by a single conic mirror with a conic constant of either k_e or $1/k_e$ where [3]

$$k_e = -\left(\frac{\sqrt{-k_1}+\sqrt{-k_2}}{1+\sqrt{-k_1}\sqrt{-k_2}}\right)^2 . \tag{6.10}$$

For each of the folded configurations shown in Figure 6.2(c)-(g), the equivalent conic is either a hyperboloid or an ellipsoid. The equivalent conic is a sphere for the special (but impractical) case of a folded system made of two concentric spheres.

The paraboloidal configurations ($k_1 = k_2 = -1$) in Figures 6.2(h) and 6.2(i) also have equivalent single-conic systems. However, the conic constants of these equivalent systems are not independent of scale. In these cases, k_e is a function of the *parameters* h_1 and h_2 of the two paraboloids and can be shown to be

$$k_e = -\left(\frac{h_1+h_2}{h_1-h_2}\right)^2 . \tag{6.11}$$

Here again, the equivalent conic can be an ellipsoid or a hyperboloid when $h_1 \neq h_2$. When the two paraboloids are identical, i.e. $h_1 = h_2$, no compression of the field of view is achieved and the equivalent conic is a sphere with the viewpoint at its center.

6.4 Optics of Folded Systems

The above designs only define the geometry of the sensor. That is, the entrance pupil of the imaging system is taken to be a pinhole and hence only the principal rays are considered. When a lens is used to gather more light, each principal ray is accompanied by a bundle of surrounding rays and a variety of optical aberrations appear that make the design of a folded system challenging.

---

[3] In equation (6.7) we see that for $k_1 \neq 0$ and $k_1 \neq -1$, $\tan\alpha|_{k_1,\theta} = -\tan\alpha|_{1/k_1,\theta}$. That is, the compression by an ellipsoid of conic constant k_1 is equivalent to the compression by a hyperboloid of conic constant $1/k_1$.

6.4.1 Pertinent optical effects

Here, we briefly describe some of the optical aberrations that are pertinent and we need to minimize in our designs. Details on these aberrations can be found in [104].

Chromatic Aberration: The refractive index of any material is a function of the wavelength of light. Hence, the focal length of any lens will vary somewhat with the "color" of the incoming light. An imaging lens will have several individual elements, the exact number depending on the purpose and quality of the lens. Each element can have a different refractive index and curvature. A part of our design procedure will be to ensure that chromatic aberrations induced by individual elements at least partially compensate for each other. In systems that use curved mirrors, other optical effects discussed below tend to be more severe than chromatic shifts.

Coma and Astigmatism: Both these aberrations are caused primarily due to the curvatures of the mirrors. In particular, since our designs use aspherical mirrors, the point blur function has non-intuitive and varying shapes over the field of view. The effect of coma is linearly dependent on the field angle (measured from the optical axis) while it is proportional to square of the aperture size. In contrast, astigmatism varies as square of the field angle while it is linear in the aperture size. Both effects cause the best focused image of a scene point to not be a single point but rather a volume (of confusion). In coaxial systems like the ones shown in Figure 6.2, these areas are somewhat umbrella shaped and point towards the center of the image (see [12] for examples). As in any conventional lens, this blur function expands with aperture size. Our design goal is to maximize aperture size (minimize F-number) while ensuring that the blur function falls within a single detector (pixel) for all points in the field of view.

Field Curvature: Since at least one of our mirrors is curved, points at infinity end up being best focused not on a plane but rather a curved surface behind the imaging lens. This curved surface is also called the Petzval surface [104]. Astigmatism causes further problems, in that, even on this curved surface, the image is not perfectly focused. Since the CCD imagers we have at our disposal are planar, the curved image surface is essentially sliced through by the planar detector. Thus, the best image quality is achieved where the curved image and the planar detector intersect. Field curvature is our most serious optical aberration. In compact systems (small mirrors with high curvatures) field curvature tends to dominate over all other aberrations. Interestingly, folded systems can come to our aid here. In a single mirror system, the image surface is curved in the same direction as the mirror itself. Hence, in a two-mirror system it is to our advantage to use a convex and a concave mirror so that the field curvatures introduced by the two mirrors serve to compensate for each other.

We have seen that the design of a folded system requires simultaneous minimization of a variety of complex aberrations. In other words, the objective function used for minimization needs to be carefully formulated and controlled during the optimization process.

6.4.2 Design Parameters

Before we describe how the optimization is performed, let us summarize the parameters at work. Since the total number of parameters is generally very large, it helps to fix some of them prior to system optimization based on what is commonly known in optics. The benefits of such early choices are obvious; the smaller the number of free parameters the greater the liklihood that the optimization will converge to the desired result.

CCD Size: A few different CCD formats are commercially available (1 inch, 1/2 inch, 1/3 inch, 1/4 inch, etc.). If the number of pixels in each CCD is more or less the same, the pixel size reduces with CCD size. Typically, the choice of the CCD format is based on the packaging and resolution requirements of the application. In our systems, the sharpest digital image is not necessarily obtained using a large or small CCD. Given the complexity of the image formation process, the best results could be obtained for any one of the above choices.

Imaging Lens: The parameters of the imaging lens are characterized by its focal length, field of view, number of elements and its speed (aperture size). While the number of elements and their basic shapes (convex, concave, meniscus, etc.) may be selected up-front by the designer, the curvatures and diameters of the lenses may be treated as free parameters. Once the optimization is done, one tries to match the resulting parameters with those of commercially available lenses. If a reasonable match is not found, a custom lens may be designed and fabricated.

Mirrors: As we have seen in section 6.3, a large number mirror shapes are feasible from the perspective of geometry. Based on the size and field of view requirements, as well as a good deal of intuition, one must select the general shapes of the mirrors to be used. Further, since we know *apriori* that the use of a convex and a concave mirror helps to reduce field curvature, such a choice can be made up-front. Once the basic shapes have been chosen, the exact shape parameters can be determined via optimization. Note that selecting mirror shapes is not equivalent to selecting the parameters of the mirrors. For instance, when using conics, the conic constants can be treated as free parameters to be optimized, with upper and lower bounds provided by the designer.

Distances: We know that to achieve a single viewpoint, the far focus of one mirror must coincide with the near focus of the other. In addition, fairly tight bounds on the distances between the individual optical components can be set based on the sensor size requirements imposed by the application. The exact distances can then be treated as free parameters in the optimization process.

6.4.3 System Optimization

In our work, the free parameters are computed using the Zemax software package from Focus Software Incorporated. The package performs iterative numerical optimization using fast ray-tracing. During each iteration, images of point sources in the scene are generated. An objective function is formulated to yield a minimum when the ray-traced point spread functions are most compact. Again, the optimization package cannot be allowed to simply run without expert guidance. Typically, scores of designs are arrived at, analyzed, and new user inputs provided before a final design is achieved.

6.5 An Example Implementation

We have experimented with a few of the folded designs discussed in this chapter. Here, as an example, we will describe a panoramic camera based on the layout shown in Figure 6.2(h), wherein two parabolic mirrors are used. Note that the secondary mirror has a significantly longer focal length than the first one. This is because the two mirrors must be adequately separated to avoid a large blindspot due to obstruction by the secondary mirror. Prior to optimization, it was decided that the complete sensor must lie within a cylinder that is 90 mm tall and 50 mm in diameter. The desired field of view was set to a hemisphere and the maximum allowable blindspot to 22 degrees when measured from the optical axis. It was also decided that a 1/3 inch CCD camera would be used. Given these constraints, the secondary mirror ends up being a small (shallow) section of a paraboloid, which is well-approximated by a spherical mirror. Using the above numbers as upper bounds, the parameters of the entire system were optimized.

Figure 6.4 shows the resulting device. The primary parabolic mirror has a focal length of 10 mm and a diameter of 40 mm. The secondary spherical mirror has a radius of curvature of 110 mm. The video camera used is a Computar EMH200 board camera that produces black-and-white images with 550 horizontal lines of resolution. The imaging lens has a focal length of 6mm and is attached to the primary mirror. This permits the user to adjust the focus setting of the lens by simply rotating the mirror. Finally, a microphone is attached to the center of the secondary mirror, pointing towards the primary mirror. This effectively maps the narrow response cone of the microphone to a panoramic one; sound waves from anywhere in the hemispherical field of view are reflected by the primary mirror into the microphone. The microphone itself does not obstruct the field of view as it lies within the blindspot created by the secondary mirror.

Figure 6.5 shows the matrix spot diagram for the above design. Each spot can be viewed as the point blur function for a specific wavelength of light (columns) and a specific angle of incidence (rows). The scale bar shown beside the top-left spot is 20 microns long. As seen, the spots vary in

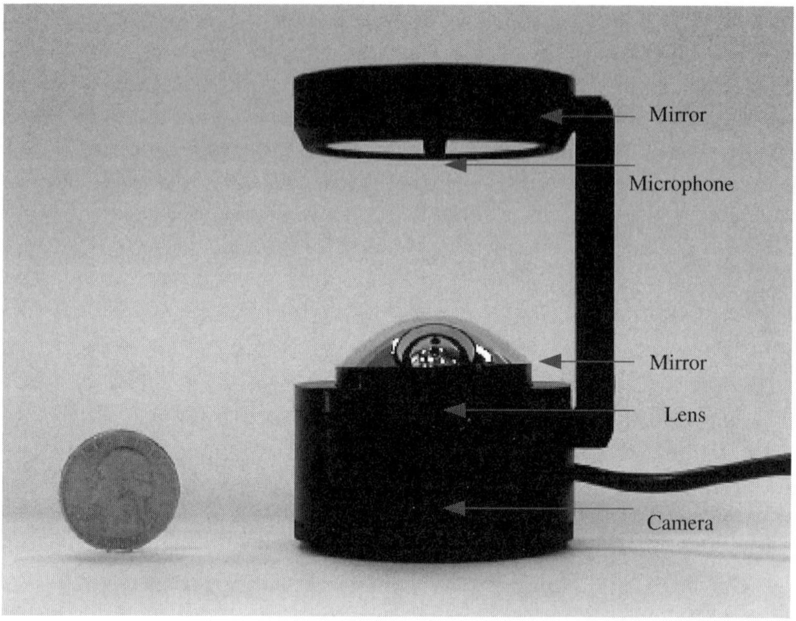

FIGURE 6.4. A folded catadioptric camera with a hemispherical field of view. The device is 90 mm tall and 50 mm wide. It includes folded optics, a video camera and a microphone.

shape quite a bit. This is due to aberrations caused by coma, astigmatism, field curvature and chromatic aberration. The goal of the optimization was to ensure that all the spots (across the different wavelengths and angles of incidence) are kept as compact as possible. Figure 6.6 shows the energy plots for the different angles of incidence. The plots convey, for each angle of incidence, the fraction of energy in the point spread function included within a circle of given radius. As the dotted lines indicate, for all angles of incidence, about 70% of the total energy in the point spread function lies within a circle of radius 4 microns. In our case, the pixel size on the CCD chip is approximately 6.4 x 7.4 microns. Hence, the above system produces an almost ideal digital image.

Figure 6.7(a) shows an image captured using the sensor. As can be seen, despite all the complex optical aberrations at work, the sensor produces a clear image that has a very large depth of field for all angles of incidence. Figures 6.7(b) and (c) show perspective and panoramic video streams that are computed from the hemispherical video.

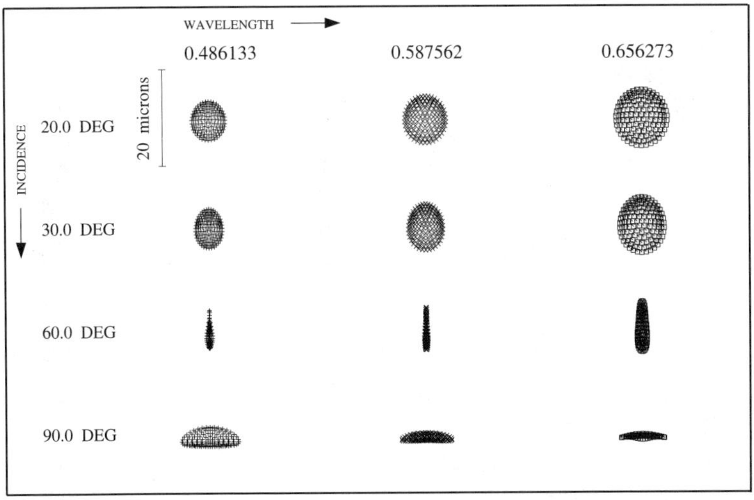

FIGURE 6.5. Spot diagrams for various wavelengths (columns) and angles of incidence (rows), computed using the optimized optical design for the camera shown in Figure 6.4.

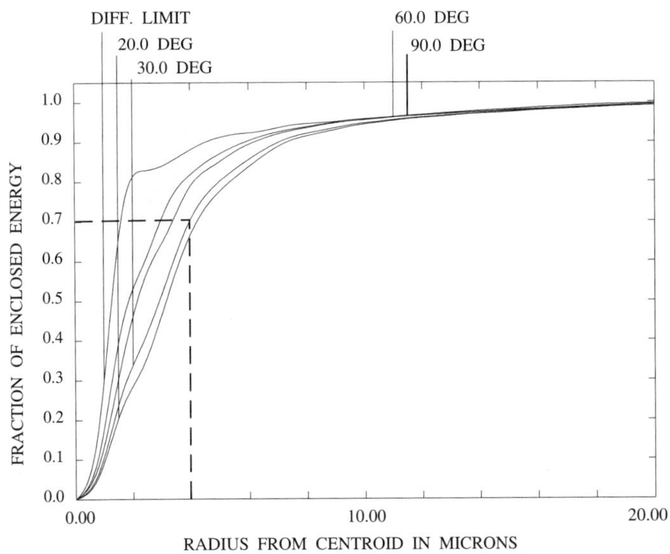

FIGURE 6.6. Encircled energy plots for different angles of incidence, for the camera shown in Figure 6.4. As indicated by the dotted lines, for all angles of incidence, 70% of the total energy in the point spread function lies within a circle of radius 4 microns. The pixel size on the 1/3 inch CCD detector used is 6.4 x 7.4 microns.

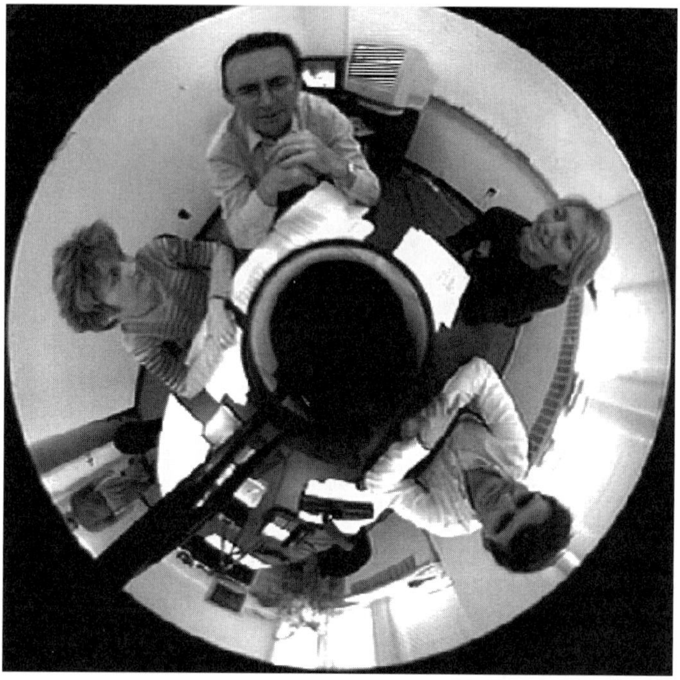

(a)

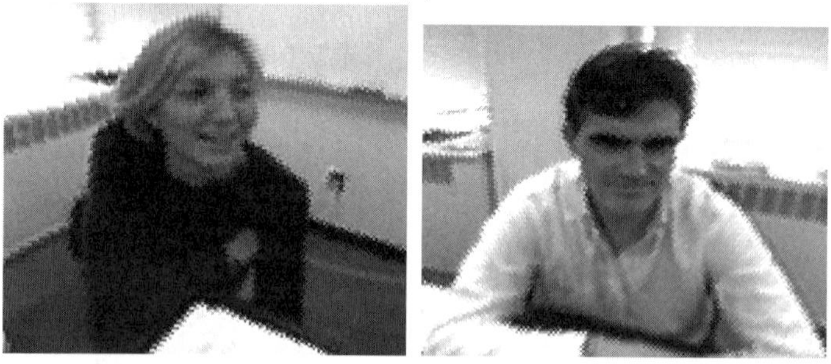

(b)

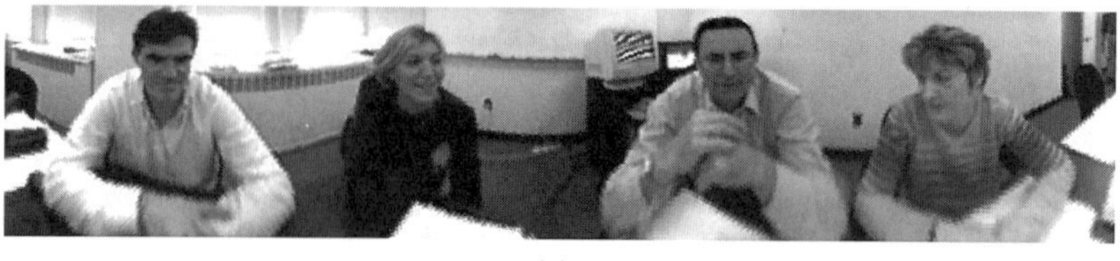

(c)

FIGURE 6.7. (a) Hemispherical video produced by the catadioptric camera shown in Figure 6.4. Software is used to map the hemispherical video to (b) perspective and (c) panoramic video streams. The jaggy artifacts are due to the low resolution (640x480) of the original video. These video streams are generated using user-selected parameters such as viewing direction and field of view.

Acknowledgment

The authors thank Sergey Trubko and Jim Korein at CycloVision Technologies for pointers to previously implemented folded systems, and Malcolm MacFarlane for the simulation results reported in this paper. Michael Oren introduced the authors to related work in microwave optics. This work was supported in parts by DARPA's Image Understanding Program, DARPA's Tactical Mobile Robots Program and an ONR/DARPA MURI grant under ONR contract No. N00014-97-1-0553. Venkata Peri is supported by CycloVision Technologies.

Section II

Panoramic Stereo Vision Systems

The previous section focusses on *central, single-capture systems.* In this section, various alternative hardware-oriented solutions to producing stereo panoramic images are described. These systems enable both wide-angle visualization with parallax and depth recovery.

Chapters 7 (Basu and Baldwin) and 8 (Peleg, Ben-Ezra, and Pritch) describe panoramic systems that capture dynamic stereo panoramic images at video rates. These systems overcome the problems associated with using a rotating camera to generate stereo panoramic images. Chapter 7 (Basu and Baldwin) describes a new approach to designing a real-time stereo panoramic imaging system using a double-lobed mirror that allows stereovision using just one camera. A technique for calibrating this panoramic stereo camera using color codes is described, as is the real-time video hardware. A mathematical model for depth estimation using the new stereo design is also derived; experimental results to validate this model are also presented.

Chapter 8 (Peleg, Ben-Ezra, and Pritch) presents another mirror-based stereo system. It introduces two possibilities for capturing stereo panoramic images using optics and without using any moving parts. In particular, it describes a mirror that is specially designed to be essentially equivalent to using a centrally-displaced rotating camera. Such a mirror enables stereo panoramic movies to be captured using just a regular video camera. The analysis of the lens and mirror for stereo panorama is also provided in this chapter; this analysis is based on curves whose caustic is a circle.

The last three chapters in this section describe the various aspects of a rotating camera system used for panoramic stereo vision. This system comprises two rotating linear cameras whose optical center is on the rotation axis. Chapter 9 (Benosman and Devars) describes the sensor and its geometry. This is followed by description of two stereo head calibration techniques in Chapter 10 (Benosman and Devars). The first calibration technique is based on rigid transformations while the second is based on projective vectors of points in the scene. Finally, Chapter 11 (Benosman and Devars) describes two real-time methods to match a pair of linear images taken using the panoramic stereo vision system.

Additional Notes on Chapters

A previous version of Chapter 9 was published in the *Journal of Electronic Imaging* in July 1996. A previous version of Chapter 10 was published in the proceedings of the *IEEE Conference on Pattern Recognition*, held on August 1996 and in *Pattern Recognition Letters* in July 1998. A previous version of Chapter 11 was published in the proceedings of the *IEEE Conference on Pattern Recognition*, held in August 1996.

7

A Real-time Panoramic Stereo Imaging System and Its Applications

A. Basu and J. Baldwin

7.1 Introduction

In the past omni-directional cameras have been designed by several researchers such as [302]. The problem with using normal cameras for vision-guided navigation is that objects from behind or the sides cannot be seen, and are thus impossible to avoid collisions with. Yagi addressed this problem by placing a mirror surface vertically on top of a normal camera. Even though the quality of the resulting image was not suitable for tasks such as object recognition, the images could be used very effectively for detecting moving and static obstacles in the scene. A robot was built with this panoramic imaging system in Osaka, Japan, and the robot could autonomously navigate in an environment cluttered with obstacles. Variations of this system have been developed by several other researchers later on.

One of the limitations of using panoramic images as viewed by a normal camera focussed on a mirror surface is that the images are distorted and not suitable for recognition or inspection type tasks. To alleviate this difficulty the images need to be warped into its proper geometric shape before being used for future tasks. One such application involved pipeline inspection using conical mirrors. Figure 7.1 shows an actual implementation of such a device [19].

Omni-directional imaging also allows users to have a full 360 degree field of view, which enables them to have the feeling of immersive presence in a "virtual" environment. This "virtual" environment is different from graphically generated scenes in the context of virtual reality in that it allows users to visualize a real environment without being physically present in it. Traditional applications of omni-directional sensing have been in autonomous vision based navigation of mobile robots, security and surveillance, and military applications. One of the future applications of panoramic sensing is in providing telepresence without the need for using moving parts or multiple cameras. A single camera system is desirable in situations where it is important to minimize the number of components in order to reduce the

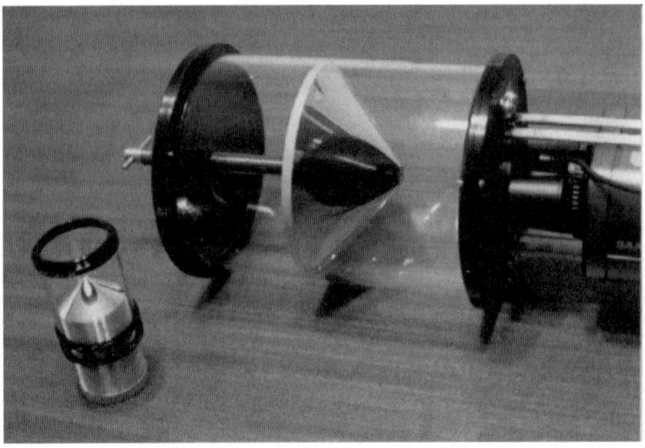

FIGURE 7.1. Omni-directional cameras. The smaller cone on the left is from a previous version of the system.

possibility of breakdowns. Consider an imaging system that is to be used in a Lunar Rover. There are two considerations for such an application:

1. **Weight:** it is very expensive to transport equipment in space. Thus it is preferable to make the system as light as possible.

2. **Redundancy and fault tolerance:** in case of breakdowns the system should have some backup so that images can still be seen. Therefore it is desirable to have individual cameras work as independent, and possibly redundant, units.

Another area in which panoramic sensors can be used is in automatic missile tracking systems that may be mounted in defence aircraft or navy vessels. A panoramic stereo device would provide a compact piece of hardware, information from which can be easily processed without the need for coordinating input from multiple cameras or the use of pan/tilt units for moving one or more cameras.

In the past, various strategies have been proposed for 3D range imaging. Some of the techniques include projection of light patterns on objects [233], photon counting [180], range from defocusing [164], and synchronized scanners [226]. Range imaging has a wide variety of applications including computer aided design, data acquisition for automated design, and manufacturing of customized orthopedic devices for the handicapped. Even though range imaging has several useful applications, it is not essential in many situations where there is a "human in the loop." Stereo imaging is often sufficient for human visualization and depth perception. The system described in this paper is intended for real-time applications that require fast response. High resolution, but not real-time, systems can be designed using other methods, such as, a vertically aligned linear sensor system described in [22].

The next section describes some past work done by us which utilized omni-directional sensing. Section 3 introduces a novel concept for designing a *stereo* panoramic sensor using a single camera. An alternative way for calibrating an arbitrary panoramic surface using a colored calibration surface is discussed in Section 4. An actual hardware design for panoramic stereo is described in Section 5; followed by snapshots of real-time video produced by the system in Section 6. Section 7 describes the mathematical modelling of panoramic stereo for depth estimation, with related experimental results vaildating the model being described in Section 8. Finally, some future improvements are outlined in Section 9.

7.2 Previous Applications

In the past we conducted research and development on using omni-directional sensors for pipe inspection. Industrial pipes carrying different kinds of fluids, as well as sewer systems, need to be routinely examined for cracks and deformities. At present, authorized inspectors make a video tape utilizing fish-eye type lenses. This type of inspection, however, can be quite subjective. It is possible to use an omni-directional camera to obtain cyclindrical image pieces of the interior surfaces of pipes. These images can then be patched together and displayed as a 3D surface using graphics tools.

FIGURE 7.2. An individual image fragment.

Experiments were conducted using real images. Images from a section of a pipe were obtained by moving the panoramic camera in small steps inside the pipe. The image pieces were then warped into rectangular sections which were registered into composite sections.

Figure 7.2 shows 1 of 25 fragments that were automatically assembled into the composite image of Figure 7.3 (left). The numbered strip on the right hand side is shown to compare the accuracy of the registered image with the actual image of the inner surface of the pipe. Note that the numbered strip was added to illustrate the correctness of the registration. The image registration algorithm was not given this portion of the images (which would have made the task considerably easier). The registration was accurate except for a small portion at the bottom of the image. This inaccuracy was caused by insufficient lighting — the light was placed at one end of the pipe, so the image got darker towards the bottom.

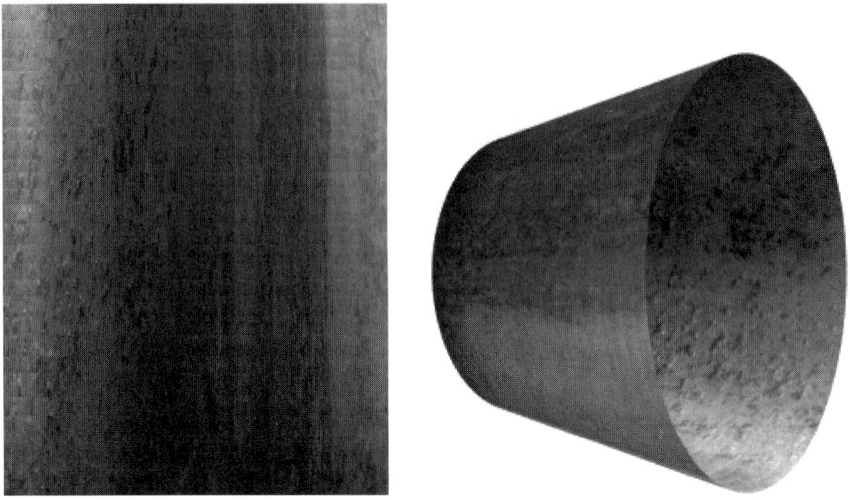

FIGURE 7.3. Registered image pieces (left) and 3D visualization of registered image (side view).

The registered images were then mapped on to a 3D model of the pipe using texture mapping techniques (Figure 7.3, right).

7.3 Stereo Design

We were motivated to develop an imaging system which is passive, yet stereoscopic and omni-directional [28]. Traditionally, work on stereo computer vision systems used multiple cameras facing in the same direction [63] [151] [205]. In addition, in order to achieve omni-directional vision articulated camera platforms were used. This was expensive, complex and slow. Our design obviates the need for multiple signals and return telemetry to the camera by using a single camera and a specially shaped, double-lobed mirror (Figure 7.4).

The mirror comprises two bi-convex lobes — a minor lobe embedded in a major lobe; the field of view of each is restricted by the geometry, but covers well over a hemisphere. At most elevations a point in the environment is reflected in both lobes and is thus represented twice on the imaging plane of the camera. Since the object has been effectively imaged from two different positions in space, the essence of a binocular imagery is present, and depth can be recovered.

Since we preferred a device with uniform characteristics over the full 360° range of azimuth, the mirror design reduces to specifying the radial profile (and the distance from the camera to the mirror). However, several related design issues hinge around this shape as outlined below.

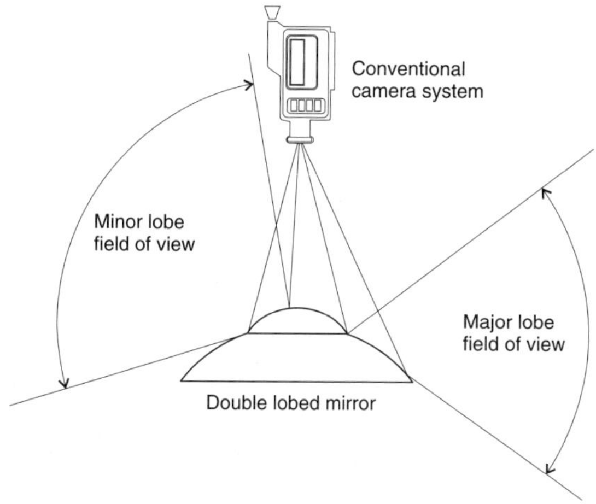

FIGURE 7.4. Concentric double convex lobes each provide an image covering the complete azimuth image, but each over a limted range of elevations. The overlapped elevation range visible to both lobes is the stereo field of the device.

7.3.1 Vertical Extent of Stereo Field of View

This is the easiest performance measure to calculate. Stereo imaging requires two viewpoints, so a point in the environment must be represented in the fields of both minor and major lobes of the mirror. For very high elevations, either the view from the minor mirror will be eclipsed by the camera body, otherwise the image from the major lobe will be lost because the minor lobe has started. It is desirable for these two events to occur at roughly the same high elevation. For very low elevations, either the minor lobe limits are violated, or the major lobe fails because the grazing reflection from its edges yield extremely poor image quality.

It is reasonable to accept conservative upper and lower limits to the stereo field and design the boundaries accordingly.

7.3.2 Effective Eye Separation

In the case of a two camera stereo arrangement with parallel axes, each camera represents an eye, and so the distance between the eyes (inter-occular distance) equals the spacing between the cameras. In the double-lobe mirror case, however, the inter-occular distance is not constant but a function of the elevation of the point of interest in the field of view. The effective eye positions are the points of reflection on the surfaces of the lobes. It is necessary to perform tests with human subjects to see just how disturbing it might be to perceive one's eyes separating when panning up, and converging again when panning down.

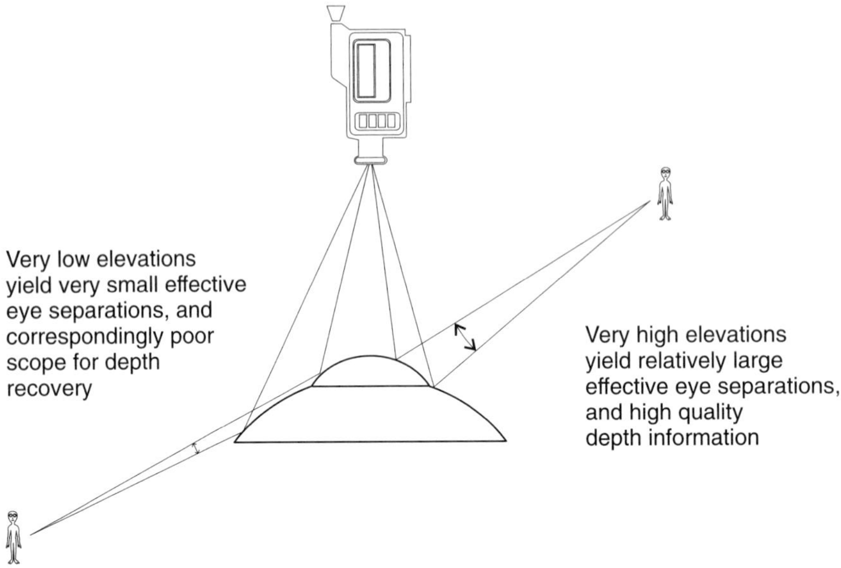

FIGURE 7.5. For typical lobe geometries, the higher the elevation, the larger the effective eye separation.

If the system downstream of the double-lobed mirror were an artificial vision system then it might be possible to factor in this deterministic effect (such that estimations of depth could take into account the eye separation). Even in this scenario it is fundamentally impossible to fully compensate for the eye separation; for example, occlusions in the scene could not be "undone" to fake a constant eye separation.

Clearly not all of these performance parameters are likely to be optimized simultaneously; we need to prioritize them. This is not easy, because it involves the performance of the human visual system, and so require tests, and iteration. The devices built thus far have been conservative designs, intended to allow us to further understand the nature of this class of imaging system. Many of the human tests can be carried out with vector or ray traced computer graphics simulations.

7.3.3 *Orientation of Eye Separation*

Two images from slightly displaced view points is the only absolute requirement of a stereo arrangement, but when attempting to interface with the human visual system, we must also consider the orientation of this separation. Human eyes are displaced horizontally, but the effective eye positions derived from our mirror are displaced vertically, if the camera/mirror axis is vertical.

This is yet another area which requires human subject testing. Note that for small rotations (say up to 45°), human eyes rotate axially when the head is tilted, so that vertical lines in the environment continue to create vertical edges on the retina. This response has likely evolved in order to facilitate stereo matching, as well as generally providing rotation invariance for small tilting of the head. When the head is tilted, the effective eye separation now has a significant vertical component, yet depth perception from stereopsis does not seem to be impaired. If the human visual system can interpret stereo image pairs despite a *purely* vertical effective eye separation, then the double-lobed mirror is best deployed in the vertical axis mode. If this separation proves to be a problem, the system can be used in a horizontal axis mode, but at a cost. The panoramic field of view develops serious blind zones and left-field/right-field asymmetry is introduced.

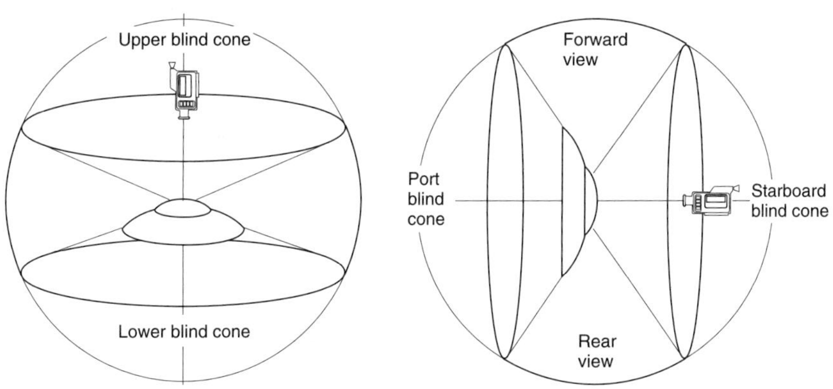

FIGURE 7.6. Left: The vertical axis system has the advantage of uninterrupted vision across the entire horizon, but suffers from vertical disparity and blind cones above and below the device. Right: The horizontal axis has the advantages of horizontal disparity and uninterrupted vision across the entire elevation range, but only for a limited azimuth range. The significant lateral blind cones and the inherent asymmetry of the configuration are drawbacks.

7.4 Device Calibration

The hardware based video transformation engine described in the next section can perform arbitrarily complex transformations because it uses a two dimensional lookup table to determine where pixels in the transformed image come from in the source image. It follows that when mirrors are changed or moved, or when cameras and lens are changed or adjusted, the resident lookup table becomes invalid. There was thus a need to provide a rapid way of re-evaluating the transformation table.

7.4.1 Analog Approach

The first approach to the calibration problem used a continuous color ramp test pattern. Calibration patterns of (say) grids were difficult to interpret automatically, especially after they have suffered an *arbitrary distortion* because of the mirror under test. With no *a priori* knowledge of the mirror, it is not possible to say anything about what the mapped image will contain. Lines in the calibration pattern cannot be assumed to map to lines in the distorted image. Additionally, the double-lobed mirrors have discontinuous profiles, and it was hard to provide smoothing functions to enhance the continuously curving surfaces without introducing undesirable chamferring at the interfaces between lobes. So, a scheme which used color and no spatial patterns at all seemed very attractive.

The idea was to produce a panoramic test scene; formed from a paper cylinder. The paper was colored using a large-scale ink jet printer, such that the intensity of green ramped from zero to saturation as we move from azimuth=0° to azimuth=360°. Red is ramped from zero to saturation as we move from azimuth=360° to azimuth=0°. Blue is ramped from zero to saturation as we move from minimum elevation to maximum elevation.

The intention of this arrangement is to arrive at an estimate of the spatial origin of each pixel by comparing the magnitudes of the three independent color components:

$$\text{azimuth estimate} = G - R \tag{7.1}$$

$$\text{elevation estimate} = B - (G + R) \tag{7.2}$$

(where R, G and B are unsigned 8 bit quantities, representing the intensities of the red, green and blue components of the pixel under consideration.)

This procedure gives an azimuth measurement of 9 bit precision, and an elevation estimate of 8 bits. The formulation of the above equations attempts to provide some illumination intensity invariance. This approach assumes nothing about the geometry of the mirror, in particular it does not require the mirror to be identical in all directions of azimuth. Just by looking at the color of an individual pixel, it is theoretically possible to deduce what azimuth and elevation it corresponds to in the environment. By evaluating these estimates from each pixel, and then applying boundary constraints and smoothing, we hoped to build up a transformation table for the system under calibration.

This approach was abandoned for two main reasons:

- The printing facilities available to us could not support 8 bits per color component, and the resultant dithering patterns resulted in very poor component isolation. Only 6 bits per color were generated by the rendering system, even after dithering.

- Even though software can apply boundary conditions and ensure that at least the full range of a given parameter is represented (e.g., the azimuth measurement is forced to correspond to a complete 360°), there is no way of detecting non-linearities in any of the color ramps. Steps in the ramp were caused by abrupt changes in the dithering patterns, and non-linear interactions between the components also generated distortions. It was also unrealistic to expect open loop linear responses from the camera system, to 8 bit precision.

Using color in this way to avoid resorting to spatial patterns was an example of a good idea that did not work in practice.

7.4.2 Digital Approach

Poor signal-to-noise ratio and signal non-linearity were the basic reasons for failure with the analog calibration approach. The calibration scheme described here uses digital signals to overcome these difficulties. In addition, we retreat from the ideal of making no assumptions about the geometry of the mirror. This algorithm assumes that the mirror's properties are invariant over azimuth; in other words the mirror is a cone, but with an arbitrary conic profile.

We are limiting ourselves to measuring how actual elevation varies as we move along a radial line from the periphery to the centre of the mirror, so we need to find a way of encoding height.

A large calibration strip is placed facing the device under test. It is tall enough to cover the entire anticipated elevation range. Vertical parallel lines in the calibration strip map to radial lines in the raw camera image, due to the conical form of the mirror.

7.4.2.1 Design of the Calibration Strip

The calibration pattern takes the form of a Grey code, which have the useful property that adjacent numbers in the Grey sequence only differ by 1 bit transition from their neighbours.

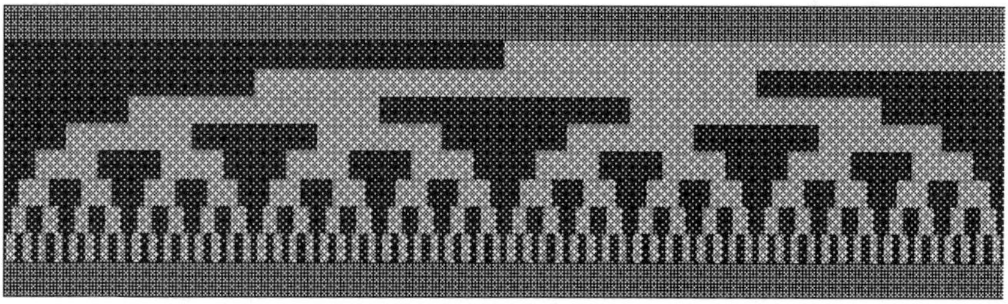

FIGURE 7.7. Color test pattern.

This property is used to provide some degree of error detection. Our pattern uses an 8 bit Grey code; 256 different samples. It is likely that the most frequently changing bits in the pattern will not be resolved by a standard video camera. The fractal nature of the pattern (Figure 7.7) allows us to recover appropriate height information. In areas of the radial images where the angular gain of the mirror is very high, we can see most of the bits of the 8 bit code at any given distance from the centre of the image. In those areas where the angular gain is relatively poor, the higher frequency bits will not be sampled correctly, but we can fall back to a level where we can comfortably resolve the height, by disregarding the higher frequency bits. In this way, the pattern has structure from which we can calibrate the device at all scales. This is more useful than (say) a regular grid pattern, which only contributes information at a single frequency. The grid could be either too coarse (in which case we do not resolve as much information as we would like) or worse, too fine, in which case the entire grid is sub-sampled and we either get no calibration information at all or misleading aliased signals.

The edges of the pattern are red [255,0,0], and the Grey coded interior uses green [0,255,0] (= binary 0) and blue [0,0,255] (= binary 1). This color scheme makes good use of the printing device to separate elements of the pattern, and does not rely on continuous grades of color.[1]

7.4.2.2 Calibration Algorithm

Having acquired an image through the mirror under test with the digital calibration strip in place, we use various signal processing algorithms to derive our calibration parameters. The details of all of these steps would take too much space, but the process can be broken down as follows :

- Determine the location of the calibration strip. This involves scanning radial lines for red, and finding the two peaks which correspond to the edge strips on the calibration pattern.
- Having determined (in azimuth) where the device resides, we find the two internal edges, and knowing the number of bits per Grey code (in our case, 8), we store the angular centre of each of the 8 sampling angles.
- Now we sample the image, gathering information for the calibration. For each bit centre, the radial trajectory is sampled, and the value of the blue intensity less the green intensity is stored in a linear array associated with each bit position.

[1] ...the native {Cyan, Magenta, Yellow} colorspace of the printer might have been chosen to prevent the need for mixing colors on the paper — however this would have simply deferred the complications to the video stage, where the primary detectors are {Red, Green, Blue}.

- We process the 8 linear blue-green signal arrays. In array i, we anticipate 2^i bit transitions. To turn our blue-green signals into arrays of binary digits, we first apply a low pass filter, then square off the signal, making use of the number of transitions we expect.

- Further post processing is used to clean the signals and remove anomalies; the Grey code single transition property allows us to detect most errors. We also make use of the fact that within the range of an interval in array i, we expect twice as many intervals in array $i + 1$. As resolution failure renders the high frequency components useless, this is detected and the bits involved are flagged so as to be ignored.

- Once the final height/distance from centre of image relationship is known, it remains to apply a trigonometric factor to convert the height reading into an elevation reading, and use the radial device characteristic to generate the transformation table, which is passed to the hardware system.

7.5 Hardware Design and Implementation

To straighten out the warped image seen by the video camera aimed at the conical mirror, a real-time, dedicated hardware system was built. The complete video system is seen running in Figure 7.8.

The incoming video is digitized, stored in a frame buffer, and an output image is generated from this stored frame using a mapping lookup table stored in erase-programmable memories. The circuit simultaneously stores the present incoming video frame, and generates the output image from the previous frame. This allows a 30 frames/second video signal to be continuously flowing out, delayed only one frame.

The video is sampled at 10 MHz to provide a 512 x 480 image with 8 bits of greyscale. There are two 256K x 8 bits frame storage buffers of fast SRAM (Static Ram) each capable of storing one frame. The data coming from the video ADC (Analog to Digital Converter) is written to one frame storage, while the other holds the previous frame and is being read from to generate data for the video DAC (Digital to Analog Converter). A 256 K x 18 bits EPROM (Eraseable Programmable Read Only Memory) array provides the X and Y coordinates of the stored pixel corresponding to each pixel in the ouput image. It is an inverse mapping, so that a single pixel in the input image can appear many times in the output image, thus producing a magnifying effect.

The frame storage buffers alternate between being written to and read from at every frame, and all the data is carried through a common bus — the most efficient implementation. This results in a bus speed of 20 MHz.

Since this circuit was realized discretely (using only standard off the shelf components), the 74F logic family was chosen for most of the logic.

A software package was written to generate and test the lookup tables in software before programming the table into the EPROM array. One program takes a lookup table and remaps a test raster image file, another takes the lookup table and generates the files needed by the EPROM programmer. A program written specifically for this application generates the remapping table used; being the only part that must be changed for arbitrary remapping.

7.6 Results Produced by System

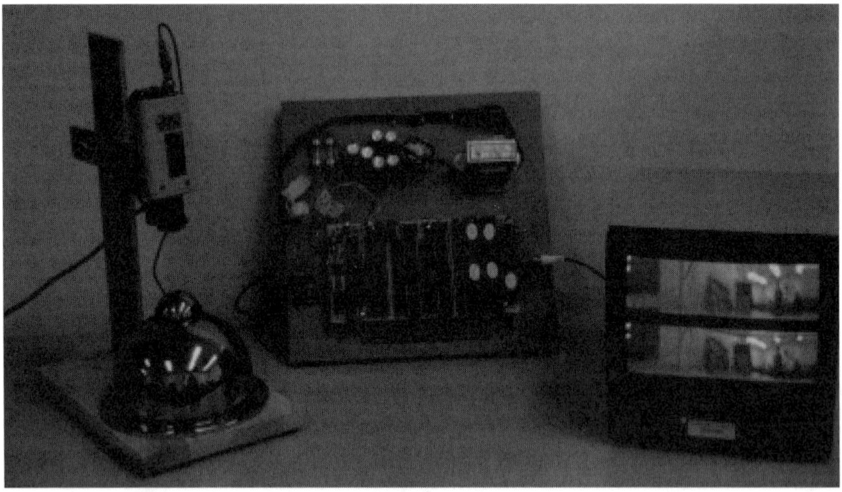

FIGURE 7.8. The camera, mirror, video hardware and final unwarped output display.

The hardware designed was first tested by placing the panoshperic stereo surface inside a box with grids drawn on it. Figure 7.9 (left) shows the resulting image obtained by a standard CCD sensor. The two stereo panoramic images extracted are shown in Figure 7.9 (right).

The hardware designed was tested with both the horizontal and vertical field of view options. Figure 7.10 (left) shows the mirror surface placed horizontally on a table. The resulting stereo output of the hardware is shown in Figure 7.10 (right).

Figure 7.11 (left) shows the mirror surface held vertically. The corresponding stereo generated by the hardware is shown in Figure 7.11 (right).

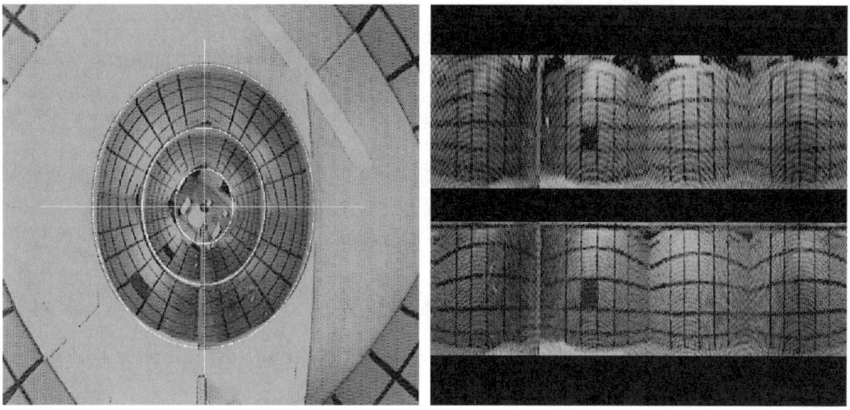

FIGURE 7.9. Grid pattern on panoramic stereo (left) and output of hardware.

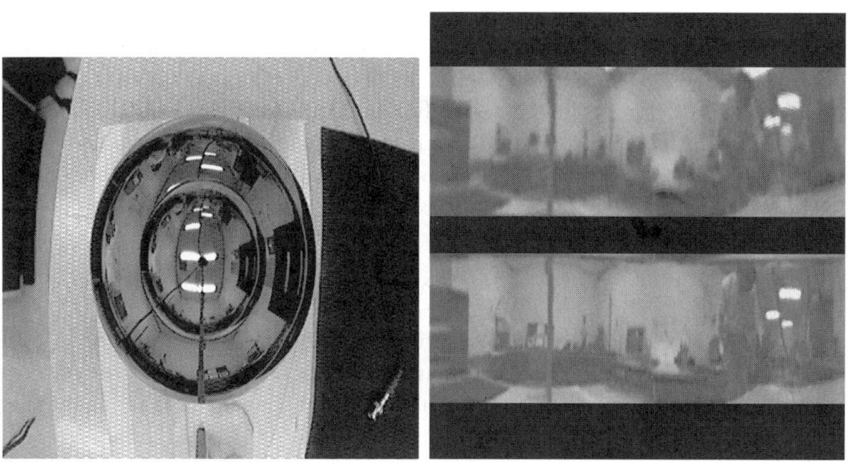

FIGURE 7.10. *Image of stereo surface (left) and horizontal strips output by hardware.*

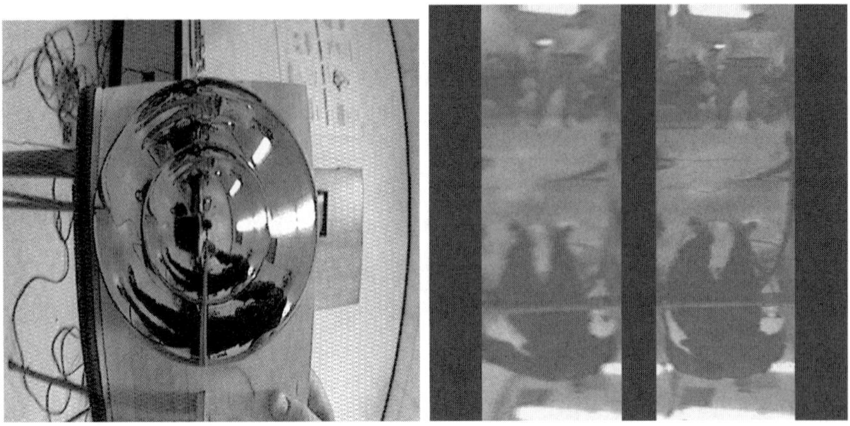

FIGURE 7.11. *Image of vertical stereo surface (left) and corresponding output of hardware.*

7.7 The Mathematics of Panoramic Stereo

In order to use the stereo panoramic images to compute 3D information it is necessary to precisely model the system and obtain solutions for 3D position from the image projections. This section formalizes the mathematical notation and obtains such a solution.

We define the coordinate system so that the focal point of the camera is at the origin (in 3D-space) and the viewing axis pointing along the y-axis (see Figure 7.12). The image plane is located at a distance f below the focal point (it can be considered to be a sub-plane of the plane $y = -f$). The mirror will be mounted such that the lowest point on the mirror is at distance d from the focal point. For uniformity of the resulting image, the mirror must be designed so that it is symmetric about the y-axis. This allows us to work in only two dimensions (instead of the normal three).

Initially, let us consider a single lobed mirror which is defined as a part of the sphere:

$$x^2 + y^2 + z^2 = r^2$$

Under our initial conditions (described above and shown in Figure 7.12), we only need to consider a circle in two dimensions. Also, since the surface is mirrored, and a light ray cannot pass through the surface, we only need to consider the lower half of the surface. This gives us the equation of a curve that represents our mirrored surface in the coordinate system defined above:

$$x^2 + (y - (d + r))^2 = r^2 \tag{7.3}$$

We wish to determine the point on the image plane where a point in space will project.

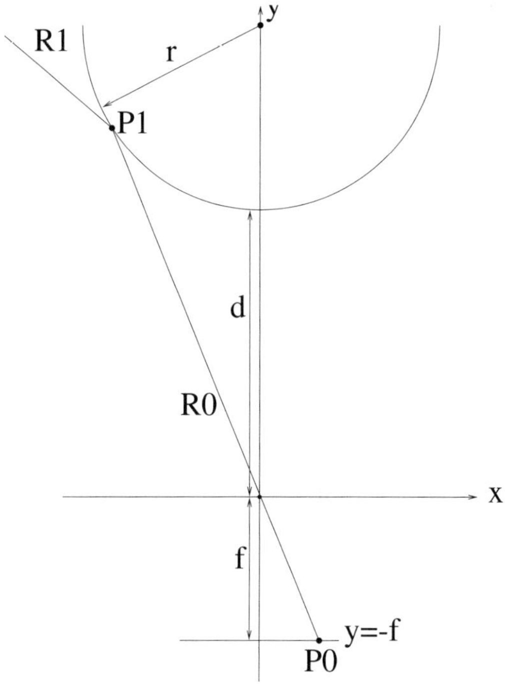

FIGURE 7.12. Single lobed mirror configuration. The image plane is at $y = -f$, the focal point is at the origin $(0,0)$, and the mirror, of radius r, is located at distance d from the origin. A point $P_0 = (x_0, -f)$ is produced from a point in space along ray R_1 using ray $R_0 := y = \frac{-fx}{x_0}$, intersecting the mirror at $P_1 = (x_1, y_1)$.

First, let us determine the ray, R_0, that corresponds to a point on the image plane. Given a point $P_0 = (x_0, -f)$ on the image plane, P generates a ray R_0 passing through the origin to intersect the surface of the mirror. The equation of ray R_0 is:

$$y = \frac{-f}{x_0} x \tag{7.4}$$

This will intersect the surface of the mirror at some point $P_1 = (x_1, \frac{-f}{x_0} x_1)$ which satisfies:

$$x_1^2 + (\frac{-f}{x_0} x_1 - (d + r))^2 = r^2$$

giving the solutions:

$$x_1 = -\frac{x_0(fd + fr - \sqrt{f^2r^2 - x_0^2d^2 - 2dx_0^2r}))}{x_0^2 + f^2} \tag{7.5}$$

$$x_1 = -\frac{x_0(fd + fr + \sqrt{f^2r^2 - x_0^2d^2 - 2dx_0^2r}))}{x_0^2 + f^2} \tag{7.6}$$

Equation 7.5 can be discarded since it represents a solution that is not feasible.

For there to be a solution to Equation 7.6, the following equation must be satisfied:

$$|x_0| \leq \frac{fr}{\sqrt{d^2 + 2dr}}$$

The case of equality in Equation 7.7 is the degenerate case of R_0 being tangential to the mirror at point P_1.

Ray R_0 in Equation 7.4 will reflect about the normal to the curve defined in Equation 7.3, the mirror, at point P_1 and generate another ray, R_1. The first object that intersects with this reflected ray R_1 will appear on the image plane at the point P_0.

This reflected ray R_1 has the equation:

$$y - y_1 = \frac{-y_1 \left[y_1 - (d+r)\right]^2 - x_1^2 \left[y_1 - (d+r)\right]}{x_1 \left[(d+r)^2 - y_1^2 - x_1^2\right]}(x - x_1)$$

For a double lobed mirror (see Figure 7.13), with lobes parameterized by r_1, d_1 and r_2, d_2, a point in space can be completely determined from two points in the image plane $(x_{10}, -f)$ and $(x_{20}, -f)$. The two points determine two mirror intersection points (one for each lobe) (x_{11}, y_{11}) and (x_{21}, y_{21}). The intersection of the two reflected rays, R_{11} and R_{21}, provides the point in space that corresponds to the two points in the image plane. The distance from the x coordinate of the intersection point provides the distance to the camera axis for the point. We can also determine the Euclidean distance of the point to the focal point in the standard way.

The point in space $P = (x, y)$ satisfies the two equations:

$$y - y_{11} = \frac{-y_{11} \left[y_{11} - (d_1 + r_1)\right]^2 - x_{11}^2 \left[y_{11} - (d_1 + r_1)\right]}{x_{11}((d_1 + r_1)^2 - y_{11}^2 - x_{11}^2)} \cdot (x - x_{11}) \tag{7.7}$$

$$y - y_{21} = \frac{-y_{21} \left[y_{21} - (d_2 + r_2)\right]^2 - x_{21}^2 \left[y_{21} - (d_2 + r_2)\right]}{x_{21}((d_2 + r_2)^2 - y_{21}^2 - x_{21}^2)} \cdot (x - x_{21}) \tag{7.8}$$

with the added constraints:

$$y_{11} = \frac{-f}{x_{10}} x_{11}$$

$$x_{11} = -\frac{x_{10}(fd_1 + fr_1 \pm \sqrt{f^2r_1^2 - x_{10}^2d_1^2 - 2d_1x_{10}^2r_1}))}{x_{10}^2 + f^2}$$

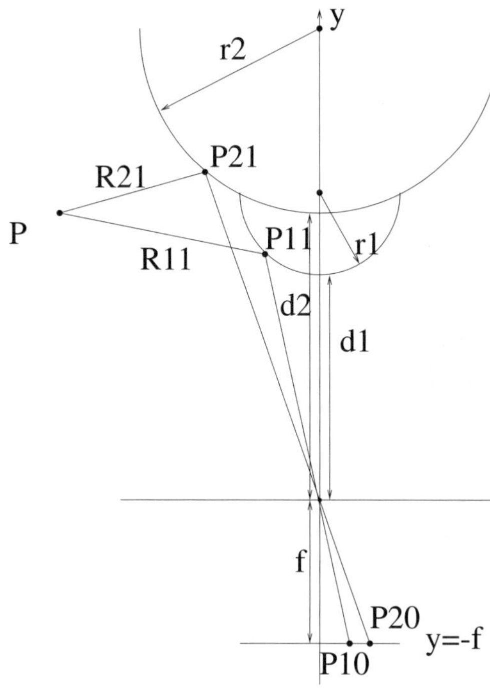

FIGURE 7.13. Double lobed mirror configuration. The image plane is at $y = -f$, the focal point is at the origin $(0, 0)$, the smaller lobe, radius r_1, located at distance d_1 from the origin, and the larger lobe, radius r_2, is located at distance d_2 from the origin. The points $P_{10} = (x_{10}, -f)$ and $P_{20} = (x_{20}, -f)$ each produce rays through the origin which intersect the mirror lobes at $P_{11} = (x_{11}, y_{11})$ and $P_{21} = (x_{21}, y_{21})$ respectively and meet at a point in space $P = (x, y)$.

$$y_{21} = \frac{-f}{x_{20}} x_{21}$$

$$x_{21} = -\frac{x_{20}(fd_2 + fr_2 \pm \sqrt{f^2 r_2^2 - x_{20}^2 d_2^2 - 2d_2 x_{20}^2 r_2}))}{x_{20}^2 + f^2}$$

7.8 Experimental Results

The size of the mirror lobes can be physically measured or is known from the manufacturing process. This gives the radius of the two lobes and an offset of the center of the smaller lobe from the larger one. This means that we only need to determine one distance (either the height of the bottom of the smaller lobe or the height of the center of the larger lobe) rather than both distances.

To determine the height of the lobes and the focal length f, the distance from the origin to the image plane, we use the principle of similar triangles.

We need to take two pictures of an object with known length, l, positioned at a known height, h, from the camera. This object projects into a measurable image. The object placed at height h may not be exactly at that distance from the origin. This means we need a small offset, o, which is added to any height measurement from a known plane (in our case, the plate which the camera is mounted to) to get the actual height values. Using the two calibration pictures and ratios from similar triangles, we can get a value for f, 618.18046 pixels, and the offset, o = 0.091400234cm. Note that these two values use different units, pixels and cm; however, this is not a problem since the pixel units cancel each other out.

We have measured the height of the centre of the large mirror lobe from the camera mounting plate. Using this value and the offset determined above, we can get the geometry of the camera and mirror system: $r_1 = 1.941$ cm, $r_2 = 5.775$ cm, $d_1 = 8.7527634$ cm, $d_2 = 10.3164$cm, and f = 618.18046 pixels. Note that focal length and image coordinates are measured in pixels, whereas other measurements are in cm. This does not cause any problem since the pixel units cancel each other resulting in ratios without any units.

Several experiments were conducted using different images. The best results were obtained using images of lights. These produced the best results because they provided the easiest means of matching points in the two images. Using bright lights allows easier matches. The first step in the calculation process is to identify an initial set estimate for the matching points. Using these initial matches, we calculate the position of the object and refine our initial match. This refinement process is necessary because of the poor resolution of the images (especially from the smaller mirror) and because we are trying to show that we can get reasonable position results not that the matching process works well (we are matching by eye, not automatically). Since the equations are based on radial symmetry, once the initial matches are made, we are only working with the radial distance from the centre of the image.

We conducted experiments using two different light positions. The results are presented in Tables 7.1 and 7.2 with the horizontal radial distance (actual and estimated), the vertical height from the plane of the origin (actual and estimated), and the Euclidean distance from the origin (actual and estimated).

distance	actual	estimate
horizontal	107.65 cm	106.976 cm
vertical	54.091 cm	46.584 cm
Euclidean	120.476 cm	116.679 cm

TABLE 7.1. For Light 1, radial distance in image: $x_{10} = 27$ pixels, $x_{20} = 168$ pixels

distance	actual	estimate
horizontal	214.5 cm	215.878 cm
vertical	43.5914 cm	51.383 cm
Euclidean	218.885 cm	221.909 cm

TABLE 7.2. For Light 2, radial distance in image: $x_{10} = 92.723$ pixels, $x_{20} = 200.5005$ pixels.

7.9 Further Improvements

The panoramic stereo device is still in the research and development stage. Several improvements to the current systems are being worked on. These include: automatically adjusting focus to make maximum use of the mirror surface, thereby increasing the resolution of the images; modifying the shape of the hemispherical surfaces to equalise the resolution of the two stereo strips; and adding image interpolation to the hardware so that the stereo images are of higher perceptual quality.

We are also working on the design and implementation of a hardware "clipper" which will select only the parts relevant to a given viewing direction and display them on a head-mounted display.

7.10 Acknowledgment

The authors would like to thank Mark Fiala and David Southwell for their work on the real-time panoramic image sensor using a double lobed hemisphere. Editorial support of Anne Nield is also gratefully acknowledged.

8

Panoramic Imaging with Horizontal Stereo

S. Peleg, M. Ben-Ezra, and Y. Pritch

8.1 Introduction

The ultimate immersive visual environment should provide three elements: (i) Stereo vision, where each eye gets a different image appropriate to its location in space; (ii) complete 360° view, allowing the viewer to look in any desired direction; (iii) allow free movement. Stereo Panoramas [137, 114, 213, 259] use a new scene to image projection that enables simultaneously both (i) stereo and (ii) a complete panoramic view. No depth information or correspondences are necessary. Viewers of stereo panoramas have the ability to freely view, in stereo, all directions. Since the scene to image projection necessary for stereo panoramic imaging cannot be done with a regular camera, stereo panoramic images were generated by mosaicing images taken with rotating cameras [137, 114, 213, 259]. As it is necessary to rotate a video camera a full circle in order to obtain a single stereo panoramic images, it was impossible to generate video-rate stereo panoramic movies. In this chapter, we present two possible camera systems, without any moving parts, that can capture stereo panoramic movies in video rate. One system uses special mirrors, and the other system uses special lenses. With such cameras it will be possible to make stereo panoramic movies of real events: sports, travel, etc. Short introductions are given in this section to panoramic imaging, stereo imaging, multiple viewpoint projections, and caustic curves.

8.1.1 Panoramic Images

A panoramic image is a wide field of view image, up to a full view of 360°. Panoramas can be created on an extended planar image surface, on a cylinder, or on a sphere. Traditional panoramic images have a single viewpoint, also called the "center of projection" [177, 49, 267]. Panoramic images can be captured by panoramic cameras, by using special mirrors [195, 149], or by mosaicing a sequence of images from a rotating camera [267, 214].

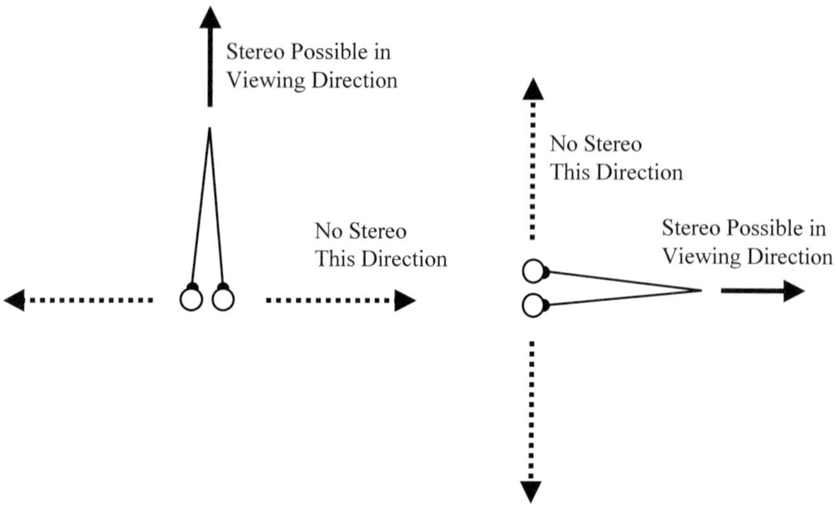

FIGURE 8.1. No arrangement of two single-viewpoint images can give stereo in all viewing directions. For upward viewing the two cameras should be separated horizontally, and for side ways viewing the two cameras should be separated vertically.

8.1.2 Visual Stereo

A stereo pair consists of two images of a scene from two different viewpoints. The disparity, which is the angular difference in viewing directions of each scene point between the two images, is interpreted by the brain as depth. Figure 8.1 shows a conventional stereo setting. The disparity is a function of the point's depth and the distance between the eyes (*baseline*). Maximum disparity change, and hence maximum depth separation, is along the line in the scene whose points have equal distances from both eyes ("principal viewing direction"). No stereo depth separation exists for points along the extended baseline.

People can perceive depth from stereo images if the viewpoints of the two cameras generate horizontal disparity in a specific range. Stereo has been obtained in panoramic images by having two viewpoints,one above the other [82]. However, since the disparity in this case is vertical, it can only be used for depth calculation, and not for viewing by humans having eyes which are separated horizontally.

8.1.3 Caustic Curves

Definition 1 *The* **envelope** *of a set of curves is a curve C such that C is tangent to every member of the set.*

Definition 2 **A caustic** *is the envelope of rays emanating from a pointsource and reflected (or refracted) by a given curve.*

A caustic curve caused by reflection is called a catacaustic, and a caustic curve caused by refraction is called a diacaustic [308]. In Figure 8.10 the catacaustic curve given the mirror and the optical center is a circle. In Figure 8.12 and Figure 8.13, the diacaustic curve given the lens and the optical center is a circle.

8.2 Multiple Viewpoint Projections

Regular images are created by perspective projections: scene points are projected onto the image surface along projection lines passing through a single point, called the "optical center" or the"viewpoint". Multiple viewpoint projections use different viewpoints for different viewing direction, and were used mostly for special mosaicing applications. Effects that can be created with multiple viewpoint projections and mosaicing are discussed in [297, 222]. Stereo panoramic imaging uses a special type of multipleviewpoint projections, *circular projections*, where both the left-eye image and the right-eye image share the same cylindrical image surface. To enable stereo perception, the left viewpoint and the right viewpoint are located on an inner circle (the "viewing circle") inside the cylindrical image surface, as shown in Figure 8.2. The viewing direction is on a line tangent to the viewing circle. The left-eye projection uses the rays on the tangent line in the clockwise direction of the circle, as in Figure 8.2(b). The right-eye projection uses the rays in the counter clockwise direction as in Figure 8.2(c). Every point on the viewing circle, therefore, defines both a viewpoint and a viewing direction of its own.

The applicability of circular projections to panoramic stereo is shown in Figure 8.3. From this figure it is clear that the two viewpoints associated with all viewing directions, using the "left-eye" projection and the "right-eye" projection, are in optimal relative positions for stereo viewing for all directions. The vergence is also identical for all viewing directions [256], unlike regular stereo that has a preferred viewing direction.

8.3 Stereo Panoramas with Rotating Cameras

Representing all stereoscopic views with only two panoramic images presents a contradiction, as depicted in Figure 8.1. When two ordinary

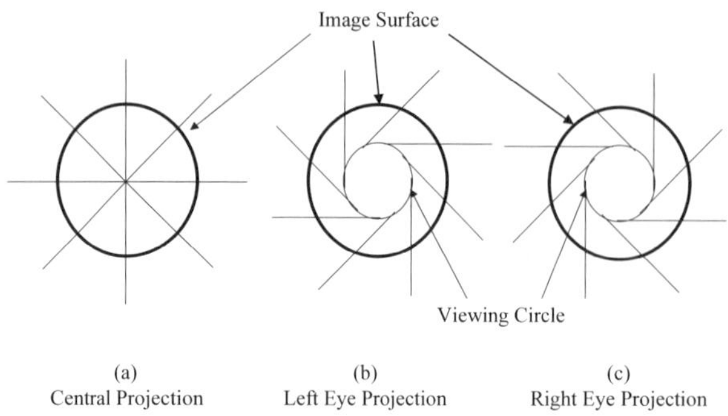

FIGURE 8.2. Circular projections. The projection from the scene to the image surface is done along the rays tangent to the viewing circle. (a) Projection lines perpendicular to the circular imaging surface create the traditional single-viewpoint panoramic image. (b-c) Families of projection lines tangent to the inner viewing circle form the multiple-viewpoint circular projections.

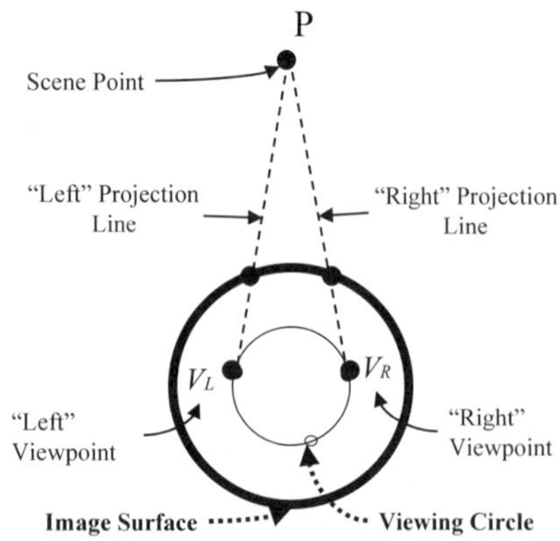

FIGURE 8.3. Viewing a scene point with "left-eye" and "right-eye" projections. The two viewpoints for these two projections are always in optimal positions for stereo viewing.

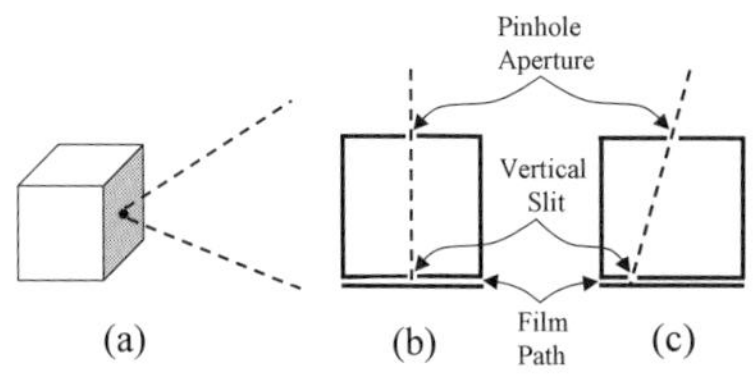

FIGURE 8.4. Two models of slit cameras. (a) Side view. (b-c) Top view from inside the camera. While the camera is moving, the film is also moving in the film path. The locations of the aperture and the slit are fixed in each camera. (b) A vertical slit at the center gives a viewing direction perpendicular to the image surface. (c) A vertical slit at the side gives a viewing direction tilted from the perpendicular direction.

panoramic images are captured from two different viewpoints, the disparity and the stereo perception will degrade as the viewing direction becomes closer to the baseline until no stereo will be apparent. Generation of image-based stereo panoramas by rotating a stereo head having two cameras was proposed in [114, 259]. A stereo head with two cameras is rotated, and two panoramic mosaics are created from the two different cameras.

8.3.1 Stereo Mosaicing with a Slit Camera

Panoramic stereo can also be performed with a single rotating camera [213, 137, 259]. This is done by simulating a "slit camera" as shown in Figure 8.4. In such cameras the aperture is a regular pinhole as shown in Figure 8.4(a), but the film is covered except for a narrow vertical slit. The plane passing through the aperture and the slit determines a single viewing direction for the camera. The camera modeled in Figure 8.4(b) has its slit fixed at the center, and the viewing direction is perpendicular to the image surface. The camera modeled in Figure 8.4(c) has its slit fixed at the side, and the viewing direction is tilted from the perpendicular direction.

When a slit camera is rotated about a vertical axis passing through the line connecting the aperture and the slit, the resulting panoramic image has a single viewpoint (Figure 8.2(a)). In particular, a single viewpoint panorama is obtained with rotations about the aperture. However, when the camera is rotated about avertical axis directly behind the camera, and the vertical slit is not in the center, the resulting image has multiple viewpoints. The moving slit forms a cylindrical image surface. All projection lines, which are tilted from the cylindrical image surface, are tangent to some *viewing circle* on which all viewpoints are located. The slit camera in Figure 8.4(c), for example, will generate the circular projection described in Figure 8.2(b). For stereo panoramas we use a camera having two slits: one slit on the right and one slit on the left. The slits, which move together with the camera, form a single cylindrical image surface just like a single slit. The two projections obtained on this shared cylindrical image surface are exactly the circular projections shown in Figure 8.2. Therefore, the two panoramic images, obtained by the two slits, enable stereo perception in all directions.

8.3.2 Stereo Mosaicing with a Video Camera

Stereo panoramas can be created with video cameras in the same manner as with slit cameras, by using vertical image strips in place of the slits [213]. The video camera is rotated about an axis behind the camera as shown in Figure 8.5. The panoramic image is composed by combining together narrow strips, which together approximate the desired circular projection on a cylindrical image surface. In manifold mosaicing [214], each image contributes to the mosaic a strip taken from its center. The width of the strip is a function of the displacements between frames. Stereo mosaicing is very similar, but each image contributes **two** strips, as shown in Figure 8.5. Two panoramas are constructed simultaneously. The left panorama is constructed from strips located at the right side of the images, giving the "left-eye" circular projection. The right panorama, likewise, is constructed from strips located at the left side of the images, giving the "right-eye" circular projection.

A schematic diagram of the process creating a pair of stereo panoramic images is shown in Figure 8.6. A camera having an optical center O and an image plane is rotated about an axis behind the camera. Strips at the left of the image are seen from viewpoints V_R, and strips at the right of the image are seen from viewpoints V_L. The distance between the two viewpoints is a function of the distance r between the rotation axis and the optical center, and the distance $2v$ between the left and right strips. Increasing the distance between the two viewpoints, and thus increasing the stereo disparity, can be obtained by either increasing r or increasing v.

8.4 Stereo Panoramas with a Spiral Mirror

Regular cameras are designed to have a single viewpoint ("optical center"), following the perspective projection. In this section, we show how to create images having circular projections using a regular camera and a spiral shaped mirror. The shape of the spiral mirror can be determined for a given optical center of the camera o, and a desired viewing circle V. The tangent to the mirror at every point has equal angles to the optical center and to the tangent to the circle (see Figure 8.7). Each ray passing through

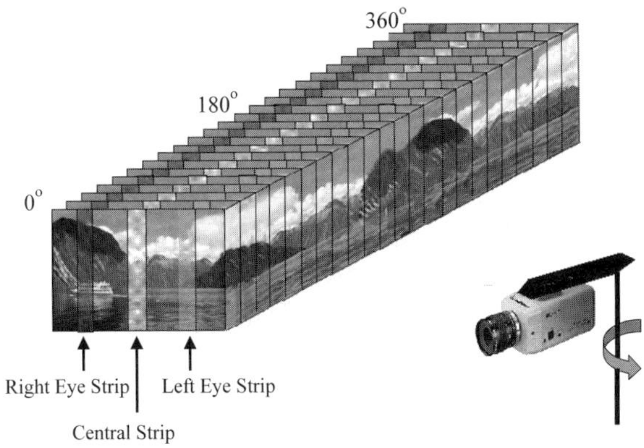

FIGURE 8.5. Stereo Panoramas can be created using images captured with a regular camera rotating about an axis behind it. Pasting together strips taken from each image approximates the panoramic image cylinder. When the strips are taken from the center of the images an ordinary panorama is obtained. When the strips are taken from the left side of each image, the viewing direction is tilted counter clockwise from the image surface, obtaining the right-eye panorama. When the strips are taken from the right side of each image, the left-eye panorama is obtained.

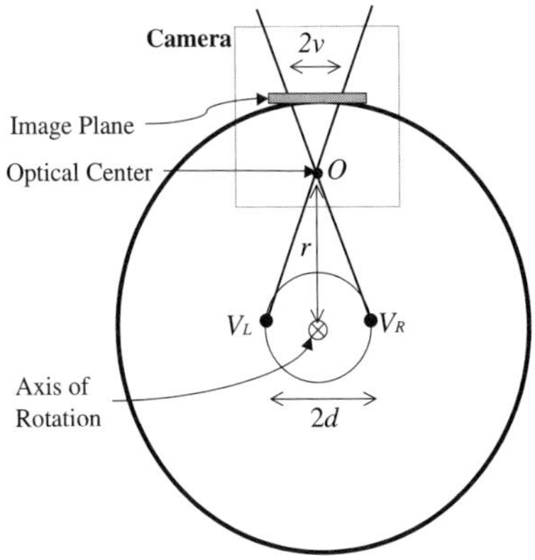

FIGURE 8.6. Schematic diagram of the system to create a pair of stereo panoramic images. A camera having an optical center "O" is rotated about an axis behind the camera. Note the "inverted" camera model, with image plane in front of the optical center.

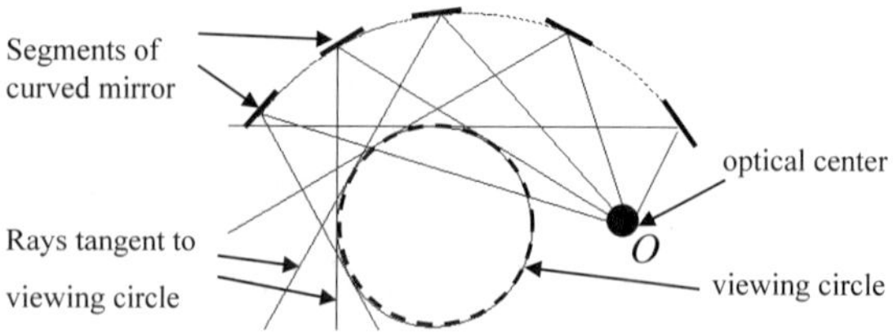

FIGURE 8.7. The spiral mirror: All rays passing through the optical center o will be reflected by the mirror to be tangent to the viewing circle V. This implies that rays tangent to the viewing circle will be reflected to pass through the optical center.

the optical center will be reflected by this mirror to be tangent to the viewing circle. This is true also in reverse: all rays tangent to the circle will be reflected to pass through the optical center. The mirror is therefore a curve whose catacaustic is a circle.

The conditions at a surface patch of the spiral shaped mirror are shown in Figure 8.8. The optical center is at the center of the viewing circle of radius R, and the mirror is defined by its distance $r(\theta)$ from the optical center. A ray passing through the optical center hits the mirror at an angle α to the normal, and is reflected to be tangent to the viewing circle. Let the radius of the viewing circle be R, and denote by $\overline{r}(\theta)$, the vector from the optical center and the mirror at direction θ (measured from the x-axis). The distance between the camera center and the mirror at direction θ will therefore be$r = r(\theta) = \| \overline{r} \|$. The ray conditions can be written as:

$$R = \| \overline{r} \| \sin(2\alpha) = \| \overline{r} \| \, 2sin(\alpha)\cos(\alpha)$$

$$\sin(\alpha) = \frac{|N \times \overline{r}|}{\|\overline{r}\| \cdot \|N\|} \tag{8.1}$$

$$\cos(\alpha) = \frac{(N,r)}{\|\overline{r}\| \cdot \|N\|}$$

using those conditions we can derive the following differential equation, where$\rho = \rho(\theta)$ is defined to be $\frac{r(\theta)}{R}$.

$$2\rho^2 \frac{\partial \rho}{\partial \theta} = (\frac{\partial \rho}{\partial \theta})^2 + \rho^2 \tag{8.2}$$

This second degree equation in $\frac{\partial \rho}{\partial \theta}$ has two possible solutions:

$$\frac{\partial \rho}{\partial \theta} = \left\{ \begin{array}{c} \rho^2 + \rho\sqrt{\rho^2 - 1} \\ \rho^2 - \rho\sqrt{\rho^2 - 1} \end{array} \right\}. \tag{8.3}$$

The curve is obtained by integration on θ. The solution which fits our case is:

$$\theta = \rho + \sqrt{\rho^2 - 1} + \arctan(\frac{1}{\sqrt{\rho^2 - 1}}) \tag{8.4}$$

With the constraint that $\rho > 1$. The spiral mirror can also be represented by a parametric equation. Given the position of the camera (p_1, p_2) and the radius R of aviewing circle centered around the origin, points $(x(t), y(t))$ on the mirror can be represented as a function of a parameter t:

$$\begin{aligned} x &= \frac{\sin(t)(R^2+{p_1}^2-R^2t^2+{p_2}^2)-2p_2R-2R^2t\cos(t)}{2(-p_2\cos(t)-Rt+\sin(t)p_1)} \\ y &= \frac{-\cos(t)(R^2+{p_1}^2-R^2t^2+{p_2}^2)+2p_1R-2R^2t\sin(t)}{2(-p_2\cos(t)-Rt+\sin(t)p_1)} \end{aligned} \tag{8.5}$$

When the camera is positioned at the origin, e.g. in the center of the viewing circle, the equations above simplify to:

$$\begin{aligned} x &= \frac{R(-\sin(t)+2t\cos(t)+t^2\sin(t))}{2t} \\ y &= \frac{-R(-\cos(t)-2t\sin(t)+t^2\cos(t))}{2t} \end{aligned} \tag{8.6}$$

A curve satisfying these conditions has a spiral shape, and Figure 8.9 shows such a curve extended for three cycles. To avoid self-occlusion, a practical mirror will use only segments of this curve.

A spiral shaped mirror where the optical center is located at the center of the viewing circle is shown in Figure 8.10.

The configuration where the optical center is at the center of the viewing circle is also convenient for imaging together the left image and the right image. Such a symmetric configuration is shown in Figure 8.11. This configuration has a mirror symmetry, and each mirror covers 132° without self occlusions. An *OmniCamera* [195, 149] can be placed at the center of the viewing circle to capture both the right image and the left image. Since this setup captures up to 132 degrees, three such cameras are necessary to cover a full 360 degrees.

8.5 Stereo Panoramas with a Spiral Lens

Circular projections can also be obtained with a lens whose diacaustic is a circle: the lens refracts the rays getting out of the optical center to be tangent to the viewing circle, as shown in Figure 8.12. A lens can cover up to 360 degrees without self-occlusion depending on the configuration. The spiral of the lens is different from the spiral of the mirror. We have not yet computed an explicit expression for this curve, and it is generated using numerical approximations. It is possible to simplify the configuration and use multiple identical segments of a spiral lens, each capturing a small angular sector. Figure 8.13 presents a configuration of fifteen lenses,

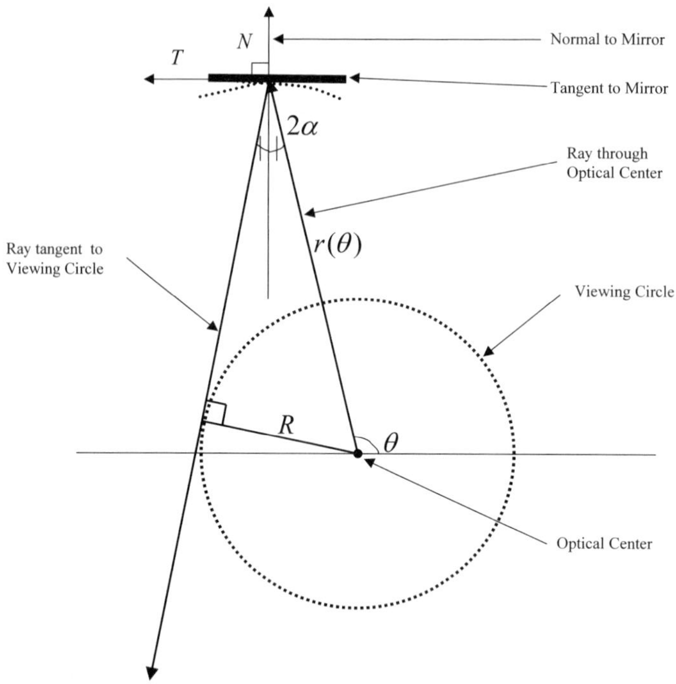

FIGURE 8.8. Differential conditions at a mirrorpatch: The optical center is at the center of the viewing circle of radius R, and the mirror is defined by its distance $r(\theta)$ from the optical center. A ray passing through the optical center hits the mirror at an angle α to the normal, and is reflected to be tangent to the viewing circle.

each covering 24°. The concept of switching from one big lens to multiple smaller lenses that produce the same optical function was first used in the Fresnel lens. In practice, a Fresnel-like lens can be constructed for this purpose having thousands of segments. A convenient way to view the entire panorama is by placing a panoramic omnidirectional camera [195, 149] at the center of the lens system as shown in Figure 8.5. A camera setup for creating two 360° panoramas simultaneously (one for each eye) is presented in Figure 8.15. This system consists of two multiple-lens systems as described in Figure 8.13. A conic beam splitter and a conic mirror areused. The beam splitter splits each of the rays to two separate identical rays. The rays which are not reflected by the beam splitter enter the lower lens system. The rays which are reflected by the beam splitter are reflected again by the mirror into the upper lens system. One lens system will produce a panoramic images using a left viewing circle, and the other lens system will produce a panoramic image using a right viewing circle.

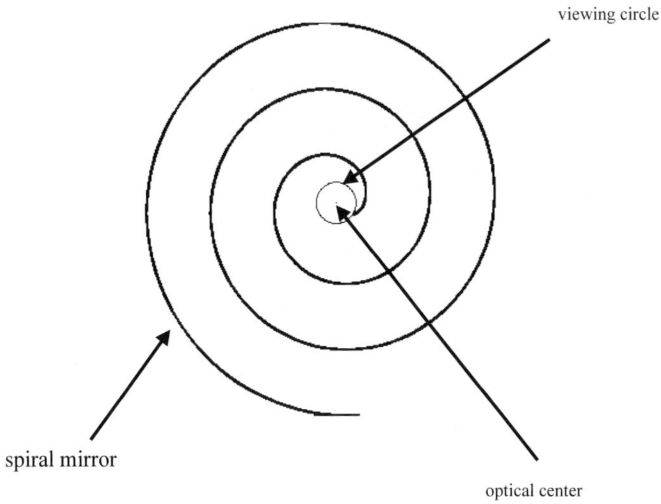

FIGURE 8.9. A spiral shaped mirror extended for three full cycles. The catacaustic curve of this spiral is the small inner circle.

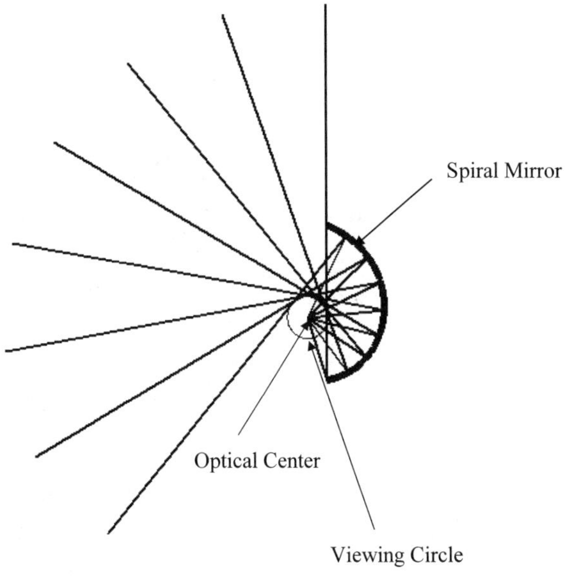

FIGURE 8.10. A spiral mirror where the optical center is at the center of the viewing circle.

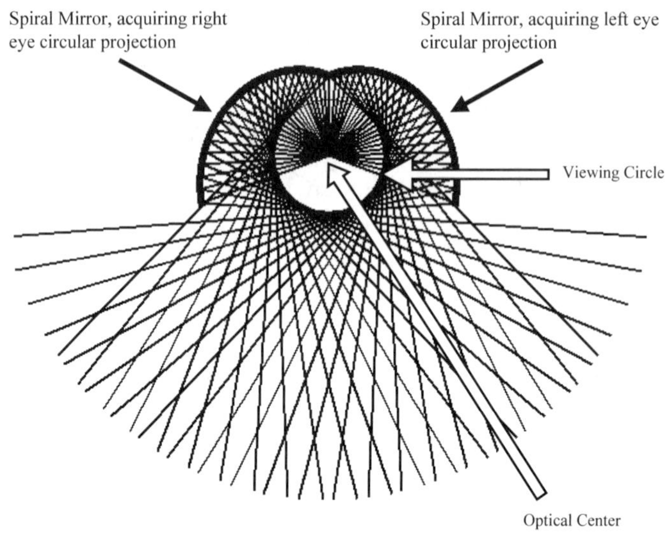

FIGURE 8.11. Two spiral shaped mirrors sharing the same optical center and the viewing circle. One mirror for the left-circular-projection and one for the right-circular-projection.

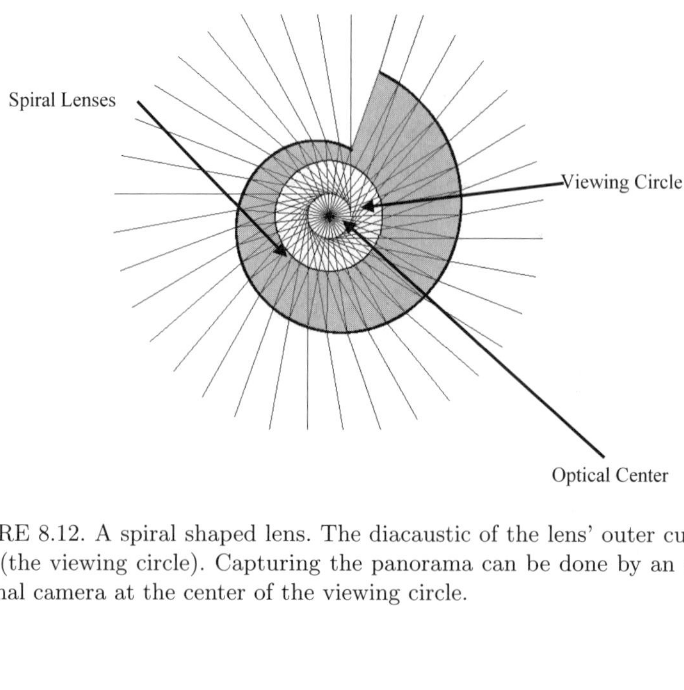

FIGURE 8.12. A spiral shaped lens. The diacaustic of the lens' outer curve is a circle (the viewing circle). Capturing the panorama can be done by an omnidirectional camera at the center of the viewing circle.

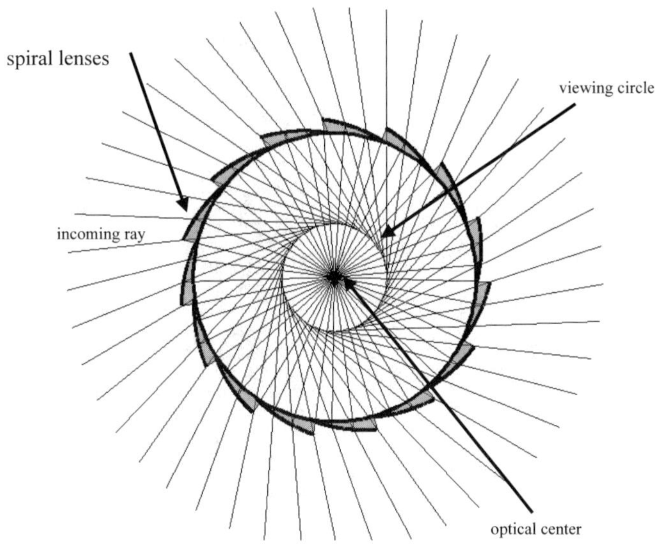

FIGURE 8.13. A collection of identical shortspiral lens positioned on a circle. A Fresnel-like lens can be built with thousands of lens segments. Capturing the panorama can be done by an OmniCamera at the center of the viewing circle.

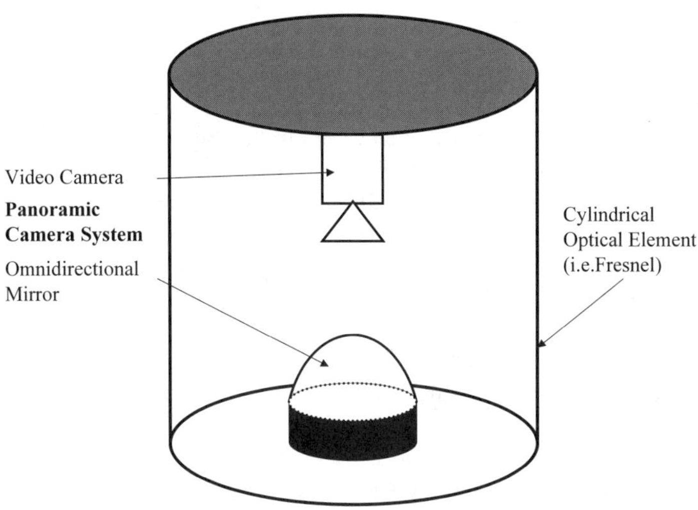

FIGURE 8.14. An omnidirectional camera at the center of the viewing circle enables the creation of a full 360 degrees left-image or a right-image.

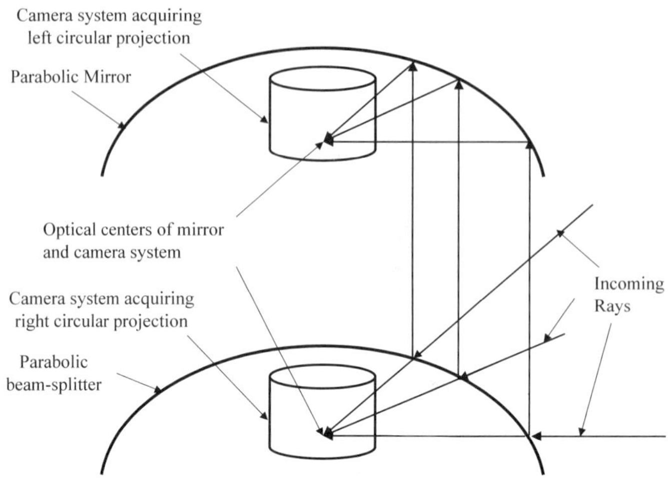

FIGURE 8.15. A setup for simultaneous capture of both left and right panoramas. A beam splitter is used to split the rays between two lens system. The horizontal rays enter into the bottom lens system for the right eye. The upward rays are reflected by a mirror into the upper lens system for the left eye.

The requirement that the cylindrical optical element (e.g., as in Figure 8.13) just bends the rays in the horizontal direction is accurate for rays that are in the same plane of the viewing circle. But this is only an approximation for rays that come from different vertical directions. Consider, for example, Figure 8.16. Let us examine the rays for viewpoint R. Ray A is in the horizontal plane that includes the viewing circle V. It is deflected by the Fresnel lens into ray a, and passes through the center O of the viewing circle, the location of the optical center of the panoramic camera. Ray B, which also passes through viewpoint R, but from a higher elevation, is also deflected by the same horizontal angle, but will not reach O. Instead, Ray B is deflected into ray d, which can intersect the horizontal plane closer or further to the Fresnel lens than O. In order that ray B will bedeflected into Ray c, that intersects O, the Fresnel lens should deflect it also in the vertical direction. Each elevation should have a different vertical deflection. A possible arrangement is that the cylindrical Fresnel lens has vertical elements on one side that take care of the horizontal deflection (which is constant), and on the other side it has horizontal elements that take care of the horizontal deflection (which is different for every elevation).

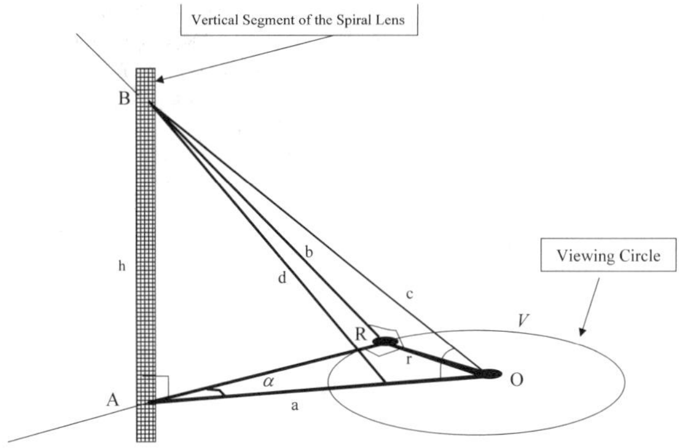

FIGURE 8.16. Vertical deflection of rays is necessary in order to assure that every viewing direction will have a single viewpoint on the viewing circle.

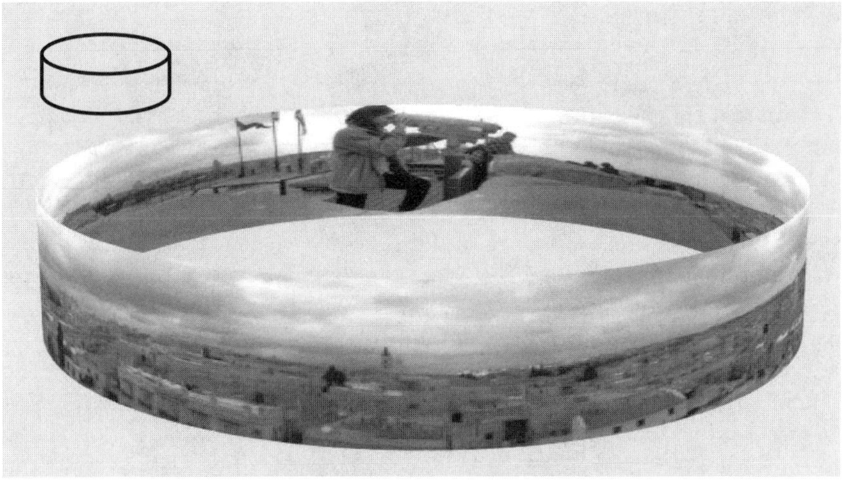

FIGURE 8.17. Cylindrical projection.

8.6 Stereo Pairs from Stereo Panoramas

When viewing the stereo panorama on a flat screen, like a computer or television monitor, or a head-mounted display, the panoramic image is projected from the cylinder onto a plane. While the cylindrical panoramic stereo images are created using circular projections (Figure 8.2(b,c)), they should be projected into the planar image surface using a central projection (Figure 8.2(a)). As seen in Figure 8.18, central projections introduce fewer distortions, and are symmetrical for the left and right images. A central projection about the center of the cylinder, with the image plane tangent to the panoramic cylinder, is a natural projection; it is symmetric for the

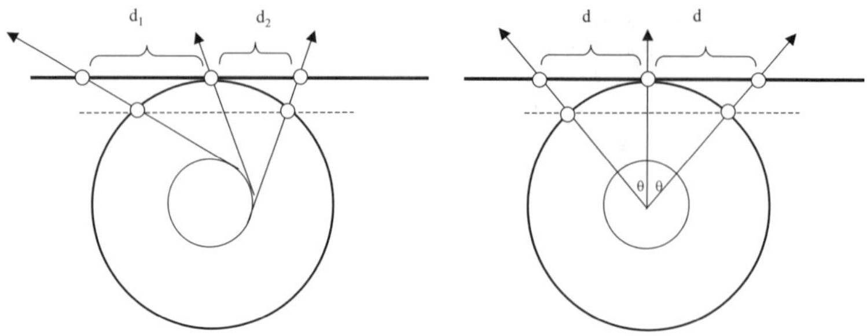

FIGURE 8.18. (a) Projecting the cylindrical panorama using the original circular projection creates a distorted planar image. (b) A central projection creates a symmetrical planar image which preserves the disparity for a viewer located at the center of the cylinder.

left side and the right side of the image as well as symmetric between the left-eye and right-eye projections. This projection also preserves the angular disparity that exists on the cylinder for a viewer located at the center of the cylindrical projection, and hence preserves the depth perception. An example of cylindrical projection is given in image 8.17.

Below is further examination of the process that generates the cylindrical panoramas using the multiple viewpoint circular projection, and creates planar images from the cylindrical panoramas using the single viewpoint central projection. Figure 8.19 describes the relation between a conventional stereo pair and cylindrical panoramic stereo having the same base line of $2d$. For a point at depth Z, the disparity of conventional stereo is 2θ, where $\theta = tan^{-1}(\frac{d}{Z})$. The disparity of stereo panorama is 2α, where $\alpha = sin^{-1}(\frac{d}{Z})$. This disparity is preserved by the central projection of the panorama onto a planar image. Since the stereo disparities that can be fused by a human viewer are small, $sin(x) \approx tan(x)$ and the disparities are practically the same.

8.7 Panoramic Stereo Movies

Unlike the case of panoramic stereo with rotating cameras, stereo panoramic cameras are capable of capturing a dynamic scene to createa movie. This movie can than be projected in a theater having a stereo projector and cylindrical screen. Each viewer, equipped with the appropriate stereo glasses, is able to view in stereo any desired direction. A more interactive experience can be obtained when an individual viewer is using a

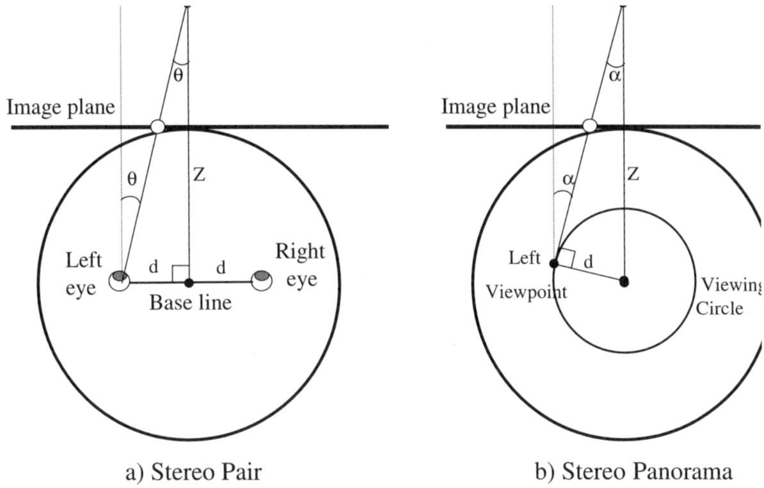

FIGURE 8.19. Comparing disparities between cylindrical panoramas and conventional stereo pairs. (a) The disparity of conventional stereo is 2θ where $\theta = tan^{-1}(\frac{d}{Z})$. (b) The disparity of stereo panorama is2α where $\alpha = sin^{-1}(\frac{d}{Z})$. This disparity is preserved by the central projection of the panorama onto a planar image.

head-mounted display. In such a case, the viewer should control the time axis as well. It is important to control the time axis in panoramic movies in order to enable repetitions that can be used to view more directions not viewed before.

8.8 Left-right Panorama Alignment (Vergence)

The imaging process introduces a shift between the left view panorama and the right view panorama. This shift is not related to the depth parallax, and in particular points at infinity may not be aligned. Since the stereo disparity of points at infinity should be zero, aligning the points at infinity will correct this shift. Figure 8.20 illustrates this process. A point P_∞ located at infinity is projected by a reference central projection into point S, and by the left circular projection into P'_∞. The angle β between these points is the misalignment of the left circular projection relative to the reference central projection. $\beta = \angle(SCP'_\infty) = \angle(CP'_\infty V_R) = \sin^{-1}(R/L)$. For vergence on points at infinity, such that they will be aligned in both panoramas, the left panorama and the right panorama should each be rotated towards the reference circular projection by β.

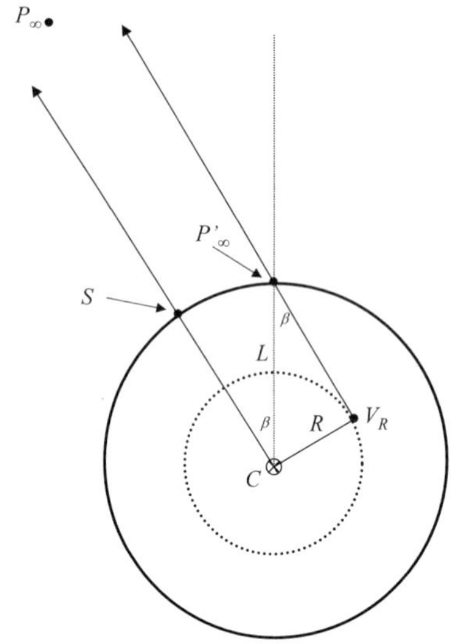

FIGURE 8.20. Vergence for left circular projection.

8.9 Concluding Remarks

Two systems, having no moving parts, were presented for capturing stereo panoramic video. One system is based on spiral mirrors, and the second system is based on spiral lenses. While not constructed yet at the time of writing this paper, these systems represent the only known possibilities to capture real-time movies having the stereo panoramic features.

8.10 Acknowledgment

The authors wish to thank Tanya Matskewich and Eisso Atzema (University of Maine) for their help in deriving the expressions defining the spiral mirror.

9

Panoramic Stereovision Sensor

R. Benosman and J. Devars

9.1 Rotating a Linear CCD

Panoramic sensors with sequential acquisition are mainly based on rotating cameras, several approaches can be found in [311, 234, 192, 136, 22, 24]. Before we conceive any panoramic sensor we have to think of a geometry that will decide of all the treatments that will be applied in the image side. The architecture of the panoramic stereovision sensor has been developed to symplifiy to the maximum the calibration stage that is 2D instead of the usual 3D and ease the features matching with an implicit epipolar geometry that becomes 1D instead of the usual 2D. When we talk about panoramic stereovision we mean observing and reconstructing an unknown scene all around the sensor. The panoramic image that describes this observation is the set of all equidistant points the optical center. The projection is then central, it can be cylindrical or spherical. In what follows the retained solution is the cylindrical one. The equivalent sensor can be looked at as a cylinder on which will be projected points of the 3D scene, as shown by Figure 9.1. Once we have defined the elementary panoramic sensor, we can establish the architecture of the panoramic stereovision sensor. The omnidirectional stereovision sensors have not been developed as a unique entity. The main drawback of these sensors is that usually they are an empirical assembly of standard elements putting all the difficulties on computation. The architecture of the system built is based on two linear CCD cameras fixed vertically one on the top of the other. They are specially designed as a part of a whole mechanical entity and accurately mounted parallel. They are rotated around a vertical axis, the distance between the two cameras is adjustable between 10 cm and 40 cm, with a 5 cm step. The linear sensors we use are Thomson 1024 pixels TH7804A, and the lenses are of 12.5 mm focal length. The motion of the system is conducted by a stepper motor and the whole system is controlled by computer (Figure 9.2).

The developed sensor shown by Figure 9.3 is equipped with a slip ring that allows continous rotation, the linear images are sent to the computer using an optical fiber rotating link that ensures continous rotation. Color images are obtained by using RGB filters that can automaticaly commute in front of the lens. Figure 9.4 shows the stereo images given by the sensor.

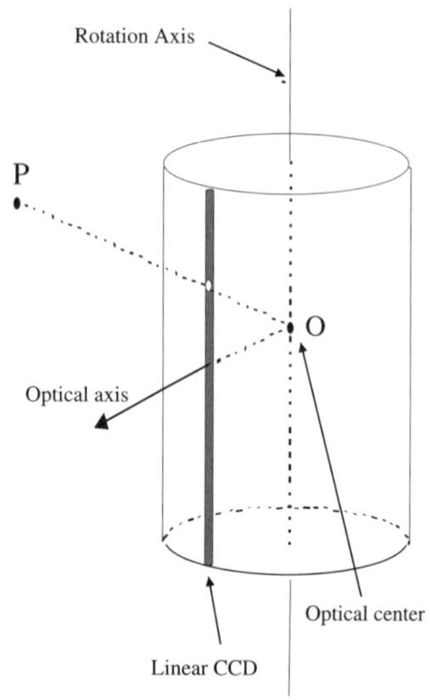

FIGURE 9.1. Elementary sensor for panoramic vision with axial cylindrical geometry.

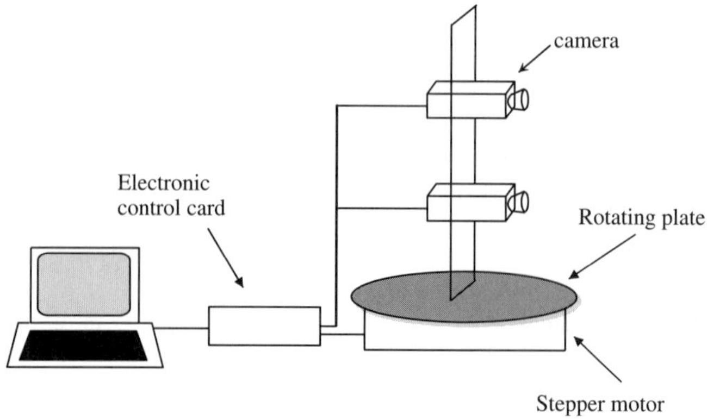

FIGURE 9.2. The panoramic sensor architecture.

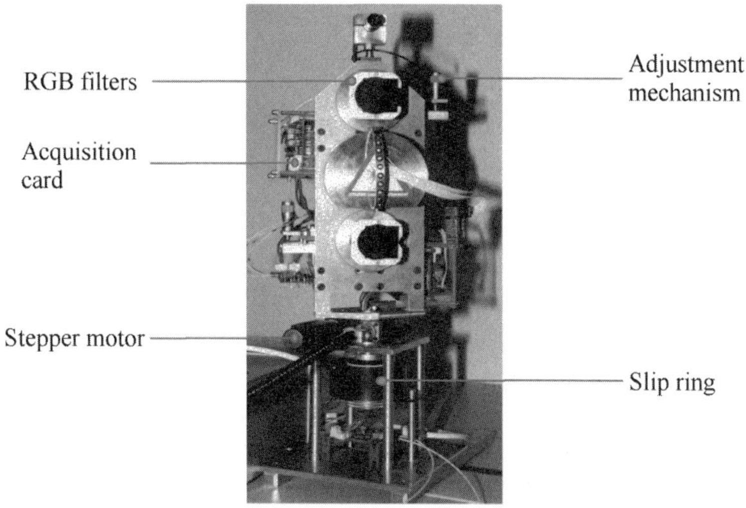

FIGURE 9.3. The panoramic stereovision sensor.

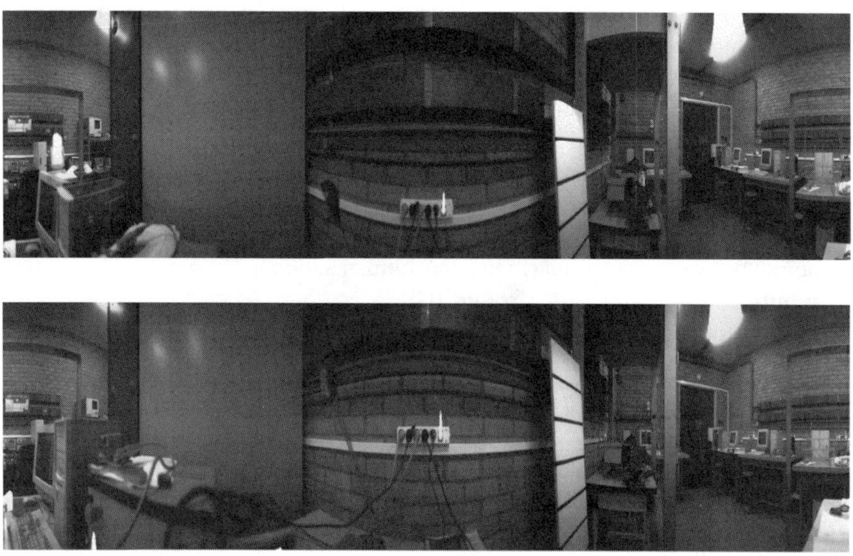

FIGURE 9.4. Panoramic stereovision upper and lower images.

9.2 System Function

The computer controls the positioning of the cameras by the stepper motor (Micro-Control UE30PP) which elementary step is $1/100°$. The maximal frequency of the increment pulse is 400 Hz. The computer controls an acquisition sequence of a column image for each camera. The information relative to the 2*1024 pixels of the image columns are stored in a RAM. Each pixel is encoded on 256 levels of gray. Figure 9.6 presents the general architecture of the system. Once the acquisition ends, the computer leads the rotation to the next position.

The rotating step is typically $1/10°$. The information stored in the memory is read by the computer during the rotation of the whole system to the next position. The architecture of the system and the obvious epipolarity of the images allow a data stream structure of the computational treatment, column by column, as they are taken. The advantages of the system come from the unusual positioning of the two linear CCD image sensor. As we built our system we took great care to insure the mechanical precision. The two linear cameras have several mechanisms which allow the adjusment of the parallelism between the two sensors. The optimization of the adjustment is controlled by the analysis of series of images of a calibration pattern composed of vertical black and white lines. In the theoretical case there is a coincidence between the rotating axis and the optical center.

The parallelism of both linear CCD is function of the angle ψ (see Figure 9.5) that characterizes the deviation regarding the vertical rotation axis of the panoramic device. We measure the effect of the adjustment by ensuring that the motif of the alignment pattern appear on the same columns in both upper and lower images. A more precise adjustment is then done by working directly on the columns where there is a transition from a black strip to a white one, and also by ensuring that all the pixels have the same values in both upper and lower images. The adjustment mechanism of the cameras exert a pressure on the support of the linear CCD deforming the fixing. Such constraints allow us to obtain a setting precision of $5 \mu m$. The spacing between the adjustment mechanisms being known, we can then compute the precision of ψ around $0.01°$.

A non-coincidence is not a critical problem, it involves an imprecision much smaller than the imprecision due to the spatial sampling of the images. The system presents lots of advantages, that come mainly from the fact that both stereo images (upper and lower) acquisitions are taken simultaneously. The stereo-matching can be made imediately after the acquisition, this will allow the matching of both linear images corresponding to the previous angular position while the acquisition of the linear images corresponding to the next position is made. The matching can be implemented on a specific ASIC that matches pixels giving 3D coordinates of the objects seen. One of the main drawback of these kind of system is their

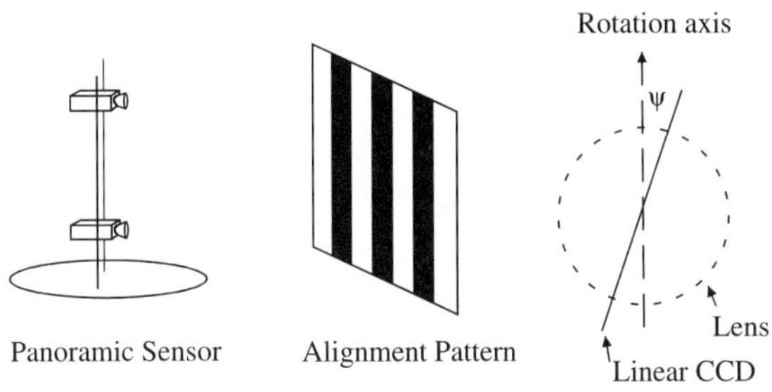

FIGURE 9.5. Alignment of both linear CCD.

difficulty of localizing vertical lines that depend on the elementary rotation step.

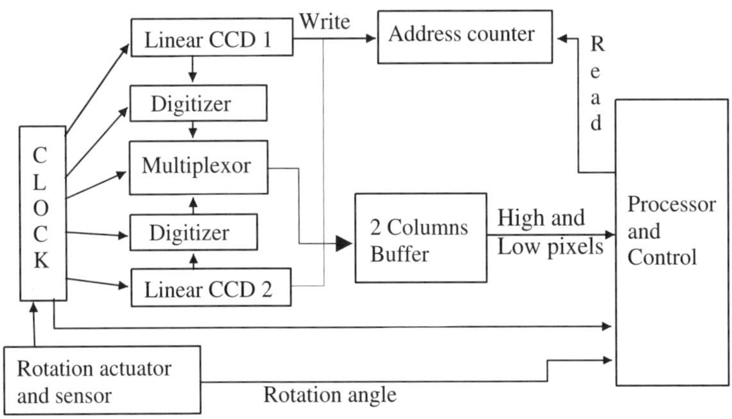

FIGURE 9.6. Global architecture of the system

The system is also limited in real time applications as the acquisition time of a complete panoramic image is connected to the exposure time of the linear CCD. We will see in what follows that a solution can be found. The presented prototype needs 6 minutes to do a complete acquisition, this time could seem long and can be explained as follows:

1) The rotation time of the stepper motor. The maximal frequency of the control card is 400Hz, as a panoramic images needs 36000 steps, the complete rotation is done in 90s

2) The exposure time is 25ms. It is necessary to wait for another cycle to start the next acquisition then the total is 50ms for a single acquisition. If we need 3600 linear images, the complete time for an acquisition is 180 seconds. Adding these two numbers gives a minimal time of 4 minutes 30 seconds, the additional 1 minute and 30 seconds, can be explained by the stopping and starting time of the stepper motor.

These results are just given as an exemple to show the problems that can be faced with these kind of sensors. The performances can be bettered using linear ccd with very short exposure time, even though they will remain too slow for real-time applications. These kind of sensors are very powerful as they produce very high and accurate reconstructions, their domain of applications are maintely the numerization of scenes for cinematographical and multimedia purposes.

9.3 Toward a Real-time Sensor?

One of the main drawback of panoramic sensors with sequential acquisition could be overcome by keeping the electronic still and applying the rotation only on the optical side. Acquisition can be made continuous to avoid the use of a stepper motor that slows the sensor. It will be then possible to use just one or two linear ccd that remain still. The problem would be then to send the rays of light toward this sensor using a rotation periscope based on mirrors (see Figure 9.7).

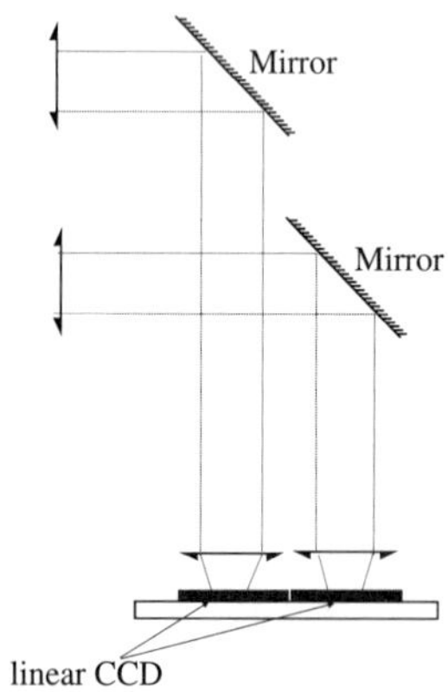

FIGURE 9.7. Optical binocular system for sending back the observed image toward the linear CCD.

The bibliographical studies show that such a system is feasible, and the reader is referred to [152]. The main drawback of the proposed periscope is that it needs the rotation of the electronical system to folllow the rotation. The solution is in the use of a double periscope with a constant field of view, that would bring both reflected images from any angular position to the same plane of view. We can find in the literature an example of such a periscope.

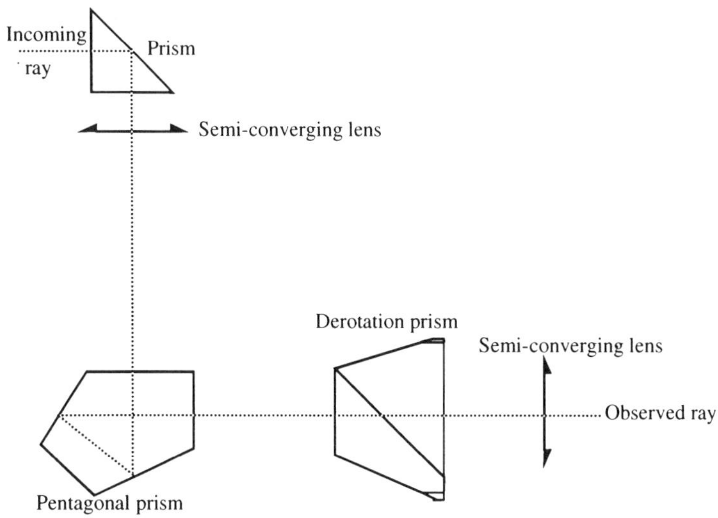

FIGURE 9.8. Layout of optical lenses for a panoramic telescope.

The principle of this non-rotation of the incident image is shown by Figure 9.7. The principle of non-rotation is explained by Figure 9.8. The solution to this problem can be found using of a double mirror represented by the dove prism introduced in Figure 9.7. If an incident image is rotated by an angle α toward left and if the double mirror is rotated by an angle $\alpha/2$ also toward left, then the reflected image seen on the double mirror has not turned. Figure 9.9 illustrates this effect of the derotation prism. The panoramic sensor using this technology would have a binocular persicope turning at a speed v with a dove prism turing at a speed v/2 that would bring the reflected images to the same agular position on the linear CCD that will remain still.

9.4 Acknowledgment

The authors thank Clause Gastaud, Thierry Maniere, Olivier Romain and Thomas Ea at University Pierre and Marie Curie for the work done on the

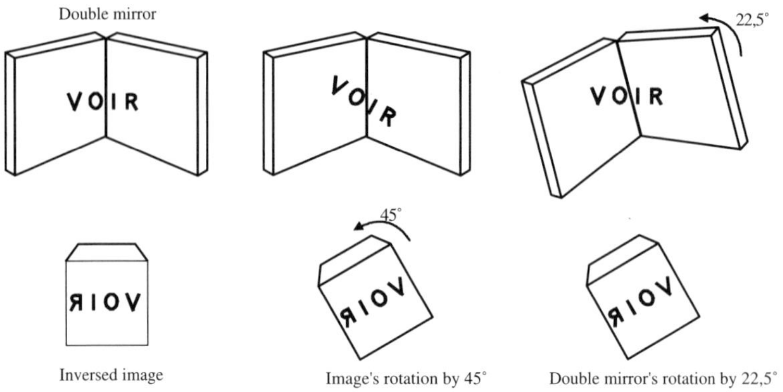

FIGURE 9.9. The non-rotation of a reflected image by a rotating double mirror.

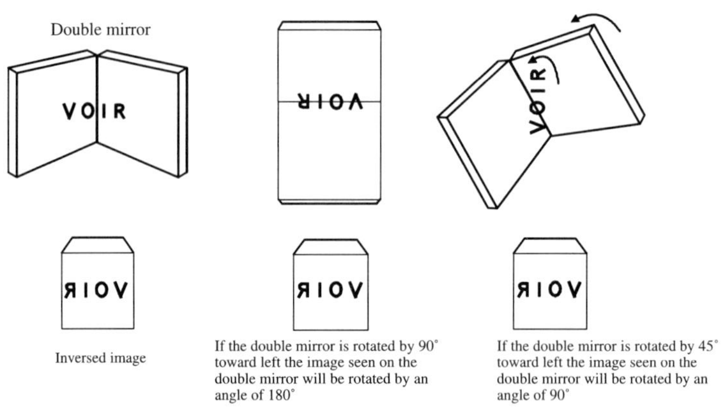

FIGURE 9.10. The rotation of the incident image is corrected by the rotation of the double mirror.

development of the panoramic stereovision sensor since 1993. This work was supported in parts by the French Department of Education.

10

Calibration of the Stereovision Panoramic Sensor

R. Benosman and J. Devars

10.1 Introduction

The Panoramic stereovision sensor introduced in the last chapter is based on two rotating linear cameras. This chapter deals with the calibration of a stereo head composed of two linear cameras. Though the calibration of CCD matrix cameras has received a lot of attention, few methods of calibration of linear CCD are described [111, 68, 23]. The following parts are organized as follows. The first part presents a calibration method of the panoramic stereovision sensor using a classical sketch of calibration. The second part introduces a more unusual calibration method based on normalized vectors to express points appearing in the scene.

10.2 Linear Camera Calibration using Rigid Transformation

10.2.1 The Pinhole Model

The model of camera used in the pinhole camera shown by Figure 10.1 A point P of the 3D space has an image p on the linear image. As a first approximation we will consider that the camera has a perfect perspective projection, O_c is the projection's center. The optical axis O_cX_c intersection the linear image at a point o which coordinate is u_0. The distance O_co is called the focal distance and will be represented by f. The camera coordinates system is $(O_cX_cY_c)$, the coordinates system of the image line (ox) is (cu). We then have the following relations:

$$\frac{u}{Y_c} = \frac{f}{X_c} \tag{10.1}$$

If we change the scaling mesure on (ox) :

$$x \Longrightarrow \frac{u}{k_u}$$

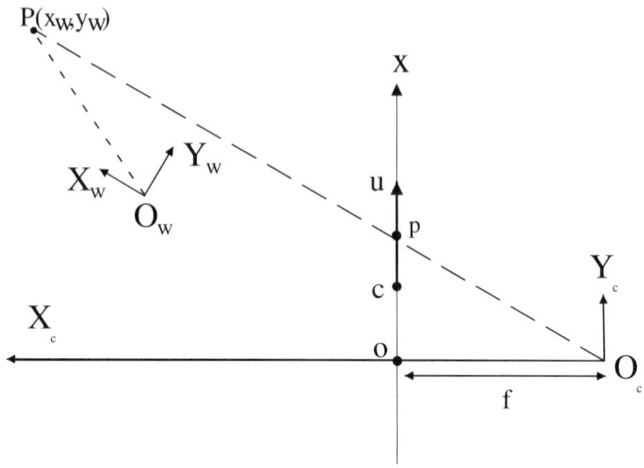

FIGURE 10.1. The pinhole model.

And if we translate the origin

$$u \Longrightarrow u - u_0$$

we obtain the following relation :

$$x = \frac{u - u_0}{k_u} \tag{10.2}$$

with $k_u > 0$,

If we set $\alpha_u = k_u . f$, (10.1) and (10.2) can be rewritten as a linear relation of homogeneous coordinates:

$$\begin{bmatrix} su \\ s \\ 1 \end{bmatrix} = \begin{bmatrix} u_0 & \alpha_u & 0 \\ 1 & 0 & 0 \\ 0 & 0 & 1 \end{bmatrix} \begin{bmatrix} x_c \\ y_c \\ 1 \end{bmatrix} \tag{10.3}$$

The physical significance of the parameters k_u, α_u, u_0 is the following:

α_u is focal length measured in pixels,

$\frac{1}{k_u}$ is the dimension of a pixel in meters ($tpix = \frac{1}{k_u}$).

u_0 is the intersection of the optical axis with the linear image and is called the center of the image.

(10.3) can be seen as follows:

$$U = MX \tag{10.4}$$

As depth can not be retrieved from a single camera, M is defined up to a scale factor, and is called the perspective transform matrix.

(10.4) can be considered under many aspects, the known and unknown parameters, if X and M are known, (10.4) gives the coordinates of a the point P, while if U and M are known, (10.4) allows a $2D$ reconstruction, the reader will notice that in this case (10.4) defines a line.

10.2.2 Applying the Rigid Transformation

A rotation R and a translation t is applied to the coordinates system (O_w, X_w, Y_w):

$$\begin{pmatrix} X_c \\ Y_c \end{pmatrix} = R \begin{pmatrix} X_w \\ Y_w \end{pmatrix} + t$$

The matrix M can be written as follows :

$$M = \begin{bmatrix} u_0 & \alpha_u & 0 \\ 1 & 0 & 0 \\ 0 & 0 & 1 \end{bmatrix} \begin{bmatrix} \cos\alpha & \sin\alpha & tx \\ -\sin\alpha & \cos\alpha & ty \\ 0 & 0 & 1 \end{bmatrix} =$$

$$\begin{bmatrix} u_0\cos\alpha - \alpha_u\sin\alpha & u_0\cos\alpha + \alpha_u\sin\alpha & \alpha_u ty + u_0 tx \\ \cos\alpha & \sin\alpha & tx \\ 0 & 0 & 1 \end{bmatrix}$$

10.2.3 Computing the Calibration Parameters

Let us assume that M has been computed and we would like now to find the values of the intrinsics and extrinsics parameters α_u, k_u, f, R and t. We have the following relation:

$$\begin{bmatrix} su \\ s \\ 1 \end{bmatrix} = M. \begin{bmatrix} x_w \\ y_w \\ 1 \end{bmatrix}$$

If we divide M by t_x, the system can be rewritten as follows:

$$\begin{bmatrix} su \\ s \\ 1 \end{bmatrix} = \begin{bmatrix} \frac{u_0\cos\alpha - \alpha_u\sin\alpha}{tx} & \frac{u_0\cos\alpha + \alpha_u\sin\alpha}{tx} & \frac{\alpha_u ty + u_0 tx}{tx} \\ \frac{\cos\alpha}{tx} & \frac{\sin\alpha}{tx} & 1 \\ 0 & 0 & \frac{1}{tx} \end{bmatrix} \begin{bmatrix} x_w \\ y_w \\ 1 \end{bmatrix}$$

Eliminating s from both equations gives us the expression for the image point u:

$$u = h_1 X + h_2 Y + h_3 uX + h_4 uY + h_5$$

with

$$h_1 = \frac{u_0\cos\alpha - \alpha_u\sin\alpha}{tx}$$

$$h_2 = \frac{u_0 \cos\alpha + \alpha_u \sin\alpha}{tx}$$

$$h_3 = \frac{\cos\alpha}{tx}$$

$$h_4 = \frac{\sin\alpha}{tx}$$

$$h_5 = \frac{\alpha_u ty + u_0 tx}{tx}$$

Under a matrix form the relation is written:

$$u = [XY - uX - uY1].H^T$$

10.2.4 Reconstruction

The equation connecting an image point to its 2D point in the scene is:

$$h_1^i X + h_2^i Y - h_3^i u^i X - h_4^i u^i Y + h_5^i - u^i = 0$$

We will consider i as the camera's index. In this case $i = 1..2$.

Computing the 2D coordinates of a point from its images on both upper and lower cameras needs to solve the following system of equations:

$$\begin{bmatrix} h_1^1 - h_3^1 u^1 & h_2^1 - h_4^1 u^1 \\ h_1^2 - h_3^2 u^2 & h_2^2 - h_4^2 u^2 \end{bmatrix} \cdot \begin{bmatrix} X \\ Y \end{bmatrix} + \begin{bmatrix} h_5^1 - u^1 \\ h_5^2 - u^2 \end{bmatrix} = 0$$

We have a high number of points to solve the system, the problem is then over-determined, we can find a solution applying a least-squares method.

10.2.5 Experimental Results

The geometry of the multidirectional device brings the calibration problem to a 2D one. As shown by Fig.10.2 the calibration will be held in the plane corresponding to a single angular position. In order to perform the calibration process we need a set of 2D reference points.

The most natural pattern is composed of two lines, assembled so that their angle is precisely 90° determining the world coordinates system (see Figure 10.3). The calibration pattern must be positioned so that when the panoramic sensor reaches the angular position where it is located, both orthogonal lines and optical centers of each camera belong to the same plane. Figure 10.4 shows the experimental device.

The reconstruction of calibration pattern's points from stereo in the camera coordinates system illustrated by Figures 10.5 and 10.6 show good result with a precision less than $10^{-3}m$.

	Lower camera	Upper camera
f en pixels	979.76	959.62
u_0 en pixels	522.67	606.06
t_x en m	3.597	3.4742
t_y en m	-0.396	-0.3589
$cos(\alpha)$	-0.4498	-0.3893
$sin(\alpha)$	-0.8931	-0.9211

TABLE 10.1. Estimating the calibration parameters

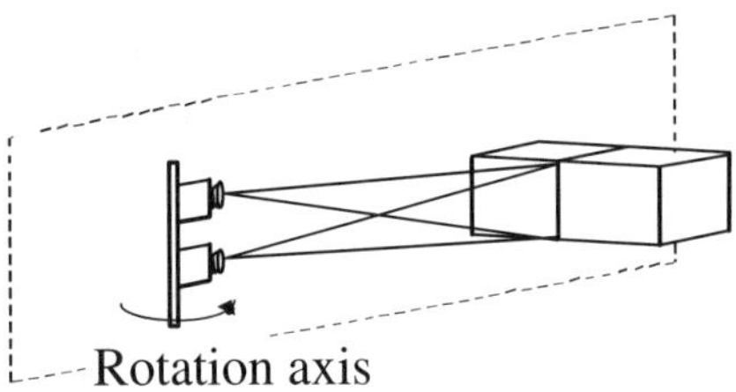

FIGURE 10.2. Calibration Plane.

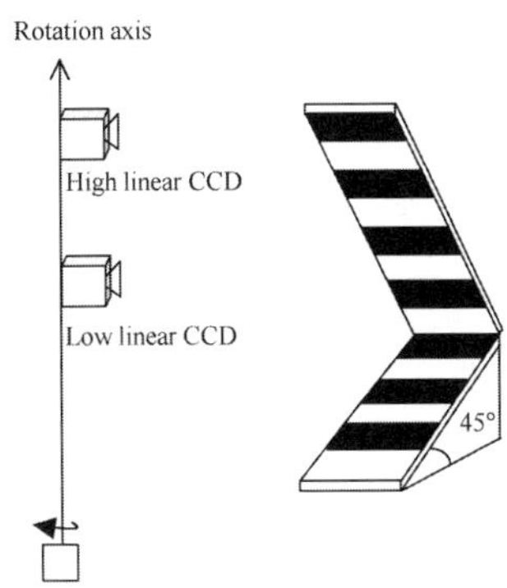

FIGURE 10.3. The calibration pattern.

10.3 Calibrating the Panoramic Sensor using Projective Normalized Vectors

10.3.1 Mathematical Preliminaries

Considering an object point P in the 3D space (see Figure 10.7), and p its projection on the image line, m_p is the vector starting from the view

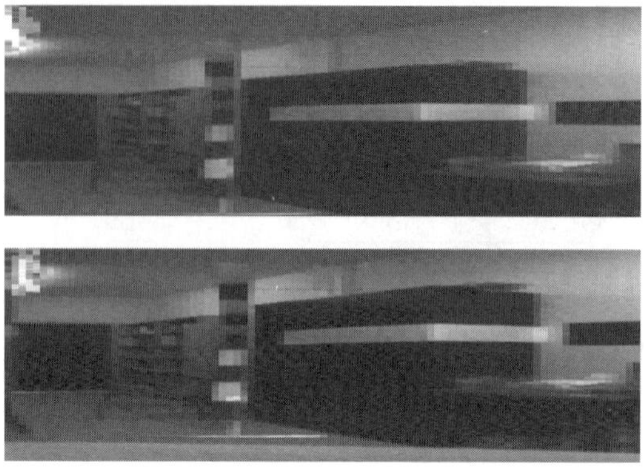

FIGURE 10.4. Observed calibration pattern.

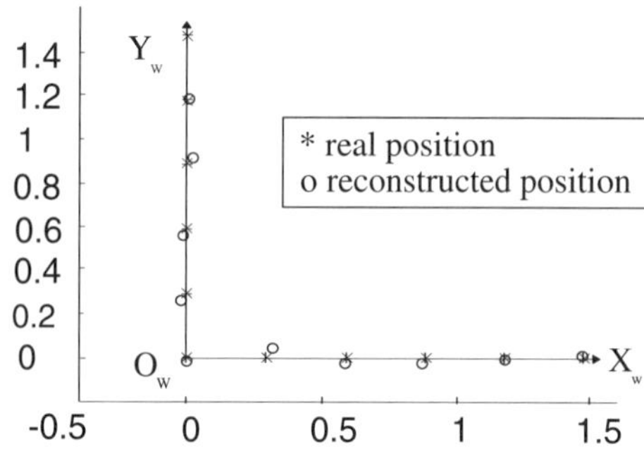

FIGURE 10.5. Reconstruction of the calibration points in the world coordinate system.

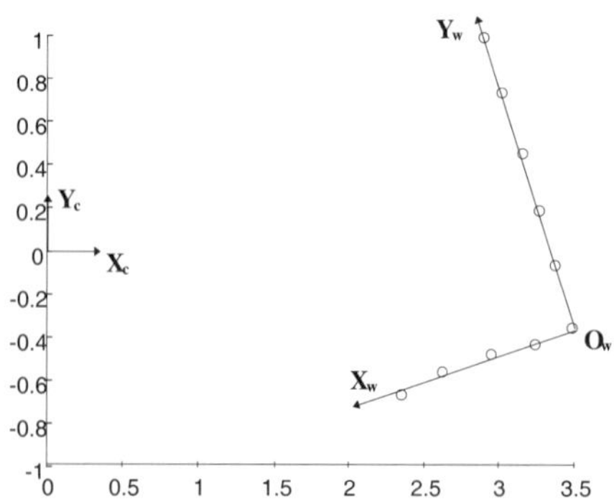

FIGURE 10.6. Reconstruction of the calibration points in the camera coordinate system.

point O and pointing towards P. If we want r_p to represent the absolute distance between O and P, we have to normalize vector m_p in order to have $\mathbf{OP} = \mathbf{r_p}.\mathbf{m_p}$.

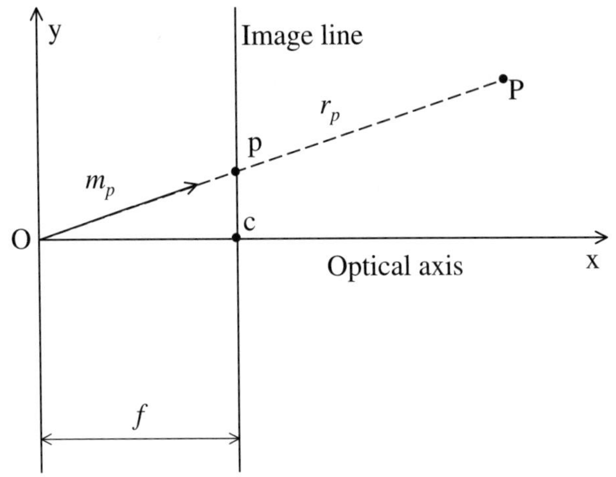

FIGURE 10.7. Normalized image vector.

The non-normalized expression of m_p^T is:

$$m_p^T = (f, (c-p)tpix)$$

where f represents the focal length, c the intersection of the optical axis with the image line and $tpix$ the vertical size of a pixel expressed in meters. Once the vector is normalized we get its new expression:

$$m_p^T = \left(\frac{f}{\sqrt{f^2 + (c-p)^2.tpix^2}}, \frac{(c-p).tpix}{\sqrt{f^2 + (c-p)^2.tpix^2}} \right)$$

To simplify the expression of normalized vector we will set:

$$\alpha = \frac{tpix}{f}, n_p = \sqrt{1 + (c-p)^2.\alpha^2}$$

Vector **OP** can be rewritten as follow:

$$\mathbf{OP} = \left(\frac{\mathbf{r_p}}{\mathbf{n_p}}, \frac{\mathbf{r_p.(c-p)}.\alpha}{\mathbf{n_p}} \right)$$

10.3.2 Camera Calibration

Considering Figure 10.8, we associate to each of the pattern points $P, Q, \overline{Q}, \overline{P}$ their corresponding normalized vectors $(m_p, m_q, m_{\overline{o}}, m_{\overline{p}}, m_{\overline{q}})$

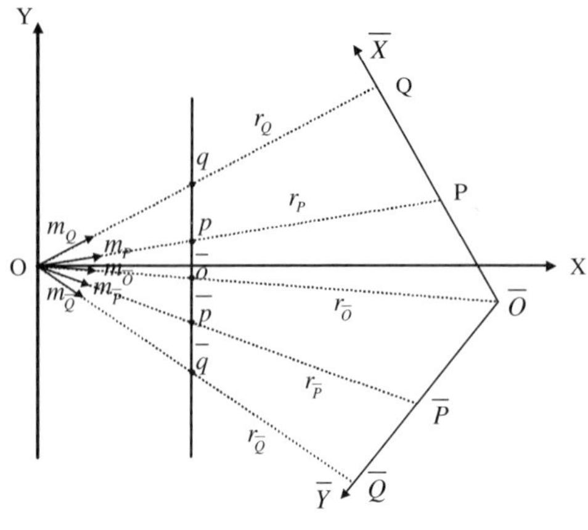

FIGURE 10.8. General calibration scheme.

starting from the view point O and pointing respectively towards their image points $(p, q, \overline{o}, \overline{p}, \overline{q})$.

The distances between $\overline{O}$ and pattern points $P, Q, \overline{Q}, \overline{P}$ are respectively noted x_P, x_Q, $x_{\overline{Q}}$, $x_{\overline{P}}$.

If we want to compute vector $\mathbf{OQ}$ we then have: $\mathbf{OQ} = \mathbf{O\overline{O}} + \mathbf{\overline{O}Q}$.

We can deduce $\mathbf{\overline{O}Q} = \mathbf{OQ} - \mathbf{O\overline{O}} = \mathbf{r_Q}.\mathbf{m_Q} - \mathbf{r_{\overline{O}}}\mathbf{m_{\overline{O}}}$, to finally give the coordinates of vector $\mathbf{\overline{O}Q}$:

$$\mathbf{\overline{O}Q} = \left(\frac{\mathbf{r_Q}}{\mathbf{n_Q}} - \frac{\mathbf{r_{\overline{O}}}}{\mathbf{n_{\overline{O}}}}, \frac{\mathbf{r_Q}}{\mathbf{n_Q}}.(\mathbf{c} - \mathbf{q}).\alpha - \frac{\mathbf{r_{\overline{O}}}}{\mathbf{n_{\overline{O}}}}.(\mathbf{c} - \overline{\mathbf{o}}).\alpha \right)$$

We can then easily deduce the expression of vectors $\overline{\mathbf{OP}}, \overline{\mathbf{OQ}}, \overline{\mathbf{OP}}$.

The pattern points P and Q are lying on the same axis vectors $\mathbf{\overline{O}Q}$ and $\mathbf{\overline{O}P}$ are then collinear to each other. Colinearity can be written as follow $\mathbf{\overline{O}Q} = \mathbf{R_{QP}}.\mathbf{\overline{O}P}$ with $R_{QP} = \frac{x_Q}{x_P}$ (inversely $R_{PQ} = \frac{x_P}{x_Q}$). Developing the colinearity relation gives the two following relations :

$$\frac{r_Q}{n_Q} = \frac{r_{\overline{O}}}{n_{\overline{O}}}.(1 - R_{QP}) + R_{QP}.\frac{r_P}{n_P} \tag{10.5}$$

and

$$\frac{r_P}{n_P} = \frac{r_{\overline{O}}}{n_{\overline{O}}}.(1 - R_{PQ}).\frac{q - \overline{o}}{q - p} \tag{10.6}$$

Points $\overline{P}$ and $\overline{Q}$ are also lying on the same axis vectors $\overline{\mathbf{OP}}$ and $\overline{\mathbf{OQ}}$ are colinear we can then deduce the same relations as (10.5) and (10.6) for points $\overline{P}$ and $\overline{Q}$.

Each of the vectors $\mathbf{\overline{O}Q}$ and $\overline{\mathbf{OQ}}$ are lying on different axes that are orthogonal to themselves. We can then apply the Pythagorean theorem to the triangle formed by the pattern points $\overline{O}, Q, \overline{Q}$ giving the following equation: $\left(OQ - O\overline{Q}\right)^2 = x_Q^2 + x_{\overline{Q}}^2$

We have then the following relation:

$$\alpha^2 \left(\frac{r_Q(c-q)}{n_Q} - \frac{r_{\overline{Q}}(c-\overline{q})}{n_{\overline{Q}}} \right)^2 + \tag{10.7}$$

$$\left(\frac{r_Q}{n_Q} - \frac{r_{\overline{Q}}}{n_{\overline{Q}}} \right)^2 = x_Q^2 + x_{\overline{Q}}^2$$

Replacing $\frac{r_Q}{n_Q}$ and $\frac{r_{\overline{Q}}}{n_{\overline{Q}}}$ by their expressions from (10.5) and (10.6) in (10.7) gives:

$$A.\left(\frac{1}{\alpha^2} + c^2\right) + B.c + C - \frac{1}{r_{\overline{O}}^2}.\left(\frac{1}{\alpha^2} + (c^2 - \overline{o})^2\right) = 0 \tag{10.8}$$

(10.8) is of form $A.x + By + z + C = 0$, where the unknown x, y and z are of expression:

$$x = (\frac{1}{\alpha^2} + c^2), y = c, z = \frac{1}{r_{\overline{O}}^2}.(\frac{1}{\alpha^2} + (c^2 - \overline{o})^2)$$

A, B, C are known and are given by :

$$A = \frac{\delta^2}{x_Q^2 + x_{\overline{Q}}^2}, \; B = \frac{2.\mu.v}{x_Q^2 + x_{\overline{Q}}^2}, \; C = \frac{v^2}{x_Q^2 + x_{\overline{Q}}^2},$$

with

$\delta = (1 - R_{QP}).\frac{p-\overline{o}}{p-q} - (1 - R_{\overline{QP}}).\frac{\overline{p}-\overline{o}}{\overline{p}-\overline{q}}$.

$v = -(1 - R_{QP}).\frac{p-\overline{o}}{p-q}.q - (1 - R_{\overline{QP}}).\frac{\overline{p}-\overline{o}}{\overline{p}-\overline{q}}.\overline{q}$.

$\mu = \beta - \gamma$, with $\beta = (1 - R_{QP}).\frac{p-\overline{o}}{p-q}$ and $\gamma = (1 - R_{\overline{QP}}).\frac{\overline{p}-\overline{o}}{\overline{p}-\overline{q}}$.

Solving such an equation needs at least 3 quartets of points P, Q, $\overline{Q}$ and $\overline{P}$ taken on the calibration pattern. To obtain a more robust solution of the equation we need to use as many quartets of calibration points as possible, combining all the existing points on the calibration pattern together. The overconstrained system is solved using a least squares method.

10.4 Handling Lens Distortions

In the case of a perfect centered lens the distortion is symmetrical according the optical axis modifying the Franke [74] polynomial form to adapt it to the 2D geometry of the problem giving the following formula limited to the $4th$ order:

$$(u^* - \delta u) = (u - \delta u).(K_1.r^2 + K_2.r^4)$$

where u is the distorted pixels coordinates, u^* is the pixels coordinates in which the camera distortion is removed, $K_1$and K_2 are the distortions coefficients and δu is the shift value to pass from the theoretical optical center to the real one. The distortion corrections shown by Figure 10.9 are those of the low sensor.

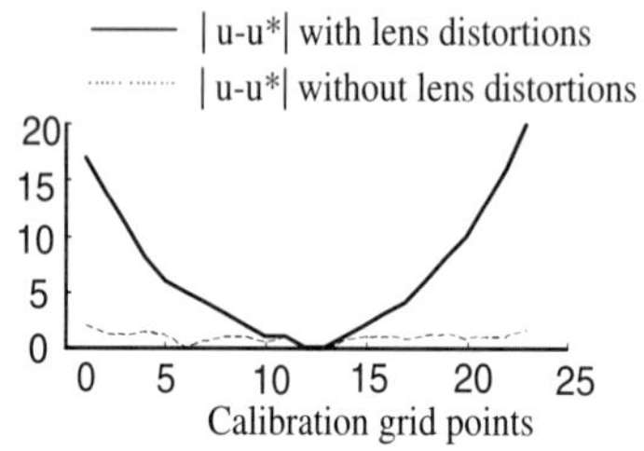

FIGURE 10.9. Lens Distortions Calibration.

10.5 Results

The detection of calibration points used in the calibration process uses an edge detection procedure that allows subpixel accuracy. The edge detection is done by thresholding the first column image derivative using the second column image derivative. Edge localization consists of finding the zero crossing, a zero crossing can be detected when two consecutive pixels are of different sign. The linear interpolation of the derivative values between pixels I and I+1 determine the position I_c that corresponds to the real position of the zero crossing. The value I_c contains the line value of edge points with an accuracy of 1/16 of the pixel size. The modified Deriche algorithm used uses a IIR recursive filter of order 2 with a causal and anticausal sweep, followed by two convolutions with FIR detection filter on 3 pixels for the first and second derivatives [77]. The identification of point $\overline{O}$ is made manually.

The experimental results where carried out using a calibration pattern shown by Figure 10.3 the points where spaced by a gap of 0.295 meters. Table 10.2 presents the estimation of intrinsic parameters. The reconstruction of the pattern calibration points in the world coordinates system $(\overline{O},\overline{X},\overline{Y})$ compared to the theoretical calibration pattern points' position is shown by Figure 10.10. While the reconstruction of the calibration pattern points in the camera coordinates system (O,X,Y) is illustrated by Figure 10.11.

The calibration pattern is placed so that both $\overline{OXY}$ and the rotation axis of the panoramic sensor are parallel, the parallelism method is similar to the one used to ensure the alignments of both linear CCD but this time the checking is done on a portion of the panoramic images containing the

	High Sensor	Low Sensor
c in pixels	522.57	606.06
$\frac{f}{tpix}$ in pixels	979.76	959.62
t_x in meters	3.697	3.5742
t_y in meters	-0.396	-0.3589
$\cos(\alpha)$ in rd	-0.4498	-0.3893
$\sin(\alpha)$ in rd	-0.8931	-0.9211

TABLE 10.2. Estimation of the calibration parameters by the calibration method based on rigid transformation.

	High Sensor	Low Sensor
c in pixels	612.6	497.2
$\frac{f}{tpix}$ in pixels	1051.6	1032.8
r_0 in meters	3.80	3.64

TABLE 10.3. Projective method estimation of the calibration parameters.

calibration pattern by checking that all pixels representing a same strip appear on the same line with the same grey levels values.

The errors of reconstructions can be lowered by bettering the optical distortions correction. It appears that the calibration method is very sensible to optical distortions, better results can be obtained using high quality optic. Compared to the method introduced in the first part of this chapter, the calibration method reaches similar reconstruction results (see Tables 10.2 and 10.3).

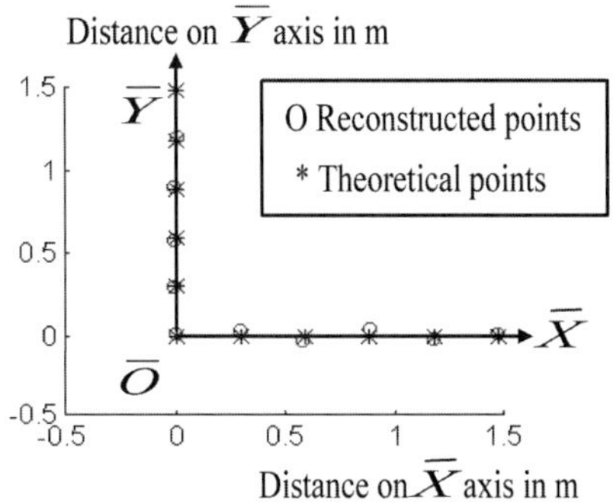

FIGURE 10.10. Reconstructed points compared to the theoretical calibration pattern points.

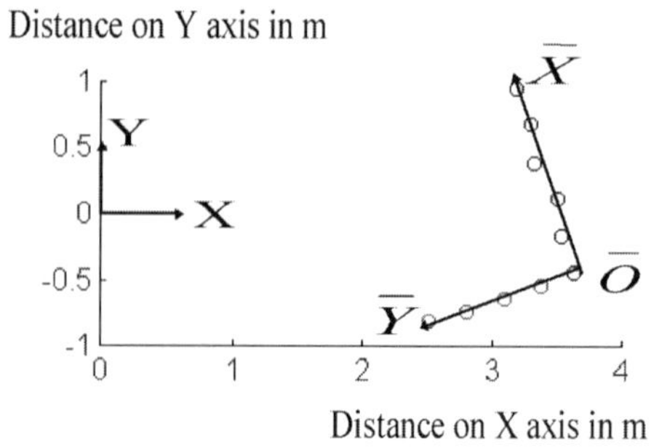

FIGURE 10.11. Reconstructed calibration reference points in the camera coordinates system.

10.6 Conclusion

The reader may wonder which method to use if a stereo head composed of two linear cameras is to be calibrated. The first method is very robust to noise and to errors in the localization of the calibration points and is quite easy to implement, whereas the second gives also good results but is very sensitive to noise and needs a subpixel accuracy in the detection of the calibration points. Both methods reach the same results if it is possible to be very accurate in the estimatation of the calibration features, but the reader may prefer the first method if the noise is too important or if the errors in the localization of the points needed by the calibration are high.

10.7 Acknowledgment

The authors thank Franck Nilusmas for developing the first sketch of the stereo-vision sensor used for our work.

11

Matching Linear Stereoscopic Images

R. Benosman and J. Devars

11.1 Introduction

The stereoscopic sensor presented in the last chapter is different from other systems due to the use of linear CCDs. The main problem is to find matching techniques to obtain a 3D reconstruction of the observed scenes directly from two linear images.

This chapter presents matching methods used to give a 3D reconstruction of unknown scenes, the main purpose is to allow real time reconstruction, we will start by analysing the geometrical properties of the sensor then we will introduce two matching algorithms both based on dynamic programing. The first method uses pixels as a feature while the second is based on regions.

11.2 Geometrical Properties of the Panoramic Sensor

The elementary panoramic sensor is a linear CCD swiveling around a vertical axis that we will call Z. The focal distance is denoted f. We have shown that the projection is cylindrical, f represents the ray of the cylinder illustrated by Figure 11.1.

The image coordinates of a $3D$ point $P = (x, y, z)$ on the cylinder are given by θ, Z_p, where θ represents the angular position of the point P, Z_p is the vertical distance between the image point and the plane containing the optical center O, the projection on the cylinder is defined as follows : $\theta = \arctan(y/x)$,with $\theta \in \left(-\frac{\pi}{2}, \frac{\pi}{2}\right)$. $Z_p = \frac{z*f}{\sqrt{x^2+y^2}}$. $\theta \in \left(-\frac{\pi}{2}, \frac{3\pi}{2}\right)$, obtained by transforming : $\theta \rightarrow \theta + \pi$. A 3D line D observed in the scene has the following equation : $D : \mathbf{x} = \begin{pmatrix} x_0 \\ y_0 \\ z_0 \end{pmatrix} + \begin{pmatrix} O \\ t \\ O \end{pmatrix}$; $\mathbf{t} \in (-\infty, +\infty)$ and it is projected on the cylinder as follows : $Zp = cos(\theta) * \left(\frac{f*z_0}{x_0}\right)$; $x_0 > 0; \theta \in \left(-\frac{\pi}{2}, \frac{\pi}{2}\right)$

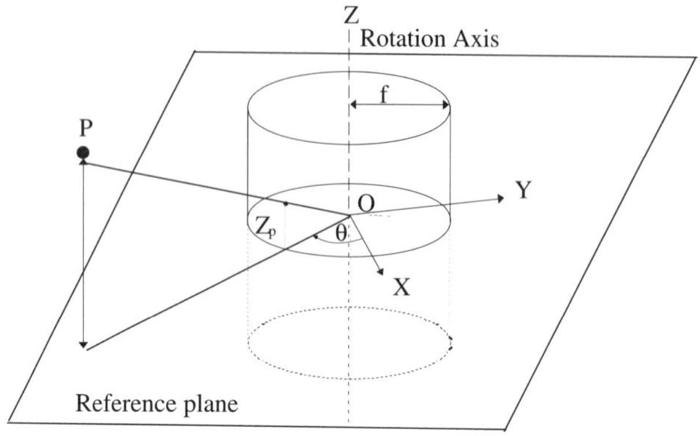

FIGURE 11.1. General scheme of cylindrical projection

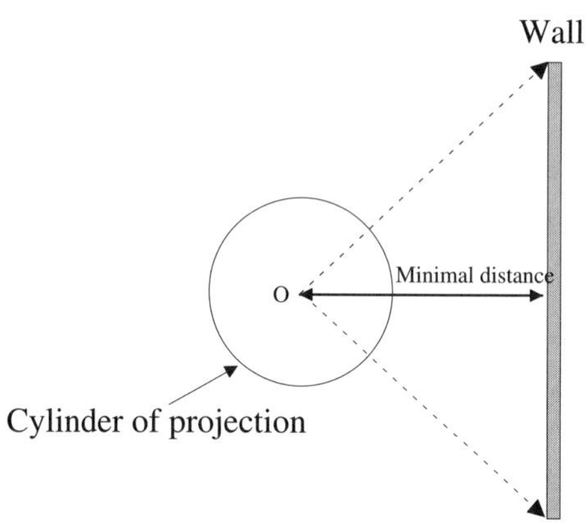

FIGURE 11.2. Curvature's maxima position.

The result shows that the vertical ridges of a wall in the scene are projected in the form of sinusoidal curves. The apex of these curves corresponds to the angular orientation of the sensor where the distance between the cameras and the wall is minimal, Figure 11.2 illustrates this principle.

Parallel lines of the form:

$$D : \mathbf{x} = \begin{pmatrix} c * x_0 \\ y_0 \\ c * z_0 \end{pmatrix} + \begin{pmatrix} O \\ t \\ O \end{pmatrix} ; \mathbf{t} \in (-\infty, +\infty); \mathbf{c} \in \mathbf{IN}$$

have the same image on the cylinder, this shows that we can not retreive any depth infromation from a single panoramic view, which is an expected result.

11.3 Positioning the Problem

Using the natural deformation of the projection of lines of the scenes is of great interest for environment modelisation. The aim of the approach is to retrieve the position of walls in the scenes. A matching algorithm based on the detection of curvature's maxima of the projected lines is used. The angular position of the apex of each line is saved and if a line apex is detected at the same angular position in both upper and lower images, a wall is then detected.

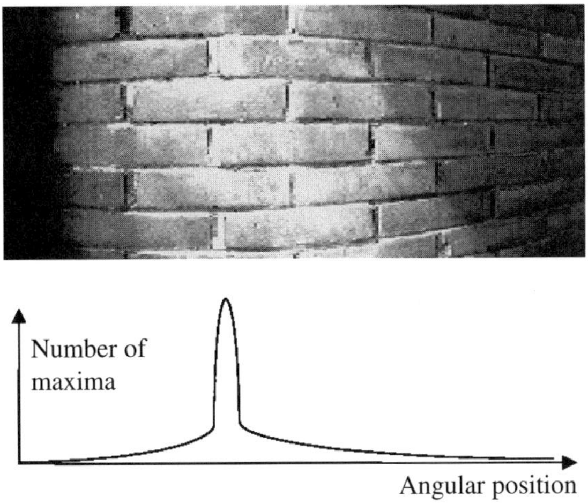

FIGURE 11.3. Wall detection.

As shown by Figure 11.3, the principle is simple. We have to detect maxima of curvature of each detected curve. An histogram of the angular occurence of these maxima shows a peak corresponding to the presence of a wall in the unknown scene [234]. The main reproach to this method is that the algorithm used to detect walls, is based on features that are strictly linked to the scene and may not appear if the scenes are too complex or if the lines are severely truncated. In some cases the rooms are assumed to be squared to simplify computation[179]. The use of the deformation of horizontal lines is a very attractive idea to solve the problem of obstacle detection and 3D reconstruction but remains too incertain, in what follows we will introduce two matching methods that give 3D reconstruction of an unknown scene, both allowing real time processing.

11.4 A Few Notions on Dynamic Programing

11.4.1 Principle

The dynamic programing can be seen as a measure of cost to transform a chain of elements that we will call the entry chain into another chain of element that we will call the reference chain. To make the entry chain correspond to the reference one, a set of editing operations are defined. The goal is to minimise the distance between the entry chain and the reference applying these edition operations.

In what follows we are interested principaly in the family of algorithms of dynamic programing allowing only operations of inserting, deletion and substitution where all the chain features are treated in the order of appearance.

11.4.2 The Family of Dynamic Programming Used

Let A and B be the entry chain and the reference chain each containing respectively n_A and n_B elements indexed from 0 à $n_A - 1$ and from 0 to $n_B - 1$. Let $d(i,j)$ be the distance between the jth element of A and the ith element of B.

The minimal cost to match the sub-chains $A(j)$, $j \in \{0..n_j - 1\}$ and $B(i)$, $i \in \{0..n_i - 1\}$, $g(n_j, n_i)$, is defined as being the distance between $A(j)$ and $B(i)$ to which we add the minimal costs :

1. $g(n_j - 1, n_i)$, inserting the element $A(n_j - 1)$ in the chain at a position n_j,
2. $g(n_j - 1, n_i - 1)$, substitution,
3. $g(n_j, n_i - 1)$, suppressing the element.

For the computation at the bounds g(0,.) and g(.,0), the costs g(-1,.) and g(.,-1) are used and are given high costs to forbid these possibilities. The path chosen by the min operator is stored and allows at the end of the processing to give the best match corresponding to the optimal path. This can be summerized by the following algorithm:

Dynamic Programing Algorithm

A, entry chain, n_A elements indexed from 0 to $n_A - 1$;
B, the reference chain, n_B elements indexed from 0 to $n_B - 1$
$g(-1, .)$ and $g(., -1)$ have a maximal cost.
for j going from 0 to $n_A - 1$ **do**
  for i going from 0 to $n_B - 1$ **do**
    compute $d(j, i)$

evaluate $g(j,i)=d(j,i)+min(g(j-1,i),g(j-1,i-1),g(j,i-1))$
store the chosen argument $argmin(j,i)$.
end for
end for

Retrieve the optimal path, i.e retreive the list of arguments matched to retrieve the optimal path going back from point (n_A-1,n_B-1) toward the origin $(0,0)$.

11.5 Matching Linear Lines

During the acquisition process of the panoramic sensor, the positionning is done by a rotating plate which elementary path is 0.01°. The linear images are stored in a temporary RAM memory. To allow online reconstruction of the observed scene the computation has to be done while the system is rotating toward its new position. It appears judicious to use the linear images while they are acquired. The matching algorithm has to be quick and also robust as it is dealing with raw linear images without any information on the previous columns, making the maching much harder.

11.5.1 Principle

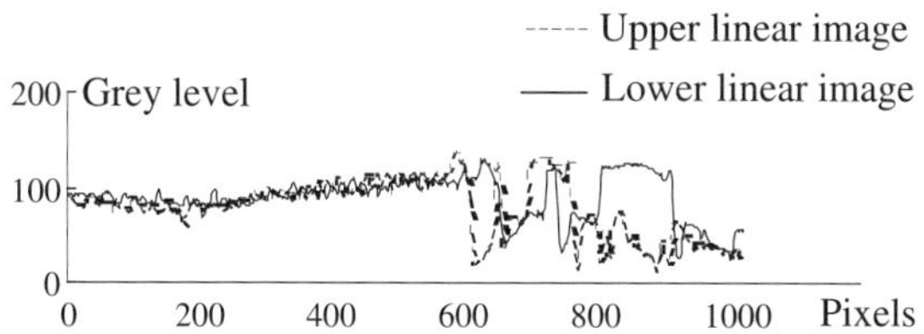

FIGURE 11.4. Linear images to be matched.

In order to fulfill the online constraint, the best matching is the one that works directly on the linear images while they are acquired. In what follows the lower linear image is called *cb* while the upper is represented by *ch*, $cb(i)$ is the grey level value of the ith pixel of the lower linear image, and we have the same for the upper sensor where $ch(j)$ is the grey level value of the jth pixel as shown by Figure 11.4. The aim is to match the pixels of both images to allow a 3D reconstruction of the environment.

11.5.2 Cost Function

The cost function evaluates the distance that separates a point from another, it must be simple in order to be computed quickly. We can consider that the difference between the grey levels of pixels values as a good cost function. In fact a scene point seen by both cameras will have the same grey level values in case of non specularity. We will call F this function which expression is

$$F(i, j) = |cb(i) - ch(j)|$$

Seen from a purely computational point of view, this cost function is simple because it uses a substraction and an absolute value, Figure 11.5 gives a 3D representation of the cost table of between two linear images.

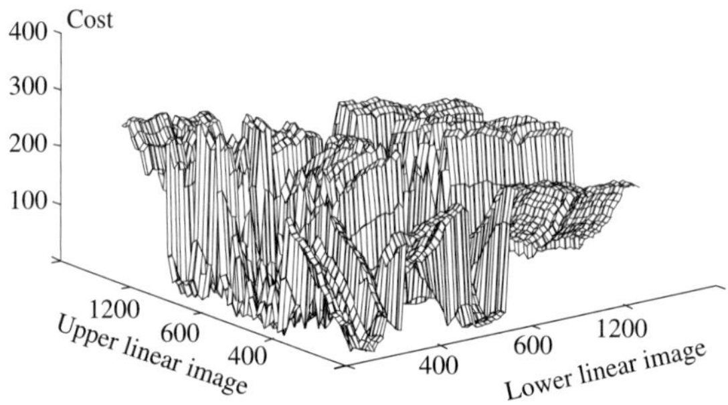

FIGURE 11.5. 3D representation of the cost table.

11.5.3 Optimal Path Retrieval and Results

Applying the dynamic programing algorithm we obtain a distance table and an optimal path corresponding to the matching illustrated by Figure 11.6.

The optimal path gives pairs of matched points, the matching of the two linear images is shown by Figure 11.7.

A filtering on matched pairs must be done, to minimise matching errors we will keep pairs of points where only both of them are edges in their images.

At this stage, the principle of the matching procedure has been explained, if we apply it directely on the linear images coming from the panoramic sensor, the number of false matches will be high. In order to lower the

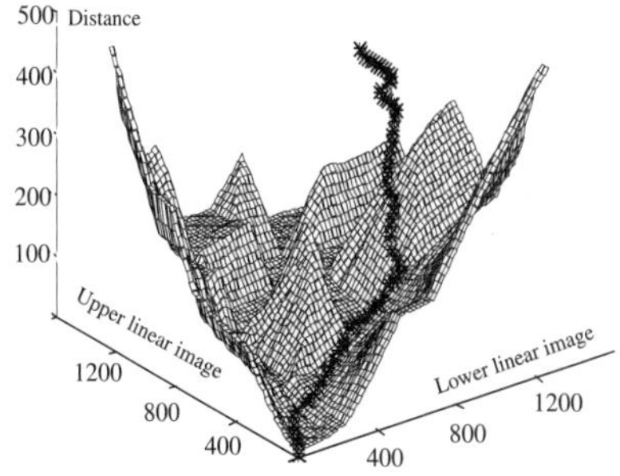

FIGURE 11.6. 3D representation of the distance table and the optimal path.

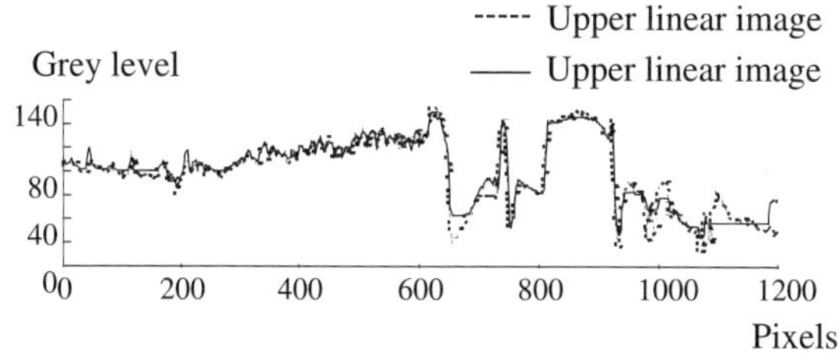

FIGURE 11.7. Matched linear images.

number of false matches we need to add several constraints that will refine the matching.

11.5.4 Matching Constraints

Local and photometric ressemblance criterions are generaly not enough restrictive to avoid false matchings. To overcome this drawback a certain number of global constraints must be added.

11.5.4.1 Geometric Constraint

This constraint is the only one that does not assume anything about the scene it derives directly from the geometry of the panoramic sensor. Linear stereovision is possible if a point is seen from both upper and lower cameras.

Let P be a point of the scene seen by both upper and lower cameras. Let i_1 the index of the pixel representing the position of its image point in the upper linear camera image and i_2 representing the same thing but for the lower linear camera. Whatever the position of points in the scene is, we will always have $i_1 > i_2$. This constraint is directly linked to the layout of the linear cameras which is of great help in this case and leads to great simpli-

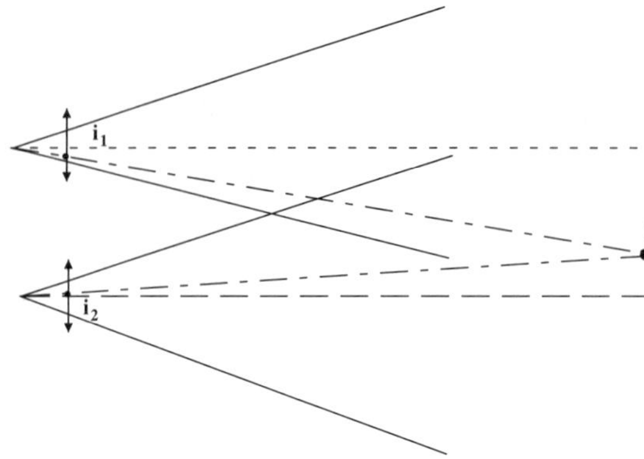

FIGURE 11.8. Geometric constraint.

fication in the matching process, appart from giving an implicit epipolar geometry the architecture of the sensor divides by two the matching space as illustrated by Figure 11.9. This constraints has also great effects on the execution time as the number of operations to be done is also divided by two.

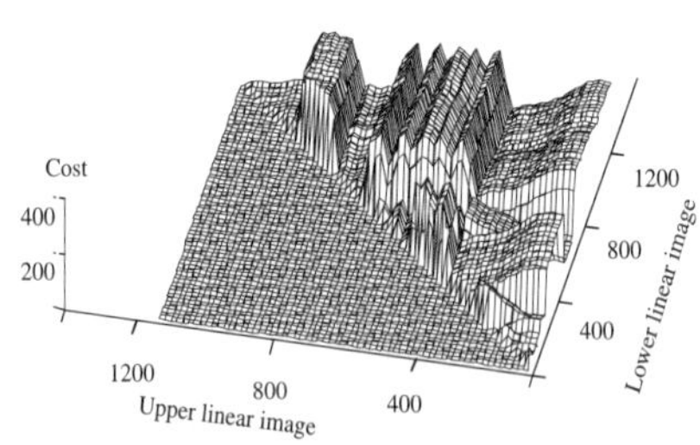

FIGURE 11.9. Influence of the geometrical constraint on the cost table.

11.5.4.2 Sign Constraint

This photometric constraint assumes that both upper and lower features corresponding to the same scene point, present localy derivatives having the same sign. A sign is affected to each point, a positive derivative corresponds to a transition from dark to light while the negative sign is due to a transition from light to dark, see Figure 11.10. The linear image is derivated applying the first derivative of Deriche [77]. The extrema correspond to the position of edge points. The position of these points is computed from the second derivative of the image to obtain a sub-pixel precision. Two edge points can be matched if their derivatives present the same sign if not they are considered as a false match.

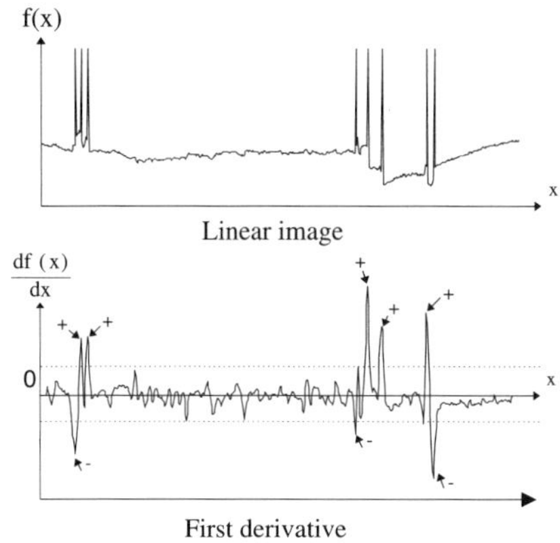

FIGURE 11.10. The sign constraint.

11.5.4.3 Conclusions and Experimental Results

The presented matching procedure uses two constraints, the geometric constraint linked to the architecture of the sensor and the photometric constraint linked to the derivative of the linear image. When points are matched after applying dynamic programing and retreiving the optimal path, two edge points are considered matched if they fullfill the geometrical and the sign constraints. Images of Figure 11.11 represent a 180° panoramic image and their reconstruction is shown by Figure 11.12. Figure 11.13 is a 360° panoramic image of a meeting room.

Some comments are useful to the interpretation of the reconstruction shown by Figure 11.14:

1. The position of the panoramic sensor, is at the center of the coordinates system of the reconstructed scene.

2. Reconstructed edges of the table,

3. Chair,

4. White screen,

5. Brick Wall, false matches are unavoidable due to the repeatitivity of the pattern,

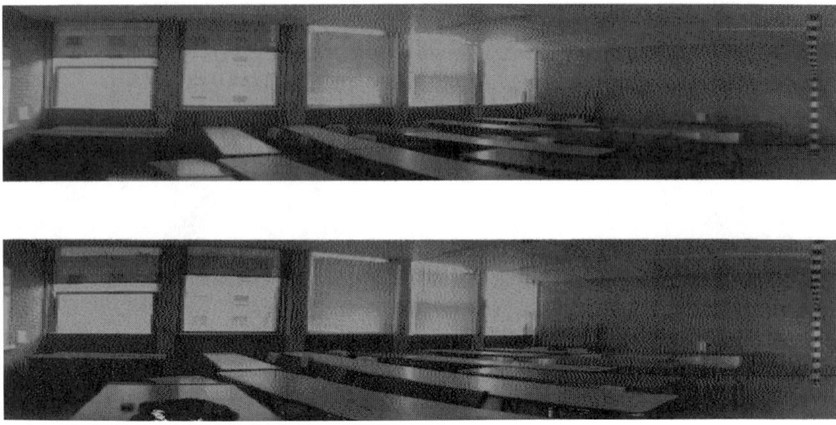

FIGURE 11.11. Panoramic images covering 180° of an indoor scene.

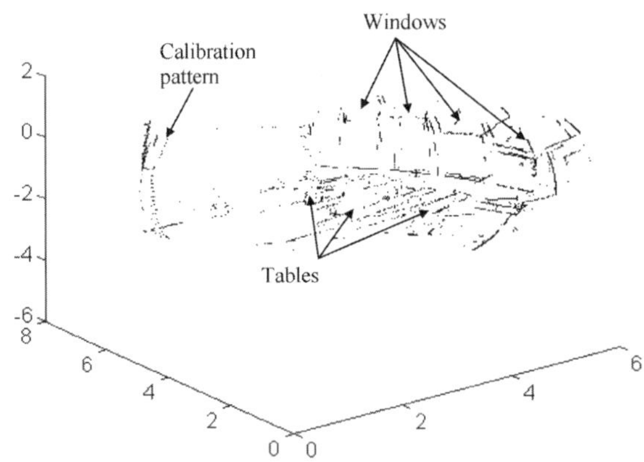

FIGURE 11.12. 3D Reconstruction on 180°.

6. Cupboard, and

7. Round table.

The meeting room contains few information to allow a good 3D reconstruction, where the geometric structure of the observed room could appear. We then added extra patterns on the walls to recover the shape as shown by Figure 11.15, figures 11.16 and 11.17 present the results of the 3D reconstruction.

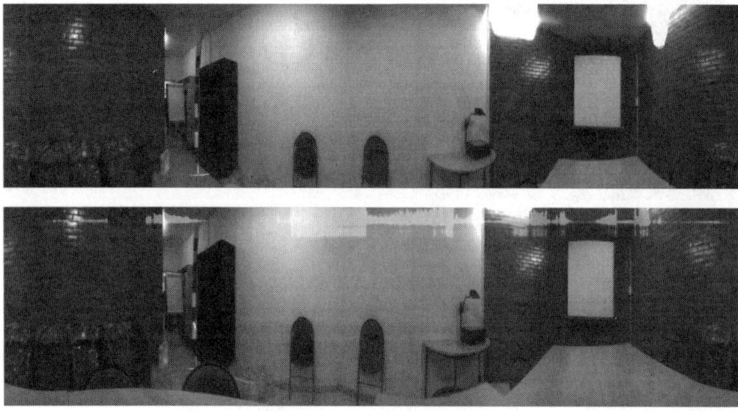

FIGURE 11.13. 360° panoramic images.

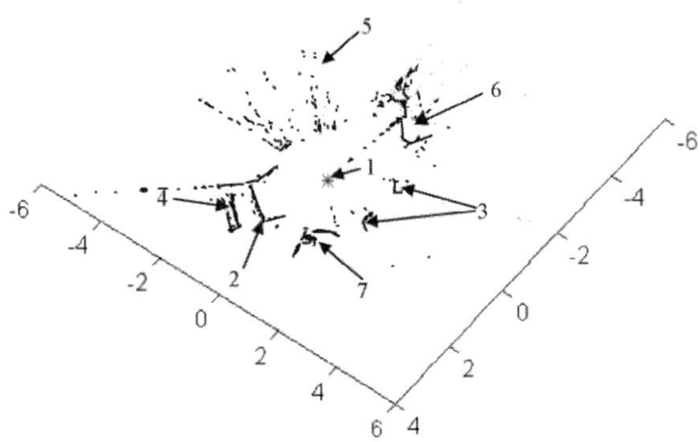

FIGURE 11.14. 3D reconstructed scene: upper view.

11.5.4.4 Conclusions

The matching results show a good reconstruction giving the shape of the observed room with very few false matched points, the added constraints enabled us to lower their number, but also to divide by two the computation time.

The presented method is very easy to implement, the unique reproach we can formulate concerns the fact that the matching procedure is based on a dynamic programming method that deals with images of resolution 1024×1024. A feasability research shows that a hardware architecture computing the dynamic programming procedure is possible, this is due to

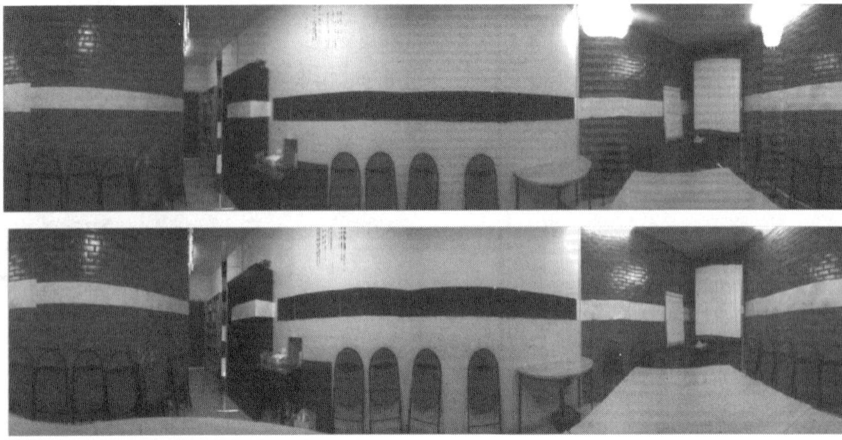

FIGURE 11.15. Meeting room with extra patterns on the walls.

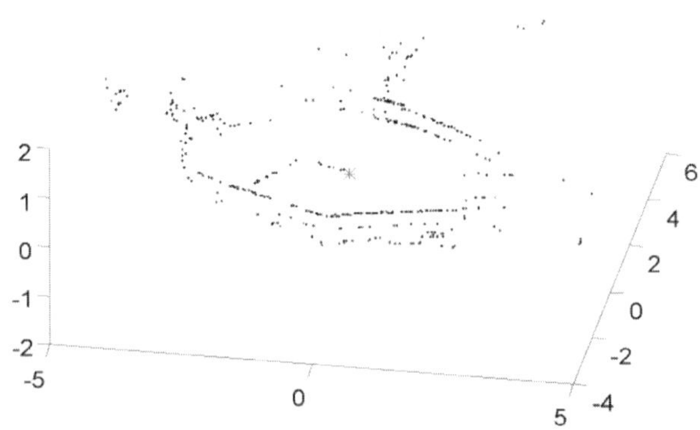

FIGURE 11.16. 3D reconstruction of the meeting room: a lateral view.

the fact that we use do not use all the image's point of the 360° image for the matching. However, to lower computation time and memory size we only use edge points as an entry to achieve the matching.

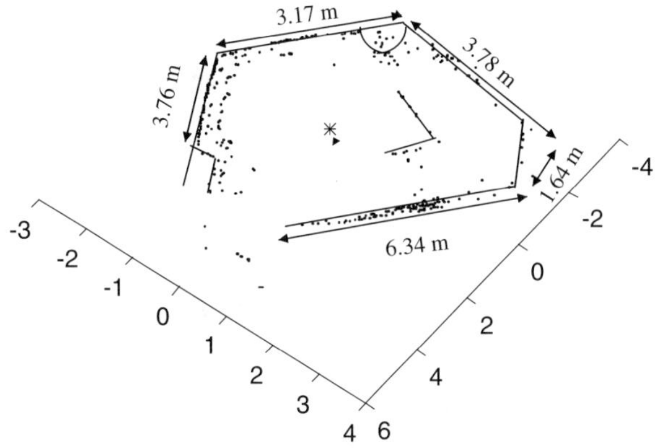

FIGURE 11.17. The recovered metric of the reconstructed room.

11.6 Region Matching

11.6.1 Introduction

The information needed by the method we will present in this section is the regions delimited by two edge points in a linear image, we are dealing with linear images, a region is simply a segment .

Matching linear images is a subject where few research has been done. The approach presented is similar to the one developped by [37], they are both based on the same principle, they differ by the fact that the presented method is not based on recursivity.

In what follows the constraints enouced in the previous sections are still valid. The sequential analysis of the linear images reduces the features matching. If we consider the order constraint of stereovision the constraints presented can be applied sequentially, a pair of matched features can determine the next matching, if two features are matched they can be used as a reference to match the following features.

11.6.2 Principle of Method

The main idea of the method is first to extract from each linear image the edge points and to assign to each point a sign corresponding to the fact that they are even a transition from light to dark or the inverse.

The algorithm uses a dynamic programming procedure that has as an entry two edge points. The fundamental principle consists of using the last matched couple as a valid match $\{H(i), B(i)\}$. The matching will always start from a valid node to find another pair to match. There is a duality between edge points and regions. Each edge point separates two regions. Let us consider an edge point $H(i+1)$ delimiting two regions $[H(i); H(i+1)]$ and $[H(i+1); H(i+2)]$. The region $[H(i+1); H(i+2)]$ is delimited by two edge points $H(i+1)$ and $H(i+2)$. It is then possible to state that if a point $H(i)$ delimitates a region R in the upper image and its homologous $B(j)$ in the lower image delimitates a region $R^{'}$ then R corresponds to $R^{'}$.

11.6.3 Computing Similarity between Two Intervals

To judge the quality of the matching between two regions, we will have to measure the similarity between two edge points of a linear image.

If we want to compute the interval defined by the edge point $H(i+k)$ with the edge point $B(i+k')$, we will consider the intervals $[H(i); H(i+k+\epsilon)]$ and $[B(i); B(i+k+\epsilon')]$ $\epsilon, \epsilon' \in \{0,1\}$ with $\epsilon + \epsilon' \neq 0$ defined by the last valid pair $\{H(i), B(i)\}$.

The two defined intervals will be used to measure the similarity, but before using them few operations are needed. The output of the upper and lower cameras have different levels of gain, it appears then the necessity to bring the pixels of each interval to a value where the mean value equals zero.

If the length of the interval is denoted by l, and the gray levels of the interval are expressed by $ndg(j)$ the mean m of the interval is defined as follows :

$$m = \frac{1}{l} \sum_{x=0}^{x=l-1} ndg(x)$$

The gray levels are modified so that they have a mean equal to zero. Let $ndg_m(x)$, be the new gray levels obtained after applying the following relation:

$$ndg_m(x) = ndg(x) - m, \ x = 0, 1..l-1$$

This modification is applied to all the intervals. The second stage concerns the length of intervals, their length has few probabilities to be equal. Comparing two intervals that do not have the same size is much too complicated. To achieve that, the pixels of the smalest interval of length l are kept unchanged. The pixels of the longest interval of length L are rescaled. We compute the rescaled interval called ndg_R as follows:

$$ndg_R(x) = H(int(\frac{x \times L}{l})), \ x = 0, 1..l-1$$

the similarity measure between two intervals associated to the feature points $H(i+k)$ $B(i+k')$ to be matched is then :

$$S[H(i+k+\epsilon), B(i+k'+\epsilon')] = \frac{1}{N} \sum_{x=0}^{N} |ndg_H(x) - ndg_B(x)|$$

N corresponds to the number of pixels in the normalized interval. S is the measure of similarity between two intervals, the more it is close to zero the more the similarity is great.

11.6.4 Matching Modulus

In what follows we will explain the matching procedure without taking into account the epipolar constraint or the sign of the gradient, to simplifiy the understanding.

We want to match the point $H(i+k)$ with the edge point $B(j+k\prime)$ taking into account the intervals $[H(i); H(i+k+\epsilon)]$ and $[B(j); B(j+k+\epsilon')]$.

To match the pair $\{H(i), B(j)\}$ we check if the pair $\{H(i+1), B(j+1)\}$ is valid. In the affirmative if the pair is valid the problem is solved, if not it starts to be more complicated. In the case where $H(i+1)$ and $B(j+1)$ is not a valid match we will compute three similarity measures :

$$S_{22} = S[H(i+2), B(j+2)]$$

$$S_{12} = S[H(i+1), B(j+2)]$$

$$S_{21} = S[H(i+2), B(j+1)]$$

S_{uv} represents a similarity measure and can be seen as a rectangle which sides are formed by the intervals $[H(i); H(i+u)]$ and $[H(j); H(j+v)]$. Figure 11.18 expresses graphicaly these similarity measures

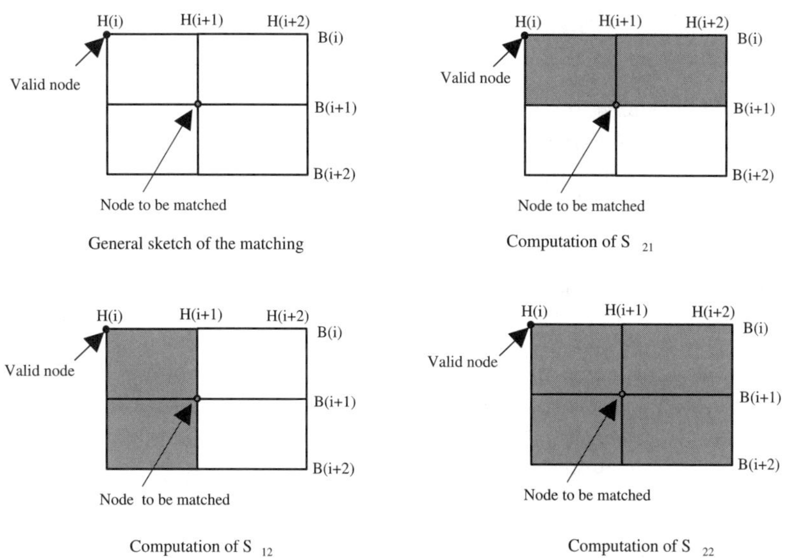

FIGURE 11.18. Computing similarities measures.

11.6.5 Matching Algorithm

We start from $\{H(i), B(j)\}$ and we want to match $\{H(i+1), B(j+1)\}$. We consider the intervals $[H(i), H(i+1+\epsilon)]$ and $[B(j), B(j+1+\epsilon')]$ with $\epsilon', \epsilon \in \{0,1\}$ and $\epsilon + \epsilon' \neq 0$.

We must compute:

$$S_{22} = S[H(i+2), B(j+2)]$$

$$S_{12} = S[H(i+1), B(j+2)]$$

$$S_{21} = S[H(i+2), B(j+1)]$$

We differentiate between the following three possible cases:

1. S_{22} is the most reliable measure : $H(i+1)$ is matched with the edge point $B(j+1)$, the matching is considered as valid. the next valid pair is then $\{H(i+1), B(j+1)\}$. We then start from the pair $\{H(i+2), B(j+2)\}$ that becomes the pair to be matched.

2. S_{21} is the most reliable measure : this means that the point $H(i+1)$ has no homologous in the lower image, it is then ignored and replaced by $H(i+2)$. The pair $\{H(i), B(j)\}$ is still the valid pair and $\{H(i+2), B(j+1)\}$ becomes the pair to be tested.

3. S_{12} is the most reliable measure : this means that the point $B(j+1)$ has no homologous in the upper image , it is then ignored and replaced by the point $B(j+2)$. The pair $\{H(i), B(j)\}$ is still valid and $\{H(i+1), B(j+2)\}$ becomes the new pair to be tested.

11.6.6 Adding Constraints

In the previous section we introduced two constraints that simplified considerabely the matching procedure, minimizing the risks of false matchings. These two constraints are the epipolar and the sign constraints linked to the derivative sign of the linear image. In what follows we are adding these two constraints in the previous matching algorithm.

11.6.6.1 Epipolar Constraint

We have shown that the index of to features in their respective images verify the following relation:

$$x_H < x_B$$

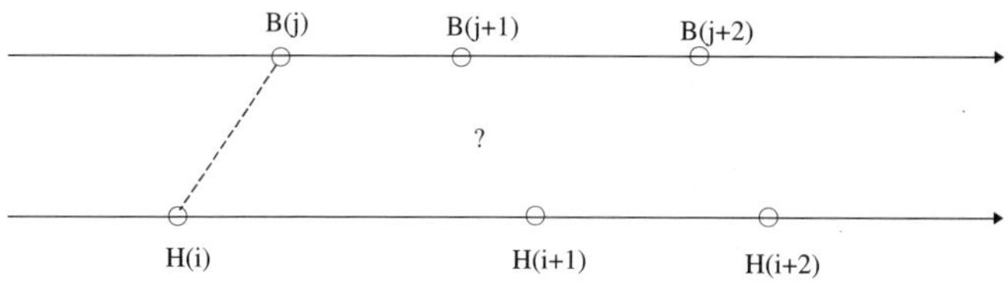

FIGURE 11.19. Verification of the epipolar constraint.

On Figure 11.19 the features of the lower and upper images are represented by two axis. Each axis symbolises a camera and the position of the features in this image.

The valid pair is $H(i)$ et $B(j)$. If $H(i+1)$ and $B(j+1)$ verify the constraints then the matching can be continued. At the contrary, the solution is to ignore feature $B(j+1)$. More generaly we need to find a feature $B(j+k)$ with $2 \leq k \leq N - j$ which verifies the constraint with the feature $H(i+1)$. If no feature $B(j+k)$ verifying the constraint is found, $H(i+1)$ has no homologous.

11.6.6.2 Sign Constraint

The sign constraint linked to the derivative of the image signal is applied right after the epipolar constraint. It consists on verifing that the pair $\{H(i+1), B(j+1)\}$ have the same sign. We start from the valid pair $\{H(i), B(j)\}$ and we try to match the pair $\{H(i+1), B(j+1)\}$.

1. If $H(i+1)$ and $B(j+1)$ have the same sign and verified the epipolar constraint, we then can apply the matching procedure described in the previous sections.

2. If $H(i+1)$ and $B(j+1)$ have different signs it means that one of the features has no homologous. We consider then the two pairs $\{H(i+1), B(j+2)\}$ and $\{H(i+2), B(j+1)\}$. We test for each pair that they fullfill the constraints and we compute the similarity measures. For the compatible pairs we apply the matching algorithm.

We obtain then four cases, the matching has been tested:

1. On the two pairs $\{H(i+1), B(j+2)\}$ and $\{H(i+2), B(j+1)\}$.
2. On only one pair $\{H(i+1), B(j+2)\}$.
3. On only one pair $\{H(i+2), B(j+1)\}$.
4. On no pair.

We will analyze the results based on the case:

Case 1:

S_{22} is not the smalest measure for any pair, we start then from pair $\{H(i+2), B(j+2)\}$.

S_{22} is the smalest measure for only one pair, according to the cases $\{H(i+1), B(j+2)\}$ (respectively $\{H(i+2), B(j+1)\}$) becomes the present valid pair. Pairs $\{H(i+2), B(j+3)\}$ (respectively $\{H(i+3), B(j+2)\}$) become the new pairs to be matched.

S_{22} is the smalest value for both pairs, we keep then the pair which value is the smalest.

Cases 2 and 3:

In these cases only one pair is valid. The matching algorithm is applied normaly. The result is taken into account only if S_{22} is the smallest measure. The new valid pair becomes $\{H(i+1), B(j+2)\}$ (respectively $\{H(i+2), B(j+1)\}$). The pair $\{H(i+2), B(j+3)\}$ (respectively $\{H(i+3), B(j+2)\}$) becomes the pair to be matched.

Case 4:

Both pairs do not fullfill the constraints, the new pair to be matched is then $\{H(i+2), B(j+2)\}$.

11.6.7 Experimental Results

Figures 11.21 and 11.22 show the results of the stereomatching on images of Figure 11.20. We can see the following objects:

1. Cupboard,
2. Postion of the panoramic stereovision system,
3. Edges of the table, and
4. White screen.

We can notice a high number of false matching due to the periodicity of the brick wall. The main objects of the scene appear, but many edge points are not correctly matched. The method is less robust than the previous one and seems to have the drawback of the classical matching method based on regions. In case of too many regions not easely distinguishable, this method reaches its limits.

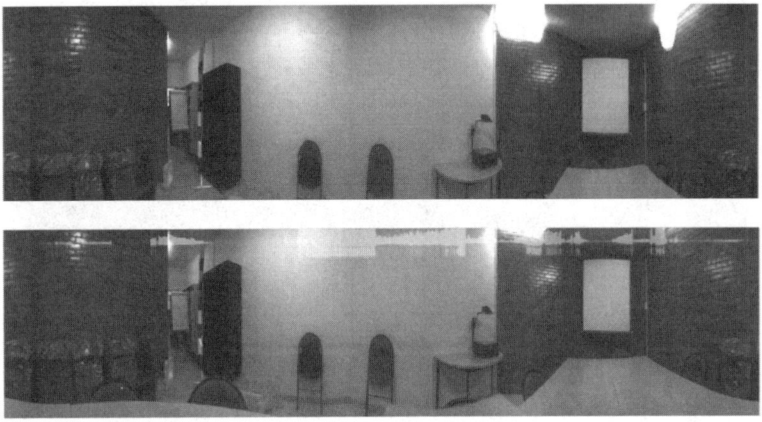

FIGURE 11.20. Panoramic stereovision images to be matched.

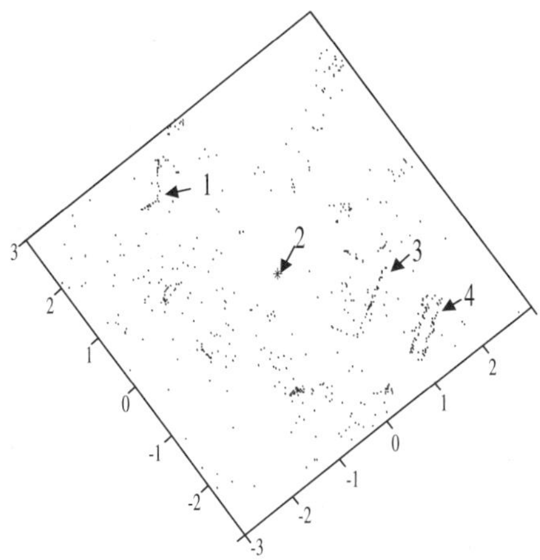

FIGURE 11.21. 3D reconstruction by matching of regions: upper view.

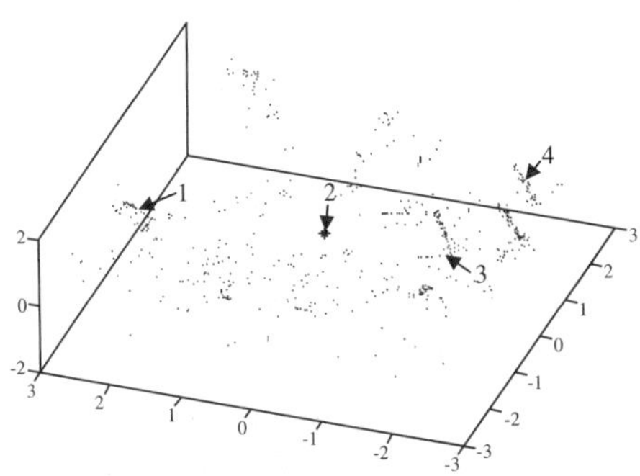

FIGURE 11.22. 3D reconstruction by matching of regions: lateral view.

Section III

Techniques for Generating Panoramic Images

The first two sections in this book describe a variety of hardware-oriented approaches for creating panoramic images. The chapters in this section, on the other hand, focus on software approaches for generating panoramic images. In addition, except for the approach described in Chapter 15 (Nayar and Karmarkar), all the other approaches use just conventional off-the-shelf cameras. The types of panoramic images described here range from cylindrical ones (with 360° horizontal field of view) to spherical ones to those with arbitrary coverage.

Chapter 12 (Kang and Weiss) examines the characterization of errors in compositing cylindrical panoramic images. The cylindrical panoramic image is created by stitching images captured while rotating the camera about a vertical axis. The cross-sectional circumference of the cylindrical panorama is called the *compositing length*. If the camera focal length is unknown, it is shown here that the error in camera focal length can be corrected by iteratively using the compositing length to compute a new and more correct focal length. This *compositing approach to camera calibration* has the advantages of not requiring both feature detection and separate prior calibration.

In Chapter 13 (Shum and Szeliski), a system for constructing full view image mosaics from sequences of images is described. The mosaic representation associates a transformation matrix with each input image, rather than explicitly projecting all of the images onto a common surface (e.g., a cylinder). In particular, to construct a full view panorama, they introduce a *rotational mosaic* representation that associates a rotation matrix with each input image. A *patch-based alignment* algorithm is developed to quickly align two images given motion models. Techniques for estimating and refining camera focal lengths are also presented. In order to reduce accumulated registration errors, they apply global alignment (*block adjustment*) to the whole sequence of images, which results in an optimally registered image mosaic. To compensate for small amounts of motion parallax introduced by translations of the camera and other unmodeled distortions, the local alignment technique of *deghosting* is used.

An *inverse texture mapping* algorithm for efficiently extracting environment maps from the panoramic image mosaics is also presented in Chapter 13 (Shum and Szeliski). By mapping the mosaic onto an arbitrary texture-mapped polyhedron surrounding the origin, the virtual environment can be explored using standard 3D graphics viewers and hardware without requiring special-purpose players.

In the first two chapters in this section, the camera internal parameters are assumed fixed while it is moved. The work described in Chapter 14 (Agapito, Hayman, Reid, and Hartley) goes a step further: while the camera is rotated, it is also allowed to zoom. The basis of the approach is to make use of the so-called *infinite homography constraint* which relates the unknown calibration matrices to the computed inter-image homographies. A number of self-calibration methods are described, namely, an iterative non-linear method, a fast linear method, and the use of an optimal Maximum Likelihood estimator.

Thus far, relatively narrow field-of-view cameras are used to acquire image data. This poses problems when computing a complete spherical mosaic. First, a large number of images are needed to capture a sphere. Second, errors in mosaicing make it difficult to complete the spherical mosaic without noticeable seams. Third, with a hand-held camera it is hard for the user to ensure complete coverage of the sphere. Chapter 15 (Nayar and Karmarkar) presents two approaches to spherical mosaicing. The first is to rotate a 360° camera about a single axis to capture a sequence of 360° strips. The unknown rotations between the strips are estimated and the strips are blended together to obtain a spherical mosaic. The second approach seeks to significantly enhance the resolution of the computed mosaic by capturing 360 slices rather than strips. A variety of slice cameras are proposed that map a thin 360° sheet of rays onto a large image area. This results in the capture of high resolution slices despite the use of a low resolution video camera. A slice camera is rotated using a motorized turntable to obtain regular as well as stereoscopic spherical mosaics. Several experimental results are presented that demonstrate the quality of the computed mosaics.

The mosaicing methods described in the first three chapters are based on projecting all images onto a pre-determined single manifold: a plane is commonly used for a camera translating sideways, a cylinder is used for a panning camera, and a sphere is used for a camera which is both panning and tilting. While different mosaicing methods should therefore be used for different types of camera motion, more general types of camera motion, such as forward motion, are practically impossible for traditional mosaicing.

In Chapter 16 (Peleg, Rousso, Rav-Acha, and Zomet), a new methodology to allow image mosaicing in more general cases of camera motion is presented. Mosaicing is performed by projecting thin strips from the images onto manifolds which are dynamically determined by the camera motion. While the limitations of existing mosaicing techniques are a result of using predetermined manifolds, the use of dynamic manifolds overcomes these limitations. With manifold mosaicing it is now possible to generate high-quality mosaicing even for the very challenging cases of forward motion and of zoom.

Additional Notes on Chapters

The material in Chapter 12 has originally appeared in the article with the same name in *Computer Vision and Image Understanding*, vol. 73, no. 2, 1999. The material in Chapter 13 has originally appeared in the article "Systems and experiment paper: Construction of panoramic image mosaics with global and local alignment," *International Journal of Computer Vision*, vol 36, no. 2, 2000. Different parts of Chapter 16 have appeared in the following articles: "Panoramic mosaics by manifold projection," *IEEE Computer Society Conference on Computer Vision and Pattern Recognition*, 1997, "Universal mosaicing using pipe projection," *International Conference on Computer Vision*, 1998, and "Rectified mosaicing: Mosaics without the curl," *IEEE Computer Society Conference on Computer Vision and Pattern Recognition*, 2000. Parts of Chapter 15 have appeared in the proceedings of the *IEEE Conference on Computer Vision and Pattern Recognition* held in June 2000.

12

Characterization of Errors in Compositing Cylindrical Panoramic Images

S.B. Kang and R. Weiss

12.1 Introduction

A cylindrical panoramic image has a 360° horizontal field of view. Panoramic images of scenes have interesting applications in computer vision and visualization because they contain full information about the scene from a given viewpoint. For example, Apple's QuickTime VR^{TM} [49] product uses panoramas for scene visualization. In computer vision, applying the stereo algorithm on multiple panoramas allows the entire 3D scene data points to be extracted (Chapter 17) and subsequently modeled [145]. In order to have metrically correct models, it is necessary to have an accurate estimate of the focal length.

A panoramic image can be produced by following a series of steps: First, a sequence of images is taken while rotating a camera about a vertical axis that approximately passes through the camera optical center. Each image in the sequence is then projected onto a cylindrical surface whose cross-sectional radius is an initially estimated focal length (see Figure 12.1). The panoramic image is subsequently created by determining the relative displacements between adjacent images in the sequence and using a refinement of phase correlation and compositing the displaced sequence of images. The length of the panoramic image is termed the *compositing length*.

There are alternatives to or variants of this approach to produce a panoramic image. Ishiguro *et al.* [136], for example, generate each panoramic image by rotating a camera about a vertical axis at very small angular increments (a fraction of a degree) and stacking the same vertical columns from the image sequence. However, while the resulting panoramic image is precise, the camera motion has to be controlled accurately, and the acquisition rate is slow. More recently, Szeliski and Shum [273] (Chapter 13) developed a technique to merge multiple images taken with a camera at different unknown tilt and pan orientations. In this case, care must be taken to ensure that the projection centers associated with all the constituent views coincide if the resulting mosaic is to be physically exact. In the case that this is not true, they [258] apply a *deghosting* technique based on image subdivision and patch alignment to minimize the effects of misregistration due to motion parallax. A more detailed survey of panoramic image generation techniques can be found in [144].

12.1.1 Analyzing the Error in Compositing Length

In this chapter, we describe the effect of errors in intrinsic camera parameters on the compositing length. We are not aware of any prior work in this specific area. In particular, we consider the focal length and the radial distortion coefficient. The camera focal length is important for two reasons: it is necessary for accurate 3D modeling, and it affects the amount of blurring in compositing the images. An important consequence of the analysis is that a much better estimate of the camera focal length can be calculated from the current compositing length. Hence by iterating the process of projecting onto a cylindrical surface (whose cross-sectional radius is the latest estimation of the camera focal length) and compositing the new sequences, we quickly arrive at the camera focal length within a specified error tolerance. We show later that the convergence towards the true focal length is exponential. This method constitutes a simple means of calibrating a camera.

12.1.2 Camera Calibration

Conventional means of camera calibration use a calibration or control pattern (e.g., points [270, 284, 291], lines [20, 42, 288]), or take advantage of feature structural constraints (e.g., roundness of spheres [215, 263], straightness of lines [34, 263]). In practice, these methods may not be desirable because they are domain dependent or require some form of intervention. There are also self-calibration techniques that do not require calibration or control patterns. One example is [64], which describes a method for self-calibration with the assumption that the direction of the camera motion is known. However, features have to be tracked, and the resulting motion sequence is not suitable for producing a panoramic image. In a more general approach, Hartley [97] uses a two-step technique, comprising projective structure recovery, followed by iterative minimization of feature projection errors in Euclidean reconstruction. Again, image mosaicking cannot be done concurrently with calibration, and selecting reliable feature points for tracking is domain dependent.

In a more related work, Hartley [98] proposes a calibration technique that uses multiple views taken with a camera rotated about its optical center. This technique uses information from image correspondence to estimate the five intrinsic camera parameters. We propose a method for featureless camera calibration based on an iterative scheme of projecting rectilinear images to cylindrical images and then compositing. In addition to determining the camera focal length, this technique results in a panoramic image (i.e., with 360° horizontal field of view) that is both physically correct (ignoring radial distortion effects) and seamlessly blended.

The basis of the compositing approach to camera calibration is the discovery that the relative compositing length error due to camera focal length error is disproportionately much less (i.e., in terms of percentages) than the relative focal length error. When a planar image is projected to a cylinder as in the compositing process, mis-estimation of the radius of the cylinder will produce an erroneous warping of the image that will affect the length of the final composite image. However, it turns out that near the center of the overlap between successive images, the amount of combined warping for both images is minimal and so is the effect of the mis-estimation. The result of this is that the percent error in length of the composite image is less than the percent error in the focal length. This makes it possible to use the composite length to recover a better estimate of the camera focal length.

The proposed technique has the advantage of not having to know the camera focal length when a panorama is to be generated from a sequence of images. This is in contrast to Apple's QuickTime VR^{TM} [49], which we believe that a reasonably good estimate of camera focal length is required *a priori*. This is also the case for McMillan and Bishop's method of creating panoramas [181]. Their method of estimating the camera focal length necessitates small panning rotations and relies on translation estimates near the image centers.

The method of calibration that is closest to ours is that of Stein's [263], in which features are tracked throughout the image sequence taken while the camera is rotated a full 360°. While this technique results in accurate camera parameters, it still requires feature detection and tracking. Our technique directly uses the given image sequence of the scene to determine camera focal length without relying on specific tracked features.

12.1.3 Motivation and Outline

The motivation for generating panoramic images is to directly recover 3D scene data points over a wide field of view using stereo for subsequent modeling and photorealistic rendering [145]. Traditional approaches to recovering 3D data of a wide scene is to take stereo snapshots of the scene at various poses and then merge these 3D stereo depth maps. This is not only computationally intensive, but the resulting merged depth maps may be subject to merging errors, especially if the relative poses between depth maps are not known exactly. The 3D data may also have to be resampled before merging, which adds additional complexity and potential sources of errors.

The outline of this chapter is as follows: Section 12.2 reviews how a panoramic image is produced from a set of images. This is followed by sec-

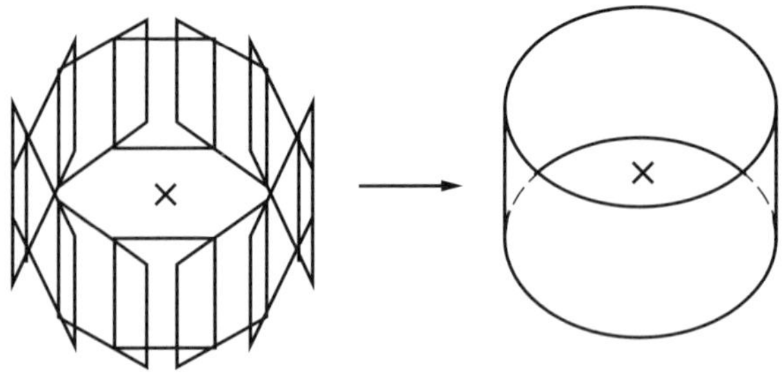

FIGURE 12.1. Compositing multiple rotated camera views into a panorama. The '×' marks indicate the locations of the camera optical and rotation center.

tion 12.3 which gives a detailed analysis of the compositing error due error in the camera focal length in Section 12.3. A consequence of this analysis is the iterative compositing approach to camera calibration. Section 12.4 looks at the effect of misestimating the radial distortion coefficient on the panoramic compositing length. We then describe the effect of errors in both focal length and radial distortion coefficient on the reconstructed 3D data in section 12.5 before summarizing in section 12.7.

12.2 Generating a Panoramic Image

A panoramic image is created by compositing a series of rotated camera image images, as shown in Figure 12.1. In order to create this panoramic image, we first have to ensure that the camera is rotating about an axis passing through its optical center, i.e., we must eliminate motion parallax when panning the camera around. To achieve this, we manually adjust the position of camera relative to an X-Y precision stage (mounted on the tripod) such that the motion parallax effect disappears when the camera is rotated back and forth about the vertical axis [263]. If the axis of rotation is not perpendicular to the camera axis, this could be detected in the alignment procedure by searching for vertical displacement. This was not necessary for obtaining good experimental results.

In previous work described elsewhere in this book, the camera was first calibrated to extract its intrinsic parameters, namely κ, the radial distortion coefficient, and f, the camera focal length. This was accomplished by taking snapshots of a calibration dot grid pattern at known spacings and using the iterative least squares algorithm described in [270]. As a result of our analysis reported here, this calibration step can be skipped if the radial distortion coefficient is insignificant, which is the case for standard commercial lenses.

A panoramic image is created using the following steps:

1. Capture a sequence of rotated camera views about a vertical axis passing through the camera optical center;
2. Undistort the sequence to correct for κ;
3. Warp the undistorted (rectilinear) sequence to produce a corresponding cylindrical-based image sequence whose cross-sectional radius is equal to the camera focal length f; and finally
4. Composite the sequence of images [267].

The compositing technique comprises two steps: rough alignment using phase correlation, and iterative local refinement to minimize overlap intensity difference between successive images (see, for example, [267]). In both steps, the translation is assumed to be in one direction only, namely in the x-direction (since the cylindrical-based images have been "flattened" or unrolled). This is a perfectly legitimate assumption, since camera motion has been constrained to rotate about a vertical axis during image sequence capture. (In practice, however, this may not be exactly true. In this chapter, we assume that any vertical camera motion that may occur is insignificant.) If the estimated focal length is exact, then the error in the composited length is due to the digitization and image resampling effects, the limit in the number of iterations during local matching, and computer truncation or rounding off effects.

The rough alignment step has been made more robust by adding the iterative step of checking the displacement corresponding to the peak—if the intensity RMS error in matching the overlap regions is high, the peak is tagged as false and the next highest peak is chosen instead.

12.3 Compositing Errors due to Misestimation of Focal Length

Compositing errors occur as a result of using a wrong value of the camera focal length in converting the rectilinear images to cylindrical-based images prior to compositing. If the correct focal length used, say f_{true}, then the expected length of the composited panoramic image[1] is

$$L = 2\pi f_{true} \tag{12.1}$$

If the focal length f used is incorrect, then the mapped cylindrical images are no longer physically correct. The compositing step will attempt to

[1]In creating the panoramic image, the order of compositing is I_1, I_2, ..., I_{N-1}, I_N, I_1, where I_k is the kth image in the sequence and N is the number of images in the sequence. The compositing length L is actually the displacement of the first frame I_1 relative to its original location.

minimize the error in the overlap region of successive images, but there is still a net error in compositing length L.

Since each column in a rectilinear image is projected to another column in the cylindrical image and translation is constrained to be along the x-direction, it suffices to consider only a scanline in our analysis. We assume for simplicity that the images are "fully textured" so that alignment of corresponding pixels is unambiguous. We also assume, for ease of analysis, that the amount of camera rotation between successive frames is the same throughout the sequence (this need not be so in practice). In our analysis, the net translation is computed by minimizing the sum of squares of the pixel displacements from their matching locations. In other words, even after translation with interpolation, the pixels in the second image will not match the pixels in the first image at the same location. Each pixel will match one at a displaced location. The translation which minimizes the sum of their squares is the one that results in zero average displacement.

12.3.1 Derivation

In order to model the displacement of each pixel $\mathbf{u}_i$ in the second cylindrical image, we map it back to $\mathbf{t}_i$ in the image plane, find the corresponding pixel $\mathbf{s}_i$ in the first image based on the actual rotation α, and map that back to $\mathbf{v}_i$ in the cylindrical image. For simplicity of analysis, we assume equal angles of rotation, but this is *not* part of the algorithm. (Note that boldface letters are used to represent the points themselves, while the same letters in italic represent their respective x-coordinates in the image.) This is illustrated in Fig. 12.2, where I_1 and I_2 are the first and second cylindrical images, respectively. $I_{1,true}$ is the true cylindrical first image while α is the amount of actual camera rotation between successive frames, i.e., $2\pi/N$, N being the number of images in the sequence. Recall that the cylindrical images are formed by warping the images into a cylindrical surface whose cross-sectional radius is the estimated focal length. The mappings are given by the following equations:

$$\begin{aligned} t_i &= f \tan\left(\frac{u_i}{f}\right) \\ s_i &= f_{true} \tan\left(\tan^{-1}\left(\frac{t_i}{f_{true}}\right) + \alpha\right) \\ v_i &= f \tan^{-1}\left(\frac{s_i}{f}\right) \end{aligned} \qquad (12.2)$$

As before, $\alpha = 2\pi/N$ and f_{true} is the correct focal length while f is the estimated focal length used.

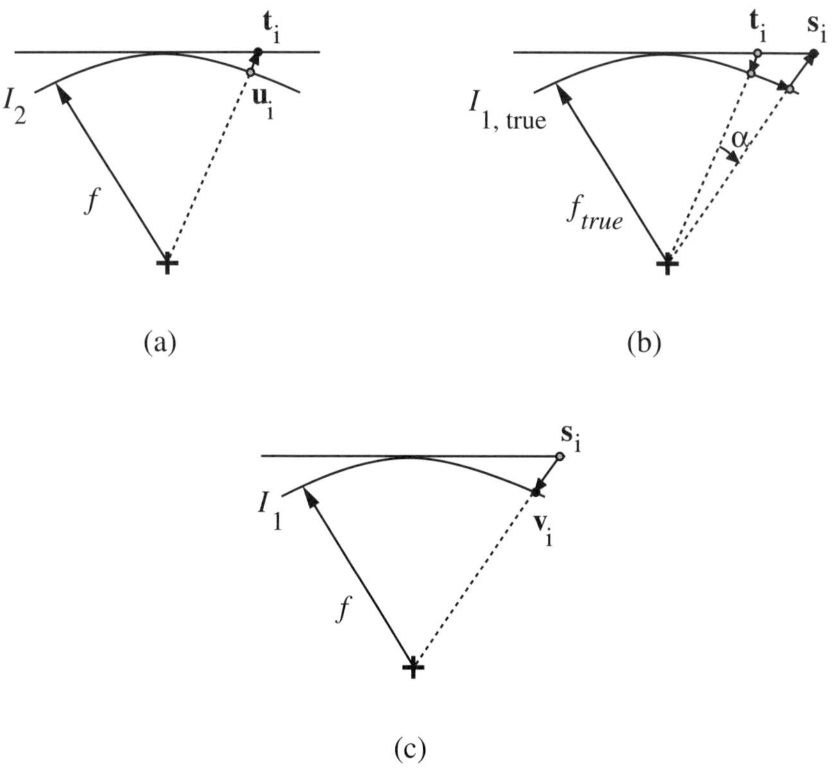

FIGURE 12.2. Effect of inexact focal length: (a) actual mapping from second cylindrical image; (b) theoretical displacement; (c) actual mapping to first cylindrical image. See text.

Using Mathematica™ [296], we find that, up to the third order in u_i and α,

$$
\begin{aligned}
v_i\,(u_i) &= u_i + \frac{f^2 f_{true}^2 + f^2 u_i^2 - f_{true}^2 u_i^2}{f^2 f_{true}}\alpha \\
&+ \frac{(f - f_{true})\,(f + f_{true})\left(3f^2 f_{true}^2 u_i + 3f^2 u_i^3 - 5f_{true}^2 u_i^3\right)}{3f^4 f_{true}^2}\alpha^2 \\
&+ \frac{(f - f_{true})\,(f + f_{true})\left(f^2 f_{true}^2 + 4f^2 u_i^2 - 6f_{true}^2 u_i^2\right)}{3f^4 f_{true}}\alpha^3
\end{aligned}
\qquad (12.3)
$$

The displacement between two successive frames at u_i is $d_i(u_i) = v_i\,(u_i) - u_i$; the plot of the variation of $d_i(u_i)$ versus u_i for $f_{true} = 274.5$ and $N = 50$ for different values of misestimated values of f is shown in Fig. 12.3. It is interesting to note that the minimum displacement due to focal length error occurs near the *center* of the overlap. The change in the displacement error distribution due to the amount of overlap (changing number of frames N)

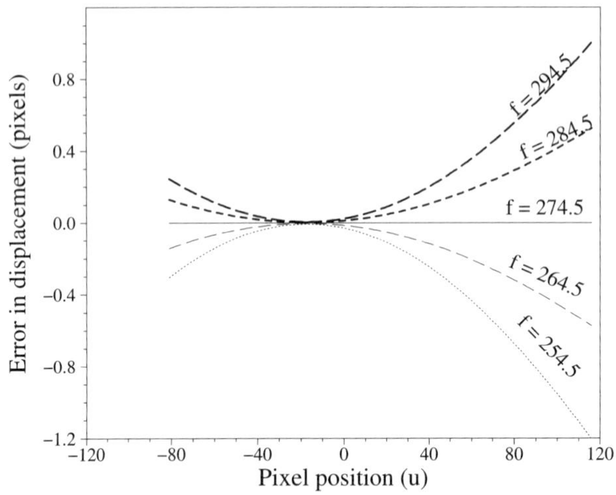

FIGURE 12.3. Graph of error in displacement vs. pixel location for varying estimated focal length f. $f_{true} = 274.5, N = 50$, and $l = 232$.

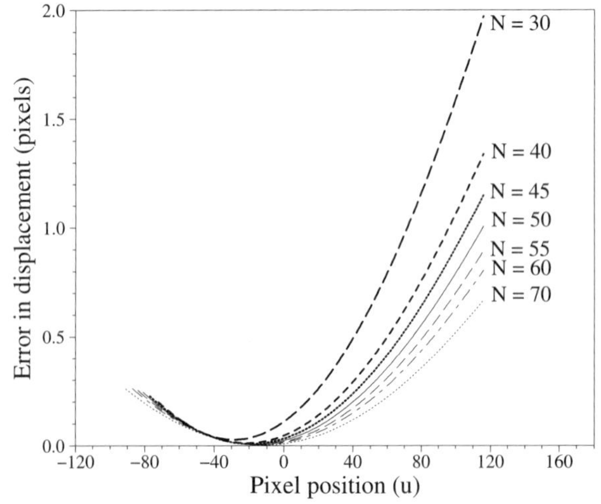

FIGURE 12.4. Graph of error in displacement vs. pixel location for varying number of frames N. $f_{true} = 274.5, f = 294.5$ and $l = 232$.

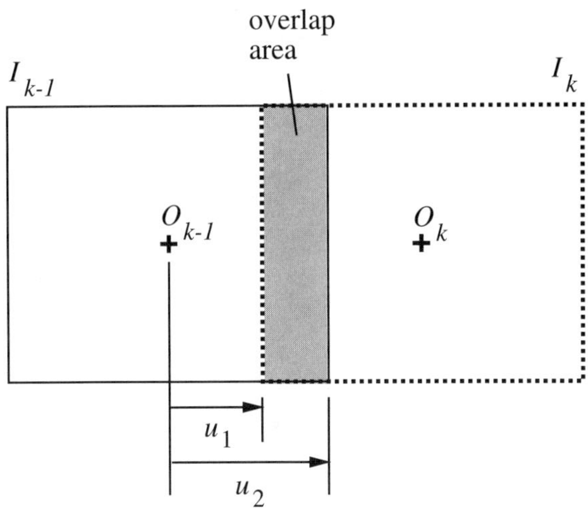

FIGURE 12.5. Overlap between successive images I_{k-1} and I_k, with centers at O_{k-1} and O_k respectively.

is shown in Fig. 12.4. As can be observed, as N increases, the amount of overlap increases, and interestingly enough, the overall error decreases. Having a large overlap is important in the alignment process but is not needed for the compositing. If everything is kept constant except for the image length l, the error distribution remains the same save for u_1 and u_2, the two end pixel locations of the overlap area (see Fig. 12.5). They shrink to decrease the amount of horizontal overlap as l decreases. The mean displacement between two successive frames is

$$\bar{D} = \frac{\sum_{u_i=u_1}^{u_2} (v_i(u_i) - u_i)}{u_2 - u_1 + 1} \tag{12.4}$$

Note that if the interframe displacement is equal throughout the sequence and that the length of each image is l, then $u_2 = l/2$ and $u_1 = 2\pi f_{true}/N - l/2$. The *mean* total displacement, i.e., the composite length, is given by

$$L = N\bar{D} \tag{12.5}$$

If N is increased and l is decreased at the same time, this results in a situation similar to that used by Ishiguro *et al.* [136], except that the rotation is recovered from the overlap.

Suppose we reestimate the focal length from the composite length, namely $f' = L/(2\pi)$. The question is: Is f' a better estimate of the focal length than f? It turns out that for initial estimates of f close to the true value, the answer can be shown to be yes. To see this, if $f \approx f_{true}$, then from (12.3), (12.4) and (12.5), we get

$$\begin{aligned}
f' &= \frac{L}{2\pi} \approx \frac{N}{2\pi} \left\{ \left[f_{true} + \left(1 - \frac{f_{true}^2}{f^2}\right) \frac{\overline{u^2}}{f_{true}} \right] \alpha \right. \\
&+ \left[\left(1 - \frac{f_{true}^2}{f^2}\right) \overline{u} - \frac{1}{3} \left(1 - \frac{f_{true}^2}{f^2}\right) \left(5 \frac{f_{true}^2}{f^2} - 3\right) \frac{\overline{u^3}}{f_{true}^2} \right] \alpha^2 \\
&+ \left. \left[\frac{1}{3} f_{true} \left(1 - \frac{f_{true}^2}{f^2}\right) - 2 \left(1 - \frac{f_{true}^2}{f^2}\right) \left(\frac{f_{true}^2}{f^2} - \frac{2}{3}\right) \frac{\overline{u^2}}{f_{true}} \right] \alpha^3 \right\} \\
&\approx f_{true} + \left(1 - \frac{f_{true}^2}{f^2}\right) \frac{\overline{u^2}}{f_{true}} \qquad (12.6) \\
&+ \left[\left(1 - \frac{f_{true}^2}{f^2}\right) \overline{u} - \frac{1}{3} \left(1 - \frac{f_{true}^2}{f^2}\right) \left(5 \frac{f_{true}^2}{f^2} - 3\right) \frac{\overline{u^3}}{f_{true}^2} \right] \alpha \\
&+ \left[\frac{1}{3} f_{true} \left(1 - \frac{f_{true}^2}{f^2}\right) - 2 \left(1 - \frac{f_{true}^2}{f^2}\right) \left(\frac{f_{true}^2}{f^2} - \frac{2}{3}\right) \frac{\overline{u^2}}{f_{true}} \right] \alpha^2
\end{aligned}$$

noting that $\alpha = 2\pi/N$, and where

$$\begin{aligned}
\overline{u} &= \frac{\sum_{i=u_1}^{u_2} i}{u_2 - u_1 + 1} \\
&= \frac{1}{2} (u_2 + u_1) = \frac{\pi f_{true}}{N}, \qquad (12.7)
\end{aligned}$$

$$\begin{aligned}
\overline{u^2} &= \frac{\sum_{i=u_1}^{u_2} i^2}{u_2 - u_1 + 1} \\
&= \frac{1}{3} \left(u_2^2 + u_1 u_2 + u_1^2 + \frac{1}{2} (u_2 - u_1) \right) \\
&= \frac{1}{3} \left((u_2 + u_1)^2 - u_2 u_1 + \frac{1}{2} (u_2 - u_1) \right) \\
&= \frac{1}{3} \left[\frac{4\pi^2 f_{true}^2}{N^2} - \left(\frac{2\pi f_{true}}{N} - \frac{l}{2} \right) \frac{l}{2} + \frac{\pi f_{true}}{N} - \frac{l}{2} \right] \qquad (12.8)
\end{aligned}$$

and

$$\begin{aligned}
\overline{u^3} &= \frac{\sum_{i=u_1}^{u_2} i^3}{u_2 - u_1 + 1} \\
&= \frac{1}{4} (u_2 + u_1) \left(u_2^2 + u_1^2 + u_2 - u_1 \right) \\
&= \frac{1}{2} \frac{\pi f_{true}}{N} \left[\left(\frac{2\pi f_{true}}{N} - \frac{l}{2} \right)^2 + \frac{l^2}{4} + \frac{2\pi f_{true}}{N} - l \right] \qquad (12.9)
\end{aligned}$$

Hence

$$
\begin{aligned}
f_{true} - f' &\approx \left\{ \frac{\overline{u^2}}{f_{true}} + \left[\overline{u} - \frac{1}{3}\left(5\frac{f_{true}^2}{f^2} - 3\right)\frac{\overline{u^3}}{f_{true}^2} \right]\alpha \right. \\
&+ \left. \left[\frac{f_{true}}{3} - 2\left(\frac{f_{true}^2}{f^2} - \frac{2}{3}\right)\frac{\overline{u^2}}{f_{true}} \right]\alpha^2 \right\} \left(\frac{f_{true}^2}{f^2} - 1\right) \\
&\approx \frac{f_{true}}{f}\frac{f_{true}+f}{2f} 2 \left\{ \frac{\overline{u^2}}{f_{true}^2} + \left(\frac{\overline{u}}{f_{true}} - \frac{2}{3}\frac{\overline{u^3}}{f_{true}^3} \right)\alpha \right. \\
&+ \left. \left(\frac{1}{3} - \frac{2}{3}\frac{\overline{u^2}}{f_{true}^2} \right)\alpha^2 \right\} (f_{true} - f) \\
&\approx 2 \left\{ \frac{\overline{u^2}}{f_{true}^2} + \left(\frac{\overline{u}}{f_{true}} - \frac{2}{3}\frac{\overline{u^3}}{f_{true}^3} \right)\alpha \right. \\
&+ \left. \frac{1}{3}\left(1 - 2\frac{\overline{u^2}}{f_{true}^2} \right)\alpha^2 \right\} (f_{true} - f) \qquad (12.10)
\end{aligned}
$$

Let

$$
\beta_1 = \frac{\overline{u}}{f_{true}} = \frac{\pi}{N}, \qquad (12.11)
$$

$$
\beta_2 = \frac{\overline{u^2}}{f_{true}^2} = \frac{1}{3}\left[\frac{4\pi^2}{N^2} - \left(\frac{2\pi}{N} - \frac{l}{2f_{true}} \right)\frac{l}{2f_{true}} + \frac{1}{f_{true}}\left(\frac{\pi}{N} - \frac{l}{2f_{true}} \right) \right] \qquad (12.12)
$$

and

$$
\beta_3 = \frac{\overline{u^3}}{f_{true}^3} = \frac{1}{2}\frac{\pi}{N}\left[\left(\frac{2\pi}{N} - \frac{l}{2f_{true}} \right)^2 + \left(\frac{l}{2f_{true}} \right)^2 + \frac{2}{f_{true}}\left(\frac{\pi}{N} - \frac{l}{2f_{true}} \right) \right] \qquad (12.13)
$$

Thus (12.10) becomes

$$
\begin{aligned}
f_{true} - f' &\approx 2\left[\beta_2 + \left(\beta_1 - \frac{2}{3}\beta_3 \right)\alpha + \frac{1}{3}(1 - 2\beta_2)\alpha^2 \right](f_{true} - f) \\
&= \eta\,(f_{true} - f) \qquad (12.14)
\end{aligned}
$$

If N is large, which is typical (in practice, N is about 50), then $|f_{true} - f'| \ll |f_{true} - f|$. This implies that the estimated focal length based on the composited length is a significantly better estimate.

12.3.2 Image Compositing Approach to Camera Calibration

The previous result suggests a direct, iterative method of simultaneously determining the camera focal length and constructing a panoramic image. This *iterative image compositing approach to camera calibration* has the advantages of not requiring both feature detection and separate prior calibration. The pseudocode associated with this method is as follows:

```
Let the initial estimate of focal length be f_0.
Determine compositing length L_0 from f_0.
Set k = 1.
    1. Calculate f_k = L_{k-1}/(2π).
    2. Determine compositing length L_k from f_k.
    3. If (|L_k - L_{k-1}| ≥ ε) {
                k ← k + 1
                Go to Step 1.
          }
          else
                f_k is the final estimated focal
  length.
```

Since we know that the iterated value of f_k converges toward f_{true}, it would be interesting to determine its rate of convergence. (12.14) can be rewritten as a recurrence equation (assuming equality rather than approximation)

$$f_{true} - f_k = \eta\,(f_{true} - f_{k-1}) \tag{12.15}$$

Rearranging, we have

$$f_k - \eta f_{k-1} = (1 - \eta) f_{true}, \tag{12.16}$$

from which the solution can be found to be

$$f_k = f_{true} + (f_0 - f_{true})\,\eta^k \tag{12.17}$$

Hence, the convergence of f_k towards f_{true} is exponential in the vicinity of the true focal length, as shown by (12.17). This also indicates that the convergence is faster if the number of frames N increases, the image length l decreases, or the true focal length f_{true} increases. As an example, for $N = 50$, $l = 232$, and $f_{true} = 274.5$, $\eta = 0.117$.

The graph in Figure 12.6 shows the convergence of estimated focal length from different initial estimates. (A sequence of the synthetic room is shown in Figure 12.7 and the corresponding composited image is shown in Figure 12.8.) It is interesting to note that the actual estimated focal lengths are *smaller* than theoretically predicted ones. One of the reasons could be due to effects of resampling using bilinear interpolation. In addition, we also make the assumption that each point is "fully textured," which is difficult to realize in practice and even in simulations. Finally, shifts greater than 1 pixel are not likely to influence the net shift correctly.

A panorama of the synthetic room is shown in Figure 12.9. As can be seen, the effect of misestimating the focal length in compositing is a blurring effect, presumably about the correct locations. When a rectilinear image is projected onto a cylindrical surface of the wrong cross-sectional radius, which is also the estimated focal length, the error in pixel placement

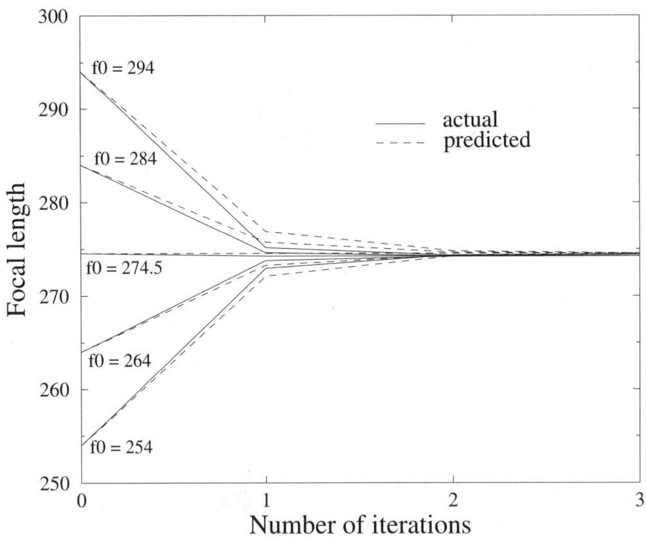

FIGURE 12.6. Graph of estimated focal length vs. number of iteration. f0 is the initial estimated focal length; the actual focal length is 274.5. The solid lines represent actual values whereas dashed lines represent predicted values.

increases away from the central image column. Having many cylindrical-converted images superimposed would thus have the effect of locally smearing the correct locations. This suggests that a good scheme of compositing many images to form a panorama is to down-weight the pixels away from the central image column during compositing. Indeed, Figure 12.10 shows the effect of using such a simple scheme. Here each pixel is weighted by a factor proportional to $|c - c_{\text{center}}|^{x_i}$, where c is the current pixel column, c_{center} the central pixel column, and $x_i = -5$. This yields a panorama that visually appears almost as good as that shown in Figure 12.8. Note, however, that the panorama in Figure 12.10 is still not quite physically correct; the *aspect ratio* is still not exact.

To further illustrate the robustness of this approach, we have also started the iterative process with the *original rectilinear images*, (i.e., $f_0 = \infty$), which would be the worst case focal length initialization. The convergence of the focal length value is: $\infty \to 281.18 \to 274.40 \to 274.24$. As before, the actual focal length is 274.5. The process arrives at virtually the correct focal length in just two iterations. This result is very significant; it illustrates that in principal, we can start without a focal length estimate.

Note that in general, the process of iterative local image registration can converge to a local minimum. This did not pose a problem to us because

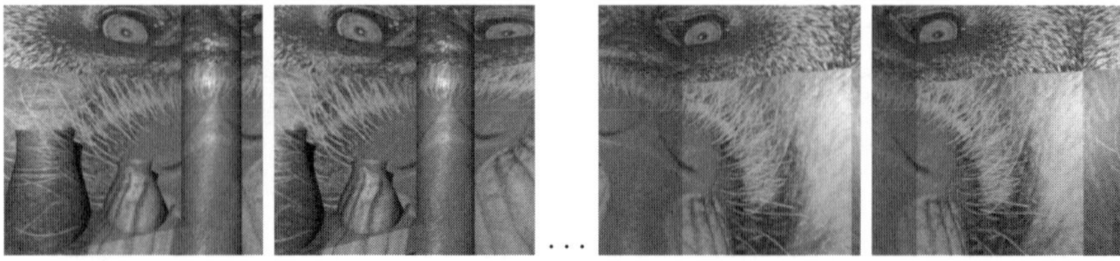

FIGURE 12.7. Example undistorted image sequence of synthetic room.

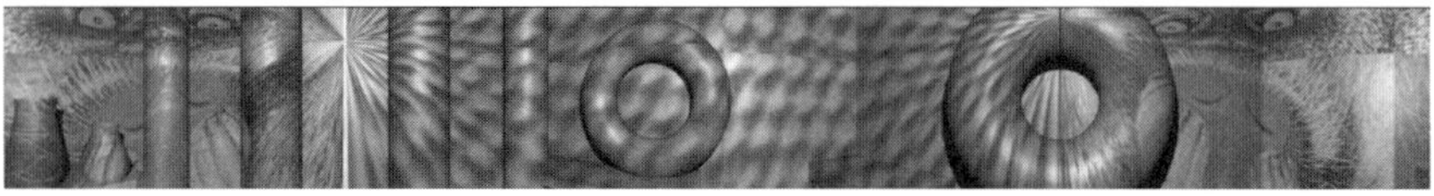

FIGURE 12.8. Panorama of synthetic room after compositing the sequence in Figure 12.7.

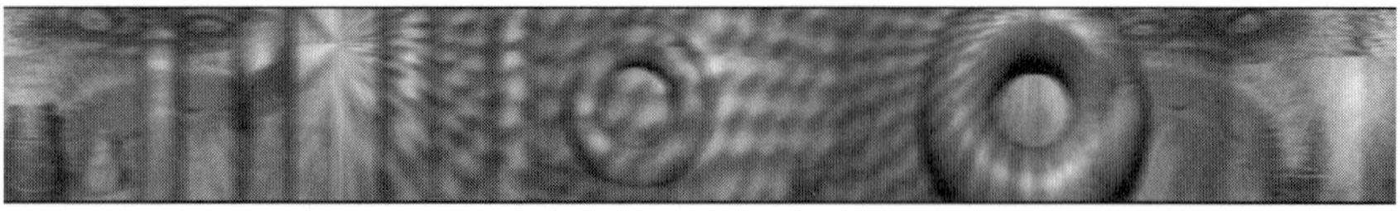

FIGURE 12.9. Panorama of synthetic room corresponding to an erroneous focal length.

the consecutive images taken have significant overlap ($> 50\%$). The reason that we start off with $f = \infty$ is to show the *rapid* rate of convergence at the worst case when converging to the right minimum.

12.4 Compositing Errors due to Misestimation of Radial Distortion Coefficient

Since we are estimating the focal length alone, it is important to show that we can ignore errors in the other intrinsic camera parameters for this process. Another intrinsic parameter that is likely to cause errors in the compositing length is the radial lens distortion. If (x_u, y_u) is the undistorted

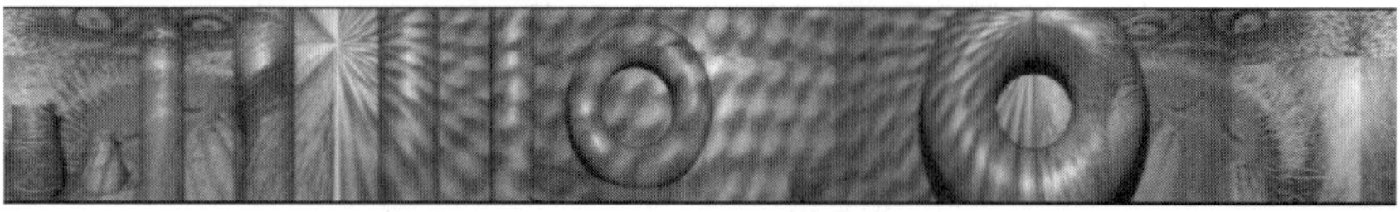

FIGURE 12.10. Panorama of synthetic room corresponding to an erroneous focal length, but using a simple weighted compositing technique.

image location and (x_d, y_d) is its radially distorted counterpart, then

$$\begin{aligned} x_u &= x_d(1 + \kappa_1 r_d^2 + \kappa_2 r_d^4 + ...) \\ y_u &= y_d(1 + \kappa_1 r_d^2 + \kappa_2 r_d^4 + ...) \end{aligned} \tag{12.18}$$

where

$$r_d = \sqrt{x_d^2 + y_d^2}$$

For our work, we use only the first radial coefficient term $\kappa = \kappa_1$:

$$\begin{aligned} x_u &= x_d(1 + \kappa r_d^2) \\ y_u &= y_d(1 + \kappa r_d^2) \end{aligned} \tag{12.19}$$

with the inverse

$$\begin{aligned} x_d &= \frac{x_u}{1 + \kappa r_d^2} \\ y_d &= \frac{y_u}{1 + \kappa r_d^2} \end{aligned} \tag{12.20}$$

where

$$\begin{aligned} r_d^2 =& \left(\sqrt{\left(\frac{1}{27\kappa^3} + \frac{r_u^2}{2\kappa^2}\right)^2 - \frac{1}{729\kappa^6}} + \frac{1}{27\kappa^3} + \frac{r_u^2}{2\kappa^2}\right)^{\frac{1}{3}} \\ &+ \frac{1}{9\left(\sqrt{\left(\frac{1}{27\kappa^3} + \frac{r_u^2}{2\kappa^2}\right)^2 - \frac{1}{729\kappa^6}} + \frac{1}{27\kappa^3} + \frac{r_u^2}{2\kappa^2}\right)^{\frac{1}{3}} \kappa^2} - \frac{2}{3\kappa} \end{aligned} \tag{12.21}$$

(12.21) is found using Mathematica^{TM} [296]. Details of lens distortion modeling can be found in [260]. Note that this analysis makes the assumption that the first radial distortion coefficient is dominant; if this is not true, then a similar analysis that includes the other significant distortion coefficients will have to be included.

The transformations required to show the effect of incorrect focal length and radial distortion coefficient are depicted in Figure 12.11. We assume that the cylindrical images are displaced by an angular amount α. To see how these transformations come about, consider the right half of the series of transformations beyond "rotate by α." We require the mapping from the correct cylindrical image point to the actual cylindrical image point, given estimates of f and κ. To generate the correct undistorted rectilinear image, we have to unproject from the cylindrical surface to the flat rectilinear surface (f_{true}^{-1}) and then radially undistort (κ_{true}^{-1}). Subsequently we perform radial distortion (κ) and cylindrical projection (f) to arrive at the estimated cylindrical image. This is similarly done for the second image.

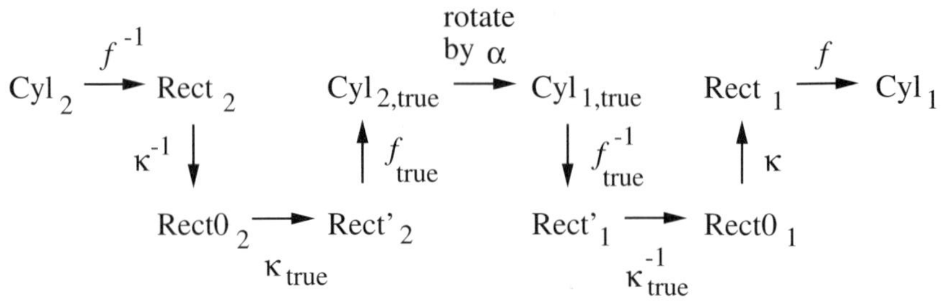

FIGURE 12.11. Mapping of pixels from the second cylindrical image to the first. The transformation f indicates mapping from cylindrical to rectilinear coordinates with focal length f while transformation κ indicates the radial distortion mapping with radial distortion factor κ. Terms with the subscript "true" represent the correct entities while those without this subscript represent estimated ones. Rect0 is the undistorted rectilinear image. See text.

Equations (12.3), (12.19), (12.20), and (12.21) are used in series to determine the theoretical displacement, as is similarly done in section 12.3. The difference is that in calculating the mean displacement, the displacements are averaged over *all* the pixels in the image. This is because radial distortion changes both x and y coordinates, while the cylindrical projection changes the x component independently of y. In addition, if the camera axis passes through the image center row, the average displacement in y is zero.

The effect of misestimating the radial distortion coefficient κ for a typical value of $f = 274.5$ and $\kappa = 2.8 \times 10^{-7}$ is shown in Figure 12.12. As can be seen, the effect is almost linear, and despite significant errors in κ, the resulting error in the effective focal length is small ($< 1\%$). This illustrates that for typical real focal lengths and radial distortion coefficients, the dominant factor in the compositing length error is the accuracy of the focal length.

The appearance of the panorama due to error in radial distortion coefficient κ is not very perceptible if the radial distortion is typically small (of the order of 10^{-7}). An extreme case that corresponds to a large error in radial distortion coefficient (by 10^{-5}) can be seen in Figure 12.13. Here, a simple scheme of compositing by direct averaging is performed, and there is a perceptible ghosting effect (note especially the area between the second and third columns in Figure 12.13). However, using the weighted compositing scheme results in a much sharper image, as shown in Figure 12.14. There is still some blurring effects, which is more pronounced away from the central horizontal row of the panorama, but this is to be expected with errors in κ.

There are two ways of measuring compositing length error: mismatch between observed compositing length and expected compositing length based

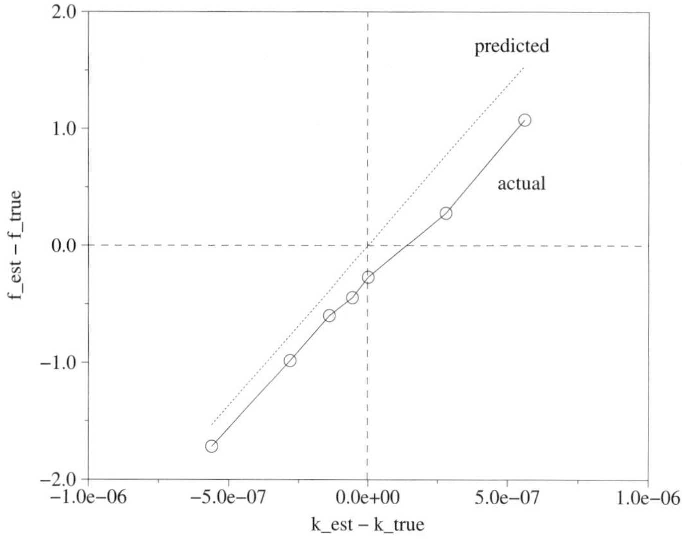

FIGURE 12.12. Graph of equivalent focal length error vs. error in κ, the radial distortion factor. The true focal length (f_{true}) is 274.5 and the true radial distortion factor (κ_{true}) is 2.8×10^{-7}.

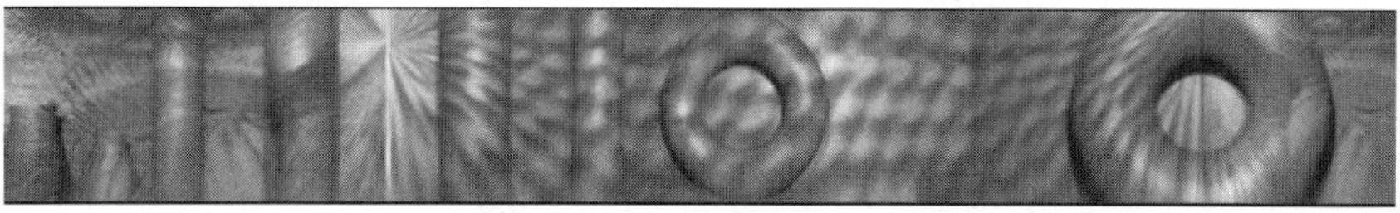

FIGURE 12.13. Another panorama of synthetic room corresponding to a large erroneous radial distortion coefficient (by 1.0×10^{-5}).

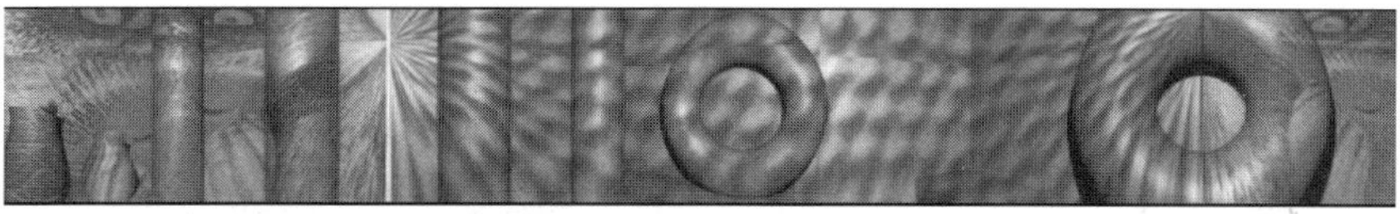

FIGURE 12.14. Panorama of synthetic room (same camera location as in Figure 12.13) corresponding to an erroneous focal length.

on estimated focal length, and mismatch between the correct compositing length and expected compositing length. The first error ($dL0$) measures the consistency between the estimated focal length and the observed composite length. The second error ($dL1$) metric measures the error due to the current estimate of the focal length, and cannot be calculated unless the true focal length is known. Figure 12.15 shows the variation of both types of compositing length error as a function of errors in estimated focal length and radial distortion coefficient. (The nominal focal length and radial distortion coefficient are 274.5 and 2.8×10^{-7} respectively.) The error $dL0$ is $L - 2\pi f$, where L is the compositing length and f is the estimated focal length. This is relevant if the estimated focal length is assumed to be correct and the composited length is adjusted to be compatible with the estimated focal length. In this case, the image displacement errors are distributed over all the frames (the simpliest method being uniform distribution). This procedure involves the least amount of computation as the images do not require reprojection onto a cylindrical surface of a difference cross-sectional radius (i.e., focal length). It may be used in the case of accurately estimated focal lengths. Meanwhile, the error $dL1$ is $2\pi(f - f_{true})$, f_{true} being the correct focal length. This is relevant in the case of using the newly estimated focal length based on the composited length. As can be observed, both types of compositing length errors are more sensitive to the error in the estimated focal length, with $dL0$ much more so.

12.5 Effect of Error in Focal Length and Radial Distortion Coefficient on 3D Data

The recovered 3D data do depend on the accuracy of the estimated focal length and radial distortion coefficient. This can be seen from Figures 12.17 and 12.18. The length and breadth of the synthetic room are 10 and 8 units respectively. Stereo data was recovered from 3 camera locations; two camera locations are $0.3\sqrt{2}$ units away from the first or reference camera location. An example of a distribution of recovered stereo data corresponding to the correct focal length of 274.5 and no radial distortion is shown in Figure 12.16. Surprisingly, despite the increased numerical errors, the recovered 3D data corresponding to the other (erroneous) focal lengths and radial distortion coefficient do not appear significantly different from that shown in Figure 12.16. This suggests that if exact reconstruction is not required and that the panorama does not have to be of high quality, then just using the estimated focal length directly would suffice.

From Figure 12.17, it can be observed that the effect of underestimating the focal length is greater than overestimating it. This is most likely due to the greater relative change in the curvature error (the curvature of the cylindrical surface being inversely proportional to the cross-sectional radius,

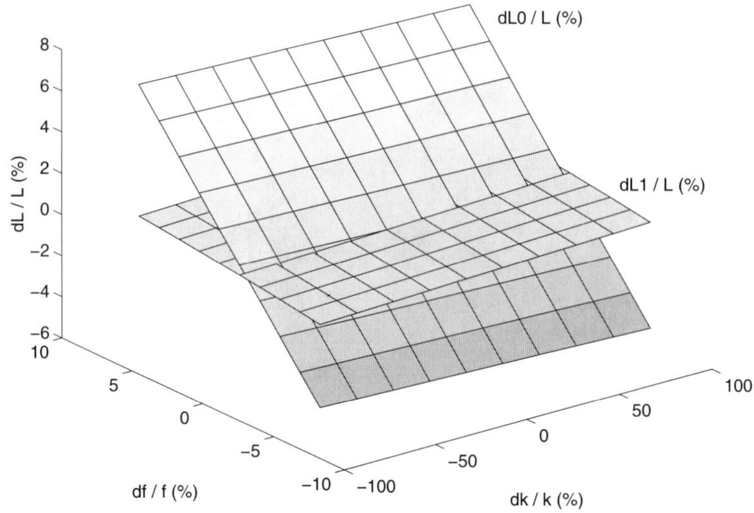

FIGURE 12.15. Variation of compositing length error vs. errors in both focal length and radial distortion coefficient. The deviations are all in terms of percentages. The nominal focal length and radial distortion coefficient are 274.5 and 2.8×10^{-7} respectively. See text for descriptions of $dL0$ and $dL1$.

which is the focal length) in underestimating the focal length. In addition, the effect of misestimating the focal length appears to be more significant on the accuracy of the reconstructed 3D points than does misestimating the radial distortion coefficient (assuming typical values of κ of the order of 10^{-7}). This suggests that as long as the field of view is not too large as to result in significant radial distortion, we can get by with a simple estimation of κ, or by assuming no radial distortion.

If necessary, κ can be determined using pairs of adjacent images and performing a bounded search to minimize the sum of residual intensity error in fitting global 2D projective transformation (we implemented Brent's 1D parabolic interpolation search [220]). Simulations have shown that the error in the recovered value of κ is less than 10% (with actual $\kappa = 5.0 \times 10^{-6}$ and the individual image size of 216×232).

12.6 An Example using Images of a Real Scene

An example of 3D recovery of a real scene is described in this section. This example is based on one of the examples in this book. One of the eight panoramic images created using the iterative compositing approach is shown in Figure 12.19. These eight panoramas were taken at about 3

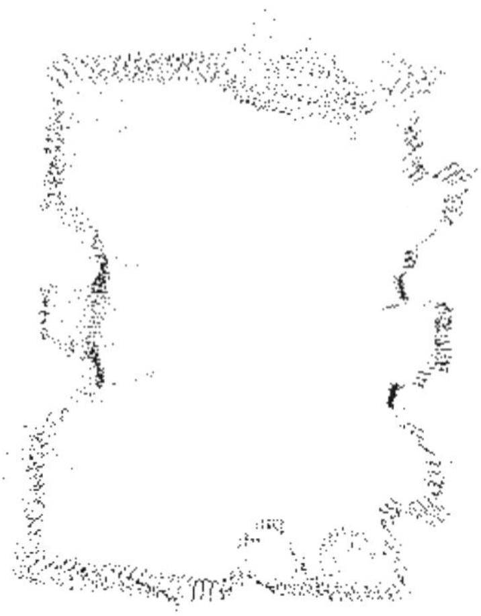

FIGURE 12.16. Example recovered 3D data (corresponding to the correct focal length of 274.5).

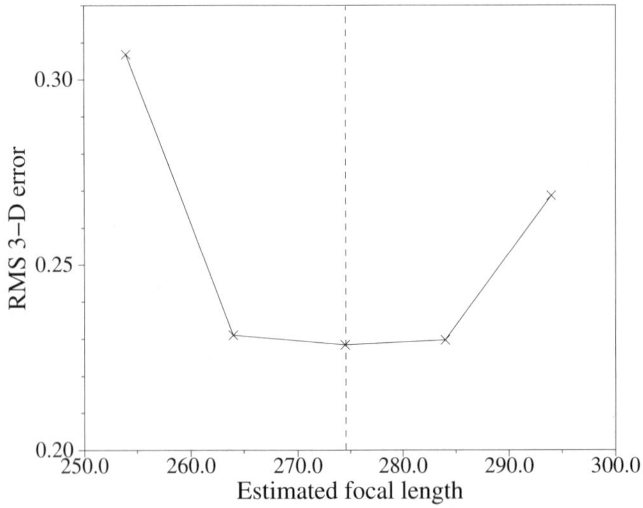

FIGURE 12.17. Graph of RMS 3D error of recovered stereo data vs. estimated focal length. The true focal length is 274.5 (indicated by the vertical dashed line).

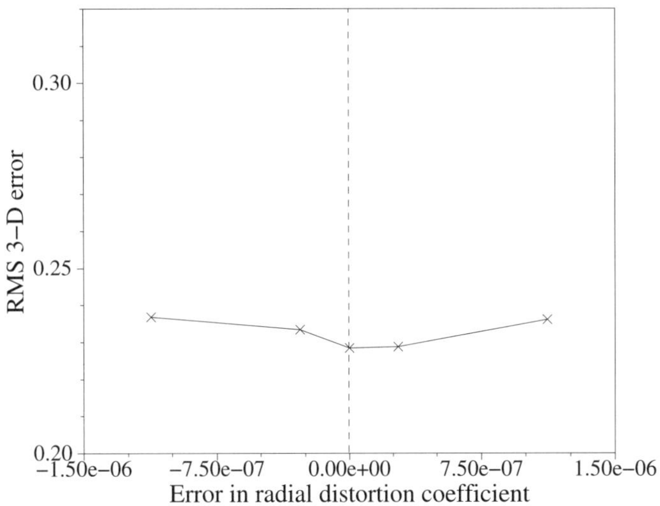

FIGURE 12.18. Graph of RMS 3D error of recovered stereo data vs. error in radial distortion coefficient κ. Typical real values of κ is of the order of 10^{-7}. The zero error in κ is indicated by the vertical dashed line.

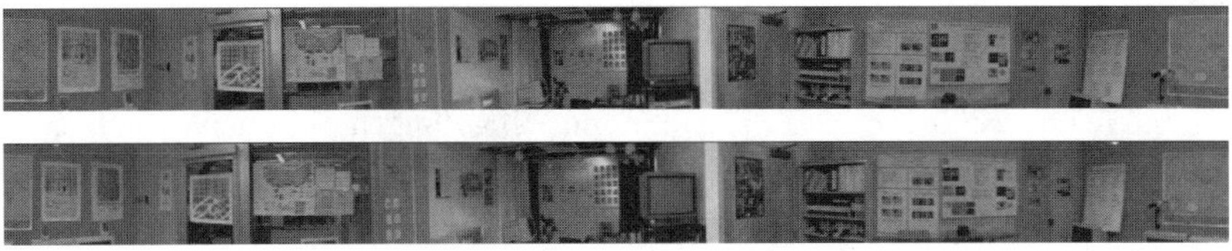

FIGURE 12.19. Two of eight composited panoramic images of the laboratory.

inches apart (ordered roughly in a zig-zag fashion) in the lab are extracted. The longest dimensions of the L-shaped lab is about 15 feet by 22.5 feet.

The 3D point distributions (original and filtered) are shown in Figure 12.20. The 3D point distribution in Figure 12.20(a) was obtained by applying multibaseline stereo on the panoramic images. As can be seen, the shape of the lab has been reasonably well recovered; the "noise" points at the bottom of Figure 12.20(a) corresponds to the positions *outside* the laboratory, since there are parts of the transparent laboratory window that are not covered. This reveals one of the weaknesses of any correlation-based algorithm (namely all stereo algorithms); they do not work well with image reflections and transparent material.

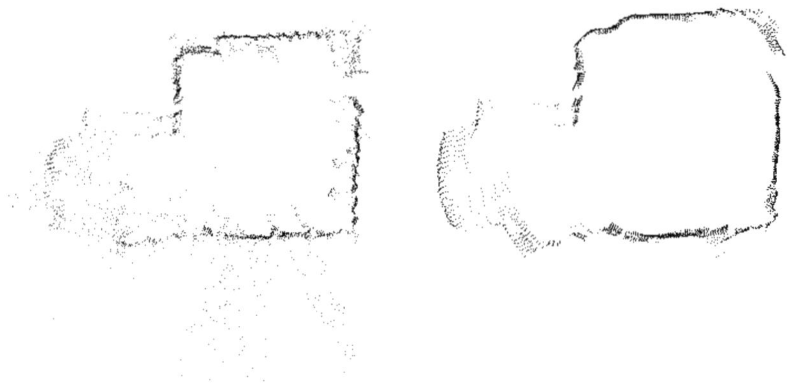

(a) After applying multibaseline stereo (b) Median-filtered version of (a)

FIGURE 12.20. Extracted 3D point distribution of a laboratory scene using six panoramic images.

12.7 Summary

We have analyzed the compositing error in terms of two intrinsic camera parameters, namely the focal length and the radial distortion coefficient. Given typical values of the radial distortion coefficient, the effect of the focal length on the compositing error is more significant than that of the radial distortion coefficient. An important discovery from this analysis is that the relative compositing length error due to camera focal length error is disproportionately much less than the relative focal length error. This enables the use of the resulting compositing length to recover a better estimate of the camera focal length, and forms the basis of the iterative compositing approach to camera calibration. This method has the advantage of not having to know the camera focal length when a panorama is to be generated from a sequence of images. In addition, it does not rely on feature detection and tracking or on a separate prior calibration process.

It has also been found that the resulting composite panorama is of a much higher visual quality if a weighted scheme in combining overlapping regions is used. Specifically, in blending images, we employ a weighting distribution of an exponential form that favors pixels closer to the central column of the image to which they belong.

Work has also been done on evaluating the effect of radial distortion on the composited length of the panorama. It turns out that for reasonably small radial distortion coefficients (of the order of 10^{-7}), the effect on the composited length is small (less than 1 percent error). We have not tried to recover the other intrinsic camera parameters, because it seemed they would have a much smaller effect on the modeling errors. In principle, the analysis presented here could be extended to some of the other intrinsic parameters.

13

Construction of Panoramic Image Mosaics with Global and Local Alignment

H.-Y. Shum and R. Szeliski

13.1 Introduction

The automatic construction of large, high-resolution image mosaics is an active area of research in the fields of photogrammetry, computer vision, image processing, and computer graphics. Image mosaics can be used for many different applications [163, 122]. The most traditional application is the construction of large aerial and satellite photographs from collections of images [186]. More recent applications include scene stabilization and change detection [93], video compression [125, 122, 167] and video indexing [240], increasing the field of view [105, 177, 266] and resolution [126, 50] of a camera, and even simple photo editing [38]. A particularly popular application is the emulation of traditional film-based panoramic photography [175] with digital panoramic mosaics, for applications such as the construction of virtual environments [181, 267] and virtual travel [49].

In computer vision, image mosaics are part of a larger recent trend, namely the study of *visual scene representations* [5]. The complete description of visual scenes and scene models often entails the recovery of depth or parallax information as well [161, 239, 271]. In computer graphics, image mosaics play an important role in the field of *image-based rendering*, which aims to rapidly render photorealistic novel views from collections of real (or pre-rendered) images [48, 181, 49, 84, 168, 144].

A number of techniques have been developed for capturing panoramic images of real-world scenes (for references on computer-generated environment maps, see [86]). One way is to record an image onto a long film strip using a panoramic camera to directly capture a cylindrical panoramic image [182]. Another way is to use a lens with a very large field of view such as a fisheye lens [298]. Mirrored pyramids and parabolic mirrors can also be used to directly capture panoramic images [195].

A less hardware-intensive method for constructing full view panoramas is to take many regular photographic or video images in order to cover the whole viewing space. These images must then be aligned and composited into complete panoramic images using an image mosaic or "stitching" algorithm [177, 266, 122, 49, 181, 267].

For applications such as virtual travel and architectural walkthroughs, it is desirable to have complete (full view) panoramas, i.e., mosaics that cover the whole viewing sphere and hence allow the user to look in any direction. Unfortunately, most of the results to date have been limited to cylindrical panoramas obtained with cameras rotating on leveled tripods adjusted to minimize motion parallax [181, 49, 263, 267, 148]. This has limited the users of mosaic building to researchers and professional photographers who can afford such specialized equipment.

The goal of our work is to remove the need for pure panning motion with no motion parallax. Ideally, we would like any user to be able to "paint" a full view panoramic mosaic with a simple hand-held camera or camcorder. In order to support this vision, several problems must be overcome.

First, we need to avoid using cylindrical or spherical coordinates for constructing the mosaic, since these representations introduce singularities near the poles of the viewing sphere. We solve this problem by associating a rotation matrix (and optionally focal length) with each input image, and performing registration in the input image's coordinate system (we call such mosaics *rotational mosaics* [273]). A postprocessing stage can be used to project such mosaics onto a convenient viewing surface, i.e., to create an *environment map* represented as a texture-mapped polyhedron surrounding the origin.

Second, we need to deal with accumulated misregistration errors, which are always present in any large image mosaic. For example, if we register a sequence of images using pairwise alignments, there is usually a gap between the last image and the first one even if these two images are the same. A simple "gap closing" technique can be used to force the first and last image to be the same, to refine the focal length estimation, and to distribute the resulting corrections across the image sequence [273, 148]. Unfortunately, this approach works only for pure panning motions with uniform motion steps. In this paper, we present a global optimization technique, derived from *simultaneous bundle block adjustment* in photogrammetry [295], to find the optimal overall registration.

Third, any deviations from the pure parallax-free motion model or ideal pinhole (projective) camera model may result in local misregistrations, which are visible as a loss of detail or multiple images (*ghosting*). To overcome this problem, we compute local motion estimates (block-based optical flow) between pairs of overlapping images, and use these estimates to warp each input image so as to reduce the misregistration [258]. Note that this is less ambitious than actually recovering a projective depth value for each pixel [161, 239, 271], but has the advantage of being able to simultaneously

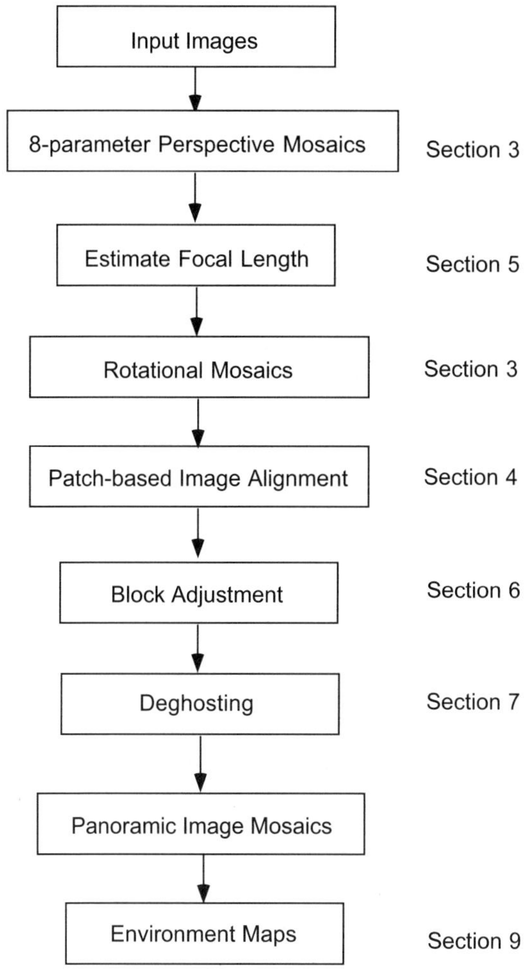

FIGURE 13.1. Panoramic image mosaicing system

model other effects such as radial lens distortions and small movements in the image.

The overall flow of processing in our mosaicing system is illustrated in Figure 13.1. First, if the camera intrinsic parameters are unknown, the user creates a small mosaic using a planar projective motion model, from which we can compute a rough estimate of the focal length (Section 13.5). Next, a complete initial panoramic mosaic is assembled sequentially (adding one image at a time and adjusting its position) using our rotational motion model (Section 13.3) and patch-based alignment technique (Section 13.4). Then, global alignment (block adjustment) is invoked to modify each image's transformation (and focal length) such that the global error across all possible overlapping image pairs is minimized (Section 13.6). This stage also removes any large inconsistencies in the mosaic, e.g., the "gaps" that might be present in a panoramic mosaic assembled using the sequential algorithm. Lastly, the local alignment (*deghosting*) algorithm is invoked to reduce any local misregistration errors (Section 13.7). The final mosaic can be stored as a collection of images with associated transformations, or optionally converted into a texture-mapped polyhedron or environment map (Section 13.9).

The structure of our paper essentially follows the major processing stages, as outlined above. In addition, we show in Section 13.2 how to construct cylindrical and spherical panoramas, which are special cases of panoramic image mosaics with a known camera focal length and a simple translational motion model. Section 13.8 presents our experimental results[1] using both global and local alignment, and Section 13.10 discusses these results and summarizes the components in our system.

13.2 Cylindrical and Spherical Panoramas

Cylindrical panoramas are commonly used because of their ease of construction. To build a cylindrical panorama, a sequence of images is taken by a camera mounted on a leveled tripod. If the camera focal length or field of view is known, each perspective image can be warped into cylindrical coordinates. Figure 13.2a shows two overlapping cylindrical images—notice how horizontal lines become curved.

To build a cylindrical panorama, we map world coordinates[2] $\mathbf{p} = (X, Y, Z)$ to 2D cylindrical screen coordinates (θ, v) using

$$\theta = \tan^{-1}(X/Z) \tag{13.1}$$
$$v = Y/\sqrt{X^2 + Z^2} \tag{13.2}$$

where θ is the panning angle and v is the scanline [267]. Similarly, we can map world coordinates into 2D spherical coordinates (θ, ϕ) using

$$\theta = \tan^{-1}(X/Z) \tag{13.3}$$
$$\phi = \tan^{-1}(Y/\sqrt{X^2 + Z^2}). \tag{13.4}$$

Once we have warped each input image, constructing the panoramic mosaics becomes a pure translation problem. Ideally, to build a cylindrical or

---

[1]Example image sequences and results are also online www.research.microsoft.com/users/hshum/ijcv99/ijcv.htm.

[2]To convert from image coordinates (x, y) to world coordinates (directions), we use $(X, Y, Z) = (x + c_x, y + c_y, f)$, where (c_x, c_y) are the coordinates of the camera's optical center, and f is the focal length measured in pixels (see Section 13.3.2).

spherical panorama from a horizontal panning sequence, only the unknown panning angles need to be recovered. In practice, small vertical translations are needed to compensate for vertical jitter and optical twist. Therefore, both a horizontal translation t_x and a vertical translation t_y are estimated for each input image.

To recover the translational motion, we estimate the incremental $\delta\mathbf{t} = (\delta t_x, \delta t_y)$ by minimizing the intensity error between two images[3],

$$E(\delta\mathbf{t}) = \sum_i [I_1(\mathbf{x}'_i + \delta\mathbf{t}) - I_0(\mathbf{x}_i)]^2, \tag{13.5}$$

where $\mathbf{x}_i = (x_i, y_i)$ and $\mathbf{x}'_i = (x'_i, y'_i) = (x_i + t_x, y_i + t_y)$ are corresponding points in the two images, and $\mathbf{t} = (t_x, t_y)$ is the global translational motion field which is the same for all pixels [25].

After a first order Taylor series expansion, the above equation becomes

$$E(\delta\mathbf{t}) \approx \sum_i [\mathbf{g}_i^T \delta\mathbf{t} + e_i]^2 \tag{13.6}$$

where $e_i = I_1(\mathbf{x}'_i) - I_0(\mathbf{x}_i)$ is the current intensity or color error, and $\mathbf{g}_i^T = \nabla I_1(\mathbf{x}'_i)$ is the image gradient of I_1 at $\mathbf{x}'_i$. This minimization problem has a simple least-squares solution,

$$\left(\sum_i \mathbf{g}_i \mathbf{g}_i^T\right) \delta\mathbf{t} = -\left(\sum_i e_i \mathbf{g}_i\right). \tag{13.7}$$

Figure 13.2b shows a portion of a cylindrical panoramic mosaic built using this simple translational alignment technique. To handle larger initial displacements, we use a hierarchical coarse-to-fine optimization scheme [25].

When blending the images into a composite mosaic, in order to reduce discontinuities in intensity and color between the images being composited, we apply a simple *feathering* algorithm, i.e., we weight the pixels in each image proportionally to their distance to the edge [267]. More precisely, for each warped image being blended, we first compute the distance map, $d(\mathbf{x})$, which measures either the city block distance [228] or the Euclidean distance [54] to the nearest transparent pixel ($\alpha = 0$) or border pixel. We then blend all of the warped images using

$$C(\mathbf{x}) = \frac{\sum_k w(d(\mathbf{x}))\tilde{I}_k(\mathbf{x})}{\sum_k w(d(\mathbf{x}))} \tag{13.8}$$

where w is a monotonic function (we currently use $w(x) = x$). An alternative to such weighted blending is to select pixels from only one image, but this can be tricky in practice [185, 214, 297, 56].

---

[3]For robust versions of this metric, see [27, 240].

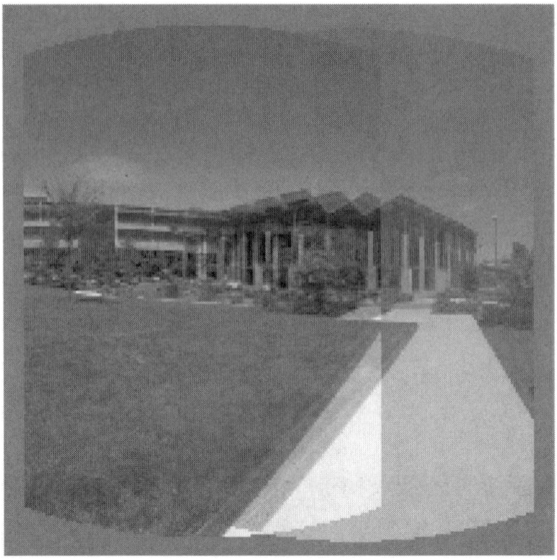

(a)

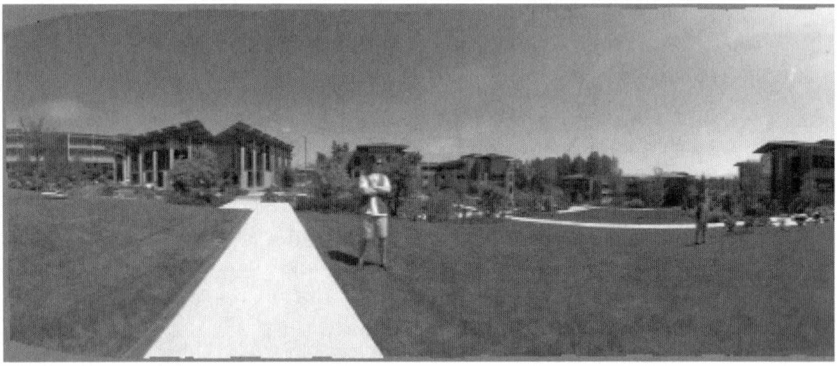

(b)

FIGURE 13.2. Construction of a cylindrical panorama: (a) two warped images; (b) part of cylindrical panorama composited from a sequence of images.

Once the alignment and blending steps are finished, we can clip the ends (and optionally the top and bottom) and write out a single panoramic image. An example of a cylindrical panorama is shown in Figure 13.2b. The cylindrical/spherical image can then be displayed with a special purpose viewer like QTVR or Surround Video. Alternatively, it can be wrapped onto a cylinder or sphere using texture-mapping. For example, the Direct3D graphics API has a `CreateWrap` primitive which can be used to wrap a spherical or cylindrical image around an object using texture-mapping. However, the object needs to be finely tessellated in order to avoid visible artifacts.

Creating panoramas in cylindrical or spherical coordinates has several limitations. First, it can only handle the simple case of pure panning motion. Second, even though it is possible to convert an image to 2D spherical or cylindrical coordinates for a known tilting angle, ill-sampling at north pole and south pole causes big registration errors[4]. Third, it requires knowing the focal length (or equivalently, field of view). While focal length can be carefully calibrated in the lab [284, 263], estimating the focal length of lens by registering two or more images is not very accurate, as we will discuss in Section 13.5.

13.3 Alignment Framework and Motion Models

In our system, we represent image mosaics as collections of images with associated geometrical transformations. The first stage of our mosaic construction algorithm computes an initial estimate for the transformation associated with each input image. We do this by processing each input image in turn, and finding the best alignment between this image and the mosaic constructed from all previous images.[5] This reduces the problem to that of parametric motion estimation [25]. We use the hierarchical motion estimation framework proposed by Bergen *et al.*, which consists of four parts: (i) pyramid construction, (ii) motion estimation, (iii) image warping, and (iv) coarse-to-fine refinement [25].

An important element of this framework, which we exploit, is to perform the motion estimation between the current new input image and a *warped* (resampled) version of the mosaic. This allows us to estimate only *incremental* deformations of images (or equivalently, *instantaneous* motion), which greatly simplifies the computation of the gradients and Hessians required in our gradient descent algorithm (e.g., compare the Hessians computed below with those presented in [267]). Thus, to register two images $I_0(\mathbf{x})$ and $I_1(\mathbf{x}')$, where $\mathbf{x}'$ is computed using some parametric motion model $\mathbf{m}$, i.e., $\mathbf{x}' = \mathbf{f}(\mathbf{x}; \mathbf{m})$, we first compute the warped image

$$\tilde{I}_1(\mathbf{x}) = I_1(\mathbf{f}(\mathbf{x}; \mathbf{m})) \tag{13.9}$$

(in our current implementation, we use bilinear pixel resampling). The task is then to find a deformation of $\tilde{I}_1(\mathbf{x})$ which brings it into closer registration with $I_0(\mathbf{x})$ and which can also be used to update the parameter $\mathbf{m}$. The warp/register/update loop can then be repeated. In the next three

---

[4]Note that cylindrical coordinates become undefined as you tilt your camera toward north or south pole.

[5]To speed up this part, we can optionally register with only the previous image in the sequence.

subsections, we describe how this can be done for two different transformation models, namely 8-parameter planar projective transformations and 3D rotations, and how this can be generalized to other motion models and parameters.

13.3.1 8-parameter Perspective Transformations

Given two images taken from the same viewpoint (optical center) but in potentially different directions (and/or with different intrinsic parameters), the relationship between two overlapping images can be described by a homography or planar perspective motion model [177, 266, 122, 267] (for a proof, see Section 13.3.2 below). The planar perspective transformation warps an image into another using

$$\mathbf{x}' \sim \mathbf{M}\mathbf{x} = \begin{bmatrix} m_0 & m_1 & m_2 \\ m_3 & m_4 & m_5 \\ m_6 & m_7 & m_8 \end{bmatrix} \begin{bmatrix} x \\ y \\ 1 \end{bmatrix}, \tag{13.10}$$

where $\mathbf{x} = (x, y, 1)$ and $\mathbf{x}' = (x', y', 1)$ are homogeneous or projective coordinates, and $\sim$ indicates equality up to scale.[6] This equation can be re-written as

$$x' = \frac{m_0 x + m_1 y + m_2}{m_6 x + m_7 y + m_8} \tag{13.11}$$

$$y' = \frac{m_3 x + m_4 y + m_5}{m_6 x + m_7 y + m_8}. \tag{13.12}$$

To recover the parameters, we iteratively update the transformation matrix[7] using

$$\mathbf{M} \leftarrow \mathbf{M}(\mathbf{I} + \mathbf{D}) \tag{13.13}$$

where

$$\mathbf{D} = \begin{bmatrix} d_0 & d_1 & d_2 \\ d_3 & d_4 & d_5 \\ d_6 & d_7 & d_8 \end{bmatrix}. \tag{13.14}$$

Resampling image I_1 with the new transformation $\mathbf{x}' \sim \mathbf{M}(\mathbf{I} + \mathbf{D})\mathbf{x}$ is the same as warping the resampled image $\tilde{I}_1$ by $\mathbf{x}'' \sim (\mathbf{I} + \mathbf{D})\mathbf{x}$,[8] i.e.,

$$x'' = \frac{(1 + d_0)x + d_1 y + d_2}{d_6 x + d_7 y + (1 + d_8)} \tag{13.15}$$

$$y'' = \frac{d_3 x + (1 + d_4)y + d_5}{d_6 x + d_7 y + (1 + d_8)}. \tag{13.16}$$

---

[6] Since the **M** matrix is invariant to scaling, there are only 8 independent parameters.

[7] To improve conditioning of the linear system and to speed up the convergence, we place the origin $(x, y) = (0, 0)$ at the center of the image.

[8] Ignoring errors introduced by the double resampling operation.

We wish to minimize the squared error metric

$$E(\mathbf{d}) = \sum_i [\tilde{I}_1(\mathbf{x}_i'') - I_0(\mathbf{x}_i)]^2 \tag{13.17}$$

$$\approx \sum_i [\tilde{I}_1(\mathbf{x}_i) + \nabla \tilde{I}_1(\mathbf{x}_i) \frac{\partial \mathbf{x}_i''}{\partial \mathbf{d}} \mathbf{d} - I_0(\mathbf{x}_i)]^2 = \sum_i [\mathbf{g}_i^T \mathbf{J}_i^T \mathbf{d} + e_i]^2 \tag{13.18}$$

where $e_i = \tilde{I}_1(\mathbf{x}_i) - I_0(\mathbf{x}_i)$ is the intensity or color error[9], $\mathbf{g}_i^T = \nabla \tilde{I}_1(\mathbf{x}_i)$ is the image gradient of $\tilde{I}_1$ at $\mathbf{x}_i$, $\mathbf{d} = (d_0, \ldots, d_8)$ is the incremental motion parameter vector, and $\mathbf{J}_i = \mathbf{J}_\mathbf{d}(\mathbf{x}_i)$, where

$$\mathbf{J}_\mathbf{d}(\mathbf{x}) = \frac{\partial \mathbf{x}''}{\partial \mathbf{d}} = \begin{bmatrix} x & y & 1 & 0 & 0 & 0 & -x^2 & -xy & -x \\ 0 & 0 & 0 & x & y & 1 & -xy & -y^2 & -y \end{bmatrix}^T \tag{13.19}$$

is the Jacobian of the resampled point coordinate $\mathbf{x}_i''$ with respect to $\mathbf{d}$.[10]

This least-squares problem (13.18) has a simple solution through the *normal equations* [220]

$$\mathbf{A}\mathbf{d} = -\mathbf{b}, \tag{13.20}$$

where

$$\mathbf{A} = \sum_i \mathbf{J}_i \mathbf{g}_i \mathbf{g}_i^T \mathbf{J}_i^T \tag{13.21}$$

is the *Hessian*, and

$$\mathbf{b} = \sum_i e_i \mathbf{J}_i \mathbf{g}_i \tag{13.22}$$

is the *accumulated gradient* or *residual.* These equations can be solved using a symmetric positive definite (SPD) solver such as *Cholesky* decomposition [220]. Note that for our problem, the matrix $\mathbf{A}$ is singular unless we eliminate one of the three parameters $\{d_0, d_4, d_8\}$. In practice, we set $d_8 = 0$, and therefore only solve an 8×8 system. A diagram of our alignment framework is shown in Figure 13.3.

Translational motion is a special case of the general 8-parameter perspective transformation where $\mathbf{J}$ is a 2×2 identity matrix because only the two parameters m_2 and m_5 are used. The translational motion model can be used to construct cylindrical and spherical panoramas if we warp each image to cylindrical or spherical coordinates image using a known focal length, as shown in Section 13.2.

The 8-parameter perspective transformation recovery algorithm works well provided that initial estimates of the correct transformation are close enough. However, since the motion model contains more free parameters

---

[9]Currently three channels of color errors are used in our system, but we can use the luminance (intensity) error instead.

[10]The entries in the Jacobian correspond to the optical flow induced by the instantaneous motion of a plane in 3D [25].

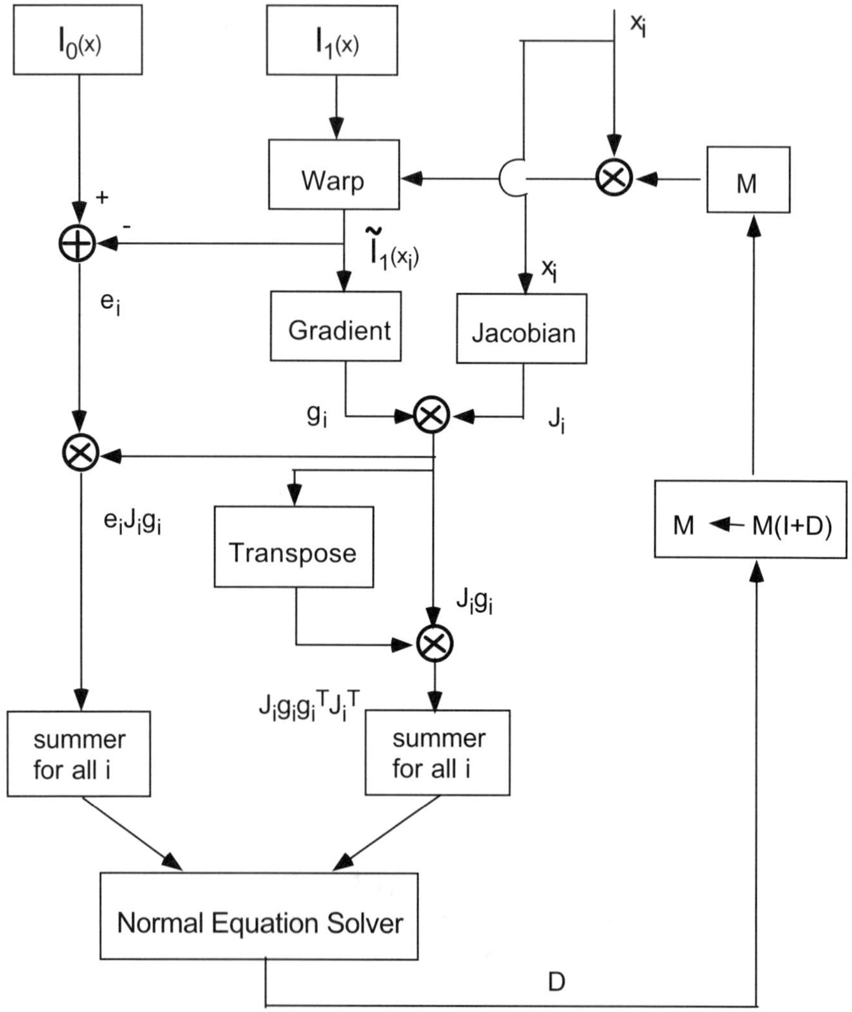

FIGURE 13.3. A diagram for our image alignment framework

than necessary, it suffers from slow convergence and sometimes gets stuck in local minima. For this reason, when we know that the camera is rotating around its optical axis, as opposed to undergoing general motion while observing a plane, we prefer to use the 3-parameter rotational model described next.

13.3.2 3D Rotations and Zooms

For a camera centered at the world origin, i.e., $(X, Y, Z) = (0, 0, 0)$, the relationship between a 3D point $\mathbf{p} = (X, Y, Z)$ and its image coordinates $\mathbf{x} = (x, y, 1)$ can be described by

$$\mathbf{x} \sim \mathbf{TVRp}, \tag{13.23}$$

where

$$\mathbf{T} = \begin{bmatrix} 1 & 0 & c_x \\ 0 & 1 & c_y \\ 0 & 0 & 1 \end{bmatrix}, \mathbf{V} = \begin{bmatrix} f & 0 & 0 \\ 0 & f & 0 \\ 0 & 0 & 1 \end{bmatrix}, \text{ and } \mathbf{R} = \begin{bmatrix} r_{00} & r_{01} & r_{02} \\ r_{10} & r_{11} & r_{12} \\ r_{20} & r_{21} & r_{22} \end{bmatrix}$$

are the image plane translation, focal length scaling, and 3D rotation matrices. For simplicity of notation, we assume that pixels are numbered so that the origin is at the image center, i.e., $c_x = c_y = 0$, allowing us to dispense with $\mathbf{T}$ (in practice, mislocating the image center does not seem to affect mosaic registration algorithms very much).[11] The 3D direction corresponding to a screen pixel $\mathbf{x}$ is given by $\mathbf{p} \sim \mathbf{R}^{-1}\mathbf{V}^{-1}\mathbf{x}$.

For a camera rotating around its center of projection, the mapping (perspective projection) between two images k and l is therefore given by

$$\mathbf{M} \sim \mathbf{V}_k\mathbf{R}_k\mathbf{R}_l^{-1}\mathbf{V}_l^{-1} = \mathbf{V}_k\mathbf{R}_{kl}\mathbf{V}_l^{-1} \tag{13.24}$$

where each image is represented by $\mathbf{V}_k\mathbf{R}_k$, i.e., a focal length and a 3D rotation.

Assume for now that the focal length is known and is the same for all images, i.e, $\mathbf{V}_k = \mathbf{V}$. Our method for computing an estimate of f from an initial set of homographies is given in Section 13.5. To recover the rotation, we perform an incremental update to $\mathbf{R}_k$ based on the angular velocity $\boldsymbol{\Omega} = (\omega_\mathbf{x}, \omega_\mathbf{y}, \omega_\mathbf{z})$,

$$\mathbf{R}_{kl} \leftarrow \mathbf{R}_{kl}\hat{\mathbf{R}}(\boldsymbol{\Omega}) \qquad \text{or} \qquad \mathbf{M} \leftarrow \mathbf{V}\mathbf{R}_{\mathbf{kl}}\hat{\mathbf{R}}(\boldsymbol{\Omega})\mathbf{V}^{-1} \tag{13.25}$$

where the incremental rotation matrix $\hat{\mathbf{R}}(\boldsymbol{\Omega})$ is given by Rodriguez's formula [8],

$$\hat{\mathbf{R}}(\hat{\mathbf{n}}, \theta) = \mathbf{I} + (\sin\theta)\mathbf{X}(\hat{\mathbf{n}}) + (1 - \cos\theta)\mathbf{X}(\hat{\mathbf{n}})^2 \tag{13.26}$$

---

[11] The above equation also assumes a unit aspect ratio, no skew, and no radial distortion.

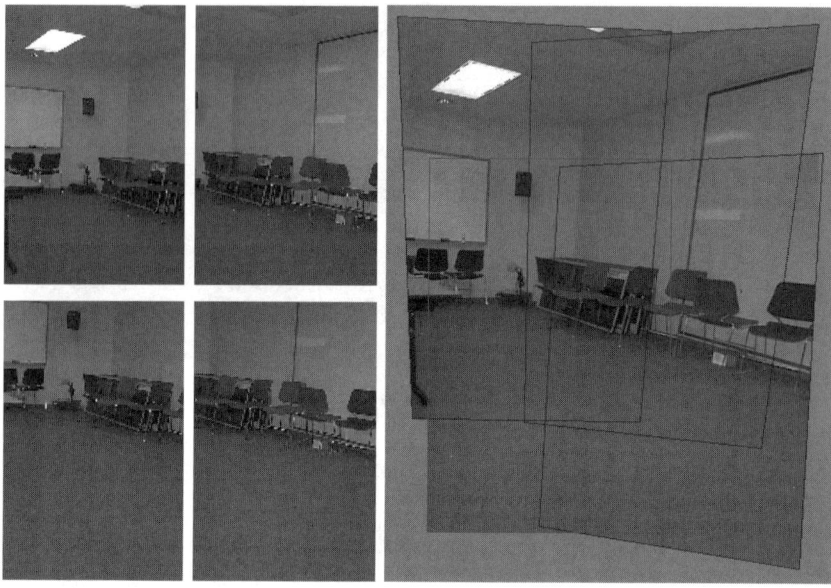

(a) (b)

FIGURE 13.4. 3D rotation registration of four images taken with hand-held camera: (a) four original pictures; (b) image mosaic using 3D rotation.

with $\theta = \|\mathbf{\Omega}\|$, $\hat{\mathbf{n}} = \mathbf{\Omega}/\theta$, and

$$\mathbf{X}(\mathbf{\Omega}) = \begin{bmatrix} 0 & -\omega_z & \omega_y \\ \omega_z & 0 & -\omega_x \\ -\omega_y & \omega_x & 0 \end{bmatrix}$$

is the cross product operator.[12] Keeping only terms linear in $\mathbf{\Omega}$, we get

$$\mathbf{M}' \approx \mathbf{V}\mathbf{R}_k\mathbf{R}_l^{-1}[\mathbf{I} + \mathbf{X}(\mathbf{\Omega})]\mathbf{V}^{-1} = \mathbf{M}(\mathbf{I} + \mathbf{D}_{\mathbf{\Omega}}), \tag{13.27}$$

where

$$\mathbf{D}_\Omega = \mathbf{V}\mathbf{X}(\mathbf{\Omega})\mathbf{V}^{-1} = \begin{bmatrix} 0 & -\omega_z & f\omega_y \\ \omega_z & 0 & -f\omega_x \\ -\omega_y/f & \omega_x/f & 0 \end{bmatrix}$$

is the deformation matrix which plays the same role as $\mathbf{D}$ in (13.13).

Computing the Jacobian of the entries in $\mathbf{D}_\Omega$ with respect to $\mathbf{\Omega}$ and applying the chain rule, we obtain the new Jacobian,[13]

$$\mathbf{J}_\Omega = \frac{\partial \mathbf{x}''}{\partial \mathbf{\Omega}} = \frac{\partial \mathbf{x}''}{\partial \mathbf{d}}\frac{\partial \mathbf{d}}{\partial \mathbf{\Omega}} = \begin{bmatrix} -xy/f & f + x^2/f & -y \\ -f - y^2/f & xy/f & x \end{bmatrix}^T. \tag{13.28}$$

---

[12]This is also called the *twist* or *exponential map* representation in robotics [193].

[13]This is the same as the rotational component of instantaneous rigid flow [25].

This Jacobian is then plugged into the previous minimization pipeline to estimate the incremental rotation vector $(\omega_x \; \omega_y \; \omega_z)$, after which $\mathbf{R}_k$ can be updated using (13.25).

Figure 13.4 shows how our method can be used to register four images with arbitrary (non-panning) rotation. Compared to the 8-parameter perspective model, it is much easier and more intuitive to interactively adjust images using the 3-parameter rotational model.[14]

13.3.3 Other Motion Models

The same general strategy can be followed to obtain the gradient and Hessian associated with any other motion parameters. For example, the focal length f_k can be adjusted by setting $f_k \leftarrow (1 + e_k)f_k$, i.e.,

$$\mathbf{M} \leftarrow \mathbf{M}(\mathbf{I} + e_k\mathbf{D}_{110}) \tag{13.29}$$

where $\mathbf{D}_{110}$ is a diagonal matrix with entries $(1, 1, 0)$. The Jacobian matrix $\mathbf{J}_{e_k}$ is thus the diagonal matrix with entries (x, y), i.e., we are estimating a simple re-scaling (dilation). This formula can be used to re-estimate the focal length in a video sequence with a variable focal length (zoom).

If we wish to update a single global focal length estimate, $f \leftarrow (1 + e)f$, the update equation and Jacobian are more complicated. We obtain

$$\mathbf{M} \leftarrow (\mathbf{I} + e\mathbf{D}_{110})\mathbf{V}\mathbf{R}_k\mathbf{R}_l^{-1}\mathbf{V}^{-1}(\mathbf{I} - e\mathbf{D}_{110}) \approx \mathbf{M}(\mathbf{I} + e\mathbf{D}_e) \tag{13.30}$$

where

$$\mathbf{D}_e = \mathbf{D}_{110} - \mathbf{M}\mathbf{D}_{110}\mathbf{M}^{-1} \tag{13.31}$$

(further simplifications of the second term are possible because of the special structure of $\mathbf{D}_{110}$). The Jacobian does not have a nice simple structure, but can nevertheless be written as the product of $\mathbf{J}_\mathbf{d}$ and $\partial\mathbf{d}/\partial e$, which is given by the entries in $\mathbf{D}_e$. Note, however, that global focal length adjustment cannot be done as part of the initial sequential mosaic creation stage, since this algorithm presupposes that only the newest image is being adjusted. We will address the issue of global focal length estimate refinement in Section 13.6.

The same methodology as presented above can be used to update any motion parameter p on which the image-to-image homography $\mathbf{M}(p)$ depends, e.g., the aspect ratio.[15] We simply set

$$\mathbf{M} \leftarrow \mathbf{M}(p + \delta p) \approx \mathbf{M}(\mathbf{I} + \mathbf{M}^{-1}\frac{\partial \mathbf{M}}{\partial p}\delta p). \tag{13.32}$$

[14] With only a mouse click/drag on screen, it is difficult to control 8 parameters simultaneously.

[15] Updating parameters such as radial distortion which affect the image formation process in a non-linear way requires a different method, i.e., directly taking derivatives of image pixel locations w.r.t. these parameters.

Hence, we can read off the entries in $\partial\mathbf{d}/\partial p$ from the entries in $\mathbf{M}^{-1}(\partial\mathbf{M}/\partial p)$.

13.4 Patch-based Alignment Algorithm

The normal equations given in the previous section, together with an appropriately chosen Jacobian matrix, can be used to directly improve the current motion estimate by first computing local intensity errors and gradients, and then accumulating the entries in the parameter gradient vector and Hessian matrix. This straightforward algorithm suffers from several drawbacks: it is susceptible to local minima and outliers, and is also unnecessarily inefficient. In this section, we present the implementation details of our algorithm which makes it much more robust and efficient [257].

13.4.1 Patch-based Alignment

The computational effort required to take a single gradient descent step in parameter space can be divided into three major parts: (i) the warping (resampling) of $I_1(\mathbf{x}')$ into $\tilde{I}_1(\mathbf{x})$, (ii) the computation of the local intensity errors e_i and gradients $\mathbf{g}_i$, and (iii) the accumulation of the entries in $\mathbf{A}$ and $\mathbf{b}$ (13.21–13.22). This last step can be quite expensive, since it involves the computations of the monomials in $\mathbf{J}_i$ and the formation of the products in $\mathbf{A}$ and $\mathbf{b}$.

Notice that equations (13.21–13.22) can be written as vector/matrix products of the Jacobian $\mathbf{J}(\mathbf{x}_i)$ with the *gradient-weighted intensity errors*, $e_i\mathbf{g}_i$, and the *local intensity gradient Hessians* $\mathbf{g}_i\mathbf{g}_i^T$. If we divide the image up into little patches $\mathcal{P}_j$, and make the approximation that $\mathbf{J}(\mathbf{x}_i) = \mathbf{J}_j$ is constant within each patch (say by evaluating it at the patch center), we can write the normal equations as

$$\mathbf{A} \approx \sum_j \mathbf{J}_j \mathbf{A}_j \mathbf{J}_j^T \qquad \text{with} \qquad \mathbf{A}_j = \sum_{i \in \mathcal{P}_j} \mathbf{g}_i \mathbf{g}_i^T \tag{13.33}$$

and

$$\mathbf{b} \approx \sum_j \mathbf{J}_j \mathbf{b}_j \qquad \text{with} \qquad \mathbf{b}_j = \sum_{i \in \mathcal{P}_j} e_i \mathbf{g}_i. \tag{13.34}$$

$\mathbf{A}_j$ and $\mathbf{b}_j$ are the terms that appear in patch-based optical flow algorithms [172, 25]. Our algorithm therefore augments step (ii) above with the accumulation of $\mathbf{A}_j$ and $\mathbf{b}_j$ (only 10 additional multiply/add operations, which could potentially be done using fixpoint arithmetic), and performs the computations required to evaluate $\mathbf{J}_j$ and accumulate $\mathbf{A}$ and $\mathbf{b}$ only once per patch.

A potential disadvantage of using this approximation is that it might lead to poorer convergence (more iterations) in the parameter estimation algorithm. In practice, we have not observed this to be the case with the small patches (8×8) that we currently use.

13.4.2 Correlation-style Search

Another limitation of straightforward gradient descent is that it can get trapped in local minima, especially when the initial misregistration is more than a few pixels. A useful heuristic for enlarging the region of convergence is to use a hierarchical or coarse-to-fine algorithm, where estimates from coarser levels of the pyramid are used to initialize the registration at finer levels [221, 4, 25]. This is a remarkably effective technique, and we typically always use 3 or 4 pyramid levels in our mosaic construction algorithm. However, it may still sometimes fail if the amount of misregistration exceeds the scale at which significant image details exist (i.e., because these details may not exist or may be strongly aliased at coarse resolution levels).

To help overcome this problem, we have added a *correlation-style search* component to our registration algorithm.[16] Before doing the first gradient descent step at a given resolution level, the algorithm can be instructed to perform an independent search at each patch for the integral shift which will best align the I_0 and $\tilde{I}_1$ images (this *block-matching* technique is the basis of most MPEG coding algorithms [166]). For a search range of $\pm s$ pixels both horizontally and vertically, this requires the evaluation of $(2s+1)^2$ different shifts. For this reason, we usually only apply the correlation-style search algorithm at the coarsest level of the pyramid (unlike, say, [4], which is a dense optic flow algorithm).

Once the displacements have been estimated for each patch, they must somehow be integrated into the global parameter estimation algorithm. The easiest way to do this is to compute a new set of patch Hessians $\mathbf{A}_j$ and patch residuals $\mathbf{b}_j$ (c.f. (13.33–13.34)) to encode the results of the search. Recall that for patch-based flow algorithms [172, 25], $\mathbf{A}_j$ and $\mathbf{b}_j$ describe a local error surface

$$E(\mathbf{u}_j) = \mathbf{u}_j^T \mathbf{A}_j \mathbf{u}_j + 2\mathbf{u}_j^T \mathbf{b}_j + c \; = (\mathbf{u}_j - \mathbf{u}_j^*)^T \mathbf{A}_j (\mathbf{u}_j - \mathbf{u}_j^*) + c' \tag{13.35}$$

where

$$\mathbf{u}_j^* = -\mathbf{A}_j^{-1} \mathbf{b}_j \tag{13.36}$$

is the minimum energy (optimal) flow estimate.

We have applied two techniques for computing $\mathbf{A}_j$ and $\mathbf{b}_j$ from the results of the correlation-style search. The first is to fit (13.35) to the discretely sampled error surface which was used to determine the best shift $\mathbf{u}_0$. Since there are 5 free parameters in $\mathbf{A}_j$ and $\mathbf{b}_j$ ($\mathbf{A}_j$ is symmetric), we can simply

---

[16] To compensate for even larger misregistration, *phase correlation* could be used to estimate a translation for the whole image [267].

fit a bivariate quadratic surface to the central E value and its 4 nearest neighbors (more points can be used, if desired). Note that this fit will implicitly localize the results of the correlation-style search to sub-pixel precision (because of the quadratic fit).

A second approach is to compute $\mathbf{A}_j$ and $\mathbf{b}_j$ using the gradient-based approach (13.33–13.34), but with image $\tilde{I}(\mathbf{x})$ shifted by the estimated amount $\mathbf{u}_0$. After accumulating the new Hessian $\hat{\mathbf{A}}_j$ and residual $\hat{\mathbf{b}}_j$ with respect to the shifted image, we can compute the new gradient-based sub-pixel estimate

$$\hat{\mathbf{u}}_j^* = -\hat{\mathbf{A}}_j^{-1}\hat{\mathbf{b}}_j. \tag{13.37}$$

Adding $\hat{\mathbf{u}}_j^*$ to the correlation-style search displacement $\mathbf{u}_0$, i.e.,

$$\mathbf{u}_j^* = \hat{\mathbf{u}}_j^* + \mathbf{u}_0 \tag{13.38}$$

is equivalent to setting

$$\mathbf{A}_j = \hat{\mathbf{A}}_j, \qquad \mathbf{b}_j = \hat{\mathbf{b}}_j - \mathbf{A}_j\mathbf{u}_0. \tag{13.39}$$

We prefer this second approach, since it results in $\mathbf{A}_j$ estimates which are non-negative definite (important for ensuring that the normal equations can be solved stably), and since it better reflects the certainty in a local match.[17]

13.5 Estimating the Focal Length

In order to apply our 3D rotation technique, we must first obtain an estimate for the camera's focal length. We can obtain such an estimate from one or more perspective transforms computed using the 8-parameter algorithm. Expanding the $\mathbf{V}_1\mathbf{R}\mathbf{V}_0^{-1}$ formulation, we have

$$\mathbf{M} = \begin{bmatrix} m_0 & m_1 & m_2 \\ m_3 & m_4 & m_5 \\ m_6 & m_7 & 1 \end{bmatrix} \sim \begin{bmatrix} r_{00} & r_{01} & r_{02}f_0 \\ r_{10} & r_{11} & r_{12}f_0 \\ r_{20}/f_1 & r_{21}/f_1 & r_{22}f_0/f_1 \end{bmatrix} \tag{13.40}$$

where $\mathbf{R} = [r_{ij}]$.

In order to estimate focal lengths f_0 and f_1, we observe that the first two rows (or columns) of $\mathbf{R}$ must have the same norm and be orthogonal (even if the matrix is scaled), i.e.,

$$m_0{}^2 + m_1{}^2 + m_2{}^2/f_0{}^2 = m_3{}^2 + m_4{}^2 + m_5{}^2/f_0{}^2 \tag{13.41}$$

$$m_0m_3 + m_1m_4 + m_2m_5/f_0{}^2 = 0 \tag{13.42}$$

[17] An analysis of the relationship between these two approaches can be found in [277].

and

$$m_0{}^2 + m_3{}^2 + m_6{}^2 f_1{}^2 = m_1{}^2 + m_4{}^2 + m_7{}^2 f_1{}^2 \qquad (13.43)$$

$$m_0 m_1 + m_3 m_4 + m_6 m_7 f_1{}^2 = 0. \qquad (13.44)$$

From this, we can compute the estimates

$$f_0{}^2 = \frac{m_5{}^2 - m_2{}^2}{m_0{}^2 + m_1{}^2 - m_3{}^2 - m_4{}^2} \quad \text{if } m_0{}^2 + m_1{}^2 \neq m_3{}^2 + m_4{}^2$$

or

$$f_0{}^2 = -\frac{m_2 m_5}{m_0 m_3 + m_1 m_4} \quad \text{if } m_0 m_3 \neq -m_1 m_4.$$

Similar result can be obtained for f_1 as well. If the focal length is fixed for two images, we can take the geometric mean of f_0 and f_1 as the estimated focal length $f = \sqrt{f_1 f_0}$. When multiple estimates of f are available, the median value is used as the final estimate.

13.5.1 Closing the Gap in a Panorama

Even with our best algorithms for recovering rotations and focal length, when a complete panoramic sequence is stitched together, there will invariably be either a gap or an overlap (due to the accumulated errors in the rotation estimates). We solve this problem by registering the same image at both the beginning and the end of the sequence.

The difference in the rotation matrices (actually, their quotient) directly tells us the amount of misregistration. This error can be distributed evenly across the whole sequence by converting the error in rotation into a quaternion, and dividing the quaternion by the number of images in the sequence (for lack of a better guess). We can also update the estimated focal length based on the amount of misregistration. To do this, we first convert the quaternion describing the misregistration into a *gap angle*, θ_g. We can then update the focal length using the equation $f' = f(1 - \theta_g/360°)$.

Figure 13.5a shows the end of registered image sequence and the first image. There is a big gap between the last image and the first which are in fact the same image. The gap is 32° because the wrong estimate of focal length (510) was used. Figure 13.5b shows the registration after closing the gap with the correct focal length (468). Notice that both mosaics show very little visual misregistration (except at the gap), yet Figure 13.5a has been computed using a focal length which has 9% error. Related approaches have been developed by [98, 181, 263, 148] to solve the focal length estimation problem using pure panning motion and cylindrical images. In next section, we present a different approach to removing gaps and overlaps which works for arbitrary image sequences.

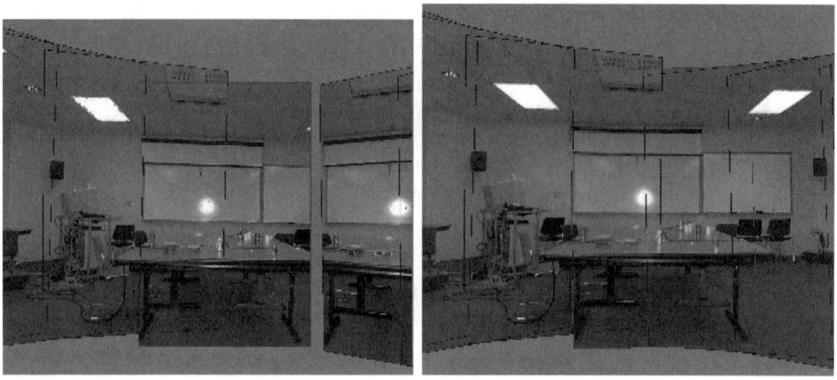

(a) (b)

FIGURE 13.5. Gap closing: (a) a gap is visible when the focal length is wrong ($f = 510$); (b) no gap is visible for the correct focal length ($f = 468$).

13.6 Global Alignment (Block Adjustment)

The sequential mosaic construction techniques described in Sections 13.3 and 13.4 do a good job of aligning each new image with the previously composited mosaic. Unfortunately, for long image sequences, this approach suffers from the problem of accumulated misregistration errors. This problem is particularly severe for panoramic mosaics, where a visible gap (or overlap) will exist between the first and last images in a sequence, even if these two images are the same, as we have seen in the previous section.

In this section, we present our global alignment method, which reduces accumulated error by simultaneously minimizing the misregistration between all overlapping pairs of images. Our method is similar to the *"simultaneous bundle block adjustment"* [295] technique used in photogrammetry but has the following distinct characteristics:

- Corresponding points between pairs of images are automatically obtained using patch-based alignment.
- Our objective function minimizes the difference between ray directions going through corresponding points, and uses a rotational panoramic representation.
- The minimization is formulated as a constrained least-squares problem with hard linear constraints for identical focal lengths and repeated frames.[18]

[18]We have found that it is easier to use certain frames in the sequence more than once during the sequential mosaic formation process (say at the beginning and at the end), and to then use the global alignment stage to make sure that these all have the same associated location.

13.6.1 Establishing the Point Correspondences

Our global alignment algorithm is *feature-based*, i.e., it relies on first establishing point correspondences between overlapping images, rather than doing direct intensity difference minimization (as in the sequential algorithm).

To find our features, we divide each image into a number of patches (e.g., 16×16 pixels), and use the patch centers as prospective feature points. For each patch center, its corresponding point in another image could be determined directly by the current inter-frame transformation $\mathbf{M}_k\mathbf{M}_l^{-1}$. However, since we do not believe that these alignments are optimal, we instead invoke the correlation-style search-based patch alignment algorithm described in Section 13.4.2. (The results of this patch-based alignment are also used for the deghosting technique discussed in the next section.)

Pairs of images are examined only if they have significant overlap, for example, more than a quarter of the image size (see [242] for a general discussion of topology inference). In addition, instead of using all patch centers, we select only those with high confidence (or low uncertainty) measure. Currently we set a threshold for the minimum eigenvalue of each 2×2 patch Hessian (available from patch-based alignment algorithm) so that patches with uniform texture are excluded [253]. Other measures such as the ratio between two eigenvalues can also be used so that patches where the aperture problem exists can be ignored. Raw intensity error, however, would not make a useful measure for selecting feature patches because of potentially large inter-frame intensity variations (varying exposures, vignetting, etc.).

13.6.2 Optimality Criteria

For a patch j in image k, let $l \in \mathcal{N}_{jk}$ be the set of overlapping images in which patch j is totally contained (under the current set of transformations). Let $\mathbf{x}_{jk}$ be the center of this patch. To compute the patch alignment, we use image k as I_0 and image l as I_1 and invoke the algorithm of Section 13.4.2, which returns an estimated displacement $\mathbf{u}_{jl} = \mathbf{u}_j^*$. The corresponding point in the warped image $\tilde{I}_1$ is thus $\tilde{\mathbf{x}}_{jl} = \mathbf{x}_{jk} + \mathbf{u}_{jl}$. In image l, this point's coordinate is $\mathbf{x}_{jl} \sim \mathbf{M}_l\mathbf{M}_k^{-1}\tilde{\mathbf{x}}_{jl}$, or $\mathbf{x}_{jl} \sim \mathbf{V}_l\mathbf{R}_l\mathbf{R}_k^{-1}\mathbf{V}_k^{-1}\tilde{\mathbf{x}}_{jl}$ if the rotational panoramic representation is used.

Given these point correspondences, one way to formulate the global alignment is to minimize the difference between screen coordinates of all overlapping pairs of images,

$$E(\{\mathbf{M}_k\}) = \sum_{j,k,l\in\mathcal{N}_{jk}} \|\mathbf{x}_{jk} - \mathcal{P}(\mathbf{M}_k\mathbf{M}_l^{-1}\mathbf{x}_{jl})\|^2 \tag{13.45}$$

where $\mathcal{P}(\mathbf{M}_k\mathbf{M}_l^{-1}\mathbf{x}_{jl})$ is the projected screen coordinate of $\mathbf{x}_{jl}$ under the transformation $\mathbf{M}_k\mathbf{M}_l^{-1}$ ($\mathbf{M}_k$ could be a general homography, or could be

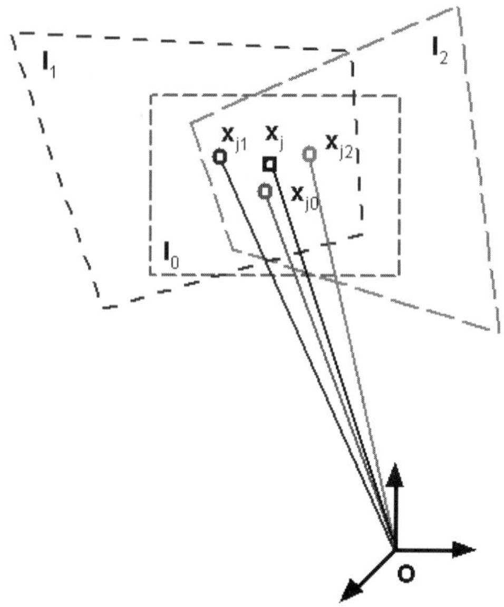

FIGURE 13.6. Illustration of simultaneous bundle block adjustment: we adjust the bundle of rays going through corresponding point features $\mathbf{x}_{jk}$ on overlapping images so that they converge to the ray going through $\mathbf{x}_j$.

based on the rotational panoramic representation). This has the advantage of being able to incorporate local certainties in the point matches (by making the above norm be a matrix norm based on the local Hessian $\mathbf{A}_{jk}$). The disadvantage, however, is that the gradients with respect to the motion parameters are complicated (Section 13.3). We shall return to this problem in Section 13.6.4.

A simpler formulation can be obtained by minimizing the difference between the ray directions of corresponding points using a rotational panoramic representation with unknown focal length. Geometrically, this is equivalent to adjusting the rotation and focal length for each frame so that the bundle of corresponding rays converge, as shown in Figure 13.6.

Let the ray direction in the final composited image mosaic be a unit vector $\mathbf{p}_j$, and its corresponding ray direction in the kth frame as $\mathbf{p}_{jk} \sim \mathbf{R}_k^{-1}\mathbf{V}_k^{-1}\mathbf{x}_{jk}$. We can formulate block adjustment to simultaneously optimize over both the pose (rotation and focal length $\{\mathbf{R}_k, f_k\}$) and structure (ray direction $\{\mathbf{p}_j\}$) parameters,

$$E(\{\mathbf{R}_k, f_k\}, \{\mathbf{p}_j\}) = \sum_{j,k} \|\mathbf{p}_{jk} - \mathbf{p}_j\|^2 = \sum_{j,k} \|\mathbf{R}_k^{-1}\hat{\mathbf{x}}_{jk} - \mathbf{p}_j\|^2 \qquad (13.46)$$

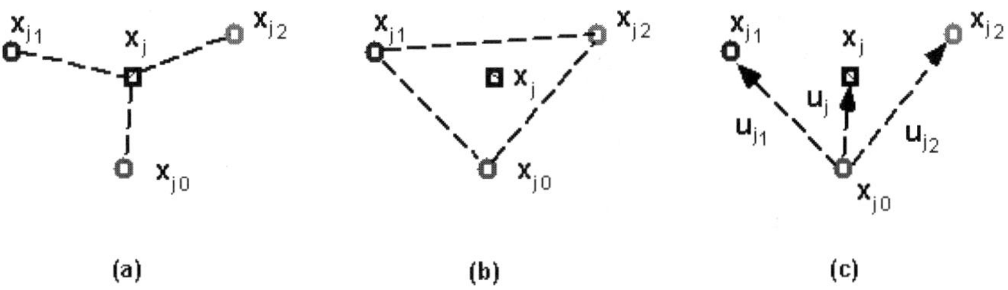

FIGURE 13.7. Comparison between two global registration methods: (a) minimizing the difference between all rays $\mathbf{p}_{jk}$ (with measured feature locations $\mathbf{x}_{jk}$) and $\mathbf{p}_j$ (at the predicted location $\mathbf{x}_j$); (b) minimizing the difference between all pairs of rays $\mathbf{p}_{jk}$ and $\mathbf{p}_{jl}$ (with feature locations $\mathbf{x}_{jk}$ and $\mathbf{x}_{jl}$ in overlapping images). (c) The desired flow for deghosting $\overline{\mathbf{u}}_{jk}$ is a down-weighted average of all pairwise flows $\mathbf{u}_{jl}$.

where

$$\hat{\mathbf{x}}_{jk} = \begin{bmatrix} x_{jk} \\ y_{jk} \\ f_k \end{bmatrix} / l_{jk} \tag{13.47}$$

is the ray direction going through the jth feature point located at (x_{jk}, y_{jk}) in the kth frame, and

$$l_{jk} = \sqrt{x_{jk}{}^2 + y_{jk}{}^2 + f_k{}^2} \tag{13.48}$$

(note that this absorbs the f_k parameter in V_k into the coordinate definition).

The advantage of the above direct minimization (13.46) is that both pose and structure can be solved independently for each frame. For instance, we can solve $\mathbf{p}_j$ using linear least-squares, $\mathbf{R}_k$ using relative orientation, and f_k using nonlinear least-squares. The disadvantage of this method is its slow convergence due to the highly coupled nature of the equations and unknowns.[19]

For the purpose of global alignment, however, it is not necessary to explicitly recover the ray directions. We can reformulate block adjustment to only minimize over pose ($\{\mathbf{R}_k, f_k\}$) for all frames k, without computing the $\{\mathbf{p}_j\}$. More specifically, we estimate the pose by minimizing the difference in ray directions between all pairs (k and l) of overlapping images,

$$E(\{\mathbf{R}_k, f_k\}) = \sum_{j,k,l \in \mathcal{N}_{jk}} \|\mathbf{p}_{jk} - \mathbf{p}_{jl}\|^2 = \sum_{j,k,l \in \mathcal{N}_{jk}} \|\mathbf{R}_k^{-1}\hat{\mathbf{x}}_{jk} - \mathbf{R}_l^{-1}\hat{\mathbf{x}}_{jl}\|^2 \tag{13.49}$$

[19]Imagine a chain of spring-connected masses. If we pull one end sharply, and then set each mass to the average of its neighbors, it will take the process a long time to reach equilibrium. This situation is analogous.

Once the pose has been computed, we can compute the estimated directions $\mathbf{p}_j$ using the known correspondence from all overlapping frames $\mathcal{N}_{jk}$ where the feature point j is visible,

$$\mathbf{p}_j \sim \frac{1}{n_{jk}+1} \sum_{l \in \{\mathcal{N}_{jk} \cup k\}} \mathbf{R}_l^{-1} \mathbf{V}_l^{-1} \mathbf{x}_{jl}. \tag{13.50}$$

where $n_{jk} = |\mathcal{N}_{jk}|$ is the number of overlapping images where patch j is completely visible (this information will be used later in the deghosting stage).

Figure 13.7 shows the difference between the above two formulations. Figure 13.7a shows how the difference being minimized (dashed lines) is between the expected feature location $\mathbf{x}_j$ (or the expected ray $\mathbf{p}_j$ going through) and all feature locations $\mathbf{x}_{jk}$ (or the rays $\mathbf{p}_{jk}$ going through), while Figure 13.7b shows minimizing the difference between all pairs of features $\mathbf{x}_{jk}$ (or the rays $\mathbf{p}_{jk}$ going through) on the overlapping images.

13.6.3 Solution Technique

The least-squares problem (13.49) can be solved using regular gradient descent method. To recover the pose $\{\mathbf{R}_k, f_k\}$, we iteratively update the ray directions $\mathbf{p}_{jk}(\mathbf{x}_{jk}; \mathbf{R}_k, f_k)$ to

$$\mathbf{R}_k^{-1} \leftarrow \hat{\mathbf{R}}(\mathbf{\Omega_k})\mathbf{R_k^{-1}} \quad \text{and} \quad \mathbf{f_k} \leftarrow \mathbf{f_k} + \delta\mathbf{f_k}. \tag{13.51}$$

The minimization problem (13.49) can be rewritten as

$$E(\{\mathbf{R}_k, f_k\}) = \sum_{j,k,l \in \mathcal{N}_{jk}} \|\mathbf{H}_{jk}\mathbf{y}_k - \mathbf{H}_{jl}\mathbf{y}_l + \mathbf{e}_j\|^2 \tag{13.52}$$

where

$$\begin{aligned}
\mathbf{e}_j &= \mathbf{p}_{jk} - \mathbf{p}_{jl}, \\
\mathbf{y}_k &= \begin{bmatrix} \mathbf{\Omega}_k \\ \delta f_k \end{bmatrix}, \\
\mathbf{H}_{jk} &= \begin{bmatrix} \frac{\partial \mathbf{p}_{jk}}{\partial \mathbf{\Omega}_k} \\ \frac{\partial \mathbf{p}_{jk}}{\partial f_k} \end{bmatrix},
\end{aligned}$$

and

$$\frac{\partial \mathbf{p}_{jk}}{\partial \mathbf{\Omega}_k} = \frac{\partial(\mathbf{I} + \mathbf{X}(\mathbf{\Omega}))\mathbf{p}_{jk}}{\partial \mathbf{\Omega}_k} = \frac{\partial}{\partial \mathbf{\Omega}_k} \begin{bmatrix} 1 & -\omega_z & \omega_y \\ \omega_z & 1 & -\omega_x \\ -\omega_y & \omega_x & 1 \end{bmatrix} \mathbf{p}_{jk} = -\mathbf{X}(\mathbf{p}_{jk}), \tag{13.53}$$

$$\frac{\partial \mathbf{p}_{jk}}{\partial f_k} = \mathbf{R}_k^{-1} \frac{\partial \tilde{\mathbf{x}}_{jk}}{\partial f_j} = \mathbf{R}_k^{-1} \begin{bmatrix} -x_{jk} f_k \\ -y_{jk} f_k \\ {l_{jk}}^2 - {f_k}^2 \end{bmatrix} / {l_{jk}}^3. \tag{13.54}$$

We therefore have the following linear equation for each point j matched in both frames k and l,

$$\begin{bmatrix} \mathbf{H}_{jk} & -\mathbf{H}_{jl} \end{bmatrix} \begin{bmatrix} \mathbf{y}_j \\ \mathbf{y}_k \end{bmatrix} = -\mathbf{e}_i \tag{13.55}$$

which leads to normal equations

$$\mathbf{A}\mathbf{y} = -\mathbf{b} \tag{13.56}$$

where the 4×4 (k, k)th block diagonal term and (k, l)th block off-diagonal term [20] of the symmetric $\mathbf{A}$ are defined by

$$\mathbf{A}_{kk} = \sum_j {\mathbf{H}_{jk}}^T \mathbf{H}_{jk} \tag{13.57}$$

$$\mathbf{A}_{kl} = -\sum_j {\mathbf{H}_{jk}}^T \mathbf{H}_{jl} \tag{13.58}$$

and the kth and lth 4×1 blocks of $\mathbf{b}$ are

$$\mathbf{b}_k = \sum_j {\mathbf{H}_{jk}}^T \mathbf{e}_j \tag{13.59}$$

$$\mathbf{b}_l = -\sum_j {\mathbf{H}_{jl}}^T \mathbf{e}_j. \tag{13.60}$$

Because $\mathbf{A}$ is symmetric, the normal equations can be stably solved using a symmetric positive definite (SPD) linear system solver. By incorporating additional constraints on the pose, we can formulate our minimization problem (13.49) as a constrained least-squares problem which can be solved using Lagrange multipliers. Details of the constrained least-squares can be found in Appendix 13.11. Possible linear constraints include:

- $\Omega_0 = 0$. First frame pose is unchanged. For example, the first frame can be chosen as the world coordinate system.
- $\delta f_k = 0$ for all N frames $j = 0, 1, ..., N - 1$. All focal lengths are known.

[20] The sequential pairwise alignment algorithm described in Section 2 and Section 3 can be regarded as a special case of the global alignment (13.56) where the off-diagonal terms $\mathbf{A}_{kl}$ (13.58) and $\mathbf{b}_l$ (13.60) are zero if frame k is set fixed.

- $\delta f_k = \delta f_0$ for $j = 1, ..., N$. All focal lengths are the same but unknown.
- $\delta f_k = \delta f_l$, $\Omega_k = \Omega_l$, Frame j is the same as frame k. In order to apply this constraint, we also need to set $f_k = f_l$ and $\mathbf{R}_k = \mathbf{R}_l$.

The above minimization process converges quickly (several iterations) in practice. The running time for the iterative non-linear least-squares solver is much less than the time required to build the point correspondences.

13.6.4 Optimizing in Screen Coordinates

Now we return to Equation (13.45) to solve global alignment using screen coordinates. If we update $\mathbf{M}_k$ and $\mathbf{M}_l$ by

$$\mathbf{M}_k \leftarrow (\mathbf{I} + \mathbf{D}_k)\mathbf{M}_k \quad \text{and} \quad \mathbf{M}_l \leftarrow (\mathbf{I} + \mathbf{D}_l)\mathbf{M}_l, \tag{13.61}$$

we get

$$\begin{aligned} \mathbf{M}_{kl} &\leftarrow (\mathbf{I} + \mathbf{D}_{kl})\mathbf{M}_{kl} \\ &= (\mathbf{I} + \mathbf{D}_k)\mathbf{M}_k\mathbf{M}_l^{-1}(\mathbf{I} - \mathbf{D}_l) \\ &= (\mathbf{I} + \mathbf{D}_k - \mathbf{M}_{kl}\mathbf{D}_l\mathbf{M}_{kl}^{-1})\mathbf{M}_{kl}. \end{aligned}$$

Because of linear relationship between $\mathbf{D}_{kl}$ and $\mathbf{D}_k$, $\mathbf{D}_l$, we can find out the Jacobians

$$\mathbf{J}_k = \frac{\partial \mathbf{d}_{kl}}{\partial \mathbf{d}_k} \quad \text{and} \quad \mathbf{J}_l = \frac{\partial \mathbf{d}_{kl}}{\partial \mathbf{d}_l}. \tag{13.62}$$

In fact, $\mathbf{J}_k = \mathbf{I}$. Since we know how to estimate $\mathbf{D}_{kl}$ from patch-based alignment, we can expand the original 8×8 system (assuming perspective case) $\mathbf{A}\mathbf{d}_{kl} = \mathbf{b}$ to four blocks of 8×8 system, much like equations (57)-(60). An example of global alignment in screen coordinates is shown in Section 13.8.

13.7 Deghosting (Local Alignment)

After the global alignment has been run, there may still be localized mis-registrations present in the image mosaic, due to deviations from the idealized parallax-free camera model. Such deviations might include camera translation (especially for hand-held cameras), radial distortion, the mis-location of the optical center (which can be significant for scanned photographs or Photo CDs), and moving objects.

To compensate for these effects, we would like to quantify the amount of mis-registration and to then locally warp each image so that the overall mosaic does not contain visible *ghosting* (double images) or blurred details. If our mosaic contains just a few images, we could choose one image as the *base*, and then compute the optical flow between it and all other images, which could then be deformed to match the base. Another possibility would be to explicitly estimate the camera motion and residual parallax [161, 239, 271], but this would not compensate for other distortions.

However, since we are dealing with large image mosaics, we need an approach which makes all of the images globally consistent, without a preferred base. One approach might be to warp each image so that it best matches the current mosaic. For small amounts of misregistration, where most of the visual effects are simple blurring (loss of detail), this should work fairly well. However, for large misregistrations, where ghosting is present, the local motion estimation would likely fail. Another approach is to select pixels from only one image at a time [185, 214, 297, 56].

The approach we have adopted is to compute the flow between all pairs of images, and to then infer the desired local warps from these computations. While in principle any motion estimation or optical flow technique could be used, we use the the patch-based alignment algorithm described in Section 13.4.2, since it provides us with the required information and allows us to reason about geometric consistency.

Recall that the block adjustment algorithm (Section 13.50) provides an estimate $\mathbf{p}_j$ of the true direction in space corresponding to the jth patch center in the kth image, $\mathbf{x}_{jk}$. The projection of this direction onto the kth image is

$$\mathbf{x}_{jk} \sim \mathbf{V}_k \mathbf{R}_k \frac{1}{n_{jk}+1} \sum_{l \in \{\mathcal{N}_{jk} \cup k\}} \mathbf{R}_l^{-1} \mathbf{V}_l^{-1} \mathbf{x}_{jl} = \frac{1}{n_{jk}+1} \left(\mathbf{x}_{jk} + \sum_{l \in \mathcal{N}_{jk}} \tilde{\mathbf{x}}_{jl} \right). \tag{13.63}$$

This can be converted into a motion estimate

$$\overline{\mathbf{u}}_{jk} = \mathbf{x}_{jk} - \mathbf{x}_{jk} = \frac{1}{n_{jk}+1} \sum_{l \in \mathcal{N}_{jk}} (\tilde{\mathbf{x}}_{jl} - \mathbf{x}_{jk}) = \frac{1}{n_{jk}+1} \sum_{l \in \mathcal{N}_{jk}} \mathbf{u}_{jl}. \tag{13.64}$$

This formula has a very nice, intuitively satisfying explanation (Figure 13.7c). The local motion required to bring patch center j in image k into global registration is simply the average of the pairwise motion estimates with all overlapping images, *downweighted* by the fraction $n_{jk}/(n_{jk}+1)$. This factor prevents local motion estimates from "overshooting" in their corrections (consider, for example, just two images, where each image warps itself to match its neighbor). Thus, we can compute the location motion estimate for each image by simply examining its misregistration with its neighbors, without having to worry about what warps these other neighbors might be undergoing themselves.

Once the local motion estimates have been computed, we need an algorithm to warp each image so as to reduce ghosting. One possibility would be to use a *forward mapping* algorithm [294] to convert each image I_k into a new image I'_k. However, this has the disadvantage of being expensive to compute, and of being susceptible to tears and foldovers.

Instead, we use an *inverse mapping* algorithm, which was already present in our system to perform warpings into cylindrical coordinates and to optionally compensate for radial lens distortions [273]. Thus, for each pixel in the *new* (warped) image I'_k, we need to know the relative distance (flow) to the appropriate source pixel. We compute this field using a sparse data interpolation technique [202]. The input to this algorithm is the set of negative flows $-\bar{\mathbf{u}}_{jk}$ located at pixel coordinates $\mathbf{x}_{jk} = \mathbf{x}_{jk} + \bar{\mathbf{u}}_{jk}$. At present, we simply place a tent (bilinear) function over each flow sample (the size is currently twice the patch size). To make this interpolator locally *reproducing* (no "dips" in the interpolated surface), we divide each accumulated flow value by the accumulated weight (plus a small amount, say 0.1, to round the transitions into regions with no motion estimates[21]).[22]

The results of our deghosting technique can be seen in Figures 13.11–13.14 along with some sample computed warp fields. Note that since the deghosting technique may not give perfect results (because it is patch-based, and not pixel-based), we may wish to iteratively apply the algorithm (the warp field is simply incrementally updated).

Even though we have formulated local alignment using rotational mosaic representation, the deghosting equation (13.63) is valid for other motion models (e.g., 8-parameter perspective) as well. We need only to modify (13.63) to

$$\mathbf{x}_{jk} \sim \mathbf{M}_k \frac{1}{n_{jk}+1} \sum_{l \in \{\mathcal{N}_{jk} \cup k\}} \mathbf{M}_l^{-1} \mathbf{x}_{jl} = \frac{1}{n_{jk}+1} \left(\mathbf{x}_{jk} + \sum_{l \in \mathcal{N}_{jk}} \tilde{\mathbf{x}}_{jl} \right). \tag{13.65}$$

13.8 Experiments

In this section we present the results of applying our global and local alignment techniques to image mosaicing. We have tested our methods on a number of real image sequences. In all of the experiments, we have used the rotational panoramic representation with unknown focal length. In general, two neighbor images have about 50% overlap.

The speed of our patch-based image alignment depends on the following parameters: motion model, image size, alignment accuracy, level of pyra-

[21]This makes the interpolant no longer perfectly reproducing.

[22]In computer graphics, this kind of interpolation is often called *splatting* [292].

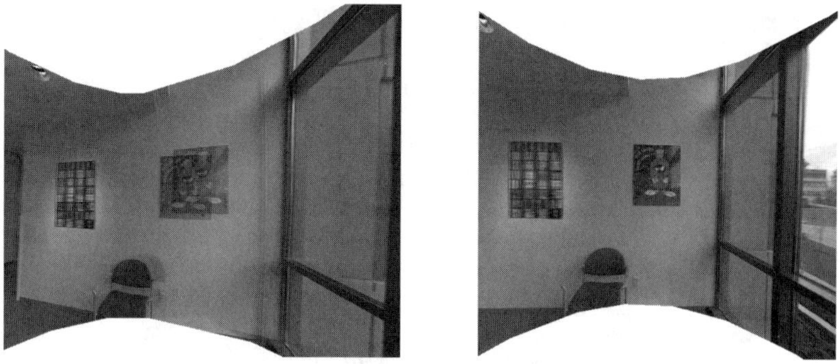

(a) (b)

FIGURE 13.8. Reducing accumulated errors of image mosaics by block adjustment. (a): image mosaics with gaps/overlap; (b): corresponding mosaics after applying block adjustment.

mid, patch size, and initial misalignment. Typically, we set the patch size 16, the alignment accuracy 0.04 pixel, and we use a 3 level pyramid. Using our rotational model, it takes a few seconds (on a Pentium 200MHz PC) to align two images of size 384×300, with an initial misregistration of about 30 pixels. The speed of global alignment and local alignment mainly depends on the correlation-style search range while building feature correspondence. It takes several minutes to do the block adjustment for a sequence of 20 images with a patch size of 16 and a search range of 4.

13.8.1 Global Alignment

The first example shows how misregistration errors quickly accumulate in sequential registration. Figure 13.8a shows a big gap at the end of registering a sequence of 24 images (image size 384×300) where an initial estimate of focal length 256 is used. The double image of the right painting on the wall signals a big misalignment. This double image is removed, as shown in Figure 13.8b, by applying our global alignment method which simultaneously adjusts all frame rotations and computes a new estimated focal length of 251.8. To reduce the search range for correspondence, we append the first image at the end of image sequence and enforce a hard constraint that the first image has to be the last one.

In Section 13.5, we proposed an alternative "gap closing" technique to handle the accumulated misregistration error. However, this technique only works well for a sequence of images with uniform motion steps. It also requires that the sequence of images follow a great circle on the viewing sphere. The global alignment method in Section 13.6, on the other hand, does not make such assumptions. For example, our global alignment method can handle the misalignment (Figure 13.9c, which is the close-up of double image on the middle left side of Figure 13.9a) of an image mosaic

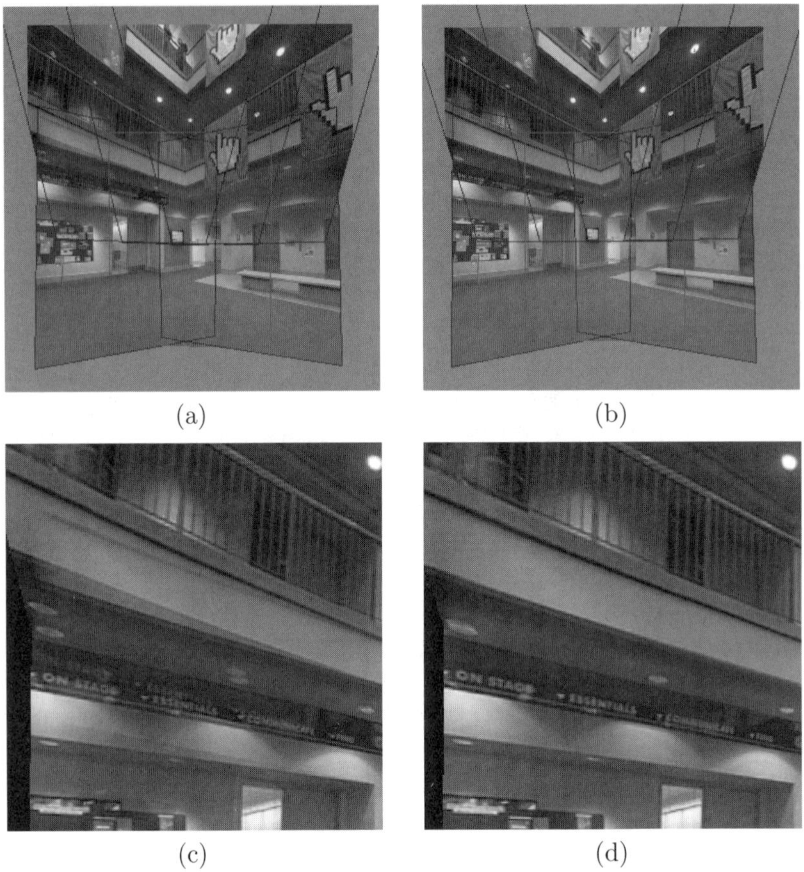

FIGURE 13.9. Reducing accumulated errors of image mosaics by block adjustment. (a): image mosaics with gaps/overlap; (b): corresponding mosaics after applying block adjustment; (c) and (d): close-ups of left middle regions of (a) and (b), respectively.

which is constructed from 6 images taken with a camera leveled and tilted up. Figures 13.9b and 13.9d (close-up) show the image mosaic after block adjustment where the visible artifacts are no longer apparent. In this example we do not enforce the constraint that the first frame has to be the last one (i.e., do not add the first image to the end of sequence), nor do the images form a great circle on the viewing sphere (only six images are used).

As discussed in Section 13.6.4, our global alignment method also works for non-rotational motion models (e.g., perspective) where optimization is formulated in screen coordinates. Figure 13.10a shows an image mosaic composed of 5 whiteboard images using 8-parameter perspective model. The double image in the top left region of Figure 13.10a (or Figure 13.10c

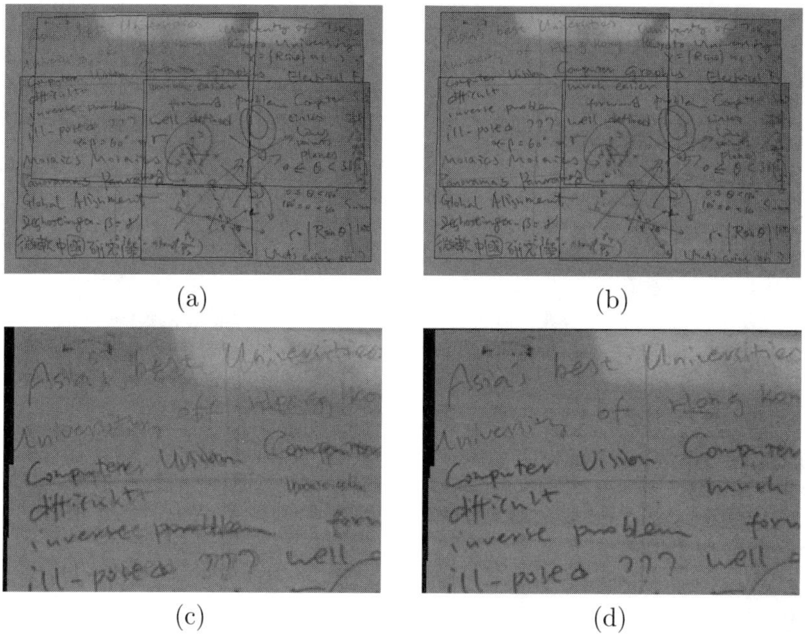

FIGURE 13.10. Reducing accumulated errors of image mosaics by global alignment in screen coordinates. (a): image mosaic with error accumulation (at the top left region); (c): corresponding mosaic after applying global alignment; (b) and (d): close-ups of (a) and (c) respectively.

for a close-up) due to accumulated registration error is significantly reduced after applying our global alignment method, as shown in Figure 13.10b and 13.10d.

13.8.2 Local Alignment

The next two examples illustrate the use of local alignment for sequences where the global motion model is clearly violated. The first example consists of two images taken with a hand-held digital camera (Kodak DC40) where some camera translation is present. The parallax introduced by this camera translation can be observed in the registered image (Figure 13.11a) where the front object (a stop sign) causes a double image because of the misregistration. This misalignment is significantly reduced using our local alignment method (Figure 13.11b). However, some visual artifacts still exist because our local alignment is patch-based (e.g. patch size 32 is used in Figure 13.11b). To overcome this problem, we repeatedly apply local alignment with successively smaller patches, which has the advantage of being able to handle large motion parallax and refine local alignment. Figure 13.11c shows the result after applying local alignment three times with patch sizes of 32, 16 and 8. The search range has been set to be half of

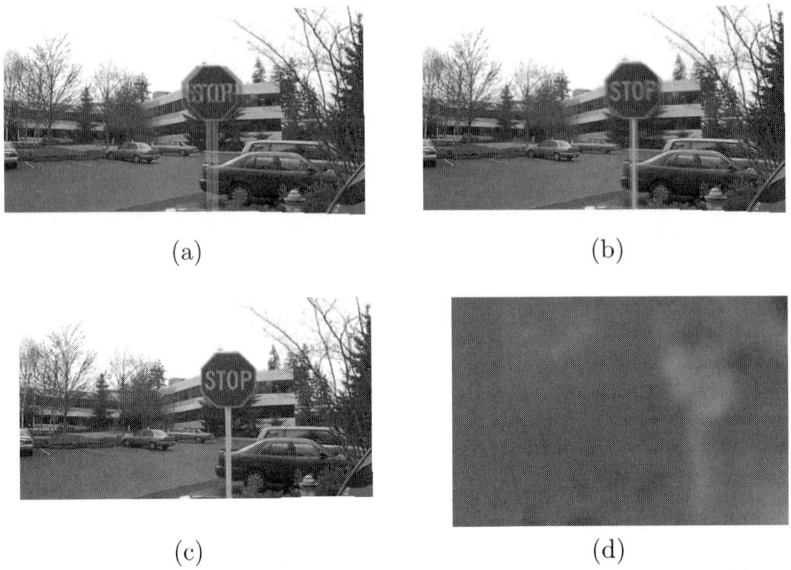

FIGURE 13.11. Deghosting an image mosaic with motion parallax: (a) image mosaic with parallax; (b) after single deghosting step (patch size 32); (c) after multiple deghosting steps (patch sizes 32, 16 and 8); (d) flow field of the left image.

the patch size for reliable patch motion estimation. Figure 13.11d shows the flow field corresponding to the left image (Figure 13.11e). Red values indicate rightward motion (e.g. the stop sign).

The global motion model is also invalid when registering two images with strong optical distortion. One way to deal with radial distortion is to carefully calibrate the camera. Another way is to use local alignment, making it possible to register images with optical distortion without using explicit camera calibration (i.e., recovering lens radial distortion).[23] Figure 13.12d shows one of two images taken with a Pulnix camera and a Fujinon F2.8 wide angle lens. This picture shows significant radial distortion; notice how straight lines (e.g., the door) are curved. The registration result is shown in Figure 13.12a. The mosaic after deghosting with a patch size 32 and search range 16 is shown in Figure 13.12b. Figure 13.12c shows an improved mosaic using repeated local alignment with patch sizes 32, 16, 8. The flow fields in Figure 13.12e–f show that the flow becomes larger towards the corner of the image due to radial distortion (bright green is upward motion, red is rightward motion). Notice however that these warp fields do *not* encode

[23]The recovered deformation field is not guaranteed, however, to be the true radial distortion, especially when only a few images are being registered. Recall that the minimum norm field is selected at each deghosting step.

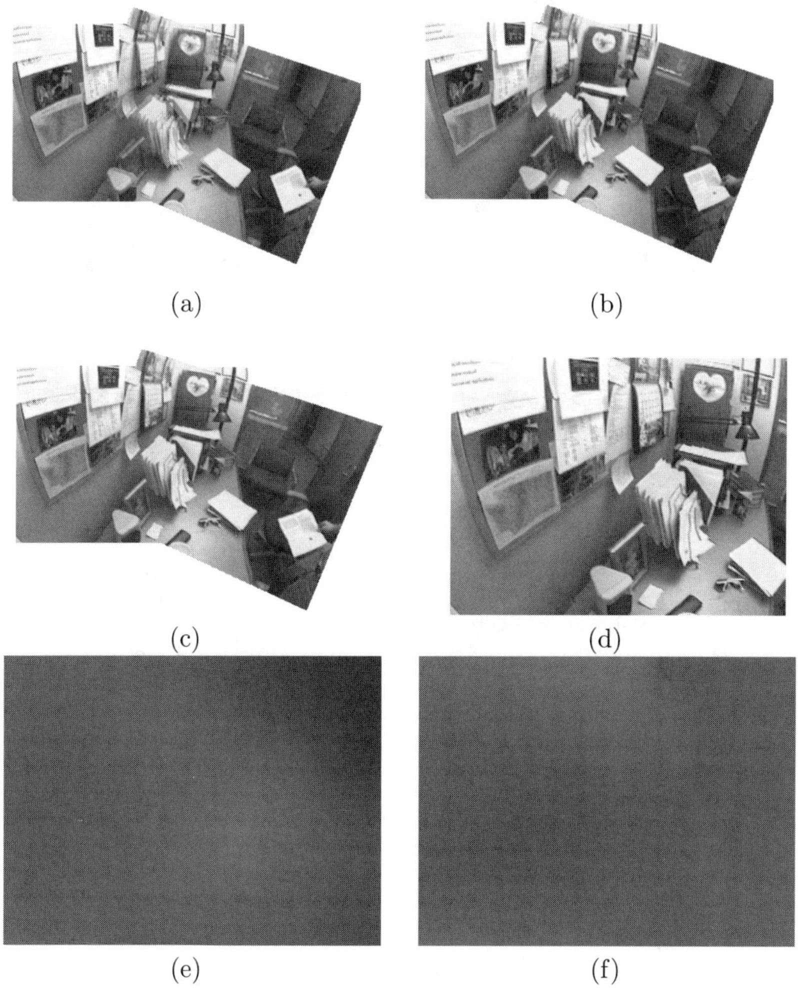

FIGURE 13.12. Deghosting an image mosaic with optical distortion: (a) image mosaic with distortion; (b) after single deghosting step (patch size 32); (c) after multiple deghosting steps (patch sizes 32, 16 and 8); (d) original left image; (e–f) flow fields of the two images after local alignment.

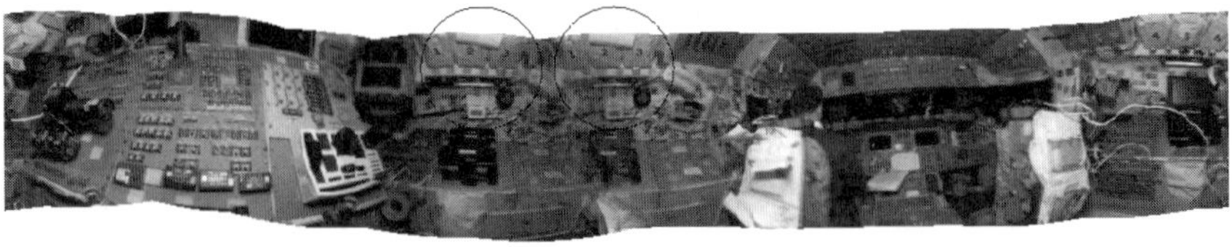

(a)

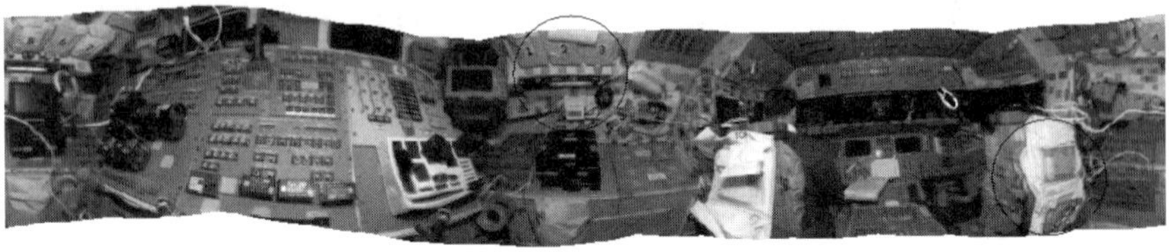

(b)

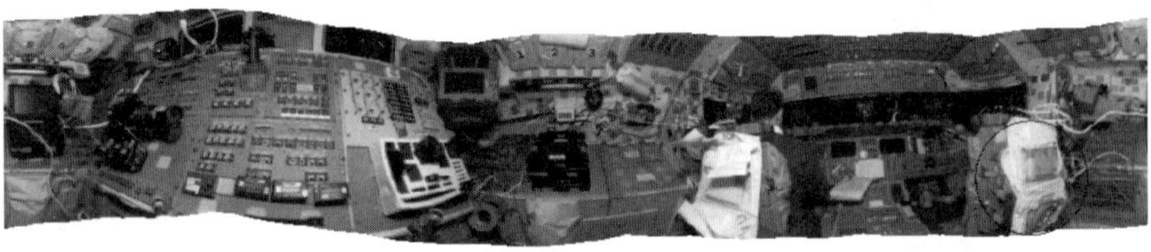

(c)

FIGURE 13.13. Panoramic image mosaics constructed from images taken with a hand-held camera: (a) significant accumulated error is visible in the center (repeated numbers 1-2-3); (b) with block adjustment, only small imperfections remain, such as the double image on the right pilot's chair; (c) with deghosting, the mosaic is virtually perfect.

the true radial distortion. A parametric deformation model (e.g., the usual quadratic plus quartic terms) would have to be used instead.

13.8.3 Additional Examples

We present two additional examples of large panoramic mosaics. The first mosaic uses a sequence of 14 images taken with a hand-held camera by an astronaut on the Space Shuttle flight deck. This sequence of images has significant motion parallax and is very difficult to register. The accumulated error causes a very big gap between the first and last images as shown in Figure 13.13a (notice the repeated "1 2 3" numbers, which should only appear once). We are able to construct a good quality panorama (Figure 13.13b) using our block adjustment technique (there is some visible ghosting, however, near the right pilot chair). This panorama is further

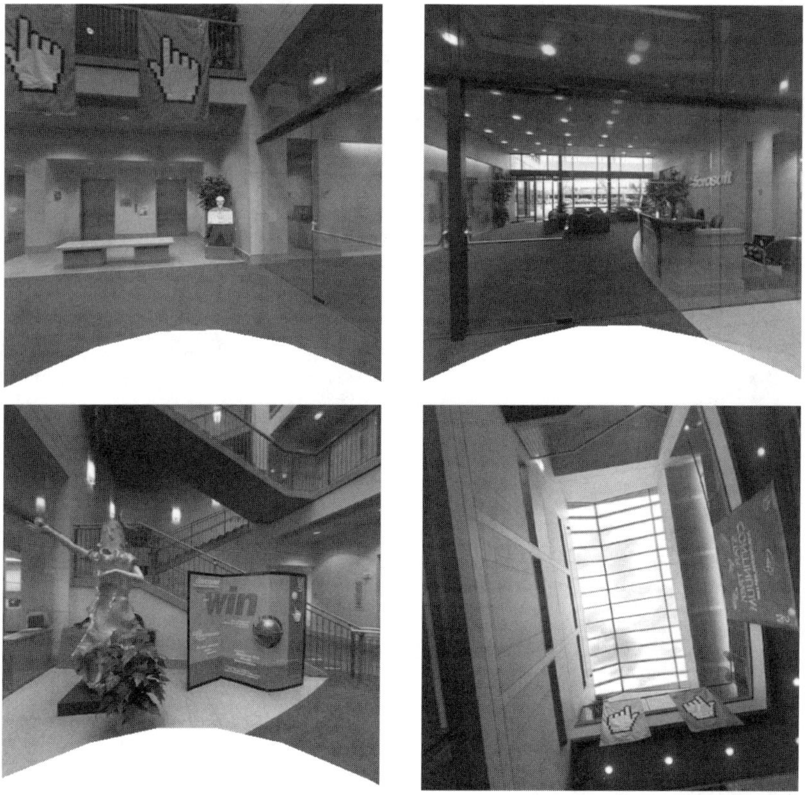

FIGURE 13.14. Four views of an image mosaic of lobby constructed from 3 sequences of 50 images.

refined with deghosting as shown in Figure 13.13c. These panoramas were rendered by projecting the image mosaic onto a tessellated spherical map.

The final example shows how to build a full view panoramic mosaic. Three panoramic image sequences of a building lobby were taken with the camera on a tripod tilted at three different angles (with 22 images for the middle sequence, 22 images for the upper sequence, and 10 images for the top sequence). The camera motion covers more than two thirds of the viewing sphere, including the top. After registering all of the images sequentially with patch-based alignment, we apply our global and local alignment techniques to obtain the final image mosaic, shown in Figure 13.14. These four views of the final image mosaic are equivalent to images taken with a very large rectilinear lens. Each view is twice as big as the input image (300×384 with focal length 268), therefore, is equivalent to vertical field of view 110 degrees. A tessellated spherical map of the full view panorama is shown in Figure 13.15. Our algorithm for building texture-mapped polyhedra from panoramic image mosaics is described in the next section.

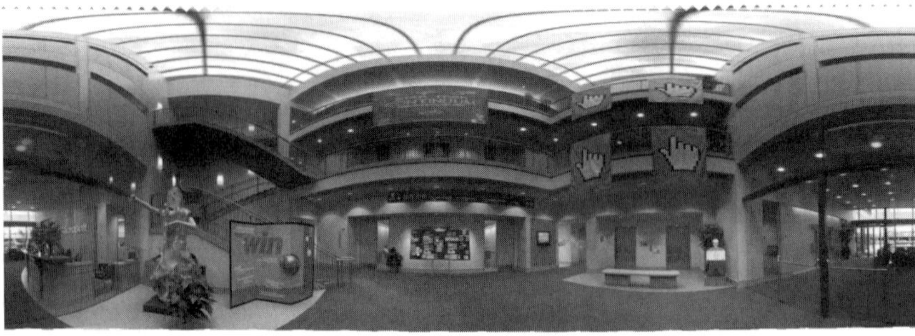

FIGURE 13.15. Tessellated spherical panorama covering the north pole (constructed from 50 images). The white triangles at the top are the parts of the texture map not covered in the 3D tessellated globe model (due to triangular elements at the poles).

13.9 Environment Map Construction

Once we have constructed a complete panoramic mosaic, we need to convert the set of input images and associated transforms into one or more images which can be quickly rendered or viewed.

A traditional way to do this is to choose either a cylindrical or spherical map (Section 13.2). When being used as an environment map, such a representation is sometimes called a latitude-longitude projection [86]. The color associated with each pixel is computed by first converting the pixel address to a 3D ray, and then mapping this ray into each input image through our known transformation. The colors picked up from each image are then blended using the weighting function (feathering) described earlier. For example, we can convert our rotational panorama to spherical panorama using the following algorithm:

1. for each pixel (θ, ϕ) in the spherical map, compute its corresponding 3D position on unit sphere $\mathbf{p} = (X, Y, Z)$ where $X = cos(\phi)sin(\theta), Y = sin(\phi)$, and $Z = cos(\phi)cos(\theta)$;

2. for each $\mathbf{p}$, determine its mapping into each image k using $\mathbf{x} \sim \mathbf{T}_k\mathbf{V}_k\mathbf{R}_k\mathbf{p}$;

3. form a composite (blended) image from the above warped images.

Unfortunately, such a map requires a specialized viewer, and thus cannot take advantage of any hardware texture-mapping acceleration (without approximating the cylinder's or sphere's shape with a polyhedron, which would introduce distortions into the rendering). For true full-view panoramas, spherical maps also introduce a distortion around each pole.

As an alternative, we propose the use of traditional texture-mapped models, i.e., environment maps [86]. The shape of the model and the embedding of each face into texture space are left up to the user. This choice can range from something as simple as a cube with six separate texture maps [86], to something as complicated as a subdivided dodecahedron, or even a latitude-longitude tessellated globe.[24] This choice will depend on the characteristics of the rendering hardware and the desired quality (e.g., minimizing distortions or local changes in pixel size), and on external considerations such as the ease of painting on the resulting texture maps (since some embeddings may leave gaps in the texture map).

In this section, we describe how to efficiently compute texture map color values for any geometry and choice of texture map coordinates. A generalization of this algorithm can be used to project a collection of images onto an arbitrary model, e.g., non-convex models which do not surround the viewer.

We assume that the object model is a triangulated surface, i.e., a collection of triangles and vertices, where each vertex is tagged with its 3D (X, Y, Z) coordinates and (u, v) texture coordinates (faces may be assigned to different texture maps). We restrict the model to triangular faces in order to obtain a simple, closed-form solution (projective map, potentially different for each triangle) between texture coordinates and image coordinates. The output of our algorithm is a set of colored texture maps, with undefined (invisible) pixels flagged (e.g., if an alpha channel is used, then $\alpha \leftarrow 0$).

Our algorithm consists of the following four steps:

1. paint each triangle in (u, v) space a unique color;
2. for each triangle, determine its $(u, v, 1) \to (X, Y, Z)$ mapping;
3. for each triangle, form a composite (blended) image;
4. paint the composite image into the final texture map using the color values computed in step 1 as a stencil.

These four steps are described in more detail below.

The pseudocoloring (triangle painting) step uses an auxiliary buffer the same size as the texture map. We use an RGB image, which means that 2^{24} colors are available. After the initial coloring, we grow the colors into invisible regions using a simple dilation operation, i.e., iteratively replacing invisible pixels with one of their visible neighbor pseudocolors. This operation is performed in order to eliminate small gaps in the texture map, and to support filtering operations such as bilinear texture mapping and MIP mapping [293]. For example, when using a six-sided cube, we set the (u, v)

[24]This latter representation is equivalent to a spherical map in the limit as the globe facets become infinitesimally small. The important difference is that even with large facets, an exact rendering can be obtained with regular texture-mapping algorithms and hardware.

coordinates of each square vertex to be slightly inside the margins of the texture map. Thus, each texture map covers a little more region than it needs to, but operation such a texture filtering and MIP mapping can be performed without worrying about edge effects.

In the second step, we compute the $(u, v, 1) \to (X, Y, Z)$ mapping for each triangle T by finding the 3×3 matrix $\mathbf{M}_T$ which satisfies

$$\mathbf{u}_i = \mathbf{M}_T \mathbf{p}_i$$

for each of the three triangle vertices i. Thus, $\mathbf{M}_T = \mathbf{U}\mathbf{P}^{-1}$, where $\mathbf{U} = [\mathbf{u}_0|\mathbf{u}_1|\mathbf{u}_2]$ and $\mathbf{P} = [\mathbf{p}_0|\mathbf{p}_1|\mathbf{p}_2]$ are formed by concatenating the $\mathbf{u}_i$ and $\mathbf{p}_i$ 3-vectors. This mapping is essentially a mapping from 3D directions in space (since the cameras are all at the origin) to (u, v) coordinates.

In the third step, we compute a bounding box around each triangle in (u, v) space and enlarge it slightly (by the same amount as the dilation in step 1). We then form a composite image by blending all of the input images j according to the transformation $\mathbf{u} = \mathbf{M}_T \mathbf{R}_k^{-1} \mathbf{V}_k^{-1} \mathbf{x}$. This is a full, 8-parameter perspective transformation. It is *not* the same as the 6-parameter affine map which would be obtained by simply projecting a triangle's vertices into the image, and then mapping these 2D image coordinates into 2D texture space (in essence ignoring the foreshortening in the projection onto the 3D model). The error in applying this naive but erroneous method to large texture map facets (e.g., those of a simple unrefined cube) would be quite large.

In the fourth step, we find the pseudocolor associated with each pixel inside the composited patch, and paint the composited color into the texture map if the pseudocolor matches the face id.

Our algorithm can also be used to project a collection of images onto an arbitrary object, i.e., to do true inverse texture mapping, by extending our algorithm to handle occlusions. To do this, we simply paint the pseudocolored polyhedral model into each input image using a z-buffering algorithm (this is called an *item buffer* in ray tracing [290]). When compositing the image for each face, we then check to see which pixels match the desired pseudocolor, and set those which do not match to be invisible (i.e., not to contribute to the final composite).

Figure 13.15 shows the results of mapping a panoramic mosaic onto a longitude-latitude tessellated globe. The white triangles at the top are the parts of the texture map not covered in the 3D tessellated globe model (due to triangular elements at the poles). Figures 13.16–13.18 show the results of mapping three different panoramic mosaics onto cubical environment maps. We can see that the mosaics are of very high quality, and also get a good sense for the extent of viewing sphere covered by these full-view mosaics. Note that Figure 13.16 uses images taken with a hand-held digital camera.

Once the texture-mapped 3D models have been constructed, they can be rendered directly with a standard 3D graphics system. For our work, we

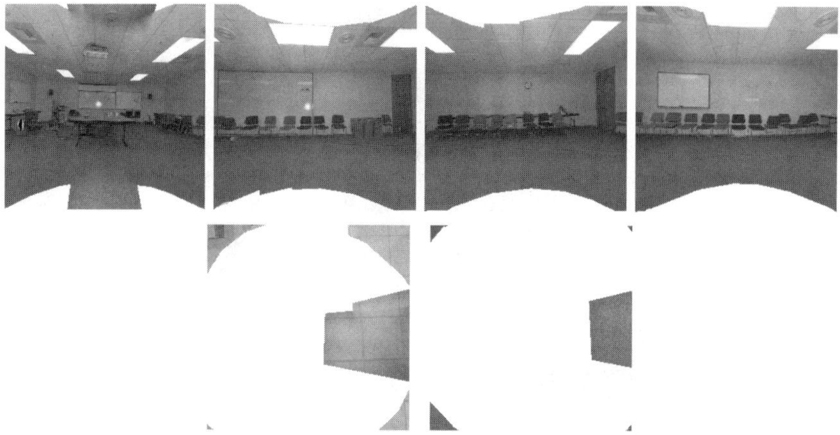

FIGURE 13.16. Cubical texture-mapped model of conference room (from 75 images taken with a hand-held digital camera).

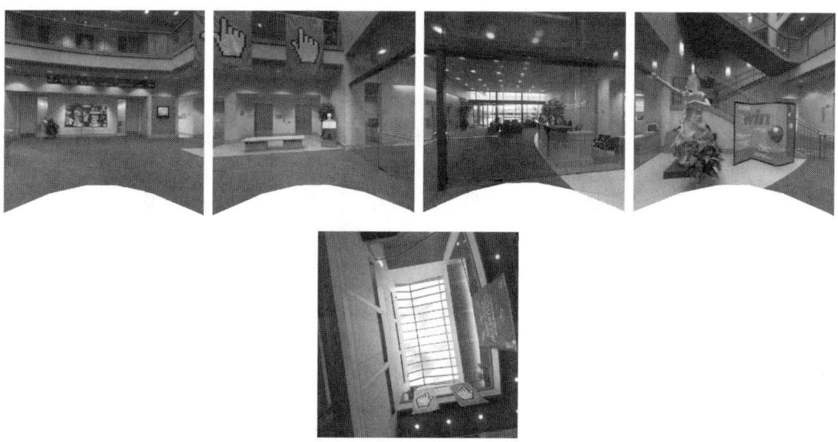

FIGURE 13.17. Cubical texture-mapped model of lobby (from 50 images).

are currently using a simple 3D viewer written on top of the Direct3D API running on a personal computer.

13.10 Discussion

In this paper, we have presented our system for constructing full view panoramic image mosaics from image sequences. Instead of projecting all of the images onto a common surface (e.g., a cylinder or a sphere), we use a representation that associates a rotation matrix and a focal length with each input image. Based on this rotational panoramic representation, we use block adjustment (global alignment) and deghosting (local alignment)

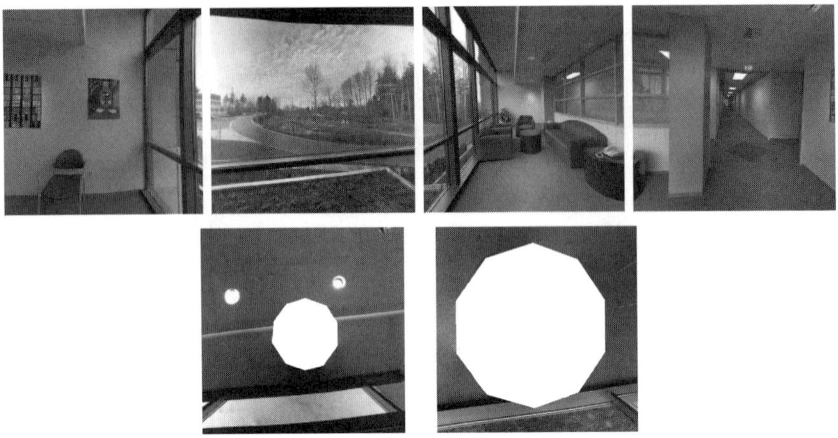

FIGURE 13.18. Cubical texture-mapped model of hallway and sitting area (from 70 images).

techniques to significantly improve the quality of image mosaics, thereby enabling the construction of mosaics from images taken by hand-held cameras.

When constructing an image mosaic from a long sequence of images, we have to deal with error accumulation problems. Our system simultaneously adjusts all frame poses (rotations and focal lengths) so that the sum of registration errors between all matching pairs of images is minimized. Geometrically, this is equivalent to adjusting all ray directions of corresponding pixels in overlapping frames until they converge. Using corresponding "features" in neighboring frames, which are obtained automatically using our patch-based alignment method, we formulate the minimization problem to recover the poses without explicitly computing the converged ray directions. This leads to a linearly-constrained non-linear least-squares problem which can be solved very efficiently.[25]

To compensate for local misregistration caused by inadequate motion models (e.g., camera translation[26] or moving object) or imperfect camera projection models (e.g., lens distortion), we refine the image mosaic using a deghosting method. We divide each image into small patches and compute patch-based alignments. We then locally warp each image so that the overall mosaic does not contain visible ghosting. To handle large parallax

[25]If we were only adjusting one rotation matrix at a time, we could use Horn's absolute orientation algorithm [112, 113, 143]. Unfortunately, this would be converge more slowly than solving a single global optimization problem.

[26]We assume in our work that the camera translation is relatively small. When camera translation is significant, a "manifold mosaic" [214] can still be constructed from a dense sequence of images using only center columns of each image. However, the resulting mosaic is no longer metric.

or distortion, we start the deghosting with a large patch size. This deghosting step is then repeated with smaller patches so that local patch motion can be estimated more accurately. In the future, we plan to implement a multiresolution patch-based flow algorithm so that the alignment process can be sped up and made to work over larger displacements. We also plan to develop more robust versions of our alignment algorithms.

Our deghosting algorithm can also be applied to the problem of extracting texture maps for general 3D objects from images [236]. When constructing such texture maps by averaging a number of views projected onto the model, even slight misregistrations can cause blurring or ghosting effects. One potential way to compensate for this is to refine the surface geometry to bring all projected colors into registration [76]. Our deghosting algorithm can be used as an alternative, and can inherently compensate for problems such as errors in the estimated camera geometry and intrinsic camera models.

To summarize, the collection of global and local alignment algorithms presented in this paper, together with our efficient patch-based implementation, make it easy to quickly and reliably construct high-quality full view panoramic mosaics from arbitrary collections of images, without the need for special photographic equipment. We believe that this will make panoramic photography and the construction of virtual environments much more interesting to a wide range of users, and stimulate further research and development in image-based rendering and the representation of visual scenes.

13.11 Appendix: Linearly-constrained Least-squares

We would like to solve the linear system

$$\mathbf{A}\mathbf{x} = \mathbf{b} \tag{13.66}$$

subject to

$$\mathbf{C}\mathbf{x} = \mathbf{q}. \tag{13.67}$$

It is equivalent to minimizing

$$\sum_i (\mathbf{A}_i^T \mathbf{x} - b_i)^2 \tag{13.68}$$

subject to

$$\mathbf{c}_j^T \mathbf{x} - q_j = 0 \tag{13.69}$$

for all j, where $\mathbf{c}_j$ are rows of $\mathbf{C}$.

13.11.1 Lagrange Multipliers

This problem is a special case of constrained nonlinear programming (or more specifically quadratic programming). Thus, it can be formulated using Lagrange multipliers by minimizing

$$e = \sum_i (\mathbf{A}_i^T \mathbf{x} - b_i)^2 + \sum_j 2\lambda_j (\mathbf{C}_j^T \mathbf{x} - q_j). \tag{13.70}$$

Taking first order derivatives of e with respect to $\mathbf{x}$ and λ, we have

$$\frac{\partial e}{\partial \mathbf{x}} = \sum_i \mathbf{A}_i \mathbf{A}_i^T \mathbf{x} - \sum_i b_i \mathbf{A}_i + \sum_j \lambda_j \mathbf{C}_j = 0 \tag{13.71}$$

and

$$\frac{\partial e}{\partial \lambda_j} = \mathbf{C}_j^T \mathbf{x}_j + q_j = 0 \tag{13.72}$$

or

$$\begin{bmatrix} \mathbf{H} & \mathbf{C}^T \\ \mathbf{C} & 0 \end{bmatrix} \begin{bmatrix} \mathbf{x} \\ \lambda \end{bmatrix} = \begin{bmatrix} \mathbf{d} \\ \mathbf{g} \end{bmatrix} \tag{13.73}$$

where $\mathbf{H} = \sum_i \mathbf{A}_i \mathbf{A}_i^T$, $\mathbf{d} = \sum_i \mathbf{A}_i b_i$, $\mathbf{x} = [x_j]$, $\lambda = [\lambda_j]$, and $\mathbf{g} = [g_j]$.

If $\mathbf{H}$ is invertible, we can simply solve the above system by

$$\begin{bmatrix} \mathbf{x} \\ \lambda \end{bmatrix} = \begin{bmatrix} \mathbf{H}^{-1} - \mathbf{KCH}^{-1} & \mathbf{K} \\ \mathbf{K}^T & -\mathbf{P} \end{bmatrix} \begin{bmatrix} \mathbf{d} \\ \mathbf{g} \end{bmatrix} \tag{13.74}$$

where

$$\begin{aligned} \mathbf{P} &= (\mathbf{CH}^{-1}\mathbf{C}^T)^{-1} \\ \mathbf{K} &= \mathbf{H}^{-1}\mathbf{C}^T\mathbf{P} \end{aligned}$$

Unfortunately, this requires additional matrix inversion operations.

13.11.2 Elimination Method

We now present a simple method to solve the linearly-constrained least-squares problem by eliminating redundant variables using given hard constraints.

If there are no hard constraints (i.e., $\mathbf{Cx} = \mathbf{q}$), we can easily solve the least-squares problem $\mathbf{Ax} = \mathbf{b}$ using normal equations, i.e.,

$$\mathbf{Hx} = \mathbf{d} \tag{13.75}$$

where $\mathbf{H} = \mathbf{A}^T\mathbf{A}$, and $\mathbf{d} = \mathbf{A}^T\mathbf{b}$. The normal equations can be solved stably using a SPD solver. We would like to modify the normal equations using the given hard linear constraints so that we can formulate new normal equations $\tilde{\mathbf{H}}\mathbf{x} = \tilde{\mathbf{d}}$ which are also SPD and of the same dimensions as $\mathbf{H}$.

Without loss of generality, we consider only one linear constraint and assume the biggest entry is $l_k = 1$. Let $\mathbf{H}_k$ be the kth column of $\mathbf{H}$, and $\mathbf{A}_k$ be the kth column of $\mathbf{A}$. If we subtract the linear constraint properly from each row of $\mathbf{A}$ so that its k-th column becomes zero, we change the original system to

$$\tilde{\mathbf{A}}\mathbf{x} = \tilde{\mathbf{d}} \tag{13.76}$$

subject to

$$\mathbf{c}^T\mathbf{x} = q \tag{13.77}$$

where $\tilde{\mathbf{A}} = \mathbf{A} - \mathbf{A}_k\mathbf{c}^T$ and $\tilde{\mathbf{d}} = \mathbf{d} - \mathbf{A}_k q$.

Because the constraint (13.77) is linearly independent of the linear system (13.76), we can formulate new normal equations with

$$\begin{aligned} \tilde{\mathbf{H}} &= \tilde{\mathbf{A}}^T\tilde{\mathbf{A}} + \mathbf{c}\mathbf{c}^T \\ &= (\mathbf{A} - \mathbf{A}_k\mathbf{c}^T)^T\mathbf{A} - \mathbf{A}_k\mathbf{c}^T + \mathbf{c}\mathbf{c}^T \\ &= \mathbf{H} - \mathbf{c}\mathbf{H}_k^T - \mathbf{H}_k\mathbf{c}^T + (1 + h_{kk})\mathbf{c}\mathbf{c}^T \end{aligned}$$

and

$$\begin{aligned} \tilde{\mathbf{d}} &= \tilde{\mathbf{A}}^T\tilde{\mathbf{d}} + \mathbf{c}q \\ &= \mathbf{d} - \mathbf{H}_k q - \mathbf{c}d_k + (1 + h_{kk})\mathbf{c}q \end{aligned}$$

where $\mathbf{H}_k$ is the kth column of $\mathbf{H}$ and $h_{kk} = \mathbf{A}_k^T\mathbf{A}_k$ is the kth diagonal element of $\mathbf{H}$.

It is interesting to note that the new normal equations are not unique because we can arbitrarily scale the hard constraint.[27] For example, if we scale Equation (13.77) by h_{kk}, we have $\tilde{\mathbf{H}} = \mathbf{H} - \mathbf{c}\mathbf{H}_k^T - \mathbf{H}_k\mathbf{c}^T + 2h_{kk}\mathbf{c}\mathbf{c}^T$ and $\tilde{\mathbf{d}} = \mathbf{d} - \mathbf{H}_k q - \mathbf{c}d_k + 2h_{kk}\mathbf{c}q$.

To add multiple constraints, we simply adjust the original system multiple times, one constraint at a time. The order of adding multiple constraints does not matter.

13.11.3 QR Factorization

The elimination method is very efficient if we have only a few constraints. When the number of constraints increases, we can use QR factorization to solve the linearly-constrained least-squares [83]. Suppose $\mathbf{A}$ and $\mathbf{C}$ are of full ranks, let

$$\mathbf{C}^T = \mathbf{Q}\begin{bmatrix} \mathbf{R} \\ 0 \end{bmatrix} \tag{13.78}$$

[27] One can not simply scale any soft constraints (i.e., the linear equations $\mathbf{A}_i x_i = b_i$) because it adds different weights to the least-squares formulation, that leads to incorrect solutions.

be the QR factorization of $\mathbf{c}^T$ where $\mathbf{Q}$ is orthorgonal, $\mathbf{Q}\mathbf{Q}^T = \mathbf{I}$. If we define $\mathbf{Q}^T\mathbf{x} = \begin{bmatrix} \mathbf{x}_1 \\ \mathbf{x}_2 \end{bmatrix}$, $\mathbf{A}\mathbf{Q} = (\mathbf{A}_1, \mathbf{A}_2)$, we can solve $\mathbf{x}_1$ because $\mathbf{R}$ is upper diagonal and

$$\begin{aligned} \mathbf{C}\mathbf{x} &= \mathbf{C}\mathbf{Q}\mathbf{Q}^T\mathbf{x} \\ &= \mathbf{R}^T\mathbf{x}_1 = \mathbf{q}. \end{aligned}$$

Then we solve $\mathbf{x}_2$ from the unconstrained least-squares $\|\mathbf{A}_2\mathbf{x}_2 - (\mathbf{b} - \mathbf{A}_1\mathbf{x}_1)\|^2$ because

$$\begin{aligned} \mathbf{A}\mathbf{x} - \mathbf{b} &= \mathbf{A}\mathbf{Q}\mathbf{Q}^T\mathbf{x} - \mathbf{b} \\ &= \mathbf{A}_1\mathbf{x}_1 + \mathbf{A}_2\mathbf{x}_2 - \mathbf{b} \\ &= \mathbf{A}_2\mathbf{x}_2 - (\mathbf{b} - \mathbf{A}_1\mathbf{x}_1). \end{aligned}$$

Finally $\mathbf{x} = \mathbf{Q}\begin{bmatrix} \mathbf{x}_1 \\ \mathbf{x}_2 \end{bmatrix}$. Note that this method requires two factorizations.

14

Self-Calibration of Zooming Cameras from a Single Viewpoint

L. de Agapito, E. Hayman, I.D. Reid, and R.I. Hartley

14.1 Introduction

A configuration that commonly occurs in many imaging applications is that in which a camera has its optic centre fixed in location but which may rotate and zoom, thus changing its internal parameters. This is the case in applications such as surveillance, broadcasting and panoramic viewing, where a wide field of view is captured from a single viewpoint by rotating a camera which is typically mounted on a tripod or a pan-tilt platform and which may also be allowed to zoom.

In this chapter we are concerned with the problem of determining the internal parameters of such a camera using unstructured visual data. The internal parameters of a camera determine the mapping from image locations to rays in 3D Euclidean space, and for this reason camera calibration has been the subject of much research from the start of the short history of machine vision.

Traditional approaches to calibration (see, e.g., [285]) made use of known scene structure such as accurately manufactured grids, and it was only relatively recently that the possibility of *self-calibration* of a camera simply by observing an unknown scene was realised and explored. The first major work to consider the problem was [70], which showed that self-calibration was theoretically and practically feasible for a camera moving through an unknown scene with constant but unknown intrinsics. Since that time numerous methods have been developed [98, 174, 282] including some that deal with special motions such as pure rotation [99] or pure translation [187].

These methods required the calibration of the camera to be fixed over a sequence of images – no zooming was allowed. Subsequently, interest in zooming cameras led to methods for self-calibration of cameras with changing internal parameters ([107, 218, 100]). Recent work in self-calibration of rotating and zooming cameras includes our own work [58, 59,

60] which we will describe in this chapter, and work by Seo and Hong [245, 246].

This chapter is organised as follows. We begin with background material, describing pinhole projection equations and discussing the specific case of zero translation (section 14.2.1). We then develop a constraint which is the basis for self-calibration (section 14.2.3). Two methods for self calibration, a non-linear and a linear method, are considered (section 14.3) and we present results for a variety of experiments with both synthetic and real data (section 14.4). We go on to consider optimal parameter estimation (section 14.5) using bundle-adjustment and we conclude with a discussion of the work and future directions (section 14.6).

14.2 The Rotating Camera

14.2.1 Camera Model

The projection of scene points onto an image by a perspective camera may be modelled by the central projection equation $\mathbf{x} = \mathtt{P}\mathbf{X}$, where $\mathbf{x} = [x\ y\ 1]^\top$ are the image points in homogeneous coordinates, $\mathbf{X} = [X\ Y\ Z\ 1]^\top$ are the world points and $\mathtt{P}$ is the 3×4 camera projection matrix. This equation only holds up to scale. The matrix $\mathtt{P}$ is a rank-3 matrix which may be decomposed as $\mathtt{P} = \mathtt{K}\,[\mathtt{R}| - \mathtt{R}\mathbf{t}]$, where the rotation $\mathtt{R}$ and the translation $\mathbf{t}$ represent the Euclidean transformation between the camera and the world coordinate systems and $\mathtt{K}$ is an upper triangular matrix which contains the internal parameters of the camera in the form

$$\mathtt{K} = \begin{bmatrix} \alpha_u & s & u_0 \\ 0 & \alpha_v & v_0 \\ 0 & 0 & 1 \end{bmatrix}. \tag{14.1}$$

The elements α_u and α_v represent the focal length of the camera expressed in horizontal and vertical pixel units respectively. The aspect ratio is $r = \alpha_v/\alpha_u$. The principal point is (u_0, v_0) and s is a skew parameter which is a function of the angle between the horizontal and vertical axes of the sensor array. Usually the axes of the sensor array may be assumed to be orthogonal in which case the skew parameter is zero.

Here we consider the problem of calibrating a camera which is fixed in location, free to rotate but not translate, and which can vary its internal parameters by zooming. Choosing the origin of the coordinate system to be located at the optic centre of the camera, common to all views, the projection matrix for each view i may be written as

$$\mathtt{P}_i = \mathtt{K}_i\,[\mathtt{R}_i|0]\,. \tag{14.2}$$

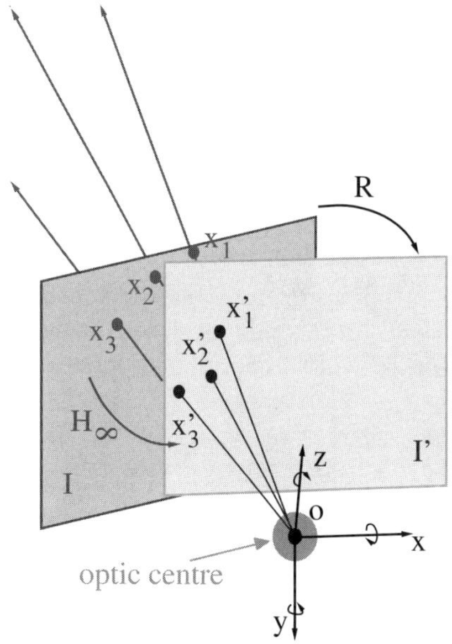

FIGURE 14.1. Corresponding image points are related by the infinite homography $\mathtt{H}_\infty$

The projection of a scene point $\mathbf{X} = [X\ Y\ Z\ 1]^\top$ onto an image point $\mathbf{x}$ may now be expressed as

$$\mathbf{x} = \mathtt{K}_i\,[\mathtt{R}_i|0] \begin{bmatrix} X \\ Y \\ Z \\ 1 \end{bmatrix} = \mathtt{K}_i\mathtt{R}_i \begin{bmatrix} X \\ Y \\ Z \end{bmatrix} = \mathtt{K}_i\mathtt{R}_i\overline{\mathbf{X}}. \tag{14.3}$$

Since the last row of the projection matrix is zero, the depth of the world points along the ray is irrelevant and we only consider the projection of 3D rays $\overline{\mathbf{X}}$. Therefore, in the case of a rotating camera, the mapping of 3D rays to image points is encoded by the 3×3 invertible projective transformation

$$\overline{\mathtt{P}}_i = \mathtt{K}_i\mathtt{R}_i. \tag{14.4}$$

14.2.2 The Inter-image Homography

Given a 3D ray $\overline{\mathbf{X}}$, its projections onto two different images will be

$$\mathbf{x}_i = \mathtt{K}_i\mathtt{R}_i\overline{\mathbf{X}} \tag{14.5}$$
$$\mathbf{x}_j = \mathtt{K}_j\mathtt{R}_j\overline{\mathbf{X}} \tag{14.6}$$

Eliminating $\overline{\mathbf{X}}$ from both equations it is easy to see that in the case of a rotating camera there exists a global 2D projective transformation (homography) $\mathtt{H}_{ij}$ that relates corresponding points in two views:

$$\mathbf{x}_j = \mathtt{H}_{ij}\mathbf{x}_i. \tag{14.7}$$

The analytic expression of this homography is

$$\mathtt{H}_{ij} = \mathtt{K}_j\mathtt{R}_j\mathtt{R}_i^{-1}\mathtt{K}_i^{-1} = \mathtt{K}_j\mathtt{R}_{ij}\mathtt{K}_i^{-1}. \tag{14.8}$$

The inter-image homographies $\mathtt{H}_{ij}$ may be calculated directly from image measurements, for instance from point or line correspondences, or direct methods, based on pixel intensity.

14.2.3 The Infinite Homography Constraint

We will now derive the constraint that relates the homographies to the calibration matrices for each view. Since $\mathtt{R}_{ij} = \mathtt{K}_j^{-1}\mathtt{H}_{ij}\mathtt{K}_i$ is a rotation matrix, it satisfies the property that $\mathtt{R}=\mathtt{R}^{-\top}$, leading to

$$\mathtt{K}_j{}^\top\mathtt{H}_{ij}^{-\top}\mathtt{K}_i^{-\top} = \mathtt{K}_j^{-1}\mathtt{H}_{ij}\mathtt{K}_i \tag{14.9}$$

and

$$\left(\mathtt{K}_j\mathtt{K}_j{}^\top\right) = \mathtt{H}_{ij}\left(\mathtt{K}_i\mathtt{K}_i{}^\top\right)\mathtt{H}_{ij}{}^\top. \tag{14.10}$$

This equation is known as the *infinite homography constraint* and it relates the camera calibration matrices to the inter-image homographies and constitutes the constraint we will use for self-calibration.

This same expression is also obtained by projecting a point on the plane at infinity, $\mathbf{X} = [X\ Y\ Z\ 0]^\top$, onto a camera with a non-zero fourth column in $\mathtt{P}_i$. The observed inter-image homographies $\mathtt{H}_{ij}$ are thus the homographies induced by the plane at infinity, i.e., the infinite homographies $\mathtt{H}_\infty$ (Figure 14.1).

This constraint may also be interpreted geometrically in terms of the absolute conic and its projection on the image plane. The absolute conic Ω_∞ is a point conic in 3 space which is invariant to Euclidean transformations. It consists of points $\mathbf{X} = [X\ Y\ Z\ 0]^\top$ on the plane at infinity such that $X^2+Y^2+Z^2 = 0$ or alternatively $\mathbf{X}^\top\mathbf{X} = 0$. This implies that its expression in the Euclidean frame is given by the identity matrix $\mathtt{I}$.

Since points on the absolute conic are on the plane at infinity they project onto the image plane following the expression $\mathbf{x} = \mathtt{KR}\overline{\mathbf{X}}$, where $\overline{\mathbf{X}} = [X\ Y\ Z]^\top$. Therefore, points on the image of the absolute conic (IAC) $\boldsymbol{\omega}$ must satisfy: $\mathbf{x}^\top(\mathtt{KK}^\top)^{-1}\mathbf{x} = 0$ and the expression of the IAC is thus given by $\boldsymbol{\omega} = (\mathtt{KK}^\top)^{-1}$. What is important to note here is that the IAC only depends on the calibration parameters of the camera, therefore determining the location of the IAC is equivalent to knowing the calibration of the camera.

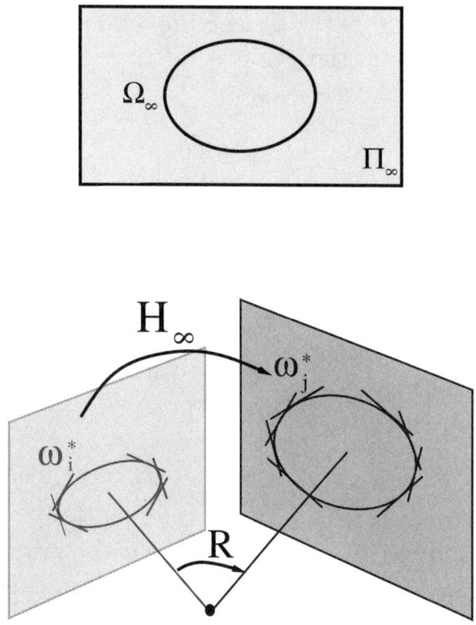

FIGURE 14.2. The absolute conic Ω_∞ is a point conic that lies on the plane at infinity Π_∞ which is invariant to euclidean transformations. It projects onto the *image of the absolute conic* (IAC) ω, which depends only on the internal parameters of the camera at each frame. Its dual space line conic is the *dual image of the absolute conic* (DIAC) ω^*. The infinite homography $\mathtt{H}_\infty$ maps the DIAC ω^* between views: $\boldsymbol{\omega}_j^* = \mathtt{H}_\infty \boldsymbol{\omega}_i^* \mathtt{H}_\infty{}^\top$.

Noting that its inverse is the dual space line conic, also called the dual image of the absolute conic (DIAC, Figures 14.2 and 14.3) $\boldsymbol{\omega}^* = \mathtt{K}\mathtt{K}^\top$, we may rewrite the infinite homography constraint (14.10) as

$$\boldsymbol{\omega}_j^* = \mathtt{H}_{ij} \boldsymbol{\omega}_i^* \mathtt{H}_{ij}{}^\top. \tag{14.11}$$

When the internal parameters of the camera are varying, the DIAC is different for each frame and the infinite homography constraint describes its mapping between image planes [174]. It relates the 2D projective transformations $\mathtt{H}_{ij}$ to the calibration matrices for each frame $\mathtt{K}_i$ and will constitute the basis for the self-calibration algorithms we will describe.

14.2.3.1 An Alternative Derivation of the Infinite Homography Constraint

In [282], Triggs introduced a clean way of expressing the self-calibration problem (in his case for a moving camera with fixed but unknown intrinsics) in terms of a quadric in $\mathcal{P}^3$ invariant under Euclidean transformations. We now show that for a rotating camera with varying intrinsics, we can derive a similar constraint, and that it is equivalent to the infinite homography constraint.

The quadric in question is the degenerate dual space disc quadric whose rim is the absolute conic in the plane at infinity. The representation of the quadric in a Euclidean frame is given by the rank-3 4×4 symmetric matrix

$$\mathtt{Q}^*_\infty = \begin{bmatrix} \mathtt{I} & 0 \\ 0 & 0 \end{bmatrix}. \tag{14.12}$$

It is easy to verify that any Euclidean transformation $\mathtt{T}$ maps $\mathtt{Q}^*_\infty$ onto itself: $\mathtt{T}\mathtt{Q}^*_\infty\mathtt{T}^\top = \mathtt{Q}^*_\infty$. Triggs's self-calibration method comprises locating the quadric in an initial projective frame and then using it to recover the transformation from projective to Euclidean structure. $\mathtt{Q}^*_\infty$ is recovered using its projection constraint: $\mathtt{Q}^*_\infty$ projects onto the dual of the image of the absolute conic (DIAC)

$$\boldsymbol{\omega}_i^* = \mathtt{K}_i\mathtt{K}_i{}^\top = \mathtt{P}_i\mathtt{Q}^*_\infty\mathtt{P}_i{}^\top \tag{14.13}$$

irrespectively of the projective basis chosen for the projection matrices $\mathtt{P}_i$.

While Triggs introduced this constraint in the context of self-calibration of a moving camera with fixed intrinsics [282], Pollefeys *et al.* extended the method to the case where the camera parameters may vary [218]. We now derive the projection constraint of $\mathtt{Q}^*_\infty$ for the case of a stationary rotating camera with varying intrinsic parameters.

Without loss of generality we may choose the first frame to be the projective basis in which the camera matrices are expressed. Therefore

$$\mathtt{P}_0 = [\mathtt{I}|0], \quad \mathtt{P}_i = [\mathtt{H}_i|0], \tag{14.14}$$

where we define $\mathtt{H}_i$ to be the infinite homography between views 0 and i, and

$$\mathtt{Q}^*_\infty = \begin{bmatrix} \mathtt{K}_0\mathtt{K}_0{}^\top & -\mathtt{K}_0\mathtt{K}_0^\top\mathbf{a} \\ -\mathbf{a}^\top\mathtt{K}_0\mathtt{K}_0^\top & \mathbf{a}^\top\mathtt{K}_0\mathtt{K}_0^\top\mathbf{a} \end{bmatrix} \tag{14.15}$$

where $\left[\mathbf{a}^\top 1\right]$ is a 4-vector describing the location of the plane at infinity Π_∞.

We can rewrite equation (14.13) as:

$$\boldsymbol{\omega}_i^* = \mathtt{K}_i\mathtt{K}_i{}^\top = \mathtt{P}_i \begin{bmatrix} \mathtt{K}_0\mathtt{K}_0{}^\top & -\mathtt{K}_0\mathtt{K}_0^\top\mathbf{a} \\ -\mathbf{a}^\top\mathtt{K}_0\mathtt{K}_0^\top & \mathbf{a}^\top\mathtt{K}_0\mathtt{K}_0^\top\mathbf{a} \end{bmatrix} \mathtt{P}_i{}^\top \tag{14.16}$$

Combining equations (14.15) and (14.16) the projection constraint becomes

$$\boldsymbol{\omega}_i^* = \mathtt{K}_i\mathtt{K}_i{}^\top = \mathtt{H}_i\mathtt{K}_0\mathtt{K}_0{}^\top\mathtt{H}_i{}^\top = \mathtt{H}_i\boldsymbol{\omega}_0^{*\top}\mathtt{H}_i{}^\top \tag{14.17}$$

Thus in the case of a rotating camera the projection constraint of $\mathtt{Q}^*_\infty$ reduces to the infinite homography constraint.

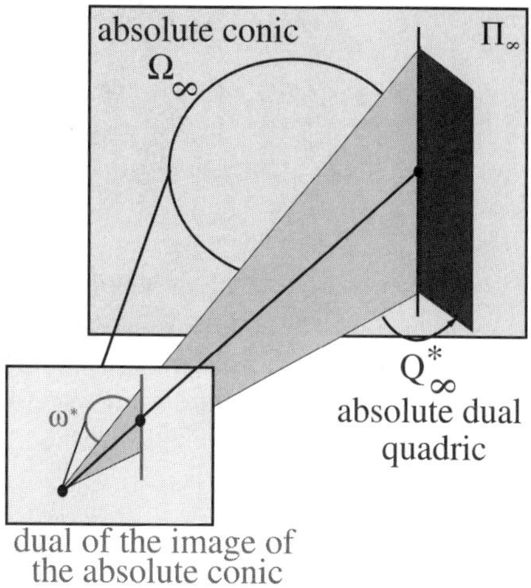

FIGURE 14.3. Q^*_∞ is the degenerate dual space disc quadric whose rim is the absolute conic Ω_∞ on the plane at infinity. It projects onto the dual image of the absolute conic (DIAC) ω.

14.3 Self-calibration of Rotating Cameras

14.3.1 Problem Formulation

The problem of self-calibrating a rotating and zooming camera is that of determining the calibration matrices for each frame, given only correspondences between views.

The infinite homography constraint

$$\mathtt{K}_j\mathtt{K}_j{}^\top = \mathtt{H}_{ij}\mathtt{K}_i\mathtt{K}_i{}^\top\mathtt{H}_{ij}{}^\top. \tag{14.18}$$

relates the calibration matrices $\mathtt{K}_j$ to the 2D projective transformations $\mathtt{H}_{ij}$ which may be computed directly from corresponding features between images. Given at least 4 point or line correspondences between views the infinite homographies $\mathtt{H}_{ij}$ may be calculated and the infinite homography constraint may be used to compute the calibration matrices $\mathtt{K}_j$.

14.3.2 Constant Intrinsic Parameters

In the case where the camera's internal parameters remain fixed throughout the sequence ($\mathtt{K}_i = \mathtt{K}, i = 1, ..., n$) the infinite homography takes the form

$$\mathtt{K}\mathtt{K}^\top = \boldsymbol{\omega}^* = \mathtt{H}_{ij}\boldsymbol{\omega}^*\mathtt{H}_{ij}{}^\top \tag{14.19}$$

Hartley demonstrated in [99] that this expression may be used to generate a set of linear equations in the entries of the dual image of the absolute conic, $\boldsymbol{\omega}^*$, which may be used to solve for $\boldsymbol{\omega}^*$, and subsequently for $\mathtt{K}$ by Choleski factorization.

14.3.3 Varying Intrinsic Parameters

Our main contribution has been to extend the self-calibration capability to the case where the internal parameters of the camera change throughout the sequence. This would be useful to self-calibrate a sequence taken by a zooming camera where the focal length and perhaps other parameters are changing between views.

Here we describe two different algorithms: a non-linear algorithm which is more versatile in the nature of the constraints which can be imposed on the intrinsic parameters of the camera, and a simple linear algorithm which is more restrictive in the type of constraints which can be imposed on the internal parameters of the camera.

14.3.3.1 Non-linear Algorithm

It is possible to use the infinite homography constraint (14.11) using an approach similar to Pollefeys *et al.* [218] to solve for the camera calibration matrices $\mathtt{K}_j$ given the set of 2D projective transformations $\mathtt{H}_{ij}$ which relate corresponding points between views. Without loss of generality we may choose the origin of the coordinate system to be aligned with the first frame such that $\mathtt{H}_{00} = \mathtt{I}$ and $\mathtt{H}_{0j} = \mathtt{H}_j$. We may now write the infinite homography constraint as

$$\mathtt{K}_j\mathtt{K}_j{}^\top = \mathtt{H}_j\mathtt{K}_0\mathtt{K}_0{}^\top\mathtt{H}_j{}^\top \tag{14.20}$$

which only holds up to scale.

If U is the number of unknown intrinsics in the first frame, and V is the number of intrinsics which may subsequently vary, then the total number of unknowns is $U + V(n-1)$ where n is the number of frames. A condition for a solution is therefore

$$U + V(n-1) \leq P(n-1) \tag{14.21}$$

where P is the number of independent equations provided by (14.20) which is clearly less than or equal to 5 since each side of the equation is a symmetric matrix defined only up to scale. We therefore require $V < 5$ (i.e. strictly less than 5), meaning that not all the intrinsic parameters may be allowed to vary throughout the sequence and therefore some constraints on the parameters must be provided. When this is the case, equation (14.20) may be solved and the calibration matrices $\mathtt{K}_j, j = 0, ..., n$ may be determined. The minimal assumption for this algorithm is that at least one parameter must remain fixed throughout the sequence.

A solution may be obtained using a non-linear least squares algorithm. In our implementation [58], a Levenberg-Marquardt algorithm is used, where the parameters to be computed are the unknown intrinsic parameters of each calibration matrix $\mathtt{K}_j$ $(\alpha_u^j, \alpha_v^j, u_0^j, v_0^j, s^j)$ and the cost function to be minimized is

$$\mathcal{D} = \sum_{j=1}^{n-1} \| \mathtt{K}_j \mathtt{K}_j^\top - \mathtt{H}_j \mathtt{K}_0 \mathtt{K}_0^\top \mathtt{H}_j^\top \|_F^2 \tag{14.22}$$

where $\mathtt{K}_j \mathtt{K}_j^\top$ and $\mathtt{H}_j \mathtt{K}_0 \mathtt{K}_0^\top \mathtt{H}_j^\top$ are normalised so that their Frobenius norms are equal to one to eliminate the unknown scale factor.

Once the calibration matrices have been determined it is straightforward to compute the rotation matrices $\mathtt{R}_j$ which express the relative orientation of each frame with respect to the reference frame using the expression $\mathtt{R}_j = \mathtt{K}_j^{-1} \mathtt{H}_j \mathtt{K}_0$. In practice we fit an orthonormal matrix to $\mathtt{R}_j$ by setting the singular values of the SVD to unity.

The interesting feature of this algorithm is the flexibility it provides to incorporate any constraints available on the intrinsic parameters since the parameterization of the calibration matrices $\mathtt{K}_j$ explicitly makes use of the intrinsic parameters of the camera. Parameters may be assumed to be known, unknown but constant throughout the sequence or varying. In particular, one may impose standard constraints such as zero camera skew or known aspect ratio or less restrictive ones such as constant but unknown skew, aspect ratio or principal point.

Another important aspect is that the initial estimate for the non-linear minimization need not be very close to the global minimum to ensure convergence. We have observed that the algorithm converges to the global minimum even when initialized far from it. In practice we use the output from the linear algorithm described below as the starting point for the non-linear minimization.

14.3.3.2 A Linear Algorithm

The use of the infinite homography constraint (14.11) does not provide a simple way of imposing minimal constraints on the calibration parameters (such as zero skew or known aspect ratio) linearly. However, it was first noticed in [313] and more recently used in [59], that a simple trick leads to some linear constraints on the intrinsic parameters, provided the skew of the camera is zero.

Taking the inverse of (14.11) gives:

$$\boldsymbol{\omega}_i = \mathtt{H}_i^{-\top} \boldsymbol{\omega}_0 \mathtt{H}_i^{-1}, \tag{14.23}$$

where now the inverse of the infinite homography constraint is expressed in terms of the image of the absolute conic, $\boldsymbol{\omega}_i = \mathtt{K}_i^{-\top} \mathtt{K}_i^{-1}$.

One may verify that if the skew of the camera is zero ($s = 0$) the form of the image of the absolute conic $\boldsymbol{\omega}_i$ in each frame is:

$$\begin{aligned} \boldsymbol{\omega}_i &= \mathtt{K}^{-\top} \mathtt{K}^{-1} \\ &= \begin{bmatrix} 1/\alpha_u^2 & 0 & -u_0/\alpha_u^2 \\ 0 & 1/\alpha_v^2 & -v_0/\alpha_v^2 \\ -u_0/\alpha_u^2 & -v_0/\alpha_v^2 & 1 + u_0^2/\alpha_u^2 + v_0^2/\alpha_v^2 \end{bmatrix} \end{aligned}$$

This assumption leads to a linear constraint in the coefficients of each $\boldsymbol{\omega}_i$: the coefficient $\omega_{12} = 0$. Some additional constraints on the camera intrinsics also lead to further linear equations. We summarize these constraints here:

1. If skew is zero then $\omega_{12} = 0$.
2. If skew is zero and aspect ratio is 1 (square-pixels constraint) then $\omega_{11} = \omega_{22}$.
3. If skew is zero and $u_0 = 0$, then $\omega_{13} = 0$. Similarly if $v_0 = 0$ then $\omega_{23} = 0$.

If the pixels have aspect ratio other than 1, or the principal point is at a different known point other than the origin, then a simple change of image coordinates converts to one of the cases above.

Each of these constraints will give one linear equation per frame in the entries of each $\boldsymbol{\omega}_i$. Equation (14.23) may be used to transfer these constraints to constraints on the image of the absolute conic only in the reference frame $\boldsymbol{\omega}_0$. Each constraint provides one linear equation in the 5 independent entries (up to scale) of $\boldsymbol{\omega}_0$ (since $\boldsymbol{\omega}$ is symmetric). For each image each condition gives one equation, and the set of all equations may be written as $\mathtt{E}\mathbf{a} = 0$, where $\mathbf{a}$ encodes the entries of $\boldsymbol{\omega}_0$, and each row of $\mathtt{E}$ represents one equation. If more than 5 equations are available the problem may be solved via least-squares by finding $\mathbf{a}$ that minimizes $||\mathtt{E}\mathbf{a}||$ subject to $||\mathbf{a}|| = 1$.

In forming these equations, one should include equations for the reference image. A (possibly inferior) alternative would be to parametrize ω in terms of only 5 entries, setting the $(1,2)$ entry to zero. Then each image other than the reference image gives one equation. The difference is that in this latter case, the computed skew will be exactly zero in the reference image but non-zero (because the equations will not be satisfied exactly) in all other images. This approach would unreasonably single out the reference image for special treatment. The same remarks apply in the square-pixels and known-principal point cases as well.

The obvious advantage of the linear algorithm is that it is a simple method that does not require an initial estimate, hence it will not have convergence problems. It is also very fast, making it suitable for real time applications. However, it has the disadvantage of not incorporating some useful constraints on the calibration parameters such as unknown but constant parameters (skew, aspect ratio, principal point). An alternative method of solving for such parameters would be to use the residual from the linear algorithm as the cost function in a linear search over a range of feasible values of the parameter to determine the value that best fits the data.

The self-calibration algorithms we have presented in this section are also applicable in the case of cameras undergoing general motion to upgrade the calibration from affine to euclidean space. Obtaining affine structure is equivalent to knowing the location of the plane at infinity. This in turn is equivalent to determining the infinite homographies. Therefore, once these are known the rest of the self-calibration problem is reduced to that of self-calibrating a non-translating camera and the infinite homography constraint may be used to determine the calibration matrix for each frame.

Indeed these self-calibration methods may also be used to guide the search for the plane at infinity. Given a choice for the location of the plane at infinity, the residual given by the self-calibration algorithm may guide the search over a range of feasible values for the plane at infinity. The result is a stratified algorithm for self calibration, applicable to cameras undergoing general motion with changing internal parameters, in which one proceeds from a projective to an affine and then to a Euclidean reconstruction. This algorithm is described in [100].

14.4 Experimental Results

14.4.1 Experiments with Synthetic Data

Experiments were first carried out on synthetic data to evaluate the performance of the linear and non-linear self-calibration algorithms using different constraints on the internal parameters. The data were created to simulate a camera with a zoom lens providing a total focal length range of 12.5 mm to 35 mm. A cloud of 1000 points was randomly generated within a confined cubic space of 3 m side lying in front of the rotating camera at a distance of 5 m. The points were projected onto each of the image planes arising from the different orientations of the camera and the location of each image point was then perturbed in a random direction by a distance governed by a Gaussian distribution with zero mean and standard deviation σ measured in pixels. The size of the image planes was 384×288 pixels. The skew of the image axes was taken to be zero, the aspect ratio of the image pixels equal to one, and the principal point was located at the centre of the image. The camera motion was such that the principal ray described a circular trajectory of radius $\theta = 5°$ measured from the positive Z axis, simulating the motion of a pan-tilt unit. The focal length of the camera increased linearly throughout the 30 frame sequence from a value of 800 pixels to 1400 pixels.

In Figure 14.4 we show the results of one run of the self-calibration algorithms for a typical noise level of $\sigma = 0.5$ pixel, comparing the performance of the different algorithms using different constraints on the intrinsic parameters. The graphs compare the results of the computation of the focal length, the principal point and the motion of the camera with the ground truth data.

The algorithms were run on two different sequences, one where the radius of motion of the camera was larger ($\theta = 5°$) and the focal length of the

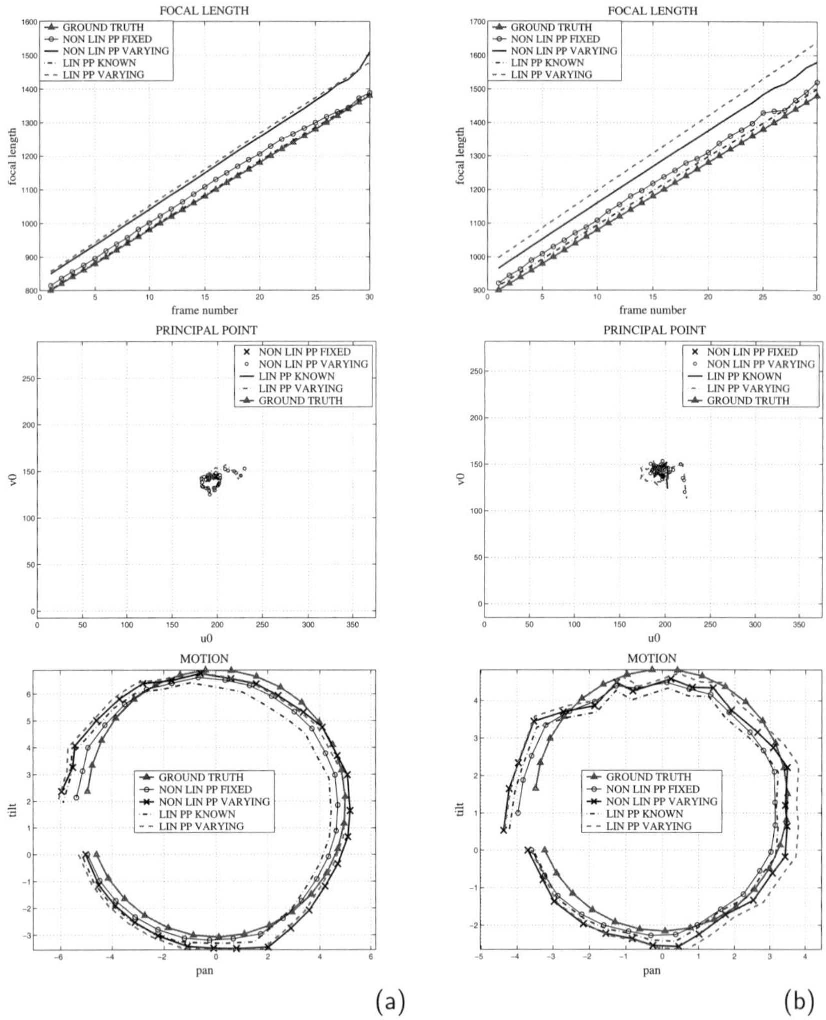

FIGURE 14.4. Calibration results with synthetic data in the presence of image noise of $\sigma = 0.5$ pixel , showing only one run of the non-linear and linear algorithms using different constraints on the intrinsic parameters. Computed values for the focal length (top), the location of the principal point (middle) and the aspect ratio (bottom) for a sequence with (a) smaller focal length and motion of 5 degrees radius and (b) a sequence with a larger focal length and smaller motion of 3.5 degrees radius.

camera was shorter and the other one where the radius was $\theta = 3.5°$ and the focal length was longer, a more ill-conditioned configuration.

More accurate results were obtained for both sequences when the principal point remained fixed in the Levenberg Marquardt non-linear minimization and when the principal point was known in the linear algorithm, while when it was allowed to vary the results were worse with both algorithms. The focal length was overestimated and the motion was underestimated. This behaviour is due to a near-ambiguity that arises in the simultaneous computation of the motion and focal length parameters. This near-ambiguity is described in depth in [101].

Note that errors in the calibration and motion parameters were larger in the sequence with longer focal length and smaller motion. In the case of the shorter focal length and larger motion sequence the error in the focal length does not exceed 4%, the error in the principal point is smaller than 50 pixels in the worse case and the error in the motion is smaller than 1°.

It is relevant to note here that motion is recovered only up to an overall rotation transformation. However, the technique described in [102] was used to determine the initial vergence of the camera in a frame aligned with the pan-tilt axes of the unit so as to decompose the recovered general rotations into the two parameter rotations described by pan-tilt units.

14.4.2 Experiments with Real Data

The image sequences used in our experiments were taken using a camera with a zoom lens mounted on our Yorick stereo head/eye platform [250]. The camera was rotated using one of the two independent vergence axes to pan the camera, and the common elevation axis to tilt it. The mechanics of our head do not permit rotations about the Z axis. This situation arises very often when using stationary cameras, since they tend to be mounted on tripods without fewer than three degrees of freedom for rotation. This type of motion exhibits a degeneracy (see [59]) and imposing only the skew zero constraint fails to solve the self-calibration problem: additional constraints must be used.

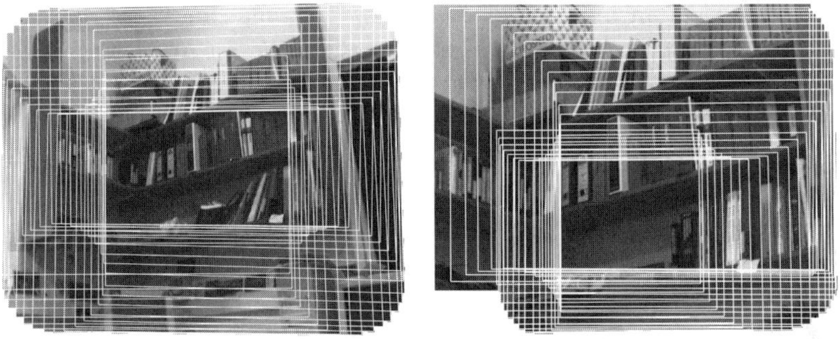

FIGURE 14.5. Mosaics constructed from the two bookshelf sequences during which the camera panned and tilted while the focal length remained fixed (left) and was varied (right).

Two image sequences were taken. In the first sequence, the focal length of the camera remained fixed, while the pan and the tilt of the camera were varied to perform a circular trajectory. In the second sequence, the focal length of the camera was set to increase linearly, using the controlled zoom lens, while the camera performed a similar circular motion. The encoders of the head/eye platform provided ground truth values for the pan and tilt angles of the camera which are accurate to 0.01 of a degree. The servo control of the zoom lens provided ground truth values of the position of the zoom lens for each frame in the image sequence. The camera was then calibrated, using an accurately machined calibration grid and a classical calibration algorithm, to obtain ground truth values for the internal parameters at each of the different positions of the zoom lens. Radial lens distortion was modelled off-line by using a single parameter and the images were appropriately warped to correct for this factor.

The homographies that relate corresponding points between views were computed in two stages. First, the inter-image homographies were computed from corresponding corners (detected and matched automatically). Second, the homographies were refined by minimizing the global image reprojection error using a bundle-adjustment technique [41]. This second stage can be essential in order to obtain accurate calibration results. Figure 14.5 shows the mosaics of both image sequences. In both sequences the aspect ratio was fixed at 1.0 and the skew at 0.0 in the self-calibration process.

Note that the value of the focal length obtained from the linear algorithm is more accurate than the LM algorithm run using the same calibration assumptions (LM-var-pp). However, in both sequences, focal length and motion estimation is largely improved by using the iterative non-linear method fixing the principal point (LM-fixed-pp).

This might appear as a contradiction since the principal point was actually varying between views. However, this behaviour is related to the fact that there exists an inherent near-ambiguity in the simultaneous computation of the focal length and the angle of rotation for a rotating camera. This ambiguity becomes much more prominent when the principal point is allowed to vary indiscriminately in the minimization process, since the principal point is a poorly conditioned parameter which tends to fit to noise. In the next section we will see how imposing a prior on the distribution of this parameter using MAP estimation will improve results.

14.5 Optimal Estimation: Bundle-adjustment

The previous self-calibration algorithms are not optimal in the statistical sense, since both the non-linear and linear algorithms minimize an algebraic error. In this section we derive an optimal estimator for the calibration and the motion parameters for the case when point correspondences are used as input data. Similar derivations may be obtained for the case where line correspondences are used or for direct approaches.

14.5.1 Maximum Likelihood Estimation (MLE)

Let us consider that the noise $\mathbf{w}$ on the measured image feature positions $\hat{\mathbf{x}}$ is additive and described by a Gaussian distribution with mean zero and standard deviation σ. The measured location $\hat{\mathbf{x}}$ is thus related to the true location by:

$$\hat{\mathbf{x}} = \mathbf{x} + \mathbf{w} = \mathtt{H}(\boldsymbol{\theta}) + \mathbf{w} \tag{14.24}$$

where $\mathbf{x} = \mathtt{H}(\boldsymbol{\theta})$ describes the model we have for the true values of the image points given an estimate of the model parameters $\boldsymbol{\theta}$. In our case, of course, this is the projection equation.

The conditional density function of the measured point $\hat{\mathbf{x}}$ given an estimate $\boldsymbol{\theta}$ is given by

$$p(\hat{\mathbf{x}}|\boldsymbol{\theta}) = \left(\frac{1}{2\pi\sigma^2}\right) \exp\left[-\frac{1}{2\sigma^2}(\hat{\mathbf{x}} - \mathtt{H}(\boldsymbol{\theta}))^\top(\hat{\mathbf{x}} - \mathtt{H}(\boldsymbol{\theta}))\right] \tag{14.25}$$

The Maximum Likelihood Estimator is then the value of $\boldsymbol{\theta}$ which maximizes $p(\hat{\mathbf{x}}|\boldsymbol{\theta})$.

Consider now a rotating camera. The projection of a 3D ray $\overline{\mathbf{X}}_j$ onto each image plane is given by the projection equation

$$\mathbf{x}_{ij} = \overline{\mathtt{P}}_i\overline{\mathbf{X}}_j = \mathtt{K}_i\mathtt{R}_i\overline{\mathbf{X}}_j. \tag{14.26}$$

where $\mathtt{K}_i$ are the calibration matrices for each frame and $\mathtt{R}_i$ describe the rotation matrices. If we assume that our measurements of image feature locations $\hat{\mathbf{x}}_{ij}$ have Gaussian noise with mean zero and standard deviation [1] σ, the joint density function of these measurements given an estimate $\boldsymbol{\theta}$ of the model is

$$p(\hat{\mathbf{x}}|\boldsymbol{\theta}) = \Pi_{n,m}\left(\frac{1}{2\pi\sigma^2}\right) \exp\left[-\frac{1}{2\sigma^2}(\hat{\mathbf{x}}_{ij} - \mathtt{K}_i\mathtt{R}_i\overline{\mathbf{X}}_j)^\top(\hat{\mathbf{x}}_{ij} - \mathtt{K}_i\mathtt{R}_i\overline{\mathbf{X}}_j)\right] \tag{14.27}$$

where n is the number of views and m is the number of points. The Maximum Likelihood estimator is therefore obtained by minimizing the sum of all the exponents:

$$\mathtt{MLE} = \arg\min_{\mathtt{K}_i\mathtt{R}_i\overline{\mathbf{X}}_j} \sum_{i=1}^{n}\sum_{j=1}^{m} \| \hat{\mathbf{x}}_{ij} - \mathtt{K}_i\mathtt{R}_i\overline{\mathbf{X}}_j \|^2 \tag{14.28}$$

---

[1] Of course it is a trivial extension to allow different σ for each point

The cost function is thus the sum of the squared distances of measured feature locations to the true image points for all points across all views. If the noise is gaussian, Maximum Likelihood estimation is optimal in the sense that it attains the Cramer Rao lower bound exactly.

The minimum of this non-linear cost function is sought using a Levenberg-Marquardt algorithm modified to take advantage of the sparse block structure of the matrices involved in the process. This method is generically termed bundle-adjustment in the computer vision and photogrammetry communities.

An attractive feature of this method is that the parameterization of the model is flexible. This permits to impose any constraints available both on the internal parameters of the camera and on the rotation parameters. If the rotations have only 2 degrees of freedom (as is the case with pan-tilt mounts) this can be reflected in the model. Available constraints on the internal parameters of the cameras such as zero skew, known aspect ratio or fixed but unknown principal point may also be imposed.

Given the large number of model parameters it is not surprising that the objective is highly non-convex and so it is crucial to provide an initial estimate for the iteration close to the global minimum for the algorithm to converge to the global minimum. In our implementation we have used the output from the non-linear iterative method described in section 14.3.3.1 to initialize the minimization.

Our overall algorithm is as follows. First compute the inter-image homographies from corresponding points between views. Then obtain an initial estimate for matrices $\mathtt{K}_i$ and $\mathtt{R}_i$ using the linear method described in section 14.3.3.2. Use this as the starting point for the non-linear method described in section 14.3.3.1. Finally, refine the estimates of the camera matrices $\mathtt{K}_i$, the rotation matrices $\mathtt{R}_i$, and the 3D rays $\overline{\mathbf{X}}_j$ using the MLE minimization.

14.5.2 Using Priors on the Estimated Parameters: Maximum a Posteriori Estimation (MAP)

Maximum a posteriori estimation allows prior information about model parameters to be incorporated with observed data in a meaningful statistical way. For instance, it is well known that the principal point varies between views when a camera is zoomed, but this variation is small and is centred around the image centre. Incorporating prior knowlegde is achieved using Bayes rule which provides the posterior density of the parameters $p(\boldsymbol{\theta}|\hat{\mathbf{x}})$ given the observed data and a prior model for the parameter vector $p(\boldsymbol{\theta})$ as the product

$$p(\boldsymbol{\theta}|\hat{\mathbf{x}}) \propto p(\hat{\mathbf{x}}|\boldsymbol{\theta})p(\boldsymbol{\theta}) \tag{14.29}$$

Maximum a Posteriori estimation chooses the maximum of this distribution as the estimate of the parameters. A Gaussian prior on the parameter vector may be expressed as

$$p(\boldsymbol{\theta}) \propto \exp\left[-\frac{1}{2}(\boldsymbol{\theta} - \mu_\theta)^\top \mathtt{P}_0^{-1}(\boldsymbol{\theta} - \mu_\theta)\right] \tag{14.30}$$

where μ_θ is the mean value and $\mathtt{P}_0^{-1}$ is the covariance matrix of the parameter vector $\boldsymbol{\theta}$. If we wish to maximize the posterior distribution (14.29) we must minimize the sum of the exponents in (14.27) and (14.30). This is achieved by minimizing the following cost function.

$$\mathcal{C}_{MAP} = \sum_{i=1}^{n}\sum_{j=1}^{m} \parallel \hat{\mathbf{x}}_{ij} - \mathtt{K}_i\mathtt{R}_i\overline{\mathbf{X}}_j \parallel^2 + (\boldsymbol{\theta} - \mu_\theta)^\top \mathtt{P}_0^{-1}(\boldsymbol{\theta} - \mu_\theta) \tag{14.31}$$

This cost function is equivalent to (14.28) with an added term that penalizes values of the parameters that are far from satisfying the prior model.

In our self-calibration algorithm we have imposed a prior on the location of the principal point. As we can observe from our ground truth graphs for the calibration of our zoom camera (see Figure 14.6), the location of the principal point varies between views but not very significantly. It is located close to the image centre and within a small radius distance.

The principal point is known to be a poorly constrained parameter which tends to fit to noise. Thus, as we observed in our experiments, permitting it to vary indiscriminately can have very deleterious effects in the computation of the other parameters. However, the use of prior knowledge about the distribution of this parameter in the MAP estimate may reduce these effects. The prior can be expressed as:

$$\sum_{i=1}^{n}(\mathbf{u}_0^i - \overline{\mathbf{u}}_0)^\top \begin{bmatrix} \sigma_x^2 & 0 \\ 0 & \sigma_y^2 \end{bmatrix}^{-1} (\mathbf{u}_0^i - \overline{\mathbf{u}}_0) \tag{14.32}$$

where $\mathbf{u}_0^i = ({u_0}^i, {v_0}^i)$ is the estimate of the principal point location for each frame, σ_x and σ_y are the uncertainties in the x and y direction of the principal point and $\overline{\mathbf{u}}_0$ is its mean value that we have taken to be at the centre of the image. This prior penalizes values of the principal point that are far away from the centre of the image.

14.5.3 Experimental Results

14.5.3.1 Real Images

Here we present the results of the bundle-adjustment refinement stage on the bookshelf sequence shown in section 14.4.2. We show results using two different starting points for the minimization: the output given by the nonlinear method imposing fixed principal point and allowing it to vary. Rotation matrices were modelled as the two parameter rotations described by pan-tilt units.

Results are shown in figure 14.7 and prove the significance of choosing a starting point for the bundle-adjustment minimization close enough to the global minimum. When the algorithm was initialized using the output from the non-linear algorithm allowing the principal point to vary (see Figure 14.7 (b)) the minimization started far from the true solution. Estimates of the focal length and motion improved, but bundle-adjustment failed to achieve convergence to the global minimum. These results show that bundle-adjustment fails to resolve the near-ambiguities described in [101]. Indeed bundle-adjustment attempts to minimize image reprojection error, however this does not prevent the process from converging to a local minimum where the ambiguity is still present. These near-ambiguities tend to occur when the viewing conditions are ill-conditioned (large focal lengths or small rotations) and are more severe when the self-calibration algorithm attempts to solve for a varying principal point. The higher the dimensionality of the parameter space the more likely ambiguities are to appear. Best results were obtained when a prior on the location of the principal point was imposed using MAP estimation.

However, when the starting point was set at the output given by the non-linear algorithm imposing the fixed principal point constraint (see Figure 14.7 (a)), bundle-adjustment started closer to the true solution. In this case, the final estimates given by bundle-adjustment were very close to the global minimum. Best results, particularly for the motion parameters, were also achieved when imposing a prior on the location of the principal point.

Note that in the bundle-adjustment process itself, different constraints may also be imposed on the intrinsic parameters. Our results show that when initialized close to the true solution applying the fixed principal point constraint or allowing it to vary did not make much difference to the result, while when initialized far away from the true solution imposing the principal point to be constant throughout the sequence provided better results. However, best results are achieved in both cases when a prior on the location of the principal point is imposed by using MAP estimation.

14.6 Discussion

In this chapter we have discussed the theory of self-calibration of rotating cameras with varying internal parameters. We have described two self-calibration algorithms (linear and non-linear) to solve for the varying intrinsic parameters of the camera given the inter-image homographies that relate corresponding points between views. The algorithms are based on the use of the *infinite homography constraint* which describes the mapping of the image of the absolute conic (or its dual) between views. Both methods require some constraints to be imposed on the calibration parameters of the camera.

The first algorithm is iterative and requires an initial estimate, however we have experienced that the global minimum is achieved over a wide range of starting points. The problem is parameterized explicitly in terms of the calibration parameters of each camera, therefore it is a very flexible algorithm in terms of the constraints that can be imposed on the intrinsics. Each calibration parameter may be assumed to be known, constant throughout the sequence or free to vary. The linear algorithm is a fast and simple method, suitable for real-time applications, but is more restrictive in terms of the constraints that can be imposed on the internal parameters of the camera. It can be used with the minimal assumption of zero camera skew, but useful constraints such as a fixed principal point or aspect ratio may not be imposed. A final bundle-adjustment algorithm where global image reprojection error is minimized has also been described. If some prior knowledge on the distribution of the parameters is known, this may be imposed via a MAP estimate.

In the experimental results we have analysed the effect of imposing different constraints on the intrinsic parameters of the camera. A relevant issue we have addressed is that, in general, best results are obtained when the principal point is assumed to be fixed throughout the sequence, even when it is known to be varying in reality. This, perhaps contradictory, effect is caused by the fact that there is an inherent ambiguity in the simultaneous computation of the rotation parameters and the focal length of the camera (described in [101]) which becomes more prominent when the principal point, a poorly conditioned parameter, is allowed to vary indiscriminately. Results improve when a MAP estimate is used to impose a prior on the location of the principal point.

An important issue we have not addressed in this chapter is the effect of radial distortion on the self-calibration process. Radial distortion can have very negative effects on the self-calibration of a rotating and zooming camera. A geometric interpretation of this effect is described in [279]. In [60] we investigate the possibility of including some radial correction parameters in the bundle-adjustment stage of the self-calibration process. However, in these experiments bundle-adjustment did not succeed to converge to the global minimum. Therefore, finding a reliable method to determine the radial distortion parameters automatically when the intrinsic parameters of the camera are varying is an important matter still under investigation.

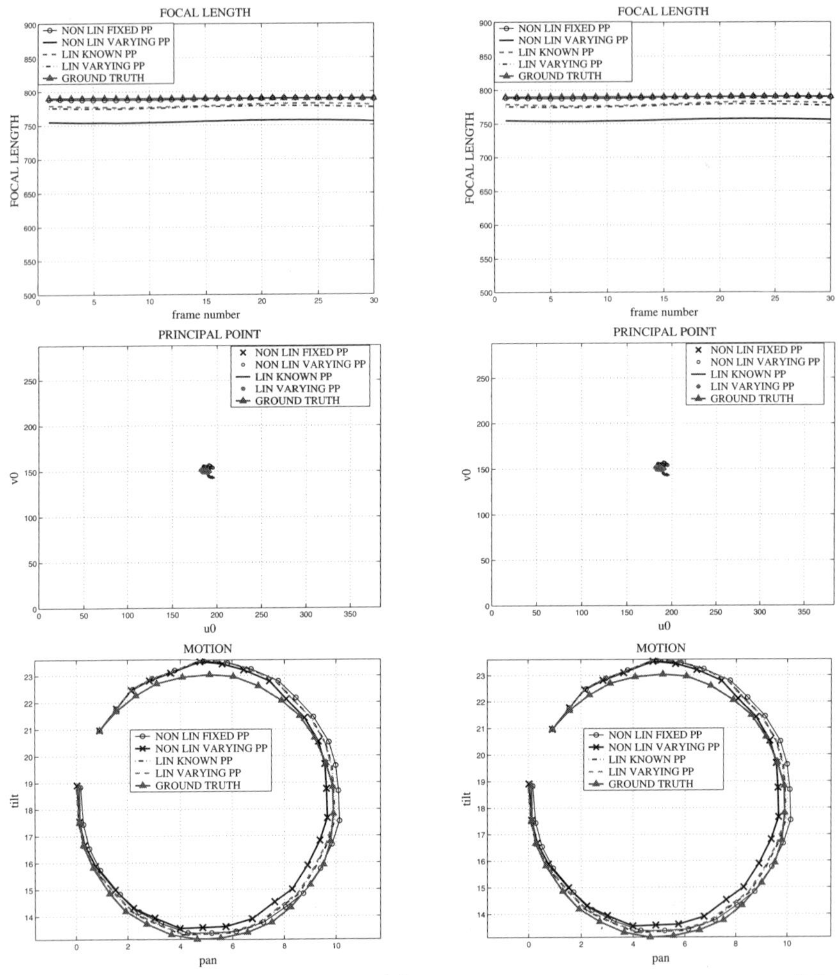

FIGURE 14.6. Ground truth and computed values for the focal length (top), the location of the principal point (middle) and the motion of the camera (bottom) for the fixed focal length (left (a)) and the variable focal length (right (b)) bookshelf sequences. Results are shown for (i) the iterative Levenberg-Marquardt algorithm imposing the square-pixels constraint (NON LIN VARYING PP), (ii) the iterative Levenberg-Marquardt algorithm imposing the square-pixels and known fixed principal point constraints (NON LIN FIXED PP), (iii) the linear algorithm imposing the square-pixels constraint (LIN VARYING PP) and (iv) the linear algorithm imposing the square-pixels and known principal point constraint (LIN FIXED PP). For visualization purposes, the motion was represented by plotting pan versus elevation angles.

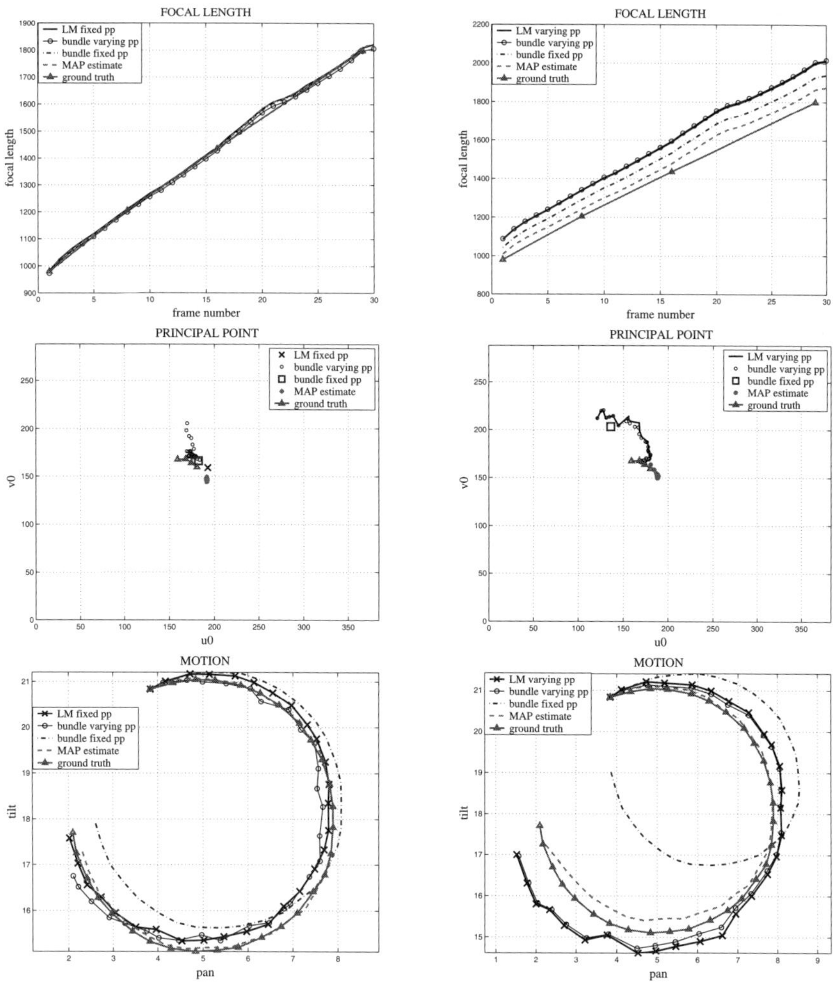

(a) (b)

FIGURE 14.7. Ground truth and computed values of the focal length, the location of the principal point and the motion of the camera for the variable focal length bookshelf sequence using the bundle-adjustment refinement. Results of the bundle-adjustment algorithm are shown using different starting points. On the left column (a) we show results using the iterative Levenberg-Marquardt algorithm imposing both the square-pixels and the fixed principal point constraints (LM fixed pp) as starting point, whereas on the right (b) the starting point was provided by the iterative Levenberg-Marquardt algorithm imposing only the square-pixels constraint, allowing the principal point to vary (LM varying pp). Results are given for (i) bundle-adjustment allowing the principal point to vary (bundle varying pp), (ii) bundle-adjustment with fixed principal point (bundle fixed pp) and (iii) maximum a posteriori estimation (MAP estimate).

15

360 x 360 Mosaics: Regular and Stereoscopic

S.K. Nayar and A.D. Karmarkar

15.1 Spherical Mosaics

A mosaic is constructed by stitching[1] together multiple images, where the individual images correspond to different views of the scene captured from approximately the same viewpoint. Several methods for image mosaicing have been proposed (for examples, see [38, 178, 312, 49, 122, 146, 214, 231, 267, 241, 158, 181, 273]). These techniques use a conventional imaging lens to capture the image sequence. Since such lenses have limited fields of view, the computation of a complete spherical mosaic requires the capture and processing of a large number of images. In addition, errors in the image projection model and errors in the estimation of motion between images makes it difficult to complete the sphere without undesirable seams in the final mosaic. Further, in the case of a hand-held camera, it is hard for the user to ensure that the complete sphere has been scanned during the capture process.

An alternative approach is to use a wide-angle imaging system such as a fish-eye lens (see [159, 298]) or a catadioptric imaging system (see [195], [300] for surveys). In both cases, a hemispherical field of view can be captured within a single image. Hence, a small number of such images can be stitched together to obtain a spherical mosaic[2]. However, this approach typically results in inadequate resolution due to the inherent trade-off between field of view and image resolution; as the field of view increases, the resolution decreases, causing the computed spherical image to be of lower quality than in the case of a conventional imaging system.

This chapter presents two efficient approaches for capturing high resolution spherical mosaics. In the first approach, a wide-angle imaging system is used to capture a sequence of 360° strips on the sphere by a single ro-

---

[1] In our definition of mosaicing, we will include both image based as well as slit (a slice through the image) based techniques. In the case of slits, the slices are not really stitched but rather concatenated together to form the mosaic.

[2] See [117] for results on the stitching of two fish-eye images to obtain a spherical mosaic.

tation of the capture device. For this, we suggest the use of a catadioptric imaging system since such a system typically produces higher resolution in the periphery of the hemispherical field of view than a fish-eye lens. The unknown rotations between the strips are estimated and used to blend the multiple strips into a single spherical mosaic. Our second approach seeks to further enhance the resolution of the computed mosaic. This is done by designing novel catadioptric sensors that capture a single 360° slice of the scene[3]. Mirror shapes are derived that enable the projection of a thin slice onto a large image area. This results in the capture of high resolution slices despite the use of a low resolution (640x480 pixel) image detector. Such a slice camera is rotated on a turntable and the captured slices are concatenated to obtain a high resolution spherical mosaic. Though a large number of images (slices) are needed to obtain a high resolution mosaic, the processing of each image is minimal and is easily done in real time.

Recently, several investigators have explored the capture of stereoscopic panoramas. Ishiguro *et al.* [135] were the first to use stereo panoramas for computing structure. Then, Huang and Hung [114] used a rotating stereo head to show that two panoramic images are sufficient to generate stereo views for any direction within the panoramas. Subsequently, Peleg and Ben-Ezra [213] showed that the rotation of a single camera provides all the information needed to obtain a stereo panorama. More recently, Shum *et al.* [256] extended these ideas to capture omnivergent stereo data, using the rotation of a camera. Shum *et al.* also showed synthetic examples of spherical stereo mosaics but did not present techniques for obtaining such data in practice. We show that our strip and slice cameras can be used to easily capture stereoscopic spherical mosaics by displacing the viewpoint of the imaging system from the axis of rotation. We conclude with examples of high resolution stereoscopic spherical mosaics, that enable a user to freely pan and tilt while perceiving the depths of objects in the scene.

15.2 360° Strips

A spherical mosaic can be represented in several ways. Without loss of generality, we will use the spherical panorama shown in Figure 15.1 as our representation of choice. This representation is convenient as it is linear in the polar angle θ and the azimuth angle ϕ. As shown in Figure 15.1, if we use only half the strip (180°), a single 360° rotation along the azimuth angle ϕ is sufficient to cover the entire sphere. If the strip is cylindrical, it maps to a bow-shaped band in the spherical panorama. Alternatively, a 180° rotation of the sensor is sufficient if full 360° strips are used.

---

[3] In [209], a 180° slice is captured by using a fish-eye lens and a high resolution line detector.

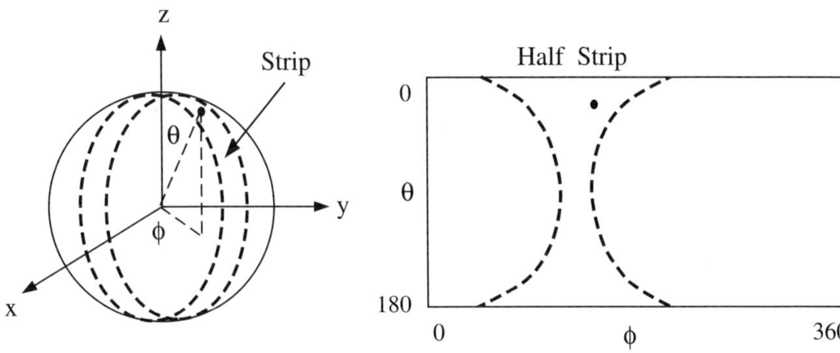

FIGURE 15.1. A single rotation of a 360° camera results in strips on the sphere that together cover the entire sphere. Half of a strip (180°) maps to a bow-shaped band in the spherical panorama.

A 360° strip can be captured using a fish-eye lens with a field of view slightly greater than a hemisphere, or a catadioptric sensor that uses a curved mirror and an imaging lens. As shown in [12], parabolic, hyperbolic and ellipsoidal mirrors will produce strips while maintaining a single viewpoint. Catadioptric sensors have a clear advantage over fish-eye lenses here, since they tend to have greater resolution in the periphery of the field of view (and hence, within the strip). It was shown in [12] that if a conic mirror with profile $z(r)$ is used with a perspective lens located at $z = c$, the resolution of the catadioptric system is:

$$\frac{dA}{d\Omega} = \frac{r^2 + z^2}{(c - z)^2 + r^2} \frac{dA}{d\omega} \tag{15.1}$$

where dA is the area of a single pixel on the image detector, $d\omega$ is the solid angle subtended by the pixel through the imaging lens and $d\Omega$ is the solid angle subtended by the pixel after reflection by the curved mirror. In the case of a parabolic system, the resolution perpendicular to the optical axis (in the middle of the strip) is approximately 4 times the resolution in the direction of the optical axis [195]. This increase in resolution (with respect to a fish-eye lens) is of course only in the ϕ dimension of the mosaic, as the maximum achievable resolution along θ is determined by the number of pixels on the image detector and is similar for all 360° imaging systems.

Typically, catadioptric systems tend to be larger than conventional optics, since the mirror and the imaging lens need to be distant from each other to minimize the blindspot of the sensor. However, since we are using only a thin (peripheral) strip, the mirror and the lens can be in close proximity to each other, allowing compact packaging of the system. In addition, folded systems with two or more mirrors can be used to facilitate further reduction in size while improving image quality, as described in [199].

Let us consider the case where the sensor is freely rotated by a human and not a controlled turntable. In this case, the rotations between consecutive frames are unknown and need to be estimated, so that all captured strips can be mapped to the coordinate frame of the spherical mosaic. To this end, the rotation matrices $\mathbf{R}_{k-1,k}$ between consecutive images k and $k-1$ are computed using a set of corresponding features, that are found using a feature tracking algorithm. We can assume that the frame of reference of the mosaic is defined with respect to the initial orientation ($k = 0$) of the sensor. Then, each strip is mapped to the mosaic by using the rotation matrix:

$$\mathbf{R}_k = \mathbf{R}_{0,1}\mathbf{R}_{1,2}....\mathbf{R}_{k-1,k} \tag{15.2}$$

When strips are mapped to the spherical panorama, they are expected to overlap with previously accumulated data. Two steps are taken to ensure a seamless mosaic. First, we note that the computed rotations between strips are expected to include small errors. Therefore, the computed rotation for a strip is only used as an initial estimate of the location of the strip with respect to the mosaic. The Euler angles $(\alpha_k, \beta_k, \gamma_k)$ corresponding to the rotation matrix $\mathbf{R}_k$ are then varied within a small search range to find the strip location on the mosaic that minimizes the sum-of-squared difference in brightness between the strip and the mosaic. Once the rotation matrix has been refined in this manner, a blending process is used to merge the strip data with the mosaic. During blending, the brightness of a point in the region of overlap between the mosaic and the strip is computed as a weighted sum of its brightnesses in the mosaic and the strip. The weights are proportional to the shortest distances of the point from the boundaries of the mosaic and the strip.

Figure 15.2 shows the catadioptric imaging system we have used for strip mosaicing. This system was described in [195] and includes a parabolic mirror and a telecentric lens. This optics is attached to a Canon Optura video camera. The imaging system is mounted on a tripod and rotated by hand, and the captured video is processed using the above mosaicing algorithm. Since the sensor was rotated by 360°, only half the strip (180○) was used for the mosaic computation. In our experiment, a strip width of 30° was used. The computed spherical mosaic (4000×2000 pixels in size) is shown in Figure 15.3(a). Using one of several image rendering softwares, one can create perspective images and freely navigate around the spherical field of view. Three examples of computed perspective images are shown in Figure 15.3(b), which reveal the resolution of the computed mosaic. While the resolution is reasonable for objects at short distances from the imaging system, it is not sufficient for distant object. Several factors contribute to the lack of resolution. First, the alignment of a strip with the mosaic is never exact and therefore the blending process low-pass filters the mosaic. More importantly, the video camera has only 640×480 pixels. Hence, though there are 2000 pixels in the θ dimension of the mosaic, these pixels are interpolated from just $\pi 240 = 753$ pixels (measurements). We will now present ways to enhance mosaic resolution, without increasing the resolution of our image detector.

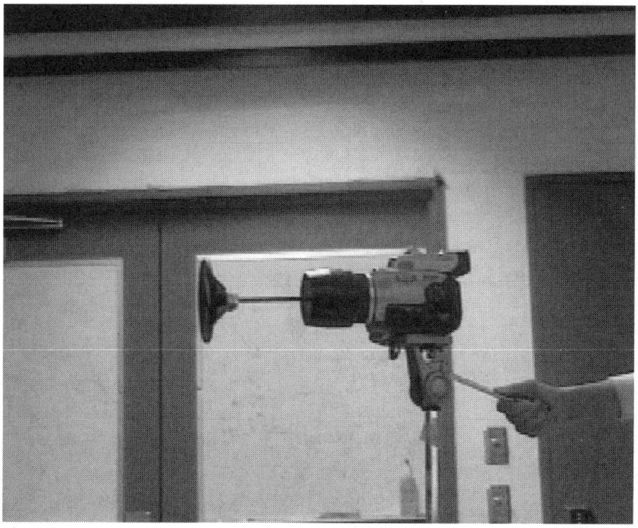

FIGURE 15.2. A panoramic camera (described in [195]) is rotated by hand on a tripod to capture a sequence of 360° strips.

15.3 360° Slices

We now introduce a new class of sensors that can image a thin 360 degree slice with higher resolution. Before we proceed to present the problem of slice imaging, it is worth comparing the use of slices with the use of strips. The advantage of strips is that for smooth rotation of the sensor, an overlap between successive frames is guaranteed and can be used for computing the rotations between frames. However, as we have seen, the resulting mosaic is limited in resolution. In the case of slices higher resolution is achieved. However, since there is no overlap between slices, the rotation of the sensor must be known. As illustrated in Figure 15.4, a 360° slice corresponds to a greater circle on the sphere and half the slice maps to a vertical line in the spherical panorama.

As shown in Figure 15.5(a), a slice camera is rotated using a motorized turntable. The turntable is spun at constant velocity as the images are captured, keeping the rotation between consecutive slices constant. As noted in [213] and [256], if the center of projection of the image sensor is displaced from the axis of rotation, a stereoscopic panorama can be captured. In the case of spherical stereo, complete 360° slices must be captured during rotation. If this is feasible, one half (180° field of view) of the slice is used to construct a left-view mosaic while the other half can be used to obtain a right-view mosaic. Clearly, we could also use a 360° strip sensor to accomplish this. However, as we have seen, the resolution is not of sufficient quality and is expected to degrade when the strip sensor is placed off-axis since this introduces a translation in addition to the rotation between frames. Both these problems can be overcome using a slice sensor.

We define a slice camera as one that projects a very thin 360° sheet of rays onto a large number of image pixels as shown in Figure 15.6(a). While a fish-eye lens or a wide-angle catadioptric sensor projects a slice of the scene onto a circle (say, of radius R_1), the slice camera projects the same slice onto a wide disc (of thickness $R_1 - R_2$). Since this disc is imaged using a rectangular grid of pixels, additional measurements along θ are obtained within the disc. Therefore, in place of the small number of measurements on a circle shown in Figure 15.6(b), we obtain a larger number of measurements as shown in Figure 15.6(c). These measurements are easily interpolated to obtain a dense, uniform sampling of the brightness function $I(\theta)$ along the slice. It may appear that the resolution in this case is proportional to the width of the image disc. Due to finite (non-zero) pixel size this is not the case. An analysis of exactly how resolution varies with disc width is currently under investigation. For now, we will simply note that a significant improvement in resolution is achievable.

15.4 Slice Cameras

We are now left with the problem of designing a slice sensor. Once again, catadioptric imaging provides the flexibility needed for such a design. As shown in Figure 15.7, the problem can be formulated as one of deriving the mirror shape that reflects only a set of parallel incoming rays towards the center of projection (pinhole) O of the imaging lens. Since this is a rotational symmetric imaging system, the problem is reduced to finding the profile $z(r)$ of the mirror. Let the pinhole of the perspective imaging lens be at $z = c$. For any point on the mirror, we denote the angle made by the normal with respect to the optical (vertical) axis by β and the angle made by the reflected ray with the horizontal axis by α. Here, we will assume that the slice is perpendicular to the optical axis, and hence $\beta + \gamma = \pi/2$. However, the formulation is general in that $\beta + \gamma$ can be set to any other angle, which would result in the imaging of a conical sheet of rays with its axis aligned with the optical axis, rather than a flat sheet.

Note that the reflecting point (z, r) is related to the angle of reflection α as:

$$\tan\alpha = \frac{c - z}{r}. \tag{15.3}$$

Since the incoming ray is specularly reflected, it is easy to show that

$$\alpha = 2\beta . \tag{15.4}$$

Also, we know that the slope of the mirror at the point of reflection is related to the angle β of the normal as

$$-\tan\beta = \frac{dz}{dr} . \tag{15.5}$$

Using the above expressions in the well-known identity

$$\tan 2\beta = \frac{2\tan\beta}{1-\tan^2\beta} , \tag{15.6}$$

we get the first-order quadratic differential equation:

$$\frac{-2\frac{dz}{dr}}{1-\frac{dz}{dr}^2} = \frac{c - z}{r} . \tag{15.7}$$

This equation is solved to obtain the mirror profile

$$z = c - 2\sqrt{k}\sqrt{|r| + k} , \tag{15.8}$$

where k is the constant of integration. If we set $z = 0$ at $r = 0$, we get $k = c/2$. The resulting mirror is shown in Figure 15.8 and has a hat-like shape. Closer examination of the manner in which this mirror reflects incoming rays, reveals that it is a surface of revolution generated by a parabolic section. For instance, the parallel sheet rays that lie in the plane of Figure 15.8 are reflected by the parabola towards its focus, where the pinhole of the imaging lens is located.

An even simpler mirror shape is obtained by using orthographic image projection. In this case, $\beta = \pi/2$ and hence (15.5) reduces to $dz/dr = -1$. The resulting mirror is a cone with a 90° angle at the apex, as shown in Figure 15.9. In [195], orthographic projection was used with a parabolic mirror and in [304] a cone was used with perspective lens. In both cases, a wide field of view was sought in both dimensions (ϕ and θ). In our case, the combination of orthographic projection and a conical mirror results in the desired image projection model for parallel rays. It is worth noting that the thickness Δz of the sheet of rays can be made arbitrarily small. For instance, if a cone with a 1 cm outer diameter is projected onto a 500x500 pixel detector, a 0.5 mm thick sheet of rays is projected onto an image disc that is 25 pixels wide.

15.5 Experimental Results

We have implemented the slice camera illustrated in Figure 15.9. A telecentric lens is used to ensure orthographic projection and a cone with a

65 mm outer diameter is attached to the lens using a transparent acrylic cylinder. This optical system is attached to a Canon Optura digital video camera, as shown in Figure 15.10. The complete imaging system is rotated using a Daedal motorized turntable. The center of projection of the imaging system is offset from the axis of rotation by 3 inches to get a stereo baseline of 6 inches. In most of our experiments, a complete 360 degree rotation of the sensor was done in 3 minutes. This results in a sequence of approximately 5000 images.

An example of an image produced by the slice camera is shown in Figure 15.11. As expected, scene features are mapped to radial strips in the image. A 4-pixel wide disc was used to obtain approximately 3000 color measurements within a 180 degree (half) slice. These measurements are interpolated to obtain 2000 uniformly distributed samples. The right half and the left half of the slice were mapped to vertical lines in the left and right spherical panoramas, respectively. Figures 15.16(a) and (b) show the left and right spherical mosaics computed for an indoor scene. Each mosaic is 4000x2000 pixels in size. It is easy to see that all scene points produce disparity in the left and right mosaics, the disparity varying with distance from the imaging system. Figures 15.16(c) and (d) show stereo pairs of perspective views for two regions of the scene. We have used a perspective viewer to enable a user to freely roam around the captured sphere, while perceiving the depths of objects using red-green eye glasses. The resulting experience is similar to freely panning and tilting one's head.

The resolution of these mosaics is significantly greater that the one in Figure 15.3 generated using a strip camera. This increase in resolution is not obvious since all mosaics have been scaled down in size prior to printing on paper. The resolution advantage of the slice camera is illustrated in Figure 15.13, where a step edge in the scene is reconstructed from the slices using image discs of 1 pixel and 4 pixel widths. In both cases, the same interpolation algorithm (a Gaussian filter with σ equal to 0.001 radians) was used. It is clear that the 4-pixel disc provides higher resolution that the 1-pixel disc. It is worth mentioning that our images were digitized using the analog output of the video camera, which is known to be of low quality compared to the digital output. Experiments using the digital camera output are underway and are expected to produce significantly better results.

15.6 Variants of the Slice Camera

We conclude by mentioning a few variants of the slice camera shown in Figure 15.10. As always, there exists an inherent trade-off between slice resolution and slice field of view. If a greater resolution is desired at the cost of field of view, the magnification of the imaging lens can be increased to image smaller sections of the cone. In Figure 15.14, two 90° sections of the cone are configured to fill the larger dimension (640 pixels in this case) of the image detector. Consequently, a further increase in resolution by a factor of two is achieved. Finally, as with wide-angle catadioptric systems, multiple mirrors can be used to reduce sensor size while possibly improving image quality (see [199]). In Figure 15.15(a), a perspective lens and a concave parabolic mirror are used to achieve orthographic projection of the conical mirror. Similarly, as shown in Figure 15.15(b), an ellipsoidal or hyperboloidal mirror can be used with a perspective lens to image the hat-shaped mirror. In this case, the near focus of the ellipsoidal or hyperboloidal mirror serves as the entrance pupil for the reflections from the hat-shaped mirror.

15.7 Summary

In this chapter we have presented several results on the capture of regular as well as stereoscopic spherical mosaics. We described two methods, one based on strips and other based on slices, to capture all the required scene information with a single rotation of the sensor. In addition, we derived a class of catadioptric slice cameras that project a thin sheet of parallel rays onto a wide disc in the image. The additional measurements provided by such a sensor were used to construct high resolution stereoscopic spherical mosaics. We are currently in the process of developing compact and portable slice cameras.

Acknowledgment

This research was conducted in the Computer Vision Laboratory (CAVE) at Columbia University. It was supported in parts by an NSF National Young Inventigator Award, by a David and Lucile Packard Fellowship, the DARPA/ONR MURI Grant N00014-95-1-0601 and the VSAM effort of the DARPA Image Understanding Program under ONR contract No. N00014-97-1-0553.

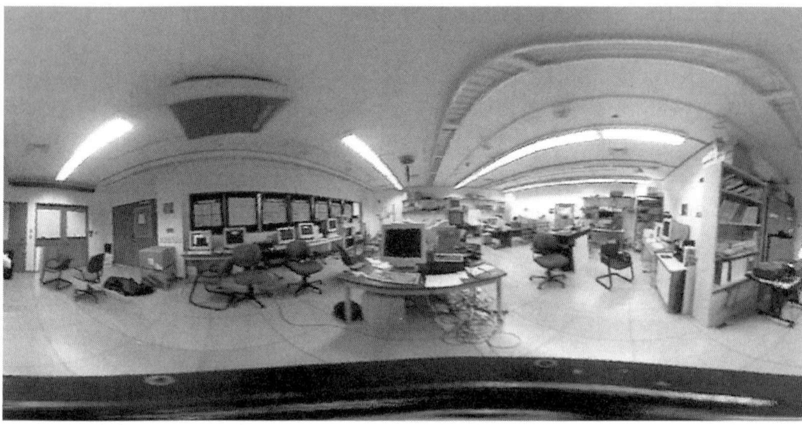

(a) Complete spherical mosaic.

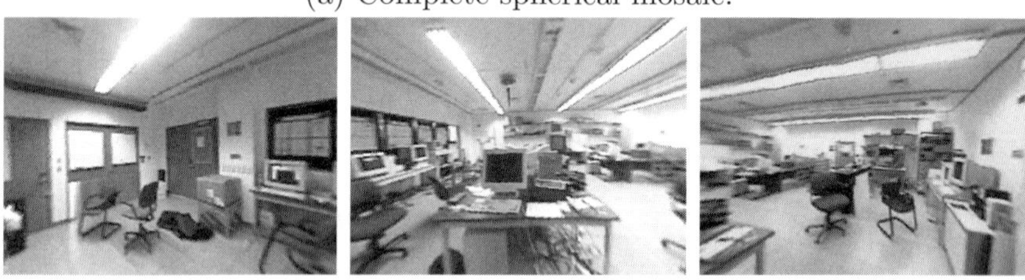

(b) Perspective views.

FIGURE 15.3. (a) The 360° camera shown in Figure 15.2 is rotated by hand to obtain a sequence of 30° strips. The unknown rotations between strips are computed from corresponding image features. The computed rotations are used to blend the strips together into a single spherical mosaic, shown here as a 4000×2000 pixel spherical panorama. (b) An interactive viewer is used to generate perspective views from the spherical mosaic.

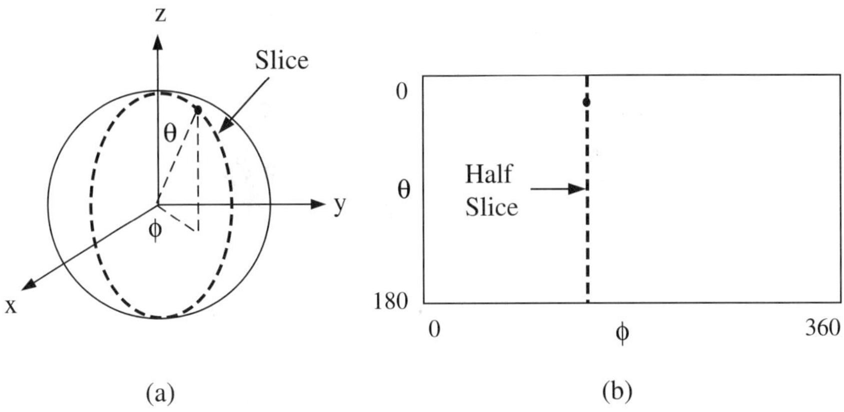

FIGURE 15.4. A single rotation of a 360° slice sensor produces a higher resolution spherical mosaic. (a) Each slice corresponds to a greater circle on the sphere. (b) Half the slice maps to a line in the spherical panorama.

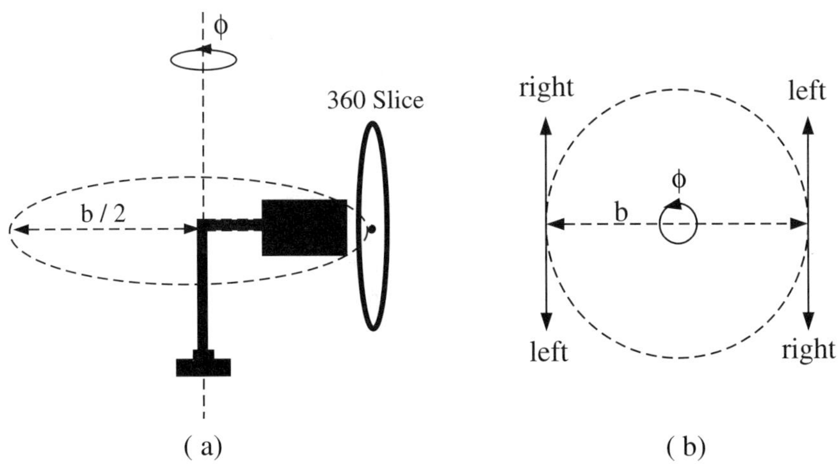

FIGURE 15.5. (a) Rotation of a slice camera with the center of projection away from the axis of rotation results in a stereoscopic spherical mosaic. (b) The two halves of the 360° slice are used to construct left and right spherical panoramas such that all scene points are seen with approximately the same baseline b. The general idea of off-axis rotation is described in detail in [213] and [256].

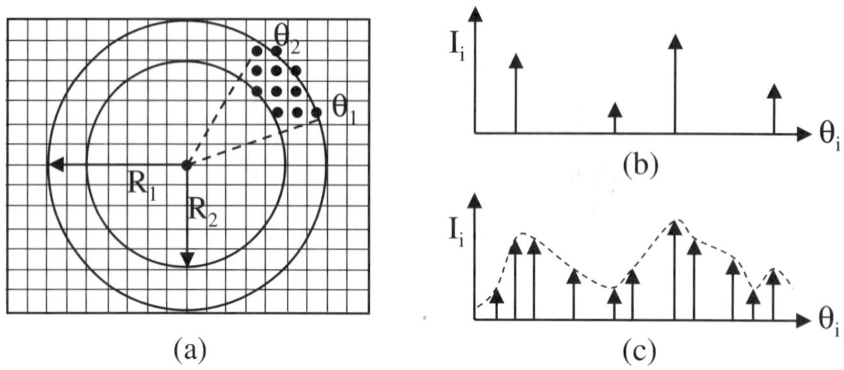

FIGURE 15.6. (a) A slice camera projects a thin 360° sheet of parallel rays onto a large disc in the image. The number of measurements within the sheet increases from (b) pixels on a circle to (c) pixels within a disc. These measurements can be interpolated to obtain a uniformly sampled high resolution slice.

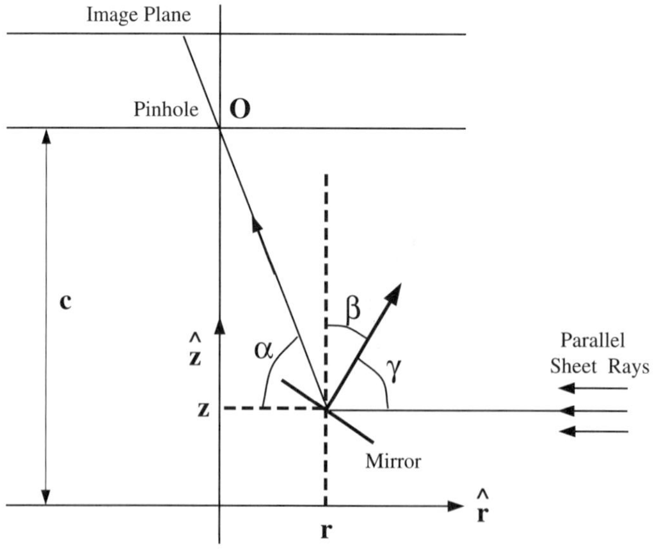

FIGURE 15.7. The mirror shape that produces a compact 360° slice is defined as one that reflects a thin sheet of parallel rays through the effective pinhole of the imaging lens.

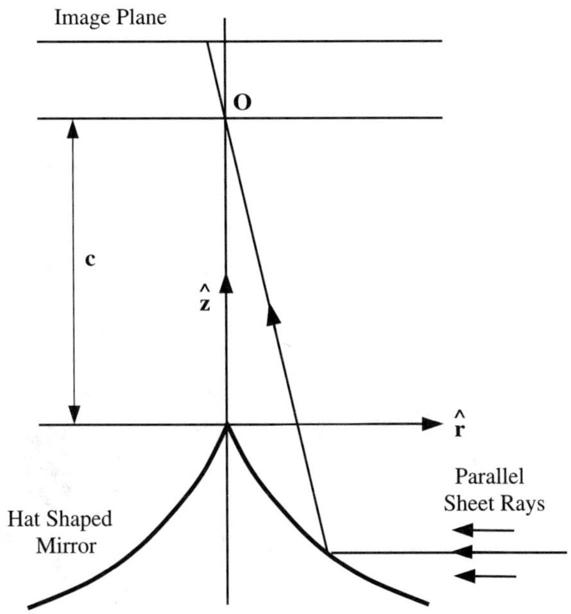

FIGURE 15.8. For perspective projection, the mirror shape that images a thin 360° sheet of parallel rays is hat-shaped and given by (15.8).

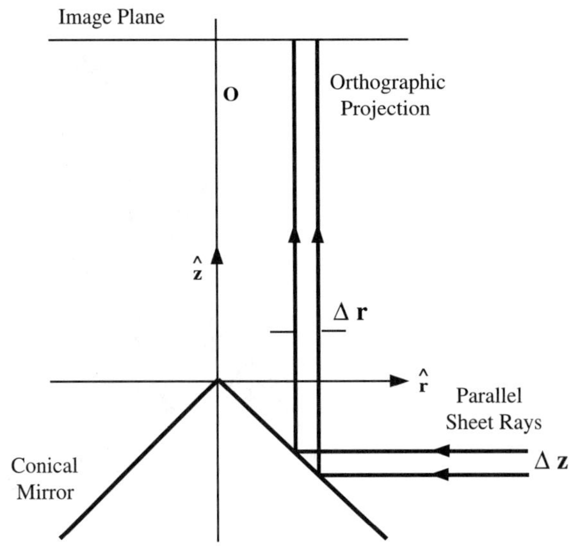

FIGURE 15.9. For orthographic projection, a conical mirror is used to image a 360° sheet of parallel rays. The thickness Δz of the sheet that maps to a given image disc can be made arbitrarily small by increasing the magnification of the orthographic lens and reducing the size of the cone.

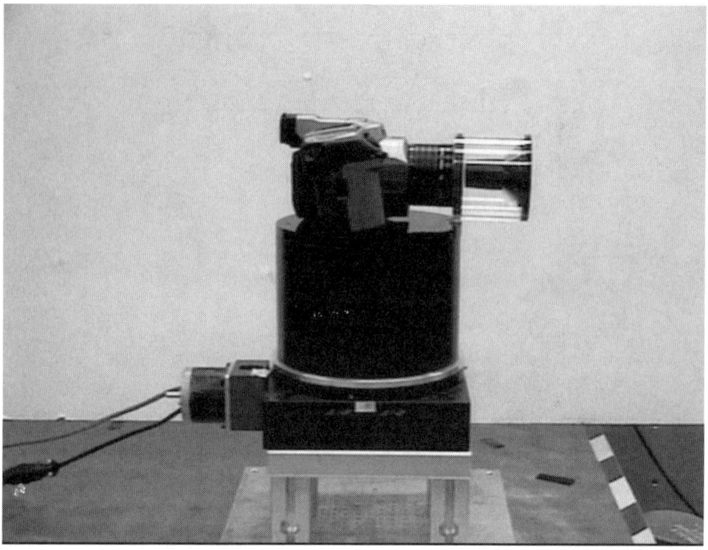

FIGURE 15.10. A slice imaging system based on the design shown in Figure 15.9. A telecentric lens and a conical mirror are attached to each other using a transparent acrylic tube. This optical system is attached to a Canon Optura video camera. The complete imaging system is rotated (off-axis for stereo) on a motorized turntable.

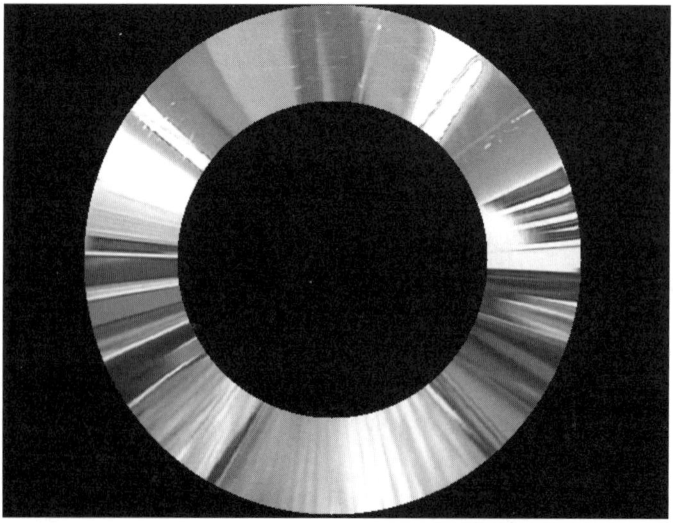

FIGURE 15.11. Example of an image produced by the slice camera shown in Figure 15.10. As expected, scene features are projected to radial strips in the image.

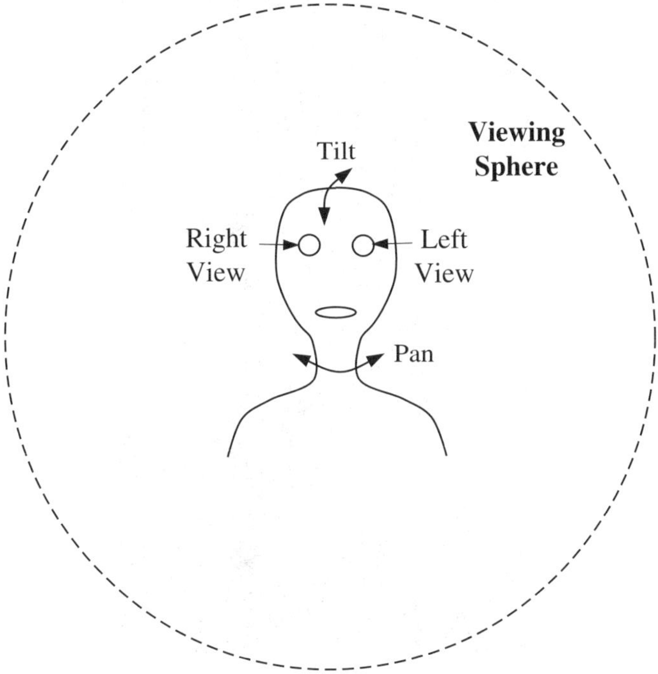

FIGURE 15.12. A 360 × 360 stereoscopic mosaic enables a user to freely pan and tilt, while viewing the world in stereo with roughly constant baseline. The resulting experience is equivalent to that of tilting and panning one's head.

(a) (b)

FIGURE 15.13. Magnified images of a step edge in the scene reconstructed using (a) an image disc of 1 pixel width and (b) an image disc of 4 pixels width. Note the effects of aliasing in (a).

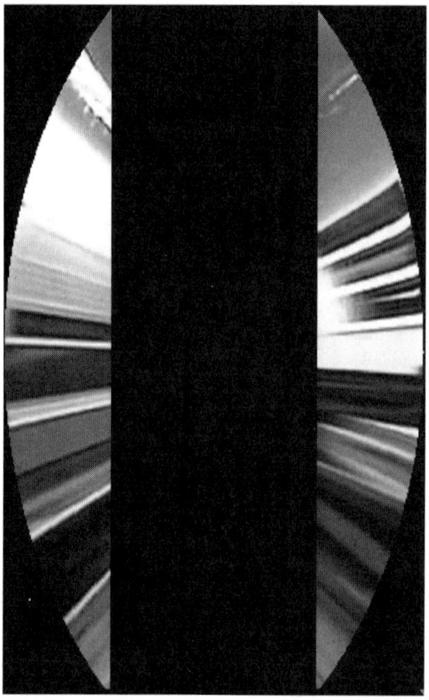

FIGURE 15.14. Two 90° sections of a cone are projected on to the larger dimension of the rectangular image. This results in a panoramic slice camera with a two-fold increase in slice resolution.

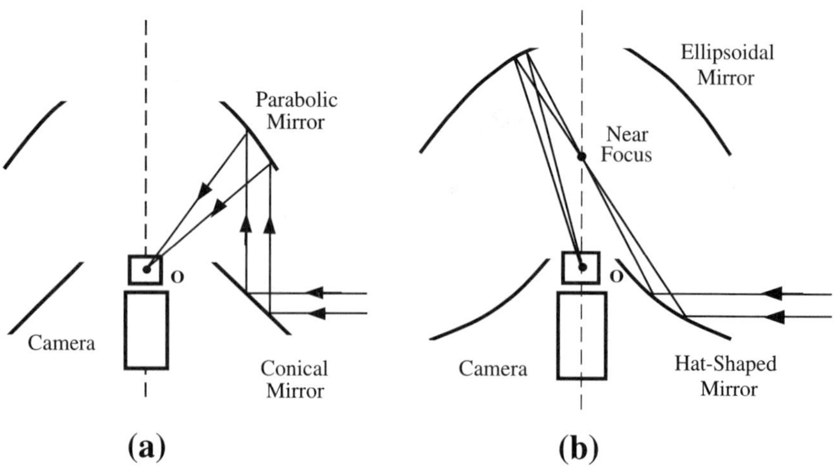

FIGURE 15.15. Optical folding can be used to further reduce the sizes of slice cameras based on (a) the conical mirror and (b) the hat-shaped mirror.

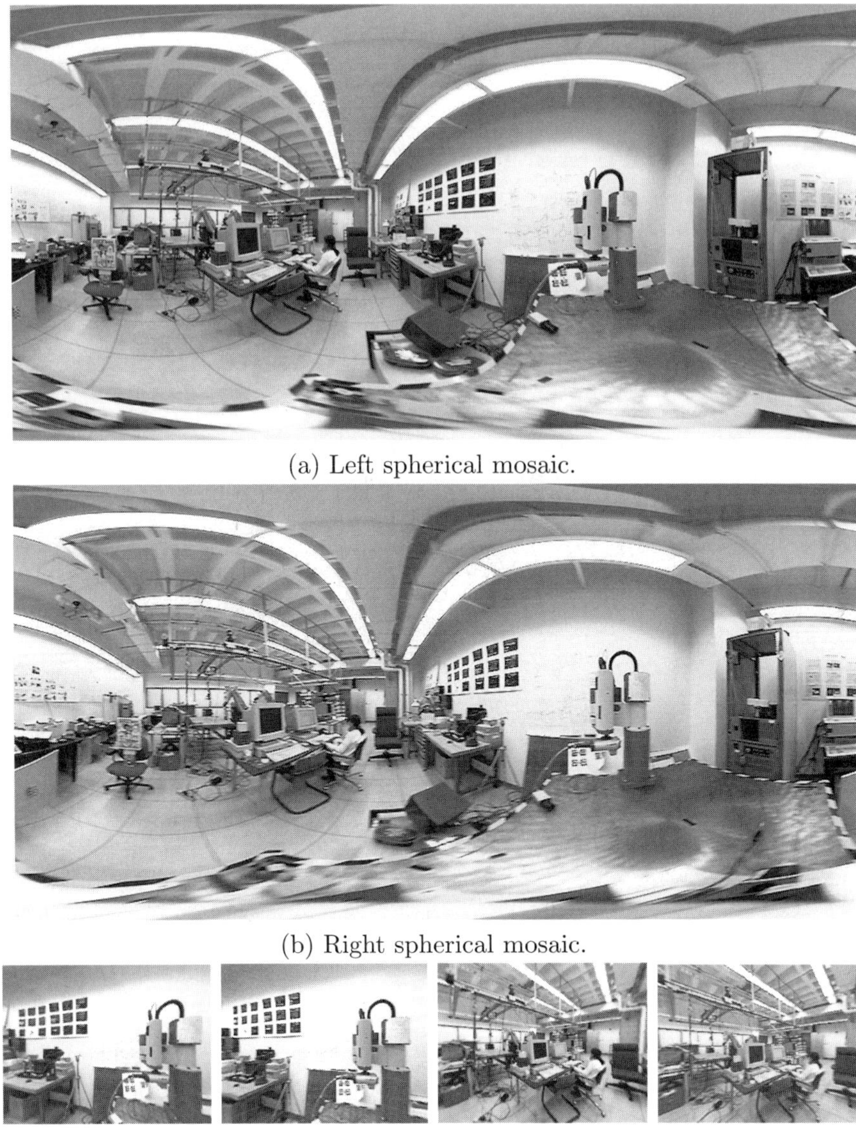

(a) Left spherical mosaic.

(b) Right spherical mosaic.

(c) Left and right perspective views. (d) Left and right perspective views.

FIGURE 15.16. The slice camera shown in Figure 15.10 was rotated with the center of projection 3 inches away from the axis of rotation to obtain the left and right spherical mosaics shown in (a) and (b). Note the horizontal disparity between the image coordinates of scene points in the left and right mosaics. Each mosaic is 4000×2000 pixels in size. (c) and (d) show left and right (stereo) perspective views for two different parts of the scene.

16

Mosaicing with Strips on Adaptive Manifolds

S. Peleg, B. Rousso, A. Rav-Acha, and A. Zomet

16.1 Introduction

Creating pictures having larger field of view, by combining many smaller images, is common since the beginning of photography, as the camera's field of view is smaller than the human field of view. In addition, some large objects can not be captured in a single picture as is the case in aerial photography. Using omnidirectional cameras [195] can sometimes provide a partial solution, but the images obtained with such cameras have substantial distortions, and capturing a wide field of view with the limited resolution of a video camera compromises image resolution. A common solution is photo-mosaicing: aligning and pasting pictures, or frames in a video sequence, to create a wider view. Digital photography enabled new implementations for mosaicing [184, 185, 212, 38, 122, 273], which were first applied to aerial and satellite images, and later used for scene and object representation.

The simplest mosaics are created by panning the camera around its optical center using a special device, in which case the panoramic image can be created on a cylindrical or a spherical manifold [177, 49, 181, 267, 158, 273]. The original images, which are a perspective projection onto an image plane, are warped to be perspectively projected into an appropriate cylinder, where they can be combined to a full 360 degrees panorama as in Fig. 16.1. While the limitations to pure sideways camera rotation enables easy mosaicing without the problems of motion parallax, this approach can not be used with other camera motions.

Simple mosaicing is also possible from a set of images whose mutual displacements are pure image-plane translations. And for somewhat more general camera motions more general transformation for image alignment can be used, like a global affine transformation or a planar-projective transformation [40, 93, 139, 241, 122]. In most cases images are aligned pairwise using the global parametric transformation, a reference frame is selected, and all images are aligned to this reference frame and combined to create the panoramic mosaic. Such methods imply the perspective projection of

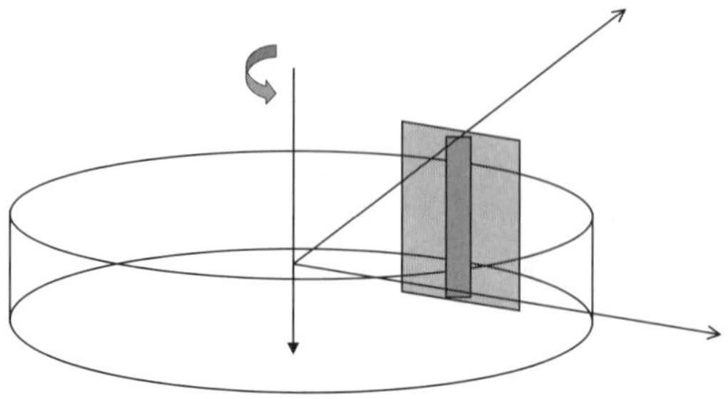

FIGURE 16.1. A panoramic image can be generated from a panning camera by combining the images on the surface of a cylinder.

all the images onto the planar manifold corresponding to the image plane of the reference frame. Using a planar manifold, and aligning all frames to a single reference frame, is reasonable only when the camera is far from the scene and its motion is mainly a translation and a rotation around the optical axis. Significant distortions are created, for example, when the camera motion includes sideway rotation.

Most restrictions on the motion of the camera used for mosaicing can be eliminated by using an adaptive manifold whose shape is determined during the mosaicing process. To enable undistorted mosaicing the selected manifold should have the property that after projecting the images onto the manifold the *optical flow*[1] vectors become approximately uniform: parallel to each other and of equal magnitude. Typical cases for this optical flow is sideways image translation, where the manifold is a plane, and a panning camera, where the manifold is a vertical cylinder, and the optical flow in a central vertical strip of the image is approximately uniform. It will also be shown that in the general case of a translating camera the manifold should be a cylinder whose axis is the direction of motion

When a perspective camera moves in a general scene, the optical flow is not uniform and depends on the scene depth. A solution for mosaicing such scenes is the "slit camera", or the "pushbroom camera", used in aerial photography [95]. This camera can be modeled as a 1-D sensor array which collects strips by "sweeping" the scene, as described in Figure 16.2.

The imaging process of the pushbroom camera can be modeled by a multi-perspective projection: For each strip the projection is perspective, while different strips may be acquired from different centers of projections. Thus in the direction of the strips, the projection is perspective, while in the direction of advance the projection is parallel. Under parallel projection, there is no parallax, so the optical flow in the result image is uniform.

[1]Image motion is represented by the optical flow: the displacement vectors associated with each image point, which specify the location of the image point in the next frame relative to its location in the current frame.

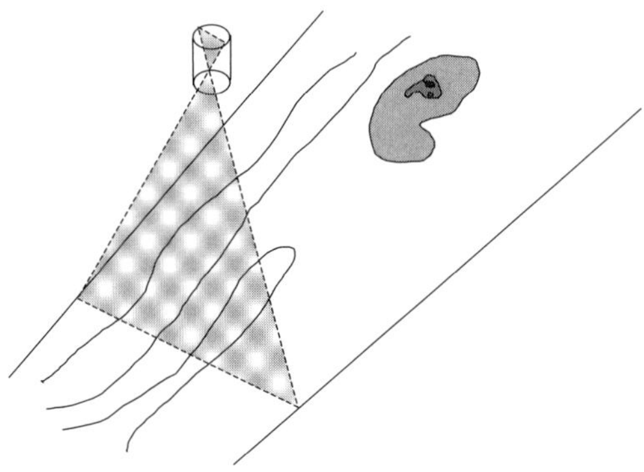

FIGURE 16.2. An aerial pushbroom camera.

The mosaicing techniques described in this paper process video sequences acquired by a standard perspective camera moving on a smooth route. They approximate the mosaic image which would have been acquired by a pushbroom camera moving on the same route. This is done by reprojecting thin strips from the images onto an adaptive manifold, such that the optical flow becomes approximately uniform: parallel and of equal magnitude. Both the adaptive manifold and the reprojection transformation are computed implicitly.

Each region in the mosaic is taken from that image where it is captured at highest resolution. While this could have been neglected in the traditional mosaicing which do not allow any scale changes, it is critical for general camera motions where, for example, a region is seen at higher resolution when closer.

A mosaicing approach which constructs for the first time multi-perspective panoramic views on general manifolds has been described in [312]. A video camera is continuously scanning the scene through a vertical "slit", and the one-dimensional vertical slits are then combined into a panoramic image. In the case of a purely panning camera the panoramic images generated by this approach are similar to the cylindrical case of Fig. 16.1, and when the slits are narrow and continuous there is no need to warp the images from a plane to a cylinder. A more general case is also presented: a camera moving on a smooth path on a horizontal plane, as described in Fig. 16.3. The mosaic is generated in this case on a more general manifold. It was assumed in [312] that the motion of the camera is measured by external devices rather than being computed from the video itself.

Practical implementations of general manifold mosaicing will be presented, based on the computed motion between the images.

Unlike other methods for multi-perspective mosaics [222, 297] the mosaics are constructed without knowing or recovering the structure of the

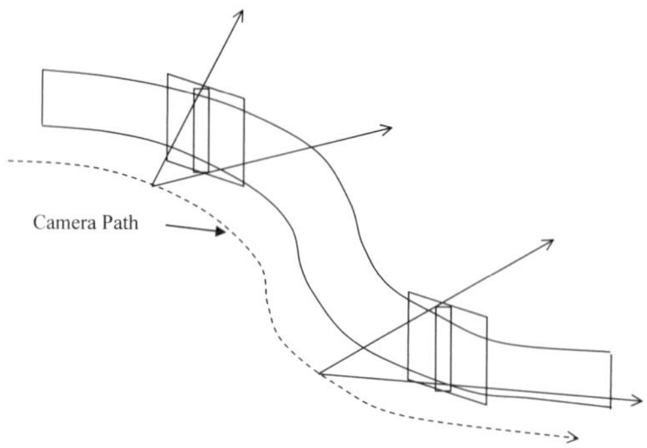

FIGURE 16.3. A panoramic image generated from a 'vertical "slit" moving on a smooth path on a horizontal plane.

scene, and without knowing explicitly the full motion and calibration of the camera.

We assume that the camera motion is a pure rotation or a pure translation. In case the camera motion comprises of both rotation and translation it is assumed that the rotation can be cancelled [229].

The method is based on building a mosaic images by collecting strips from the images, satisfying the following conditions:

- The width of the strips should be proportional to the motion.
- The collected strips should be warped and pasted into the panoramic image such that after warping, their optical flow becomes parallel to the direction in which the panoramic image is constructed, and of equal magnitude.
- In order to avoid global resizing, each image strip includes a feature (the *anchor*) which does not change under the warping. This anchor determines the form of the "broom".
- It is recommended to have *the anchor* perpendicular to the optical flow. This maximizes the information collected by the virtual 1-D sensor array.

Examples of manifold mosaicing using strips will be given for cases of almost uniform image translations caused by a panning camera [214], for 2D planar projective transformation caused from a forward moving camera [232], and for 2D planar projective transformation caused by a tilted panning camera, or a tilted camera translating in a planar scene. Mosaics generated in this manner can be considered as similar to the vertical "slits" [312] or the"linear push-broom cameras" [95]. However, unlike the straight "slit" or "broom", the broom in manifold mosaicing will adapt its shape from a straight line to a circular arc, to become mostly perpendicular to the optical flow.

In cases where strips are wide, it is possible to reduce the parallax and simulate the parallel projection by generating intermediate views [244, 48]. The introduction of intermediate views simulates a denser image sequence, where the strips are narrower, with smaller discontinuities due to motion parallax.

16.2 Mosaicing with Strips

Most existing mosaicing systems align and combine full images or video frames [273, 122, 241, 163]. The combination of full frames into mosaics introduces some difficulties:

- It is almost impossible to align accurately complete frames due to lens distortion, motion parallax, moving objects, etc. This results in "ghosting" or blurring when the mosaic is constructed.
- It is difficult to determine the mosaicing manifold. E.g., If all images are aligned to one reference image, different reference images will give different mosaics. In the case of a projection onto a cylinder it is important that the camera motion is a pure sideways rotation.

In order to overcome the above difficulties, we propose to use mosaicing with strips. A preliminary system was proposed in [312], where the strip was a vertical "slit", and the camera motion was limited to sideways camera translations and rotations measured by external devices. In this simple case vertical sections were taken from each image and pasted side by side (see Fig. 16.3. The same vertical slit is useless with vertical image motion, as the optical flow is parallel to the scanning slit (Fig. 16.5.b). No mosaic will be created as no image area will pass through the slit. Optimal mosaics are achieved only with a slit which is perpendicular to the optical flow.

An example for the determination of the shape of the slit is given for image motion generated by a pure translation of the camera, as shown in Fig. 16.4. In this case the image motion can be described by a radial optical flow emanating from the focus of expansion (FOE), and the field of view of the camera (FOV) can be described as a circle on the image plane. The optimal slit will be the longest circular section having its center at the FOE and passing through the FOV. This is the longest curve in the FOV that is perpendicular to the optical flow.

The definition of the scanning slit as perpendicular to the optical flow is very simple for some cases.

- In sideways image motion the optimal slit is vertical (Fig. 16.5.a).
- In image scaling (zoom), and in forward motion, the optimal slit is a circle (Fig. 16.5.c).

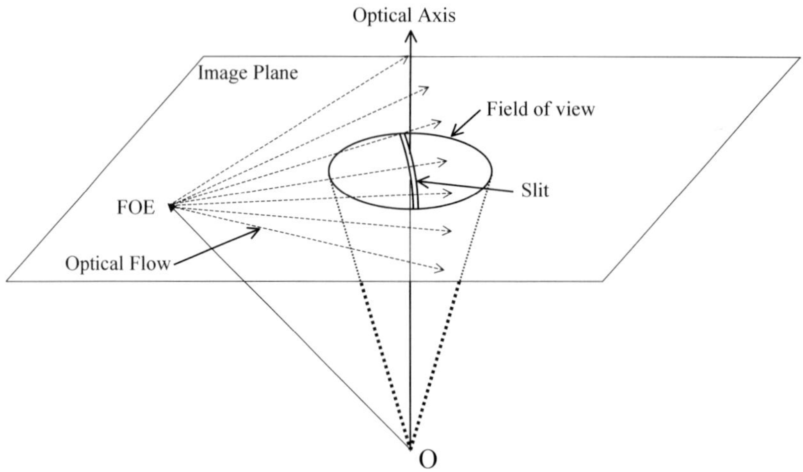

FIGURE 16.4. Determining the shape of the slit with camera translation. In this case the optimal slit will be the longest circular section having its center at the FOE and passing through the field of view. This is the longest curve in the FOV that is perpendicular to the optical flow.

- In image motion generated by camera translation, the optimal slit is a circular arc (Fig. 16.5.d).

Image motion is usually more general than these simple special cases. However, in most cases circular or elliptic curves are sufficient for mosaicing.

The shape of the slit determines the shape of the manifold on which the mosaic is created. The circular slit, for example (Fig. 16.5.c), can be combined on a cylindrical manifold.

16.3 Cutting and Pasting of Strips

The mosaic is constructed by pasting together strips taken from the original images. The shape of the strip, and its width, depend on the image motion. After choosing the strip, it should be warped such that the optical flow becomes parallel and of equal magnitude to allow for mosaicing. This section describes how to select and to warp these strips.

16.3.1 Selecting Strips

In order to determine the strip to be taken from Image I_n, the preceding frame, I_{n-1}, and the succeeding frame, I_{n+1}, should be considered.

Let $\mathcal{A}_n$ be the transformation relating points $p_n = (x_n, y_n)$ in Image I_n to the corresponding points $p_{n-1} = (x_{n-1}, y_{n-1})$ in Image I_{n-1}, and

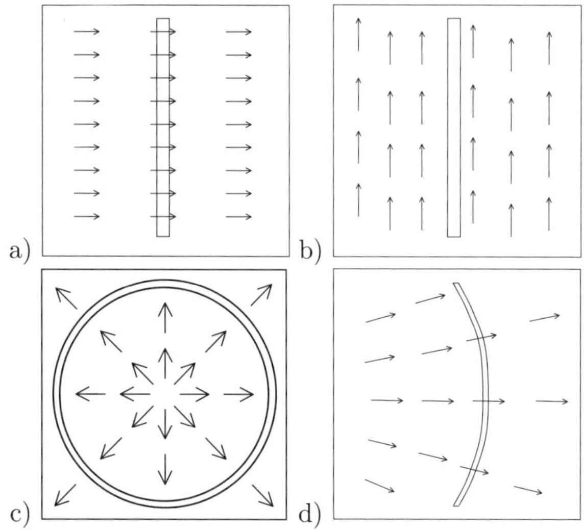

FIGURE 16.5. The mosaicing process and the direction of the optical flow. (a) A vertical slit is optimal when the optical flow is horizontal. (b) A vertical slit is useless when the optical flow is vertical. (c) A circular slit is optimal when the optical flow is radial. (d) For general motion optimal slits should be perpendicular to the optical flow, and bent accordingly.

let $\mathcal{A}_{n+1}$ be the transformation relating points p_{n+1} in Image I_{n+1} to the corresponding points p_n in Image I_n.

Given the transformations $\mathcal{A}_n$ and $\mathcal{A}_{n+1}$, the lines $\mathcal{F}_n(x_n, y_n) = 0$ and $\mathcal{F}_{n+1}(x_{n+1}, y_{n+1}) = 0$ are selected respectively (see Fig. 16.6.a-c). The line $\mathcal{F}_n(x_n, y_n) = 0$ in I_n corresponds to the line $\mathcal{F}'_n(x_{n-1}, y_{n-1}) = 0$ in I_{n-1} using the transformation $\mathcal{A}_n$. In the same way, the line $\mathcal{F}_{n+1}(x_{n+1}, y_{n+1}) = 0$ in I_{n+1} corresponds to the line $\mathcal{F}'_{n+1}(x_n, y_n) = 0$ in I_n using the transformation $\mathcal{A}_{n+1}$.

The strip that is taken from the image I_n is bounded between the two lines $\mathcal{F}_n(x_n, y_n) = 0$ and $\mathcal{F}'_{n+1}(x_n, y_n) = 0$ in I_n (see Fig. 16.6.a-c).

Line $\mathcal{F}_n$ will be the first boundary of the strip, and will be orthogonal to the optical flow with regard to the previous image. Line $\mathcal{F}'_{n+1}$ will be the second boundary of the strip, which is the projection of line $\mathcal{F}_{n+1}$ onto image I_n.

This selection of the boundaries of the strip ensures that no information is missed nor duplicated along the strip collection, as the orthogonality to the optical flow is kept.

16.3.2 Pasting Strips

Consider the common approach to mosaicing where one of the frames is used as a reference frame, and all other frames are aligned to the reference

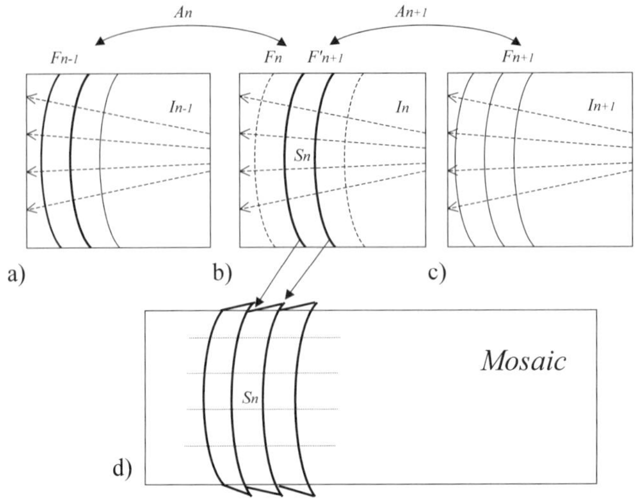

FIGURE 16.6. Cutting and pasting strips.
(a)-(c) Strips are perpendicular to the optical flow. (d) Strips are warped and pasted so that their back side is fixed and their front side is warped to match the back side of the next strip.

frame before pasting. In term of strips, the first strip is put in the panoramic image as is. The second strip is warped in order to match the boundaries of the first strip. The third strip is now warped to match the boundaries of the *already warped* second strip, etc. As as result, the mosaic image is continuous. However, major distortions may be caused by the accumulated warps and distortions. Large sideways rotations can not be handled, and cases such as forward motion or zoom usually cause unreasonable expansion (or shrinking) of the image.

To create continuous mosaic images while avoiding accumulated distortions, the warping of the strips should depend only on an adjacent original frame, independent of the history of previous warpings.

for example, we may choose the anchor as the back side of each strip. This is the side of the strip which corresponds to the boundary between image I_{n-1} and image I_n and is defined by $\mathcal{F}_n$. In this case, the front side of the strip is warped to match the back side of the next strip defined by $\mathcal{F'}_{n+1}$.

In the example described in Fig. 16.6.d, we warp the strip from image I_1 such that its left side does not change, while its right side is warped to match the left side of the strip coming from image I_2. In the second strip, the left side does not change, while the right side is warped to match the left side of the third strip, etc.

The warping done when strips are pasted together, which is necessary in order to get a continuous mosaic, is actually the projection of the strips onto the mosaicing manifold. This is done without the explicit computation of that manifold. After that warping, the original optical flow becomes parallel to the direction in which the panoramic mosaic is constructed. No accumulative distortions are encountered, as each strip is warped to match just another original strips, avoiding accumulative warps. Having an anchor in the strip prevents change of scale in the warping. The anchors are placed parallel along the mosaic, completing a parallel projection in the direction of the motion of the camera. Assuming the motion between successive frames is small, canceling the parallax by some smooth interpolation of the coordinates is a satisfying approximation for the narrow gaps between the anchors. In case the strips are wide, and the gaps between the anchors are big, view interpolation can be used, as described in 16.6.

16.4 Examples of Mosaicing Implementations

In this section two implementations of manifold mosaicing are described. The simplest implementation uses only straight slits, and the other implementation uses curved slits. Implementation issues, like strip cut and paste, and color merging across seams, are also described.

16.4.1 Strip Cut and Paste

Combination of the sequence of aligned image frames into a single panoramic mosaic can be done in several ways. In those cases where image alignment is close to perfect, it is possible to use all overlapping images to produce the mosaic.

The most common approach to combine the overlapping parts of the images is averaging. Averaging, however, may result in blurring when the alignment is not perfect. In this case it is preferred to select only one of the input images to represent a region in the mosaic. Such a selection should be done to minimize effects of misalignment. The most logical selection is to select from each image the strip closest to its center. There are two reasons for that selection:

- Alignment is usually better at the center than at the edges of the pictures.
- Image distortion is minimal at the center of the images

This selection corresponds to the Voronoi tessellation [7], and is shown in Figure 16.7. Using the Voronoi tessellation for image cut-and-paste also serves to minimize visible misalignment due to lens distortions. Voronoi tessellation causes every seam to be at the same distance from the two corresponding image centers. As lens distortions is a radial effect, features

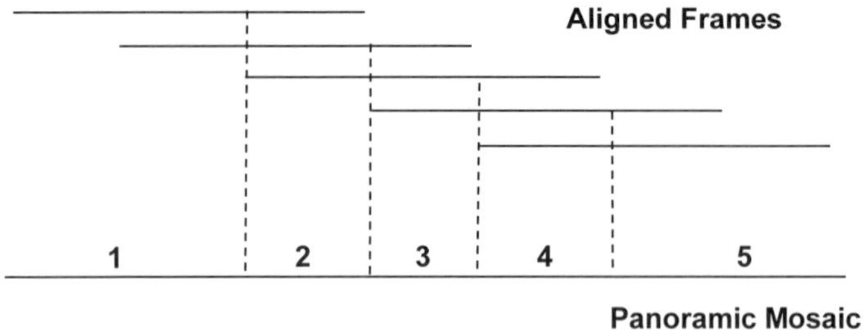

FIGURE 16.7. Pixel values in the panoramic mosaic are taken from a single image whose center, after alignment, is closest to the corresponding pixel. All pixels in Region 2 of the mosaic are therefore taken from the strip at the center of Image 2, etc. This constructions corresponds in 2D to the Voronoi tessellation.

that are perpendicular to the seam will be distorted equally on the seam, and therefore will remain aligned regardless of lens distortion.

16.4.2 Color Merging in Seams

Changes in image brightness, usually caused by the mechanism of automatic gain control (AGC), cause visible brightness seams in the mosaic between regions covered by different images. These seams should be eliminated in order to get a seamless panorama.

The process of blending the different images into a seamless panorama must smooth all these illumination discontinuities, while preserving image sharpness. A method that fulfills this requirement is described in [38]. In this approach, the images are decomposed into band-pass pyramid levels, and then combined at each band-pass pyramid level . Final reconstruction of the images from the combined band-pass levels give the desired panorama.

16.4.3 Mosaicing with Straight Strips

Manifold mosaicing can be implemented very efficiently when the optical flow is approximately parallel, as in camera translations or sideways rotation. In this case a simple 2D rigid image alignment (only image translations and rotations) can be used, and the strips can be straight. Construction is very fast, and has been demonstrated live on a PC [214]. Results are impressive in most cases, and have the desired feature of manifold mosaicing: each object in the mosaic appears in the same shape and size as it appears in the video frames, avoiding any scaling, and therefore avoiding distortions and loss of resolution. In this system, the manifold is defined to follow the center strip of the images as seen in Fig. 16.1 and Fig. 16.3. Mosaicing was done without the explicit assumption of pure rotation, and without the need to project the images onto a cylinder before mosaicing.

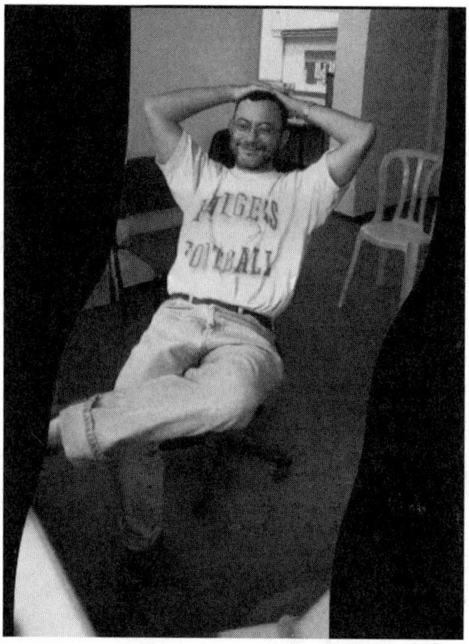

FIGURE 16.8. Manifold mosaicing with vertical scanning. The curved boundary is created by the unstabilized motion of the hand-held camera.

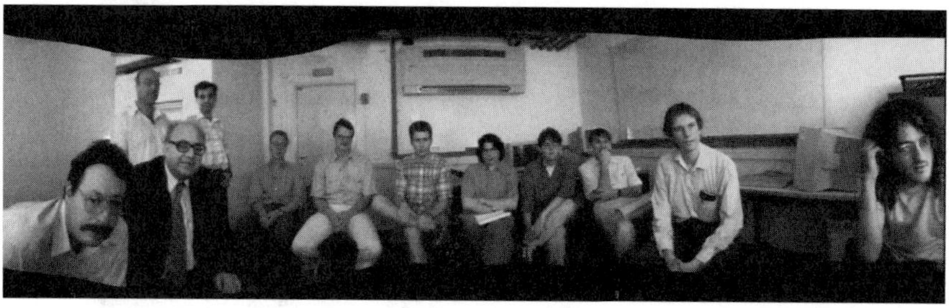

FIGURE 16.9. An example of panoramic imaging using manifold mosaicing with straight strips. The curved boundary is created by the unstabilized motion of the hand-held camera.

Fig. 16.9 and Fig. 16.8 show panoramic mosaic images created with an implementation of the manifold mosaicing on the PC [214].

16.4.4 Mosaicing with Curved Strips: Forward Motion

Mosaicing of images from forward moving cameras can be done using the more general manifold mosaicing. In Fig. 16.10 the camera was moving and looking forward inside a small canyon. The computed image motion was an homography, and the slit was an elliptic shape.

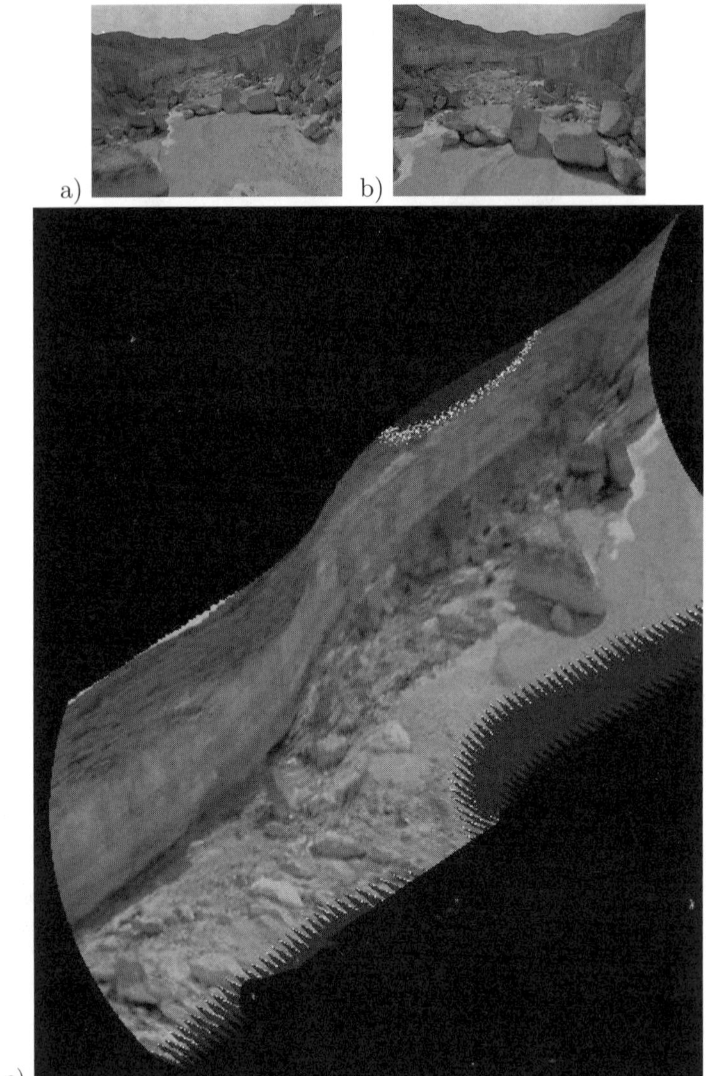

FIGURE 16.10. Forward motion in a small canyon.
(a-b) Two original frames. (c) Mosaic generated from curved strips.

16.5 Rectified Mosaicing: A Tilted Camera

The mosaicing algorithm described in Sect. 16.4 handles flawlessly the following two cases:

- A panning camera, when the optical axis is perpendicular to the rotation axis. E.g. - When a camera is panning from left to right with a vertical rotation axis, its optical axis must be horizontal.

- A translating camera scanning a planar scene, when the viewing direction is in the plane defined by the direction of motion and the normal to the plane. E.g. - The camera may look normal to the plane or have a forward view.

When the camera motion and the viewing directions are different, e.g. when the camera is tilted, this mosaicing algorithm constructs a curled mosaic. In this section we describe an algorithm for the mosaicing of sequences when the camera is tilted, and the two conditions above are not satisfied. The algorithm comes in two variants, one uses asymmetric strips, and the other uses symmetric strips. The image motion model used is a homography, which is assumed to be computed by one of many methods (e.g. [25]).

For the simplicity of explanation, we assume that the optical flow is close to parallel and close to horizontal, and therefore we simulate a pushbroom camera having a vertical straight slit. Therefore the "anchor", which is a feature in the strip that does not change with the warping of the strip, will also be a vertical straight line. The method can be easily adapted to more general motions using the methodologies described earlier in this paper.

In the first variant of the algorithm one side of the strip is taken as the anchor. In the second variant the anchor will be a vertical straight line at the center of the strip.

Examples for rectified mosaicing in the cases of a translating camera is shown in Fig. figure:translation, and in the case of a panning camera in Fig. figure:panning.

In the first algorithm, one of the borders of the strip is used as the anchor. It is simpler than the second algorithm, and useful when the borders of the strips are close to the borders of the image, which is recommended when the motion induces significant changes of scale in the image. In the second algorithm, a vertical line in the middle of the strip is used as the anchor. When the anchor is the central vertical line of the image, this algorithm is less sensitive to lens distortion, and less dependent on the direction of motion. For methodological reasons, we assume for both algorithms that the camera is translating to the right in front of a planar scene. In order to follow the technical details, we recommend the reader to use figures , .

16.5.1 Asymmetrical Strips

Assuming the camera motion is to the right, we use the left border of the strip as the anchor (Fig. 16.11). We mark the intersection of the anchor with the top and bottom image borders by P_k and Q_k. Given the homography H_k between Image I_k and Image I_{k+1}, let $\tilde{Q_k} = H_k^{-1}(Q_{k+1})$ and $\tilde{P_k} = H_k^{-1}(P_{k+1})$. $\tilde{Q_k}$ and $\tilde{P_k}$ are the mapping onto Image I_k of the anchor edges in Image I_{k+1}.

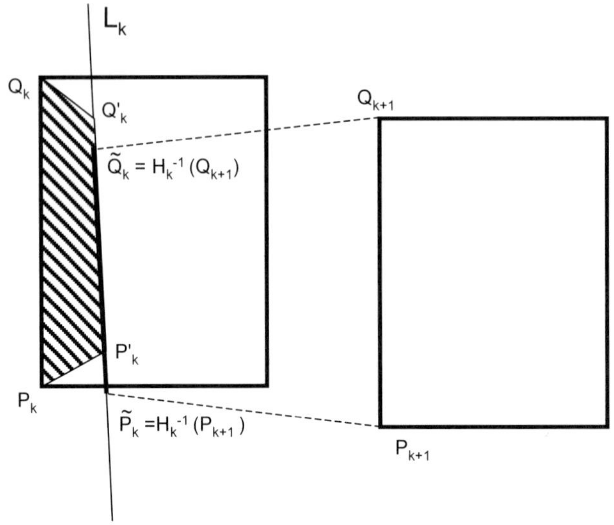

FIGURE 16.11. Non symmetric strip. The anchor is the left border of the strip.

Let L_k be the line passing through $\tilde{Q}_k$ and $\tilde{P}_k$. We find on the line L_k two points Q'_k and P'_k such that their distance is like the distance between $\tilde{Q}_k$ and $\tilde{P}_k$, and their centroid is on the middle row of the image. The region in the image to be warped to a strip in the mosaic is defined by the quadrangle $\tilde{Q}_k\tilde{P}_kP_kQ_k$. The warping is done by smooth (e.g. bilinear) interpolation of the coordinates of $\tilde{Q}_k, \tilde{P}_k, P_k, Q_k$. The use of an interpolation is needed for strip alignment, and this is an approximation to the real transformation which is unknown. As the strips are very narrow, this approximation is satisfying.

The next strip in the mosaic is placed with vertical offset of $\| \tilde{Q}_k - Q'_k \|_2 * \frac{h}{\|Q'_k - P'_k\|_2}$ from the current strip, where h is the image height.

16.5.2 Symmetrical Strips

We assume similar imaging conditions as in 16.5.1.

We mark the vertical line at the center of the image as C_k, and its intersection with the top and bottom image borders by P_k and Q_k.

We would like to choose a region which is approximately symmetrical around C_k, to reduce lens distortion. (This is the reason for choosing C_k as the anchor, in general any other line an be used). This region is illustrated in Fig. 16.12

Given the homography H_{k-1} between Image I_k and Image I_{k-1}, Let O_{k-1} be the center of image I_{k-1}, and let d be the vertical offset between O_{k-1} and $H_{k-1}(O_{k-1})$. Let P'_k be a point shifted from P_k by d, and Let Q'_k be a point vertically shifted from Q_k by d. Based on the homography

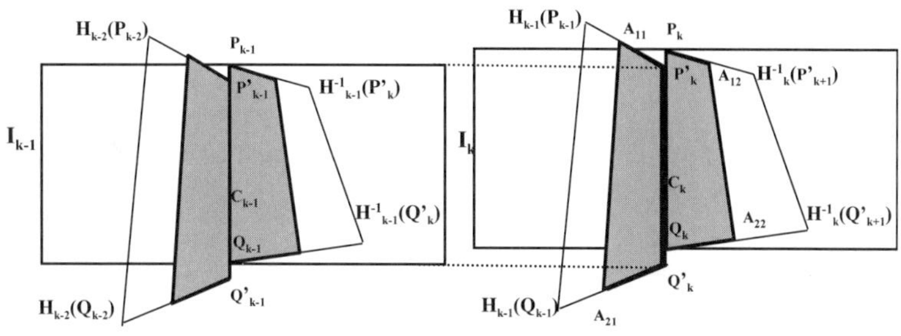

FIGURE 16.12. Mosaicing with symmetrical strips. A rectangular strip in the mosaic is mapped to the grey polygonal region in the image.

H_k between Image I_{k+1} and Image I_k, we apply a similar process between images I_k and I_{k+1}.

We now use the homographies to map points P'_{k+1} and Q'_{k+1} from Image I_{k+1}, and points P_{k-1} and Q_{k-1} from Image I_{k-1}, to Image I_k. We then find the middle points: Let F_L be the homography mapping an arbitrary rectangle UVWX to the points $H_{k-1}(P_{k-1}), P'_k, Q'_k, H_{k-1}(Q_{k-1})$ respectively, and Let F_R be the homography mapping UVWX to the points $P_k, H_k^{-1}(P'_{k+1}), H_k^{-1}(Q'_{k+1}), Q_k$ respectively. The region borders are defined by:

$$A_{11} = F_L(\frac{U+V}{2}), A_{21} = F_L(\frac{W+X}{2}),$$

$$A_{12} = F_R(\frac{U+V}{2}), A_{22} = F_R(\frac{W+X}{2})$$

The polygonal region in the image is comprised of two quadrangles: the left quadrangle, with the corners at P'_k, Q'_k, A_{11}, and A_{21}, and the right quadrangle, with the corners at P_k, Q_k, A_{12}, and A_{22}. Each of these quadrangles is mapped to a rectangle in the mosaic. We warp the left quadrangle to a rectangle in the mosaic by some smooth (e.g. bilinear) interpolation of the coordinates of the corners like in the asymmetric case. We apply a similar process to the right part of the strip (rectangle) and the right part of the region.

We place the left part of the strip at the same vertical offset as the right part of the previous strip, and the right side of the strip with vertical offset of d from the left part.

16.6 View Interpolation for Motion Parallax

Taking strips from different images when the width of the strips is more than one pixel would work fine only without parallax. When motion parallax is involved, no single transformation can be found to represent the optical flow in the entire scene. As a result, a transformation that will

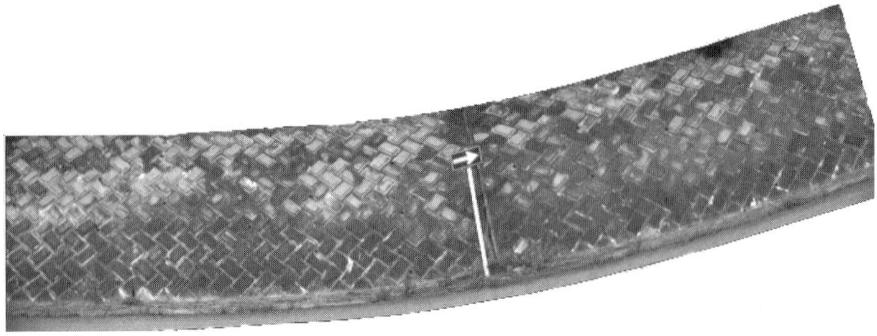

FIGURE 16.13. A translating camera mosaicing a slanted wall. Regular mosaicing results in a curled image, while rectified mosaicing results in a straight mosaic.

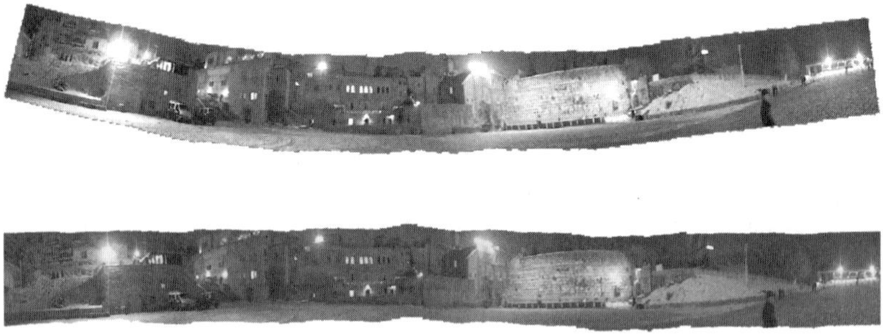

FIGURE 16.14. Mosaicing from a panning camera which is slightly tilted upward. Regular mosaicing results in a curled image, while rectified mosaicing results in a straight mosaic.

align a close object will duplicate far objects, and on the other hand, a transformation that will align a far object will truncate closer objects.

In order to overcome the problems of motion parallax in general scenes, instead of taking a strip with a width of N pixels, we can synthetically generate intermediate images, and use narrower strips. For example, we can take a collection of N strips, each with a width of one pixel, from interpolated camera views in between the original camera positions. In order to synthesize new views we can use various methods, such as optical flow interpolation [48, 244], trilinear tensor methods [229], and others. In most cases approximate methods will give good results. The creation of the intermediate views can involve only view interpolation, as in this application view extrapolation is not needed.

The use of intermediate views for strips collection gives the effect of orthographic projection, which avoids discontinuities due to motion parallax. This strategy can be combined with the methods that were described in the previous sections as a preliminary stage, such that a complete solution is given for general motion in general scenes.

16.7 Concluding Remarks

Mosaicing on a surface of a manifold, which adapts to the motion of the camera, has been introduced. Strips from the images are reprojected onto the manifold using multi-perspective projection.

Manifold mosaicing can be performed by computing the manifold explicitly from the ego motion of the camera, and projecting the images onto that manifold. Alternatively, this projection can be done implicitly by the process of cutting and warping strips, and without explicit computation of the manifold.

Manifold mosaics represent the entire environment of a video shot in a single, static, image. This single image can be used as a summary of the video clip for video browsing, or as a compressed representation of the shot which can be approximately re-generated from the mosaic given the stored motion parameters.

Acknowledgment

This research was partially funded by DARPA through ARL Contract DAAL01-97-0101 and by the European ACTS project AC074 "Vanguard".

Section IV

Applications

In this final section, we present a diverse sample of applications that makes use of or are faciliated by panoramic imaging. The areas covered by these applications are not only computer vision, but robotics and image/video processing as well. More specifically, the applications detailed here are 3D environment modeling, identification and recognition of robots, human tracking, and video representation.

A traditional approach to extracting geometric information from a large scene is to compute multiple 3D depth maps from stereo pairs or direct range finders, and then to merge the 3D data. However, the resulting merged depth maps may be subject to merging errors if the relative poses between depth maps are not known exactly. In addition, the 3D data may also have to be resampled before merging, which adds additional complexity and potential sources of errors.

Chapter 17 (Kang and Szeliski) describes a means of directly extracting 3D data covering a very wide field of view, thus by-passing the need for numerous depth map merging. The cylindrical panoramic images are obtained using the method described in Section III (Chapter 12). By taking such image panoramas at different camera locations, 3D data of the scene can be recovered using a set of simple techniques: feature tracking, an 8-point structure from motion algorithm, and multibaseline stereo.

One of the trends in computer vision is development of systems using multiple vision sensors. Such use of multiple omni-directional vision sensors (ODVSs) opens up a new application area of computer vision with their wide range of view. Chapter 18 (Sogo, Ishiguro, and Trivedi) describes a real-time human tracking system using multiple ODVSs. This system locates people using omni-directional images taken with the ODVSs and by applying N-ocular stereo, which is an extension of trinocular stereo.

N-ocular stereo can handle the correspondence problem among multiple targets without explicitly using visual features. In addition, several error compensation methods are introduced for accurate localization of targets in N-ocular stereo. The system has been shown to robustly track people in real time.

In the more esoteric area of robotics, the development of multiple robot systems which solve complex and dynamic problems in a parallel and distributed manner is a key issue. Such multiple robot systems require robust methods for identifying robots and to enable collaborative behaviors. Chapter 19 (Ishiguro, Kato, and Barth) describes a method for identifying and localizing robots; here, each robot has an omnidirectional vision sensor as its visual system. The method allows the different robots to be identified, even if they look alike. It is based on the simple internal angle constraint within a triangle, i.e., summing to 180°. For each robot, itself and any other two robots within its field of view constitute the vertices of the triangle. Simulation and real experimental results validate this method.

The standard way of representing video as a sequence of frames is adequate for viewing it in a movie mode. However, it does not support the type of interaction with video information required by emerging Web-based applications. Chapter 20 (Irani and Anandan) presents a new approach for efficient access, storage, and manipulation of video data. This approach capitalizes on the very high temporal redundancy in video data. The video data is transformed from a sequential *frame-based* representation into a single common *scene-based* representation, to which each original frame can be directly related. This representation then allows direct and immediate access to the scene information, such as static locations and dynamically moving objects. Because it eliminates the redundancy between the different views of the scene contained in the frames, it results in a highly efficient and compact representation of the video information. This chapter provides details on how the scene-based representation can be extracted from video without any information about the camera parameters or the scene.

Additional Notes on Chapters

The material in Chapter 17 has originally appeared in the article "3D scene data recovery using omnidirectional multibaseline stereo," *International Journal of Computer Vision*, vol. 25, no. 2, 1997. Chapter 18 has recently appeared in *IEEE Workshop on Omnidirectional Vision* held in June 2000, while Chapter 19 has been presented in *IEEE/RSJ International Conference on Intelligent Robots and Systems* in 1999.

17

3D Environment Modeling from Multiple Cylindrical Panoramic Images

S.B. Kang and R. Szeliski

17.1 Introduction

A traditional approach to extracting geometric information from a large scene is to compute multiple (possibly numerous) 3D depth maps from stereo pairs, and then to merge the 3D data [71, 109, 210, 255]. This is not only computationally intensive, but the resulting merged depth maps may be subject to merging errors, especially if the relative poses between depth maps are not known exactly. The 3D data may also have to be resampled before merging, which adds additional complexity and potential sources of errors. 3D data registration and merging are very much simplified if the motion of the stereo pair is known. One simple instance of this is fixing the location of the center of the reference camera of a stereo pair and constraining the motion of the stereo pair to rotation about the vertical axis. However, unless a motorized rotary table is used to control the amount of rotation, the rotation between successive stereo views still has to be estimated. There is still the same (but much more constrained) problem of registration and 3D resampling, albeit with only one rotational degree of freedom.

This paper provides a means of directly extracting 3D data covering a very wide field of view, thus by-passing the need for numerous depth map merging. In our work, cylindrical images are first composited from sequences of images taken while the camera is rotated 360° about a vertical axis. By taking such image panoramas at different camera locations, we can recover 3D data from the scene using a set of simple techniques: feature tracking, 8-point direct and iterative structure from motion algorithms, and multibaseline stereo.

There are several advantages to this approach. First, the cylindrical image mosaics can be built quite accurately, since the camera motion is very restricted. Second, the relative pose of the various camera locations can be determined with much greater accuracy than with regular structure from motion applied to images with narrower fields of view. Third, there is no need to build or purchase a specialized stereo camera whose calibration may be sensitive to drift over time—any conventional video camera on a tripod will suffice. Our approach can be used to construct models of building interiors, both for virtual reality applications (games, home sales, architectural remodeling), and for robotics applications (navigation).

In this paper, we describe our approach to generate 3D data corresponding to a very wide field of view (specifically 360°), and show results of our approach on both synthetic and real scenes. We first review relevant work in Section 17.2 before delineating our basic approach in Section 17.3. The method to extract wide-angle images (i.e., *panoramic images*) is described in Section 17.4. Section 17.5 reviews the 8-point algorithm and shows how it can be applied to cylindrical panoramic images. Section 17.6 describes two methods for extracting 3D point data: the first relies on unconstrained tracking and uses an 8-point structure from motion algorithm, while the second constrains the search for feature correspondences to epipolar lines (traditional stereo). We briefly outline our approach to modeling the data in Section 17.7—details of this are given elsewhere [145]. Finally, we show results of our approach in Section 17.8 and close with a discussion and conclusions.

17.2 Relevant Work

There is a significant body of work on range image recovery using stereo (good surveys can be found in [16, 63]). Most work on stereo uses images with limited fields of view. One of the earliest work to use panoramic images is the omnidirectional stereo system of Ishiguro [136], which uses two panoramic views. Each panoramic view is created by one of the two vertical slits of a camera image sweeping around 360°; the cameras (which are displaced in front of the rotation center) are rotated by very small angles, typically about 0.4°. One of the disadvantages of this method is the slow data acquisition, which takes about 10 minutes. The camera angular increments must be approximately $1/f$ radians, and are assumed to be known *a priori*.

Murray [192] generalizes Ishiguro *et al.*'s approach by using all the vertical slits of the image (except in the paper, he uses a single image raster). This would be equivalent to structure from known motion or motion stereo. The advantage is more efficient data acquisition, done at lower angular resolution. The analysis involved in this work is similar to Bolles *et al.*'s [29] spatio-temporal epipolar analysis, except that the temporal dimension is replaced by that of angular displacement.

Another related work is that of plenoptic modeling [181]. The idea is to composite rotated camera views into panoramas, and based on two cylindrical panoramas, project disparity values between these locations to a given

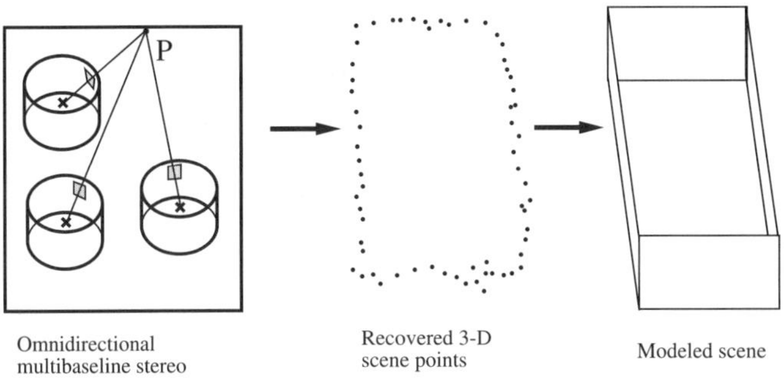

FIGURE 17.1. Generating scene model from multiple 360° panoramic views.

viewing position. While a disparity value is estimated for each pixel in each cylindrical panorama, no explit 3D model is ever constructed.

Our approach is similar to that of [181] in that we composite rotated camera views to panoramas as well. However, we go a step further by reconstructing 3D feature points and modeling the scene based upon the recovered points. We use multiple panoramas for more accurate 3D reconstruction.

17.3 Overview of Approach

Our ultimate goal is to generate a photorealistic model to be used in a variety of scenarios. We are interested in providing a simple means of generating such models. We also wish to minimize the use of CAD packages as a means of 3D model generation, since such an effort is labor-intensive [274]. In addition, we would like to generate our 3D scene models using off-the-shelf equipment. In our case, we use a workstation with framegrabber (real-time image digitizer) and a standard 8-mm camcorder.

Our approach is straightforward: at each camera location in the scene, we capture sequences of images while rotating the camera about the vertical axis passing through the camera optical center. We composite each set of images to produce panoramas at each camera location. We use stereo to extract 3D data of the scene. Finally, we model the scene using these 3D data input and render it with textures extracted from the input 2D images. Our approach is summarized in Figure 17.1.

Using panoramic images, we can directly extract 3D data covering a very wide field of view, thus by-passing the need for numerous depth map merging. Multiple depth map merging is not only computationally intensive, but the resulting merged depth maps may be subject to merging errors, especially if the relative poses between depth maps are not known exactly. The 3D data may also have to be resampled before merging, which adds additional complexity and potential sources of errors.

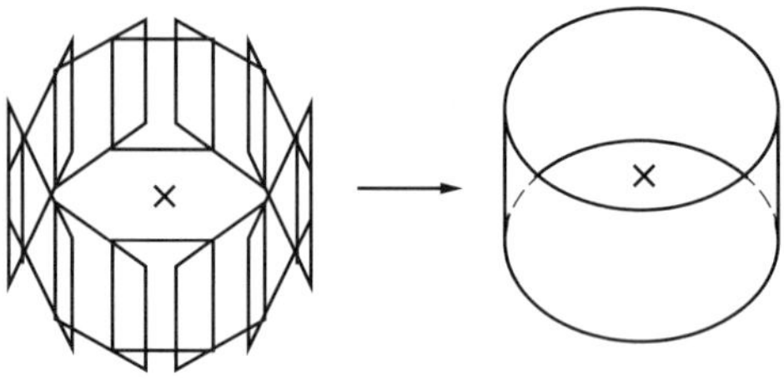

FIGURE 17.2. Compositing multiple rotated camera views into a panorama. The '×' marks indicate the locations of the camera optical and rotation center.

Using multiple camera locations in stereo analysis significantly reduces the number of ambiguous matches and also has the effect of reducing errors by averaging [206, 147]. This is especially important for images with very wide fields of view, because depth recovery is unreliable near the epipoles[1], where the looming effect takes place, resulting in very poor depth cues.

17.4 Extraction of Panoramic Images

A panoramic image is created by compositing a series of rotated camera images, as shown in Figure 17.2. In order to create this panoramic image, we first have to ensure that the camera is rotating about an axis passing through its optical center, i.e., we must eliminate motion parallax when panning the camera around. To achieve this, we manually adjust the position of camera relative to an X-Y precision stage (mounted on the tripod) such that the motion parallax effect disappears when the camera is rotated back and forth about the vertical axis [263].

Prior to image capture of the scene, we calibrate the camera to compute its intrinsic camera parameters (specifically its focal length f, aspect ratio r, and radial distortion coefficient κ). The camera is calibrated by taking multiple snapshots of a planar dot pattern grid with known depth separation between successive snapshots. We use an iterative least-squares algorithm (Levenberg-Marquardt) to estimate camera intrinsic and extrinsic parameters (except for κ) [270]. κ is determined using 1D search (Brent's parabolic interpolation in 1D [220]) with the least-squares algorithm as the black box.

The steps involved in extracting a panoramic scene are as follow:

- At each camera location, capture a sequence while panning camera around 360°.

[1]For a pair of images taken at two different locations, the epipoles are the location on the image planes which are the intersection between these image planes and the line joining the two camera optical centers. An excellent description of the stereo vision is given in [67].

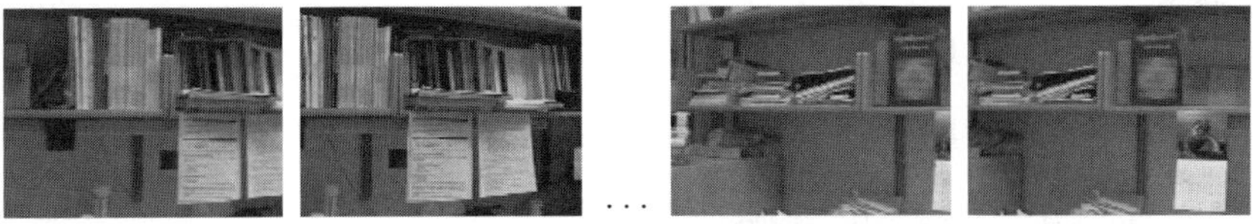

FIGURE 17.3. Example undistorted image sequence (of an office).

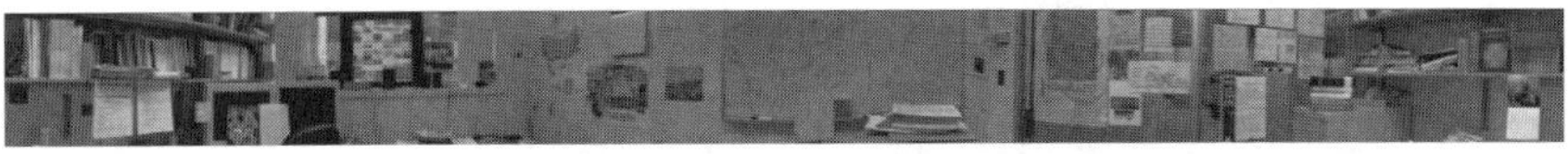

FIGURE 17.4. Panorama of office scene after compositing.

- Using the intrinsic camera parameters, correct the image sequence for r, the aspect ratio, and κ, the radial distortion coefficient.
- Convert the (r, κ)-corrected 2D flat image sequence to cylindrical coordinates, with the focal length f as its cross-sectional radius. An example of a sequence of corrected images (of an office) is shown in Figure 17.3.
- Composite the images (with only x-directional DOF, which is equivalent to motion in the angular dimension of cylindrical image space) to yield the desired panorama [266]. The relative displacement of one frame to the next is coarsely determined by using phase correlation [160]. This technique estimates the 2D translation between a pair of images by taking 2D Fourier transforms of both images, computing the phase difference at each frequency, performing an inverse Fourier transform, and searching for a peak in the magnitude image. Subsequently, the image translation is refined using local image registration by directly comparing the overlapped regions between the two images [266, 267].
- Correct for slight errors in the resulting length (which in theory equals $2\pi f$) by propagating residual displacement error equally across all images and recompositing. The error in length is usually within a percent of the expected length.

An example of a panoramic image created from the office scene in Figure 17.3 is shown in Figure 17.4.

17.5 Recovery of Epipolar Geometry

In order to extract 3D data from a given set of panoramic images, we have to first know the relative positions of the camera corresponding to the panoramic images. For a calibrated camera, this is equivalent to determining the epipolar geometry between a reference panoramic image and every other panoramic image.

The epipolar geometry dictates the *epipolar constraint*, which refers to the locus of possible image projections in one image given an image point in another image. For planar image planes, the epipolar constraint is in the form of straight lines [67]. For cylindrical images, epipolar curves are sinusoids [181].

We use the 8-point algorithm [170, 94] to extract the *essential matrix*, which yields both the relative camera placement and the epipolar geometry. This is done pairwise, namely between a reference panoramic image and another panoramic image. There are, however, four possible solutions [170, 94]. The solution that yields the most *positive* projections (i.e., projections away from the camera optical centers) is chosen.

17.5.1 8-point Algorithm: Basics

We briefly review the 8-point algorithm here. If the camera is calibrated, i.e., its intrinsic parameters are known, then for any two corresponding image points (at two different camera placements) $(u, v, w)^{\mathrm{T}}$ and $(u', v', w')^{\mathrm{T}}$ in 3D, we have

$$(u', v', w')E \begin{pmatrix} u \\ v \\ w \end{pmatrix} = 0 \tag{17.1}$$

The matrix E is called the *essential matrix*, and is of the form $E = [\mathbf{t}]_\times R$, where R and $\mathbf{t}$ are the rotation matrix and translation vectors, respectively, and $[\mathbf{t}]_\times$ is the matrix form of the cross product with $\mathbf{t}$.

If the camera is not calibrated, we have a more general relation between two corresponding image points (on the image plane) $(u, v, 1)^{\mathrm{T}}$ and $(u', v', 1)^{\mathrm{T}}$, namely

$$(u', v', 1)F \begin{pmatrix} u \\ v \\ 1 \end{pmatrix} = 0 \tag{17.2}$$

F is called the fundamental matrix and is also of rank 2, $F = [\mathbf{t}]_\times A$, where A is an arbitrary 3×3 matrix. The fundamental matrix is the generalization of the essential matrix E, and is usually employed to establish the epipolar geometry and to recover projective depth [69, 251].

In our case, since we know the camera parameters, we can recover E. Let $\mathbf{e}$ be the vector comprising e_{ij}, where e_{ij} is the (i,j)th element of E. Then for all the point matches, we have from (17.1)

$$\begin{aligned} uu'e_{11} \quad + \quad & uv'e_{21} + uw'e_{31} + vu'e_{12} + vv'e_{22} + \\ & vw'e_{32} + wu'e_{13} + wv'e_{23} + ww'e_{33} = 0, \end{aligned} \tag{17.3}$$

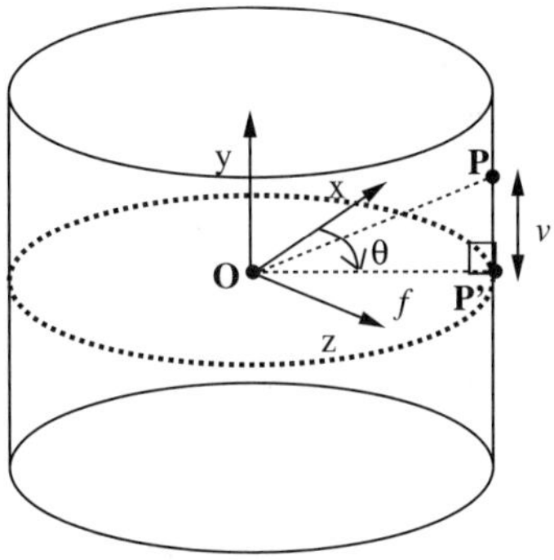

FIGURE 17.5. Cylindrical coordinate system. **P** is any point on the cylindrical surface while **P**' is the point projected on the x-z plane. θ is the angle subtended by the x-axis and the line segment **O-P**', **O** being the center of the coordinate frame. f is the camera focal length while v is the height of point **P**.

from which we get a set of linear equations of the form

$$\mathcal{A}\mathbf{e} = 0. \tag{17.4}$$

If the number of input points is small, the output of algorithm is sensitive to noise. On the other hand, it turns out that *normalizing* the 3D point location vector on the cylindrical image reduces the sensitivity of the 8-point algorithm to noise. This is similar in spirit to Hartley's application of isotropic scaling [94] prior to using the 8-point algorithm (though Hartley's algorithm is for recovering the fundamental matrix and not the essential matrix). The 3D cylindrical points are normalized according to the relation

$$\mathbf{u} = (f \sin\theta, v, f\cos\theta) \rightarrow \hat{\mathbf{u}} = \mathbf{u}/|\mathbf{u}|, \tag{17.5}$$

i.e., we normalize each vector so that it is a unit direction in space. The coordinate system used for the cylinder is shown in Figure 17.5.

With N panoramic images, we solve for $(N-1)$ sets of linear equations of the form (17.4). The kth set corresponds to the panoramic image pair 1 and $(k+1)$. Notice that the solution for $\mathbf{t}$ is defined only up to an unknown scale. In our work, we measure the distance between camera positions; this enables us to recover the scale. However, we can relax this assumption by carrying out the following steps:

- Fix camera distance of first pair (pair 1), to, say unit distance. Assign camera distances for all the other pairs to be the same as the first.
- Calculate the essential matrices for all the pairs of panoramic images, assuming unit camera distances.
- For each pair, compute the 3D points.

- To estimate the relative distances between of camera positions for pair $j \neq 1$ (i.e., not the first pair), find the scale of the 3D points corresponding to pair j that minimizes the distance error to those corresponding to pair 1. Robust statistics is used to reject outliers; specifically, only the best 50% are used. Note that outlier rejection is performed at this step of relative scale recovery only. Once the relative scales is recovered, *all* of the scaled points are used in determining the optimal merged 3D positions.

17.5.2 Tracking Features for 8-point Algorithm

The 8-point algorithm assumes that feature point correspondences are available. Feature tracking is a challenge in that purely local tracking fails because the displacement can be large (of the order of about 100 pixels, in the direction of camera motion). To mitigate this problem, we use spline-based tracking, which attempts to globally minimize the image intensity differences. This yields estimates of optic flow, which in turn is used by a local tracker to refine the amount of feature displacement.

The optic flow between a pair of cylindrical panoramic images is first estimated using spline-based image registration between the pair [269, 272]. In this image registration approach, the displacement fields $u(x, y)$ and $v(x, y)$ (i.e., displacements in the x- and y- directions as functions of the pixel location) are represented as two-dimensional *splines* controlled by a smaller number of displacement estimates which lie on a coarser *spline control grid.*

Once the initial optic flow has been found, the best candidates for tracking are then chosen. The choice is based on the minimum eigenvalue of the local Hessian, which is an indication of local image texturedness. Subsequently, using the initial optic flow as an estimate displacement field, we use the Shi-Tomasi tracker [253] with a window of size 25 pixels $\times$ 25 pixels to further refine the displacements of the chosen point features.

Why did we use the approach of applying the spline-based tracker before using the Shi-Tomasi tracker? This approach is used to take advantage of the complementary characteristics of these two trackers, namely:

1. The spline-based image registration technique is capable of tracking features with larger displacements. This is done through coarse-to-fine image registration; in our work, we use 6 levels of resolution. While this technique generally results in good tracks (sub-pixel accuracy) [272], poor tracks may result in areas in the vicinity of object occlusions/disocclusions.

2. The Shi-Tomasi tracker is a local tracker that fails at large displacements. It performs better for a small number of frames and for relatively small displacements, but deteriorates at large numbers of

frames and in the presence of rotation on the image plane [272]. We are considering a small number of frames at a time, and image warping due to local image plane rotation is not expected. The Shi-Tomasi tracker is also capable of sub-pixel accuracy.

The approach that we have undertaken for object tracking can be thought of as a "fine-to-finer" tracking approach. In addition to feature displacements, the measure of reliability of tracks is available (according to match errors and local texturedness, the latter indicated by the minimum eigenvalue of the local Hessian [253, 272]). As we will see later in Section 17.8.1, this is used to cull possibly bad tracks and improve 3D estimates.

Once we have extracted point feature tracks, we can then proceed to recover 3D positions corresponding to these feature tracks. 3D data recovery is based on the simple notion of stereo.

17.6 Omnidirectional Multibaseline Stereo

The idea of extracting 3D data simultaneously from more than the theoretically sufficient number of two camera views is founded on two simple tenets: statistical robustness from redundancy and disambiguation of matches due to overconstraints [206, 147]. The notion of using multiple camera views is even more critical when using panoramic images taken at the same vertical height, which results in the epipoles falling *within* the images. If only two panoramic images are used, points that are close to the epipoles will not be reliable. It is also important to note that this problem will persist if all the multiple panoramic images are taken at camera positions that are collinear. In the experiments described in Section 17.8, the camera positions are deliberately arranged such that all the positions are *not* collinear. In addition, all the images are taken at the same vertical height to maximize view overlap between panoramic images.

We use three related approaches to reconstruct 3D from multiple panoramic images. 3D data recovery is done either by (1) using just the 8-point algorithm on the tracks and directly recovering the 3D points, or (2) proceeding with an iterative least-squares method to refine both camera pose and 3D feature location, or (3) going a step further to impose epipolar constraints in performing a full multiframe stereo reconstruction. The first approach is termed as *unconstrained tracking and 3D data merging* while the second approach is *iterative structure from motion.* The third approach is named *constrained depth recovery using epipolar geometry.*

17.6.1 Reconstruction Method 1: Unconstrained Feature Tracking and 3D Data Merging

In this approach, we use the tracked feature points across all panoramic images and apply the 8-point algorithm. From the extracted essential matrix and camera relative poses, we can then directly estimate the 3D positions.

The sets of 2D image data are used to determine (pairwise) the essential matrix. The recovery of the essential matrix turns out to be reasonably stable; this is due to the large (360°) field of view. A problem with the 8-point algorithm is that optimization occurs in function space and not image space, i.e., it is not minimizing error in distance between 2D image point and corresponding epipolar line. Deriche *et al.* [61] use a robust regression method called *least-median-of-squares* to minimize distance error between expected (from the estimated fundamental matrix) and given 2D image points. We have found that extracting the essential matrix using the 8-point algorithm is relatively stable as long as (1) the number of points is large (at least in the hundreds), and (2) the points are well distributed over the field of view.

In this approach, we use the same set of data to recover Euclidean shape. In theory, the recovered positions are only true up to a scale. Since the distance between camera locations are known and measured, we are able to get the true scale of the recovered shape. Note, however, that this approach does not depend critically on knowing the camera distances, as indicated in Section 17.5.1.

Once we have recovered the camera poses, i.e., the rotation matrices and translation vectors, we use the following method for estimating the 3D point positions $\mathbf{p}_i$. Let $\mathbf{u}_{ik}$ be the ith point of image k, $\hat{\mathbf{v}}_{ik}$ be the unit vector from the optical center to the panoramic image point in 3D space, Λ_{ik} be the corresponding line passing through both the optical center and panoramic image point in space, and $\mathbf{t}_k$ be the camera translation associated with the kth panoramic image (note that $\mathbf{t}_1 = \mathbf{0}$). The equation of line Λ_{ik} is then $\mathbf{r}_{ik} = \lambda_{ik}\hat{\mathbf{v}}_{ik} + \mathbf{t}_k$. Thus, for each point i (that is constrained to lie on line Λ_{i1}), we minimize the error function

$$\mathcal{E}_i = \sum_{k=2}^{N} \|\mathbf{r}_{i1} - \mathbf{r}_{ik}\|^2 \tag{17.6}$$

where N is the number of panoramic images. By taking the partial derivatives of $\mathcal{E}_i$ with respect to λ_{ij}, $j = 1, \ldots, N$, equating them to zero, and solving, we get

$$\lambda_{i1} = \frac{\sum_{k=2}^{N} \mathbf{t}_k^{\mathrm{T}} \left(\hat{\mathbf{v}}_{i1} - \left(\hat{\mathbf{v}}_{i1}^{\mathrm{T}}\hat{\mathbf{v}}_{ik}\right)\hat{\mathbf{v}}_{ik}\right)}{\sum_{k=2}^{N} \left(1 - \left(\hat{\mathbf{v}}_{i1}^{\mathrm{T}}\hat{\mathbf{v}}_{ik}\right)^2\right)}, \tag{17.7}$$

from which the reconstructed 3D point is calculated using the relation $\mathbf{p}_{i1} = \lambda_{i1}\hat{\mathbf{v}}_{i1}$. Note that a more optimal manner of estimating the 3D point is to minimize the expression

$$\mathcal{E}_i = \sum_{k=1}^{N} \|\mathbf{p}_{i1} - \mathbf{r}_{ik}\|^2 \tag{17.8}$$

A detailed derivation involving (17.8) is given in Appendix 17.10. To simplify the inverse texture-mapping of the input images onto the recovered 3D mesh of the estimated points, the projections of the estimated 3D points have to coincide with the 2D image locations in the reference image. This can be justified by saying that since the feature tracks originate from the reference image, it is reasonable to assume that there is no uncertainty in feature location in the reference image (see [11] for a discussion of similar ideas).

An immediate problem with the approach of feature tracking and data merging is its reliance on tracking, which makes it relatively sensitive to tracking errors. It inherits the problems associated with tracking, such as the aperture problem and sensitivity to changing amounts of object distortion at different viewpoints. However, this problem is mitigated if the number of sampled points is large. In addition, the advantage is that there is no need to specify minimum and maximum depths and resolution associated with multibaseline stereo depth search (e.g., see [206, 147]). This is because the points are extracted directly analytically once the correspondence is established.

17.6.2 Reconstruction Method 2: Iterative Panoramic Structure from Motion

The 8-point algorithm recovers the camera motion parameters directly from the panoramic tracks, from which the corresponding 3D points can be computed. However, the camera motion parameters may not be optimally recovered, even though experiments by Hartley using narrow view images indicate that the motion parameters are close to optimal [94]. Using the output of the 8-point algorithm and the recovered 3D data, we can apply an iterative least-squares minimization to refine both camera motion and 3D positions *simultaneously*. This is similar to work done by Szeliski and Kang on structure from motion using multiple narrow camera views [270].

As input to our reconstruction method, we use 3D *normalized* locations of cylindrical image points. The equation linking a 3D normalized cylindrical image position $\mathbf{u}_{ij}$ in frame j to its 3D position $\mathbf{p}_i$, where i is the track index, is

$$\mathbf{u}_{ij} = \mathcal{P}\left(\mathbf{R}_j^{(k)}\mathbf{p}_i + \mathbf{t}_j^{(k)}\right) = \mathcal{F}\left(\mathbf{p}_i, \mathbf{q}_j, \mathbf{t}_j\right) \tag{17.9}$$

where $\mathcal{P}()$ is the projection transformation; $\mathbf{R}_j^{(k)}$ and $\mathbf{t}_j^{(k)}$ are the rotation matrix and translation vector, respectively, associated with the relative pose of the jth camera. We represent each rotation by a quaternion $\mathbf{q} = [w, (q_0, q_1, q_2)]$ with a corresponding rotation matrix

$$\mathbf{R}(\mathbf{q}) = \begin{pmatrix} 1 - 2q_1^2 - 2q_2^2 & 2q_0q_1 - 2wq_2 & 2q_0q_2 + 2wq_1 \\ 2q_0q_1 + 2wq_2 & 1 - 2q_0^2 - 2q_2^2 & 2q_1q_2 - 2wq_0 \\ 2q_0q_2 - 2wq_1 & 2q_1q_2 + 2wq_0 & 1 - 2q_0^2 - 2q_1^2 \end{pmatrix} \quad (17.10)$$

(alternative representations for rotations are discussed in [9]).

The projection equation is given simply by

$$\begin{pmatrix} u \\ v \\ w \end{pmatrix} = \mathcal{P}\begin{pmatrix} x \\ y \\ z \end{pmatrix} \equiv \frac{1}{\sqrt{x^2 + y^2 + z^2}}\begin{pmatrix} x \\ y \\ z \end{pmatrix} \quad (17.11)$$

In other words, all the 3D points are projected onto the surface of a 3D unit sphere.

To solve for the structure and motion parameters simultaneously, we use the iterative Levenberg-Marquardt algorithm. The Levenberg-Marquardt method is a standard non-linear least squares technique [220] that works well in a wide range of situations. It provides a way to vary smoothly between the inverse-Hessian method and the steepest descent method.

The merit or objective function that we minimize is

$$\mathcal{C}(\mathbf{a}) = \sum_i \sum_j c_{ij} \left|\mathbf{u}_{ij} - \mathcal{F}\left(\mathbf{a}_{ij}\right)\right|^2, \quad (17.12)$$

where $\mathcal{F}()$ is given in (17.9) and

$$\mathbf{a}_{ij} = \left(\mathbf{p}_i^{\mathrm{T}}, \mathbf{q}_j^{\mathrm{T}}, \mathbf{t}_j^{\mathrm{T}}\right)^{\mathrm{T}} \quad (17.13)$$

is the vector of structure and motion parameters which determine the image of point i in frame j. The weight c_{ij} in (17.12) describes our confidence in measurement $\mathbf{u}_{ij}$, and is normally set to the inverse variance σ_{ij}^{-2}. We set $c_{ij} = 1$.

The Levenberg-Marquardt algorithm first forms the approximate Hessian matrix

$$\mathbf{A} = \sum_i \sum_j c_{ij} \left(\frac{\partial \mathcal{F}(\mathbf{a}_{ij})}{\partial \mathbf{a}}\right)^{\mathrm{T}} \frac{\partial \mathcal{F}(\mathbf{a}_{ij})}{\partial \mathbf{a}} \quad (17.14)$$

and the weighted gradient vector

$$\mathbf{b} = -\sum_i \sum_j c_{ij} \left(\frac{\partial \mathcal{F}(\mathbf{a}_{ij})}{\partial \mathbf{a}}\right)^{\mathrm{T}} \mathbf{e}_{ij}, \quad (17.15)$$

where $\mathbf{e}_{ij} = \mathbf{u}_{ij} - \mathcal{F}(\mathbf{a}_{ij})$ is the image plane error of point i in frame j. Given a current estimate of $\mathbf{a}$, it computes an increment $\delta\mathbf{a}$ towards the local minimum by solving

$$(\mathbf{A} + \lambda\mathbf{I})\delta\mathbf{a} = -\mathbf{b}, \quad (17.16)$$

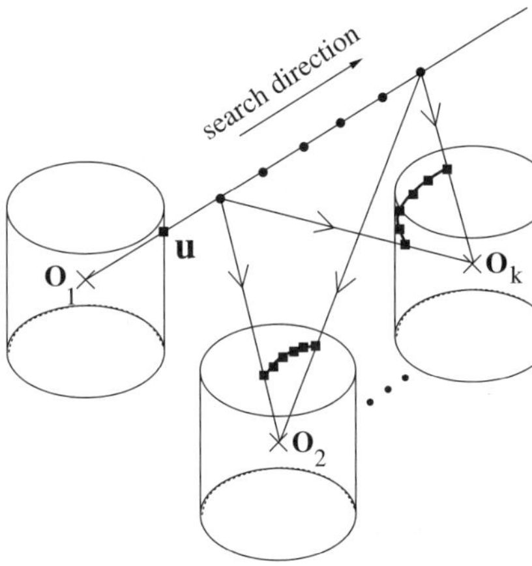

FIGURE 17.6. Principle of omnidirectional multibaseline stereo. $\mathbf{O}_1$ ... $\mathbf{O}_k$ represent the centers of the panoramic images 1 to k, respectively, with panoramic image 1 taken to be the reference image.

where λ is a stabilizing factor which varies over time [220]. Note that the matrix $\mathbf{A}$ is an approximation to the Hessian matrix, as the second-derivative terms are left out. As mentioned in [220], inclusion of these terms can be destabilizing if the model fits badly or is contaminated by outlier points.

To compute the required derivatives for (17.14) and (17.15), we compute derivatives with respect to each of the fundamental operations (perspective projection, rotation, translation) and apply the chain rule. The equations for each of the basic derivatives are given in Appendix 17.11. The derivation is exactly the same as in [270], except for the projection equation.

17.6.3 Reconstruction method 3: Constrained Depth Recovery using Epipolar Geometry

As a result of the first reconstruction method's reliance on tracking, it suffers from the aperture problem and hence limited number of reliable points. The approach of using the epipolar geometry to limit the search is designed to reduce the severity of this problem. Given the epipolar geometry, for each image point in the reference panoramic image, a constrained search is performed along the line of sight through the image point. Subsequently, the position along this line which results in minimum match error at projected image coordinates corresponding to other viewpoints is chosen. Using this approach results in a denser depth map, due to the epipolar constraint. This constraint reduces the aperture problem during search (which theoretically only occurs if the direction of ambiguity is along the epipolar line of interest). The principle is the same as that described in [147].

The principle of multibaseline stereo in the context of multiple panoramic images is shown in Figure 17.6. In that figure, take panoramic image with center $\mathbf{O}_1$ as the reference image. Suppose we are interested in determining the depth associated with image point $\mathbf{u}$ as shown in Figure 17.6. Given minimum and maximum depths as well as the depth resolution, we then project hypothesized 3D points onto the rest of the panoramic images (six points in our example). For each hypothesized point in the search, we find the sum of squared intensity errors between the local windows centered at the projected image points and the local window in the reference image. The hypothesized 3D point that results in the minimum error is then taken to be the correct location. Note that the 3D points on a straight line are projected to image points that lie on a sinusoidal curve on the cylindrical panoramic image. The window size that we use is 25×25. The results do not seem to change significantly with slight variation of the window size (e.g., 23×23 and 27×27). There was significant degradation in the quality of the results for small window sizes (we have tried 11×11).

While this approach mitigates the aperture problem, it suffers from a much higher computational demand. In addition, the recovered epipolar geometry is still dependent on the output quality of the 8-point algorithm (which in turn depends on the quality of tracking). The user has to also specify minimum and maximum depths as well as resolution of depth search.

An alternative to working in cylindrical coordinates is to project sections of cylinder to a tangential rectilinear image plane, rectify it, and use the rectified planes for multibaseline stereo. This mitigates the computational demand as search is restricted to horizontal scanlines in the rectified images. However, there is a major problem with this scheme: reprojecting to rectilinear coordinates and rectifying is problematical due to the increasing distortion away from the new center of projection. This creates a problem with matching using a window of a fixed size. As a result, this scheme of reprojecting to rectilinear coordinates and rectifying is not used.

A point can be made of using the original image sequences in the projection onto composite planar images to get scan-line epipolar geometry for a speedier stereo matching process. There are the questions as to what the optimal projection directions should be and how many projections should be used. The simpliest approach, as described in the previous paragraph, would be to project subsets of images to pairwise tangent planes. However, because the relative rotation within the image sequence cannot be determined *exactly*, one would still encounter the problem of constructing composite planar images that are not exactly physically correct. In addition, one would still have to use a variable window size scheme due to the varying amount of distortion across the composite planar image (e.g., comparing a local low-distortion area in the middle of one composite planar image with another that has high distortion near a side of another composite planar image). Our approach to directly use the cylindrical images is mostly out of expediency.

17.7 Stereo Data Segmentation and Modeling

Once the 3D stereo data has been extracted, we can then model them with a 3D mesh and texture-map each face with the associated part of the 2D image panorama. We have done work to reduce the complexity of the resulting 3D mesh by planar patch fitting and boundary simplification. Our simplification and noise reduction algorithm is based on a segmentation of the input surface mesh into surface patches using a least squares fitting of planes. Simplification is achieved by extracting, approximating, and triangulating the boundaries between surface patches. The displayed models shown in this paper are rendered using our modeling system. A more detailed description of model extraction from range data is given in [145].

17.8 Experimental Results

In this section, we present the results of applying our approach to recover 3D data from multiple panoramic images. We have used both synthetic and real images to test our approach. As mentioned earlier, in the experiments described in this section, the camera positions are deliberately arranged so that all of the positions are not collinear. In addition, all the images are taken at the same vertical height to maximize overlap between panoramic images.

17.8.1 Synthetic Scene

The synthetic scene is a room comprising objects such as tables, tori, cylinders, and vases. One half of the room is textured with a mandrill image while the other is textured with a regular Brodatz pattern. The synthetic objects and images are created using Rayshade, which is a program for creating ray-traced color images [155]. The synthetic images created are free from any radial distortion, since Rayshade is currently unable to model this camera characteristic. The omnidirectional synthetic depth map of the entire room is created by merging the depth maps associated with the multiple views taken around inside the room.

The composite panoramic view of the synthetic room from its center is shown in Figure 17.7. From left to right, we can observe the vases resting on a table, vertical cylinders, a torus resting on a table, and a larger torus. The results of applying both reconstruction methods (i.e., unconstrained search with 8-point and constrained search using epipolar geometry) can

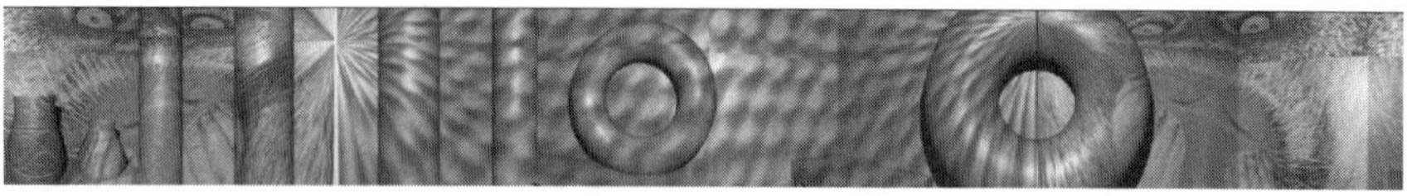

FIGURE 17.7. Panorama of synthetic room after compositing.

be seen in Figure 17.8. We get many more points using constrained search (about 3 times more), but the quality of the 3D reconstruction appears more degraded (compare Figure 17.8(b) with (d)). This is in part due to matching occurring at integral values of pixel positions, limiting its depth resolution. The dimensions of the synthetic room are 10(length) $\times$ 8(width) $\times$ 6(height), and the specified resolution is 0.01. The quality of the recovered 3D data appears to be enhanced by applying a 3D median filter.

The median filter works in the following manner: For each feature point in the cylindrical panoramic image, find other feature points within a certain neighborhood radius (20 in our case). Then sort the 3D depths associated with the neighborhood feature points, find the median depth, and *rescale* the depth associated with the current feature point such that the new depth is the median depth. As an illustration, suppose the original 3D feature location is $\mathbf{v}_i = d_i\hat{\mathbf{v}}_i$, where d_i is the original depth and $\hat{\mathbf{v}}_i$ is the 3D unit vector from the camera center in the direction of the image point. If d_{med} is the median depth within its neighborhood, then the filtered 3D feature location is given by $\mathbf{v}'_i = (d_{\text{med}}/d_i)\mathbf{v}_i = d_{\text{med}}\hat{\mathbf{v}}_i$. However, the median filter also has the effect of rounding off corners.

The mesh in Figure 17.8(h) and the three views in Figure 17.9 are generated by our 3D modeling system described in [145]. As can be seen from these figures, the 3D recovered points and the subsequent model based on these points basically preserved the shape of the synthetic room. While shape distortions can be easily seen at the edges, texture-mapping tends to reduce the visual effect of incorrectly recovered shapes away from the edges.

In addition, we performed a series of experiments to examine the effect of both "bad" track removal and median filtering on the quality of recovered depth information of the synthetic room. The feature tracks are sorted in increasing order according to the error in matching[2]. We continually remove tracks that have the worst amount of match error, recovering the 3D point distribution at each instant.

From the graph in Figure 17.10, we see an interesting result: as more tracks are taken out, retaining the better ones, the quality of 3D point recovery improves—up to a point. The improvement in the accuracy is not

[2]Note that in general, a "worse" track in this sense need not necessarily translate to a worse 3D estimate. A high match error may be due to apparent object distortion at different viewpoints.

	constrained(n=10040)	8-pt(n=3057)	8-pt(n=1788)
original	0.315039	0.393777	0.302287
med.-filtered	0.266600	0.364889	0.288079

TABLE 17.1. Comparison of 3D RMS error between unconstrained and constrained stereo results (n is the number of points).

surprising, since the worse tracks, which are more likely to result in worse 3D estimates, are removed. However, as more and more tracks are removed, the gap between the amount of accuracy demanded of the tracks, given an increasingly smaller number of available tracks, and the track accuracy available, grows. This results in generally worse estimates of the epipolar geometry, and hence 3D data. Concomitant to the reduction of the number of points is the sensitivity of the recovery of both epipolar geometry (in the form of the essential matrix) and 3D data. This is evidenced by the fluctuation of the curves at the lower end of the graph. Another interesting result that can be observed is that the 3D point distribution that has been median filtered have lower errors, especially for higher numbers of recovered 3D points.

As indicated by the graph in Figure 17.10, the accuracy of the point distribution derived from just the 8-point algorithm is almost equivalent that that of using an iterative least-squares (Levenberg-Marquardt) minimization, which is statistically optimal near the true solution. This result is in agreement with Hartley's application of the 8-point algorithm to narrow-angle images [94]. It is also worth noting that the accuracy of the iterative algorithm is best at smaller numbers of input points, suggesting that it is more stable given a smaller number of input data.

Table 17.1 lists the 3D errors of both constrained and unconstrained (8-point only) methods for the synthetic scenes. It appears from this result that the constrained method yields better results (after median filtering) and more points (a result of reducing the aperture problem). In practice, as we shall see in the next section, problems due to misestimation of camera intrinsic parameters (specifically focal length, aspect ratio and radial distortion coefficient) causes 3D reconstruction from real images to be worse. This is a subject of on-going research.

17.8.2 Real Scenes

The setup that we used to record our image sequences consists of a DEC Alpha workstation with a J300 framegrabber, and a camcorder (Sony Handycam CCD-TR81) mounted on an X-Y position stage affixed on a tripod stand. The camcorder settings are made such that its field of view is maximized (at about 43°).

To reiterate, our method of generating the panoramic images is as follows:

- Calibrate the camcorder using an iterative Levenberg-Marquardt least-squares algorithm [270].
- Adjust the X-Y position stage while panning the camera left and right to remove the effect of motion parallax; this ensures that the camera is then rotated about its optical center.
- At each camera location, record onto tape an image sequence while rotating the camera, and then digitize the image sequence using the framegrabber.
- Using the recovered camera intrinsic parameters (focal length, aspect ratio, radial distortion factor), undistort each image.
- Project each image, which is in rectilinear image coordinates, into cylindrical coordinates (whose cross-sectional radius is the camera focal length).
- Composite the frames into a panoramic image. The number of frames used to extract a panoramic image in our experiments is typically about 50.

We recorded image sequences of two scenes, namely an office scene and a lab scene. A panoramic image of the office scene is shown in Figure 17.4. We extracted four panoramic images corresponding to four different locations in the office. (The spacing between these locations is about 6 inches and the locations are roughly at the corners of a square. The size of the office is about 10 feet by 15 feet.) The results of 3D point recovery of the office scene is shown in Figure 17.11, with three sample views of its model shown in Figure 17.12. As can be seen from Figure 17.11, the results due to the constrained search approach looks much worse. This may be directly attributed to the inaccuracy of the extracted intrinsic camera parameters. As a consequence, the composited panoramas may actually be not exactly physically correct. In fact, as the matching (with epipolar constraint) is in progress, it has been observed that the actual correct matches are not exactly along the epipolar lines; there are slight vertical drifts, generally of the order of about one or two pixels.

Another example of a real scene is shown in Figure 17.13. A total of eight panoramas at eight different locations (about 3 inches apart, ordered roughly in a zig-zag fashion) in the lab are extracted. The longest dimensions of the L-shaped lab is about 15 feet by 22.5 feet. The 3D point distribution is shown in Figure 17.14 while Figure 17.16 shows three views of the recovered model of the lab. As can be seen, the shape of the lab has been reasonably well recovered; the "noise" points at the bottom of Figure 17.14(a) corresponds to the positions *outside* the laboratory, since there are parts of the transparent laboratory window that are not covered. This reveals one of the weaknesses of any correlation-based algorithm (namely all stereo algorithms); they do not work well with image reflections and transparent material. Again, we observe that the points recovered using constrained search is worse.

The errors that were observed with the real scene images, especially with constrained search, are due to the following practical problems:

- The auto-iris feature of the camcorder used cannot be deactivated (even though the focal length was kept constant). As a result, there may be in fact slight variations in focal length as the camera was rotated.
- The camera may not be rotating exactly about its optical center, since the adjustment of the X-Y position stage is done manually and there may be human error in judging the absence of motion parallax.
- The camera may not be rotating about a unique axis all the way around (assumed to be vertical) due to some play or unevenness of the tripod.
- There were digitization problems. The images digitized from tape (i.e., while the camcorder is playing the tape) contain scan lines that are occasionally horizontally shifted; this is probably caused by the degraded blanking signal not properly detected by the framegrabber. However, compositing many images averages out most of these artifacts.
- The extracted camera intrinsic parameters may not be very precise.

As a result of the problems encountered, the resulting composited panorama may not be physically correct. This especially causes problems with constrained search given the estimated epipolar geometry (through the essential matrix). We actually widened the search a little by allowing search as much as a couple of pixels away from the epipolar line. The results look only slightly better, however; while there is a greater chance of matching the correct locations, there is also a greater chance of confusion. This relaxed mode of search further increases the computational demand and has the effect of loosening the constraints, thus making this approach less attractive.

17.9 Discussion and Conclusions

We have shown that omnidirectional depth data (whose denseness depends on the amount of local texture) can be extracted using a set of simple techniques: camera calibration, image compositing, feature tracking, the 8-point algorithm, and constrained search using the recovered epipolar geometry. The advantage of our work is that we are able to extract depth data within a wide field of view simultaneously, which removes many of the traditional problems associated with recovering camera pose and narrow-baseline stereo. Despite the practical problems caused by using unsophisticated equipment which result in slightly incorrect panoramas, we are still able to extract reasonable 3D data. Thus far, the best real data results come from using unconstrained tracking and the 8-point algorithm (both direct and iterative structure from motion). Results also indicate that the application of 3D median filtering improves both the accuracy and appearance of stereo-computed 3D point distribution.

In terms of the differences between the three reconstruction methods, reconstruction methods 1 (8-point and direct 3D calculation) and 2 (iterative structure from motion) yield virtually the same results, which suggests that the 8-point algorithm applied to panoramic images gives near optimal camera motion estimates. This is consistent with the intuition that widening the field of view with the attendant increase in image resolution results in more accurate estimation of egomotion; this was verified experimentally by Tian *et al.* [278]. One can then deduce that the iterative technique is usually not necessary. In the case of reconstruction method 3, where constrained search using the epipolar constraint is performed, denser data are obtained at the expense of much higher computation. In addition, the minimum and maximum depths have to be specified *a priori*. Based on real data results, the accuracy obtained using reconstruction method 3 is more sensitive to how physically correct the panoramas are composited. The compositing error can be attributed to the error in estimating the camera intrinsic parameters, namely the focal length and radial distortion factor [148].

To expedite the panorama image production in critical applications that require close to real-time modeling, special camera equipment may be called for. One such possible specialized equipment is Ahuja's camera system (as reported in [75, 158]), in which the lens can be rotated relative to the imaging plane. However, we are currently putting our emphasis on the use of commercially available equipment such as a cheap camcorder.

Even if all the practical problems associated with imperfect data acquisition were solved, we still have the fundamental problem of stereo—that of the inability to match and extract 3D data in textureless regions. In scenes that involve mostly textureless components such as bare walls and objects, special pattern projectors may need to be used in conjunction with the camera [147].

Currently, the omnidirectional data, while obtained through a 360° view, has limited vertical view. We plan to extend this work by merging multiple omnidirectional data obtained at both different heights and at different locations. We will also look into the possibility of extracting panoramas of larger height extents by incorporating *tilted* (i.e., rotated about a horizontal axis) camera views. This would enable scene reconstruction of a building floor involving multiple rooms with good vertical view. We are currently characterizing the effects of misestimated intrinsic camera parameters (focal length, aspect ratio, and the radial distortion factor) on the accuracy of the recovered 3D data.

In summary, our set of methods for reconstructing 3D scene points within a wide field of view has been shown to be quite robust and accurate. Wide-angle reconstruction of 3D scenes is conventionally achieved by merging multiple range images; our methods have been demonstrated to be a very attractive alternative in wide-angle 3D scene model recovery. In addition, these methods do not require specialized camera equipment, thus making commercialization of this technology easier and more direct. We strongly feel that this development is a significant one toward attaining the goal of creating photorealistic 3D scenes with minimum human intervention.

Acknowledgment

We would like to thank Andrew Johnson for the use of his 3D modeling and rendering program and Richard Weiss for helpful discussions.

17.10 Appendix: Optimal Point Intersection

In order to find the point closest to all of the rays whose line equations are of the form $\mathbf{r} = \mathbf{t}_k + \lambda_k \hat{\mathbf{v}}_k$, we minimize the expression

$$\mathcal{E} = \sum_k \|\mathbf{p} - (\mathbf{t}_k + \lambda_k \hat{\mathbf{v}}_k)\|^2 \tag{17.17}$$

where $\mathbf{p}$ is the optimal point of intersection to be determined. Taking the partials of $\mathcal{E}$ with respect to λ_k and $\mathbf{p}$ and equating them to zero, we have

$$\frac{\partial \mathcal{E}}{\partial \lambda_k} = 2\hat{\mathbf{v}}_k^T(\mathbf{t}_k + \lambda_k \hat{\mathbf{v}}_k - \mathbf{p}) = 0 \tag{17.18}$$

$$\frac{\partial \mathcal{E}}{\partial \mathbf{p}} = -2\sum_k(\mathbf{t}_k + \lambda_k \hat{\mathbf{v}}_k - \mathbf{p}) = 0. \tag{17.19}$$

Solving for λ_k in (17.18), noting that $\hat{\mathbf{v}}_k^T \hat{\mathbf{v}}_k = 1$, and substituting λ_k in (17.19) yields

$$\sum_k \left(\mathbf{t}_k - \hat{\mathbf{v}}_k(\hat{\mathbf{v}}_k^T \mathbf{t}_k) - \mathbf{p} + \hat{\mathbf{v}}_k(\hat{\mathbf{v}}_k^T \mathbf{p})\right) = 0,$$

from which

$$\mathbf{p} = \left[\sum_k \mathbf{A}_k\right]^{-1} \left[\sum_k \mathbf{A}_k \mathbf{t}_k\right]$$

$$= \left[\sum_k \mathbf{A}_k\right]^{-1} \left[\sum_k \mathbf{p}_k^*\right], \tag{17.20}$$

where

$$\mathbf{A}_k = \mathbf{I} - \hat{\mathbf{v}}_k \hat{\mathbf{v}}_k^T$$

is the perpendicular projection operator for ray $\hat{\mathbf{v}}_k$, and

$$\mathbf{p}_k^* = \mathbf{t}_k - \hat{\mathbf{v}}_k(\hat{\mathbf{v}}_k^T \mathbf{t}_k) = \mathbf{A}_k \mathbf{t}_k$$

is the point along the viewing ray $\mathbf{r} = \mathbf{t}_k + \lambda_k \hat{\mathbf{v}}_k$ closest to the origin.

Thus, the optimal intersection point for a bundle of rays can be computed as a weighted sum of adjusted camera centers (indicated by $\mathbf{t}_k$'s), where the weighting is in the direction perpendicular to the viewing ray.

A more "optimal" estimate can be found by minimizing the formula

$$\mathcal{E} = \sum_k \lambda_k^{-2} \|\mathbf{p} - (\mathbf{t}_k + \lambda_k \hat{\mathbf{v}}_k)\|^2 \tag{17.21}$$

with respect to $\mathbf{p}$ and λ_k's. Here, by weighting each squared perpendicular distance by λ_k^{-2}, we are downweighting points further away from the camera. The justification for this formula is that the uncertainty in $\hat{\mathbf{v}}_k$ direction defines a *conical* region of uncertainty in space centered at the camera, i.e., the uncertainty in point location (and hence the inverse weight) grows linearly with λ_k. However, implementing this minimization requires an iterative non-linear solver.

17.11 Appendix: Elemental Transform Derivatives

The derivative of the projection function (17.11) with respect to its 3D arguments and internal parameters is straightforward:

$$\frac{\partial \mathcal{P}(\mathbf{x})}{\partial \mathbf{x}} = \frac{1}{D} \begin{pmatrix} y^2 + z^2 & -xy & -xz \\ -xy & x^2 + z^2 & -yz \\ -xz & -yz & x^2 + y^2 \end{pmatrix},$$

where

$$D = \left(x^2 + y^2 + z^2\right)^{\frac{3}{2}}$$

The derivatives of an elemental rigid transformation (17.9)

$$\mathbf{x}' = \mathbf{R}\mathbf{x} + \mathbf{t}$$

are

$$\frac{\partial \mathbf{x}'}{\partial \mathbf{x}} = \mathbf{R}, \qquad \frac{\partial \mathbf{x}'}{\partial \mathbf{t}} = \mathbf{I},$$

and

$$\frac{\partial \mathbf{x}'}{\partial \mathbf{q}} = -\mathbf{R}\mathbf{C}(\mathbf{x})\mathbf{G}(\mathbf{q}),$$

where

$$\mathbf{C}(\mathbf{x}) = \begin{pmatrix} 0 & -z & y \\ z & 0 & -x \\ -y & x & 0 \end{pmatrix}$$

and

$$\mathbf{G}(\mathbf{q}) = 2\begin{pmatrix} -q_0 & w & q_2 & -q_1 \\ -q_1 & -q_2 & w & q_0 \\ -q_2 & q_1 & -q_0 & w \end{pmatrix}$$

(see [247]). The derivatives of a screen coordinate with respect to any motion or structure parameter can be computed by applying the chain rule and the above set of equations.

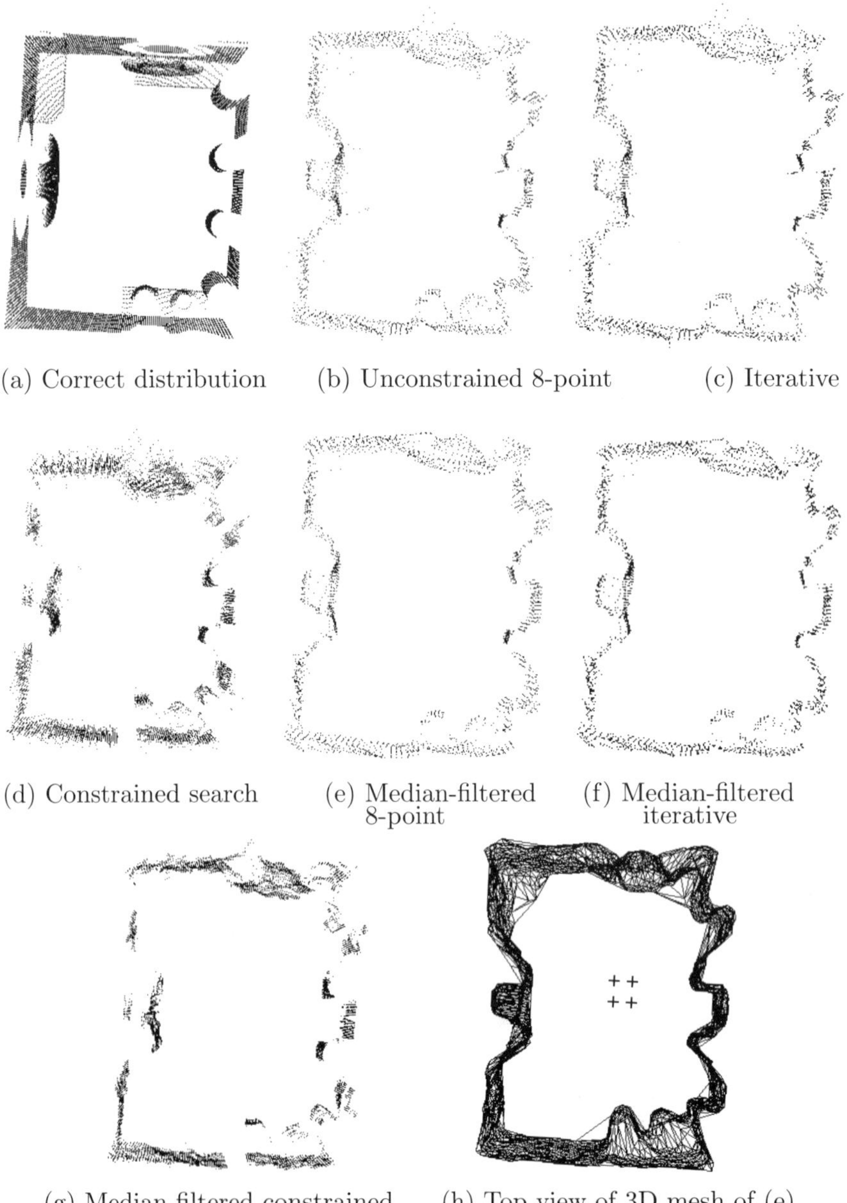

FIGURE 17.8. Comparison of 3D points recovered of synthetic room. The four camera locations are indicated by +'s in (h).

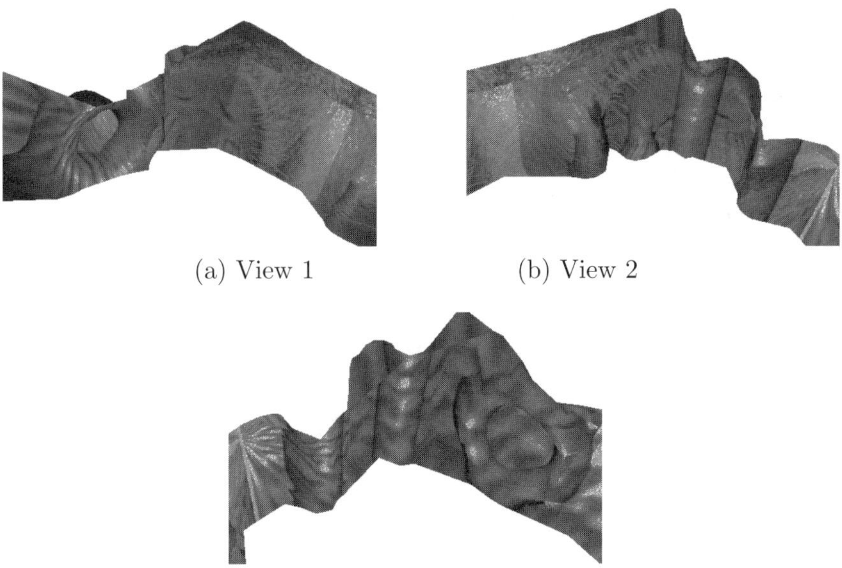

(a) View 1 (b) View 2

(c) View 3

FIGURE 17.9. Three views of modeled synthetic room of Figure 17.8(h). Note the distorted shape of the torus in (c) and the top parts of the cylinders in (b) and (c) that do not look circular.

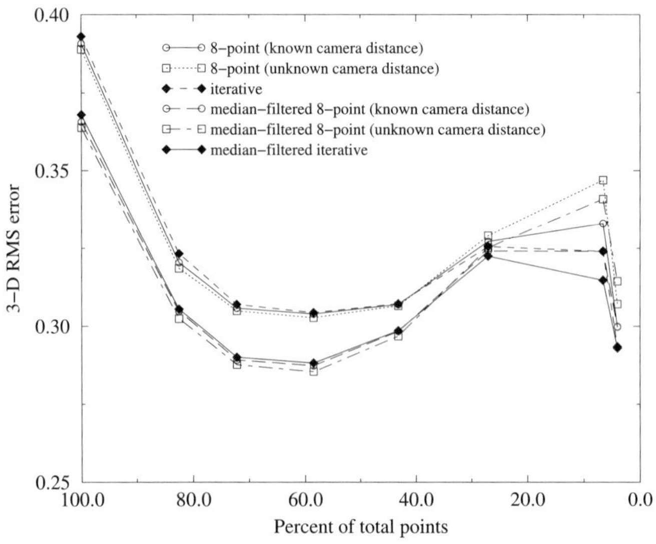

FIGURE 17.10. 3D RMS error vs. number of points. The original number of points (corresponding to 100%) is 3057. The dimensions of the synthetic room are 10(length) $\times$ 8(width) $\times$ 6(height). Note that by "8-point," we mean the reconstruction method 1, with the application of the 8-point algorithm and direct 3D position calculation. The "iterative" method is reconstruction method 2. The results of reconstruction method 3 is not represented here because the selected points (2D location and sample size) are different.

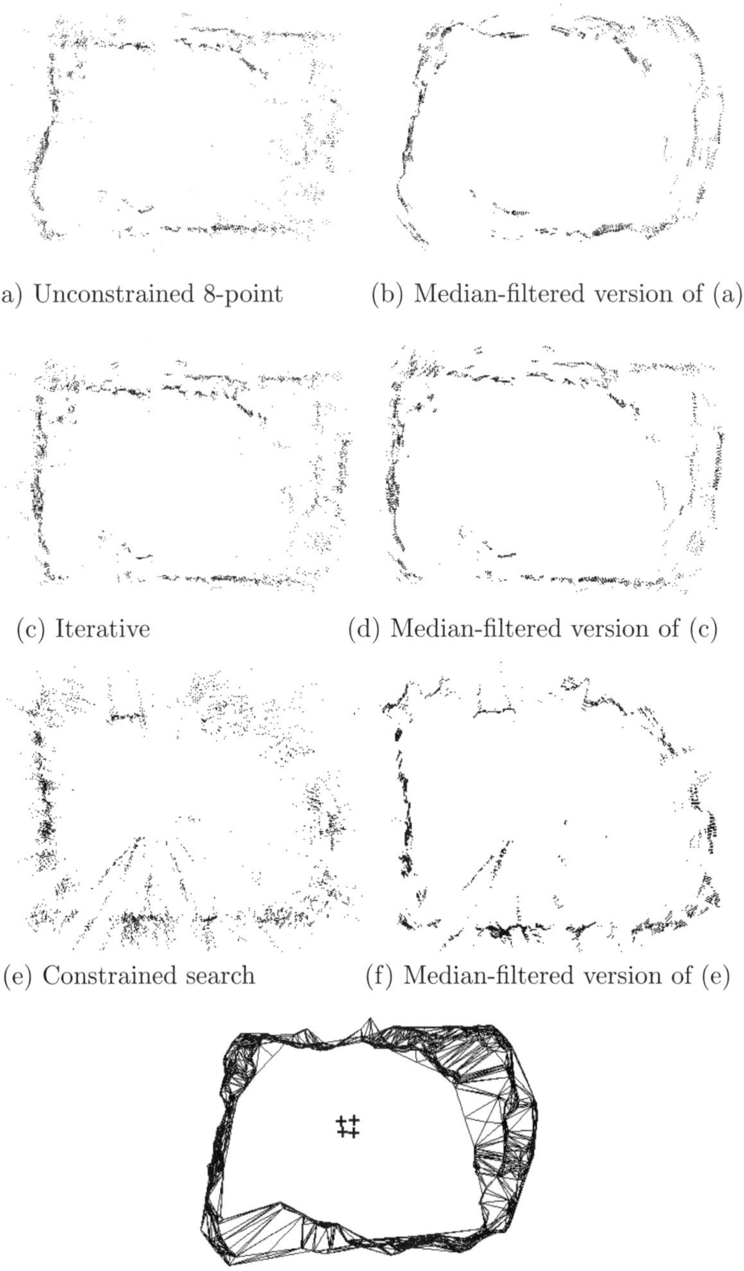

(a) Unconstrained 8-point (b) Median-filtered version of (a)

(c) Iterative (d) Median-filtered version of (c)

(e) Constrained search (f) Median-filtered version of (e)

(g) 3D mesh of (b)

FIGURE 17.11. Extracted 3D points and mesh of office scene. Notice that the recovered distributions shown in (c) and (d) appear more rectangular than those shown in (a) and (b). The camera locations are indicated by +'s in (g).

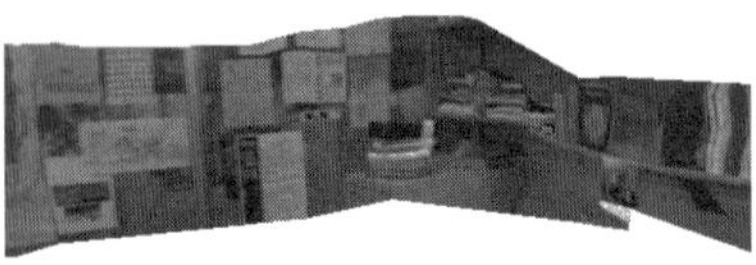

(a) View 1

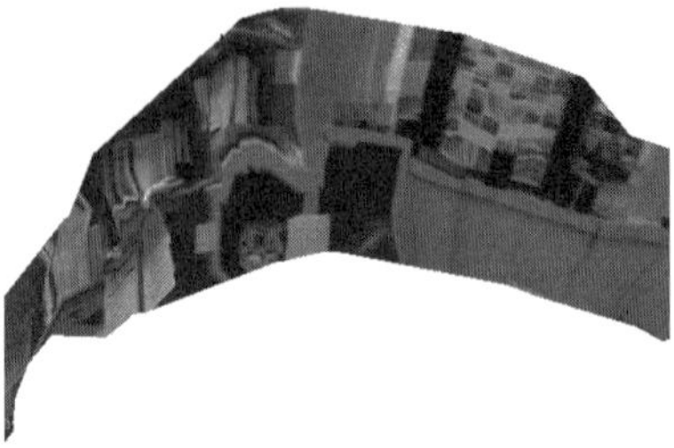

(b) View 2

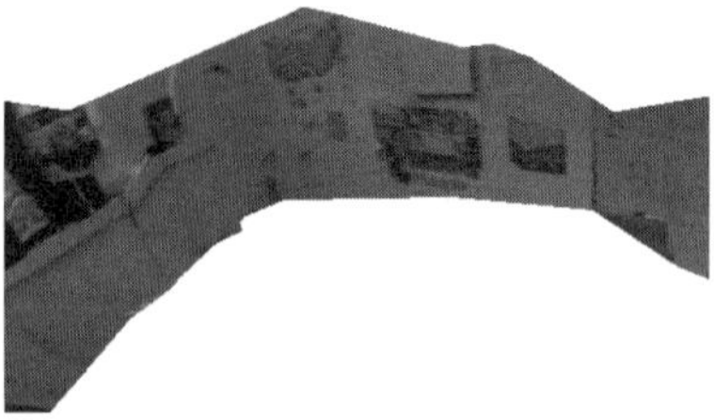

(c) View 3

FIGURE 17.12. Three texture-mapped views of the modeled office scene of Figure 17.11(g)

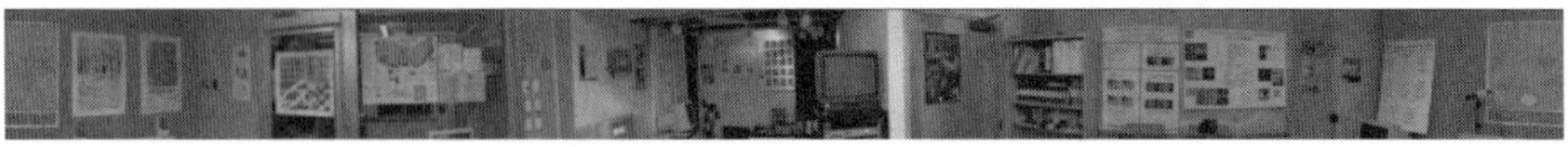

FIGURE 17.13. Panorama of laboratory after compositing.

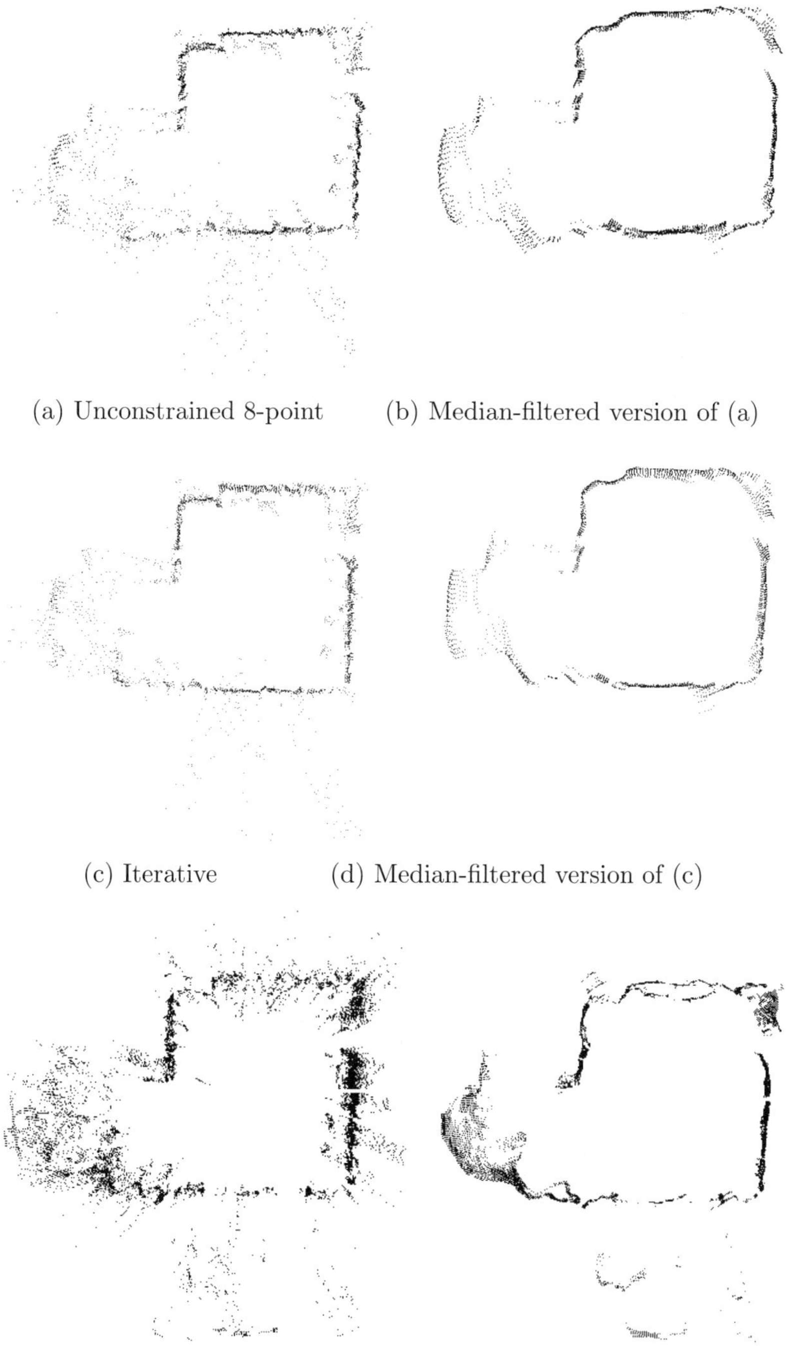

(a) Unconstrained 8-point (b) Median-filtered version of (a)

(c) Iterative (d) Median-filtered version of (c)

(e) Constrained search (f) Median-filtered version of (e)

FIGURE 17.14. Extracted 3D points and mesh of laboratory scene.

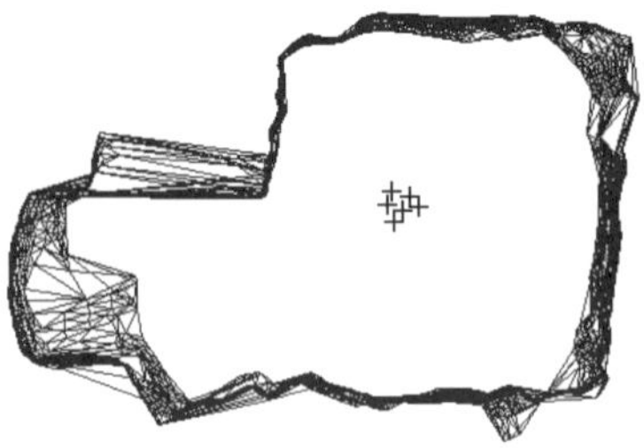

FIGURE 17.15. 3D mesh and extracted camera locations for Figure 17.14(b). Each camera location is indicated by +.

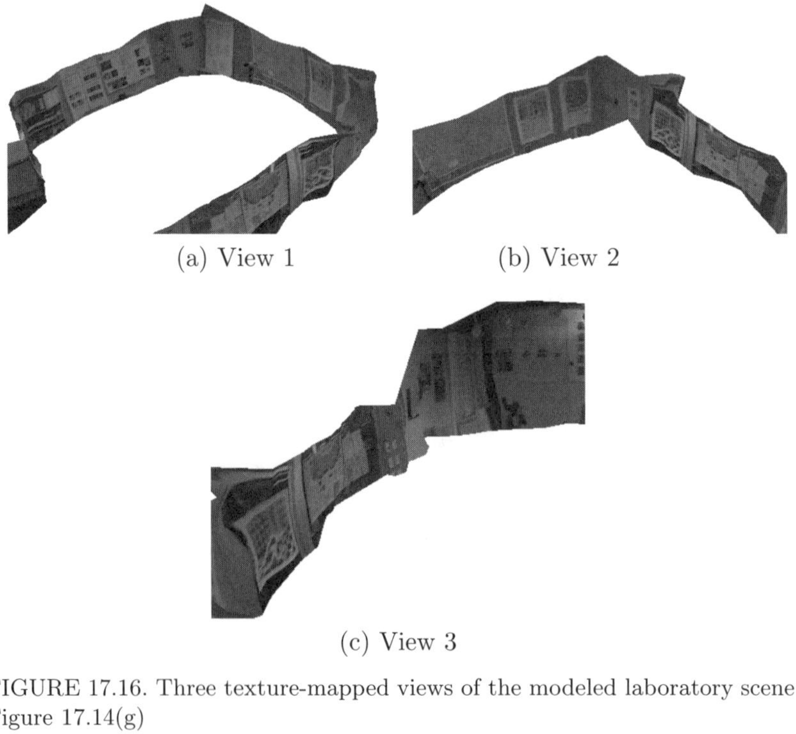

FIGURE 17.16. Three texture-mapped views of the modeled laboratory scene of Figure 17.14(g)

18

N-Ocular Stereo for Real-Time Human Tracking

T. Sogo, H. Ishiguro, and M.M. Trivedi

18.1 Introduction

In recent years, various systems using multiple vision sensors have been proposed in the area of computer vision. For example, several systems track people or automobiles in the real environment with multiple vision sensors [32, 141, 169, 51, 189] while other systems analyze their behaviors [89]. Compared with systems using a single vision sensor [243, 116, 140, 156], these systems are able to observe a moving target in a large space for a long time. However, they need to use many vision sensors to seamlessly cover the entire space, since a single standard vision sensor itself has a narrow range of view. On the other hand, an omnidirectional vision sensor (ODVS) provides a wide field of view of up to a 360° at a time. In addition, use of multiple ODVSs provide rich and redundant visual information, which enables robust recognition of the targets. Thus, multiple ODVSs opens up a new application area of computer vision with their wide range of view.

As an application of such vision systems, we propose a real-time human tracking system using multiple ODVSs. We have originally developed low-cost and compact ODVSs as shown in Figure 18.1 [131] which are used for this research. The system detects people and measures azimuth angles with the ODVSs fixed at a height of approximately 1m, and localizes them by triangulation as shown in Figure 18.2(a). In applying stereo on ODVSs, called omnidirectional stereo, the following problems should be considered:

- Correspondence problem among multiple targets, and
- Measurement precision of target locations

The first problem occurs in conventional stereo using two or more vision sensors [189, 206, 142] as well as in omnidirectional stereo. However, in omnidirectional stereo it is more difficult to verify the correspondence of targets with visual feature, since the baseline of ODVSs in our work is much longer than that of conventional stereo. The second problem is that the measurement precision of a target location becomes very low when the target is located along the baseline of two sensors [136]. For example, the target B in Figure 18.2(a) is located on the baseline of sensors 1 and 2,

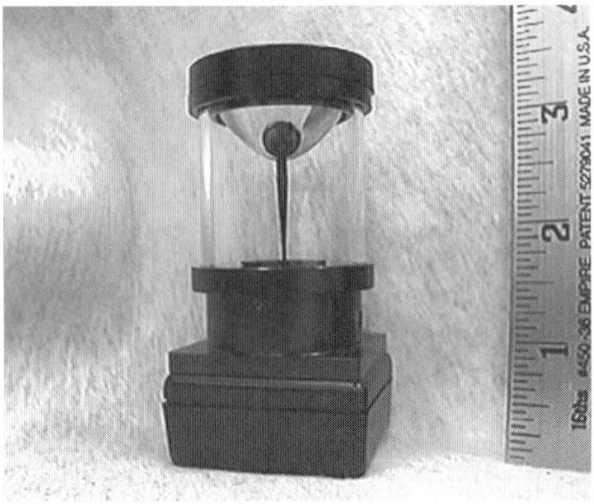

FIGURE 18.1. Omnidirectional vision sensor.

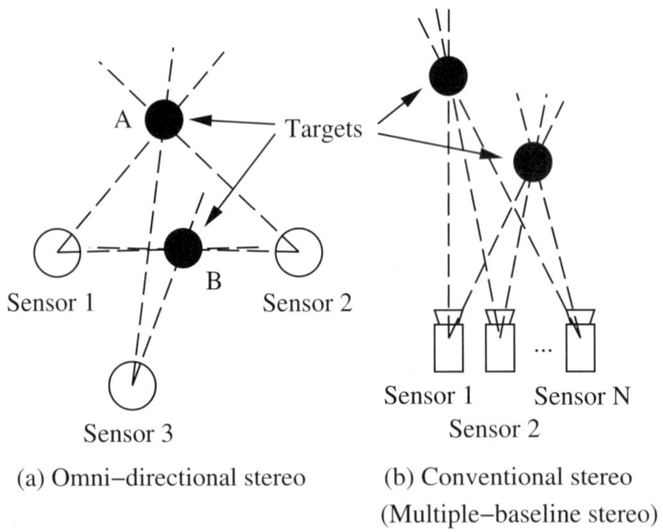

FIGURE 18.2. Omnidirectional stereo and conventional stereo.

so that the target location measured by them is unstable. This problem does not occur in conventional stereo, but in omnidirectional stereo, since omnidirectional stereo assumes arbitrary locations of sensors and targets. Furthermore, in the real-time human tracking system, human body deformations should be properly handled.

In order to solve the above problems, we use an extended version of trinocular stereo [299, 90]. The extended method, which we called *N-ocular stereo*, verifies correspondence of multiple targets without visual features. In addition, we have developed several compensation methods for observation errors in order to measure target locations more robustly and accurately.

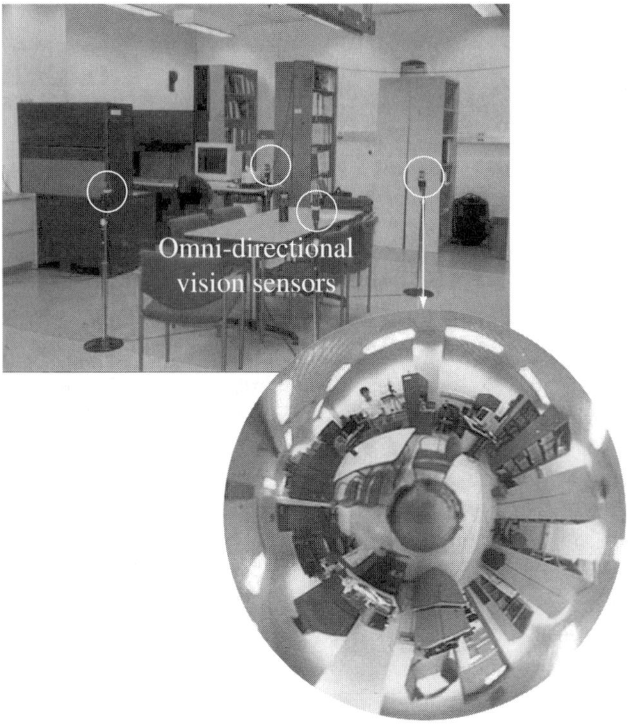

FIGURE 18.3. An image taken with the omnidirectional vision sensor.

In the following, N-ocular stereo is explained, which measures target locations using multiple ODVSs. Then, the simplified N-ocular stereo and error compensation methods are introduced for real-time processing. Finally, we show experimental results of tracking people by the real-time human tracking system.

18.2 Multiple Camera Stereo

18.2.1 The Correspondence Problems and Trinocular Stereo

In order to detect targets and measure their locations, our system uses multiple omnidirectional vision sensors (ODVSs, shown in Figure 18.1). Since each ODVS is fixed in the environment, the system can detect targets in omnidirectional images as shown in Figure 18.3 by background subtraction. Then, it measures the azimuth angles of the targets (the details are described in Section 18.5.2). If the locations and the orientations of the ODVSs are known, the locations of the targets can be measured from the azimuth angles by triangulation (see Figure 18.4).

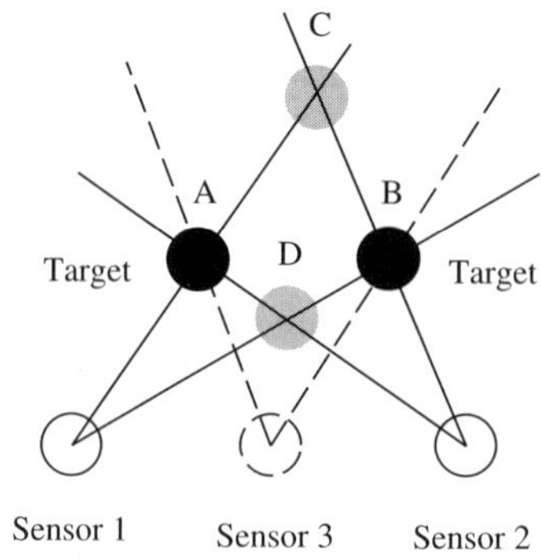

FIGURE 18.4. The correspondence problem and trinocular stereo.

In triangulation, multiple targets in the environment cause the correspondence problem. In Figure 18.4, for example, there are two targets (the black circles indicate actual target locations); however, from azimuth angles observed by the sensors 1 and 2, it is estimated by triangulation that the targets may exist at A through D in Figure 18.4. In general, this correspondence problem can be solved by using visual features of the targets. In our system, however, it is difficult to verify the correspondence of targets with visual features, since ODVSs observe targets from various points of view and their visual features may differ. Alternatively, the correspondence problem can also be solved by using three or more sensors. In Figure 18.4, the locations C and D are verified with the sensor 3, then they are eliminated since the sensor 3 does not observe the targets in these directions. This technique is known as *trinocular stereo* [299, 90], and it can be applied to our system for verifying the target correspondence.

18.2.2 Problems of Previous Methods

18.2.2.1 Observation Errors

When applying trinocular stereo to actual systems, observation errors should be considered. In Figure 18.4, for example, the lines indicating azimuth angles of the target A and B exactly intersect at one point. In practice, however, they do not intersect in this manner because of observation errors. In this case, clusters of intersections are considered as target locations [211, 249, 235].

Unfortunately, information derived from vision systems is significantly noisier compared with that of radar systems. Furthermore, our system cannot precisely detect the azimuth angles of targets because of the following reasons:

- If targets locate near sensors, they are widely projected on the ODVSs.
- Targets are humans which have bodies that can deform. In addition, each vision sensor observes the target from various points of view.

The previous methods for localizing targets do not consider these problems. In addition, binocular stereo using ODVSs has a low-precision problem with respect to targets locating along the baseline of the sensors [136]. These problems should be carefully considered in our approach.

18.2.2.2 Computational Costs

In order to solve the correspondence problems and to measure target locations properly, each azimuth angle of the targets detected by the sensors should have an association with at least one of measured locations. Assignment of azimuth angles is an optimization problem that is NP-hard [211]. Several methods for solving it have been proposed so far [211, 249], but these methods require many iterations (more than 10 or 300 times). As a result, a more efficient method is needed for real-time processing.

The aim of the N-ocular stereo proposed in this chapter is to solve the correspondence problem with low computational cost within acceptable quality of solutions, rather than to compute optimal ones.

18.3 Localization of Targets by N-ocular Stereo

18.3.1 Basic Algorithm

In trinocular stereo, three vision sensors are used to measure the target location and to verify the correspondence. On the other hand, in N-ocular stereo, more than three vision sensors are used. This is based on the idea that observation errors are reduced by using more visual information.

The basic process of N-ocular stereo is as follows:

1. Measure the location of a target from azimuth angles detected by a pair of arbitrary vision sensors as shown in Figure 18.4 (binocular stereo).
2. Check if another sensor observes the target at the location measured with $(N-1)$-ocular stereo. If so, the location is considered as a result of N-ocular stereo (see A and B in Figure 18.4). Iterate this step from $N = 3$ to N =number of sensors.
3. Finally, the locations measured with only two sensors (C and D in Figure 18.4) are considered as wrong matchings, and removed from the list of candidates.

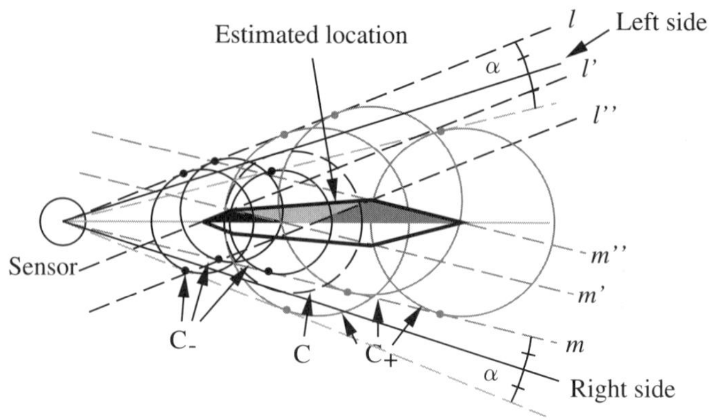

FIGURE 18.5. Localization of a target considering observation errors.

18.3.2 Localization of Targets and Error Handling

As described in Section 18.2.2, observation errors of azimuth angles should be considered when measuring people's locations, since the human body can deform over time and is widely projected on the ODVSs. Here, we suppose the human body is represented with a circle of a constant radius, and the location of a person is represented as the center of the circle. The errors in the model matching can be handled with the following two parameters:

- α: Detection errors of the right and left side of a target
- β: An error of the human model, i.e., the error of the circle's radius

With the parameters α and β, the center of the circle is localized within the hexagon as shown in Figure 18.5. It is computed as follows: suppose that a target C with a radius r is observed from the sensor, and the detection error of the right and left side of the target is α, as shown in Figure 18.5. First, a circle C_- with a radius $(r - \beta)$ is considered. The black region in Figure 18.5 indicates a possible region for the center location of the circle C_-, on condition that the right and left side of the circle C_- are projected within $\pm\alpha$ from those of the target C, respectively. Here, the straight lines l and m are parallel to l' and m', respectively, and the black region indicates only the upper half of the possible region for the circle C_-. In the same way, the dark gray region indicates a possible region for the center location of a circle C_+ with a radius $(r + \beta)$. Here, the straight lines l'' and m'' are parallel to l and m, respectively. Hence, the center of the circle whose radius is from $(r - \beta)$ to $(r + \beta)$ exists in the merged region of the black, the dark gray and the light gray regions (Figure 18.5 shows only the upper half of the region). This region indicates the location of the target C.

In the above method, target matchings can be verified by checking if the hexagons overlap each other. Then, in the first step of N-ocular stereo, the target is localized at the overlapped region of two hexagons as shown in

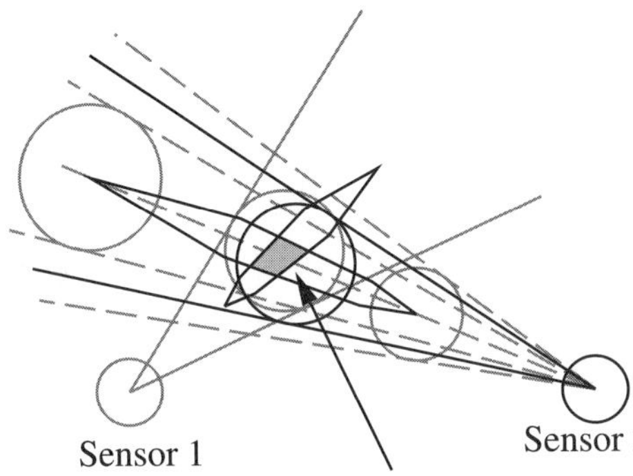

FIGURE 18.6. Localization of a target by binocular stereo.

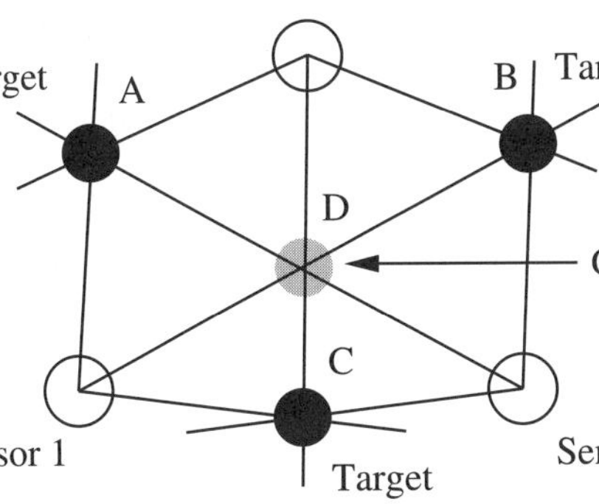

FIGURE 18.7. False matchings in N-ocular stereo.

Figure 18.6. In the same way, in the second step, the target is localized at the overlapped region of N hexagons. If let α and β smaller, the overlapped region also becomes smaller; and when it finally becomes a point, it can be considered as the location of the target.

18.3.3 False Matchings in N-ocular Stereo

While N-ocular stereo can solve the correspondence problems of multiple targets in most cases, it fails for a particular arrangement of targets. In Figure 18.7, for example, it is estimated by N-ocular stereo that targets exist at up to four locations of A through D, including a false one (called a ghost target). In general, there is no way to eliminate the ghost target except to observe the motion of the intersections for a while [249].

The false matching in N-ocular stereo occurs when an azimuth angle of a target is associated with multiple locations (in Figure 18.7, an azimuth angle observed by sensor 1 is used for the locations B and D). Therefore,

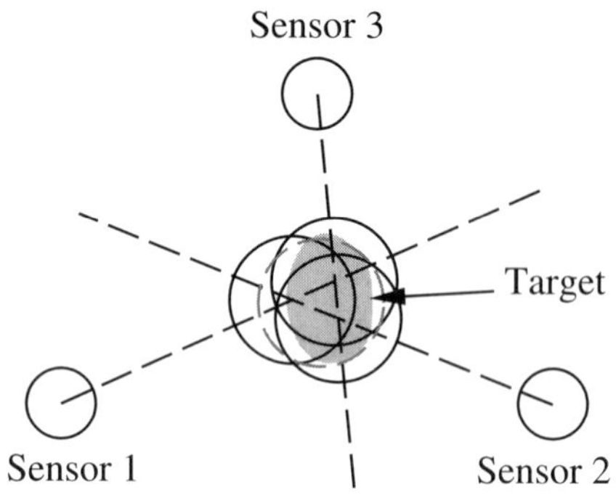

FIGURE 18.8. Simplified N-ocular stereo

if all of azimuth angles which are used for measuring a target location are also used for other locations, it is estimated that the location may be a false matching (the location D in the case of Figure 18.7).

In the implemented system, the false matchings are considered in the process of target tracking. In the process, each of the measured locations is related to the nearest one of previously measured locations, and the locations of false matchings are checked after those of correct matchings.

18.4 Implementing N-ocular Stereo

18.4.1 Simplified N-ocular Stereo

In N-ocular stereo described in the previous section, the verification costs of overlapped regions of hexagons and that of convergent operations are very high, making it difficult to run in real-time. Therefore, we have simplified N-ocular stereo as follows:

1. In the first step (binocular stereo), place a circle at the intersection of the azimuth angles detected by arbitrary two sensors, and consider the circle as the target location (see three black circles shown in Figure 18.8). Here, the radius of the circle is assumed to be 30cm since the targets are people.

2. In the second step (N-ocular stereo), check if the circles overlap each other to verify if the Nth sensor observes the target. If the circles overlap each other, place a new circle with a radius of 30cm at the center of gravity of the circles. It is considered as the target location measured with N sensors.

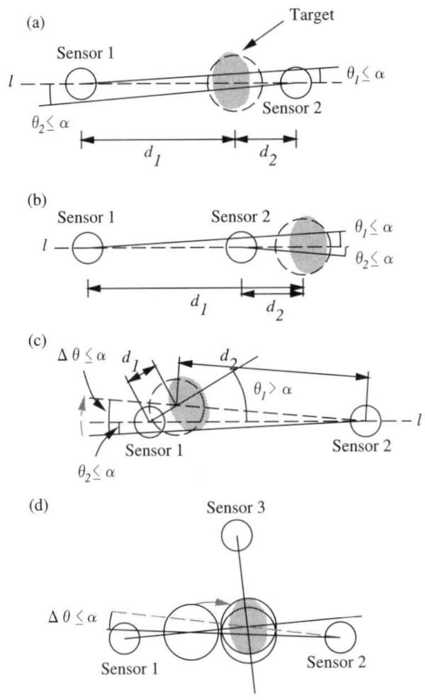

FIGURE 18.9. Error compensation.

18.4.2 Error Handling in the Simplified N-ocular Stereo

In the simplified N-ocular stereo, errors α and β described in Section 18.3.2 are handled as follows.

18.4.2.1 α: Detection Errors of the Right and Left Sides of a Target

As described in Section 18.2.2, binocular stereo using ODVSs has a low-precision problem with respect to targets locating along the baseline of the sensors [136]. In the simplified N-ocular stereo, this causes the following problems: Figure 18.9 (a), (b) and (c) show examples in the step of binocular stereo, where there is a target whereas no circle is placed since there is no intersection on account of observation errors of azimuth angles. Figure 18.9 (d) shows another example in the step of N-ocular stereo, where the target cannot be localized since the circles which are placed in the step of $(N-1)$-ocular stereo do not overlap each other on account of observation errors.

Here, we introduce the following techniques to cope with the above problems.

When there is no intersections with respect to two lines:

If the angle between the baseline l of the two sensors and each of azimuth angles detected by the sensors (let these be θ_1 and θ_2) are equal to or less than α (see Figure 18.9 (a) and (b)), consider that a

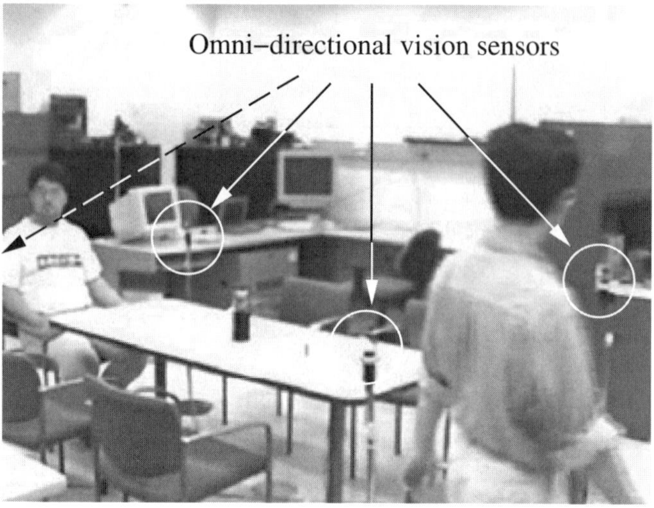

FIGURE 18.10. Overview of the real-time human tracking system.

target exists on the baseline l. Then, locate the target in such a way that the ratio of the distances between the target and each sensor (let this be $d_1 : d_2$) matches that of the apparent sizes of the target observed by the sensors. If one of the azimuth angles (let this be θ_2) is equal to or less than α, consider that a target exists on the line representing the other azimuth angle (θ_1). Then, correct the azimuth angle (θ_2) with $\Delta\theta$ ($\Delta\theta \leq \alpha$), and locate the target in such a way that the ratio of the distances $d_1 : d_2$ is close to that of the apparent sizes of the target.

When two circles do not overlap each other: If the circles overlap each other by correcting one of the azimuth angles with $\Delta\theta$ ($\Delta\theta \leq \alpha$), consider that they overlap each other (see Figure 18.9 (d)).

18.4.2.2 β: An Error of the Human Model

After the target is localized, the apparent size of the target reflected on each sensor can be computed from the distance between the sensor and the measured target location. If it differs by more than β from the actual size observed by the sensor, consider that the measured location is a false matching.

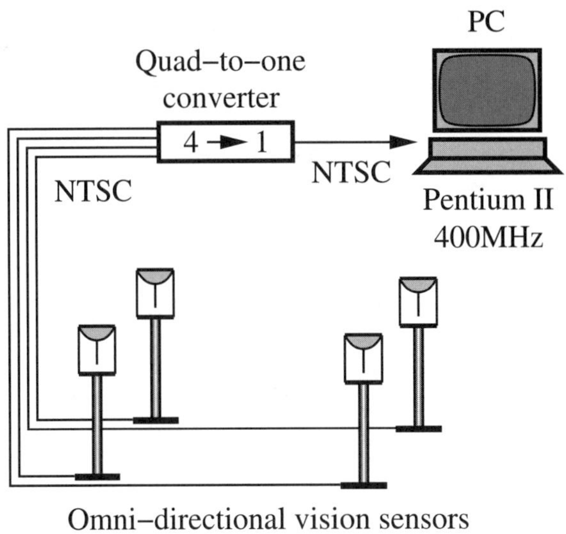

FIGURE 18.11. Hardware configuration.

18.5 Experimentation

18.5.1 Hardware Configuration

We have developed a real-time human tracking system (Figure 18.10), which measures people's locations based on N-ocular stereo and tracks them in real time. Figure 18.11 shows a hardware configuration. The system consists of four ODVSs, and omnidirectional images taken with the sensors are merged into one image with the quad-to-one video converter, then sent to a standard image capture card (Matrox Meteor, 640×480 pixels) on a PC (Pentium II 400MHz with 128MB memory). The four ODVSs are arranged in the center of a room (9m×7m) at a height of approximately 1m. In this system, the locations and the orientations of the sensors are precisely measured before tracking.

18.5.2 Detecting Azimuth Angles of Targets

Since the sensors are fixed in the environment, the system can detect targets in the omnidirectional images by background subtraction. An azimuth angle from a sensor to a target is directly given with the target location on the omnidirectional image as follows:

1. Unwrap the omnidirectional image taken by the sensor (see the top of Figure 18.12).

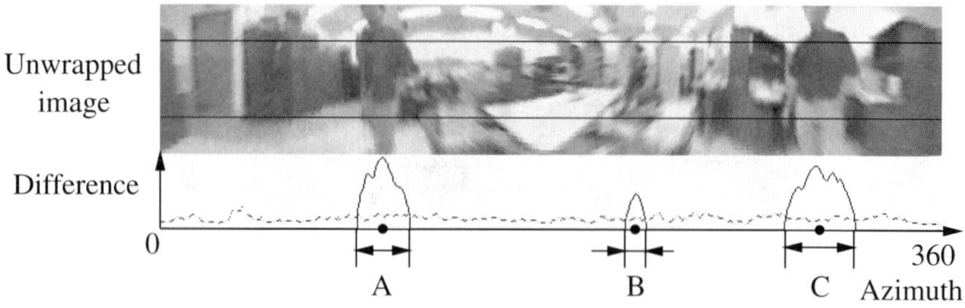

FIGURE 18.12. Detecting targets by background subtraction.

2. Compute the difference of the luminance between the current image and the reference image at each pixel (the reference image is taken in advance), then add the difference values in the vertical direction (shown as the solid line in the bottom of Figure 18.12).

3. Detect as a target where the difference exceeds a threshold (A, B and C in the bottom of Figure 18.12). Here, we have taken 10 frames to determine the threshold (it is shown as a broken line in the bottom of Figure 18.12).

4. Determine the center of the detected target as an azimuth angle of the target.

18.5.3 Precision of N-ocular Stereo

In this experiment, the resolution of the omnidirectional image as shown in Figure 18.3 is approximately 400 pixels along the circumference of the image, and that of the unwrapped image as shown in Figure 18.12 is 640 pixels. Hence, the ODVS has approximately a resolution of 1°. Figure 18.13 shows uncertainty of binocular stereo with a resolution of 1°. The arrangement of sensors is same through the experimentation in this section. Each circle indicates the error range of binocular stereo at that location using two sensors which give the best precision (the diameter of the circles in Figure 18.13 is twice of the actual error range). In Figure 18.13, the minimum error range is approximately 0.7cm and the maximum is approximately 5cm. We can find that multiple ODVSs provide fine precision in a wide area.

Figure 18.14 shows the error range of target locations measured by the system. Here, we used a white cylinder with a diameter of 30cm as a target, and placed it at precisely measured marks on the floor. The circles A through N in Figure 18.14 indicate the locations of the marks and the '+' marks indicate cylinder locations measured by the system over 100 frames. Thus, the distribution of the measured locations (Figure 18.14) is analogous to that of the uncertainty of binocular stereo (Figure 18.13). Table 18.1 shows averages and errors (distances between measured and actual

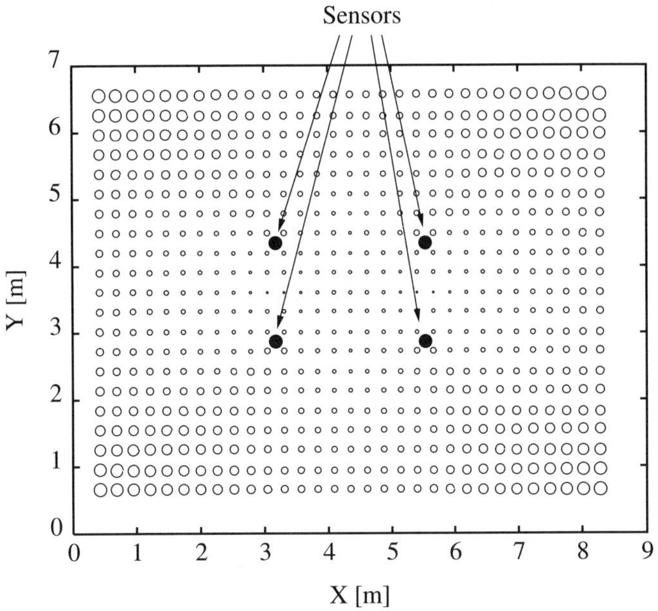

FIGURE 18.13. Uncertainty of binocular stereo.

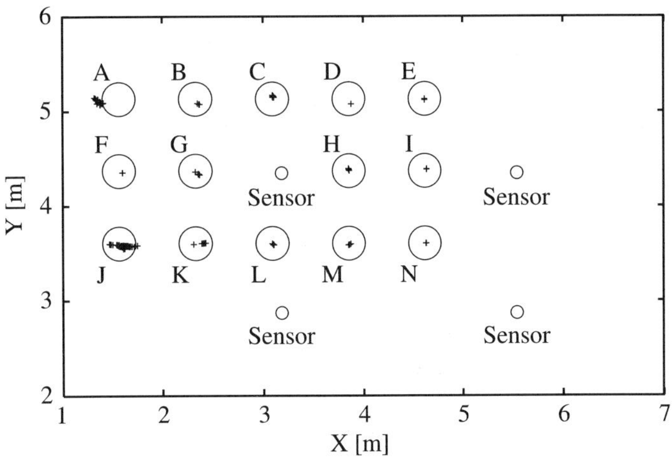

FIGURE 18.14. Precision of localization.

target locations) of the measured locations. The maximum error is 0.17m of the location A.

In Figure 18.14, we can find that the target locations are measured within 5cm if the target locates within 3m from three sensors (in N-ocular stereo, at least three sensors need to simultaneously observe the same target for measuring its location). However, the precision depends on the number

TABLE 18.1. Averages and errors of the measured locations.

Loc.	Average [m]	Error [m]
A	(1.35, 5.11)	0.170
B	(2.37, 5.07)	0.098
C	(3.10, 5.15)	0.056
D	(3.88, 5.08)	0.086
E	(4.61, 5.12)	0.041
F	(1.60, 4.35)	0.077
G	(2.36, 4.34)	0.077
H	(3.85, 4.38)	0.043
I	(4.63, 4.38)	0.061
J	(1.61, 3.58)	0.092
K	(2.40, 3.61)	0.114
L	(3.10, 3.59)	0.053
M	(3.85, 3.59)	0.047
N	(4.63, 3.61)	0.056

of sensors, the arrangement of the sensors, the precision of background subtraction, and so on.

18.5.4 Tracking People

Figure 18.15 shows trajectories of a walking person for one minute, with the same arrangement of sensors as the experiment in Section 18.5.3. The solid lines show the trajectories, and dots on the lines show the person's locations at intervals of 1/2 second. As shown in Figure 18.15, the system could track the person without loosing sight. In this experimentation, the person's location measured by N-ocular stereo is smoothed during 1/2 second, so that there is a delay of about 1/4 second.

The broken lines in Figure 18.15 indicate the person's locations at every frame before smoothing. There are large errors around A and B. This is because (1) binocular stereo using ODVSs has a low-precision problem with respect to targets locating along the baseline of the sensors (this corresponds A in Figure 18.15), and (2) the result of background subtraction becomes noisy if the color of person's clothes is similar to that of the background (this corresponds B in Figure 18.15). In the latter case, general noise filtering techniques such as the Kalman filter may not be able to successfully eliminate the noise, since the noise is different from white noise. It is effective to add additional sensors to cope with this kind of noise.

In this implementation, the system could simultaneously track three people at video rate (30 fps). The experimental results show that the system completely tracked one person, and correctly tracked two persons for 99%

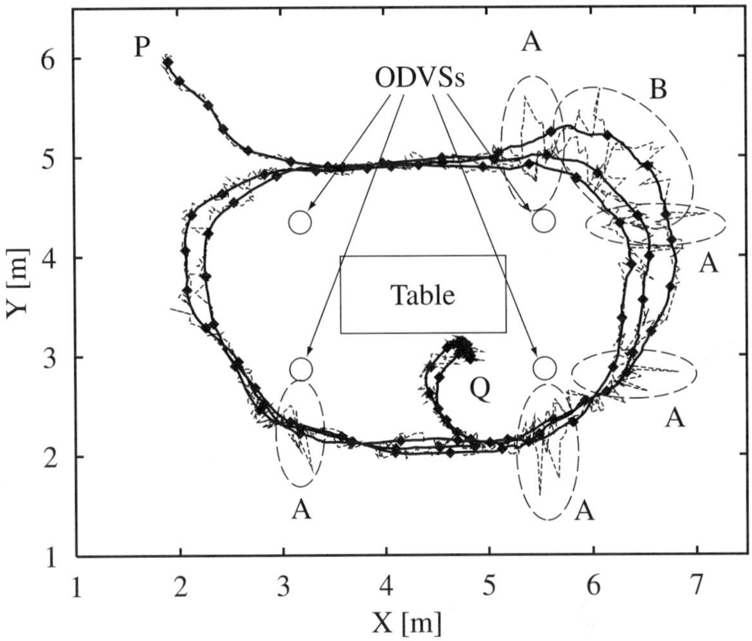

FIGURE 18.15. Trajectories of a walking person.

of the time, and three persons for 89% of the time. Tracking errors occured in the following cases:

- When two or more people moved closer with each other, the system recognized them as one person in background subtraction, or could not correctly identify them in the tracking phase.
- When a person moved behind another person, the system could not measure its location.

In order to solve the former error, a more sophisticated method is needed for detecting people. The latter error will be solved by adding ODVSs into the environment.

18.5.5 Application of the System

As shown in Figure 18.16, the implemented system can also show live images of tracked people. The images are taken with the ODVSs, and zoomed in and out according to the distance between the people and the sensor. The side views of the people also enable the system to identify the people with the colors of their clothes, to recognize their behaviors by observing motions of their head and arms, and so on. In addition, more robust recognition will be achieved by using redundant visual information taken from various points of view with multiple ODVSs.

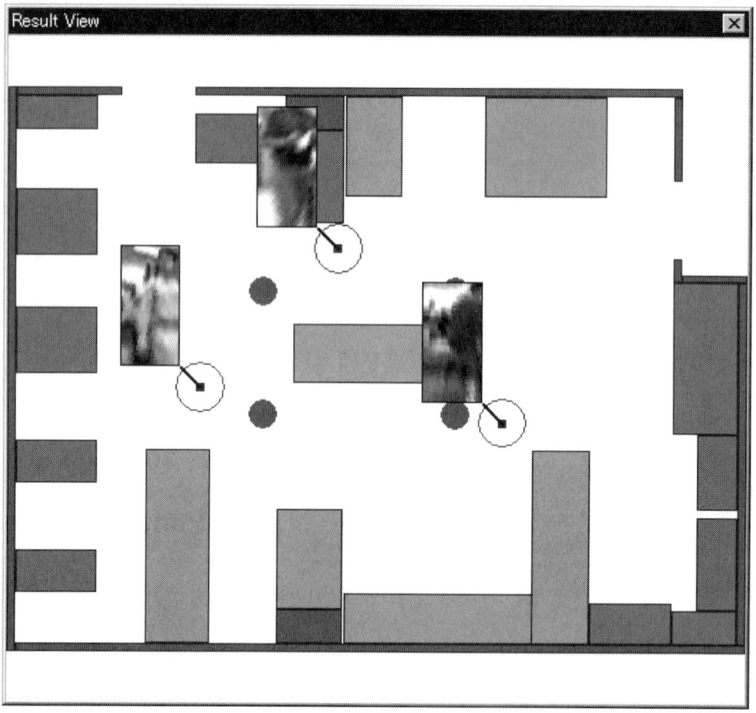

FIGURE 18.16. Display of people's locations and their images.

There are various application systems which take the above advantages. For example, the system can record people's trajectories and their behaviors, so that it is useful for a monitoring system. It is also useful for analyzing people's behaviors, since it can automatically collect an enormous amount of people's trajectories. Furthermore, in gesture recognition [305], information of people's locations and trajectories will be useful for correct gesture recognition.

18.6 Conclusion

In this chapter, we have proposed N-ocular stereo for verifying the correspondence among multiple targets and measuring their locations, using multiple omnidirectional vision sensors (ODVSs). In addition, several methods have been developed for compensating observation errors, in order to cope with the precision problem in omnidirectional stereo. We have developed a real-time human tracking system with four ODVSs using these techniques, and shown that the system can robustly track people in real time only with visual information.

In the current implementation, target tracking is realized by relating each of the current locations to the nearest one of those previously measured, as described in Section 18.3.1. As a future work, this should be improved. For tracking multiple targets in a noisy environment, several methods have been proposed so far [261, 188, 15, 225], which can be applied to our system. In addition, a method for compensating measurement errors of locations and orientations of ODVSs is essential for the system when extending it to use a large number of sensors.

19

Identifying and Localizing Robots with Omnidirectional Vision Sensors

H. Ishiguro, K. Kato, and M. Barth

19.1 Introduction

There has been a good deal of research activity in the field of multi-agent robotics (sometimes called *distributed robotic system* (DRS)) in the last several years. This research is driven by the fact that many large-scale tasks can be performed more effectively and efficiently by multiple, simplistic robots rather than by a single, sophisticated robot. Multiple robots can coordinate their actions in order to solve problems that would be difficult to solve using a single machine.

The most significant difference between the multiple robot system and a single sophisticated robot is in the observation. The single robot needs to build up an environment model for recognizing it and perform given tasks. On the other hand, robots in the multiple robot system share the observations by communicating each other. Obviously, the environmental representation which the robots for the multiple robot system need is simpler than that for the single sophisticated robot.

One of the critical research components of multi-agent robotics focuses on how the robots cooperate to perform various tasks. In the majority of multi-agent robotic concepts developed to date, this cooperation is predicated on a communication scheme between robots. However, a good deal of cooperation between robots can also be achieved through sensing, which can reduce the communication bandwidth demand. In particular, it is possible to use omnidirectional sensing techniques to perform tasks such as relative localization and environmental mapping [17].

When a single mobile robot navigates in its environment, it typically depends on sensing to perform localization within its environment. By localizing itself, the robot knows where it is with respect to its environment and this knowledge is used in carrying out various tasks (e.g., obstacle detection and avoidance, goal seeking, etc.). In a multiple mobile robot scenario, localization can be performed in a similar fashion. However, for cooperative tasks it is much more useful to perform relative localization, i.e., each robot locates itself with respect to the society of robots. A robot's behavior can then be influenced by the relative localization information, thus providing a means of cooperation based solely on observation of the other robots.

In this chapter, we focus on the problems of identification and relative localization for multi-agent robotics. One of the key underlying functionalities that is required for these problems is to have omnidirectional sensing ability. We introduce an omnidirectional vision sensor developed for the multi-agent robotic systems, followed by a description of a new identification/localization algorithm. And then, experimental results are given, followed by a discussion and conclusion.

19.2 Omnidirectional Vision Sensor

Omnidirectional sensing is a powerful capability for any mobile robot. Several omnidirectional vision techniques and hardware exist and are outlined in [131]. The techniques are categorized into two types: swiveling a camera by using a rotating table (sequential capture) and capture omnidirectional images using a mirror (single capture).

As a vision system for a robot behaving in a dynamic environment, the mirror-based methods are more suitable. One such method is used in the experiments here which obtains a 360° image by pointing a camera coaxially towards a spherical mirror, as is shown in Figure 19.1(a). The image that is formed is shown in Figure 19.1(b), where the outer edge of the image corresponds to the high horizon shown in Figure 19.1(a), and the inner circle corresponds to the low horizon.

The ODVS shown in Figure 19.1(a) has been developed by us for multi-agent robot systems. In the previous work, the researchers have developed the ODVSs as prototypes and investigated properties of ODIs taken by the ODVSs. Therefore, the developed ODVSs were not so compact and their costs were high. In order to develop practical vision systems, we have designed original low-cost and compact ODVSs [131].

19.3 Identification and Localization Algorithm

In previous work, it is assumed that each robot has a unique visual identifier such that any other robot could easily identify it [17]. Furthermore, it is assumed that relative localization can be performed simply by measuring the azimuth angles and relative distances to other robots using some type of binocular imaging technique. However, when using a mirror technique for acquiring an ODI it is difficult to calculate relative distances, although azimuth angle measurements are still possible. Below we introduce a new

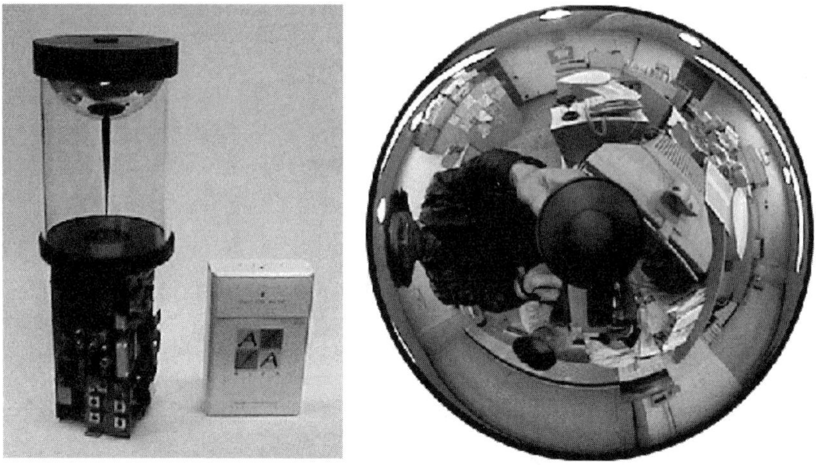

(a) (b)

FIGURE 19.1. (a) An omnidirectional vision sensor (ODVS), and (b) an omnidirectional image (ODI).

algorithm for performing relative localization based on measured azimuth angle and each robot communicating those distances to each other.

19.3.1 Methodology

Given N robots located randomly within a region, the overall goal is to identify all of the robots and to know the relative positions between them. Prior to describing the details of the algorithm, several assumptions must be stated:

1. Each robot has an ODVS and can view other robots;
2. All robots have the same body that can readily be found in the environment;
3. Each robot cannot precisely measure the distance to other robots (although rough distance measurements may be possible by viewing the robot image size);
4. The observation azimuth angles of the different robots can be shared so that each robot can localize itself within the robot society.

Each robot observes the other robots using its ODVS and determines the azimuth angle to each relative to some base viewing angle. These data can be represented as:

$$
\begin{gathered}
r_1(d_1, d_2, \ldots, d_{N_1}) \\
r_2(d_1, d_2, \ldots, d_{N_2}) \\
\cdots \\
r_N(d_1, d_2, \ldots, d_{N_N})
\end{gathered}
$$

where r_i is the robot ID, and d_n is the azimuth angle to the nth robot (for N_n observable robots). From these data, the following angles between two observed robots can be determined:

$$
\begin{gathered}
\theta^1_{1,2}, \theta^1_{1,3}, \ldots, \theta^1_{1,N_1}, \theta^1_{2,3}, \theta^1_{2,4}, \ldots, \theta^1_{2,N_1}, \ldots, \theta^1_{N_1-1,N_1} \\
\theta^2_{1,2}, \theta^2_{1,3}, \ldots, \theta^2_{1,N_2}, \theta^2_{2,3}, \theta^2_{2,4}, \ldots, \theta^2_{2,N_2}, \ldots, \theta^2_{N_2-1,N_2} \\
\cdots \\
\theta^N_{1,2}, \theta^N_{1,3}, \ldots, \theta^N_{1,N_N}, \theta^N_{2,3}, \theta^N_{2,4}, \ldots, \theta^N_{2,N_N}, \ldots, \theta^N_{N_N-1,N_N}
\end{gathered}
$$

where the superscript represents the ID of the observing robot and the subscripts index the observed robots. For each observing robot, the angles between all of the observed robot combinations are represented. Note that the algorithm does not assume that each robot can see an equal number of other robots, therefore N_i represents the total number of observed robots for robot i. This angle representation can be simplified as follows:

$$
\begin{array}{ccccccccc}
\theta^1_1 & , & \theta^1_2 & , & \ldots & , & \theta^1_{m_1} & , & \ldots & , & \theta^1_{M_1} \\
\theta^2_1 & , & \theta^2_2 & , & \ldots & , & \theta^2_{m_2} & , & \ldots & , & \theta^2_{M_2} \\
 & & & & & \cdots & & & & & \\
\theta^N_1 & , & \theta^N_2 & , & \ldots & , & \theta^N_{m_N} & , & \ldots & , & \theta^N_{M_N}
\end{array}
$$

In this case, the single subscripts index the observed robot combinations. m_i is the index and M_j is the total number of observed robot combinations for observing robot j.

19.3.2 Triangle Constraint

At this point, we want to look at different combinations of these angles. One of the key constraints that is used in the algorithm is the fact that the relative angles between three robots always add up to 180○, as shown in Figure 19.2. Each robot represents a vertex in a triangle, and the angles between robots must add up to 180○. We refer to this as the triangle constraint.

For all combinations of three robots (r_i, r_j, r_k), all observed robot combinations are checked. The resulting triplet combinations that satisfy the triangle constraint will allow us to compute the relative positions of the robots.

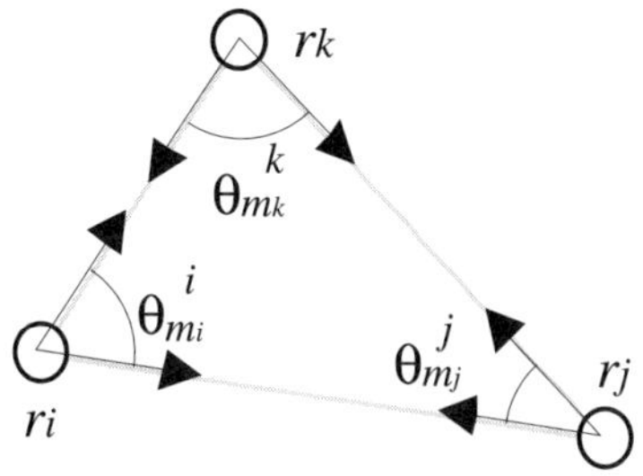

FIGURE 19.2. Triangle constraint

19.3.3 Triangle Verification

The resulting triplets from the previous step may contain impossible triangles. These impossible triangles can be classified into four different types, as shown in Figure 19.3. In order to eliminate these impossible triangle combinations, additional processing must be carried out on the triplets generated from the previous step. This processing involves evaluating neighboring triangle candidates generated from the triangle constraint. The procedure is as follows:

1. Each triangle from the candidate list is selected;
2. For a particular triangle, each edge is examined. An edge of a triangle is represented by the two angles on each end. All of the other candidate triangles are then examined to see if they contain the same edge. As an example, refer to Figure 19.4. Triangle candidates that share the same edge are paired.
3. For all pairs of triangle candidates that share an edge, check to see if other triangle candidates exist that contain the opposite edge, and one of the common vertices of the original triangle pair.

If such triangles exist and all angles observed by all robots are different from each other, the triangles

$$(r_i, r_j, r_k), (r_i, r_j, r_l), (r_i, r_k, r_l), (r_j, r_k, r_l)$$

are uniquely determined. When the triangles are uniquely determined, the projections (directions) of other robots are identified between images taken by the robots, and at the same time, the positions can be computed. That is, this method solves the identification problems for the projections, and then determines the locations. Further, the locations are precisely computed with sufficient information, since all of the robots can observe each other with the omnidirectional vision sensors.

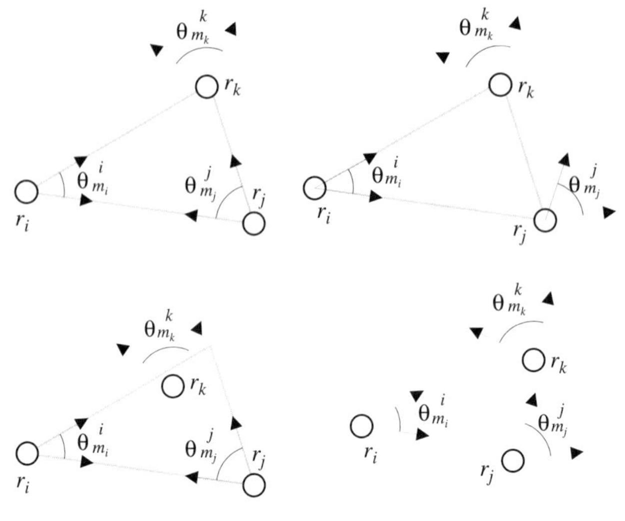

FIGURE 19.3. Impossible triangles

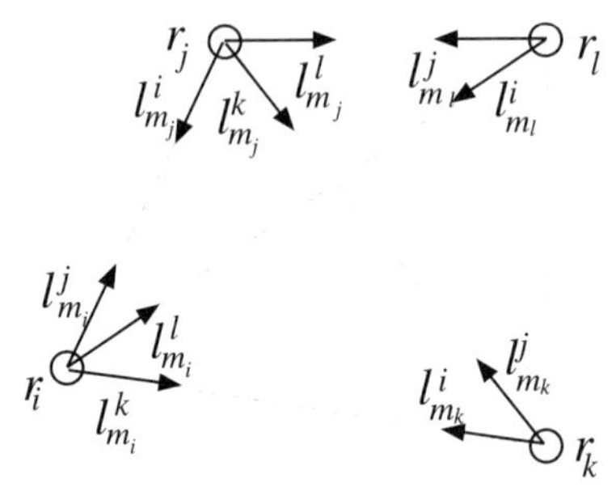

FIGURE 19.4. Neighboring triangles

19.3.4 Error Handling

Three major difficulties arise in actual situations:

1. Some of the robots may have identical angles and corresponding combinations as shown in Figure 19.5. In such cases, the triangle verification technique does not identify the robot projections;

2. Some of the angles belonging to an observing robot may have significant errors, and as a result the triangle constraint may not be met;

3. In a real environment, obstacles may exist which obstruct the robot views of each other.

In order to handle these problems, the triangle constraint can be applied allowing for an error δ in the angle observations. If δ is too large, then

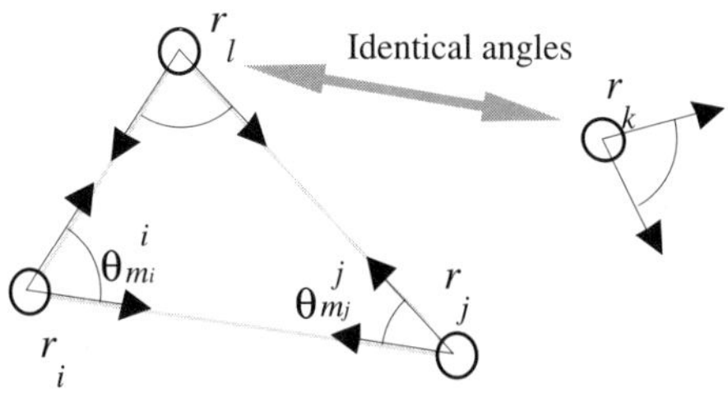

FIGURE 19.5. A case where the single triangle verification method does not correctly identify the angles

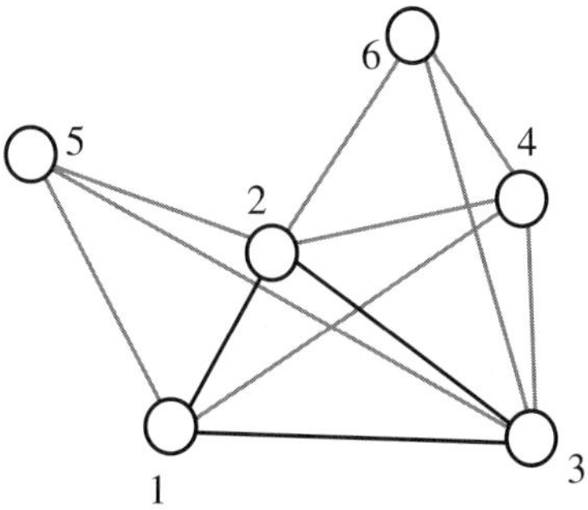

FIGURE 19.6. Iterative verification

it is possible to apply again the triangle verification technique described previously. Figure 19.6 is an example of this. In this figure, consider triangle (1,2,3) as the reference triangle. With neighbor triangles (1,2,4) and (1,3,4), we can identify projections between robots 1, 2, 3, and 4. With neighboring triangles (2,3,5) and (1,3,5), we can identify projections between robots 1, 2, 3, and 5. Further, by considering the verification triangle (2,3,4) as a new reference triangle, we can identify projections between robots 2, 3, 4, and 6 with neighboring triangles (2,3,6) and (3,4,6). We apply this process to all triangle candidates acquired using the triangle constraint and sum up the number of verification triangles.

However, this "best" solution may not be unique since there could be several solutions that have an equal maximum number of verification triangles. In order to overcome this problem, positioning information can be used. Given a single solution, the relative positions of the robots can be determined from a set of reference triangles. For each reference triangle, the position information can also be calculated from the associated verification triangles. With noisy observations, this position information will be slightly different than the reference-triangle-based positions.

The robot positions are determined by a least-square method. First, we select two robots as reference robots for determining a global coordinate system. Then, each robot position is computed relative to the global coordinate system.

19.3.5 Computational Cost

The method proposed in this paper filters out possible solutions using the triangle verification technique and selects the solution that has the minimum positioning error. The process is summarized as follows:

Step 1: List up all triplet combinations that satisfy the triangle constraints;

Step 2: Apply the triangle verification technique to all of the triplets and eliminate invalid triplets from the list;

Step 3: Estimate the positioning error for all of the remaining candidates and select the solution which has the minimum error.

In the process, suppose a unique solution is acquired at the end of Step 1. The computational cost will be

$$_NC_3 = O(N^3)$$

If a unique solution is acquired at the end of Step 2, the maximum computation cost (in the case where all triplets remain from Step 1) will be

$$_NC_3 \bullet (N-3) \bullet 3 = O(N^4)$$

Theoretically, the computational cost is high. However, Step 1 typically filters out most of the candidates. The few candidates left are then further culled using the triangle verification step. Based on our experimentation (see next section), the computation for up to 10 robots can be achieved reliably for a near real-time robotic system.

19.4 Experimental Results

In order to verify our method, both simulation and real-world experiments were carried out.

19.4.1 Simulation Experiments

A simulation program randomly place ODVS-equipped robots within a region. For each robot, the azimuth directions to the other robots are determined. From these data, the angles between observed robots (i.e., $\theta^i_{m_i}$)

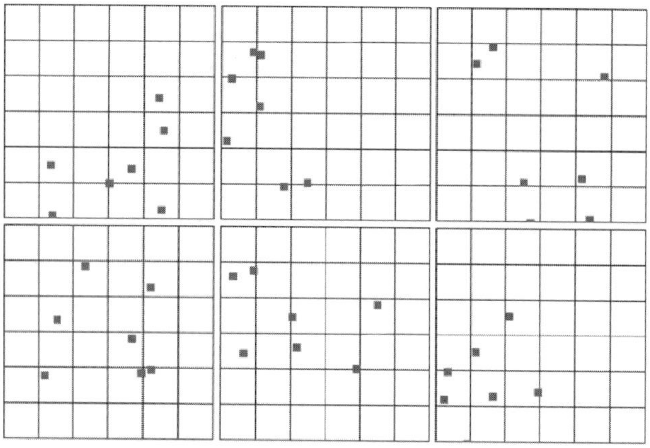

(a) Ground truth robot locations

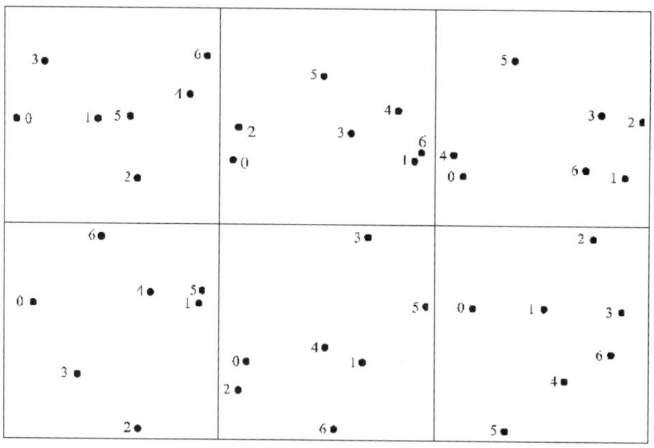

(b) Identified robots and their positions

FIGURE 19.7. Simulation results for verification of the algorithm

are calculated. The algorithm described in the previous section is then performed.

Figure 19.7 shows six simulation results for the case where all robots can precisely observe all of the other robots in the region. For each simulation, the robot locations have been randomly generated. Figure 19.7(a) shows the ground truth robot locations and Figure 19.7(b) shows the reconstructed positions. Since the reconstructed positions are computed based on relative positions of robots 0 and 1, their scale and orientation is different from that of the ground truth. However, it has been verified that the distributions of reconstructed and correct positions are displaced, scaled versions of each other.

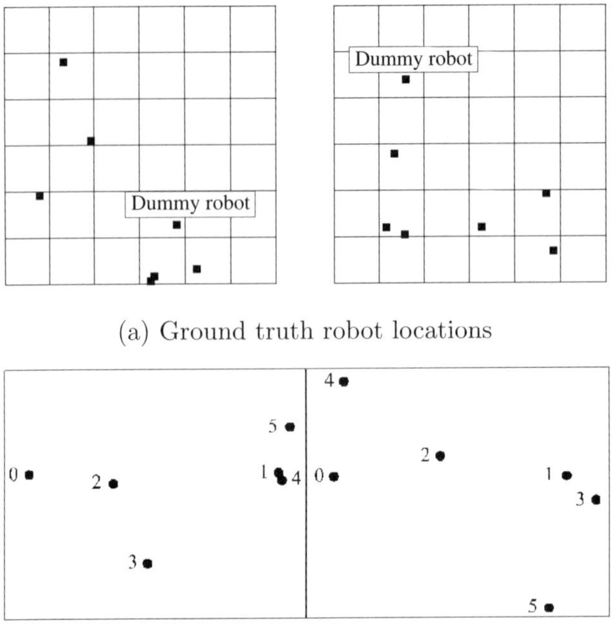

(a) Ground truth robot locations

(b) Identified robots and their positions

FIGURE 19.8. Simulation results in cases there are similar objects to the robot

TABLE 19.1. Performance of the method and its computational time

Robots	Triangles	Triangle constraint	Propagation	Computational time
4	686	678	4	0 sec.
5	4394	4370	14	0 sec.
6	18522	18458	44	1 sec.
7	59582	59284	263	5 sec.
8	159014	157902	1056	37 sec.
9	370386	366584	3718	6 min 38 sec.
10	778034	767110	10804	20 min 31 sec.

In another simulation case, observation errors are introduced. A misidentified robot is added to the observation angles of the robots. In this case, all the robots still observe each other, but they also observe an object that is misidentified as a robot. As before, the observation angles are generated and processed. The results are shown in Figure 19.8. Figure 19.8(a) displays the ground truth robot positions while Figure 19.8(b) shows the reconstructed results. Once again the robot positions were correctly recovered. In Figure 19.8(b), there are six robots and an object which seems like a robot.

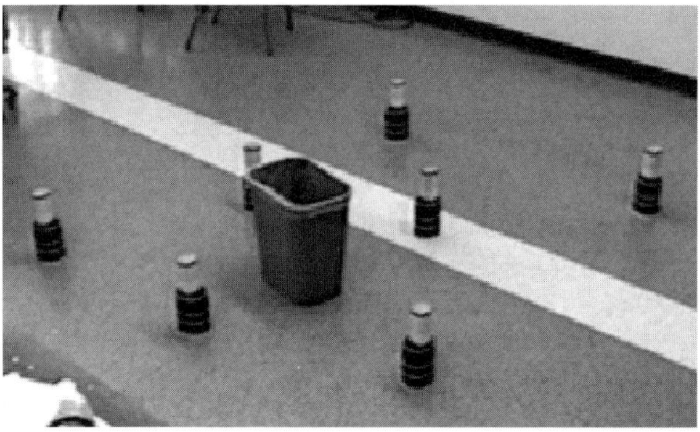

FIGURE 19.9. Seven omnidirectional sensor platforms in a real environment.

Table 19.1 shows the performance of the proposed method. In the table, the labels *Robot, Triangles, Triangle constraints* and *Propagation* refer to the number of robots, the number of possible triangles without identifying the robots, the number of triangles filtered out with the triangle constraint, and the number of triangles filtered out by propagating the triangle verification, respectively.

The computational time is small for up to seven robots. In the case where the system consists of seven robots or where the robots can be divided into small groups, each of which having at most seven robots, this algorithm solves the identification and localization problems in real time.

19.4.2 Real-world Experiment

A real-world experiment was carried out using seven identical platforms equipped with ODVSs. These platforms were placed randomly on the floor of our laboratory in a region approximately 4 x 4 meters, as shown in Figure 19.9. In addition to the robots, a trash can was placed among the robots in order to occlude the views of some robots. In this experiment, the ground truth positions of the platforms were carefully measured.

Seven ODIs were acquired at each platform location (see Figure 19.11). As an example, Figure 19.10(a) shows the ODI of robot 1. In order to determine the azimuth angles to the observed robots, the robots must first be detected in the images. Because all of the ODV-equipped platforms are set on the level floor and all are of equal height, the images of the observed platforms will fall within a very narrow, circular band in the ODV, as shown in Figure 19.10(a). Therefore, we constrain our image processing to this narrow region. Within the circular band; here we perform a simple region-based segmentation algorithm that uses connectivity analysis. The result of the segmentation are distinct "blobs" within the image region. Simple features of these blobs are used to detect the ODV platforms. The

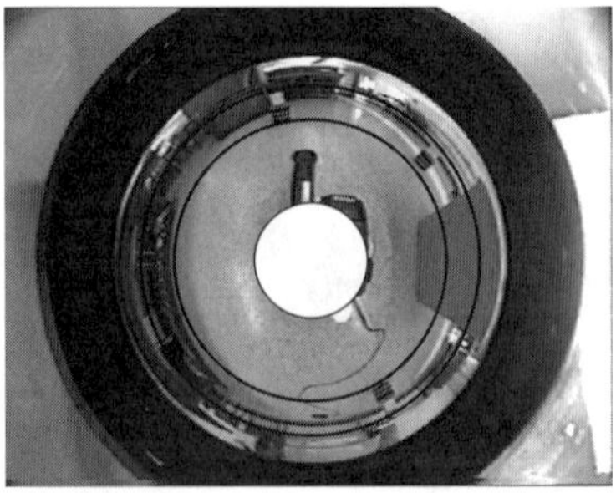

(a) ODI taken by a robot

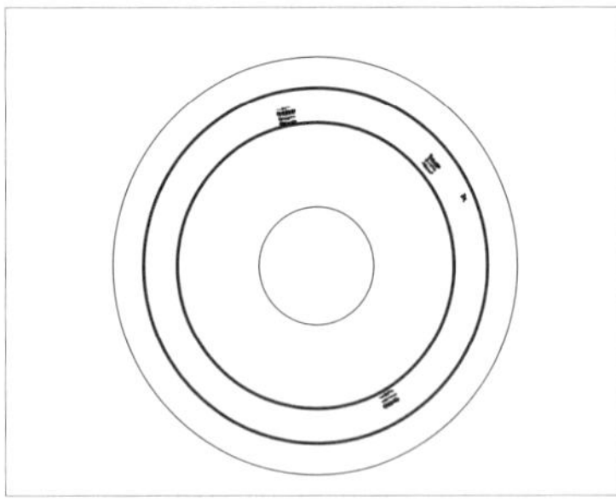

(b) Detected robots in the ODI

FIGURE 19.10. Image processing for detecting robots in an omnidirectional view.

TABLE 19.2. Observed azimuth angles for each observing platform.

Robot ID	Directions to other robots
1	110.83, 196.64, 212.80, 274.89
2	221.41, 282.07, 290.04, 179.49
3	144.76, 228.17, 295.65, 319.15, 39.09
4	260.59, 278.51, 312.00, 323.09, 0.48
5	349.12, 0.00, 15.51, 42.75, 48.58, 96.83
6	130.79, 180.00, 338.52, 33.66, 115.74
7	103.40, 138.63, 158.21, 169.02, 95.16

platforms are dark compared to their background, and have a distinctive square shape. Once the ODV platforms are detected within the image, the center of gravity of the platform blobs are used to determine the azimuth angle to each observed platform. The ODVs for all of the platforms with the processed viewing directions are shown in Figure 19.11. The observed azimuth angles to the other identified platforms are given Table 19.2.

The angles between observed robots are used as input to the positioning algorithm. The algorithm does not require all angles between observed

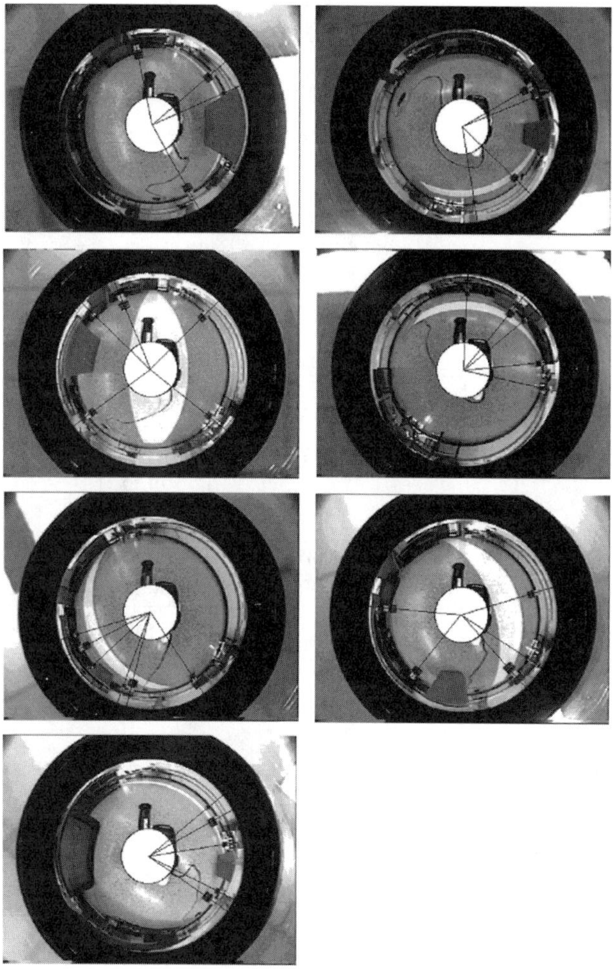

FIGURE 19.11. Omnidirectional views taken by the robots.

platforms. The subset of angles actually observed is given in Table 19.2. It is interesting to note that while platform 4 misidentified a platform (at approximately 260°), the algorithm has automatically eliminated the mistaken platform from the candidate list since no other platform misidentified this object. In order to compare the reconstructed platform positions with the ground truth data, a common coordinate system must be used.

In this experiment, platform 5 is selected as the coordinate system origin. The coordinate system orientation and scale were determined by having platform 6 lie on the x-axis with an interval of one unit length away from platform 5.

If the ground truth positions are scaled and oriented around the same coordinate system origin, it is possible to illustrate both the ground truth

TABLE 19.3. Angles between robots that are used in the algorithm.

Robot ID	Observed angles
1	6.16, 62.09
2	41.92, 60.66
3	67.48, 23.50, 79.95, 105.67, 83.40
4	37.39, 44.58
5	10.88, 48.58, 15.51, 48.25
6	158.52, 146.34, 55.14, 64.26,137.22
7	10.81, 63.05, 19.57, 6, 35.24

TABLE 19.4. X, Y coordinate results of positioning algorithm.

Robot ID	X	Y
1	1.849722	0.565838
2	1.427011	1.421890
3	0.627623	0.772362
4	-0.159063	1.328027
5	0.000000	0.000000
6	1.000000	0.000000
7	1.954834	-0.375734

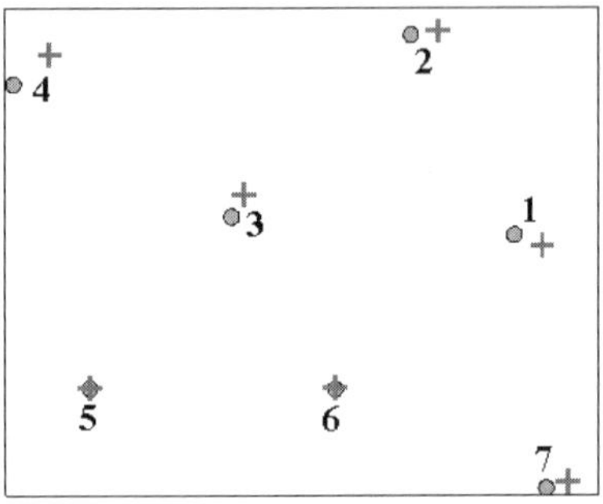

FIGURE 19.12. Comparison of ground truth platform positions and algorithm results.

positions and algorithm positions together, as shown in Figure 19.12. As can be seen, the positioning errors are approximately 10% or less.

19.5 Conclusions

In this chapter, a relative localization algorithm has been developed for ODVS-equipped robots. A key assumption for this algorithm is that robots can view other robots, but they cannot distinguish the robots among themselves. The algorithm is based on identifying potential triangles between any three robots using the simple triangle constraint that all three angles of a triangle must sum up to 180o. Once potential triangles are identified, they are subsequently validated using information from additional existing triangles. The results of the algorithm are the relative positions of all the observable robots.

The relative localization algorithm has been verified using numerous simulation experiments. Furthermore, a real-world experiment has been carried out using static platforms equipped with mirror-based ODVSs. Specific image processing routines were developed and used to pre-process the input to the localization algorithm. Both simulation and real-world results have shown that the algorithm performs well, even under noisy and ill-formed observation conditions.

20

Video Representation and Manipulations Using Mosaics

P. Anandan and M. Irani

20.1 Introduction

Video data is becoming ubiquitous. Video cameras are cheap, lightweight, and easy to use, and video provides a simple, affordable, and convenient way to record visual events. The most common usage of video is to record temporal events, however, its flexibility in usage has has led to it being used a quick way to visually capture the spatial layout of a scene by looking around and moving around with a video camera.

With the advent of the web as the medium of information flow, especially for communication, commerce, and entertainment, the role of video as a means of recording and processing visual information has rapidly grown. These information based applications of video require efficient representations of large video streams, and efficient and natural methods of accessing static and dynamic visual content in video, and effective means of visualizing the information contained in the video data.

While the standard manner of representing video as a sequence of frames is adequate for viewing it in a movie mode, it does not support the type of interaction with video information required by the emerging applications. Currently the only way to access the information of interest is by sequentially scanning the video. Even methods that search based on visual content have to repeat the search for each new frame. The only way to manipulate, annotate, or edit the video is by processing the video frame-by-frame. This process is both slow and tedious.

This chapter presents a new approach for efficient access, storage, and manipulation of video data. Our approach is based on the fact that a video sequence contains many views of the same *scene* taken over time, either from a moving or a stationary camera. Hence, the information that is common to all the frames is the scene itself. However, this information is distributed over many frames, at the cost of very high temporal redundancy, and is found only implicitly in the video data. We transform the video data from a sequential *frame-based* representation, in which this common scene information is *distributed* over many frames, into a single common *scene-based* representation to which each frame can be *directly* related. This representation then allows *direct* and *immediate* access to the *scene* information, such as static locations and dynamically moving objects. Because it eliminates the redundancy between the different views of the scene contained in the frames, it results in a highly efficient and compact representation of the video information. Hence, the scene-based representation forms the basis for direct and efficient access to and manipulation of the video information, and supports efficient storage and transmission of the video data.

The scene-representation is composed of three components: (i) *extended spatial information*: this captures the appearance of the entire scene imaged in the video clip, and is represented in the form of a few (often just one) panoramic mosaic images constructed by composing the information from the different views of the scene in the individual frames into a single image, (ii) *extended temporal information*: this captures the motion of independently moving objects in the scene (e.g., in the form of their trajectories), and (iii) *geometric information*: this captures the 3D scene structure, as well as the geometric transformations which are induced by the motion of the camera and map the frames to the common mosaic image. Taken together, these three components provide a *compact* description of the video data.

We construct the common scene-based representation by measuring and interpreting the image motion within the video clip. Regions of the video frames, corresponding to the static and dynamic portions of the scene are determined. The geometric transformations and the 3D scene structure are recovered as a part of this process. This process is done automatically, without any information about the camera calibration or the scene.

Once the common scene-based representation is constructed, it forms the basis for direct and efficient browsing, indexing, manipulation, and storage and transmission of the video data. *Browsing* is done by skimming a collection of images that "summarize" the video data. We refer to these images as *visual summaries*. These summaries visually describe the video information in a compact and succinct fashion, and can serve as a *visual table-of-contents* for the video. Moreover, since the mosaics capture the information that is common to all the frames, they provide the means to *directly* index into and manipulate the individual frames. Both the static and dynamic portions of the video sequence can be accessed this way. These indexing methods are based on *geometric* and *dynamic* information contained in the video. These complement the more traditional approach to "content-based indexing" which utilizes image *appearance* information (namely color and texture properties) [73, 106, 138, 223], but are considerably simpler to achieve and are computationally highly efficient. The existing appearance-based methods themselves can also be used more efficiently within the scene-based representation, when applied directly to the mosaic image (i.e., to the appearance component of our representation), rather than to the individual video frames one-by-one.

The efficiency of the scene-based representations naturally facilitate high degree of compression of the video data. We describe two types of video compression methods using mosaic representations, one for transmission purposes and other for efficient storage and retrieval.

The integration of all the various views of a scene contained in the video into a single scene-based representation also allows us to create enhanced still images and enhanced video sequences of the scene. The mosaic images provide an efficient way to perform such video enhancement and to produce higher-resolution imagery.

This chapter summarizes the work on mosaic based representations which has been previously described in various papers (e.g., see [121, 125, 122, 119]. The remainder of the paper is organized as follows: Section 20.2 presents the common and compact scene-based representation, to which each frame are *directly* related. Section 20.3 explains how to use the scene-based representation to efficiently and rapidly browse, index, manipulate, enhance, store and transmit video data. Section 20.4 reviews the techniques used for constructing the scene-based representation from raw video sequences. Section 20.5 concludes the paper.

20.2 From Frames to Scenes

To bring out the *common* scene information contained in the video and make it more directly accessible, we first transform the video from its *implicit* and *redundant* frame-based representation, to an *explicit* and *compact* scene-based representation. In this section we introduce the scene-based representation. In Section 20.4 we explain how this representation is constructed from the video data.

The video stream is first *temporally* segmented into *scene segments*, which are sub-sequences of the input video sequence. A beginning or an end of a scene segment is automatically detected wherever a scene-cut or scene-change occurs in the video. The scene cuts are characterized typically by *drastic* changes in the frame content, which is directly refelected in the distribution of color and the greylevels in the image, or in the image motion (e.g., see [73, 310]). These changes are relatively simple to detect.

Each scene segment is subsequently parsed into the three fundamental components of video (see Section 20.1), namely, the *extended spatial information* which captures the static background scene, the *extended temporal information* which captures the dynamic moving objects, and the *geometric information*. These three components are organized as described below.

20.2.1 The Extended Spatial Information: The Panoramic Mosaic Image

The extended spatial view of the entire scene visible in the video clip, is assembled into a single (or sometimes few) "mosaic" image (e.g., see Figure 20.1). This image captures the appearance of the *static* portions of the scene.

The mosaic image is constructed by first aligning all the frames with respect to the common coordinate system (which becomes also the mosaic coordinate system), and then integrating all these frames to form a single image. Different methods of integration can be employed (e.g., temporal average, temporal median, super-resolution, etc). These are described in more detail in Section 20.4.

The mosaic representation removes the redundancy contained in the overlap between successive frames, as it represents each spatial point only once (as opposed the original video sequence, where each scene point is observed multiple times in multiple frames). Mosaics have been previously used as an effective way of creating panoramic views of a scene from video sequences primarily for enhanced visualization of the scene [177, 267, 275, 122, 163, 121, 10]. However, here and in some of our previous papers (e.g., [121, 119]) they are used as an information component within a scene-based representation, which provides direct and efficient access to video data.

We present a *hierarchy* of such mosaic representations. The different levels of the hierarchy correspond to increasing levels of complexity in the camera motion and in the 3D scene structure. The techniques used for estimating and constructing these mosaic representations are described in Section 20.4.

1. **The 2D mosaic:** The simplest representation is a mosaic image constructed by aligning all the frames to a single coordinate system using 2D parametric coordinate transformations. We refer to such a mosaic as a *2D parametric mosaic image*. The cases when the camera induced motion can be modeled as a 2D parametric transformation can be divided broadly into three categories (see Section 20.4.1.1): (i) when the translational motion of the camera is negligible, i.e., camera motion can be approximated by only 3D rotations and zooms, (ii) when the scene is planar, or (iii) when the 3D scene is sufficiently distant from the camera, such that it can be approximated by a nearly flat 2D surface. We refer to these scenarios as *2D scenes*.

   In Section 20.3, we described some examples from this class of scenarios. For example, the baseball sequence (Figure 20.2) was captured by a panning camera (i.e., pure rotation), while the other sequences shown in that section (Figures 20.1, 20.4, and 20.5) were taken by an *airborne* camera, hence the scene was sufficiently distant from the camera and could be well approximated by a flat 2D surface.

2. **The plane+parallax mosaic:** The next level of complexity arises when the 3D deviations from the 2D planar surface approximation (when combined with the camera translation) results in measurable parallax image motion relative to the planar surface. In this case, the visual appearance of the scene is still captured by a *mosaic image* as in the previous case, while the geometric component of the representation also encodes the 3D parallax relative to the planar surface (see Section 20.4.1.2). The parallax information is captured in the geometric component of the representation and is taken into account while combining the different frames into a single mosaic [121, 163]. We refer to this representation as the *plane+parallax* representation [161, 130]. The estimation of the parallax motion is briefly described in Section 20.4.1.2. An example of such a mosaic image constructed from a real video sequence is shown in [121, 163].

3. **Layers of plane+parallax:** The third level of complexity involves using multiple *layers* of *plane+parallax* representations to handle scenes that may contain surfaces at different depths. Each layer captures a collection of points in the scene that when taken together can be approximated by a planar surface with small fluctuations [14]. Points that are not on the planes are associated with one of the layers based on their proximity in the 3D scene to those planes. The visual appearance of each layer is captured by a *plane+parallax* mosaic image as in the case above. The layered representation can also be used to handle reflections and transparency [268].

20.2.2 The Geometric Information

The geometric information relates the different video frames to the mosaic coordinate system. This information allows us to map back and forth between the panoramic mosaic image(s) and the individual frames. Corresponding to the hierarchy of the panoramic mosaic representations, there exists a hierarchy of representations of the geometric information. These range from global parametric 2D transformations to more complex 3D transformations. Below we briefly summarize this component of the representation. The details of their estimation are described in Section 20.4.1.2.

1. **2D parametric transformations:** For the 2D parametric mosaic, the geometric information consists of the *2D parametric transformations* that align each frame to the mosaic. These transformations capture the effect of rotations, translations, and zooms of the camera relative to a planar surface. They can be described by 6 or 8 parameters per frame. The estimation of these transformations is reviewed in Section 20.4.1.1.

2. **3D parallax:** The plane+parallax representation requires, in addition to the parametric transformation that aligns a dominant plane in the scene, the information required to describe the *3D parallax* of the points that deviate from the plane. The residual parallax displacements after 2D alignment, depend both on the 3D distance ("height") of the scene points from the plane, as well as the translational motion of the camera. These can be represented in terms of a pointwise "relative structure" measure (e.g., heights of points with respect to the dominant plane) and the coordinates of the camera epipoles with respect to the panoramic view. The relative structure is once again a property of the scene, which is common to all frames, and therefore represented only once in the same coordinate system as the mosaic. This is reviewed in Section 20.4.1.2.

3. **Layers:** In the multiple layer case, the geometric information for each layer consists of the following: (i) the parametric transformations associated with the dominant plane corresponding to that layer, (ii) a layer "ownership" map (typically a binary image) that indicates which points "belong" to that layer, and (iii) the 3D relative structure of the points relative to the plane. The camera translation is common to all the layers, and can be represented in a number of different ways. Since the number of layers is usually small, it is usually convenient to repeat it for each layer.

20.2.3 The Dynamic Information

The **dynamic information** refers to the information about moving objects, which are not captured by the static panoramic mosaic image. Moving object information is captured by representing the extended time trajectories of those objects, as well as their appearance. For indexing and annotation purposes, the trajectory information alone is sufficient. For these purposes, the trajectory of the center-of-mass of each detected moving object (i.e., a single image-point per moving object per frame) is maintained. These trajectories are represented in the coordinate system of the mosaic image, which is common to all the frames. In the common coordinate system, time continuity, continuous tracking, and the temporal behavior of the moving object, can be analyzed more effectively (see Figures 20.3 and 20.5).

For applications such as video compression, a representation of the visual appearance of the moving objects is also needed, in order to allow the reconstruction of the entire video sequence from the coded bit-stream. This is done by maintaining a more complete (but compressed) representation of the "residual" differences between the individual video frames and their predictions from the mosaics.

Thus, the three components of our scene-based representation form a *compact* representation of the video clip. The compactness results from the fact that every scene point is presented *only once* in the mosaic image, while in the original video clip it is observed in multiple frames.

The three levels of the representation described above can capture the vast majority of situations effectively and efficiently[1]. However, there are situations for which our current representation may not suffice, i.e., it will not produce compact or visually meaningful representation. Such situations arise when a a camera is moving around an object (or equivalently an object is rotating in front of the camera), or when the scene contains significant 3D clutter, with many objects at many different depths. These situations require further study and treatment. An example of the type of representations that may be useful in the future to handle such scenarios is the "manifold mosaic" method described in [214, 230].

Section 20.3 describes how this representation can be used for visually summarizing the video, for efficiently indexing to portions of interest, for annotation and manipulation, for video enhancement, and for very-low bit rate compression. Section 20.4 describes the methods for constructing the scene-based representation.

20.3 Uses of the Scene-based Representation

In this section we outline several applications of the scene-based representations described in the previous sections. These include: (i) creation of visual summaries of the video sequence, (ii) indexing and annotation of the video based on location (geometric) based information and dynamic (moving-object) information, (iii) video enhancement, and (iv) video compression. Note that the examples shown in this section address only the case of the 2D mosaic. An example of a mosaic image based on the plane+parallax representation can be found in [121, 163].

20.3.1 Visual Summaries: A Visual Table of Content

Once a video sequence is transformed from the *frame-based* representation to the *scene-based representation*, it forms the basis for the user's interaction with the video. The user can initially preview the video by browsing through *visual summaries* of the various video clips. These visual summaries can serve as a *visual table-of-contents* of the video data. When a

[1]Although the examples included in Section 20.3 of this paper only address the case of the 2D mosaic.

scene of interest is detected by the user, he/she can either request to view only that portion of the video, or can further index into individual video frames. The detected frames of interest can then be either *viewed* or *manipulated* by the user.

There are two types of visual summaries of video clips that a user can browse through. These are captured by two types of mosaic images which are constructed from the video clip of a scene:

- **The static background mosaic:**
  The video frames of a single video segment (clip) are aligned and integrated into a single mosaic image. This image provides an extended (panoramic) spatial view of the entire static background scene viewed in the clip in a single "snapshot" image and represents the scene better than any single frame. This image does not include any moving objects. The user can visually browse through the collection of such mosaic images to select a scene (clip) of interest.

  Figures 20.1 and 20.2 display some examples of static background mosaic images.

- **The synopsis mosaic:**
  While the static mosaic image effectively captures the background scene, it contains no representation of the dynamic events in the scene. To provide a summary of the events, we create a new type of mosaic called the *synopsis* mosaic. This is constructed by overlaying the trajectories of the moving objects on top of the background mosaic. This single "snapshot" image provides a visual summary of the entire dynamic foreground *event* that occurred in the video clip.

  Figure 20.2.c provides a summary of the entire event in the baseball video clip.

  Figure 20.3 graphically illustrates the notion of a synopsis mosaic containing the trajectory of a moving object.

  Figures 20.4 and 20.5 provide visual summaries of airborne (UAV) video clips each with multiple moving objects. Figure 20.4 shows a flying airplane and a moving car on the road. Figure 20.5 shows a flying airplane, three parachuters that were dropped from the plane, and a moving car. To allow for comprehensive display of multiple trajectories (corresponding to multiple moving objects), the trajectory of each moving object is uniquely color coded.

20.3.2 Mosaic-based Video Indexing and Annotation

The natural mode of operation for the user is to first browse through the visual summary mosaics to identify a few scenes of interest. Once the

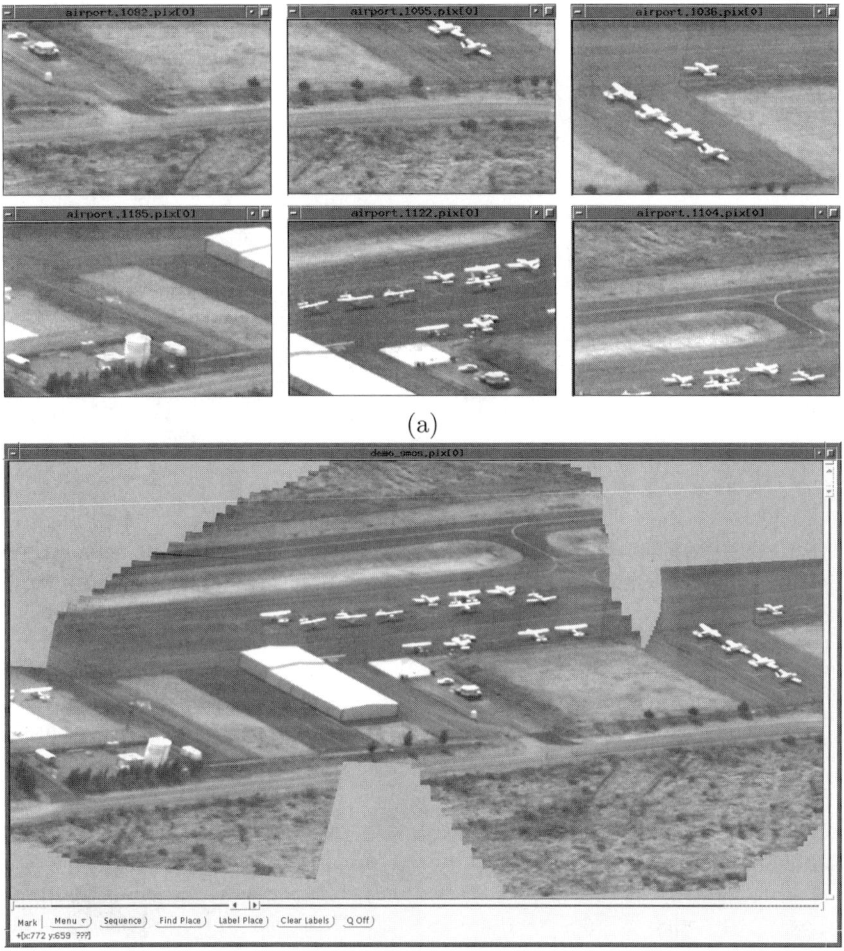

(a) (b)

FIGURE 20.1. Static background mosaic of an airport video clip. (a) A few representative frames from the minute-long video clip. The video shows an airport being imaged from the air with a moving camera. The scene itself is static (i.e., no moving objects). (b) The static background mosaic image which provides an extended view of the entire scene imaged by the camera in the one-minute video clip.

user has identified a scene (i.e., mosaic) of interest, he proceeds to directly access and/or manipulate individual video frames associated with only a *portion* of the scene which is of interest to him. The scene-based representation supports this type of indexing. Two new types of indexing methods are presented: (i) indexing based on *location* (geometric) information, and (ii) indexing based on *dynamic* information. These are made possible directly via the geometric coordinate transformations that relate

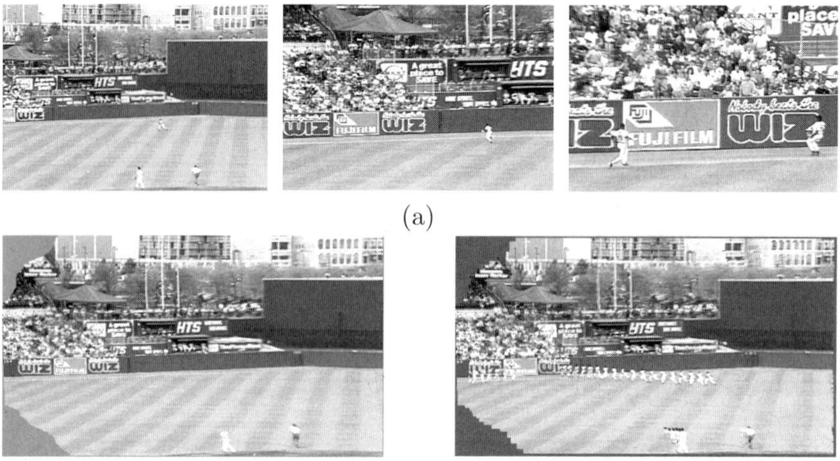

(a)

(b) (c)

FIGURE 20.2. Visual summaries of a baseball video clip.
(a) A few representative frames from the video clip. The video shows two outfielders running, while the camera is panning to the left and zooming on the two baseball players. (b) The static background mosaic image which provides an extended view of the entire scene captured by the camera in the video clip. The "missing" regions at the top-left and bottom-left were never imaged by the camera, because at that point it was zoomed on the two players (e.g., frame 80). (c) The synopsis mosaic which provides a visual summary of the entire event. It shows the trajectories of the two outfielders in the context of the mosaic image.

the different frames to the mosaic image, and through the moving objects information which was estimated in the formation of the mosaic-based scene representation (Section 20.2). The access and manipulation of selected video frames is done directly from the mosaic-based visual summaries. These location and dynamic indexing methods complement the more traditional approach to "content-based indexing", which utilizes image appearance information (e.g., color and texture) [73, 106, 138, 223]. However, our methods are considerably simpler to achieve and are highly computationally efficient.

The remainder of this section describes these modes of video indexing and manipulation.

20.3.2.1 Location (Geometric) Based Indexing

Once a few scenes of interest (in the form of visual summaries) have been selected, the user proceeds to access the video frames themselves. The user selects a scene point (or several points) in the mosaic image. The geometric coordinate transformations map the selected scene point(s) from the mosaic image to its location in the coordinate system of each of the video frames. All frames containing the selected scene point inside their field of view are

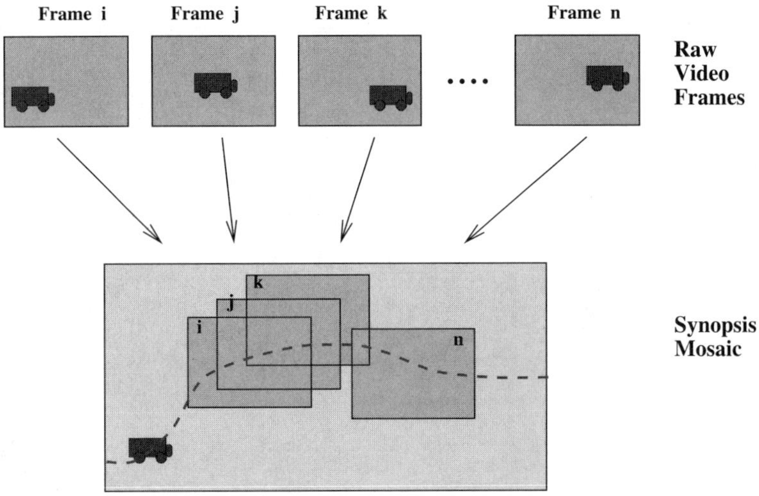

FIGURE 20.3. Synopsis of a moving object.
The trajectory of the moving object is depicted in the synopsis mosaic. This shows the motion of the moving object, after cancellation of the background (camera-induced) motion. With each point on the trajectory is associated a frame number (i.e., the "time" when the moving object was at that location).

therefore instantaneously determined. The user can view the sub-sequence of the video that contains only the frames with the selected scene point (or points). When these frames are not consecutive in time (e.g., if the selected portion of the scene was revisited by the camera multiple times), then multiple sub-sequences (corresponding to *consecutive* frame groups) are displayed to the user.

Figure 20.6 demonstrates an indexing process. Selection of a scene point in the mosaic image generates a display of all frames whose field of view contains the selected scene point. These are frames i, j, and k. In the figure, these frames are displayed as a collection of frames, but in reality, they are displayed as a video sequence.

In addition to manual scene-point selection, this representation also provides a basis for *efficiently* indexing into the video using existing *automatic* detection methods. For example, if a region is searched using an appearance-based detection method (e.g., template correlation, or search based on color or texture attributes [73, 106, 138, 223]), then instead of applying these search methods individually to each frame, it can be applied just *once* to the common mosaic image. Once it is detected in the mosaic image, the location-based indexing mechanism can be used to retrieve the corresponding frames.

Editing and annotation: The compact mosaic representation can be used not only to access video frames, but also to edit, annotate, and manipulate these frames. For example, the same mechanism used for indexing is also

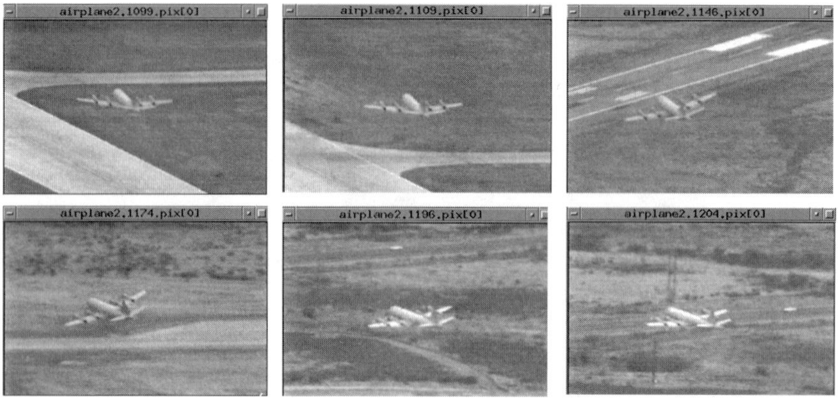

(a)

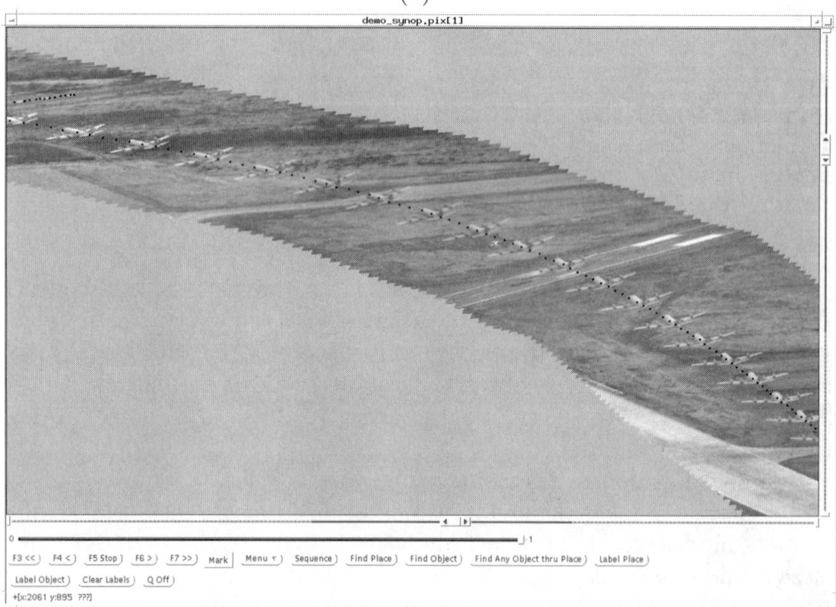

(b)

FIGURE 20.4. The visual summary of a flying plane video clip. (a) A few representative frames from the minute-long video clip. The video shows an airplane flying from right to left (during takeoff). A car driving on a road is visible for a few frames. (b) The synopsis mosaic which provides a visual summary of the entire video clip, showing the trajectories of all moving objects in the context of the mosaic image.

used to efficiently inherit annotations from the mosaic image onto scene locations in the video frames.

The annotation is specified by the user just *once* on the mosaic image, rather than tediously specifying it for each and every frame. This can be

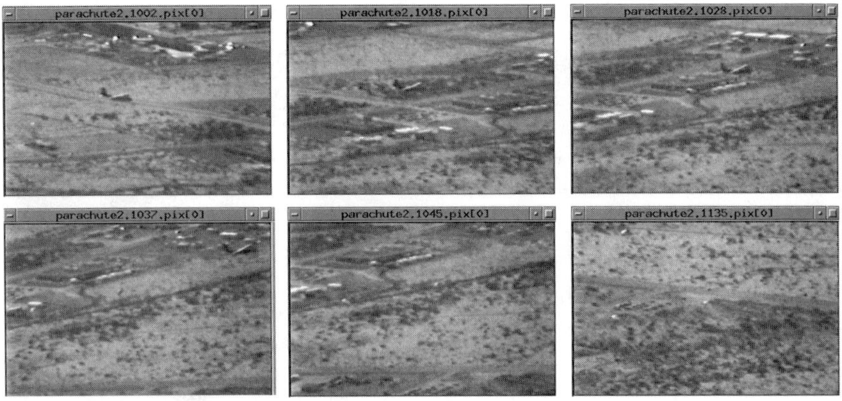

(a)

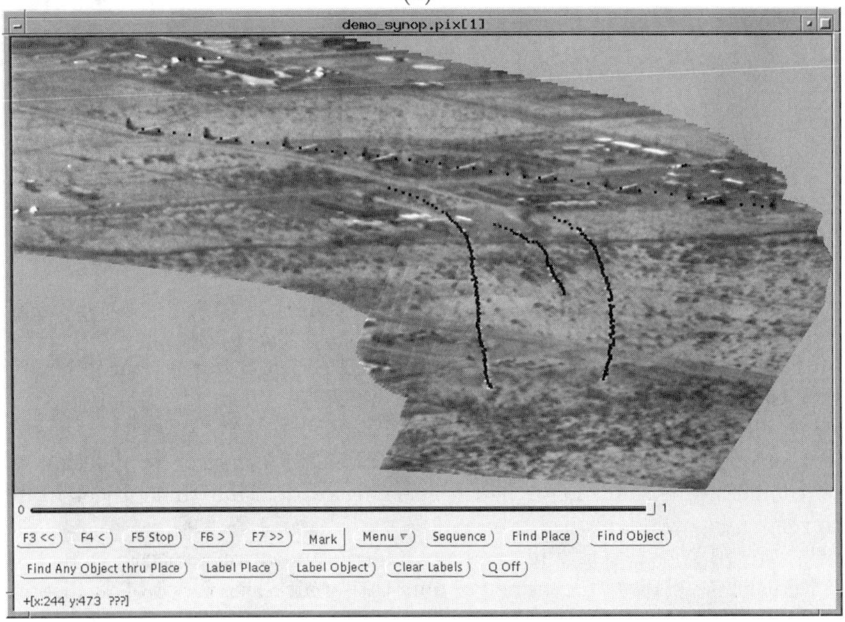

(b)

FIGURE 20.5. The visual summary of a parachuters video clip. (a) A few representative frames from the 30-second-long video clip. The video shows an airplane flying from left to right, dropping three parachuters. A car driving on a road is visible for a few frames. The parachuters are very small (tiny white dots) and difficult to see in a static image, but they are easily detectable in video, as they have different motion than the background. They are depicted in the synopsis mosaic by the black trajectories. In the video sequence, they become visible gradually, as their parachutes open – first the left parachuter, then the right one, and last the middle one. This becomes clearer in the annotated video displayed in Figure 20.10. (b) The synopsis mosaic which provides a visual summary of the entire video clip, showing the trajectories of all moving objects in the context of the mosaic image.

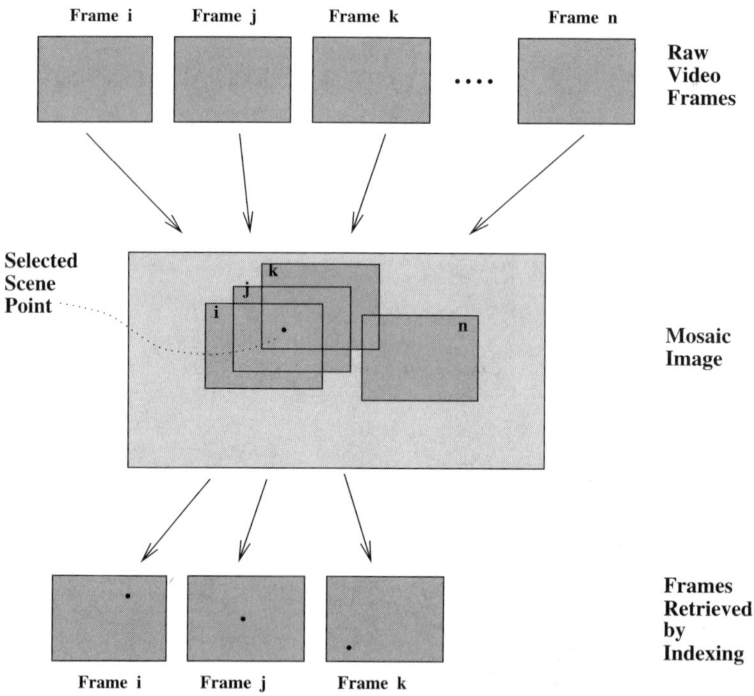

FIGURE 20.6. Location Based Indexing.
Selection of a scene point in the mosaic image generates a display of all frames whose field of view contains the selected scene point. These are frames i, j, and k. In the figure, these frames are displayed as a collection of frames, but in reality, they are displayed as a video sequence.

further extended to efficiently edit video clips, by inserting or deleting an object in the mosaic image, hence inserting or deleting that object in all corresponding video frames.

Figure 20.7 graphically illustrates a video annotation process.

Figure 20.8 shows an example of annotating airborne video of an airport scene.

20.3.2.2 Dynamic (Moving-objects) Based Indexing

Since the *synopsis* mosaic provides a snapshot view of an entire dynamic event, it can be used for indexing based on temporal events. In the synopsis mosaic, the motion of an object is represented as a trajectory in the common coordinate system, hence, the temporal event has been transformed into a spatial representation. Marking a segment on the trajectory is thus equivalent to marking a time interval, which enables access and display of all frames in this time interval.

More specifically, all frames containing a selected moving object can be immediately determined and accessed, as well as the location of the mov-

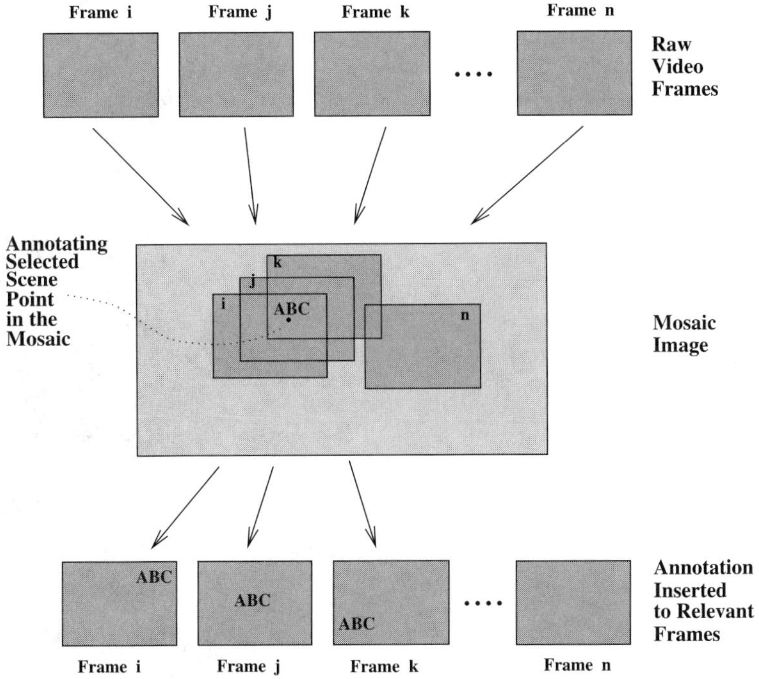

FIGURE 20.7. Location Based Annotation.
Annotation of a selected scene point in the mosaic image leads to automatic annotation of all relevant frames (i, j, and k) with the selected annotation, and at the appropriate image coordinate, i.e., that which corresponds to the selected scene point in each of the frames.

ing object in each of these frames. The user can select an object of interest whose track is marked on the synopsis mosaic. Since the trajectories of the moving objects in the mosaic coordinate system are precomputed (as well as which point on the trajectory corresponds to which frame), all frames containing that object are immediately accessed and viewed. The location of that object in each frame is estimated through the basic geometric coordinate transformations (the ones that correspond to the camera-induced motion). In a similar manner, the moving objects in the video frames are efficiently annotated or manipulated by annotating the synopsis mosaic, without the need for the user to repeatedly perform the operation on a frame-by-frame basis.

Figure 20.9 shows an example of annotating moving objects using the plane video, whose synopsis mosaic was shown in Figure 20.4. The figure displays the selected annotations on the synopsis mosaic. Representative output frames are shown, in which the annotations are automatically inherited from the mosaic. Note that the annotations "move" together with the moving objects.

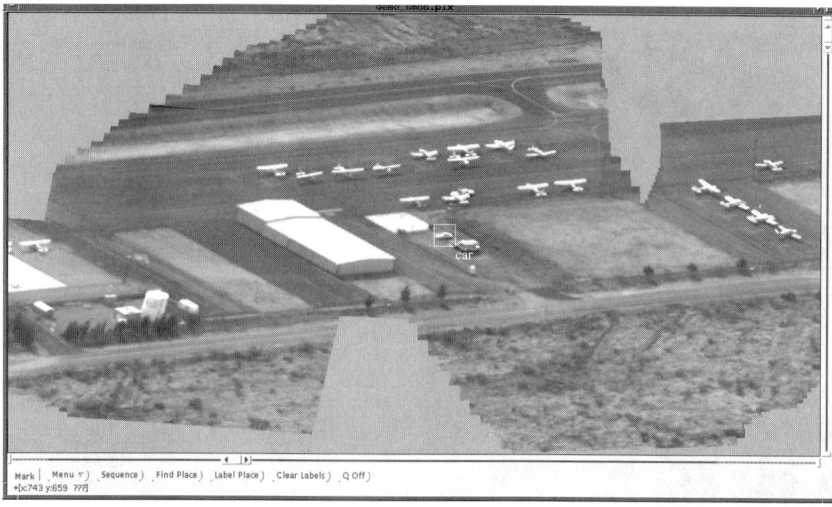

(a)

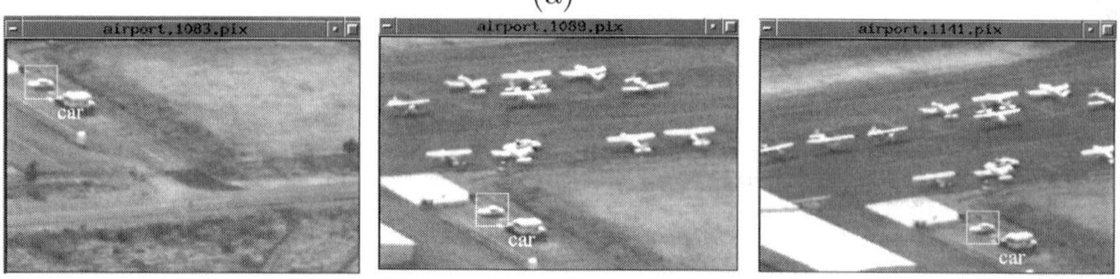

(b)

FIGURE 20.8. Annotation of the airport video clip. (a) A stationary car is annotated *once* on the mosaic image ("car"). (b) A few representative frames from the video clip with the annotations inherited from the mosaic image. The annotations are incorporated into the video frames *automatically* and *instantly* through the geometric coordinate transformations that map each frame onto the mosaic image. Some video frames from the raw video clip are displayed in Figure 20.1.

Figure 20.10 shows an example of video annotation using the airborne parachuters video. The figure displays the selected annotations on top of the synopsis mosaic image. Both moving objects and stationary scene points are annotated. Representative frames from the automatically-annotated video clip are also displayed. Note that annotations of moving objects "move" together with the moving objects, while annotations of static scene points (e.g., "building") remain stationary with respect to the background scene (i.e., they preserve the background motion induced by the moving camera).

20.3.3 Mosaic-based Video Enhancement

Mosaic representations can serve as a useful and efficient tool for producing *high quality stills* from video as well as enhancing an entire video sequence.

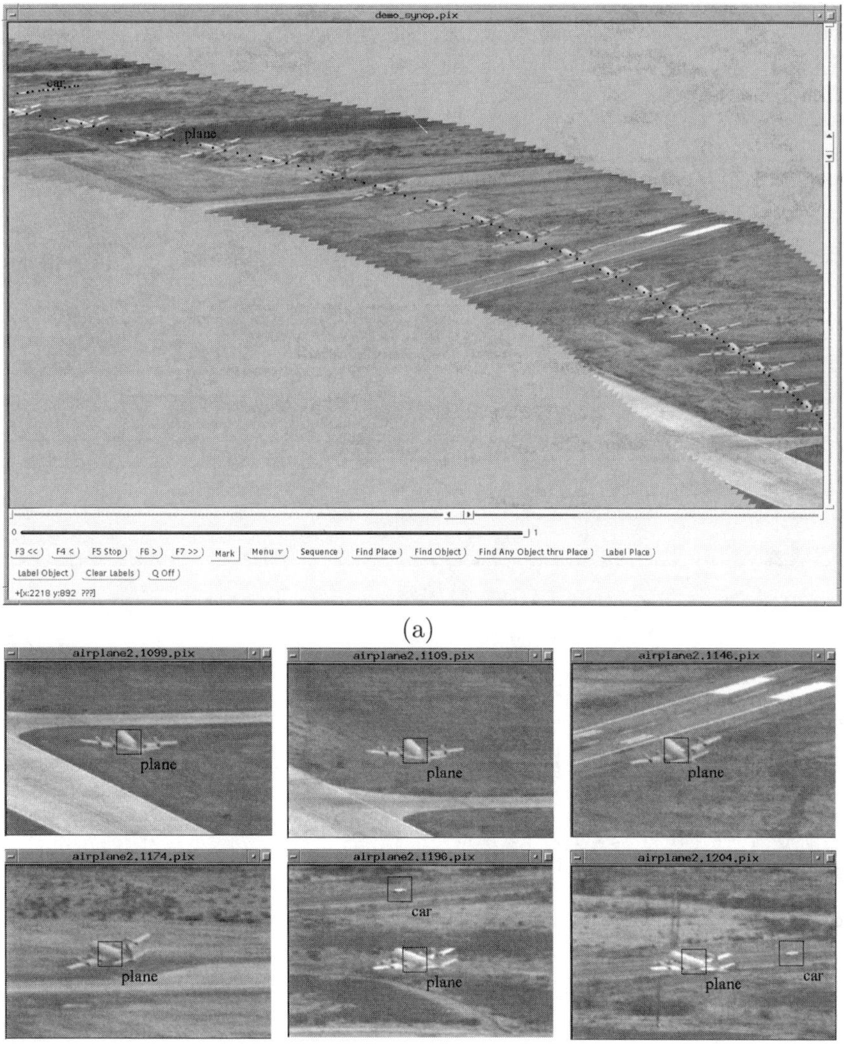

FIGURE 20.9. Annotation of the flying plane video clip. (a) The annotations are defined *once* on the synopsis mosaic image. The moving objects are being annotated ("plane" and "car"). (b) A few representative frames from the video clip with the annotations inherited from the mosaic image. The original video frames are displayed in Figure 20.4. The annotations are incorporated into the video frames *automatically* and *instantly* through the geometric coordinate transformations that map each frame onto the mosaic image.

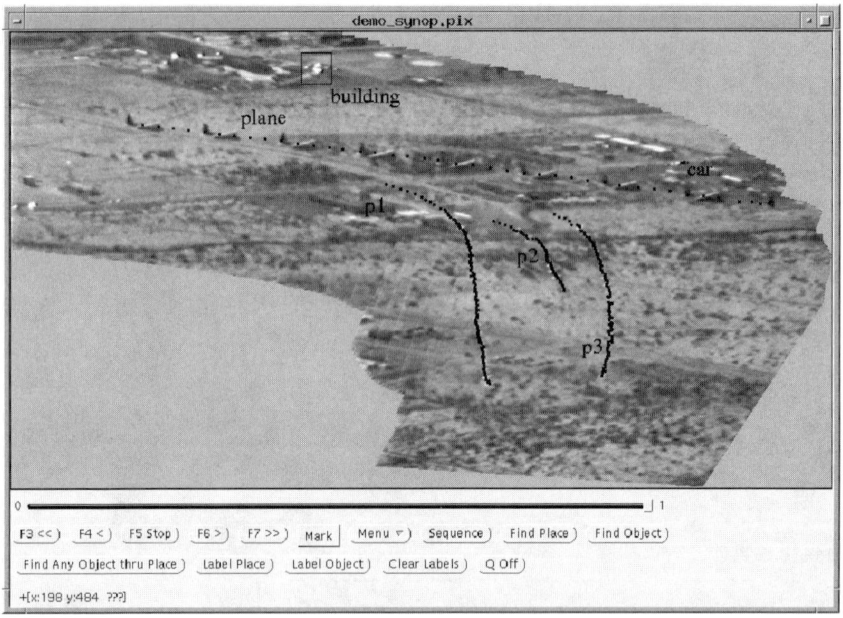

(a)

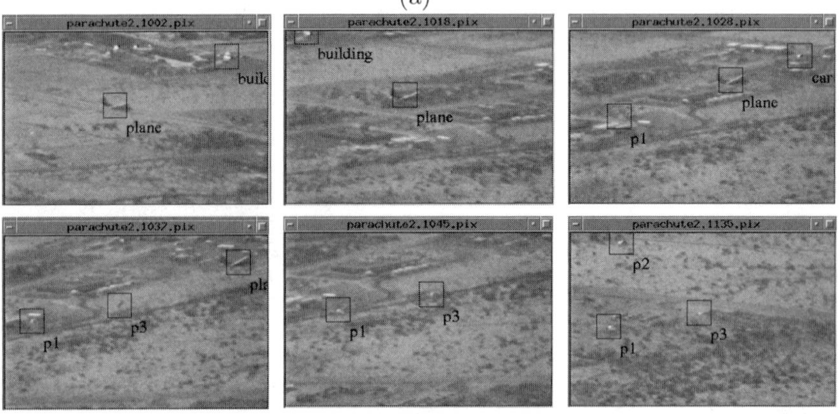

(b)

FIGURE 20.10. Annotation of the parachuters video clip. (a) The annotations are defined *once* on the synopsis mosaic image. Both static scene points ("building") and dynamic scene points ("plane", "car", "p1", "p2", "p3") are being annotated. (b) A few representative frames from the video clip with the annotations inherited from the mosaic image. The original video frames are displayed in Figure 20.5. The annotations are incorporated into the video frames *automatically* and *instantly* through the geometric coordinate transformations that map each frame onto the mosaic image. The parachuters become visible one-by-one, as their parachutes open: first the left parachuter, then the right one, and last the middle one.

The resolution of an image is determined by the physical characteristics of the camera: the optics, the density of the detector elements, and their spatial response. Resolution improvement by modifying the camera can be prohibitive. An increase in the sampling rate could, however, be achieved by obtaining more samples of the imaged scene/object from a sequence of images in which the scene/object appears moving at subpixel displacements. Therefore, aligning the sequence frames over a *finer* mosaic grid can provide higher sampling rate of the background scene, and hence integrating over that grid provides higher spatial resolution. When the blur function of the camera is also known or can be computed and used for deblurring, the increase in resolution is even more pronounced. This method is known as Super-resolution [126, 127, 177]. In [150] this idea was incorporated into a framestore of an MPEG like coder.

The *efficiency* of using *mosaics* for *video* enhancement is due to the fact that the mosaic is an *efficient* representation of the video sequence. Rather than enhancing the frames one-by-one (as is suggested in [127]), the enhancement of the entire sequence (or layer) is done in a single step within the mosaic coordinate system, and only then are the enhanced frames retrieved from the enhanced mosaic.

Figure 20.11 shows an enhanced frame from a sequence of thirty frames of a deserted truck imaged from a remote helicopter surveillance video. In this example, all the input frames were of very poor quality and very noisy. The sequence contained a single static scene that could be completely aligned using 2D alignment. The entire video sequence was enhanced by constructing a single enhanced 2D static mosaic, and then retrieving the frames from the mosaic back into their original coordinate systems (according to the inverse 2D parametric transformations).

20.3.4 Mosaic-based Video Compression

Since mosaics provide an efficient means of representing a video sequence, the most natural application to consider is video image compression. We consider two types of compression applications – video storage (e.g., for video databases and servers) and video transmission. In this section, we briefly describe how to use the scene based representations for these two classes of compression applications.

In either case, the basic approach is the following: The panoramic mosaic image, together with the geometric transformation relating each frame to the mosaic, does the bulk of the job of predicting each frame. To obtain the complete frame, the significant missing residuals between the input frame and the mosaic based prediction are coded. These usually correspond to dynamic changes in the scene. Of course, the geometric transformation should also be coded, and stored or transmitted (as the case may be) along with the residuals.

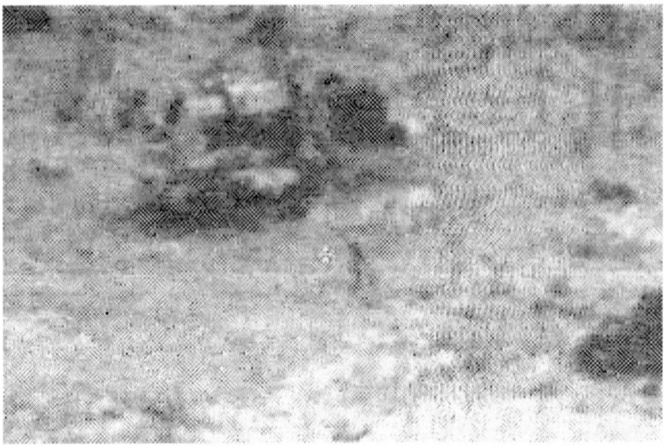

(a)

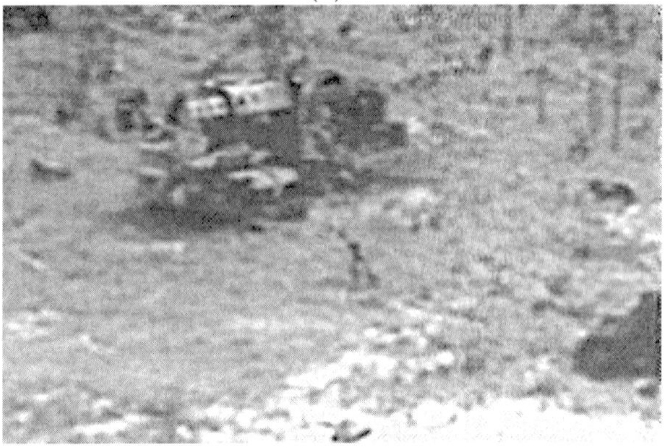

(b)

FIGURE 20.11. Mosaic-based video enhancement from a surveillance sequence of a deserted truck. (a) One out of 30 frames (all frames are of the same quality). (b) The corresponding enhanced frame in the enhanced video sequence. All the frames in the enhanced video are of the same quality.

The residuals are compressed using a lossy spatial coder based on semantic and perceptual criteria. The various ways of computing the significance measure and using them is described in greater detail in [125].

The Storage Codec:

For storage applications, it is important to provide random access to individual frames. The scene-based representation can be applied more-or-less directly to this problem. Figure 20.12 illustrates the storage codec using static mosaic for storage applications. The sequence is processed in batch mode, with the major steps being: mosaic construction, residual estimation for each frame, significance analysis, and spatial coding and decoding of the mosaic image and the individual residuals. During retrieval, the decoded individual residuals are composed with the decoded mosaic and after

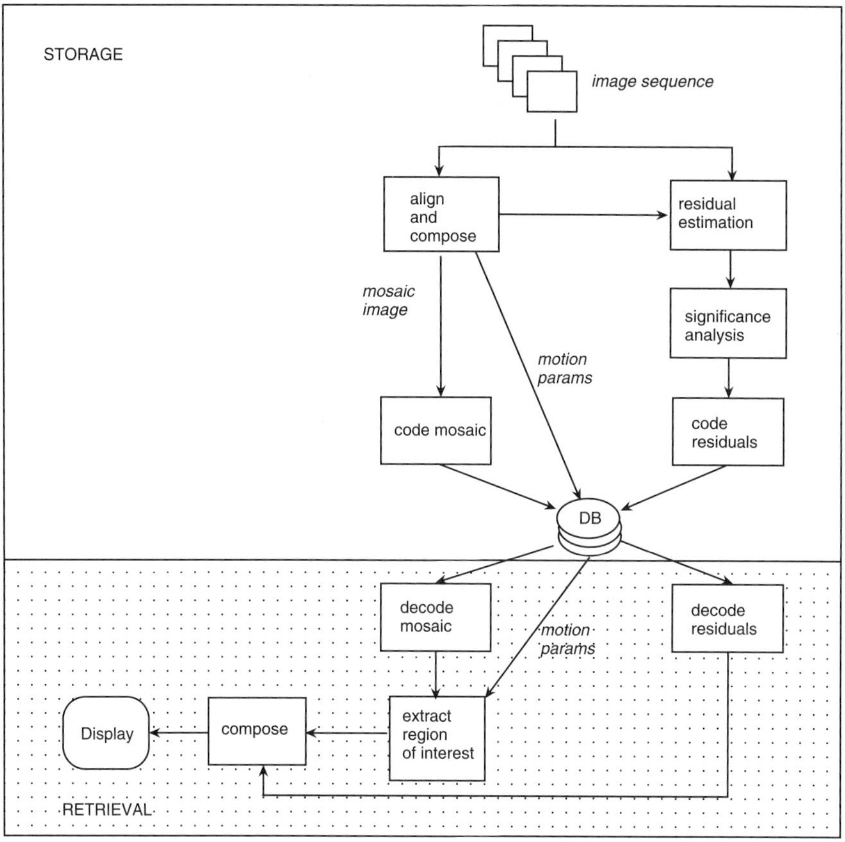

FIGURE 20.12. The codec for mosaic based video compression for video database storage

performing appropriate inverse motion transformation and image window selection the individual frames can be displayed.

The Transmission Codec:

Compression for transmission introduces two new requirements on mosaic based compression. One is the obvious requirement of real-time on-line processing. The other is the fact that the information maintained in the mosaic must be dynamic. This leads to a slight modification of the coding approach described for storage compression. First, the on-line requirement (as opposed to "batch" processing) means that the mosaic construction has to be an incremental process. As a result, the mosaic will dynamically change over time. Second, as is typical of any predictive coding system, the coder should maintain a decoder within itself in order to be in synchrony with the receiver. Figure 20.13 describes at a high level the codec

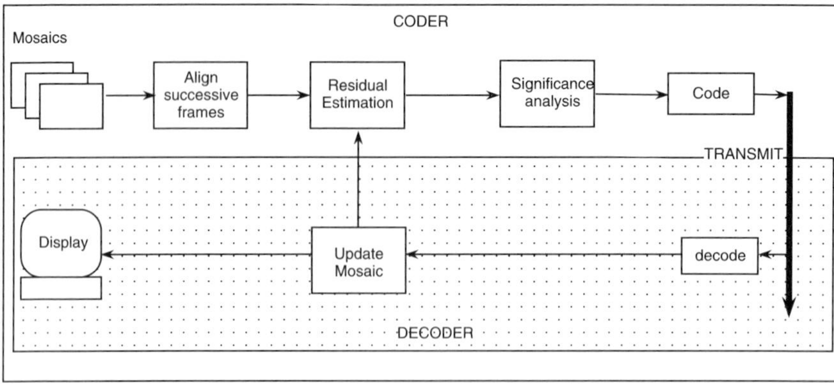

FIGURE 20.13. The codec for mosaic based video compression for real-time transmission

for real-time transmission applications. The major steps in the process are *incremental* mosaic construction, incremental residual estimation by comparison to the reconstructed mosaic from the previous time instance, the computation of significance measures on the residuals, and spatial coding and decoding.

For either class of applications, the spatial coding of the images and the residuals can be based on any available technique, e.g., Discrete Cosine Transform (DCT) or wavelets. The example shown here used a DCT based coder which is a part of an MPEG simulation software system, and included additional motion compensation at a block level. This exploits temporal correlations of "residual" objects moving with respect to the background motion, and proved to be more efficient than other existing spatial coders.

For the sake of brevity, we include only one example of video compression using the scene based representations. Figure 20.14.a shows some representative frames of a surveillance video of a storage building viewed from a flying helicopter. This example was selected partly because mosaic based compression is ideally suited for such an application, since usually the same scene is viewed over an extended period of time from a moving platform (or a stationary one with a panning camera). In these applications, typically only very low bitrate channels are available. Accordingly, the video sequence was spatially subsampled at quarter of the original resolution, and *temporally* sampled by four (i.e., 7.5 frames/sec). The sequence was then coded at the constant bit rate of 32 Kbits/sec using mosaic based compression with DCT spatial coding of the first frame and of the detected residuals (Figure 20.14.b). For comparison, the sequence was compressed by MPEG (without mosaic pre-processing), which is the existing standard video compression method to date, at the *same bitrate* (Figure 20.14.c), which resulted in significantly poorer visual quality. Note that the soldiers

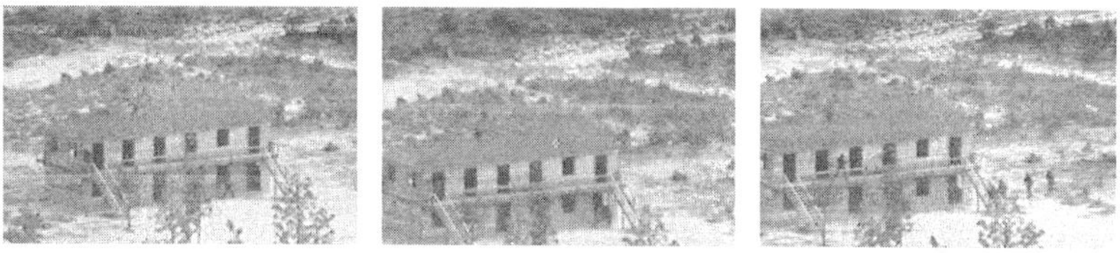

(a) Original frames

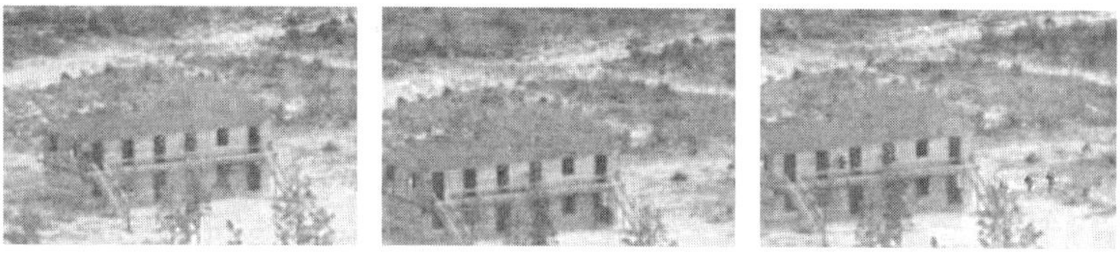

(b) Reconstructed frames using dynamic mosaic-based-compression at 32 Kbits/sec

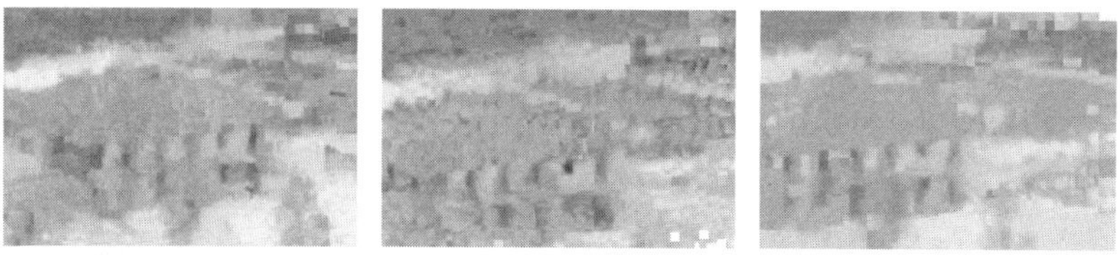

(c) Reconstructed frames using standard MPEG at 32 Kbits/sec

FIGURE 20.14. Transmission compression: results of dynamic mosaic-based-compression vs. standard MPEG compression on a storage-house surveillance sequence. (a) Some representative frames of a 24 second sequence. The sequence was constructed of SIF size images, and temporally sampled by four (i.e., 7.5 frames/sec). (b) The reconstructed frames after using dynamic mosaic-based-compression at a constant bit rate of 32 Kbits/sec. (c) For comparison: The reconstructed frames after using standard MPEG compression of the sequence at the same bit rate, i.e., 32 Kbits/sec. Note the differences in the reconstructed quality of the running soldiers in the images of the right column.

that are running in the scene on the right hand side of the building are visible in the mosaic-based compression results (Figure 20.14.b), but are invisible in the MPEG compression results (Figure 20.14.c). More experimental results are found in our paper on mosaic based video compression [125].

20.4 Building the Scene-based Representation

In Section 20.2 we introduced the basic components of the scene-based representation. In this section review the method used for its construction. The key steps involved in this process are the estimation of the geometric coordinate transformations that bring the frames into alignment (see Section 20.4.1), the alignment and the integration of the frames into a seamless mosaic (see Section 20.4.2), and the detection of independently moving objects and the recovery of their trajectories over time (see Section 20.4.3).

20.4.1 Estimating the Geometric Transformations

To relate each frame to a common representation, we need to determine the geometric coordinate transformations between the video frames. This is based on analyzing and interpreting the image motion between the video frames.

Existing methods for interpreting image motion can broadly be classified into two groups: (i) 3D techniques [3, 165, 280, 281], which try to model and interpret the camera-induced motion in terms of the 3D components (namely, 3D camera motion components R and T and the 3D scene structure $Z(x, y)$), and (ii) 2D techniques [129, 26, 39, 55, 254, 183, 287, 10], which do *not* try to decompose the image motion into its 3D components, but instead model the camera induced motion as a single global 2D *parametric* transformation (e.g., 2D affine, 2D quadratic, or 2D projective).

2D techniques have been proven to be very robust, even in the presence of independently moving objects in the scene [129]. As explained earlier (see Section 20.2), these are, however, good models for the camera induced motion only in a restricted set of scenarios ("2D scenes").

3D techniques, on the other hand, can handle general "3D scenes", but their estimation is more difficult [276]. They require *dense* 3D information in the scene (i.e., lots of depth variations), the frames need to be taken with a large baseline (i.e., large camera translation), and are less robust in presence of moving objects. More importantly, if applied to the 2D scenarios, they fail, since these become singular cases in the 3D analysis.

Our hierarchy of mosaic representations matches scenarios that gradually increase in their complexity from 2D to 3D. The same approach of progressive complexity analysis applies also to our estimation process. Our analysis of a video clip always starts with 2D analysis. We first estimate the *dominant* 2D geometric transformation between frames (see Section 20.4.1.1). Such alignment completely compensates for the camera induced motion in 2D scenes. In 3D scenes, it locks and compensates for the image motion of a dominant planar surface in the scene. The residual parallax motion of the points that are not on the dominant plane is then estimated via a 3D plane+parallax estimation process (see Section 20.4.1.2). Thus our overall estimation approach consists of two major steps: (i) the estimation of

2D parametric transformations, and (ii) the estimation of residual planar parallax displacements. When the scene is composed of several layers at a few distinct depths, multiple 2D models with residual 3D parallax may be required. The layered alignment is achieved via recursive 2D alignment [129].

20.4.1.1 The Estimation of 2D Parametric Transformation

The instantaneous image motion of a general 3D scene can be expressed as [171, 2]:

$$\begin{bmatrix} u(x,y) \\ v(x,y) \end{bmatrix} = \begin{bmatrix} -(\frac{T_X}{Z}+\Omega_Y)+x\frac{T_Z}{Z}+y\Omega_Z-x^2\Omega_Y+xy\Omega_X \\ -(\frac{T_Y}{Z}-\Omega_X)-x\Omega_Z+y\frac{T_Z}{Z}-xy\Omega_Y+y^2\Omega_X \end{bmatrix} \quad (20.1)$$

where $(u(x,y), v(x,y))$ denotes the image velocity at image location (x,y), $T = (T_X, T_Y, T_Z)^t$ denotes the translational motion of the camera, $R = (\Omega_X, \Omega_Y, \Omega_Z)^t$ denotes the camera rotation, and Z denotes the depth of the scene point corresponding to (x,y).

Although, strictly speaking, the above equations represent instantaneous image velocity fields, they are very good approximations of interframe displacements even in discretely time sampled images, provided the following requirements concerning the camera motion and the 3D scene are satisfied: (i) the field-of-view of the camera is small (e.g., less than 30°), (ii) the rotational motion between the frames is small (within a few degrees), and (iii) the translational motion component along the optical axis (T_Z) is small relative to Z. Note that these conditions are often satisfied in real video sequences sampled at 15 or 30 frames/sec.

The instantaneous image motion (Equation 20.1) can often be approximated by a single 2D parametric transformation of the form,

$$\begin{bmatrix} u(x,y) \\ v(x,y) \end{bmatrix} = \begin{bmatrix} a+b\cdot x+c\cdot y+g\cdot x^2+h\cdot xy \\ d+e\cdot x+f\cdot y+g\cdot xy+h\cdot y^2 \end{bmatrix} \quad . \quad (20.2)$$

This approximation is valid under the following conditions associated with the scene geometry and/or camera motion: (i) *A planar scene ($Z(X,Y) = A + B \cdot X + C \cdot Y$):* in this case, the parameters (a,b,c,d,e,f,g,h) are functions of the camera motion and the planar surface parameters (A,B,C) (see [120]), (ii) *Distant Scene:* i.e., when the scene is very distant from the camera (i.e., $Z \to \infty$), or when the deviations from a planar surface are small relative to the overall distance of the scene from the camera ($\Delta Z \ll Z$), (iii) *Camera Rotation*–i.e., when the camera undergoes a pure rotational motion (i.e., $T = 0$) or when the camera translation is negligible ($|T| \ll Z$); the rotation will not have any effect on the parameters b and f, and (iv) *Camera Zoom* – when the camera zooms in or out, the image undergoes a dilation. The resulting image motion field can be still be modeled by Equation 20.2; the zoom will influence the parameters b and f.

We refer to scenes that satisfy any combination of the abovementioned conditions (and hence Equation (20.2) is applicable), as *2D scenes*.

Under these conditions, we can use a previously developed method [25, 129] in order to compute the $2D$ parametric motion. This technique "locks" onto a "dominant" parametric motion between an image pair, even in the presence of independently moving objects. It does not require prior knowledge of their regions of support in the image plane (see [129]). This computation provides only the $2D$ motion parameters of the camera-induced motion, but no explicit $3D$ shape or motion information. To make this paper self-contained, we briefly outline the technique below.

We will refer to the two image frames (whose image motion is being estimated) by the names "inspection" image and "reference" image, respectively. A Laplacian pyramid is first constructed from each of the two input images and then estimates the motion parameters in a coarse-fine manner. Within each level the Sum of squared difference (SSD) measure integrated over regions of interest (which is *initially* the entire image region) is used as a match measure. This measure is minimized with respect to the unknown 2D image motion parameters.

The SSD error measure for estimating the image motion within a region is:

$$E(\boldsymbol{\alpha}) = \sum_{\mathbf{x}} \left(I(x, y, t) - I(x - u(x, y; \boldsymbol{\alpha}), y - v(x, y; \boldsymbol{\alpha}), t - 1)\right)^2 \qquad (20.3)$$

where I the (Laplacian pyramid) image intensity, $\boldsymbol{\alpha} = (a, b, c, d, e, f, g, h)$ denotes the parameters of the quadratic transformation (Equation 20.2), $(u(x, y; \boldsymbol{\alpha}), v(x, y; \boldsymbol{\alpha}))$ denotes the image velocity at the location (x, y) induced by the quadratic transformation with parameters $\boldsymbol{\alpha}$. The sum is computed over all the points within the region, often the entire image.

The objective function E given in Equation (20.3) is minimized w.r.t. the unknown parameters (a, b, c, d, e, f, g, h) via the Gauss-Newton optimization technique. Let $\boldsymbol{\alpha}_i = (a_i, b_i, c_i, d_i, e_i, f_i, g_i, h_i)$ denote the current estimate of the quadratic parameters. After warping the inspection image (towards the reference image) by applying the quadratic transformation based on these parameters, an incremental estimate $\boldsymbol{\delta\alpha} = (\delta a, \delta b, \delta c, \delta d, \delta e, \delta f, \delta g, \delta h)$ can be determined. After iterating a few times within a pyramid level, the process continues at the next finer level. We refer to this process as the *iterative warp estimation* process.

With the above technique, the reference and inspection images are registered so that the desired image region is aligned, and the quadratic transformation (20.2) is estimated. The above estimation technique is a least-squares based approach and hence possibly sensitive to outliers. However, as reported in [26] this sensitivity is minimized by doing the least-squares estimation over a pyramid. The pyramid based approach locks on to the dominant image motion in the scene.

A robust version of the above method [129] handles scenes with multiple moving objects. It incorporates a gradual refinement of the complexity of the motion model (ranging from pure translation at low resolution levels, to a 2D affine model at intermediate levels, to the 2D quadratic model at the highest resolution level). Outlier rejection is performed before each refinement step within the multiscale analysis. This robust analysis further enhances the locking property of the abovementioned algorithm onto a single *dominant* motion. The outlier rejection process computes a real-valued outlier mask which indicates the degree to which a pixel is considered to be inconsistent with the recovered dominant motion [129, 128].

20.4.1.2 Residual 3D Parallax Motion Estimation

The key observation that enables us to extend the 2D parametric registration approach to general 3D scenes is the following: the plane registration process (using the dominant 2D parametric transformation) removes all effects of camera rotation, zoom, and calibration, *without explicitly computing them* [130, 161, 238, 252]. The residual image motion after the plane registration is due only to the *translational* motion of the camera and to the *deviations* of the scene structure from the planar surface. Hence, the residual motion is an *epipolar flow field.* This observation has led to the so-called "plane+parallax" approach to 3D scene analysis [154, 130, 161, 238, 252, 118, 123, 124].

It can be shown (see [162, 130, 238, 252]) that the displacement $\mathbf{u}$ of a pixel can be decomposed as follows:

$$\mathbf{u} = \mathbf{u_p} + \boldsymbol{\mu}, \tag{20.4}$$

where $\mathbf{u_p}$ denotes the *planar* part of the *2D* image motion (which aligns a reference plane Π in the scene). As noted earlier, $\mathbf{u_p}$ can be described by a quadratic transformation as in Equation 20.2. $\boldsymbol{\mu}$ denotes the residual *planar parallax* displacement[2]:

$$\boldsymbol{\mu} = \gamma \frac{T_z}{d'_{\mathbf{p}}}(\mathbf{e} - \mathbf{p_w}) \tag{20.5}$$

where $\mathbf{p_w}$ denotes the image point (in homogeneous coordinates) in the first frame which results from warping the corresponding point $\mathbf{p'}$ in the second image, by the 2D parametric transformation of the reference plane Π. We will refer to the first frame as the *reference frame.* Also, $d'_{\mathbf{p}}$ is the perpendicular distance from the second camera center to the reference plane

[2]When $T_z = 0$, the parallax motion $\boldsymbol{\mu}$ has a slightly different form: $\boldsymbol{\mu} = \frac{\gamma}{d'_{\mathbf{p}}}\mathbf{t}$, where $t = (T_X, T_Y)$.

Π, and $\mathbf{e}$ denotes the epipole (or FOE), which is the point of intersection of the translational motion vector with the reference image plane. γ is a measure of the 3D shape of the point $\mathbf{P}$. In particular, $\gamma = \frac{H}{Z}$, where H is the perpendicular distance from the $\mathbf{P}$ to the reference plane Π, and Z is the "range" (or "depth") of the point $\mathbf{P}$ with respect to the first camera. We refer to γ as the relative 3D structure of point $\mathbf{P}$, as it provides 3D structure relative to the plane Π.

Equation 20.5 indicates that at each image point, the residual planar parallax displacement is a function of the 3D relative structure γ of the point, and the camera translation (as denoted by the epipole $\mathbf{e}$). For points belonging to the static background scene, the relative structure γ is constant over the entire sequence, hence common to all the frames, whereas the epipole $\mathbf{e}$, and the scale factor $\frac{T_z}{d'_{\mathbf{p}}}$ is unique to each frame (but common to all the points in the frame). Hence, the geometric transformation due to the 3D parallax motion for the entire sequence relative to the dominant plane, can be represented by two components: (i) a map $\gamma(x, y)$ of the relative structure, which is a "structure" mosaic (aligned with the panoramic mosaic image) that represents the extended geometric information, and (ii) for each frame, the epipole $\mathbf{e}$ and the scale factor $\frac{T_z}{d'_{\mathbf{p}}}$.

The estimation of the camera translation (namely the epipole) by analyzing the residual parallax motion is described in [130], and the estimation of the 3D projective structure γ together with the epipole is described in [161]. The estimation technique is similar to the 2D parametric estimation technique in that, (i) a multi-resolution coarse-to-fine estimation strategy is used, (ii) at each pyramid level, an SSD measure is used as a minimization criterion (however in this case, the measure is a function of the unknown $\gamma(x, y)$ map and the epipole vector $\mathbf{e}$, as opposed to the parameter vector α) in Equation 20.3, and (iii) the *iterative warp-refine estimation* strategy is used for obtaining the solution. At each step of the iterative process, the epipole vector $\mathbf{e}$, and the projective structure map $\gamma(x, y)$ are refined via the Gauss-Newton minimization technique.

20.4.2 Sequence Alignment and Integration

The previous section described the methods to estimate the geometric coordinate transformation that aligns pairs of frames. In order to combine the information from all the frames of the sequence the entire sequence needs to be aligned and integrated into a single seamless mosaic. In this section we describe these steps:

20.4.2.1 Sequence Alignment

The alignment of *all* image frames in the sequence to form the mosaic can be performed in three ways:

Frame to Frame:

The alignment parameters are first computed between *successive* frames for the entire sequence. These parameters can then be composed to obtain the alignment parameters between any two frames of the sequence.

When constructing a mosaic, all the frames are aligned to a fixed coordinate system. If the mosaic coordinate system that is selected is that of a particular frame (called the "reference" frame), then all other images are aligned to that frame. If a *virtual* coordinate system is selected, then the transformation between the virtual coordinate system and one of the input frames (the reference frame) needs to be given. In this case, this additional transformation is simply composed with the transformations required to align each frame to the reference frame.

Note that the sequence alignment process requires only one pass on the sequence (for computing adjacent alignment transformations, and then sequentially composing these transformations for warping the image frames to the mosaic coordinate system).

Frame to Mosaic:

One problem with frame to frame alignment is that errors may accumulate during the repeated composition of alignment parameters. The alignment can be further refined by directly refining the transformation between each image frame and the mosaic image. To handle the problem of large displacements between the mosaic image and the new image frames, the alignment parameters computed between the previous frame and the mosaic image are used as an initial estimate. A more advanced approach would be to combine simultaneous multi-frame paramter estimation (such as the one in [237]) with the mosaic construction using the frame to frame parameters as initial guesses.

Mosaic to Frame:

The frame to mosaic alignment is appropriate when the mosaic is constructed with respect to a static coordinate system. However, in some dynamic applications such as real-time video transmission, it is important to maintain the images in their input coordinate systems. In this case, it is more useful to align the mosaic to the current frame. In this case the transformation between the most recent mosaic and the current frame is identical to the transformation between the previous frame and the new frame.

20.4.2.2 Image Integration

Once the frames are aligned (or, in the dynamic case, the current mosaic and new frame are aligned), they can be integrated to construct the mosaic image. There are two classes of image integration methods, corresponding to the the two basic mosaic types, namely the *static background mosaic* and the *synopsis mosaic*:

Image Integration for the Background Mosaic –

The background mosaic represents the static portions of the background scene, while removing the dynamic information. Given a sequence of aligned video frames, there are several ways to integrate these frames into a single static background mosaic image:

- An ordinary temporal average or a temporal median filtering of the intensity values of the aligned images. Both a temporal average and a temporal median, when applied to a registered scene sequence will produce a panoramic image of the dominant "background" scene, where moving objects either disappear or leave "ghost-like" traces. (Temporal averages usually result in blurrier mosaic images than those obtained by temporal medians, but are computationally less expensive.) This integration scheme was used for generating the background mosaic images shown in Figure 20.1b and 20.2b.
- The pixels can be weighted in various ways in order to achieve different effects. For example, a weighted temporal average where the weights correspond to the outlier rejection maps computed in the motion estimation process of the dominant "background" (Section 20.4.1.1). This scheme prefers the dominant "background" data over "foreground" data in the mosaic construction, and therefore gives less "ghost-like" traces of "foreground" objects, and a more complete image of the dominant "background" scene (see [121, 128]). Alternatively, the weights may decrease with the distance of a pixel from the center of the frame. This reduces the effect of image alignment inaccuracies near the border of the frames due to use of low order 2D parameteric transformations. A special case of this leads to a mosaic of the type developed by Peleg, *et al.* [214].

Image Integration for the Synopsis Mosaic –

A simple way to construct the synopsis mosaic is to weight the pixels according to the *inverse* of the outlier rejection maps computed in the motion estimation process of the dominant "background" (Section 20.4.1.1). This scheme prefers the *non*-dominant "foreground" data over "background" data in the mosaic construction. Hence, the mosaic image constructed by applying such an integration method would contain a panoramic image not only of the scene, but also of the *event* that took place in that scene sequence (e.g., see Figure 20.2c and 20.4b) (see [121] for more details).

Image Integration for Enhancement –

Alternative integration schemes for image enhancement, such as Super-resolution [126, 41] can be used to produce mosaic image whose resolution and image quality surpasses those of any of the original image frames. See more details in Section 20.3.3.

20.4.3 Moving Object Detection and Tracking

The geometric coordinate transformations that relate the frames to the mosaic image (and to each other) describe the *dominant* detected motion. The dominant motion is assumed to be that of the static portions of the scene (i.e., only due to camera motion). This is a strong assumption which requires treatment in future work. However, this is a valid assumption in a wide range of scenario scenarios, when the camera is not zoomed in on a moving object. This is especially true in airborne video or remote surveillance type of applications.

After dominant-motion alignment, all static portions of the scene are in full alignment, and the only remaining misaligned portions of the image are those that move due to *independent* motion. This is used for detecting potential moving objects [129]. To verify the hypothesis and distinguish moving objects from noise, these image regions are tracked over time. The tracking is performed at a symbolic level, based on "blobs" that represent the misaligned regions. No template correlation or flow estimation is used. This has the benefit that it can effectively track even very small moving objects (e.g., objects that may be a few pixels in size), textureless objects, and non-rigidly moving objects. The objects are required to be detected and tracked over a minimum time period – typically a few (say 6) consecutive frames – before they are believed to be moving objects.

Note also that estimating the trajectories of moving objects in the common mosaic coordinate system allows more reliable detection and tracking of moving objects, even when they are very small (such as the three parachuters in Figure 20.5). This is because a "temporal coherence" constraint can be used during moving object detection and tracking after removal of the background motion. Assuming that object sizes and velocities do not change too rapidly, the detection of moving objects within each frame can be guided by the trajectory of the objects in a few previous frames. This leads to better separation between small moving objects and noise, as well as enables recovery from losing an object for a few frames (e.g., due to occlusion or bad detection). It also allows handling multiple moving objects with intersecting trajectories. The missing portion of each trajectory is smoothly interpolated/extrapolated from the neighboring frames.

20.5 Conclusion

This chapter described a new approach for efficient access, storage, and manipulation of video data. Our approach is based on transforming the video data from a sequential *frame-based* representation, in which the common scene information is *distributed* over many frames, into a single common *scene-based* representation to which each frame can be *directly* related. This representation then allows direct and immediate access to the scene information, such as static locations and dynamically moving objects. It also eliminates the redundancy between the different views of the scene contained in the frames, thereby allowing a high degree of data compression without loss of visual quality of the images.

As part of the scene-based representation, panoramic mosaic images are created, which provide a snapshot view of the information available in the video data. Two types of mosaics are described: a *static* mosaic, which captures the appearance of the static background portions of the scene, and a *synopsis* mosaic, which in addition visually captures the trajectories of moving objects. These mosaics allow the user to rapidly browse through a large collection of video sequence, and can serve as *visual table-of-contents* for a video database.

This chapter also described two new types of indexing methods, based on *geometric* and *dynamic* scene information. While the major research effort in the area of content-based video indexing is based on appearance information (e.g., texture and color), the two methods described in this chapter have been overlooked. These methods are complementary to the appearance based methods, and are substantially simpler to achieve. The existing appearance-based methods themselves can also be used more efficiently within the scene-based representation, when applied directly to the mosaic image (i.e., to the appearance component of our representation), rather than to the individual video frames one-by-one. The mosaic construction process can also be used to enhance the images, and to increase the resolution of the image information, by integrating the multiple views of the same scene elements.

The scene-based representation described in this chapter is intended to apply to all types of scenarios. However, there are situations for which our current methods for constructing panoramic views may not suffice, i.e., it will not produce compact or visually meaningful representation. Such situtations arise when a camera is moving around an object (or equivalently an object is rotating in front of the camera), or when the scene contains significant 3D clutter, with many objects at many different depths. These situations require further study and treatment.

Bibliography

[1] E. H. Adelson and J. R. Bergen. The plenoptic function and elements of early vision. *Computational Models of Visual Processing*, 1991.

[2] G. Adiv. Determining three-dimensional motion and structure from optical flow generated by several moving objects. *IEEE Trans. on Pattern Analysis and Machine Intelligence*, 7(4):384–401, July 1985.

[3] Y. Aloimonos, editor. *Active Perception*. Erlbaum, 1993.

[4] P. Anandan. A computational framework and an algorithm for the measurement of visual motion. *International Journal of Computer Vision*, 2(3):283–310, January 1989.

[5] P. Anandan et al., editors. *IEEE Workshop on Representations of Visual Scenes*, Cambridge, Massachusetts, June 1995. IEEE Computer Society Press.

[6] J. Arnspang, H. Nielsen, M. Chritensen, and K. Henriksen. Using mirror cameras for estimating depth. *Conference on Computer Analysis of Images and Patterns*, pages 711–716, 1995.

[7] F. Aurenhammer. Voronoi diagrams: A survey of a fundamental geometric data structure. *ACM Computing Surveys*, 23(3):345–405, September 1991.

[8] N. Ayache. *Vision Stéréoscopique et Perception Multisensorielle*. InterEditions, Paris, 1989.

[9] N. Ayache. *Artificial Vision for Mobile Robots: Stereo Vision and Multisensory Perception*. MIT Press, Cambridge, Massachusetts, 1991.

[10] S. Ayer and H. Sawhney. Layered representation of motion video using robust maximum-likelihood estimation of mixture models and mdl encoding. In *International Conference on Computer Vision*, pages 777–784, Cambridge, MA, June 1995.

[11] A. Azarbayejani and A. P. Pentland. Recursive estimation of motion, structure, and focal length. *IEEE Transactions on Pattern Analysis and Machine Intelligence*, 17(6):562–575, June 1995.

[12] S. Baker and S. K. Nayar. Catadioptric image formation. *International Conference on Computer Vision*, January 1998.

[13] S. Baker and S. K. Nayar. A theory of single-viewpoint catadioptric image formation. *International Journal of Computer Vision*, 35(2):1–22, November 1999.

[14] S. Baker, R. Szeliski, and P. Anandan. A layered approach to stereo reconstruction. In *IEEE Conference on Computer Vision and Pattern Recognition*, pages 434–441, Santa Barbara, June 1998.

[15] Y. Bar-Shalom. Tracking methods in a multitarget environment. *IEEE Transactions on Automatic Control*, 23(4):618–626, 1978.

[16] S. T. Barnard and M. A. Fischler. Computational stereo. *Computing Surveys*, 14(4):553–572, December 1982.

[17] M. Barth and H. Ishiguro. Distributed panoramic sensing in multiagent robotics. In *IEEE International Conference on Multisensor Fusion and Integration for Intelligent Systems*, pages 739–746, 1994.

[18] A. Basu and S. Licardie. Alternative models for fish-eye lenses. *Pattern Recognition Letters*, 16(4):433–441, 1995.

[19] A. Basu and D. Southwell. Omni-directional sensors for pipe inspection. *IEEE SMC Conference*, pages 3107–3112, October 1995.

[20] P. Beardsley and D. Murray. Camera calibration using vanishing points. In D. Hogg and R. Boyle, editors, *British Machine Vision Conference*. Springer-Verlag, September 1992.

[21] Behere, 1999.

[22] R. Benosman, T. Maniere, and J. Devars. Multidirectional stereovision sensor, calibration and scenes reconstruction. *International Conference on Pattern Recognition*, A:161–165, August 1996.

[23] R. Benosman, T. Maniere, and J. Devars. Panoramic sensor calibration. *Pattern Recognition Letters*, pages 483–490, July 1998.

[24] R. Benosman, T. Maniere, and J. Devars. Panoramic stereovision sensor. *International Conference on Pattern Recognition*, pages 767–769, August 1998.

[25] J. R. Bergen, P. Anandan, K. J. Hanna, and R. Hingorani. Hierarchical model-based motion estimation. In *Second European Conference on Computer Vision*, pages 237–252, Santa Margherita Liguere, Italy, May 1992. Springer-Verlag.

[26] J. R. Bergen, P. J. Burt, R. Hingorani, and S. Peleg. A three frame algorithm for estimating two-component image motion. *IEEE Trans. on Pattern Analysis and Machine Intelligence*, 14:886–896, September 1992.

[27] M. J. Black and A. Rangarajan. On the unification of line processes, outlier rejection, and robust statistics with applications in early vision. *International Journal of Computer Vision*, 19(1):57–91, 1996.

[28] S. Bogner. Introduction to panoramic imaging. In *IEEE SMC Conference*, pages 3100–3106, Vancouver, Canada, October 1995.

[29] R. C. Bolles, H. H. Baker, and D. H. Marimont. Epipolar-plane image analysis: An approach to determining structure from motion. *International Journal of Computer Vision*, 1:7–55, 1987.

[30] M. Born and E. Wolf. *Principles of Optics.* Pergamon, London, 1965.

[31] T. Boult. Remote reality via omnidirectional imaging. *DARPA Image Understanding Workshop*, 1998.

[32] J. E. Boyd, E. Hunter, P. H. Kelly, L.-C. Tai, C. B. Phillips, and R. C. Jain. MPI-Video infrastructure for dynamic environments. In *IEEE International Conference on Multimedia Computing and Systems*, pages 249–254, 1998.

[33] T. Brodsky, C. Fermuller, and Y. Aloimonos. Directions of motion fields are hardly ever ambiguous. *European Conference on Computer Vision*, 2:119–128, 1996.

[34] D. C. Brown. Close-range camera calibration. *Photogrammetric Engineering*, 37:855–866, 1971.

[35] A. M. Bruckstein and T. J. Richardson. Method and system for panoramic viewing with curved surface mirrors. *U.S. Patent No. 5,920,376*, July 1999.

[36] D. R. Buchele and W. M. Buchele. Unitary catadioptric objective lens systems. *U.S. Patent No. 2,638,033*, May 1953.

[37] J. C. Burie and J. L. Bruyelle. Detection and tracking of obstacles in front of a moving car with a linear stereovision system. *CESA*, pages 443–448, 1996.

[38] P. J. Burt and E. H. Adelson. A multiresolution spline with applications to image mosaics. *ACM Transactions on Graphics*, 2(4):217–236, October 1983.

[39] P. J. Burt, R. Hingorani, and R. J. Kolczynski. Mechanisms for isolating component patterns in the sequential analysis of multiple motion. In *IEEE Workshop on Visual Motion*, pages 187–193, Princeton, New Jersey, October 1991.

[40] P.J. Burt and P. Anandan. Image stabilization by registration to a reference mosaic. In *ARPA Image Understanding Workshop*, pages 457–465, Monterey, California, November 1994. Morgan Kaufmann.

[41] D. Capel and A. Zisserman. Automatic mosaicing with super-resolution zoom. In *IEEE Conference on Computer Vision and Pattern Recognition*, pages 885–891, Santa Barbara, CA, June 1998.

[42] B. Caprile and V. Torre. Using vanishing points for camera calibration. *International Journal of Computer Vision*, 4(2):127–139, March 1990.

[43] J. S. Chahl and M. V. Srinivasan. Range estimation with a panoramic visual sensor. *Journal of Optical Society of America-A*, 14(9):2144–2151, September 1997.

[44] J. S. Chahl and M. V. Srinivassan. Reflective surfaces for panoramic imaging. *Applied Optics*, 36(31):8275–8285, November 1997.

[45] J. R. Charles. Converting panoramas to circular images and vice versa - without a computer! *http://www.eclipsechaser.com/eclink/astrotec/panconv.htm*, 1976.

[46] J. R. Charles. Portable all-sky reflector with "invisible" camera support. *Riverside Telescope Makers Conference*, pages 74–50, 1988.

[47] J. R. Charles, R. Reeves, and C. Schur. How to build and use an all-sky camera. *Astronomy Magazine*, April 1987.

[48] S. Chen and L. Williams. View interpolation for image synthesis. *Computer Graphics (SIGGRAPH'93)*, pages 279–288, August 1993.

[49] S.E. Chen. QuickTime VR – An image-based approach to virtual environment navigation. *Computer Graphics (SIGGRAPH'95)*, pages 29–38, Aug. 1995.

[50] M.-C. Chiang and T. E. Boult. Efficient image warping and super-resolution. In *IEEE Workshop on Applications of Computer Vision*, pages 56–61, Sarasota, Florida, December 1996.

[51] R. T. Collins, Y. Tsin, J. R. Miller, and A.J. Lipton. Using a DEM to determine geospatial object trajectories. In *DARPA Image Understanding Workshop*, 1998.

[52] T. Conroy and J. Moore. Resolution invariant surfaces for panoramic vision systems. *International Conference on Computer Vision*, pages 392–397, 1999.

[53] S. Cornbleet. *Microwave and Optical Ray Geometry.* John Wiley and Sons, 1984.

[54] P. E. Danielsson. Euclidean distance mapping. *Computer Graphics and Image Processing*, 14:227–248, 1980.

[55] T. Darrell and A. Pentland. Robust estimation of a multi-layered motion representation. In *IEEE Workshop on Visual Motion*, pages 173–178, Princeton, New Jersey, October 1991.

[56] J. Davis. Mosaics of scenes with moving objects. In *IEEE Conference on Computer Vision and Pattern Recognition*, pages 354–360, Santa Barbara, June 1998.

[57] J. E. Davis, M. N. Todd, M. Ruda, T. W. Stuhlinger, and K. R. Castle. Optics assembly for observing a panoramic scene. *U.S. Patent No. 5,627,675*, May 1997.

[58] L. de Agapito, E. E. Hayman, and I. Reid. Self-calibration of a rotating camera with varying intrinsic parameters. In *British Machine Vision Conference*, pages 105–114, Southampton, England, 1998.

[59] L. de Agapito, R. I. Hartley, and E. Hayman. Linear calibration of a rotating and zooming camera. In *IEEE Conference on Computer Vision and Pattern Recognition*, pages 15–21, Fort Collins, CO, 1999.

[60] L. de Agapito, E. Hayman, and I. Reid. Self-calibration of rotating and zooming cameras. Technical Report OUEL 0225/00, Department of Engineering Science, University of Oxford, 2000.

[61] R. Deriche, Z. Zhang, Q.-T. Luong, and O. Faugeras. Robust recovery of the epipolar geometry for an uncalibrated stereo rig. In *Third European Conference on Computer Vision (ECCV'94)*, volume 1, pages 567–576, Stockholm, Sweden, May 1994. Springer-Verlag.

[62] R. Descartes and D. T. Smith. *The geometry of René Descartes, (originally published in Discours de la Methode, 1637).* Dover, 1954.

[63] U. R. Dhond and J. K. Aggarwal. Structure from stereo—A review. *IEEE Transactions on Systems, Man, and Cybernetics*, 19(6):1489–1510, November/December 1989.

[64] L. Dron. Dynamic camera self-calibration from controlled motion sequences. In *IEEE Conference on Computer Vision and Pattern Recognition*, pages 501–506, New York, NY, June 1993.

[65] D. Drucker and P. Locke. A natural classification of curves and surfaces with reflection properties. *Mathematics Magazine*, 69(4):249–256, October 1996.

[66] Edmund Scientific Company, New Jersey. *Optics and Optical Components Catalog*, 1996.

[67] O. Faugeras. *Three-dimensional computer vision: A geometric viewpoint.* MIT Press, Cambridge, MA, 1993.

[68] O. Faugeras, L. Quan, and P. Sturm. Self-calibration of a 1D projective camera and its application to the self-calibration of a 2D projective camera. In *European Conference on Computer Vision*, pages 36–52, Freiburg, Germany, June 1998.

[69] O. D. Faugeras. What can be seen in three dimensions with an uncalibrated stereo rig? In *Second European Conference on Computer Vision (ECCV'92)*, pages 563–578, Santa Margherita Liguere, Italy, May 1992. Springer-Verlag.

[70] O. D. Faugeras and M. Hebert. The representation, recognition, and locating of 3-D objects. *International Journal of Robotics Research*, 5(3):27–52, 1992.

[71] F. P. Ferrie and M. D. Levine. Integrating information from multiple views. In *IEEE Workshop on Computer Vision*, pages 117–122. IEEE Computer Society, 1987.

[72] M. M. Fleck. Perspective projection: The wrong imaging model. *Research report 95-01*, 1995.

[73] M. Flickner, H. Sawhney, W. Niblack, J. Ashley, Q. Huang, B. Dom, M. Gorkani, J. Hafner, D. Lee, D. Petkovic, D. Steele, and P. Yanker. Query by image and video content: The QBIC system. *Computer*, 28(9):23–32, 1995.

[74] G. Francke. *Physical optics in photography.* The local press, London, New York, 1966.

[75] D.H. Freedman. A camera for near, far, and wide. *Discover*, 16(48):48, November 1995.

[76] P. Fua and Y. G. Leclerc. Using 3–dimensional meshes to combine image-based and geometry-based constraints. In *European Conference on Computer Vision*, volume 2, pages 281–291, Stockholm, Sweden, May 1994.

[77] F. Garcia Lorca. *Filtres recursifs temps reel pour la detection de contours: Optimisations algorithmiques et architecturales.* PhD thesis, University of Paris sud, November 1996.

[78] T. Geb. Real-time panospheric image dewarping and presentation for remote mobile robot control. *IEEE Transactions on Robotics and Automation*, 1998.

[79] C. Geyer and K. Daniilidis. Catadioptric camera calibration. *International Conference on Computer Vision*, pages 398–404, September 1999.

[80] J. Gluckman and S. K. Nayar. Ego-motion and omnidirectional cameras. *International Conference on Computer Vision*, pages 999–1005, January 1998.

[81] J. Gluckman and S. K. Nayar. Planar catadioptric stereo: Geometry and calibration. *IEEE Conference on Computer Vision and Pattern Recognition*, pages 22–28, June 1999.

[82] J. Gluckman, S. K. Nayar, and K. J. Thoresz. Real-time omnidirectional and panoramic stereo. *DARPA Image Understanding Workshop*, pages 299–303, November 1998.

[83] G. Golub and C. F. Van Loan. *Matrix Computation, third edition.* The John Hopkins University Press, Baltimore and London, 1996.

[84] S. J. Gortler, R. Grzeszczuk, R. Szeliski, and M. F. Cohen. The lumigraph. In *Computer Graphics (SIGGRAPH'96)*, pages 43–54, New Orleans, August 1996.

[85] A. Goshtasby and W. A. Gruver. Design of a single-lens stereo camera system. *Pattern Recognition*, 26(6):923–937, 1993.

[86] N. Greene. Environment mapping and other applications of world projections. *IEEE Computer Graphics and Applications*, 6(11):21–29, November 1986.

[87] M. V.-P. Greguss. Centric minded imaging in space research. *International Workshop on Robotics in Alpe–Adria–Danube Region*, pages 121–126, June 1998.

[88] P. Greguss. Panoramic imaging block for three-dimensional space. *U.S. Patent No. 4,566,763*, January 1986.

[89] W. E. L. Grimson, C. Stauffer, R. Romano, and L. Lee. Using adaptive tracking to classify and monitor activities in a site. In *IEEE Conference on Computer Vision and Pattern Recognition*, pages 22–29, 1998.

[90] E. Gurewitz, I. Dinstein, and B. Sarusi. More on the benefit of a third eye. In *International Conference on Pattern Recognition*, pages 966–968, 1986.

[91] Z. Hall and E. L. Cao. Omnidirectional viewing using a fish eye lens. *SPIE Optics, Illumination, and Image Sensing for Machine Vision*, 728:250–256, October 1986.

[92] F. Hamit. New video and still cameras provide a global roaming viewpoint. *Advance Imaging*, pages 50–52, March 1997.

[93] M. Hansen, P. Anandan, K. Dana, G. van der Wal, and P. Burt. Real-time scene stabilization and mosaic construction. In *IEEE Workshop on Applications of Computer Vision*, pages 54–62, Sarasota, FL, December 1994.

[94] R. Hartley. In defence of the 8-point algorithm. In *International Conference on Computer Vision*, pages 1064–1070, Cambridge, MA, June 1995.

[95] R. Hartley and R. Gupta. Linear pushbroom cameras. In *European Conference on Computer Vision*, pages 555–566, Stockholm, Sweden, May 1994.

[96] R. I. Hartley. Estimation of relative camera positions for uncalibrated cameras. *European Conference on Computer Vision*, pages 579–587, May 1992.

[97] R. I. Hartley. An algorithm for self calibration from several views. In *Conference on Computer Vision and Pattern Recognition*, pages 908–912, Seattle, WA, June 1994.

[98] R. I. Hartley. Self-calibration from multiple views of a rotating camera. In *European Conference on Computer Vision*, volume 1, pages 471–478, Stockholm, Sweden, May 1994.

[99] R. I. Hartley. Self-calibration of stationary cameras. *International Journal of Computer Vision*, 22(1):5–23, February 1997.

[100] R. I. Hartley, E. Hayman, L. de Agapito, and I. D. Reid. Camera calibration and the search for infinity. In *International Conference on Computer Vision*, pages 510–517, Kerkyra, Greece, September 1999.

[101] E. Hayman, L. de Agapito, I. D. Reid, and D. W. Murray. The role of self-calibration in Euclidean reconstruction from two rotating and zooming cameras. In *European Conference on Computer Vision*, Dublin, Ireland, July 2000.

[102] E. Hayman, J. G. Knight, and D. W. Murray. Self-alignment of an active head from observations of rotation matrices. In *International Conference on Pattern Recognition*, Barcelona, Spain, September 2000.

[103] E. Hecht. *Optics*. Schaum Outline Series, McGraw, 1975.

[104] E. Hecht and A. Zajac. *Optics*. Addison-Wesley, 1974.

[105] P. Heckbert. Fundamentals of texture mapping and image warping. Master's thesis, University of California at Berkeley, June 1989.

[106] D. J. Heeger and J. R. Bergen. Pyramid-based texture analysis/synthesis. In *SIGGRAPH*, pages 229–238, 1997.

[107] A. Heyden and K. Astrom. Euclidean reconstruction from image sequences with varying and unknown focal length and principal point. In *IEEE Conference on Computer Vision and Pattern Recognition*, pages 438–443, June 1997.

[108] A. R. Hicks and R. Bajscy. Reflective surfaces as computational sensors. *IEEE Workshop on Perception for Mobile Agents*, June 1999.

[109] K. Higuchi, M. Hebert, and K. Ikeuchi. Building 3-D models from unregistered range images. Technical Report CMU-CS-93-214, Carnegie Mellon University, November 1993.

[110] J. Hong. Image based homing. *International Conference on Robotics and Automation*, May 1991.

[111] R. Horaud, R. Mohr, and B. Lorecki. Linear-camera calibration. In *International Conference on Robotics and Automation*, pages 1539–1544, Nice, France, May 1992.

[112] B. K. P. Horn. Closed-form solution of absolute orientation using unit quaternions. *Journal of the Optical Society of America A*, 4(4):629–642, 1987.

[113] B. K. P. Horn, H. M. Hilden, and S. Negahdaripour. Closed-form solution of absolute orientation using orthonormal matrices. *Journal of the Optical Society of America A*, 5(7):1127–1135, 1988.

[114] H. C. Huang and Y. P. Hung. Panoramic stereo imaging system with automatic disparity warping and seaming. *Graphical Models and Image Processing*, 60(3):196–208, May 1998.

[115] M. Inaba, T. Hara, and H. Inoue. A stereo viewer based on a single camera with view-control mechanism. *IEEE/RSJ International Conference on Robots and Systems*, pages 1857–1864, July 1993.

[116] S. S. Intille, W. Davis, and A. F. Bobick. Real-time closed-world tracking. In *IEEE Conference on Computer Vision and Pattern Recognition*, pages 697–703, 1997.

[117] IPIX. http://www.ipix.com/, 1999.

[118] M. Irani and P. Anandan. Parallax geometry of pairs of points for 3D scene analysis. In *European Conference on Computer Vision*, pages 17–30, Cambridge, UK, April 1996.

[119] M. Irani and P. Anandan. Video indexing based on mosaic representations. *Proceedings of the IEEE*, 86(5):905–921, May 1998.

[120] M. Irani and P. Anandan. A unified approach to moving object detection in 2D and 3D scenes. In *IEEE Trans. on Pattern Analysis and Machine Intelligence*, to appear.

[121] M. Irani, P. Anandan, J. Bergen, R. Kumar, and S. Hsu. Efficient representations of video sequences and their application. *Signal Processing: Image Communication*, 8(4), 1996.

[122] M. Irani, P. Anandan, and S. Hsu. Mosaic based representations of video sequences and their applications. In *International Conference on Computer Vision*, pages 605–611, Cambridge, MA, June 1995.

[123] M. Irani, P. Anandan, and D. Weinshall. From reference frames to reference planes: Multi-view parallax geometry and applications. In *European Conference on Computer Vision*, Freiburg, June 1998.

[124] M. Irani, M. Cohen, and P. Anandan. Direct recovery of planar parallax from multiple frames. In *Workshop on Vision Algorithms: Theory and Practice*, Corfu, Greece, September 1999.

[125] M. Irani, S. Hsu, and P. Anandan. Video compression using mosaic representations. *Signal Processing: Image Communication*, 7:529–552, 1995.

[126] M. Irani and S. Peleg. Improving resolution by image registration. *Graphical Models and Image Processing*, 53(3):231–239, May 1991.

[127] M. Irani and S. Peleg. Using motion analysis for image enhancement. *Journal of Visual Communication and Image Representation*, 4(4):324–335, December 1993.

[128] M. Irani, B. Rousso, and S. Peleg. Detecting and tracking multiple moving objects using temporal integration. In *European Conference on Computer Vision*, pages 282–287, Santa Margarita Ligure, May 1992.

[129] M. Irani, B. Rousso, and S. Peleg. Computing occluding and transparent motions. *International Journal of Computer Vision*, 12(1):5–16, January 1994.

[130] M. Irani, B. Rousso, and S. Peleg. Recovery of ego-motion using image stabilization. In *IEEE Conference on Computer Vision and Pattern Recognition*, pages 454–460, Seattle, WA, June 1994.

[131] H. Ishiguro. Development of low-cost compact omnidirectional vision sensors and their applications. In *International Conference on Information Systems, Analysis and Synthesis*, pages 433–439, 1998.

[132] H. Ishiguro, T. Sogo, and T. Ishida. Human behavior recognition by a distributed vision system. *Proc. DiCoMo Workshop (In Japanese*, pages 615–620, 1997.

[133] H. Ishiguro and S. Tsuji. Image-based memory of environment. *International Conference on Intelligent Robots and Systems*, pages 634–639, November 1996.

[134] H. Ishiguro, K. Ueda, and S. Tsuji. Omnidirectional visual information for navigating a mobile robot. *International Conference on Robotics and Automation*, pages 799–804, 1993.

[135] H. Ishiguro, H. Yamamoto, and S. Tsuji. Omnidirectional stereo. *IEEE Trans. on Pattern Analysis and Machine Intelligence*, 14:257–262, 1992.

[136] H. Ishiguro, M. Yamamoto, and S. Tsuji. Omni-directional stereo. *IEEE Trans. on Pattern Analysis and Machine Intelligence*, 14(2):257–262, 1992.

[137] H. Ishiguro, M. Yamamoto, and S. Tsuji. Omni-directional stereo. *IEEE Trans. on Pattern Analysis and Machine Intelligence*, 14(2):257–262, February 1992.

[138] C. E. Jacobs, A. Finkelstein, and D.H. Salesin. Fast multiresolution image querying. In *SIGGRAPH*, pages 277–286, 1995.

[139] P. Jaillon and A. Montanvert. Image mosaicking applied to three-dimensional surfaces. In *International Conference on Pattern Recognition*, pages 253–257, Jerusalem, Israel, October 1994.

[140] N. Johnson and D. Hogg. Learning the distribution of object trajectories for event recognition. *Image and Vision Computing*, 14(8):609–615, 1996.

[141] T. Kanade, T. Collins, A. J. Lipton, P. Anandan, P. Burt, and L. Wixson. Cooperative multi-sensor video surveillance. In *DARPA Image Understanding Workshop*, volume 1, pages 3–10, 1997.

[142] T. Kanade, A. Yoshida, K. Oda, H. Kano, and M. Tanaka. A stereo machine for video-rate dense depth mapping and its new applications. In *IEEE Conference on Computer Vision and Pattern Recognition*, pages 196–202, 1996.

[143] K. Kanatani. Analysis of 3-D rotation fitting. *IEEE Trans. on Pattern Analysis and Machine Intelligence*, 16(5):543–549, May 1994.

[144] S. B. Kang. A survey of image-based rendering techniques. In *Videometrics VI (SPIE Inter. Symp. on Electronic Imaging: Science and Technology)*, volume 3641, pages 2–16, San Jose, CA, January 1999.

[145] S. B. Kang, A. Johnson, and R. Szeliski. Extraction of concise and realistic 3-D models from real data. Technical Report 95/7, Digital Equipment Corporation, Cambridge Research Lab, October 1995.

[146] S. B. Kang and R. Szeliski. 3-D scene data recovery using omnidirectional multibaseline stereo. *IEEE Conference on Computer Vision and Pattern Recognition*, pages 364–370, June 1996.

[147] S. B. Kang, J. Webb, L. Zitnick, and T. Kanade. A multibaseline stereo system with active illumination and real-time image acquisition. In *International Conference on Computer Vision*, pages 88–93, Cambridge, MA, June 1995.

[148] S. B. Kang and R Weiss. Characterization of errors in compositing panoramic images. In *IEEE Conference on Computer Vision and Pattern Recognition*, pages 103–109, San Juan, Puerto Rico, June 1997.

[149] T. Kawanishi, K. Yamazawa, H. Iwasa, H. Takemura, and N. Yokoya. Generation of high-resolution stereo panoramic images by omnidirectional sensor using hexagonal pyramidal mirrors. *International Conference on Pattern Recognition*, pages 485–489, August 1998.

[150] R. Kermode. Building the BIG picture: Enhanced resolution from coding. MSc thesis, MIT, June 1994.

[151] Y. C. Kim and J. K. Aggarwal. Positioning 3-D objects using stereo images. *IEEE Journal of Robotics and Automation*, RA-3(4):361–373, August 1987.

[152] R. Kin. *Applied Optics and Optical Engineering.* Ed. Rudolf Kingslake, II and V, 1969.

[153] R. Kingslake. *Optical System Design.* Academic Press, 1983.

[154] J. J. Koenderink and A. J. van Doorn. Representation of local geometry in the visual system. *Biol. Cybern.*, 55:367–375, 1987.

[155] C. E. Kolb. *Rayshade User's Guide and Reference Manual*, August 1994.

[156] D. Koller, J. Weber, T. Huang, J. Malik, G. Ogasawara, B. Rao, and S. Russell. Towards robust automatic traffic scene analysis in real-time. In *International Conference on Pattern Recognition*, volume 1, pages 126–131, 1994.

[157] K. G. Konolige and R. C. Bolles. Extra set of eyes. *DARPA Image Understanding Workshop*, pages 25–32, 1998.

[158] A. Krishnan and N. Ahuja. Panoramic image acquisition. In *IEEE Computer Society Conference on Computer Vision and Pattern Recognition (CVPR'96)*, San Francisco, California, June 1996.

[159] D. P. Kuban, H. L. Martin, S. D. Zimmermann, and N. Busico. Omniview Motionless Camera Surveillance System. *U.S. Patent No. 5,359,363*, October 1994.

[160] C. D. Kuglin and D. C. Hines. The phase correlation image alignment method. In *IEEE Conference on Cybernetics and Society*, pages 163–165, New York, September 1975.

[161] R. Kumar, P. Anandan, and K. Hanna. Direct recovery of shape from multiple views: A parallax based approach. In *International Conference on Pattern Recognition*, pages 685–688, October 1994.

[162] R. Kumar, P. Anandan, and K. Hanna. Shape recovery from multiple views: A parallax based approach. In *DARPA IU Workshop*, Monterey, CA, November 1994.

[163] R. Kumar, P. Anandan, M. Irani, J. R. Bergen, and K. J. Hanna. Representation of scenes from collections of images. In *IEEE Workshop on Representations of Visual Scenes*, pages 10–17, Cambridge, MA, June 1995.

[164] S. Lang et al. Characterization and testing of the biris range sensor. In *IEEE Instrumentation and Measurement Technology Conference*, pages 459–464, 1993.

[165] J. M. Lawn and R. Cipolla. Robust egomotion estimation from affine motion parallax. In *European Conference on Computer Vision*, pages 205–210, May 1994.

[166] D. Le Gall. MPEG: A video compression standard for multimedia applications. *Communications of the ACM*, 34(4):44–58, April 1991.

[167] M.-C. Lee, W.-G. Chen, C.-L. Lin, C. Gu, T. Markoc, S. I. Zabinsky, and R. Szeliski. A layered video object coding system using sprite and affine motion model. *IEEE Transactions on Circuits and Systems for Video Technology*, 7(1):130–145, February 1997.

[168] M. Levoy and P. Hanrahan. Light field rendering. *Computer Graphics (SIGGRAPH'96)*, pages 31–42, August 1996.

[169] A. J. Lipton, H. Fujiyoshi, and R. S. Patil. Moving target classification and tracking from real-time video. In *DARPA Image Understanding Workshop*, pages 115–122, 1998.

[170] H. C. Longuet-Higgins. A computer algorithm for reconstructing a scene from two projections. *Nature*, 293:133–135, 1981.

[171] H. C. Longuet-Higgins. Visual ambiguity of a moving plane. *Proceedings of The Royal Society of London B*, 223:165–175, 1984.

[172] B. D. Lucas and T. Kanade. An iterative image registration technique with an application in stereo vision. In *Seventh International Joint Conference on Artificial Intelligence (IJCAI-81)*, pages 674–679, Vancouver, 1981.

[173] Q.-T. Luong, R. Deriche, O. Faugeras, and T. Papadopoulo. On determining the fundamental matrix: Analysis of different methods and experimental results. *Research Report 1894, INRIA*, April 1993.

[174] Q.-T. Luong and T. Viéville. Canonical representations for the geometries of multiple projective views. *Computer Vision and Image Understanding*, 64(2):193–229, September 1996.

[175] H. E. Malde. Panoramic photographs. *American Scientist*, 71(2):132–140, March-April 1983.

[176] P. L. Manly. *Unusual Telescopes*. Cambridge University Press, 1991.

[177] S. Mann and R. W. Picard. Virtual bellows: Constructing high-quality images from video. In *International Conference on Image Processing*, volume I, pages 363–367, Austin, TX, November 1994.

[178] S. Mann and R. W. Picard. Virtual bellows: Constructing high quality stills from video. In *International Conference on Image Processing*, November 1994.

[179] M. Maresch and P. Uray. Automatic camera orientation using panoramic images of a rotating linear CCD array in indoor environment. In *Workshop of Austrian Association for Pattern Recognition*, pages 227–236, 1996.

[180] J. S. Massa, M. Umasuthan, A. M. Wallace, G. S. Buller, and A. C. Walker. Range finding using time correlated single photon counting. *International Conference on Recent Advances in 3-D Digital Imaging and Modeling*, pages 36–43, May 1997.

[181] L. McMillan and G. Bishop. Plenoptic modeling: An image-based rendering system. *Computer Graphics (SIGGRAPH'95)*, pages 39–46, August 1995.

[182] J. Meehan. *Panoramic Photography*. Watson-Guptill, 1990.

[183] F. Meyer and P. Bouthemy. Region-based tracking in image sequences. In *European Conference on Computer Vision*, pages 476–484, Santa Margarita Ligure, May 1992.

[184] D. L. Milgram. Computer methods for creating photomosaics. *IEEE Transactions on Computers*, C-24:1113–1119, 1975.

[185] D. L. Milgram. Adaptive techniques for photomosaicking. *IEEE Transactions on Computers*, C-26(11):1175–1180, November 1977.

[186] F. H. Moffitt and E. M. Mikhail. *Photogrammetry*. Harper & Row, New York, 3 edition, 1980.

[187] T. Moons, L. van Gool, M. van Diest, and A. Oosterlinck. Affine structure from perspective image pairs under relative translations between object and camera. Technical Report KUL/ESAT/M12/9306, Departement Elektrotechniek, Katholieke Universiteit Leuven, Belgium, 1993.

[188] C. L. Morefield. Application of 0-1 integer programming to multitarget tracking problems. *IEEE Transactions on Automatic Control*, 22(3):302–312, 1977.

[189] T. Mori, Y. Kamisuwa, H. Mizoguchi, and T. Sato. Action recognition system based on human finder and human tracker. In *International Conference on Intelligent Robots and Systems*, pages 1334–1341, 1997.

[190] M. Muhlich and R. Mester. The role of total least squares in motion analysis. *European Conference on Computer Vision*, pages 305–321, June 1998.

[191] J. R. Murphy. Application of panoramic imaging to a teleoperated lunar rover. *IEEE SMC Conference*, pages 3117–3121, October 1995.

[192] D.W. Murray. Recovering range using virtual multicamera stereo. *Computer Vision and Image Understanding*, 61(2):285–291, 1995.

[193] R. M. Murray, Z. X. Li, and S. S. Sastry. *A Mathematical Introduction to Robotic Manipulation.* CRC Press, 1994.

[194] V. S. Nalwa. A true omnidirectional viewer. *Technical Report, Bell Laboratories*, February 1996.

[195] S. K. Nayar. Catadioptric omnidirectional camera. In *IEEE Conference on Computer Vision and Pattern Recognition*, pages 482–488, San Juan, Puerto Rico, June 1997.

[196] S. K. Nayar. Omnidirectional video camera. *DARPA Image Understanding Workshop*, May 1997.

[197] S. K. Nayar. Sphereo: Recovering depth using a single camera and two specular spheres. *Proceedings of SPIE: Optics, Illumumination, and Image Sensing for Machine Vision II*, November 1998.

[198] S. K. Nayar and S. Baker. Catadioptric image formation. *DARPA Image Understanding Workshop*, pages 1431–1437, May 1997.

[199] S. K. Nayar and V. Peri. Folded catadioptric cameras. *IEEE Conference on Computer Vision and Pattern Recognition*, 2:217–223, June 1999.

[200] R. C. Nelson and Y. Aloimonos. Finding motion parameters from spherical flow fields. *Workshop on Computer Vision*, pages 145–150, 1987.

[201] S. A. Nene and S. K. Nayar. Stereo with mirrors. *International Conference on Computer Vision*, pages 1087–1094, January 1998.

[202] G. M. Nielson. Scattered data modeling. *IEEE Computer Graphics and Applications*, 13(1):60–70, January 1993.

[203] T. Nishimura, T. Mukai, and R. Oka. Spotting recognition of gestures performed by people from a single time-varying image. *International Conference on Robots and Systems*, pages 967–972, 1997.

[204] S. J. Oh and E. L. Hall. Calibration of an omnidirectional vision navigation system using an industrial robot. *Optical Engineering*, 28(9):955–962, September 1989.

[205] Y. Ohta and T. Kanade. Stereo by intra- and inter-scanline search using dynamic programming. *IEEE Trans. on Pattern Analysis and Machine Intelligence*, PAMI-7(2):139–154, March 1985.

[206] M. Okutomi and T. Kanade. A multiple baseline stereo. *IEEE Trans. on Pattern Analysis and Machine Intelligence*, 15(4):353–363, April 1993.

[207] M. Oren and S. K. Nayar. A theory of specular surface geometry. *International Journal of Computer Vision*, 24(2):105–124, 1996.

[208] T. Pajdla. Bcrf - binary illumination coded range finder: Reimplementation. *ESAT MI2 Technical Report Nr. KUL/ESAT/MI2/9502*, April 1995.

[209] PanoScan. http://www.panoscan.com/, 1999.

[210] B. Parvin and G. Medioni. B-rep from unregistered multiple range images. In *International Conference on Robotics and Automation*, pages 1602–1607, May 1992.

[211] K. R. Pattipati, S. Deb, Y. Bar-Shalom, and R. B. Washburn. A new relaxation algorithm and passive sensor data association. *IEEE Transactions on Automatic Control*, 37(2):198–213, 1992.

[212] S. Peleg. Elimination of seams from photomosaics. *Computer Graphics and Image Processing*, 16:90–94, May 1981.

[213] S. Peleg and M. Ben-Ezra. Stereo panorama with a single camera. In *IEEE Conference on Computer Vision and Pattern Recognition*, pages 395–401, Fort Collins, CO, June 1999.

[214] S. Peleg and J. Herman. Panoramic mosaics by manifold projection. In *IEEE Conference on Computer Vision and Pattern Recognition*, pages 338–343, San Juan, Puerto Rico, June 1997.

[215] M.A. Penna. Camera calibration: A quick and easy way to determine the scale factor. *IEEE Trans. on Pattern Analysis and Machine Intelligence*, 13(12):1240–1245, 1991.

[216] V. Peri and S. K. Nayar. Generation of perspective and panoramic video from omnidirectional video. *DARPA Image Understanding Workshop*, May 1997.

[217] R. Petty, M. Robinson, and J. Evans. 3D measurement using rotating line-scan sensors. *Measurement Sciences and Technology*, 9(3):339–346, March 1998.

[218] M Pollefeys, R. Koch, and L. van Gool. Self-calibration and metric reconstruction in spite of varying and unknown internal camera parameters. In *International Conference on Computer Vision*, pages 90–95, Bombay, India, January 1998.

[219] I. Powell. Panoramic lens. *U.S. Patent No. 5,473,474*, December 1995.

[220] W. H. Press, B. P. Flannery, S. A. Teukolsky, and W. T. Vetterling. *Numerical Recipes in C: The Art of Scientific Computing*. Cambridge University Press, Cambridge, England, second edition, 1992.

[221] L. H. Quam. Hierarchical warp stereo. In *Image Understanding Workshop*, pages 149–155, New Orleans, LA, December 1984. Science Applications International Corporation.

[222] P. Rademacher and G. Bishop. Multiple-center-of-projection images. *Computer Graphics (SIGGRAPH'98)*, pages 199–206, July 1998.

[223] S. Ravela, R. Manmatha, and E. M. Riseman. Image retrieval using scale space matching. In *European Conference on Computer Vision*, volume I, pages 273–282, 1996.

[224] D.W. Rees. Panoramic television viewing system. *U.S. Patent No. 3,505,465*, April 1970.

[225] D. B. Reid. An algorithm for tracking multiple targets. *IEEE Transactions on Automatic Control*, 24(6):843–854, 1979.

[226] M. Rioux. Laser range finder based on synchronized scanners. *Applied Optics*, pages 3837–3844, 1984.

[227] G. R. Rosendahl and W. V. Dykes. Lens systems for panoramic imagery. *U.S. Patent No. 4,395,093*, July 1983.

[228] A. Rosenfeld and A. C. Kak. *Digital Picture Processing*. Academic Press, New York, New York, 1976.

[229] B. Rousso, S. Avidan, A. Shashua, and S. Peleg. Robust recovery of camera rotation from three frames. In *IEEE Conference on Computer Vision and Pattern Recognition*, pages 796–802, San Francisco, CA, June 1996.

[230] B. Rousso, S. Peleg, and I. Finci. Generalized panoramic mosaics. In *DARPA IU Workshop*, 1997.

[231] B. Rousso, S. Peleg, and I. Finci. Mosaicing with generalized strips. In *DARPA Image Understanding Workshop*, pages 255–260, New Orleans, LA, May 1997.

[232] B. Rousso, S. Peleg, I. Finci, and A. Rav-Acha. Universal mosaicing using pipe projection. In *International Conference on Computer Vision*, pages 945–952, Bombay, India, January 1998.

[233] H. O. Saldner and J. M. Huntley. Shape measurement of discontinuous objects using projected fringes and temporal phase unwarping. In *International Conference on Recent Advances in 3-D Digital Imaging and Modeling*, pages 44–50, May 1997.

[234] K. Sarachik. Characterizing an indoor environment with a mobile robot and uncaliblated stereo. *International Conference on Robotics and Automation*, pages 984–989, 1989.

[235] C.R. Sastry, E. W. Kamen, and M. Simaan. An efficient algorithm for tracking the angles of arrival of moving targets. *IEEE Transactions on Signal Processing*, 39(1):242–246, 1991.

[236] Y. Sato, M. Wheeler, and K. Ikeuchi. Object shape and reflectance modeling from observation. *Computer Graphics (SIGGRAPH'97)*, pages 379–387, August 1997.

[237] H. Sawhney and R. Kumar. True multi-image alignment and its application to mosaicking and lens distortion correction. In *IEEE Conference on Computer Vision and Pattern Recognition*, pages 450–456, San Juan, Puerto Rico, June 1997.

[238] H. S. Sawhney. 3D geometry from planar parallax. In *IEEE Conference on Computer Vision and Pattern Recognition*, pages 929–934, Seattle, WA, June 1994.

[239] H. S. Sawhney. Simplifying motion and structure analysis using planar parallax and image warping. In *International Conference on Pattern Recognition*, volume A, pages 403–408, Jerusalem, Israel, October 1994.

[240] H. S. Sawhney and S. Ayer. Compact representation of videos through dominant multiple motion estimation. *IEEE Trans. on Pattern Analysis and Machine Intelligence*, 18(8):814–830, August 1996.

[241] H. S. Sawhney, S. Ayer, and M. Gorkani. Model-based 2D & 3D dominant motion estimation for mosaicing and video representation. In *International Conference on Computer Vision*, pages 583–590, Cambridge, MA, June 1995.

[242] H. S. Sawhney, S. Hsu, and R. Kumar. Robust video mosaicing through topology inference and local to global alignment. In *European Conference on Computer Vision*, pages 103–119, Freiburg, Germany, June 1998.

[243] J. Segen and S. Pingali. A camera-based system for tracking people in real time. In *International Conference on Pattern Recognition*, volume 3, pages 63–67, 1996.

[244] S. Seitz and C. Dyer. Physically valid view synthesis by image interpolation. In *IEEE Workshop on Representation of Visual Scenes*, pages 18–25, Cambridge, MA, June 1995.

[245] Y. Seo and K. Hong. Auto-calibration of a Rotating and Zooming Camera. In *IAP Workshop on Machine Vision Applications*, pages 17–19, Chiba, Japan, November 1998.

[246] Y. Seo and K. Hong. About the self-calibration of a rotating and zooming camera: Theory and practice. In *International Conference on Computer Vision*, pages 183–189, 1999.

[247] A. A. Shabana. *Dynamics of Multibody Systems*. J. Wiley, New York, 1989.

[248] S. Shah and J. Aggarwal. Intrinsic parameter calibration procedure for a (high-distortion) fish-eye lens camera with distortion model and accuracy estimation. *Pattern Recognition*, 29(11):1775–1788, November 1996.

[249] S. Shams. Neural network optimization for multi-target multi-sensor passive tracking. *Proceedings of IEEE*, 84(10):1442–1457, 1996.

[250] P. M. Sharkey, D. W. Murray, S. Vandevelde, I. D. Reid, and P. F. McLauchlan. A modular head/eye platform for real-time reactive vision. *Mechatronics*, 3(4):517–535, 1993.

[251] A. Shashua. Projective structure from uncalibrated images: Structure from motion and recognition. *IEEE Trans. on Pattern Analysis and Machine Intelligence*, 16(8):778–790, August 1994.

[252] A. Shashua and N. Navab. Relative affine structure: Theory and application to 3D reconstruction from perspective views. In *IEEE Conference on Computer Vision and Pattern Recognition*, pages 483–489, Seattle, WA, June 1994.

[253] J. Shi and C. Tomasi. Good features to track. In *IEEE Conference on Computer Vision and Pattern Recognition*, pages 593–600, Seattle, WA, June 1994.

[254] M. Shizawa and K. Mase. Principle of superposition: A common computational framework for analysis of multiple motion. In *IEEE Workshop on Visual Motion*, pages 164–172, Princeton, NJ, October 1991.

[255] H.-Y. Shum, K. Ikeuchi, and R. Reddy. Principal component analysis with missing data and its application to object modeling. In *IEEE Conference on Computer Vision and Pattern Recognition*, pages 560–565, Seattle, WA, June 1994.

[256] H.-Y. Shum, A. Kalai, and S. M. Seitz. Omnivergent stereo. In *International Conference on Computer Vision*, pages 22–29, Kerkyra, Greece, September 1999.

[257] H.-Y. Shum and R. Szeliski. Panoramic image mosaicing. Technical Report MSR-TR-97-23, Microsoft Research, September 1997.

[258] H.-Y. Shum and R. Szeliski. Construction and refinement of panoramic mosaics with global and local alignment. In *International Conference on Computer Vision*, pages 953–958, Bombay, India, January 1998.

[259] H.-Y. Shum and R. Szeliski. Stereo reconstruction from multiperspective panoramas. *International Conference on Computer Vision*, pages 14–21, 1999.

[260] C. C. Slama, editor. *Manual of Photogrammetry*. American Society of Photogrammetry, Falls Church, Virginia, fourth edition, 1980.

[261] P. Smith and G. Buechler. A branching algorithm for discriminating and tracking multiple objects. *IEEE Transactions on Automatic Control*, 20:101–104, 1975.

[262] D. Southwell, A. Basu, M. Fiala, and J. Reyda. Panoramic stereo. *International Conference on Pattern Recognition*, A:378–382, August 1996.

[263] G. Stein. Accurate internal camera calibration using rotation, with analysis of sources of error. In *International Conference on Computer Vision*, pages 230–236, Cambridge, MA, June 1995.

[264] T. Svoboda. Central panoramic cameras design, geometry, egomotion. *PhD Thesis, Center for Machine Perception, Czech Technical University*, 1999.

[265] T. Svoboda, T. Pajdla, and V. Hlavac. Epipolar geometry for panoramic cameras. *European Conference on Computer Vision*, pages 218–232, June 1998.

[266] R. Szeliski. Image mosaicing for tele-reality applications. In *IEEE Workshop on Applications of Computer Vision (WACV'94)*, pages 44–53, Sarasota, FL, December 1994.

[267] R. Szeliski. Video mosaics for virtual environments. *IEEE Computer Graphics and Applications*, pages 22–30, March 1996.

[268] R. Szeliski, S. Avidan, and P. Anandan. Layer extraction from multiple images containing reflections and transparency. In *IEEE Conference on Computer Vision and Pattern Recognition*, Hilton Head Island, NC, June 2000.

[269] R. Szeliski and J. Coughlan. Hierarchical spline-based image registration. In *IEEE Conference on Computer Vision and Pattern Recognition*, pages 194–201, Seattle, WA, June 1994.

[270] R. Szeliski and S. B. Kang. Recovering 3D shape and motion from image streams using nonlinear least squares. *Journal of Visual Communication and Image Representation*, 5(1):10–28, March 1994.

[271] R. Szeliski and S. B. Kang. Direct methods for visual scene reconstruction. In *IEEE Workshop on Representations of Visual Scenes*, pages 26–33, Cambridge, MA, June 1995.

[272] R. Szeliski, S. B. Kang, and H.-Y. Shum. A parallel feature tracker for extended image sequences. In *IEEE International Symposium on Computer Vision*, pages 241–246, Coral Gables, FL, November 1995.

[273] R. Szeliski and H.-Y. Shum. Creating full view panoramic image mosaics and environment maps. *Computer Graphics (SIGGRAPH'97)*, pages 251–258, August 1997.

[274] C. J. Taylor, P. E. Debevec, and J. Malik. Reconstructing polyhedral models of architectural scenes from photographs. In *European Conference on Computer Vision*, volume 2, pages 659–668, Cambridge, England, April 1996.

[275] L. Teodosio and W. Bender. Salient video stills: Content and context preserved. In *ACM International Conference on Multimedia*, pages 39–46, 1993.

[276] W. B. Thompson and T. C. Pong. Detecting moving objects. *International Journal of Computer Vision*, 4:29–57, 1990.

[277] Q. Tian and M. N. Huhns. Algorithms for subpixel registration. *Computer Vision, Graphics, and Image Processing*, 35:220–233, 1986.

[278] T.Y. Tian, C. Tomasi, and D.J. Heeger. Comparison of approaches to egomotion computation. In *IEEE Conference on Computer Vision and Pattern Recognition*, pages 315–320, San Francisco, CA, June 1996.

[279] B. J. Tordoff and D. W. Murray. Violating rotating camera geometry: The effect of radial distortion on self-calibration. In *International Conference on Pattern Recognition*, 2000. To appear.

[280] P. H. S. Torr and D. W. Murray. Stochastic motion clustering. In *European Conference on Computer Vision*, pages 328–337, May 1994.

[281] P. H. S. Torr, A. Zisserman, and S. J. Maybank. Robust detection of degenerate configurations for the fundamental matrix. In *International Conference on Computer Vision*, pages 1037–1042, Cambridge, MA, June 1995.

[282] B. Triggs. Autocalibration and the absolute quadric. In *IEEE Conference on Computer Vision and Pattern Recognition*, pages 609–614, San Juan, Puerto Rico, June 1997.

[283] S. Trubko. Personal communication, August 1998.

[284] R. Y. Tsai. A versatile camera calibration technique for high-accuracy 3D machine vision metrology using off-the-shelf TV cameras and lenses. *IEEE Journal of Robotics and Automation*, RA-3(4):323–344, 1987.

[285] R. Y. Tsai and R. K. Lenz. A new technique for fully autonomous and efficient 3D robotics hand/eye calibration. *IEEE Transactions on Robotics and Automation*, 5(3):345–358, June 1989.

[286] V. S. V. Nalwa. His camera won't turn heads. *http://www.lucent.com/ideas2/innovations/docs/nalwa.html*, 1996.

[287] J. Wang and E. Adelson. Layered representation for motion analysis. In *IEEE Conference on Computer Vision and Pattern Recognition*, pages 361–366, New York, June 1993.

[288] L. L. Wang and W. H. Tsai. Camera calibration by vanishing lines for 3-D computer vision. *IEEE Trans. on Pattern Analysis and Machine Intelligence*, PAMI-13(4):370–376, April 1991.

[289] M. Watanabe and S. K. Nayar. Telecentric optics for computational vision. *European Conference on Computer Vision*, April 1996.

[290] H. Weghorst, G. Hooper, and D. P. Greenberg. Improved computational methods for ray tracing. *ACM Transactions on Graphics*, 3(1):52–69, January 1984.

[291] J. Weng, P. Cohen, and M. Herniou. Camera calibration with distortion models and accuracy evaluation. *IEEE Trans. on Pattern Analysis and Machine Intelligence*, 14(10):965–980, October 1992.

[292] L. Westover. Footprint evaluation for volume rendering. *Computer Graphics (SIGGRAPH'90)*, 24:367–376, August 1990.

[293] L. Williams. Pyramidal parametrics. *Computer Graphics (SIGGRAPH'83)*, 17(3):1–11, July 1983.

[294] G. Wolberg. *Digital Image Warping*. IEEE Computer Society Press, Los Alamitos, CA, 1990.

[295] P. R. Wolf. *Elements of photogrammetry.* McGraw-Hill, New York, 1974.

[296] S. Wolfram. *Mathematica™, A System for Doing Mathematics by Computer.* Addison-Wesley, 1991.

[297] D. N. Wood, A. Finkelstein, J. F. Hughes, C. E. Thayer, and D. H. Salesin. Multiperspective panoramas for cel animation. *Computer Graphics (SIGGRAPH'83)*, pages 243–250, August 1997.

[298] Y. Xiong and K. Turkowski. Creating image-based VR using a self-calibrating fisheye lens. In *IEEE Conference on Computer Vision and Pattern Recognition*, pages 237–243, San Juan, Puerto Rico, June 1997.

[299] M. Yachida. 3-D data acquisition by multiple views. In *3rd International Symposium on Robotics Research (ISRR'85)*, pages 11–18, London, 1986. The MIT Press.

[300] Y. Yagi. Omnidirectional sensing and its applications. *IEICE Transactions*, E82-D(3), March 1999.

[301] Y. Yagi and S. Kawato. Panoramic scene analysis with conic projection. *International Conference on Robots and Systems*, 1990.

[302] Y. Yagi, S. Kawato, and S. Tsuji. Real-time omnidirectional image sensor copis for vision-guided navigation. *IEEE Transactions on Robotics and Automation*, 10(11):11–22, February 1994.

[303] Y. Yagi, Y. Nishizawa, and M. Yachida. Map-based navigation for a mobile robot with omnidirectional images sensor copis. *IEEE Transaction on Robotics and Automation*, 11(5):634–648, October 1995.

[304] Y. Yagi and M. Yachida. Real-time generation of environmental map and obstacle avoidance using omnidirectional image sensor with conic mirror. In *IEEE Conference on Computer Vision and Pattern Recognition*, pages 160–165, June 1991.

[305] J. Yamamoto, J. Ohya, and K. Ishii. Recognizing human action in time-seqential images using hidden markov models. In *IEEE Conference on Computer Vision and Pattern Recognition*, pages 379–387, 1992.

[306] K. Yamazawa, Y. Yagi, and M. Yachida. Omnidirectional imaging with hyperboloidal projection. In *International Conference on Robotics and Automation*, pages 1029–1034, July 1993.

[307] K. Yamazawa, Y. Yagi, and M. Yachida. Obstacle detection with omnidirectional image sensor hyperomni vision. In *International Conference on Robotics and Automation*, pages 1062–1067, 1995.

[308] R. C. Yates. *A Handbook on Curves and Their Properties, rev. ed.* National Council of Teachers of Mathematics, 1952, reprinted 1974.

[309] N. Yokoya, H. Iwasa, K. Yamazawa, T. Kawanishi, and H. Takemura. Generation of high-resolution stereo panoramic images by omnidirectional imaging sensor using hexagonal pyramidal mirrors. *International Conference on Pattern Recognition*, page SA14, 1998.

[310] H.-J. Zhang, A. Kankanhalli, and S. W. Smoliar. Automatic partitioning of full-motion video. *Multimedia Systems*, 1(1):10–28, 1993.

[311] J. Y. Zheng and S. Tsuji. From anorthscope perception to dynamic vision. *International Conference on Image Processing*, 2:775–779, 1989.

[312] J. Y. Zheng and S. Tsuji. Panoramic representation for route recognition by a mobile robot. *International Journal of Computer Vision*, 9:55–76, 1992.

[313] A. Zisserman, D. Liebowitz, and M. Armstrong. Resolving ambiguities in auto-calibration. *Philosophical Transactions of the Royal Society of London, Series A*, 356(1740):1193–1211, 1998.